E. Brooks Holifield is Charles Howard Candler Professor of American Church History, Candler School of Theology, Emory University. He is former president of the American Society for Church History and the author of several books on American religious history, including *The Covenant Sealed: The Development of Puritan Sacramental Theology in Old and New England*, published by Yale University Press, and *Era of Persuasion: American Thought and Culture, 1521–1680*.

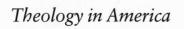

Theology in America

E. BROOKS HOLIFIELD

Theology in America

CHRISTIAN THOUGHT FROM
THE AGE OF THE PURITANS
TO THE CIVIL WAR

Yale University Press
New Haven
& London

BT
30
.U6
H65
2003

Published with assistance from the Annie Burr Lewis Fund and Emory University.
Copyright © 2003 by Yale University.
All rights reserved.
This book may not be reproduced, in whole or in part, including illustrations, in any form (beyond that copying permitted by Sections 107 and 108 of the U.S. Copyright Law and except by reviewers for the public press), without written permission from the publishers.

Set in Sabon type by Keystone Typesetting, Inc.
Printed in the United States of America by Sheridan Books, Ann Arbor, Michigan

Library of Congress Cataloging-in-Publication Data
Holifield, E. Brooks.
Theology in America: Christian thought from the age of the Puritans to the Civil War / E. Brooks Holifield.
p. cm.
Includes bibliographical references and index.
ISBN 0-300-09574-0 (alk. paper)
1. Theology, Doctrinal — United States — History. I. Title.
BT30.U6H65 2003
230′.0972 — dc21
2003042289

A catalogue record for this book is available from the British Library.

The paper in this book meets the guidelines for permanence and durability of the Committee on Production Guidelines for Book Longevity of the Council on Library Resources.

10 9 8 7 6 5 4 3 2 1

JESUIT - KRAUSS - McCORMICK - LIBRARY
1100 EAST 55th STREET
CHICAGO, ILLINOIS 60615

Contents

Preface

My intention in this book is to argue that one important feature of Christian religious life in early America was an extensive tradition of theological reflection and that this tradition engaged American writers from multiple religious backgrounds in a vast conversation that linked them to a trans-Atlantic world. I do not propose to reveal the meaning of America, to insist that theology preoccupied ordinary Americans, or to suggest that theological texts unlock the meaning of American religious experience. I try simply to show that Christian theology in America was part of a community of discourse that stretched back to the first century and across the Atlantic to Europe and that certain persisting themes and questions created a set of issues that reappeared for more than three centuries, drawing theologians from the nineteenth century into a conversation not only with each other but also with their predecessors. Among those questions, none was more important than that of the reasonableness of theology and of Christianity itself.

More than forty years ago, my graduate school mentor, Sydney Ahlstrom, surveyed the history of Christian theology in America from the seventeenth to the mid-twentieth century in about a hundred pages of subtle interpretation. My book has a more restricted temporal range, from about 1636 to around 1865, but it expands considerably the scope, drawing mainly from 282 North American writers who represented more than twenty-five movements, traditions, and schools of thought. Like Ahlstrom, I underscore the trans-Atlantic context, but in my emphasis on evidential Christianity, rationality, practicality, ethics, denominations, persistent Calvinism, and the distinction between populist and academic theologians, I go in different directions from those Ahlstrom traveled.

In his brief survey, Ahlstrom declined quite appropriately to explore what he called a "folk-theology" that he recognized as part of the nineteenth-century scene. In my account, "populist" theologians of various kinds prominently enter the picture. The historian must take them seriously because they created for themselves a place at the theological table and forced the academic theologians to take them seriously in order to counter their influence. While the term "populist" suggests for American readers a later nineteenth-century political and social movement, its appearance in this book recalls a usage current as early as the eighth century, when Alcuin, adviser of Charlemagne and abbot of Tours, cautioned against the proverb that the *"vox populi"* was the *"vox Dei."* The appeal to the "people" as a source of authority became entangled with the medieval "plowman" tradition — praise of the religious insight of the simple uneducated plowman. The two themes helped form the theological landscape in America.[1]

Even more prominent in this account, however, are the trained theologians who prevailed in the schools and in the early American denominations. I have written this book during an era in which most students of American religion have turned their attention away from literate elites, the history of ideas, the abstractions of intellectuals, and the activities of leaders. This turn has produced a rich bounty of knowledge about lived religion, women in American religious communities, African-American Christianity, and ethnic diversity. It has virtually redefined American religious history. Yet knowledge of the theological heritage can still inform readers interested in American history, early American religion, American literature, intellectual history, the theological disciplines, and religious studies. Rare was the discourse in early America in which theology had no role.

Theological ideas have always had multivalent meanings and functions. They have expressed social impulses and group tensions, they have manifested the psychological dynamics of their authors, and they have provided slogans for maintaining group identity. The same language can change in force and meaning from one context to another, and no synoptic overview can excavate the multiple levels operative even in a local religious community. But theologians have also brought to expression ancient yearnings to know the truth about mysteries that have puzzled the greatest intellects. They have tried to interpret the text of the Christian and Jewish scriptures accurately, to represent traditions consistently, and to rethink the language of a past era in changing historical times. Even when I have noted how theological ideas embodied tensions with social and economic dimensions, I have read them as the ideas of people who were attempting to clarify the rationality of what they usually took to be a unique revelation.

During the years in which I have labored over this manuscript, I have accumulated more debts than I can ever hope to repay. I am grateful to the National Endowment for the Humanities for research fellowships that enabled me to spend two sabbatical years working on the book. The Pew Endowment and the Louisville Institute for the Study of American Religion provided funding for a third year of research and writing. Emory University gave me leave time to complete the manuscript. The staff of the Pitts Theology Library at Emory was consistently helpful. Eerdmans Publishing Company granted me permission to use portions of my chapter on Charles Hodge in *Charles Hodge Revisited: A Critical Appraisal of His Life and Work,* edited by John W. Stewart and James Moorhead.

I am grateful, as well, to readers who have generously given their time to the reading and criticism of earlier drafts. David D. Hall offered both encouragement and incisive criticism at a crucial stage. I am indebted to the criticisms and insights of Robert Bruce Mullin, Conrad Cherry, Mark Noll, Jonathan Strom, Glenn Hinson, Kim Boykin, Ted Smith, Paula Shakelton, Michael Turner, Hendrikus Boers, Stephen Gunter, Gregory Wills, Philip Thompson, Stacia Brown, Paul Thompson, Liberty Stewart, Remalian Cocar, Tom Burke, and my colleagues in the Historical Studies program of the Graduate Division of Religion at Emory University.

Introduction:
Theology in America

For more than a century in early colonial America, theologians ruled the realm of ideas. America's first learned class consisted largely of Protestant clergy, and the relatively small number of pastors who published books of theology, or "divinity," attained the status of the most learned of the learned. Until almost the dawning of the American Revolution, theologians exercised a singular authority in American print culture. Until late in the eighteenth century, they were, in each decade, the most-published authors in America. Their position of eminence faded after the Revolution, but even throughout the early nineteenth century, theology continued to command respect in American intellectual circles at the same time that it provided a vocabulary that informed the lived religion of ordinary Americans. When the Presbyterian minister Robert Baird interpreted American religion for European readers in 1843, he could boast of "a vast number of publications in every department of Christian theology," and he might have added that American theological journals were the most scholarly publications in the culture.[1]

Theologians were the keepers of a language that flowed over into other fields of discourse. Confident that philosophy, rightly construed, supported theological truth, they crafted most of the early American philosophical texts. They were the primary expositors of the new discipline of "mental science," the chief proponents of "moral science," and avid participants in the formation of "natural philosophy," which would eventually transform itself into natural science. Poets and novelists — including Herman Melville, Nathanial Hawthorne, Harriet Beecher Stowe, Emily Dickinson, and Ralph Waldo Emerson — struggled with, and often against, the pronouncements of the theologians to such an extent that one can hardly hope to understand the nineteenth-century literary renaissance without knowing something about the theological ideas current in the culture. In an era when the common law allowed free latitude to local judges, theology often figured prominently in American legal decisions. American politicians spoke a public language that drew amply on theological conceptions. Notions of sin and redemption suffused the rhetoric of nineteenth-century social reformers. For almost three centuries, theologians enjoyed a position of substantial authority in the intellectual life of America.

At the same time, the language of theology informed the piety of Americans who never immersed themselves in learned and artistic productions. Through the sermons and tracts of local Protestant and Catholic clergy, the ideas of theologians reached an audience that knew little of science or philosophy. Early American theologians were themselves usually local pastors, speaking weekly to congregations as well as writing treatises for the learned. When an African-American servant named Jarena Lee wrote her *Religious Experience and Journal* in 1849, she described her religious experience — using words like "guilt," "pardon," "conversion," and "sanctification" — in ways that followed the informal rules of her Methodist theological background. She had learned to make distinctions that defined religious experience as Methodists understood it. For Jarena Lee, as for countless other American Christians, theological language drew boundaries around practices and institutions and provided markers of communal identity.[2]

Interested observers, then and now, have debated about the extent of popular interest in theology. More than one observer of Christian theology in early nineteenth-century America noted the disinclination of Americans to rally around speculative systems, including the systems of theologians who ventured too deeply into complexity. The French aristocrat Alexis de Tocqueville, who toured the country during 1831–32, said that it was hard to find Americans who devoted themselves to "the essentially theoretical and abstract portion of human knowledge" and that "doctrine" occupied a secondary place in the religious landscape. A reviewer in the New England journal *The Spirit of the Pilgrims* reached a similar conclusion in 1832 about popular habits of thought: "The spirit of religion in this country is active rather than contemplative. The nature of our institutions gives full scope to action, and the bustling character of our population is more favorable to doing than to thinking. Everything is submitted to the judgment of the people; the standard of excellence is fixed by them; and they can more justly appreciate the active laborer than the profound thinker." More than a decade later, Edwards Amasa Park at Andover Theological Seminary tried to counter the charge of German divines that Americans had "no taste for theological science" or for any other study "save that of the laws of steam and of political government," but Park had to concede that both ministers and laypeople often lacked the time to read, that publishers respected only market demand, and that theologians found it hard to speak clearly and winsomely to institutions of a "popular character."[3]

Such descriptions illumine one side of a complex story. Tocqueville was also struck by the "enormous quantity of religious works," including books of "controversial divinity," that he found in the booksellers' shops. The Connecticut minister Horace Bushnell claimed to have grown up in a village whose residents often discussed the complexities of "free will, fixed fate, foreknowledge absolute, trinity, redemption, special grace, eternity." Harriet Beecher Stowe created in her novels an imaginative world in which such conversations punctuated the routine of daily life. In 1850, the Unitarian George Burnap marveled at the extent of popular theological interest. He found knowledge of both the Bible and of "different theological systems" to be "generally diffused." Even the "most illiterate, on hearing a doctrine advanced," were able "immediately to recur to those texts of Scripture, which seem to be inconsistent with it," and people of "common education" could discuss the "metaphysical" side of theology with "no small amount of ingenuity and acuteness." Through the popular institution of oral debate, nineteenth-century Americans treated theology as a form of popular entertainment, and celebrated debaters attracted large audiences to contests that extended over days.[4]

We simply do not know the extent of popular interest in the writings of theologians in early America or the degree to which formal theology guided religious practice. Many American Christians had a rudimentary theological knowledge even though presumably only a few occupied themselves with intricate distinctions. Although Americans sometimes bristled at the idea that theology was the preserve of a learned elite, some conceded that it was a form of discourse distinct from the language of worship and devotion. "Religion is for the people," wrote Josiah Willard Gibbs at Yale, "theology is for the schools. Theology is difficult to obtain; sources are in ancient and obscure books; it treats of invisible objects; in inculcates many things ungrateful to our natural feelings."[5]

In early America, theology was normally understood to be a discipline that combined biblical interpretation with one or another form of background theory. What distinguished theology from devotional or inspirational writing or narratives of religious experience was its interdependence with various branches of philosophy, whether logic, metaphysics, epistemology, hermeneutics, rhetoric, or mental science, or of history, especially the historical study of the books of the Bible. The standard text used at seventeenth-century Harvard, *The Marrow of Theology* (1623) by the English divine William Ames, defined theology as the "doctrine of living to God" and insisted that it was derived from "divine revelation" rather than human inquiry, but he explained that any understanding of this revelation required "skill and experience in logic, rhetoric, grammar, and the languages." When the late seventeenth-century New England Puritan Samuel Willard described "the Study of Divinity" to young scholars, he said that scripture was its sole source but that it required grammar, rhetoric, and logic to get the "theological truth," and he commended as well the mastery of natural philosophy and history. Two hundred years later, the Princeton theologian Charles Hodge defined "systematic theology" as a science that related biblical "facts" not only to each other but also "to cognate disciplines." The southern Wesleyan Thomas Ralston explained that theologians derived their truths from the "inspired volume" but that part of their duty was to show that scripture, properly understood, was consistent with "the principles of sound philosophy and correct reason." Henry Tappan, the chancellor of the University of Michigan, wrote in 1856 that theology, in "form," grounded itself in "the sacred writings" but that it "called in philosophy as an adjunct authority, and to aid in interpretation and exposition." Such definitions did not escape criticism, but they represented a rough consensus that endured for more than two hundred years.[6]

The definitions were always sufficiently broad to include a variety of genres, such as sermons and popular tracts, and any history of theology in America must consider such sources. Seventeenth-century sermons, in any event, usually presented biblical themes in accord with formulas defined by sixteenth-century logicians and rhetoricians. Nineteenth-century tracts often reflected the assumptions of eighteenth-century Scottish philosophy. Such productions, as well as technical books and journal articles, joined biblical interpretation to a background theory, explicit or implicit, in a way that constituted "theology."

The overarching theme of this book is the claim that a majority of theologians in early America shared a preoccupation with the reasonableness of Christianity that predisposed them toward such an understanding of theology. The book interweaves this claim about the quest for reasonableness with five other themes that amplify and qualify it: the continued insistence on theology's "practicality" and its ethical functions, the importance of Calvinism, the interplay between Americans and Europeans, the denominational setting of theology, and the distinction between academic and populist strands of thought.

Reasonableness: The Evidential Temper

The quest for theological rationality found its earliest expression among seventeenth-century New England Calvinists who employed concepts of Aristotelian and Platonic philosophy derived from Protestant scholasticism and who organized their thought with the aid of rhetorical schemes borrowed from the sixteenth-century humanist reform of logic. The second generation of New England theologians expanded the interest in rationality, partly in response to the earliest English deists and partly in harmony with English natural philosophy, and during the eighteenth century, their successors adopted an understanding of reason in religion that can best be designated as "evidential." Deeply informed by parallel patterns of thought in England and on the European continent, this evidentialist position consisted of the claim that rational evidence confirmed the uniqueness and truth of the biblical revelation. Such a claim stood behind the rise of "evidential Christianity," a form of theology different in important ways from either the scholastic thought of the medieval church or the theologies of revelation that came out of the Protestant reform.

One feature of evidential Christianity was the importance accorded to natural theology, a mode of Christian thinking that arose as early as the second century and had a continuous history in the church but assumed unprecedented importance during the eighteenth century. The claim of the natural theologian was that reason, reflecting on either the visible world or the workings of the human mind, could produce evidence for the existence of a transcendent God apart from the revelation in scripture or the tradition of the church. What distinguished natural theology from "natural religion," the religious ideal of eighteenth-century deists, was the further claim that natural theology pointed toward and confirmed truths above the capacity of reason to discover — truths accessible only through special revelation.

By the end of the thirteenth century, natural theology had assumed two distinguishable forms. The first, rooted in Platonic and Neoplatonic philosophies and exemplified by Augustine of Hippo (354–430), found evidence for divine transcendence within the depths of human consciousness, for when the mind turned inward toward the ideas implicit within its own thinking, it discovered the presence of eternal truths, including the idea of truth itself, which had an eternal reality transcending time and space. Such ideas suggested the reality of a supraindividual, eternal, divine mind. The second, rooted in Aristotelian thought and exemplified by Thomas Aquinas (ca. 1225–74), found evidence for God by reflection on the existence and order of the natural creation. The physical world pointed toward a cause sufficient to explain its creation and a designer adequate to explain its order. The growing interest in the natural world in late-seventeenth-century natural philosophy advanced the prestige of the argument from natural order, and most American theologians never abandoned it.

A second feature of evidential Christianity was the degree of importance given to the time-honored "evidences for revelation." Like the tradition of natural theology, this evidential tradition also extended back into Christian antiquity. The letter to the Hebrews in the New Testament claimed that God attested to truth by signs, wonders, and miracles (Heb. 2:4), and by the second century, Christian apologists regularly appealed to the miracles of Jesus and his fulfillment of Old Testament prophecies to prove that he was who Christians said he was. What began as an argument for the divinity of Christ, however, became by the thirteenth century an argument for the authenticity of the Christian revelation in general and the Christian scriptures in particular. The argument became increasingly elaborate, and by the fourteenth century, theologians distinguished between extrinsic or external evidences (the appeal to miracle and fulfilled prophecy) and internal evidences based on the intrinsic credibility of Christian teaching, the internal consistency of the Bible, and the consistency of biblical truths with moral and religious experience.

Such argumentation briefly fell out of favor in the early Protestant Reformation. Martin Luther contended that it was a form of self-righteousness to attempt to demonstrate the rational probability of revelation, and John Calvin allowed the proofs only to confirm the inner testimony of the Spirit to the authority of scripture. By the seventeenth century, however, both Lutheran and Calvinist theologians employed evidential reasoning to prove the infallibility of the biblical account, and Catholics like Jacques Bossuet in France used the same arguments to demonstrate the infallible authority of both scripture and the church.[7]

It was the battle against deism, under way by the late seventeenth century, that elevated evidentialism to the place of high status it would bear among early American theologians. After Edward, Lord Herbert of Cherbury (1583–1648), argued in 1624 that every human being entertained common religious notions about the existence and honor of a supreme power—"common notions" that were accessible even apart from any specific written revelation—Christian thinkers turned their attention increasingly to the defense of the Bible as a unique and necessary revelation. When John Locke employed the evidences in his *On the Reasonableness of Christianity* (1695), he confirmed the authority of evidential reasoning for a generation newly engaged with questions about the historical veracity and credibility of the Bible. Evidentialist arguments had American proponents in the seventeenth century, but not until a domestic form of deism drew wide attention in the late eighteenth century did the evidences become a common prolegomenon to theology.[8]

In establishing the place of natural theology and the evidences, American theologians in the antebellum era found theoretical support especially in the eighteenth-century Scottish philosophical theories collectively known as Common Sense Realism. Grounded in the writing of Thomas Reid at Glasgow and Dugald Stewart at Edinburgh, Scottish Realism offered a defense of rational theology against the skepticism of David Hume and yet provided a safeguard against excessive rationalism by emphasizing also the limits of reason. The Scottish defense of reason made natural theology and an alliance with natural science seem useful and plausible; the warnings against rationalism seemed to confirm the need for revelation. By grounding their conclusions in the analysis of human "consciousness," moreover, the Scots helped to make the new discipline of "mental science" a virtual subdiscipline of theology. The admiration of the Scottish philosophers for the sixteenth-century Elizabethan courtier Francis Bacon prompted Americans to describe their defense of empirical reason as Baconian.

By the 1830s, the Baconian form of evidentialist thinking encountered resistance from a small company of thinkers weary of enlightenment rationalism. Although they shared no consensus about the substantive claims of either theology or philosophy, they tried to minimize natural theology and evidentialism altogether or they turned toward the Augustinian rather than the more empirical forms of natural theology. From Emerson and the transcendentalists to the Catholic convert Orestes Brownson, from the Mercersburg theologians Philip Schaff and John Williamson Nevin to the Connecticut pastor Horace Bushnell and the Lutheran confessionalists of the Midwest, the critics of the evidential temper sought alternative ways to understand the reasonableness of Christianity. Some of them, like the traditionalist Lutherans, preferred confessional fidelity rather than rational proofs. Others, like the transcendentalists, discovered conceptions of "intuitive" reason and gave them far more authority than a traditional Christian theologian could ever accept. A number of theologians turned to intuitive reason as a way of dismissing the conventional evidences as peripheral or even irrelevant and "rationalist." Their disillusion with the evidences marked one of the most serious divides in antebellum religious thought.

The critics of the evidential strategy never attained a dominant voice. By the mid-nineteenth century, evidential arguments continually held sway. The clergy preached on the evidences. The evidential strategy often governed oral debates. When the reformer Alexander Campbell debated the utopian skeptic

Robert Owen on the evidences of Christianity in Cincinnati in 1832, the crowd averaged twelve hundred a day for eight days. Well-endowed lecture-ships in Boston allowed Unitarian clergy to present lecture series on the evidences. Church newspapers printed popular articles that made the evidences plain for the laity. College presidents taught regular courses on the evidences. Seminary journals refined the arguments for learned readers. For many, evidential reasoning became an essential component of theology.[9]

Advocates of the evidential strategy could point to examples of success. In 1820, for instance, a young apprentice bookmaker in Boston named Thomas Whittemore told the Universalist preacher Hosea Ballou that he was skeptical of the truth of the Bible. Ballou persuaded him to read the *Evidences of Christianity* written by the English theologian William Paley. As he was reading, Whittemore also listened to Ballou's sermons on "the force of prophecy, as affecting the truth of the Bible," and he began to feel that the evidences provided "good and substantial reasons for the truth of the Christian religion." The books of the New Testament were genuine and accurate, Jesus performed miracles and prophesied future events, and eyewitnesses gave testimony to the truth of New Testament narratives. The result was his conversion: "Christianity, I said, is true."[10]

Practicality and Ethics

In 1855 the Presbyterian theologian Henry Boynton Smith noted in his inaugural lecture as the professor of systematic theology at Union Theological Seminary in New York that "theology, unlike philosophy, is a practical as well as a theoretical science." No statement about theology was more frequent in early America. The demand that theology be practical reflected not only the imperatives of revivalist religion and widespread assumptions about the relation between theology and ethics but also a long history of reflection that had its roots in ancient philosophy.[11]

In trying to convince fifth-century Athenians that the political life was not the highest good, Plato had distinguished between theoretical and practical knowledge, defining *theoria* (contemplation) as reflection on unchanging truths, which brought the greatest possible happiness. Aristotle also contrasted theory and practice, arguing, like Plato, that theoretical knowledge came from the contemplation of unchanging realities, while practical knowledge consisted of the principles that guided choices and actions. When Christian theologians adopted the distinction in the third century, they used it at first to reflect on the way in which specific practices, or good works, might help prepare one for the highest end of the contemplation of God. By the twelfth century, they were using it to define theology itself.[12]

To say that theology was speculative or theoretical meant that its aim was the beholding of God as an end in itself, an intrinsic good. To call it practical meant that it consisted of knowledge that led to a good beyond itself, specifically to the end of blessedness and union with God. Most theologians believed that the discipline was both speculative and practical, but they differed in emphasis. Thomas Aquinas in the thirteenth century viewed it as primarily, though not exclusively, speculative or theoretical because it dealt more with divine things than with human acts. His younger contemporary Duns Scotus viewed it as mainly practical, arguing that revelation was given chiefly as a guide to salutary conduct that would enable believers to attain their final end.[13]

By the seventeenth century, a few theologians defined theology as entirely practical, designed only to teach the faithful how to live piously and well and to attain blessedness through the light of God's divine truth. This was the position of Jacobus Arminius, the Dutch theologian whose criticisms of one form of Calvinism became an inspiration for various later "Arminian" rejections of Calvinist theology. An understanding of theology as fully practical, however, also attracted such Calvinist scholastics as Bartholomaus Keckermann in Heidelberg, who contended that everything in theology was directed toward the end of "living well" and loving God in a saving manner. Most thought, however, that theology was both theoretical (speculative), providing knowledge of God as an end in itself, and practical, teaching the truths that enabled the faithful to "live unto God."[14]

An understanding of theology as practical governed the discipline in America from the outset. Influenced especially by the French Protestant Petrus Ramus, who defined theology as entirely practical, the covenant theologians of seventeenth-century Europe and America would emphasize its function as a guide to living unto God. American theologians drew, moreover, on another tradition extending back into the third century, in which "speculation" referred to a vain curiosity extending beyond permitted limits. Some would follow in the path set by Martin Luther, who defined the "speculative" as a form of knowing that lacked an inner experience of the truths known. Others, also in the tradition of the Protestant reformers, would define it as any effort to go beyond biblical revelation. Gradually, theologians in America would use the term speculative only to dismiss a position with which they disagreed.[15]

The meanings assigned to the concept of the practical in America would vary. Some retained the medieval sense that the whole of theological truth could be viewed as a practical guide to salvation. Others restricted the use of the term to religious teachings about repentance, regeneration, and the Christian life. The practical doctrines described Christian experience. Still others restricted the term even further, referring to doctrines as practical only if their lively presentation from the pulpit could elicit conversion or guide ethical decisions.

Almost from the beginning, theologians in America emphasized the close connection between the practical and the moral, and even though some — usually designated by their critics as "antinomians" — questioned the closeness of the connection, the ethical side of theology became increasingly prominent. By the eighteenth century, some redefined the practicality of theology to mean simply its usefulness as a guide to a life of virtue, and even those who retained older notions of the practical became engrossed in the issues presented by the emergence of moral philosophy. By the mid-nineteenth century, it was common among theologians to include a section on moral philosophy within theology textbooks.

The emphasis on practicality merged almost seamlessly with the prevailing conceptions of theological rationality. Edwards Amasa Park noted by the mid-nineteenth century that several of the American "systems" of divinity were "in the form of sermons," and he argued that theology in America was "eminently practical" because everyone agreed that "the theological system, which is best fitted to be preached, is on that account most entitled to be believed." Park came close to saying that practical usefulness was itself a criterion of rational truthfulness. The harmony of the rational and the practical was especially visible in the evidentialist argument that the consistency of biblical teaching with the highest moral insights of humanity provided evidence that the Bible was a divine book. Even more important as a sign of the unity of the rational and the practical, however, was the confidence that the evidences had the power to generate conversions. The proofs of evidential Christianity functioned as arguments against deism, but they functioned also as means of converting the unconvinced. The experience of Thomas Whittemore, converted by evidential arguments, exemplified the ideal blending of the rational and the practical.[16]

The Importance of Calvinism

A substantial part of the history of theology in early America was an extended debate, stretching over more than two centuries, about the meaning and the truth of Calvinism. Historians of American religion have departed from earlier assumptions that the Calvinist clergy of New England deserve a place of special privilege in the national religious narrative, but New England Calvinism, and other forms of Calvinist theology elsewhere, attained to such a position of dominance in highly respected institutions, from denominations to colleges and seminaries, that most subsequent theological movements had to define themselves in relation to the Calvinist traditions. In a history of American theology, the Calvinists loom large.

By the mid-nineteenth century, the two largest Calvinist denominations in colonial America, the Congregationalists and the Presbyterians, could no longer claim predominance in membership, and the Dutch Reformed had ascendancy only in regional ethnic enclaves. The Baptists stepped in to spread Calvinist theology to a large segment of the population, however, so Calvinism remained a flash point for theological controversy throughout the nation. In attempting to refute the varied forms of American Calvinism, its opponents altered the tone and emphasis of their own theological traditions. In their efforts at defense, Calvinists altered the meaning and force of Calvinism. Opponents claimed that Calvinism was, in the most negative sense of the word, speculative; Calvinists insisted it was eminently practical.

It would be more precise to refer to the "Reformed" rather than merely to the "Calvinist" tradition, for the French Protestant reformer of sixteenth-century Geneva, John Calvin, was only one important source of the theological tradition that so often bore his name. From early in the sixteenth century, the adherents of that tradition chose to designate themselves as Reformed, a name designed to distinguish them from Catholics, Lutherans, and the early Anabaptists. American Reformed thinkers took their cues not merely from Calvin and his Zurich contemporary Ulrich Zwingli but also from late-sixteenth-century European Calvinists who gave the theology a more systematic form, seventeenth-century Protestant scholastics who formulated it in ways amenable to teaching in the classroom, and generations of European theologians who revised it in response to continued criticism.

The defining mark of Reformed theology was its regard for the glory of God, which entailed a pronounced insistence on divine sovereignty. Calvin had taught that no event occurred apart from the all-powerful direction of God and that salvation depended entirely on the divine will. Convinced by scripture that God had chosen only a select number — the elect — for salvation, Calvin and his followers committed themselves to defend the doctrine of predestination, or election, against critics who charged that it implied an arbitrary and unjust God. While predestination was by no means the central theme of Reformed thought, it figured prominently in the debates between Calvinists and their opponents. But Reformed theologians themselves were more likely to write about the crippling effects of original sin and depravity, the power of grace to transform the sinful heart, the value of divine law as a guide to the Christian life, the insistence that saving truth came through scripture alone, and the necessity that the church order its ministry and structure in close accord with scriptural instruction. Each of these topics, however, could assume different nuances of meaning as the tradition changed over time.

One example is the debate within Reformed thought about the nature of human freedom. Despite often being associated with a simple denial of free will, Reformed theologians always insisted that human beings had sufficient freedom to make them responsible for their actions, though theologians continually redefined the meaning of freedom. In the early seventeenth century, American Calvinist preachers defined human beings as "causes by counsel," meaning that the human will and intellect always participated in any decision, whatever its ultimate cause might be. By the eighteenth century, Jonathan Edwards drew on British philosophy to define freedom as one's ability to do what one pleases, even though the will was always determined. In his distinction between moral and natural inability — the former situated within the will and the latter imposed from outside the will — Edwards helped define a style of reflection on the issue that divided Reformed theologians but proved sufficiently flexible to accommodate the needs of Reformed revivalists and to counter the charge that they were simple determinists. In its understanding of freedom, as of many other topics, the Reformed tradition proved to be flexible, able to absorb change without abandoning its identity.

The first century and a half of theology in America consisted largely of debates internal to the Reformed tradition. While seventeenth-century Quaker thought and eighteenth-century Anglicanism provided alternatives, the Reformed theologians, especially in New England, virtually monopolized theological publication and discussion. The opening chapters of this book give the impression that New England entirely dominated the colonial story, but that impression fades as other traditions later come into view. William Penn and Francis Daniel Pastorius in Pennsylvania, the Anglicans Thomas Bray and Devereux Jarratt, the Lutherans Justus Falckner and Henry Melchior Muhlenberg, the Universalists George de Benneville and John and Judith Murray, along with scores of other colonial figures, eventually speak their piece. They speak not as isolated figures, as they would in a strictly chronological narrative, but as participants in the traditions that later claimed them as founding figures. And yet even they often have to speak in opposition to the continuing power of Reformed theology in the religious culture.

By the early nineteenth century, Reformed theologians defended their views against an even wider array of critics. Some, like the New England "theologians of virtue" and the early Unitarians, emerged from within the Reformed tradition itself. But a host of other traditions attained greater self-definition by positioning themselves against the Calvinists. Catholics, Lutherans, Episcopalians, Methodists, Disciples, Freewill Baptists, Quakers, and Mormons represented the variety of theological traditions that, with the increasing of American religious diversity, began to present themselves as alternatives to Calvinist thought and piety.

The European Context

The interest in evidential Christianity did not distinguish Americans from Europeans. In the half century after Locke published *On the Reasonableness of Christianity*, the topic of theological rationality consumed theologians in England, and it continued to occupy European theologians well into the nineteenth century. Americans looked to Europe for refinements of evidential arguments and for expertise in every field of theology. Robert Baird assured Europeans that America provided a better market for their theology, particularly "works of a practical character," than their own regions. He thought that some of the best English treatises, for example, had "a wider circulation in the United States than in England itself." When Americans wrote their own theological texts, they usually entered a conversation that extended beyond American shores.[17]

The borrowing of ideas normally proceeded in only one direction, for only a small number of Americans attained a reputation in Europe and England. Among the few exceptions who drew an English readership were some of the seventeenth- and eighteenth-century New England Calvinists, especially Jonathan Edwards and Jonathan Dickinson, who attracted British attention. In the nineteenth century, such immigrant theologians as the German-educated Swiss Reformed historian Philip Schaff became known in Germany largely through his efforts to interpret American thought to German audiences, and on occasion an American, such as the liberal James Warley Miles of South Carolina, received the pleasant news that a German publisher had translated and reprinted his book. Baird had to concede that American theology was rarely "known beyond the country itself," though he named more than a dozen theologians who he thought would be recognized by European students of theology.[18]

Nonetheless, one of the characteristic features of American theology was its cosmopolitan ethos. American theologians knew the work of their European counterparts. Baird noted that the libraries of the learned — and of American colleges and seminaries — contained an ample "stock of such books imported from Europe." The constant influx of immigrants, including immigrant clergy, ensured that almost every nuance of European theology would have an admirer somewhere in America, and since Americans often traveled to Europe for theological study, they kept one another informed about biblical and theological scholarship there. The appearance of theological journals in the 1830s furnished a means through which Americans constantly interpreted and responded to European thought.[19]

Institutions: Theology as a Profession

It is no accident that most theological movements in nineteenth-century America must be described with denominational labels. To write the history of American theology during that period without reference to the denominations would be to tell a story detached from the self-understanding of most of the theologians. Denominational categories structure much of the organization of this book for the period after 1800. They were not the only categories that defined theological self-understanding, for theologians also represented traditions, such as Reformed or Lutheran, that could overflow particular denominational boundaries. They also participated in "schools" of thought, such as the New England theology, the New Haven theology, the Oberlin theology, the Princeton theology, or the Mercersburg theology. But neither the category of "tradition" nor that of "school" is adequate to grasp the function of theology in early America, which must be located within the institutional setting of denominationalism.

By the end of the eighteenth century, most American theologians understood themselves as advocates for a particular denomination. They wrote, for example, as Presbyterians, Baptists, or Catholics, and in debates the denominational identifications pushed toward the forefront. Debates also occurred within denominational boundaries, as competing factions strove to impose definitions on each other, but theological concepts and slogans usually functioned to distinguish one denomination from another in the religious marketplace. This emphasis on the institutional setting of theology highlights the fragmentation of Christian theology in America. To take theology seriously, and to recognize its denominational locus, is to emphasize the extent to which theological differences could separate Americans from each other, creating local tensions and disrupting national religious organizations.

To advance this argument is not to disregard the importance of localism — and therefore of the local religious congregation — as an important secondary institutional location for theology. Theologians thought of themselves as addressing the topics important for local congregations, and most early American theologians spent most of their lives serving a congregation. Questions of parish ministry often stood in the background of what the theologians wrote. This book draws its conclusions chiefly from the writings of 282 authors active between 1636 and 1865. Eighty-nine percent of them had experience as local ministers and priests. Twenty-three percent of the authors who published their books before 1789 spent some time teaching in colleges, but 90 percent of the authors for that period served in parishes. For the next seventy-five years after 1789, they still moved back and forth from parishes to schools, with 88 percent laboring for at least a portion of their careers as parish clergy.

On the whole, the clergy were among the most educated people in their communities. Between 1636 and 1718, 90 percent of the theologians had a collegiate education, and the same pattern continued for the next seventy-five years, when about 73 percent had college training. Even during the decades between 1789 and 1865, when populist theologians made their most successful efforts to break theology away from the educated, 70 percent of the theologians in this book studied in colleges, 32 percent in seminaries, and 5 percent in graduate institutions beyond the seminary.

After the American Revolution, theologians spent more of their time teaching in the academy. Between 1789 and 1865, 36 percent taught in colleges and 22 percent taught in seminaries, even though they still moved back and forth from the academy to the parish. The professionalization of theology as a calling distinguishable from parish ministry began symbolically with the creation of the first chairs of divinity at Harvard in 1721 and Yale in 1755, but it intensified after the Dutch Reformed founded a small seminary at New Brunswick (1784), the Catholics founded St. Mary's in Baltimore (1791), and the Congregationalists founded Andover in Massachusetts (1808).

The seminary — an institution designed to educate ministers and priests — soon rivaled the parish as a center of theological production. Between 1784 and 1859, the Protestant churches founded at least thirty-nine seminaries and the Catholics founded even more. Schaff reported in 1854 that "almost every responsible denomination and sect has one such seminary or more." Most were academically insignificant, with one or two faculty members teaching ten to twenty students, and Schaff echoed a common complaint when he wrote that "the tendency to multiply them is, in truth, only too strong," creating weak institutions that could barely be sustained.[20]

From Schaff's perspective, it seemed that the "honor of a theological professor" in America was "not very enviable," but he did note that some of the older schools, such as Andover and Princeton, had large endowments, faculties of four or five, fine libraries, and "literary energy." He thought that the seminary enabled "scientific theology" to find a "more genial soil," with the result that American theologians during the 1820s and 1830s "accomplished proportionally more" than their counterparts in England and Scotland.[21]

As theology became more professional, it became more specialized. Andover set the pattern for Protestants by adopting the fourfold curriculum of biblical, historical, systematic, and pastoral studies, and Park in 1844 called for more "division of labor" among theological professors on the grounds that no one could "treat so extensive a class of themes" as teachers at seminaries were expected to treat. Yet Park also lamented that the theologians at Andover had already become so specialized in their reading that "an individual theologian is often thoroughly versed in but a small part of the whole science," and that the specialists could not always get along with each other: "Every single department comes, in this way, to have its partizan-admirers . . . apt to become indifferent to all the others, if not openly opposed to them."[22]

The advance of specialization encouraged the formation of the quarterly journal, which by the 1830s became one of the chief means of scholarly theological debate. In the journals the theologians had free rein to explore what to most Americans would have been esoteric and obscure subjects, and the journal article soon rivaled the sermon and the monograph as the vehicle of influence and celebrity within educated theological circles. Between 1730 and 1830, Americans founded some 590 religious periodicals and newspapers, and their editors set the agenda for theological writing. At least 31 percent of the authors in this book who were active between 1789 and 1865 edited a religious journal. Some of the journals — like the *Biblical Repertory* (1825) at Princeton Seminary, *Bibliotheca Sacra* (1843) at Andover, the *Christian Spectator* (1826) at Yale Divinity School, the *Christian Examiner* (1831) at Harvard, the *Southern Presbyterian Review* (1847) at Columbia Seminary in South Carolina, the *Mercersburg Review* (1849) at Mercersburg, and *Brownson's Quarterly Review* (1838), which became after 1844 the leading Catholic journal — were among the most learned periodicals in America.

The Theological Populists

Theologians of the academy felt confident that theological learning would serve the cause of the church. From the beginnings of the seminary movement, however, its proponents had to contend with an opposition convinced that the preacher called and taught by God needed "no human instruction." Even some educated and socially prominent pastors, like the powerful New York Presbyterian Gardiner Spring, worried that the seminaries would promote "the ideal of a learned rather than a spiritual and useful ministry." Within the Presbyterian churches, which had large numbers of affluent and educated lay members, such a wariness of seminaries remained muted, but even there it could be troublesome. In making a plea in 1821 for the support of the seminary at Princeton, the Presbyterian Philip Lindsley voiced astonishment at the "general prejudice against learning" among "multitudes" of Americans: "I am aware that some notions are prevalent in our country which perhaps do not obtain to the same degree in any other. . . . It is fashionable to believe that learning is a dangerous thing in any hands. That the people can be better served without it than with it." Lindsley was contending with critics who claimed that seminaries were "better calculated to make mere scholars and fine gentlemen than hardy soldiers of the cross." Some of those critics would offer alternatives to the theology of the academy.[23]

Philip Schaff observed, with dismay, the popularity in America of self-educated theologians, unexposed to the traditions of the academy, who presumed to establish themselves as authorities in matters of religious truth. He lamented that "every theological vagabond and peddler may drive here his bungling trade, without passport of license, and sell his false ware at pleasure." George Burnap also regretted the presumption of these "illiterate" theologians and urged the educated clergy to combat them, but the tension between academic theologians, often located in seminaries and colleges, and populist theologians who were prone to ridicule the necessity for academic learning, created divisions that marked the course of theology in America especially after the eighteenth-century Revolution.[24]

Schaff tended to identify populist presumption with the American ethos, but he was identifying a pattern that had long been part of Christian tradition. When the Apostle Paul, in his letter to first-century Christians in Corinth, wrote that God had chosen the weak, the low, and the despised to confound the mighty and that God's truth rendered foolish the wisdom of the world, he produced a text that would continually embolden the unlearned to challenge the authority of the learned, including the learned theologians (1 Cor. 1:18, 26–27). The Pauline distinctions helped create a tradition within the church, represented sometimes even by learned theologians, like Tertullian in third-century North Africa, who contrasted the gospel with "human wisdom" and claimed that Jerusalem had nothing to do with Athens or the church with the academy. Tertullian was opposing certain forms of theological heresy, but it was easy to turn Paul's words against any learned theologians.[25]

Distrust of learned theologians perpetually bubbled up throughout the history of the church, and the *vox populi vox Dei* idea had a powerful appeal throughout the Middle Ages, but it became especially prominent in certain periods. The Lollards of fourteenth-century Britain, followers of the reformer John Wycliffe, attacked the learned clergy in a manner that received expression through the "plowman" tradition of poetry and protest. Sometimes drawing on Thomas Langland's fourteenth-century poem *Piers Plowman,* but also giving expression to a broader cultural sensibility, the champions of the plowman trope elevated the wisdom of the simple plowman, plain of speech, above the learning of the clergy. The tradition informed the anticlericalism of the sixteenth century, and it still flourished in the seventeenth century, when radical reformers such as William Dell in England, himself an educated college master, could declare that he would "rather hear a plain countryman speak in the church, that came from the plough, than the best orthodox minister."[26]

By then the image could merge with another trope, that of the "Mechanick" preacher, who stood in contrast to the "learned Academick" by virtue of an ability to be "intelligible unto all." Appropriating the Puritan defense of a "plain style" of preaching, the lay preachers of the civil war era in England claimed that they could proclaim the gospel more faithfully than the learned clergy. No small degree of the appeal of the English Quaker movement was its assertion of the authority of the unlearned. The Quaker founders George Fox and James Nayler presented the populist viewpoint in 1653 when they asserted that the true ministry was a gift of Jesus Christ and needed "no addition of human help and learning." They used the standard argument that Jesus "chose herdsmen, fishermen, and plowmen" as his disciples and "fitted them immediately without the help of man." The Quakers felt confident that their lack of academic theological training was an aid to the discovery of truth, not a disadvantage.[27]

This populist tradition rose to the surface in seventeenth-century New England, and it formed part of the rhetoric that supported lay exhorting in the eighteenth-century revivals. It appeared with special force, however, after the American Revolution. Inspired in part by the Revolution's egalitarian rhetoric, an enterprising company of religious leaders threw off any remnants of deference to the educated and powerful, including the educated theologians of the schools, seminaries, and fashionable pulpits. They spoke of their weariness of "subtle arguments" and their dislike of "obscure erudition" and insisted that the gospel of the New Testament had been intended not for "learned doctors" but for the "common people." They took up the ancient refrain that true Christian knowledge did not require academic learning and that the Bible was as clear to the uneducated farmer as to the genteel professor, indeed, that the learned and fashionable had lost sight of the gospel. Combining religious fervor with egalitarian social protest, they often broke away from established denominations and created alternative institutions, sometimes voicing an anticlerical animus, sometimes following authoritative clerical leaders, but always insisting that the "right of private judgment" made everyone a theologian. They promoted a theology of the common people.[28]

By no means did they reject theology. What made the populist groups important for the history of theology in America was that they produced their own theologians, who in the fluid and free atmosphere of religious disestablishment could also become the leaders of mass movements. John Murray and Hosea Ballou led a "Universalist" movement directed against Calvinist theology. Sharing some of the same complaints as the more literate Unitarians, they espoused a form of theological liberalism that appealed to small farmers and laboring people. Spreading outward from the middle colonies, an upstart Methodist movement employed a similar populist rhetoric, boasting that Methodists offered a theology for the common people. They had broken away from the Church of England in 1784, and on most questions they agreed doctrinally with the American Episcopalians, but they spoke in a different accent.

The populist theme found a home in the Baptist movement, but it became even more prominent in the "Christian" enthusiasm sparked in New England by the former Baptists Elias Smith and Abner Jones, who promised that a return to primitive Christianity would overcome denominational divisions and shatter unchristian innovations like theological seminaries. In Pennsylvania and Virginia, other "restorationists," led by Alexander Campbell and Barton W. Stone, employed the same populist theme as part of their movement to restore New Testament Christianity. Debates over theological populism left a lasting mark on African-American traditions. And the populist impulse also led in unconventional directions, as converts poured into Shaker, Hicksite Quaker, and Mormon communities that stretched the boundaries of traditional Christian understandings. Rather than reject theology, however, the populist movements promoted it, sometimes insisting that they alone had discovered the theological truth.

It did not take long for the populist groups to emulate the established denominations, build colleges, create seminaries, produce textbooks in systematic theology, and begin scholarly journals. Alexander Campbell's *Millennial Harbinger* (1830), the *Methodist Quarterly Review* (1840), the *Universalist Quarterly and General Review* (1844), and the *Quarterly Review of the Methodist Episcopal Church, South* (1846) would eventually become indistinguishable in style and format from the journals connected to the seminaries. In fact, the theologians who wrote for those journals, whether self-educated or trained at the new denominational schools, adopted many of the ideas, as well as the institutions, of the academic theologians.

Both groups — the professionals and the populists — advertised the practicality of theology and shared in the quest for the reasonable. The populists scorned the academics as elitists, but rather than rejecting the academic interest in the reasonableness of revelation they announced the superior rationality of their own convictions. The academics deplored the upstarts, but they and their populist opponents had a similar understanding of what reasonableness meant. And the populists rarely questioned the underlying assumptions of the academic rational orthodoxy. With the exception of the majority of Baptists, they usually opposed the Calvinism that held sway in the Reformed schools, but they normally accepted the evidential logic, the confidence in natural theology, and the commonsense philosophy that guided much of the academic quest for reasonableness.

The Argument

The structure of this book reflects the interweaving themes of the argument. Part 1 treats primarily the early Reformed traditions. Part 2 explores theologians and traditions that employed the Baconian evidentialist style. Part 3 looks at theologians who moved away from the Baconian form of evidentialism, especially its assumption that miracle and prophecy — the older external arguments — sufficed as proofs of a divine revelation. Within Part 2, the organization of the chapters reflects both an institutional and a cultural argument. By organizing this part of the book according to denominational traditions, these chapters advance the claim that denominationalism remained the setting for most theological writing in antebellum America. In the juxtaposition of the chapters in this section, moreover, the book tries to suggest the importance of the cultural attitudes that marked the self-understanding of theologians. A chapter on Unitarians, who valued a learned clergy, leads into a chapter on Universalists, who distrusted such learning. A chapter on Episcopal thought, again representing a tradition that sought a learned clergy, stands beside the chapter on the theology of the early Methodists, who employed the rhetoric of populism as part of their movement away from their Anglican heritage. The subsequent chapters on Baptists, Christians, African-Americans, Quakers, Shakers, and Mormons continue to explore groups that defined themselves in part with populist rhetoric, even though the Baptists and Christians, like the Methodists, produced early leaders who pushed toward theological learning and an educated clergy.

When the book reaches the chapters on Lutheran and Catholic thought, it begins to treat groups that raised serious questions about Baconian evidentialism as it was generally understood, even though many theologians in both traditions continued to use evidential arguments. By the time we reach the transcendentalists, Horace Bushnell, the Mercersburg theologians, and Orestes Brownson in his Catholic period, however, we have moved beyond Baconian evidentialist assumptions toward religious thinkers who proposed more intuitive modes of evidence and rationality.

The book moves from around 1636, when New England Calvinists fell into serious theological controversy, to a symbolic terminus around 1865, when the Civil War came to a close. It could seem strange to conclude a history of theology with a war that had little to do with theological matters, but the end point is not arbitrary. The antislavery dispute that helped to bring on that war also raised questions for theology and the theologians, even though Charles Darwin's *Origin of Species,* published in 1859, would later overshadow them. The postwar era introduced challenges to theology from science, historical criticism, and philosophical understandings of metaphysics and historical development, but the southern proslavery literal reading of scripture and the northern abolitionist search for its deeper principles would long compete as alternatives for understanding what theology was to mean in American religion.

PART I

Calvinist Origins

2

The New England Calvinists

Theology as an enterprise of sustained reflection on claims of Christian truth began in America with the Calvinist clergy of seventeenth-century New England. Long before their arrival, European Catholics and English Anglicans had conducted a Christian mission to the New World, but it was the coming of the English Calvinists to New England that produced the first substantial corpus of theological writings — literature that would set the agenda for a debate that continued more than three centuries.

They thought of theology as a delicate balance of human reasoning and divine biblical revelation, an appeal to "the evidence of scripture and reason." They aspired to give reason its due credit while subordinating it always to the revealed Word. What allowed this aspiration was the Calvinist doctrine of God's accommodation to human finitude, which was also an accommodation to reason. John Calvin had employed the idea of accommodation to designate God's willingness to adapt both his self-revelation and his saving activity to the capacities of the finite and sinful creature. It provided for Calvinist theologians a religious warrant for drawing on philosophical insight, but it required that reason acknowledge its limited scope. The effort to maintain this balance would become a permanent feature of most early American theology.[1]

The New England Calvinists also stood in the tradition that saw theology as practical. Thomas Hooker in Connecticut expressed a consensus when he explained that theology was a discipline of "godliness," which produced not only insight into "the nature of things," but also "practicall wisdome." Thomas Shepard in Cambridge argued that a speculative knowledge alone — or a "notional" or "discursive" knowledge that satisfied the understanding without altering the will — remained insufficient. The aim of divinity required the enlightening of the understanding, but it served "chiefly" as "the art and rule of the will." It taught how "to live to God."[2]

The Theologians

In early New England, the theologians were preachers who assumed that the pastoral office required theological learning, and a respectable number of them wrote texts in theology. During the seventeenth century, 34 percent of the New England clergy published at least one tract or treatise. A small group — comprising 5 percent of clergy — each published ten or more works. Most of them wrote short pieces designed for polemical or devotional purposes; only 8 percent of the seventeenth-century publications exceeded one hundred pages. Sixty-nine percent were sermons. In the first half of the century only Samuel Stone, the minister in Hartford, wrote a "Whole Body of Divinity" covering all the standard topics in a systematic fashion. He completed it in 1656, but he never had it printed.[3]

These publications began a tradition that would make New England the center of theological writing in America for more than a century. Only in the mid-eighteenth century would significant numbers of clergy from other regions gain access to resources that would support theological scholarship and writing. Entry into theological debate at levels beyond the local required printing presses, easy means of transporting manuscripts to printers abroad, or the intellectual interchange that was possible only where populations were sufficiently dense to allow networks of conversation. While the middle and southern colonies produced a few isolated instances of seventeenth-century theology, most of it came from New England. Throughout the century, moreover, most Americans who read theology imported it from abroad, and even the New England clergy depended heavily on theologians in Britain and on the continent.

In the first generation, six theologians assumed the dominant voices in the theological debates. Of the six, none was more brilliant — or more erratic — than John Cotton (1584–1652), one of two in the first generation of immigrant clergy to hold the Bachelor of Divinity degree, attesting to seven years of study beyond the two liberal arts degrees. Admired as a linguist and biblical scholar, he had attracted the "high applause of Academical wits" at the university of Cambridge before he decided to ally himself with the church reformers who were becoming known as Puritans. His admirers claimed to know "scarce any that excelled him in the knowledge of the Arts and Tongues, and in all kind of learning divine and humane." After he fled from England to Boston in 1633, his English opponent Thomas Edwards conceded that Cotton had to be "the prime man of them all in New England."[4]

Some would have given the title to another Cambridge graduate, Thomas Hooker (ca. 1586–1647). Suspended and hounded from his Essex pulpit by Archbishop William Laud, who despised his notions of church reform, Hooker had spent two years in Holland, where he met the best-known scholar among the English émigrés, the theologian William Ames, who said later that "though he had been acquainted with many scholars of divers nations, yet he had never met with Mr. Hooker's equal, either for preaching or disputing." Hooker came to America in the same year and on the same boat as John Cotton, and both men drew attention for their books defending the New England churches, but within three years they found themselves on opposite sides in theological controversies.[5]

Thomas Shepard (1604–49), who arrived in the Massachusetts Bay colony in 1635 and became the minister to the congregation in New Town (Cambridge), would never have ranked himself as the intellectual equal of either Cotton or Hooker. Despite his Cambridge degree, he bemoaned his weakness of presence and utterance, and he struck observers as "a poor, weak, pale-complexioned man." He was introspective, a worrier, and easily discouraged, but he was fully as influential as Cotton or Hooker. During the 1630s he became the colony's most effective critic of Cotton's theological position, and his critique retained its authority among New England theologians for fully a century.[6]

When the elders needed someone to answer the queries of Dutch theologians about the polity of the colonial churches, they chose John Norton (1606–63), the teacher in the Ipswich congregation, who also published in 1654 the most technical of the early New England theological treatises, *The Orthodox Evangelist*. Another Cambridge graduate, who left England because he hated the Anglican ceremonies, Norton attained a certain celebrity — and notoriety — through his mordant polemic against the Quakers, but he also had a knack for theological precision that made him a valuable ally during the debates of the 1630s, when he stood with the majority against John Cotton. He admired Cotton, however, and later defended him by insisting that he had been the innocent victim of "heterodox spirits" who had deceived him. By that time, Norton had succeeded Cotton as the teacher of the church in Boston.[7]

Peter Bulkeley (1583–1659), the pastor in Concord, might have had the educational credentials to match Cotton's; some evidence suggests that he also earned the Bachelor of Divinity degree at Cambridge. In any event, he had both the confidence and the acumen to confront Cotton, and his colleagues chose him, along with Hooker, to moderate the 1637 synod that settled New England's first crucial theological division. His important work — *The Gospel Covenant* (1651) — came from his immersion in the controversy, but it had staying power in New England theology because apart from Cotton's publications it was the most detailed treatise on covenant doctrine to be written in the colonies.[8]

Finally, Richard Mather (1596–1669), the teacher at Dorchester, wrote the first draft of the "Cambridge Platform" (1646), the document that defined the early New England church order. Though he stayed only six months at Oxford University, Mather mastered the linguistic and technical skills to join the theological leaders in the colonies, and his *Church-Government and Church-Covenant Discussed* (1643) offered the first elaborate defense of the New England Way of church polity. Respected as a "mighty man," with a powerful voice and impressive physical presence, he made his mark locally as a theologian through his *Summe of Certain Sermons,* still another response to the issues of the 1630s.[9]

All six were Puritan reformers of the church who wrote theology for a popular audience, a vernacular theology composed not in the Latin of the university disputations but in English. The turn from Latin to the vernacular as the language of theology marked a momentous transition in western theological history, and it had implications beyond those envisioned by its first proponents. The Puritan preachers also communicated their theology mainly in sermons, delivered in a "plain style" calculated to ensure that the largest possible audience would understand. Theology was a discipline for the people.[10]

It was decidedly not, however, a discipline of the people. Most of the New England clergy were graduates of Cambridge; all were unusually learned by the community standards of New England, and all of them thought that theology demanded such learning. No calling, Norton said, required "more Abilities, or a larger measure of humane knowledge." The best theologians would know Hebrew, Latin, Greek, history, the Bible, and "encyclopedia," the discipline that grounded and organized the liberal arts. Theology was, in their estimation, a practical art, its wisdom available even to the unlearned, but it required of the theologian the ability to combine two worlds of discourse — one biblical, the other grounded in reason. Only the theologically educated had the logical and exegetical skills to maintain the balance without falling into error.[11]

Scripture

In his *Institutes of the Christian Religion,* John Calvin taught that a true knowledge of God and of human nature came only through the revelation in scripture. Calvin agreed with the medieval Catholic tradition that the created order contained innumerable signs of God's reality and presence — signs that reason should have recognized — but he thought that the mind was so limited by its finitude and so darkened by sin that its efforts to attain knowledge of God apart from the biblical revelation led only to idolatry. In scripture, God provided the correcting lenses that rescued reason from its fallen state. Among New England theologians, this conclusion was accepted as axiomatic.

The aim in New England was a biblical theology, bound at every point to the teachings of scripture. The clergy agreed that the biblical revelation opened the eyes of understanding "far above the capacity of Reason." They thought of the scriptures as divinely inspired, and they assumed that the inspiration preserved the biblical authors from all error. If the "holy pen-men" were inspired, asked Shepard, "how could they erre"?[12]

The Puritan clergy also brought to America an attitude toward the authority of scripture that distinguished them from the Anglican establishment in England. They read the Bible as a source of binding precedents that were to determine the shape of the church. They were biblical "primitivists," eager to discard "human inventions" — from vestments and ceremonies to bishops and deans — for which they could find no biblical precedent. "No new traditions," said Cotton, "must be thrust upon us." They were bound to the "first institution" of God, the church as it was described in scripture. They were determined to "walk in the old way," by which they meant the biblical way.[13]

They believed, therefore, that all theological doctrines had to flow from scriptural exegesis, and they accepted the customary Calvinist tenet that scripture interpreted itself. To understand difficult passages, the interpreter had to read them in the light of clearer ones. This maxim produced a primary reliance on what they called the literal or "historical" reading of the text. Unlike medieval exegetes, who also read the Bible as an allegory, a repository of hidden moral truths, and a catalog of references to the New Jerusalem, the New England clergy always appealed primarily to what Hooker called "the letter" — the grammatical meaning of the text read literally.[14]

They did not deny, however, that the same text could bear complex meanings, so in addition to searching for express commandments and propositions, they also used other principles of interpretation. Their second approach was to employ the "exemplary" reading of the Bible, the interpretation of scriptural examples as "patterns for imitation." They often read biblical episodes as precedents that permitted or required a course of action. Critics of Puritan reform in England had argued that it was wrong "to argue *a facto ad jus* (of a deed or example to make a law)," but Thomas Shepard thought that biblical examples could easily be refined into general laws that prescribed perfect rules for even "the most petty occasions of our lives."[15]

A third method of biblical reading was to practice the ancient method of typological interpretation. A type, everyone agreed, was "some outward or sensible thing ordained of God under the Old Testament, to represent and hold forth something of Christ in the New." Noah, for example, who saved his household in the ark, typified Christ, who saved his people through the church; and the Jewish exodus from Egypt prefigured the Christian deliverance from bondage to sin and Satan. The clergy usually drew a clear distinction between typical and exemplary readings. Types were outward signs of future spiritual realities; examples were not. Types pointed beyond themselves; examples bore their meanings on the surface. The visible types were abolished when they found fulfillment in their Christian antitypes; examples endured as perpetual models.[16]

Yet almost everyone agreed that some types could be partially exemplary and some examples partially typical. A synod at Cambridge in 1646 took note of the claim that the Jewish kings in the Old Testament were types and therefore were no longer "of force for our imitation." They conceded that if Israel's rulers were types "strictly taken," they only "shadow[ed] out Christs kingly power," providing no exemplary model for future magistrates. But they concluded that a ruler like Solomon might be a type of Christ in his kingly office over the temple but not in "all the Kingly offices" he performed. In some of his offices, Solomon provided exemplary precedents for New England magistrates. John Cotton made a similar distinction when he defended the singing of psalms in New England churches. If the psalms of Israel had been merely ceremonial types, then Christians could no longer sing them, for with the coming of Christ the types would have been abolished; but the Jewish psalms had been both types and examples, and their exemplary features warranted their continuation.[17]

The literal, exemplary, and typological readings held the New England theologians close to the biblical text, but a fourth interpretive method helped them link the language of the Bible to the conclusions of reason. John Cotton explained that the exegete might discern the revelation of God's will in scripture "by Proportion, or deduction, by Consequence, as well as by expresse Commandment, or Example." This "proportional" way of reading allowed the interpreter to combine two fields of discourse: when one part of a syllogism came from the Bible, Cotton explained, the conclusion embodied a "divine proposition" even though the other premise came from "our human knowledge." A truth could be grounded in the Word in two ways, wrote Thomas Hooker: "Either in the letter, or included in the sense," and the sense could include any "rational inference" that might be "brought out of the Scripture by necessary circumstance." Cotton's formulation suggested that the art of divinity combined the languages of scripture and the other arts; Hooker's offered reassurance that nonbiblical expressions might still fittingly convey the biblical sense.[18]

Reason

The rule for the proportional reading of scripture suggested a place for reason in theology, and the New England clergy combined two different ways of understanding rationality. Both the Protestant scholastic recovery of Aristotle — and of philosophy, more generally — and the sixteenth-century humanist reform of logic offered grounds for thinking of reason as a guide alongside the biblical revelation. The Puritans derived some of their ways of thinking about theology from both Aristotelian scholasticism and sixteenth-century humanism.

The clergy bore a debt to scholastic traditions. They read not only medieval Catholic scholastic theologians but also the contemporary Reformed, Lutheran, and Catholic writers who had cast theology into a form suitable for instruction in academies and universities. Designed to impress a confessional identity on competing Christian groups, this Protestant "school theology" emerged in the late sixteenth century under the guidance of academics who wrote manuals of theology for classroom use, employed philosophical concepts to explain theological ideas, and guarded against error by emphasizing precise distinctions and the interconnections between doctrines. In their own university education, the New England clergy had learned their theology through scholastic techniques, especially through oral disputations, and had absorbed a scholastic vocabulary. They carried on their debates with Platonic and Aristotelian ideas of substance, accident, potency, act, matter, and form. When precision became necessary, they turned to such scholastic distinctions as those between God's ordained and absolute power, habit and act, efficiency and sufficiency, immanent and transient acts, and material, formal, efficient, and final causes.

Like the scholastics, therefore, the New England theologians employed the customary rational arguments to demonstrate the authenticity of the scriptural revelation. They began the long tradition in American theology of justifying Christian faith by appeal to the time-honored evidences. Shepard pointed out that even Calvin tried "to prove the Scripture to be the Word of God by reason," and while Cotton cautioned that the faith wrought by the Spirit was higher than "any science gotten by demonstration," he laid out the historical evidences for the authenticity of scripture.[19]

It would be misleading, however, to describe the New England Calvinists merely as students of scholastic theology. They drew also on other sources, including especially the logical reforms of the French humanist Petrus Ramus (1515–72), a critic of scholasticism who reviled, revised, and simplified Aristotle in order to generate a new method for learning and teaching "easily and clearly." Ramus and his admirers taught the New Englanders how to envision theology as the apex of the arts and then how to organize their theological reflections according to the clear canons of "method."[20]

They did this first through the discipline of *technometria*, also known as *technologia* or encyclopedia, a philosophical attempt to define the arts and determine their relations to each other and their practical uses. It was axiomatic to Ramists that all the arts — logic, grammar, rhetoric, mathematics, physics, and divinity — had a practical aim. Ramus defined logic, for example, as the art of discoursing well, grammar as the art of speaking well, and rhetoric as the art of expressing oneself well. All of these arts were subservient to a larger practical end — the end of "living well" — and this was the domain of theology. Each art was distinct, with its own rules, and yet all the arts were interrelated. No conclusion in physics or mathematics could be devoid of significance for theology. Every art had the aim of *eupraxia* — well-doing — and theology taught the highest *eupraxia*.

Ramus outlined the method for ensuring that theology attained its end. Like every other art, theology required logic, the most general of the arts. But it did not require the subtleties of Aristotelian logic as it was understood in seventeenth-century universities. Ramist logic was a discipline designed to "invent" and then to "dispose" arguments, which were in Ramist logic any conceptual "elements" employed in thought — or as Ramus explained, "an argument is that which is affected to argue anything." What counted as an argument depended on what was being argued — an argument could be as general as the principle of causation or as particular as an observation about the visible world — but to "invent" an argument was simply to discover it, whether through observation and experience or by accepting the testimony of others.[21]

It was the second step — disposition or "judgment" — that made Ramist logic distinctive. To dispose an argument was first to give it a clear definition and then to analyze it by discovering the conceptions implicit within it. Ramus believed that every argument could be subdivided into at least two more specific ideas, which in turn could also be analyzed into further dichotomies, in a chain that moved continually from the general toward the specific. Having defined and dichotomized the arguments, the Ramist could then combine them, either in syllogisms or, better, in axioms linked in a self-evident chain of argumentation that could be displayed in an outline chart making the point manifestly clear. These procedures Ramus called "method," and they reappeared in theological argumentation in New England for more than a century.[22]

The theologians assumed that the truths revealed in scripture would be consistent with the truths conveyed by all the arts, and their notions of technologia implied a natural theology that had its roots in Platonic philosophy. The Ramists often taught that Art was a term for the wisdom of God; it therefore constituted the law by which God created the world. Through the act of creation, the archetype in the divine mind expressed itself in the created order as the *entype,* the essence of a thing, which could be taken into the human mind as an *ectype* — a conceptual idea — that not only grasped the entype in the creature but also dimly recognized the traces of the archetype in the divine mind. To perceive the world rightly was to recognize something about the *ens primum,* the Prime Being, from which everything else has come.[23]

With technologia in the background, the New England preachers could insist that "the book of the creatures," legible by the reason, provided a real knowledge of God. Thomas Hooker noted the reach of this natural theology: "There are some things of God that are revealed in the creation of the world. . . . A man that looketh into the fabrike of the world, and seeth the making of the earth, and the Sea, and all things therein, hee cannot say but God hath beene here, an infinite wisdom, and an almightie power hath been here. . . ." Thomas Shepard recited the familiar arguments for God's existence — design and order and the need for a sufficient cause to account for the world — and he thought that the "workmanship" of the creation should prove to any rational person the reality of a God worthy of worship.[24]

The clergy invariably added, however, that this natural knowledge remained insufficient, even misleading, without the revelation of God in scripture. The book of the creatures said nothing of God as reconciled, or of Christ as redeemer, or of the mercies of grace. Natural truth, as Norton put it, might be found in the creature, moral truth in the law of nature, and legal truth in the law written in the conscience, but the evangelical truth of God's merciful grace in Christ was revealed only in the Bible. However revealing nature might be, it remained a "dark" book. Only the Bible discovered God "in all his glorious attributes."[25]

To make matters more complicated, the ministers also agreed that the deepest knowledge of God came only through the motions of the Spirit that elicited a true faith. A true knowledge of God was no simple matter of the understanding. When Shepard as a young man suffered the mental agony of skepticism, he discovered that "strength of reason would commonly convince my understanding that there was a God, but I felt it utterly insufficient to perswade my will of it unlesse it was by fits." Hooker told his readers that the understanding might discern the "excellency" in God but that only the will could taste the "goodness" in God. To know God was not merely to entertain correct thoughts; the true knowledge of God was a passionate knowledge, a form of knowing that embraced the heart and will.[26]

Calvin had said that the internal witness of the Spirit certified the authority of the biblical Word, and it became a standard Calvinist tenet that Word and Spirit stood in a polar relation: scripture truly became Word as the Spirit led the reader into its depths, and the Spirit never dispensed revelations independent of the Word. This was a safeguard against fanatics who might boast of direct revelations from God. "Gods Spirit goes alwaies," said Hooker, "with the word." Shepard taught that to seek the Spirit "without or beside the word" was to stand on the "precipice of all delusion."[27]

Long before Cotton left England, he defined the distinction between the two forms of theological knowledge: to believe "that" a God exists, he wrote, was an act of the understanding, but to believe "on" God was an act also of the will, which required an altering of the disposition by the inner movement of the Spirit. The theologian's task as Cotton saw it was to promote both forms of knowledge while helping readers and hearers press beyond a "superficial" knowledge, consisting simply of "opinion," toward a more profound form of knowing, grounded in the will as well as the understanding, that Cotton called "acquaintance." It was his way of saying that theology was useless unless it was practical.[28]

Accommodation

Underlying Calvinist reflection on reason, revelation, and practicality in the seventeenth century was Calvin's idea of accommodation. Through the incarnation in Christ, through scripture, through the provision of visible and tangible means of grace that were adapted to the embodied nature of the creature, and through a willingness to respect the integrity and order of the creation, God continually displayed an accommodation to creatureliness. Unlike Calvin, New England Calvinists rarely used the word "accommodation" — Norton, for example, preferred the term "condescension" — but they employed the idea in precisely the ways that Calvin had.[29]

Divine accommodation was necessary because of human finitude, sinful-

ness, and inability. The creature could not conceive the essence of God "because of the great distance between him and us." Finitude alone ensured the
inconceivability of infinitude. Sinfulness imposed further limits on unaided
human reason. Following the teaching of the Apostle Paul in the New Testament that every human being was born full of sin, with no power to do
anything good, Calvinists taught that sinfulness distorted any seeming knowledge of God.[30]

They thought of sin as both original and actual. It was original because the
race had fallen when Adam fell. Because Adam had been their representative,
God had "imputed" his sin to his heirs: "We are all in Adam," Shepard explained, "as a whole country in a parliament man; the whole country doth
what he doeth." The original sin then gave rise to an incessant round of actual
sins. In asserting the doctrine of imputation as an explanation of original sin
and guilt — and the true ground of condemnation — the New Englanders employed a concept, linked to a particular reading of Paul's letter to the Romans
(Rom. 5:12–13), that came into prominence in the late sixteenth century. The
idea that universal guilt for Adam's sin resulted from God's "imputing" it to
Adam's posterity originated among late medieval interpreters of Paul, but it
found its main support among a few sixteenth-century Catholics, a larger
number of Lutherans, and a wide array of Calvinists, including Theodore Beza
(1519–1605), Calvin's successor in Geneva. Debates over imputation would
divide theologians in America for three centuries, but for the New England
Calvinists the doctrine helped explain the need for divine accommodation.[31]

By the seventeenth century, Calvinists talked about accommodation with
precise distinctions made possible by scholastic refinements. The New England ministers recovered, first, the medieval distinction between the *potentia
dei absoluta* (the absolute power of God) and the *potentia dei ordinata* (the
ordained power of God). According to God's absolute power, God might have
done — or might do — anything consistent with the divine nature, even provide
salvation apart from redemption in Christ. But God had determined, Norton
observed, to work with finite creatures "not according to his absolute Power,
but according to the nature of the subject." By revealing the scheme of salvation in scripture and by entering into finite existence as a human being, God
had so ordered his activity as to accept a self-limiting of the divine power. God
had, in effect, promised to act always in accord with that limitation, ordaining
limits on his own actions by declaring that he would conform them to the
pattern revealed in Christ.[32]

The first-generation ministers spoke of Christ with the standard concepts of
Reformed Christology. To them Christ was the incarnation of the second
Person of the Trinitarian God. They understood him in accord with the way

they understood the Trinity as the inner life of a God whom they described as "increated being," "a Being that is not from any Being," infinite, eternal, unchanging. This increated Being was without all internal composition — since composition and succession implied lack and imperfection — but its eternal perfection comprised three internal relations or "Persons." Norton warned readers, however, not to be misled by the term Person, which was merely a similitude.[33]

The ministers sometimes tried to show that the three Persons were necessary in this unique kind of Being: an eternal Being with understanding had to understand something even when nothing else existed. The first Person, then, was God understanding himself; the second was God understood of himself, and the third was God beloved of himself. The three Persons — Father, Son, Spirit — therefore shared the same essence, the same Godhead, but they subsisted in different relations: the Father begot the Son, the Son was begotten of the Father, the Spirit proceeded from the Father and the Son. The language came from the Christological controversies of the early church, but to the New England clergy it seemed a natural inference from the texts of the New Testament.[34]

Trinitarian speculation in Calvinist orthodoxy could become highly abstract, and the New England ministers read and cited the Trinitarian doctrines of such scholastic theologians as Francis Junius and Bartholomaus Keckermann, but in their sermons they appealed to Trinitarian themes mainly when they wanted to explain the practical doctrines of salvation. What was important for their congregations to know was that the glory of the Father consisted in creation and election, the glory of the Son in redemption, and the glory of the Spirit in "the great work of application." The drama of salvation began when the Father and Son agreed to redeem the creation from the effects of the fall. The ministers sometimes described this inter-Trinitarian agreement as a covenant of redemption.[35]

They explained redemption, as well, through recourse to the standard formulas of Calvinist orthodoxy. The Son became incarnate in the God-man, Jesus Christ, whose dual nature as human and divine made him a fit mediator. He accomplished his mediation through his three "offices": as prophet (by teaching divine truth), priest (by sacrificing himself and interceding with the Father), and king (by governing the church and reigning at God's right hand). Through these offices he effected his mediatorial "humiliation" and "exaltation." The humiliation consisted of his perfect obedience, active and passive. Through the active obedience he fulfilled the law that Adam and his progeny had broken; through the passive he offered himself as a sacrifice on the cross. The exaltation was his resurrection, ascension to heaven, and eventual return in judgment. To explain the significance of all this, the clergy returned to the explanation that Anselm of Canterbury had formulated in the twelfth century: because Jesus Christ was both a human being and the increated God, his obedience counted as a human satisfaction of an infinite debt beyond the capacity of any other human being to pay.[36]

This incarnation in Christ therefore represented a divine condescension to human understanding. In choosing self-revelation by becoming incarnate in a human being, God revealed himself, as Norton put it, "according to our manner and measure." Incarnation meant a decision to respect the integrity, the capacities, and the limits of the natural human creature.[37]

A second instance of the divine accommodation was manifest in the ordering of the world through "second causes." The New England Calvinists taught that God normally governed the world through "ordinary wayes and means," second causes, defined as natural and historical events that caused other events to occur. They distinguished between this ordinary providence and the "extraordinary" providence — the miraculous — by which God intervened directly in the world without employing secondary means. Because Catholics claimed that miracles in the history of the church confirmed the truth of Catholic doctrines, Protestants routinely argued that extraordinary providences designed to confirm church teaching had ceased after the apostolic period. It was true, Hooker conceded, that God could still use "extraordinary" means, and Shepard's autobiography contained reports of "miraculous" providences. Arguing against Catholics, Cotton claimed that the ministry of "one poore Protestant Minister" could evince "bundels of miracles." Normally, however, Puritan theologians looked for God in the "ordinary way of his providence."[38]

Critics of Calvinism felt that the doctrine of predestination belied the idea of divine accommodation to human capacities because it seemed to negate the significance of the human will and understanding. One critic was a pastor and professor of theology at Leyden in Holland, Jacobus Arminius (1559–1609), who set himself in opposition to the "high Calvinism" of the Reformed scholastics. Against their doctrine of particular election, the view that God had eternally elected particular persons to salvation, he proposed that God decreed to save all believers and that Christ died for all people, so that grace sufficient for faith was given to all. He believed that faith was the fruit of grace and that the will had no power to believe unless empowered by grace, but the sinful will could resist, and the sinner bore the responsibility for the sin. The Synod of Dort in Holland (1618–19), which condemned Arminius, set one standard of Calvinist orthodoxy with its teaching that all human beings were totally depraved, that divine election was unconditional, that Christ died only for the elect, that saving grace was irresistible, and that true elect saints never fell away.[39]

The New England preachers subscribed to the tenets of Dort. The salvation of the elect and the reprobation of the damned resulted from an eternal decree of God, before time began, logically prior to any foresight of good or evil in the creature, prior to the decree to create a world, prior to the decree to permit the fall, prior to the decree to send the Son to redeem the world. Shepard said that he was willing to accept this belief even if it meant that only one in a thousand had been chosen to escape God's wrath. Cotton had some reservations during the 1620s, but the English scholastic theologian William Twisse set him straight.[40]

The doctrine seemed a proper inference from the New Testament. According to Paul, God would either harden the heart or display mercy on whomever he chose, molding the clay as he wished, to show either his wrath or his mercy (Rom. 9:19–25). God had "destined" the saints for adoption "according to the good pleasure of his will" (Eph. 1:5–6). Jesus had announced that no one could come to him unless "drawn by the Father" (John 6:44). Dozens of texts appeared to Calvinist theologians to confirm predestinarian doctrine, which also affirmed that saving grace came entirely as a gift.

Calvinist theologians were intent, however, on showing that predestination did not negate human volition and clerical exhortation to the unsaved. They turned, therefore, as a further implication of the idea of accommodation, to the doctrine of the means of grace. By assuming human nature, Norton said, God had declared an intention to deal with human beings through "external means" adapted to human capacities. Christ had made use of audible words, visible actions, and tangible objects like bread and wine "for the calling home and building up of his Elect." He still called and nurtured the elect through such means.[41]

"Because we are reasonable creatures," the clergy taught, "God proceeds with us in the use of means." Accommodation meant that God dealt with men and women not as "stocks or senseless creatures" but as creatures of will, understanding, and affection. This meant that regeneration usually began through an appeal to the understanding, since the will could "imbrace nothing but what the understanding presents to it." But the point of exhortation was to reach the will; the understanding was only the "underling of the will." This was Hooker's view: "For howsoever faith be begun in the understanding, yet the perfection of it is from the will." In the commencement disputations at Harvard, some students argued that the will always obeyed the dictates of the understanding; others argued for a voluntarist position that accorded the will both autonomy and self-direction. In sermons, the ministers blurred such neat distinctions, for they dealt there with the fallen will and understanding. Yet they still assumed that both faculties were active in salvation because the means of grace were designed to appeal to them.[42]

God's accommodation implied a certain kind of human freedom. One could speak of compulsion, Hooker noted, only if the will were forced against its own inclination, but God never compelled the will to act against its inclination. God rather changed the inclination. The point allowed the ministers to think of the human being as a "cause by counsel," a creature who acted "according to the free-motion of his own will." As long as people acted without external constraint, and according to their own will, human liberty remained intact, even though without divine grace the will inevitably chose evil. The determinism of sovereign grace also imposed no external necessity on the will; it rather inclined the will, Norton said, "according to the nature and liberty of it": God determineth the Will sutably and agreeably to its own Nature, i.e., freely. He so determineth the Will, as the Will determineth it self. . . . The Efficiency of God offereth no violence, nor changeth the nature of things, but governeth them according to their own natures." As Hooker put it, God would not save men and women "against their will." The will was "determined and undoubtedly carried to its object," but it never consented against its inclination.[43]

Covenant

To maintain the paradoxes implicit in the idea of accommodation, the preachers drew on the doctrine of the covenant. From God's "special way of governing rational creatures," wrote William Ames in his *Marrow of Sacred Divinity*, "there arises a covenant between God and them." Calvin had used the notion of covenant to emphasize the unity of the Old and New Testaments and to interpret the meaning of the sacraments, but the New England theologians drew especially on a tradition of covenantal thought that originated in Germany. In 1562 a German Reformed theologian at Heidelberg, Zacharias Ursinus, began to distinguish between the legal covenant *(foedus naturae)* made with Adam, requiring obedience to moral law as a condition of salvation, and a covenant of grace *(foedus gratiae)*, made known by revelation to Abraham, that offered salvation as a gift to faith alone. The distinction appealed to the English Puritan refugee Thomas Cartwright, who visited Heidelberg in 1573, and when Cartwright's friend Dudley Fenner, who already cherished Ramist dichotomies, published in Geneva in 1585 his *Sacra Theologia*, he described in English for the first time a covenant of grace and a covenant of works. By that time, the idea of the dual covenants was attracting other Reformed theologians in Germany, Holland, France, and England. The influential Puritan preacher at Great St. Andrews in Cambridge, William Perkins, made the idea a commonplace among the learned clerical reformers in the Church of England.[44]

In New England, Peter Bulkeley's *Gospel Covenant* defined a covenant as an agreement with mutual conditions. In the covenant of works with Adam, he explained, God promised eternal happiness on the condition of perfect obedience. Adam's fall broke that covenant, though without annulling its demands. These demands, evident both in the natural law engraved on the conscience and in the moral laws of scripture, still required obedience, but it could no longer earn salvation. In the covenant of grace made with Abraham, however, the promise of eternal happiness rested on the condition of faith alone.[45]

At one level, the idea of dual covenants functioned as a warning against reliance on good works for salvation. Since such an error would "disanull the nature of the Covenant of grace, and turn it into a covenant of works," the preachers emphasized the differences. The covenant of works required obedience for salvation; the covenant of grace required only faith in Christ and commanded good works only "that thereby we should glorifie God, and manifest it that we are made righteous by faith." The first covenant cast men and women on their own abilities; the second provided the grace of the Spirit. The first could ensure an orderly society, but only the second could ensure an eternal place in the kingdom of God. To preach the covenant of grace was to restate the Protestant conviction that salvation came from grace alone.[46]

Yet the covenant of works remained in effect, and this meant, on another level, that preachers could issue ethical appeals and urge moral reforms. The preachers could say, with Hooker, that the "legal covenant" was "not continued with us . . . not required at our hands" as a means of salvation but that everyone stood under its command. Bulkeley reminded readers that God's purpose was immutable and that the "first covenant" also remained unchangeable. This meant, first, that New Englanders whom God had not yet called effectually into salvation remained entirely under a covenant of works and subject to its moral restraints. It meant also, according to Cotton, that the burden of moral expectation should drive the sensitive conscience to Christ. It was "the usuall manner of God to give a Covenant of Grace by leading men first into a Covenant of works." Living under the covenant of works, Shepard explained, they would discover their sinfulness, and their "terrors, and fears, and hopes" would turn them to Christ. And it meant, third, that even Christians safely within the covenant of grace remained subject to the moral substance of the first covenant. Abolished as a "covenant of life," Shepard said, the law still remained as a "Rule of Life." These were the traditional three uses of the law in Reformed theology; covenantal language provided a lively way to restate them.[47]

The ambiguities of covenantal thought allowed it to preserve conflicting religious values. This became especially evident in the distinctions with which the preachers refined the doctrine. They argued, for instance, that a covenant was both conditional and absolute. The language of conditionality permitted the preachers to urge their hearers to seek faith. "Labor to get faith," Hooker said. "Labor to yield to the . . . condition of the promises." In a similar way, it allowed them to comfort the troubled by showing them how to "test their estate." Since God promised salvation on the condition of faith, worried saints could seek signs of faith and obedience in themselves as grounds of assurance that they had met the condition.[48]

The language of conditionality could sound as if it subverted the absoluteness of God's promise to the elect. Cotton granted the other ministers their right to "speak of conditions," but he admonished them to remember that "the Lord doth undertake both for his own part and for our parts also." The effectual calling of the elect was not "built upon any Conditionall Promise" but rested on the "absolute free Promise unto the Soule" of the saint. But despite Cotton's implication to the contrary, the other ministers agreed that everything depended on God's free grace. Shepard taught that the covenant of grace was "absolute": God had "undertaken to fulfill the Covenant absolutely" for his elect. Hooker spoke often of covenant conditions, but he added that "the Lord, as he requires the condition of thee, so he worketh the condition in thee." Bulkeley insisted that the God who required the conditions also fulfilled them "for us."[49]

Bulkeley pointed out the advantage of the equivocal language. By saying that the covenant was conditional, the preachers reminded the faithful and faithless that salvation would "not be brought to pass but by means, in which mans care is required." By saying that the covenant was absolute, they reaffirmed the Reformed doctrine that the promise of salvation would "certainely be fulfilled" through the sovereign grace of God. Covenantalism was a way of affirming both things at the same time.[50]

The covenant language had a broad scope. It encompassed not only the intricacies of salvation but also the institutional arrangements of colonial society. The theologians defined the church as a covenanted community of visible saints, and they published during the 1630s and 1640s at least a dozen books, treatises, and sermons defending New England's way of organizing churches through public covenants. But covenantalism also interpreted other New England social institutions. "Whatever power one hath over another, if it be not by way of conquest or naturall relation, (as the father over the childe)," wrote Thomas Shepard, "it is by covenant." This meant, said Hooker, that covenants made through "natural free engagements" governed the relationships between prince and people, husbands and wives, masters and servants, all confederations, and all corporations. Every social relationship grounded in mutual free consent presupposed a covenant, whether implicit or explicit.[51]

The allure of covenant thought was that it maintained tensions. It reconciled conflicting themes in the biblical accounts and conflicting social impulses in the community. But the harmony that it was designed to produce, whether conceptual or social, proved elusive. From one perspective, it makes sense to speak of a "New England Mind" among the learned. They shared common convictions about a host of matters. But it is equally accurate to depict the history of theology in seventeenth-century New England as a troubled progression marked by continual dispute, often grounded in disagreements about the covenant.

Conflict

PREPARATION

Shortly after 1633 the churches in New England began to insist that candidates for membership give a credible narration of their conversion; the church voted on the credibility. This meant that social practice in New England intensified a clerical interest that had emerged among such English Puritans as William Perkins and Richard Rogers in the late sixteenth century as an attempt to deal with the pastoral problems connected to the doctrine of predestination. It focused attention on the *ordo salutis,* the order of salvation, or the stages of the spiritual life. The notion of an "order" of salvation reflected the idea of accommodation — the sense that God had "freely bounded himself" to observe the order revealed in scripture. It proved to be a troublesome notion.[52]

Among the colonial analysts of the order of salvation, Thomas Hooker was the most prolific. Several of his books described the stages of regeneration: first the preparatory stages of conviction and humiliation for sin, and then vocation (God's effectual gracious call through which the decree of election took effect in the prepared soul), faith (the soul's responsive act of trust), justification (God's imputing to the soul the merits of Christ, acquitting and accepting the sinner as righteous), ingrafting or union with Christ (a participation in the spiritual good of Christ), adoption (by which Christ gave the believer his Spirit), sanctification (the gracious creation of holy dispositions and inclinations that restored the image of God), and glorification (the final blessedness of the saints in heaven). Hooker could devote an entire book to a single stage, and though his vocabulary shifted in the three decades between his brief essay introducing John Rogers's *Doctrine of Faith* in 1627 and his grand summation in *The Application of Redemption* in 1656, he was consistent throughout his career.

Along with other New England ministers, Hooker received both praise and criticism for the emphasis he placed on the preparatory stage. "Preparation" meant driving the soul to contrition and humiliation, and most of the New Englanders agreed that it was necessary. John Cotton, preaching in England, said that "the Spirit of grace will not come but into an heart in some measure prepared," and he continued after moving to New England to insist that God prepared sinners by dashing their worldly confidence. Bulkeley thought it possible that faith might be created "without any preparation," but he too pointed out that God's "usuall course" was to break the heart before scattering the seeds of faith. The idea of preparation captured the sense of the biblical texts that described a feeling of bondage and brokenness as preliminary to grace.[53]

Hooker believed that preparation required a ministry that would uncover sin. That meant preaching the law. Cotton agreed: "There are a generation of preachers," he complained in an English sermon, "that would now have no Law preached, but onely to draw men on to Christ, by the love of Christ." Such smooth and comforting sermons were worthless; the heart had to be wounded unto death.[54]

Thomas Shepard therefore tried, one of his hearers recalled, "to pound our hearts all to pieces." This dismayed Giles Firmin, who lived about fifteen years in New England before becoming a Presbyterian minister in England. Firmin thought it was a mistake "to preach and print of such strong convictions, such dreadful legal terrors, deep sorrows and humblings, as being the common road through which men go that come to Christ," and he charged that Shepard's sermons cast people into despair and distraction, but Shepard held to his position that the heart had to be "prepared" for conversion. What especially offended Firmin was the contention that the unregenerated soul should, using Hooker's phrase, be "content to bear the extent of damnation." Firmin thought that only a saint could be that unselfish, but he also thought the idea odd even for saints. Hooker and Shepard replied that a soul "truly prepared and empty" would willingly abandon itself to be damned.[55]

Hooker thought that such "legal humiliations" were the harbingers of faith, but he also went a step further, arguing that self-denial of that magnitude suggested "a saving worke of Christ" in the soul even before the onset of faith. It followed that troubled souls might find in their very despair a sign of "special" grace. But when Hooker tried in 1636 to persuade his colleagues in New England, most of them seem to have demurred. One observer reported that this was only "Hooker's position, the rest of the Ministers do not concurr with him." John Cotton suggested that others — though not he — shared Hooker's view, but neither Shepard nor Bulkeley accepted the doctrine of "saving pre-paratives," and Norton made it clear that for him preparation was a matter of "common grace," not of the "special grace" that imparted "saving qualifications."[56]

Neither Hooker nor the other ministers ever meant to suggest that sinners could prepare their own hearts. The doctrine of preparation referred to divine activity, not to natural human effort. "Nothing but grace doth all, workes all, prepares all," Hooker wrote. "He that doth prepare is the Lord; he that doth receive the work, and is prepared, is the soules of those whom God hath elected to salvation." Preparation was not a matter of human striving. "These saving preparations," he wrote, "are no acts of mine, therefore not my fruit. . . . They are wrought in me, not by me." To the New England clergy, any suggestion that human beings might prepare their own hearts for salvation would have suggested the error of Arminius, who contended that the natural will, aided only by common grace, could accept or reject the divine offer of salvation. They ridiculed such a "naked Arminian illumination and persuasion."[57]

ANTINOMIANS

Sometime in 1634 Anne Hutchinson, a prominent Bostonian, charged that the ministers themselves relied on a covenant of works. In weekly meetings of sixty or more of the faithful, she dissected the ministers' sermons and disparaged their doctrines. She began with meetings of women; before long she organized a second meeting for men. Having traveled to New England with her family in order to remain under the ministry of John Cotton, she told her classes that in New England Cotton alone taught the true gospel. The others were "legalists" who taught people to look to good works as evidence for their sound spiritual estate.

The result was a dispute that called into question the accepted assumptions about the order of salvation and produced a flurry of theological writing. Thomas Shepard wrote his *Theses Sabbaticae* and his *Parable of the Ten Virgins Opened* partly to confute the Hutchinsonians. Richard Mather's *Summe of Certain Sermons,* John Norton's *Orthodox Evangelist,* and Peter Bulkeley's *Gospel-Covenant* emerged out of the crisis. The emotions overflowed outside clerical studies and into the streets. At one point the dispute became so intense that the magistrates disarmed Anne Hutchinson's Boston followers. It was so politically charged that it led to the defeat of Governor Henry Vane.

At one level the quarrel was over a single question: whether sanctification provided evidence of justification. But the answer bore implications for almost every stage in the order of salvation, for the quarrel was also about what it meant to "close with Christ." Cotton remarked in later years that "it was the judgment of some of place, in the Countrey, that such a Doctrin of union [with

Christ], and evidencing of Union, as was held forth by mee, was the Trojan Horse, out of which all the erroneous Opinions and differences of the Country did issue forth." Union with Christ was a pivotal moment in the order of salvation, and a dispute over closing with Christ raised questions about the equilibrium of nature and grace in New England theology.[58]

In sermons delivered around 1636 but published about two decades later as *The New Covenant* (1654) and *A Treatise of the Covenant of Grace* (1659), Cotton told his congregation that all spiritual gifts sprang immediately from union with the Person of Christ and the Holy Spirit; that the exercise of those gifts was really the activity of the Spirit, who "Acteth the gifts given to us"; and that without first discerning the presence of Christ in them, Christians could not discern either their justification or their sanctification. Instead of telling his people to look to their sanctification as evidence of true faith or of union with Christ, he told them that they had to discern their justifying faith and union with Christ before they could know whether their sanctification was genuine. This discernment could occur only through "the revelation of the holy Ghost," the immediate Seal of the Spirit, a power "above" even the biblical Word.[59]

To Thomas Shepard, who heard Cotton lecture in Boston, Cotton sounded like the sixteenth-century English Familists, who had claimed immediate revelations. He wrote asking Cotton whether he really thought that troubled saints doubtful of their conversion had to wait for an immediate "revelation of the spirit" rather than taking comfort in biblical promises. Shepard believed, as did the other ministers, that when doubtful Christians found in themselves the works of holiness to which biblical promises of salvation had been made, they could have some assurance of saving grace. But Cotton replied that Christians must "close" with Christ before they could rely on any promise. He added that although the revelation of the Spirit was never against the biblical Word, it still had a power "above, and beyond the letter of the word."[60]

To Peter Bulkeley, the problem lay in Cotton's suggestion that all spiritual gifts, including faith, sprang from a prior union with Christ. In the standard Reformed position, which Bulkeley shared, justifying faith, a human act made possible by grace, preceded the union with Christ. Empowered by an infused principle of grace, the soul could move through trust into unity with Christ. Like most of the other ministers, Bulkeley assumed distinctions among a habit of faith infused into the soul by the Spirit, an act of faith that realized and perfected the habit, and a "faith of assurance" that discerned both the gift and the response. The habit and the act preceded union with Christ; the faith of assurance followed it. Such a doctrine enabled Reformed theologians to affirm the priority of an irresistible grace (faith as an infused habit) without surrendering the idea that a human activity (faith as an act) served as the "instrumental" (not the "efficient") cause of union with Christ. But when Bulkeley raised the issue, Cotton replied that the habit of faith infused by the Spirit was itself the union with Christ and that the act of faith was merely the believer's "consenting" to this union. What Cotton called the act of faith was what the other ministers called the "faith of assurance"—the faith by which the faithful trusted that they had been justified.[61]

In December, the ministers confronted Cotton with sixteen questions, and his reply raised other questions. They argued that justifying faith preceded justification as its instrumental cause. In that sense they could speak of faith as a condition of entry into the covenant of grace. In Cotton's view, however, faith followed justification: it was "justifying" only in that it apprehended the prior justifying act of God. He was wary of making it sound as if any human activity—even an act of faith made possible by irresistible grace—might merit justification. He disliked speaking of faith as a condition of the covenant. "All the conditions," he said, "are fulfilled in Christ," who was himself the "first and last condition."[62]

Cotton also disliked the common view of what it meant to be sanctified. The other ministers thought of sanctification as the presence within the justified believer of "habits"—infused by the Spirit—that issued in holy acts. Such habits subsisted in the believer; they were "inherent" in the soul, the means by which Christ could be said to dwell within the believer. But Cotton thought of sanctification as the indwelling not of created graces, as means by which Christ lived in the believer, but of Christ himself, immediately through his Spirit.[63]

The other ministers were accustomed to telling their congregations to look to the conditional promises affixed to the sanctifying graces. They could "trust" that were among the elect if they kept the commandments, loved their neighbors, and found dispositions of joy and peace in their souls. But Cotton noted—and his opponents conceded—that hypocrites could seem to have all the right dispositions. Although he used the conditional promises for exhortation, he thought they had no place in discerning justification. The immediate witness of the Spirit to the soul was the only ground for assurance: "No man can see his gifts and duties of sanctification in himself, but hee must first have seen Christ by faith."[64]

In his initial rejoinder to the other ministers, Cotton appealed to the authority of John Calvin, and some interpreters have viewed the controversy as the result of Cotton's attempt to defend the original Calvinist vision from creeping Arminianism. But the disputants were arguing about questions that Calvin had not asked and with a vocabulary that Calvin had not used. This was a debate conducted with the philosophical distinctions of Reformed scholasticism, and to the extent that new language reshapes old thoughts, both sides departed from Calvin. But in spirit, Cotton departed the farthest, for he cast aside the fragile equilibrium that both Calvin and most of his Reformed successors, committed to the idea of God's accommodation to the creature, had tried to maintain between nature and grace. In the theology that Cotton preached in 1636, the Spirit overwhelmed the creature.

The dispute might have been only a technical argument among theologians had not Anne Hutchinson accused the colonial ministers of preaching a covenant of works. Here was a layperson — a woman, at that — presuming to teach both men and women that most of the theologians were wrong. She drew the support of at least 187 men and perhaps a greater number of women, if we can so infer from John Winthrop's complaint that the Hutchinsonians "commonly laboured to worke first upon women, being (as they conceived) the weaker to resist." Her followers described the ministers as "Popish Factors, Scribes, Pharisees, and Opposers of Christ."[65]

Anne Hutchinson's true convictions lie hidden beneath documents written and preserved by her opponents, but Cotton said eventually that she had gone beyond him. Like Cotton, she exalted union with Christ above all else. "The foundation she laid," Winthrop noted later, "was (or rather seemed to be) Christ and Free-Grace." But she lacked Cotton's inclination to wrap the piety in scholastic distinctions. Because she accused the ministers of legalism and disparaged the covenant of works, she and her party came to be known as antinomians.[66]

Cotton said that the saints were spiritually active only when Christ acted within them; Hutchinson reportedly taught that "Christ was all, did all, and the soule remained alwayes as a dead Organ." Cotton denied that obedience to the law could signify a gracious state; she may have taught that "the law is no rule of life to a Christian." Cotton identified habitual faith and the union with Christ; she was accused of saying that the Christian lived not by faith in Christ but by the "faith of Christ." Whatever Cotton said, her rhetoric seemed to take her one step further — or so it appeared to her antagonists.[67]

Cotton had said that the witness of the Spirit transcended the letter of the scripture; Hutchinson was charged with having said that "the whole Scripture in the Letter of it held forth nothing but a Covenant of works." She seems to have meant that only the saints who received an immediate witness of the Spirit could discern the meaning of the biblical text. Thomas Leverett, the ruling elder of the Boston church, quoted her as saying that until the New England ministers "received the witness of the spirit they could not preach a covenant of grace so clearly." She implicitly subordinated scripture to the Spirit; some of her followers were more explicit.[68]

She further upset the ministers by denying the natural immortality of the soul. Drawing on two scriptural passages, she distinguished between a natural soul that perished with the body and an immortal spirit, redeemed by Christ, that returned to God (Eccles. 3:13–21; Heb. 4). When she debated the issue with the ministers at her trial before the Boston church, she changed her mind several times about crucial definitions, but her main point, that the "naturall" had to be sharply distinguished from the spiritual, remained consistent with her views in the debate over nature and grace.[69]

Her great mistake before the magistrates was to claim immediate revelations. Under pressure from her judges she asserted that she could distinguish between the voice of Christ and the voice of Moses in scripture by means of "an immediate revelation" from God, "the voice of his own spirit to my soul." Some of the magistrates believed that she and her followers were saying that "their owne revelations of particular events were as infallible as the Scripture." Fearing the consequences of spiritist immediacy, the magistrates banished her.[70]

By this time, Cotton claimed that the antinomians had misunderstood and deceived him. In 1637 he declared himself ready to say that "the Spirit doth Evidence our Justification in both wayes, sometime in an absolute Promise, sometime in a conditionall." Shepard thought that he still equivocated. He commented in 1639 that "Mr. Cotton repents not, but is hid only." The English Presbyterian Robert Baylie believed that the New Englanders let matters drop "to save Mr. Cotton's credit," but by the 1640s the New England chronicler Edward Johnson expressed a common opinion when he wrote that Cotton's disciples misrepresented him. Cotton's polemics against Baptists in 1647 enhanced his reputation. Second-generation ministers admired Cotton, but they also took care not to repeat his mistakes.[71]

THE END TIMES

Within three years of the Hutchinson trial, Cotton returned to the forefront of theological innovation, this time as a herald of an imminent era of glory for the church. He had studied the biblical prophecies ever since he delivered in England, sometime between 1624 and 1632, the sermons later published in his *Brief Exposition of the Whole Book of Canticles, or Song of Solomon* (1642), in which he read the Hebrew love poem as a prophetic history of the church from the time of Solomon to the judgment. Read typologically, the poem revealed to him, through its figures and similitudes, the "approaching days of Reformation" that would lead to a glorious transformation "of Church and State, according to the Rule and Pattern of the Word of God."[72]

Between 1639 and 1642 Cotton amplified his millennialism in lectures that he eventually turned into four books on the "prophetic" reading of history. His congregation in Boston undoubtedly interpreted them, as did Cotton, with an eye cast toward political turbulence in Scotland and England. They dealt not only with the future millennium but also with other "prophetic" and eschatological topics that explained the course of history as divine plan. They uncovered the hidden meanings of such events as the invasion of Rome by Goths and Vandals, the imperial policies of Justinian and Charlemagne, and the troubles of monarchs from Theodosius to Elizabeth.[73]

Cotton believed that the world stood on the verge of a millennial age — a period, foreshadowed in Revelation 20:6, during which Satan would be restrained, the true churches would triumph, and the Catholics would be "damned from the face of the churches." These events would follow a spiritual coming of Christ — not yet the "personall bodily presence" of the final return — who would use both magistrates and ministers to build the New Jerusalem "on earth." It would mark the "resurrection" (Rev. 20) of the churches, enabling them to restore fully the ordinances and practices of the primitive churches through which they could ready themselves for the final judgment when Christ came for the last time. Cotton predicted that future events around 1655 might inaugurate the "further gradual accomplishment and fulfilling of the prophecies." New England had no special function in these final events; most of the action would take place in Arabia, Assyria, and Egypt. But he told his listeners that the time was hastening fast — "many of you may live to see it."[74]

Speculation about the end time and the return of Christ had perennially recurred in Christian theology, but it had not usually taken millennial forms. Before 1640 all Reformed theologians expected a return of Christ at the time of the last judgment, but most ignored or disparaged millennial theories, which predicted an extended earthly reign of Christ and the saints, lasting roughly a thousand years during which an earthly "New Jerusalem" would oversee the flourishing of the church. John Foxe in the sixteenth century, for instance, popularized eschatological topics in his *Actes and Monuments,* relating world history to the biblical prophecies in order to show the imminence of the second coming of Christ. But Foxe described the New Jerusalem as a heavenly, not a terrestrial, reality, and he hinted only vaguely at the doctrine that God would establish a new, transformed, historical order on this earth.[75]

The main source in the background of Cotton's theory of the end time was the English theologian Thomas Brightman (1562–1607), who had initiated renewed millennial interest by arguing in his *Revelation of the Apocalyps* (1609) and other commentaries on Daniel and Canticles that Christ, through his brightness and power, would bring about a supernatural transformation of earthly society, a golden age, an earthly New Jerusalem, long before his second coming and the end time. Recovering ideas that went back to Joachim of Fiore and the Franciscans, Brightman contended that this Middle Advent, an effusion of Christ's supernatural power, perhaps beginning in 1650, would unite the church and the state in a holy commonwealth that would flourish until Christ returned about six hundred years later to judge the living and the dead and translate this ideal kingdom into heaven.

Brightman had no monopoly on millennial speculation. The Cambridge scholar Joseph Mede (1586–1638) and the German theologian John Henry Alsted also predicted in 1627 an imminent millennial reign. Mede thought that it would follow the second coming and last judgment, Alsted that it would precede them. Other theologians who took up the theme in the late 1630s also reached conflicting conclusions. Seventeenth-century theologians could attain no common understanding of the biblical language referring to the final events. But the English civil wars of the 1640s issued in a flurry of millennial speculation, and Cotton was caught up in the excitement.[76]

Cotton's sermons probably helped generate the flurry of interest to which Thomas Lechford referred in 1640 when he observed that people in the Bay Colony talked of "nothing but Antichrist and the Man of Sin," but he failed to generate any consensus about the details of the end time. Anne Bradstreet during the 1640s wrote poetry about the impending destruction of Turkey, but she did not link the event to any explicit millennialism. Thomas Parker in Newbury expounded the prophecies of Daniel, but he repudiated Brightman's scenario and predicted an earlier time for the second coming. Thomas Shepard agreed that Christ would return twice, first to call the Jews, gather the gentiles, and destroy the Antichrist through the "brightness of the truth" and then, much later, to judge the good and the bad at the final resurrection. Nonetheless, his *Parable of the Ten Virgins Opened*, written between 1636 and 1640, concentrated more on the second coming than on the millennial era. In 1647, Shepard did cite Brightman when he announced that recent conversions of American Indians might be a preparative for the "brighter day."[77]

A few wondered whether the "first fruits" of the millennium might be visible in New England, and Captain Edward Johnson of Woburn pleaded with English Presbyterians to change their policies, on the grounds that New England governance and discipline foreshadowed the millennial kingdom, but no theologian attached that much significance to New England. Some New Englanders became uneasy about millennial speculation. Around 1650, John Eliot, the minister in Roxbury and a disciple of Cotton, composed in his *Christian Commonwealth* an elaborate description of the social and political order of the coming New Jerusalem. In 1661 the General Court suppressed it because the restoration of Charles II made it unwise to promote utopian political commonwealths. The most popular description of the end time in colonial New England, Michael Wigglesworth's poetic "Day of Doom," made no reference to an earthly millennial kingdom.[78]

The potential for conflict about the millennium became clear after Roger Williams (1603–83) arrived in Boston in 1631 as a separatist minister questing for purity. Because the congregation in Boston "would not make a public declaration of their repentance for having communion with the churches of England," Williams promptly moved to Salem and became a teacher in the separatist Salem church. Millennialism was not Williams's primary interest. His references to it were infrequent. But his theological struggles with John Cotton displayed the ways in which New Englanders could use millennial ideas for conflicting purposes.[79]

During his two-year stay in Salem, Williams accused the other ministers and churches of inconsistency and impurity. They were inconsistent because they left the English parishes without conceding that they were separating from false churches; they were impure because they allowed — even compelled — the unclean to touch holy things. They made the ungodly take oaths, even though oaths were holy acts of worship, forbidden to the unclean. They encouraged the unregenerate to pray, even though prayer was an act of worship reserved for the holy. They encouraged prayer in New England families, even though the presence of unconverted family members would profane the prayers. After he left Salem, Williams would argue that the unregenerate had no more right to hear sermons than to receive the Lord's Supper, for sermons too were among the holy things that could be profaned by the unclean.[80]

Williams's case for separation from the Church of England rested on his primitivist interpretation of the Bible. He thought that "the first *Churches of Christ Jesus*" had established "the *lights, patternes and precedents*" for "all succeeding Ages." For Williams, biblical precedent required Christians to separate themselves from uncleanness, and his debate over separatism with John Cotton, which began with an exchange of letters in 1636, consisted mainly of commentary on biblical precedents: Paul told the Corinthians to separate from idolaters (2 Cor. 6:17); John conveyed angelic admonitions for Christians to come out of Babylon (Rev. 18:4); Ephesian Christians confessed all their sins when they entered the church (Acts 19:18).[81]

His debate with Cotton over liberty of conscience also dealt largely with how to interpret the Bible. Williams condemned religious persecution mainly because scripture taught that Christ was "King alone over conscience." The precepts of the primitive church confirmed him in that judgment. Christ said that the anti-Christian tares should be allowed to grow up with the godly wheat until the harvest at the final judgment (Matt. 13), and he reproved his disciples when they wanted fire from heaven to destroy his enemies (Luke 9:54–55). In the same spirit, Paul taught the early church that the weapons of spiritual warfare were not carnal but only spiritual (2 Cor. 10:4).[82]

When Cotton argued that magistrates had protected Israel's worship, Williams countered with typology. The magistrates of Israel, he said, were types of Christ; their swords of steel prefigured the spiritual swords of Christ's ministers. Cotton used typological exegesis too, but he pressed the point that some types had an exemplary force. The kings of Israel were typical in some respects, exemplary in others. Williams replied that Israel had been a holy church and nation only as a type to foreshadow the incarnation. After the coming of Christ, who brought the types to fulfillment, holy nations and sanctified princes no longer existed.[83]

After 1639, when Williams became a Baptist for a few months, he decided that true churches also existed no longer. The church's apostasy under Constantine in the fourth century had cut off the succession of true churches and true ministers, inaugurating a 1,260-year reign of the Antichrist (Rev. 11:3–12), a period lacking any order of ministry that conformed to "the first *Institution of the Lord Jesus*." Neither the ministry nor the church had been restored. During the "wilderness" period, which extended from the time of the apostasy into the present, God's truth depended on "witnesses" (Rev. 11:3–12) who would testify against "Inventions" that subverted the "true Pattern" of the primitive past. Williams probably viewed himself as such a witness.[84]

The witnesses, however, could not hope to restore the true church or to convert the Jews, the Indians, or the Irish. All this had to await God's restoration of his "apostles," who would appear only after the conclusion of the "great businesse" between Christ and the Antichrist and the reestablishing of "Zion and Jerusalem." Williams anticipated a "thousand year raign of Christ" and a "flourishing of the new Jerusalem upon the earth (Rev. 20:21–22) before the end of the world," but he saw those events as entirely discontinuous with the work of the false ministers and false churches that now represented Christendom. Only after a dreadful "slaughter of the Witnesses" would the millennium commence. For now, Williams could only testify to the truth and wait as a seeker for the true church that was not yet here.[85]

Both Cotton and Williams agreed that the millennium would restore the primitive New Testament church, but while Cotton expected it to validate the New England ecclesiastical order, Williams thought it would overthrow New England's institutions. Thomas Shepard could see evangelism as preparing the way for the millennium; Williams thought such evangelism futile, since it brought people into churches that would be revealed at the millennium to be no churches at all. Cotton and Shepard thought that millennial prophecies encouraged ministers and magistrates to work together to stamp out irreligion; Williams thought that governmental coercion in religion contradicted the millennial future and that even in the millennial age Christ would allow the irreligious to flourish in the society, though not to worship in the true church.

On one additional point, Williams disagreed with the New England clergy. By 1652 he had decided that part of the problem of the churches was that they sought educated theologians, trained in "Seminaries for the Ministry," as their leaders. Convinced that it was wrong for the churches to defer to men with "superstitious Degrees and Titles of Divinity," he excoriated a "hireling ministry" that exalted itself over common Christians. Without dismissing the value of human learning, Williams became convinced that churches erred when they insisted on the human learning of the universities as a precondition for ministry. He insisted that God chose men of "low degree," not the "Wise" and "Noble," as his ambassadors. Like some of the followers of Anne Hutchinson, Williams concluded that true wisdom might lie with the uneducated. It was a sentiment that would recur repeatedly in the history of American theology.[86]

BAPTISM

Calvinists considered sacraments as prime examples of the means of grace expressive of the divine accommodation, but from the beginning the ideal of the covenanted church raised sacramental questions. Most of the ministers agreed that baptism, for instance, sealed the church covenant; they agreed also that it sealed the covenant of grace. But as Calvinists they had to avoid the appearance of suggesting that every baptized soul had an automatic claim to God's mercy, so they had to make some distinctions. It proved difficult to attain a consensus on what those distinctions implied.

Baptism, they said, depended entirely on "the efficacy of the covenant." Its "utmost power" was "to signifie, seale, and exhibit" the spiritual good of the covenant of grace. The sacrament did not create the covenant; it did not enter infants into the covenant, for the covenant holiness of the children of covenanted saints existed prior to their baptism; and it did not seal to every infant all the covenant promises.[87]

The covenant of grace, Hooker explained, could be distinguished into a "double covenant": "an inward and an outward." In the inward covenant stood the faithful elect, who by baptism were sealed for salvation. For others, however, the sacrament sealed only an external covenant membership, and since Hooker held that "covenant grace is one thing, and saving grace is another," he was able to protect himself from insinuations that he overstated the efficacy of the sacrament.[88]

It sometimes appeared that the ministers could say only that baptism was a pledge and engagement to obedience, but they never intended to deny that baptism was a means of grace, and in the Cambridge Platform of 1648, they asserted explicitly that covenanted, baptized children were "in a more hope-full way of attayning regenerating grace." John Cotton could caution that baptism was annexed only to an outward covenant and then turn around and proclaim that the outward covenant entitled the children of the faithful to the means by which the elect among them would eventually experience "the grace of the new birth." Shepard could even say that the external covenant, sealed by baptism, was in some sense "absolute" and that therefore its baptismal seal also had an absolute quality. It was wrong to suppose that "Circumcision and Baptism seal only conditionally." God gave to "many" baptized children "such hearts as they shall not be able to refuse the good" of the means of grace.[89]

Puritan parents therefore wished to present their children for baptismal sealing, hopeful that it would eventuate later in conversion. But the theology created practical problems, which emerged as early as 1634, when Cotton allowed a grandfather — a church member — to claim the right of baptism for his grandchild, whose parents stood outside the church covenant. Cotton insisted that the grandfather promise to raise the child, but his action was an exception to his normal rule that an infant's right to baptism ordinarily came from the covenant of "the next immediate parents (or of one of them at least)." The clergy reached no consensus, and the problems intensified when many of the baptized grew to adulthood without attesting that God had converted their hearts. Could they bring their own infants for baptism? Or did their inability to testify to conversion indicate that they been cast from the cove-nant? Were their children to have no title to the means of grace? In 1657 the Court of Massachusetts convened the elders, who affirmed the permanent membership of children baptized in New England churches. The elders ac-corded such baptized but unconverted members the right, upon becoming parents, to have their offspring baptized.[90]

The decision so disturbed traditionalists that the court called a synod in 1662 to determine a final solution. The gathering reaffirmed the earlier deci-sion. Only the regenerate could receive the Lord's Supper; only regenerate males could vote on church matters. But the baptized retained some church privileges even when they remained unregenerate: they could stand under the "Watch, Discipline, and Government" of the church, and they could present their children for baptism. The synod's defenders viewed the policy as the only way to maintain a commitment to both infant baptism and the principle of regenerate membership, which reserved the Lord's Supper for the converted. Critics of the decision would later charge the synod with having created a "Half-Way Covenant."[91]

In the ensuing debates, three issues divided the ministers. Proponents of the synod claimed that baptism sealed a permanent "personal" membership. Richard Mather, who wrote the major apologia, said that since the parents in question were "regularly baptized in their own persons," they remained "Church members in their own persons." Unless expelled for notorious sins, they therefore retained a right to at least some church privileges. But John Davenport of New Haven replied that "personall" members had to take hold of the covenant through "personall faith made visible." He thought that baptized children were only "mediate" members, whose standing in the church was incomplete and provisional until they underwent conversion. Their baptism alone conferred no right to bring their children for baptismal sealing.[92]

Proponents pointed out that baptism signified a promise. Jonathan Mitchell, successor to Thomas Shepard in Cambridge, reminded the dissenters that baptism sealed "unto the party baptized, all the good of the Covenant to be in season communicated and enjoyed." At the very least, added John Allin of Dedham, one had to assume that the promise was still extended to the unregenerate second generation: "Yea are they not Baptized into Christ? Are not the Blood and Benefits of Christ Sealed up to them in Baptism?" But Davenport replied that the Spirit was a "voluntary Agent, and therefore likened to the wind which bloweth where it listeth," impervious to coercion by covenants and covenant seals. He emphasized not the promise but the obligation signified by baptism: it bound "the infant-seed of Confederates to various Gospel duties." Under a strong "obligation" to perform their baptismal duties, the unregenerate children of the second generation had failed.[93]

Defenders of the synod responded with typological exegesis. Since circumcision was a type for baptism, and since the circumcision with which Abraham sealed his covenant with God had continued through posterity, then baptism also conveyed a title to church privileges that did not evaporate over time. But some of the dissenters were no longer impressed by typological warrants. Charles Chauncy, the president of Harvard College, dismissed the "similitude." Even if the sacrament had been implicitly instituted in the rite of circumcision, he said, the typological analogy was worthless without an additional "explicit and plain" command. Increase Mather opposed the synodical theologians on their own typological grounds, but Davenport shared Chauncy's skepticism: the types no longer convinced.[94]

The New England churches struggled over the halfway covenant for more than a century. The covenant theology divided them as much as it united them. But covenantalism, and the idea of accommodation implicit within it, balanced the principles of exclusion and inclusion within the church, nature and grace in the doctrine of salvation, and reason and revelation in the understanding of theological knowledge. Their scholastic maxim that revelation remained reasonable even as it stood always above reason and their definition of theology as a practical discipline represented the initial statement in America of assumptions that would define the course of American theology.

3

Rationalism Resisted

In the late seventeenth century, the New England theologians expanded their scope. The expansion had two sources, the first grounded in the practices of congregations, the second situated within a larger intellectual and cultural world. The congregational stimulus for change came especially through the employment of a religious genre — the catechism — that emphasized system and comprehensiveness. The growing use of the catechism within the churches of a provincial society impelled a number of New England clergy to write catechetical exercises that functioned as theological compendia for a popular audience. The change also reflected the continuing engagement of colonial theology with English and continental thought. Transitions abroad drew some of the theologians of the second generation to engage topics that the first generation had largely ignored. By the second part of the century, they attended to questions of natural science and natural theology that were pressed upon them largely by discussions in England. They began to write about meteors and comets as well as conversion.

Breadth of vision did not translate into openness toward innovation. For almost half a century, the overriding clerical aim in New England was to maintain Calvinism and to resist innovations that might promote the Arminian and rationalist trends that the clergy saw overtaking theology in England. The outcome was an insistent Calvinist orthodoxy and a concerted drive to maintain the purity of the New England churches. Yet the resistance to change was not the sole story. The effort to defend a Calvinist piety of conversion led to innovations in sacramental thought and the doctrine of the church. And the defense of Calvinist tradition against perceptions of rationalist subversion led to both an expanded emphasis on the reasonableness of Christian doctrine and a heightened supernaturalism. Like most forms of conscious conservatism, the clerical allegiance to the past subtly altered the shape of the tradition that the clergy were trying to defend.

The Flight from Calvinism

When they looked toward England after 1660, the New England clergy saw little but disheartening change. One consequence of the restoration of Charles II to the English throne in 1660 was a continuing eclipse of Calvinism as a force within the Church of England. The turbulence of the civil wars and of the Commonwealth under Oliver Cromwell had already provoked during the 1650s a reaction against a theology that some now associated with political instability as well as religious error. The punitive laws enacted after 1662 pushed large numbers of Puritan clergy with Calvinist views out of the established church. They became dissenters, exiled from Anglican parishes and subjected to humiliation. An aggressive company of Anglican thinkers now dismissed them, along with all other Calvinists, as antinomians and dogmatists.

The depiction of Calvinism as antinomian, as disregardful of the need for moral obedience to God, appeared especially in the writings of the Anglican theologians who subscribed to the theology of "holy living" popularized by the Bishop of Down and Connor in Ireland, Jeremy Taylor (1613–67). Convinced that Calvinist doctrine undercut Christian morality, leading Anglican churchmen like Herbert Thorndike (1598–1672) and George Bull (1634–1710) became wary even of talk about justification by faith alone, insisting that justification required both faith and good works. Instead of asserting, like earlier English reformers and contemporary Calvinists, that the "formal cause" of justification was the righteousness of Christ imputed to the believer, they began to say that the formal cause — "that which makes a thing what it is" — was the faith and moral obedience of the justified believer. It was a seemingly abstruse point, but it registered the change in the status of Calvinist theology in the Church of England.[1]

Even in dissenting circles, prominent figures called for revision. While John Owen (1616–83), the vice chancellor of Oxford until his expulsion in 1658, would continue to expound a traditional Calvinist theology that enjoyed broad support among English dissenters, the disaffection with orthodoxy could be seen in no less a figure than Richard Baxter (1615–91), the dissenting pastor at Kidderminster who struggled to secure cooperation among conflicting parties. Like the theologians of holy living, Baxter argued that faith included obedience and that the formal cause of justification was not the imputation of Christ's righteousness to the believer but rather the reckoning of the believer's obedient faith as righteous. His critics charged him with Arminian error. Even in English dissenting groups, therefore, it could not be taken for granted that older forms of Calvinism would prevail.[2]

Among English Independents — the counterparts of the New England Congregationalists — a small company of theologians who saw themselves as the true Calvinists reacted against Arminian tendencies, a reaction that led after 1690 to alarming disputes over the old questions of the civil war era: whether faith could be described as a condition of the covenant of grace and whether obedience to the moral law had any bearing on salvation. The evangelistic campaign of the Independent preacher Richard Davis that began in Northamptonshire in 1690 drew on the contributions of enthusiastic but uneducated shoemakers, weavers, and farmers who preached a rigorous Calvinism that seemed dangerously antinomian even to the more staid dissenters of Presbyterian sentiment.[3]

On the European continent, the orthodoxy of the Synod of Dort maintained its hold in the Calvinist schools, but important voices there also argued for revision. In France, Protestant theologians at the Academy in Saumur raised objections to Dortian doctrines as early as the 1630s. Moïse Amyraut (1596–1664) disputed the claim that Christ died only for the elect. In Amyraut's "hypothetical universalism," Christ's death was "efficient" only for the elect, but it was "sufficient" for every human being. To some this seemed a distinction without a difference, since only the elect benefited, but the language disturbed more traditional Calvinists. Amyraut supplemented this idea with a distinction between the sinner's moral and natural ability: the sinful could respond (they had the natural ability) but they would not (they inevitably lacked the will to do it). Neither proposal could be considered Arminian, but both represented a slight softening of the public presentation of Calvinist doctrine.[4]

Amyraut's colleague Josué de la Place added an objection to the doctrine of imputation. Rather than accept the orthodox view that the imputation of Adam's guilt to the human race logically preceded their natural depravity, la Place reversed the order and argued that God imputed guilt to the sinful as a result of their innate depravity. His position came to be known as the doctrine of "mediate imputation," and American Calvinists would still debate about it in the mid-nineteenth century. Most French Calvinists rejected all of these innovations, but the academy at Saumur existed until 1685, the ideas originating there stirred up conflict even after its closing, and theologians in New England felt obliged to offer refutations.[5]

The drift away from Calvinism in England coincided with a new appreciation for reason in religion. As early as the 1640s, a gifted group of theological professors at Cambridge University proposed that reason, illuminated by revelation, was "the very voice of God" and that in a reasonable religion doctrines like predestination could have no place. Convinced that the enjoyment of God consisted in "the use of Reason and the exercise of virtue," these Cambridge Platonists—John Smith (1618–52), Henry More (1614–87), Ralph Cudworth (1617–88), and Benjamin Whichcote (1609–83)—battled against the materialism of Thomas Hobbes on the one side and the determinism of the Calvinists on the other. In the two decades following the Restoration they propagated the message that reason, as "the candle of the Lord," could test and verify scriptural revelation, that ethical ideals came not simply from the divine will but from the eternal nature of things, and that dogmatism had no place in religion.[6]

In demanding a reasonable religion, the Cambridge Platonists defined reason not only as the capacity to unify the materials of sense perception but also, more importantly, as the operation of innate ideas, of principles prior to sensory experience, or of intuitions able to grasp supersensuous truths. They thought, for example, that the mind could not recognize empirical events as causes and effects unless it operated with an innate conception of causation that had to be prior to any given sensory experience. Human knowledge, argued Cudworth, could not be the mere product of "sensible things and singular bodies existing without." Reason participated in universal and eternal ideas that could have their grounding only in the eternal mind of God. Human reason participated in divine reason. The Platonists, therefore, minimized proofs and evidences that depended on sensory experience. They illustrated a way of viewing reason that a small number of Americans would later employ to criticize the dominant American conceptions of rationality.[7]

The mood typified by the Cambridge Platonists characterized a broad range of the younger Anglican clergy, who began in the 1650s to turn away from what they described as a misguided Puritan "solafidianism"—reliance on faith alone and disregard of ethical conditions for salvation—and to rehabilitate both the notion of morality in religion and the rationality of faith. Wary Calvinists labeled them as "latitudinarians." The term had no precise meaning and functioned chiefly as an abusive label, but it indicated the unease among Calvinists about the directions of Anglican thought. A number of younger Anglican clergy wished to see themselves as more moderate, impartial, and rational than earlier polemicists, and they helped form the clerical generation that set the tone for Restoration Anglicanism. Joseph Glanvill (1636–80), rector in Bath and a member of the Royal Society, which was formed in 1662 to promote the study of nature, exemplified that generation's interest in natural theology. Edward Stillingfleet (1635–99), dean of St. Paul's in London, typified their investment in moral rather than dogmatic questions and their opinion that reason should confirm and interpret scripture. While some of them shared the epistemology of the Cambridge Platonists, others maintained the older Thomist interest in religious truths derived from the data of sensory experience.[8]

The clerical interest in the Royal Society signaled the importance for theology of the more empirical understandings of rationality. John Wilkins (1614–72), the bishop of Chester, served as the first secretary of the Society and wrote treatises on planets and mathematics as well as essays on natural religion. The naturalists and clerics who joined the Society contributed to a theological trend that would reach its apex when the naturalist John Ray (1628–1705) published *The Wisdom of God Manifested in the Works of Creation* (1691) and the Anglican cleric William Derham (1675–1735) published his *Physico-Theology* (1713). Ray and Derham employed empirical observation to argue that design in the creation — illustrated in planetary orbits, the topography of the earth, the adaptations of birds and fishes, the intricacies of the human body, and a vast catalogue of other natural phenomena — proved both the reality and the benevolence of God.[9]

A handful of British and continental writers concluded that such rational arguments alone were sufficient for a natural religion, and their confidence in reason drew them toward deism. The French writer Pierre Viret used the term "deism" in 1564 to designate a belief in God that did not depend on a special Christian revelation, and Blaise Pascal used it in 1660 to describe the views of people who sought to ground religion on reason alone. Later authors employed it in such a wide variety of ways that it would lose any fixed meaning, but when Lord Herbert of Cherbury (1583–1648), the soldier and philosopher who served as the ambassador to Paris, proposed in 1624 that no special revelation was essential, and the political pamphleteer Charles Blount (1654–93) charged in 1679 that claims of special revelation cloaked imposture and economic interest, the deist attitude began to assume a more fixed meaning. Blount's *Summary Account of the Deists Religion* (1686) set the English deist controversy into motion with the insistence that "the Morality in Religion is above the Mystery of it."[10]

New Englanders observed these changes in the midst of their own distress over political and religious change closer to home. Royal pressure from England after the Restoration made it more difficult for them to maintain uniformity of religious practice, and growing royal interference in New England reached a decisive peak in 1684, when the king annulled the charter of the Bay Colony. Two years later, James II appointed a royal governor. The political interference had religious consequences in a region already divided over the halfway covenant of 1662. The crown pressed for religious toleration, and New Englanders found themselves debating Quakers and Baptists whom they once would have banished. Equally distressing to the Congregational clergy, James II sent an Anglican priest to Massachusetts Bay and compelled New England to accept an Anglican congregation in Boston.

Insofar as the New England Congregational clergy devoted themselves to the defense of Calvinism, their conservatism signified, therefore, resistance to changes both religious and political. To defend Calvinism was to defend not only biblical truth but also assumptions about the proper ordering of a religious and political culture that seemed threatened. Convinced, moreover, that New England was undergoing religious decline from within — a conviction announced explicitly in the Reforming Synod of 1679 — the New England clergy called for a public reassertion of the older theology. Their 1680 "Confession of Faith" reaffirmed their allegiance to the Calvinist theology of the "Reformed Churches."[11]

Insofar as they engaged in the debate about the scope of reason, they followed mainly the empirical rather than the Platonic path. By the end of the century, the Cambridge Platonist Henry More gained the attention of a few theologians in Boston, but they were more interested in his ethics than in his epistemology. None followed up on the implications of the Platonist insistence that a priori principles of reason made coherent sensory experience possible and linked the human mind to the mind of God. They felt drawn rather to the English theologians and naturalists who connected empirical claims about the natural world to the interpretation of scripture. They tried to make certain that reason remained in the service of scriptural revelation and that the heterodoxy of the deists not take hold in the American colonies.

Catechetical Calvinism

The conservatism also reflected more immediate pastoral concerns. Theologians were still local pastors, and their lamentations bemoaning decline from an earlier age of purity were part of a broader attempt by the churches to preserve the faith by forming the children of the second and third generations in Puritan belief and experience. Apart from the sermon and the exercise of church discipline, they made special use after 1662 of the catechism, the summation of doctrine designed to instruct children and new members in the fundamentals of the faith.

Between 1641 and 1660, the New England clergy wrote and published at least fourteen catechisms — some reflecting expectations that young Christians could master scholastic distinctions — and New England presses also printed four editions of the catechisms prepared by the Westminster Assembly in England. The clergy intended for parents to use them in catechizing their children, but by 1660 the ministers were themselves assuming the catechetical duties in the churches — a trend that left a lasting imprint on theology in New England when Samuel Willard in Boston produced his *Compleat Body of Divinity* as a compilation of his nineteen years of catechetical lectures between 1687 and 1706. After its posthumous publication in 1726, the *Compleat Body* became an authoritative text in American Reformed theology for the next half century.[12]

In teaching the catechism, the clergy regularly engaged in a form of systematic thinking reminiscent of the older orthodox systems. Unlike a sermon, the catechism comprehended all the foundational Christian doctrines and organized them in their proper relation to one another. Although it remained sketchy and allusive, it moved toward systematic and comprehensive thinking. Since a catechism was a miniature systematic theology, a summary of catechetical teaching provides an angle of vision on the Calvinist theological scheme in the second half of the century.

The catechisms displayed the practical cast of New England Calvinist theology. Continuing to define theology as "the doctrine of godliness, or living unto God," or the doctrine of "living well," or the doctrine of "godly life," they usually taught that it had two parts, designated as either "faith and obedience" or "doctrine and observance." This bipartite division foreshadowed a persistent dichotomizing, the result partly of scholastic precedent, partly of Ramist method. The movement from faith to obedience — from doctrine to observance — illustrated the practical purpose of theology in the religious culture.[13]

The doctrinal part of the catechism normally began with the distinction between God's sufficiency (the internal attributes and Trinitarian nature of God) and God's efficiency. The efficiency comprised two forms of divine action: the immanent, or the eternal divine decrees, and the transient, which made the decrees effective in the temporal world. These transient acts had a twofold expression: as creation and as providence. Creation included constant natures, like angels, who were created perfect, and inconstant natures, like human beings, animals, and the material world, all needing to be perfected by degrees. Providence was also twofold — it both conserved and governed the world, in a manner either ordinary, in which God worked through "second causes," or extraordinary, requiring immediate divine intervention. Some catechists also distinguished between providence as general, overseeing the whole creation, and as special, governing particular events. Special providence included the two covenants of works and grace, which were made necessary by human finitude and human sin.

Such dichotomies reappeared throughout the catechetical accounts of sin and salvation. The fall offended both God's holiness and God's justice and brought both guilt and punishment. The punishment was sin and death. The sin was both original (by which human nature swerved from the divine rule) and actual (by which human actions flouted the rule); the death was both physical and spiritual. Guilt was transmitted in two ways: both by union with Adam, through natural descent, and by communion with Adam, as humanity's federal representative. The communion manifested itself in both the imputation of Adam's guilt and the sharing in its consequences.

The only salvation came through Christ, who could be the mediator because his Person joined two natures. As mediator he held the three offices of prophet, priest, and king, but his mediation comprised his two states — of humiliation and of exaltation — and resulted from his twofold obedience, the active, by which he fulfilled the moral law, and the passive, by which his vicarious suffering satisfied God's wrath. The application of redemption came through the Spirit, who called the elect through both preparation, which convinced them of their sin, and infusion, which worked faith in them. Infusion occurred through vocation (the effectual calling through which the individual Christian was drawn into faith) and the creation of justifying faith. Both preparation and infusion resulted from divine grace, received in a manner both passive, through the generating of a new principle in the will, and active, through the operation of the infused faith. The process conveyed the benefits of Christ by imputation, entailing adoption and justification, and by the infusion of gracious qualities, entailing sanctification and glorification. And all of this signified a twofold relation to Christ: the union brought about by faith and the communion in Christ's benefits.

The discussion of communion usually led to the second part of the catechetical systems, which treated the observance and obedience of the sanctified believer, both through piety in the church and through moral obedience in the world. The teaching on observance and obedience continued the typical Reformed emphasis on the biblical law, and it exemplified the Reformed conviction that theological belief had manifest implications for moral practice. The core of moral theology in the catechetical tradition was the exposition of the ten commandments, which the clergy interpreted to comprehend all the duties attendant upon "the several places and relations" that linked men and women to superiors, inferiors, and equals. Adding instruction from the New Testament, they used the catechisms to make the point that true belief in the doctrines in the first half of the system should lead seamlessly to the practices of morality and piety outlined in the second half.[14]

They supplemented their catechetical teaching with moral handbooks and manuals on "cases of conscience" resolving specific issues of moral perplexity. Cotton Mather's *Bonifacius* (1710), in which he argued that the great end of human life was "to do good," followed the time-honored casuistic method of defining the duties that followed from social relations (husband and wife, parents and children, masters and servants) and from offices (ministers, magistrates, physicians, lawyers, soldiers). For most, including Mather, ethics meant explication of biblical laws. By the 1680s, however, ethics could mean more than that. In 1686, Charles Morton, a teacher at Harvard and minister in Charlestown, drew up a system of "Ethicks" that combined biblical teaching with Aristotelian virtues. Mather would eventually complain in his diary about "the employing of so much Time upon *Ethicks* in our Colledges. A vile Peece of Paganism." But his concern was simply that the young should "Study no other Ethics, but what is in the Bible," a position that accorded with the maxims of the revered William Ames.[15]

The catechisms were the conceptual maps that laid out, for a lay audience, the internal relations of Calvinist doctrines. The persistent bipartite division in the theology made it easy to memorize — one of the prime motives behind Ramist dichotomy — and gave it a simple logical clarity. Since the sermons employed the same dichotomies as the catechisms, the catechetical instruction also enabled congregations to locate sermonic ideas within the larger conceptual system, and the more technical and polemical works of theology always presupposed the catechetical scheme. The ideal was more the transmission of a tradition than any adaptation of theological ideas to changes in the culture. It was not an ideal designed to promote theological innovation. Its purpose was conservation.

The Tenacity of Calvinism

Four New England ministers dominated the theology of the era. All of them had an interest in new ideas among religious writers in Europe and England, but all resisted any change in the fundamentals of Calvinist thought. They thought of themselves as conserving the Calvinist tradition even as they revealed the extent to which theological change could occur as part of a conservative impulse.

Samuel Willard (1640–1707) transformed the genre of the catechism into the first published colonial effort at a comprehensive Calvinist theology. Willard was the teacher of the Old South Church in Boston from 1676 to 1707, and for the final six years of his career the acting president of Harvard. He produced more than fifty published works and attained a reputation as a man who "excelled in eminent degree in the Knowledge of the most abstruse parts of Theology." He also introduced into New England a form of exposition, widely practiced in Reformed churches in Europe, known as the catechetical lecture. In 1687 he began to lecture in Boston on the Shorter Catechism of the Westminster Assembly. By the time he stopped he had delivered 220 lectures and written twenty-six more, an undertaking that ended only when his health broke in 1706. His *Compleat Body of Divinity* was a folio-sized book of 914 pages, the only systematic theology published in America until Samuel Hopkins wrote his *System of Doctrines* in 1793. Willard's knowledge in "Systematic Divinity," wrote his friend Ebenezer Pemberton, was "celebrated by all," but his book was simply the catechism on a grand scale.[16]

In addition to acting on his desire to write a comprehensive and systematic Calvinist theology, Willard expressed on more than one occasion the defining aim of his thought: "the way lyes very narrow between Antinomian and Arminian errors," he wrote, "and therefore needs the greater exactness in cutting the thread true." He complained of the "invectives" directed against New England theologians by critics in England. While some accused them of antinomianism because of their Calvinism, others charged them with Arminianism because they expected the faithful to be obedient to the law. Willard's most characteristic shorter works — *Covenant-Keeping the Way to Blessedness* (1682) and *The Law Established by the Gospel* (1694) — were attempts to maintain a predestinarian Calvinism emphasizing the grace of election while also distinguishing Calvinist doctrine from antinomian error.[17]

Willard joined the high Calvinists who defended the doctrine of supralapsarian predestination. God both elected some to salvation and consigned others to reprobation, and Willard agreed with the supralapsarian position that the logically primary divine decree — prior even to the divine decision to create a world — was the decree of election, an argument cast in opposition to the infralapsarian position that the decree to save the elect logically followed the decree to create a world and to permit the fall. The purpose of the supralapsarian argument was to preserve the utter freedom of God and to reassert the unconditional gratuity of salvation. It was a way of affirming that the purpose of the creation itself was the display of God's glory through the free salvation of the elect.[18]

Willard dealt with abstruse matters, but he still thought of theology as a practical discipline. He devoted sixty-five of his lectures to the moral life, arguing that morality was obedience to the divine will, revealed to Adam in the natural law and repeated in substance in the "moral law" of the Old Testament and the teachings of Jesus in the New. Even his most arcane lectures concluded with a listing of the practical uses to which his truths could be put. His aim was to show men and women "what they were made for" so that they would not "live in vain."[19]

The second theologian of unusual prominence, Solomon Stoddard (1643–1729), was a Harvard graduate who became the pastor in 1672 of the Congregational church in Northampton, Massachusetts, where he remained for fifty-seven years. A powerful personality who attained a reputation as the pope of the Connecticut Valley, Stoddard continued to pursue the agenda of the first generation, concentrating all his enormous intellectual energy on the questions about salvation that had marked New England theology since the beginning. For Stoddard, as for Willard, the center of interest was still conversion.

In the pursuit of that interest, he was willing to innovate. In his understanding of the church, he proposed a move away from a strict congregational covenant theology, with its assumption that church membership had to be limited to regenerate visible saints and their children. Stoddard preferred an inclusive church that contained both regenerate and unregenerate members. In 1677, he argued from the pulpit that no church could, in fact, distinguish the converted from the unconverted. The absence of a "certain rule given in Scripture" ensured that the guides of the church would always lack "certain knowledge who have Sanctifying Grace." He expected converts to recognize grace in their own hearts, but he thought that even they might be unable to detect the grace within. They should not for that reason be excluded from the church.[20]

Neither should they be excluded from the sacraments. Arguing from the Protestant position that the Lord's Supper was the Word made visible, he contended that it was a converting ordinance. He drew the idea from dissenting theologians in England who argued that the sacramental symbols had the power to produce conversion by moving the mind to consent. Stoddard distinguished two kinds of conversion, the first a merely formal assent to the truth of Christian doctrine, the second an inward consent to the gospel. He argued that the Lord's Supper presupposed the first but could produce the second.[21]

The cornerstones of Stoddard's theology were the doctrines of preparation and conversion, and his life task was to show that both were necessary and that human effort could accomplish neither. He instructed the New England clergy that their duty was to serve as instruments of the Spirit's preparatory motions by preaching "the threatening of the law, Man's Insufficiency, and God's Sovereignty." They were to make their listeners sensible of "the terrours of the law" and "the danger of Damnation." He conceded that preparation did not always

require unremitting terror: "God leads men through the whole work of preparation partly by fear and partly by hope." But Stoddard believed that the Spirit
normally prepared the heart by convicting it of sin and revealing the judgment
to come, and he warned against offering any premature comfort.[22]

In 1687 Stoddard produced his masterpiece, *The Safety of Appearing at the
Day of Judgment in the Righteousness of Christ,* an essay in covenant thought
designed to show that, because Christ had fulfilled the covenant of works and
had borne the curse and assumed the guilt for original sin, believers should
cast themselves entirely on his righteousness. The book treated themes that
Stoddard would pursue for the next four decades: the demand of the law, the
sovereign will of a God under no obligation to show mercy, the merciful
decision of God to bring himself "under bonds" by entering into "a solemn
covenant" of grace to save the elect, the necessity that the elect undergo the
"preparatory work of humiliation" as a prelude to faith, and the imputed
righteousness of Christ as the ground for salvation. He always described both
preparation and conversion in terms entirely consistent with Calvinist orthodoxy. The special grace that drew the elect into salvation differed from every
kind of "common grace" that the nonelect might have been granted, and it
produced a love of Christ for his intrinsic excellence that the reprobate could
never attain.[23]

Stoddard's doctrines brought him into conflict with the most formidable
opponents he could have found: the Mathers of Boston. For intellectual
breadth, no one could match the Mathers, and no theologians made a greater
effort than they to preserve Calvinism. They agreed with Stoddard about the
truth of Calvinist doctrine; they thought, however, that he had often failed to
draw proper conclusions from it.

Increase Mather (1639–1723), the son of the founder Richard Mather,
presided over Boston's Second Church (North Church) for more than half a
century, oversaw the fortunes of Harvard College as its president for sixteen
years, and assumed a commanding role in almost every political and religious
movement in the colony. He wrote around 130 books and pamphlets on
theology, history, politics, and natural philosophy, speaking almost always in a
conservative voice that resisted theological innovation.

His battle with Stoddard came over the nature of the church and the sacraments. Increase Mather struggled relentlessly for the purity of the church,
which meant that he continued to insist that church membership required the
presumption of saving faith. After years of opposition to the halfway covenant, he gradually came by 1671 to accept it, but in his mind this made it all
the more important to restrict full membership—and access to the Lord's
Supper—to church members who could give evidence of the work of saving

grace in their souls. Just as the Jews of ancient Israel required fidelity to the covenant on the part of parents who presented their children for circumcision, so the church, the antitype of Israel, must require faithful adherence to the covenant of grace on the part of its adult members.[24]

He opposed both Stoddard's open invitation to the Lord's Supper and his description of the sacrament as a converting ordinance. If the sacrament sealed the covenant of grace, then no one should receive it who rejected the covenant itself: "But an Unregenerate and an Unbeliever does reject the Covenant of God, and of Life." In Mather's view, to administer the elements to the unregenerate was to "set the Lords Seal to a Blank." He spoke for most of the clergy of New England when he argued that the sacrament nourished rather than created the principle of spiritual life.[25]

On the essentials of Calvinist doctrine, however, Mather and Stoddard agreed. Mather taught that salvation rested on the "Sovereign Grace of God in the Salvation of the Elect," and he had no sympathy for even the mild revisions of Calvinist thought that Amyraut had attempted in France. He tried to soften somewhat Stoddard's severe doctrine of preparation for salvation; in the preface to one of Stoddard's own books he aligned himself with Giles Firmin's earlier criticisms of Hooker and Shepard for insisting too much on the Spirit's preparatory humiliation of the elect. He also reassured the parents of New England that the children of the covenant, baptized and nurtured by faithful parents and churches, had a special "promise of converting grace." God, he said, had "cast the line of Election" so that it ran for the most part "through the loyns of godly parents." These concessions signified a rhetorical domesticating of the doctrine of election, but Mather resisted any further softening of Calvinist views.[26]

So also did his son Cotton Mather (1663–1728), who served for thirty-eight years at North Church alongside his father, whom he approached in influence and exceeded in international celebrity. Cotton Mather shared his father's reservations about Stoddard's innovations. An untiring writer, he also had something to say about almost every topic in theology. His *Magnalia Christi Americana* (1702) traced the history of the church in New England; his *Free Grace* (1706) defended Calvinism and laid out the order of salvation; his *Bonifacius* (1710) assessed critically the growing interest in ethics; his *Christian Philosopher* (1721) sought to reconcile theology and natural science. And these were but four of more than four hundred books, treatises, and sermons. Since many of these works displayed a fascination with enlightenment ideas, Mather has gained a reputation as a precursor of the liberal temper in theology. In fact, his consistent intention was to preserve the old ways, and he never departed from Calvinist orthodoxy.[27]

In 1702 he published his *Seasonable Testimony to the Glorious Doctrines*, a critique of English Arminianism and a defense of total depravity, unconditional election, irresistible grace, the bondage of the will, and justification by faith through the imputation of the righteousness of Christ. He urged the clergy to defend predestinarian doctrine and to include it in their sermons. Like his father, he emphasized that the Spirit's preparation of the elect could occur in various ways, but he still assumed that the contrition and humiliation that it normally produced as a prelude to conversion came as a gift of the sovereign Spirit. He insisted that the "cannot" which bound the unregenerate will was a "will not," a moral rather than a physical inability, but he still insisted on the bondage of the will. He tried to affirm and to urge a human striving for salvation, but he explained its occurrence as a result of the divine decree.[28]

Mather increasingly emphasized a view of theology as practical. He told the German Pietist Bartholomew Ziegenbalg that "the Christian religion is nothing other than the doctrine of living unto God through Christ; and further, that it is more a practical than a theoretical science, of which the goal is the animation of real, solid, living piety." This emphasis probably helped Mather develop a tolerance for theological disagreement. He read widely in German Pietism and corresponded with the Pietists at Halle, especially August Hermann Francke, and he shared their interest in promoting Christian unity around a few essential doctrines. In 1716 he proposed fourteen; the next year he reduced them to three maxims of piety: belief in the Trinity, complete reliance on Christ for salvation, and the love of the neighbor for the sake of Christ. He told a French Arminian that though they must differ they could work together to reform the Reformation. But it was Calvinism, he thought, that most clearly grasped the truth. Mather's theology exemplified the tenacity, not the fragility, of Calvinist doctrine in New England in the late seventeenth and early eighteenth centuries.[29]

Conservatism and Change

In defending orthodoxy, however, the theologians changed it. They maintained the older doctrines, but the altered intellectual ethos of the era brought new ideas to the forefront. In trying to defend tradition against what they saw as rationalistic reduction, they of necessity accentuated the function of reason in theology. In trying to defend traditional notions of providence and divine sovereignty against trends toward naturalistic explanation in England, they veered toward a heightened supernaturalism. What defined the era was the combination of the two impulses: an insistence on the rationality of Christianity and a reassertion of supernatural mysteries that transcended reason.

Already by 1688 Samuel Willard was lecturing on the evidences that proved the Bible to be a unique divine revelation, and this turn toward evidentialism became increasingly pronounced as New Englanders sensed the danger of deism. In 1700 Cotton Mather's *Reasonable Religion* derided the deists and employed evidential arguments to validate the scriptures. Two years later, Increase Mather published *A Discourse Proving that the Christian Religion is the Only True Religion,* one of the earliest American treatises directed solely against thinkers like Benedict Spinoza in Holland and Charles Blount in England who would own "no Scripture nor any Revealed Religion." In 1712, Cotton Mather was still occupied with the deists. When a colonist asked him for a treatise to "Spread about the Country, before Deistical Notions grow Epidemical," he responded with another polemic, *Reason Satisfied and Faith Established,* in which he tried to validate the accounts of Christ's resurrection.[30]

The antideist polemic revealed the extent to which the argument against rationalism drew the theologians toward more rational forms of argumentation. They argued that the teachings of scripture were credible because they coincided with the dictates of reason. They pointed out that reason alone could demonstrate God's existence and the duty of obeying the moral law, and since the biblical revelation taught the same truths, it manifestly taught more than "cunningly devised Fables." The heart of the antideist case came in arguments long employed to validate the Bible: its confirmation by miracles and prophecies, its effects on the heart, its use of eyewitness testimony, and its improbable preservation through the centuries. Anglican theologians in England argued unceasingly after about 1660 that reason could prove the authority of the Bible. The case made by the Mathers represented the first significant publications in what would become an American evidentialist tradition.[31]

The corollary to the case against deism was the defense of classical Christology. The catechetical tradition preserved the traditional doctrine that the second Person of the Trinity was incarnate in Jesus of Nazareth who satisfied the divine law of justice for the elect by paying a ransom through his perfect life and sacrificial death. The second-generation New Englanders defended the familiar categories of Reformed Christology. Increase Mather recalled in 1686 that throughout his ministry he had "preached concerning Christ more than any other subject." When he felt himself approaching the end of his life in 1715, he repeated the same claim.[32]

Part of the stimulus for the renewed accent on Christology came from the Quakers, whose distinction between the external Christ and the Christ within appeared both to diminish the Jesus of the biblical narrative and to question his divine status. Willard criticized the Quakers for subverting the offices of Christ, and in 1688 he and other ministers debated the Scottish immigrant

Quaker George Keith, whose preaching of the inward Christ seemed to them to replace biblical revelation with subjective feeling. Increase Mather linked the Quakers to deists and Socinians — followers of Fausto Socinius, an Italian who in 1562 had denied the doctrine of the Trinity.[33]

A further stimulus to Christological interests came from the worship practices of New England congregations. An effort to promote sacramental piety, for instance, led John Eliot of Roxbury in 1678 to publish *The Harmony of the Gospels,* the first American attempt to harmonize the gospel accounts, which Eliot envisioned as reading in preparation for receiving the Lord's Supper. Increase Mather's *Mystery of Christ Opened and Applyed* (1686), Christological sermons on the covenant of redemption, originated for the same reason. Eliot and Mather both saw reflection on Christ as a fitting prelude to receiving the symbols of his body and blood.[34]

A third motive came from anxiety about what the New England clergy saw as a wave of English Socinianism. During the 1670s, Increase Mather lamented the unprecedented "opposition" to "the person and glory of Christ," and he wrote some of his essays on Christ in order to counter the "pretence of . . . Reason" that prompted such opposition. In the early eighteenth century, the theology known as Arianism — the view that Christ was a created being — won support in England through the writings of the English divines William Whiston and Samuel Clarke. Cotton Mather preached and wrote against these Arian views for more than a decade, especially after English dissenting ministers meeting in 1719 at Salters Hall in London divided over the question of subscribing to a Trinitarian creed.[35]

Even as they defended traditional Christology against various forms of rationalism, however, the New Englanders continued to claim the authority of reason. Another sign of this, in addition to their evidentialism, was their interest in natural theology. Willard conceded that reason could discover only "*that* God is but not *what* God is," and he reasserted the view that this rational knowledge remained insufficient because it taught neither what God required nor how God saved. Yet he mirrored the fashion of his age by drawing special attention to the design, symmetry, and harmony of the creation, from the vast "composure" of the cosmos to the exquisiteness of the world of insects. He found a clue to the divine purpose in "the curious contrivances in each part" of the natural world — a world "in which the least Fly is full of wonders."[36]

Willard's peers shared his confidence in the possibility of a rational natural theology. Convinced that right reason supported the Christian gospel, Cotton Mather could praise the powers of rationality: "if we do not keep Reason in the Throne, we go to Dethrone the infinite God Himself. . . . The voice of Reason, is the Voice of God." Such trust in the rationality of faith enabled the second-generation clergy to appropriate English natural philosophy in the service of New England's Calvinist theology.[37]

The first generation of New England clergy had shown little interest in natural philosophy. John Cotton conceded that Christ did not "mislike" the study of nature, but he also warned against spending too much time on "the study of creatures" because their instability left the mind restless. The students at Harvard were more enthusiastic, and by the 1650s some of them defended Copernicus's heliocentric theory of the universe, which they publicized in the New England almanacs. Zechariah Brigden announced in the almanac of 1659 that Copernicus had discovered "the true and genuine Systeme of the world" and that the Old Testament appeared to diverge from it only because the scriptural accounts, designed for "the capacity of the rudest mechanick, as of the ablest Philosophers," did not intend "exactness." In matters of philosophical truth, he wrote, "the proper literal sense" of the Bible was "subservient to the casting vote of reason."[38]

Some New England ministers — including John Cotton — rejected the Copernican universe. Others withheld judgment in the manner of John Davenport at New Haven, who replied, upon hearing Brigden's views, that the student could "injoy his opinion" but that he would rest in what he had learned until "more cogent arguments be produced than I have hitherto met with." By the second generation, however, Copernicus had clerical admirers, including the Mathers.[39]

Cotton Mather had a better grasp of English natural philosophy than any other New England minister. Scientific topics had attracted his interest ever since he was a twelve-year-old student at Harvard College. In 1683, when he was twenty, he and his father helped form a Boston Philosophical Society to keep the educated up-to-date on natural philosophy, and although it folded after five years, Cotton Mather's enthusiasm never waned. In 1693 he began writing his "Biblia Americana," a vast scriptural commentary (for which he never found a publisher) in which he struggled to harmonize the scientific and the biblical cosmology. He revealed the extent to which he granted natural philosophy an implicit authority in theology when he read Genesis as an exposition of the atomistic theory of matter and labored to provide a natural explanation of the biblical flood.[40]

In 1721 he published *The Christian Philosopher,* the premier colonial exposition of natural philosophy, as a means to expound the catechism's doctrine of creation: "The Works of the Glorious GOD in the Creation of the World," he wrote, "are what I now propose to exhibit." The book summarized dozens of English and European naturalists, especially the English physico-theologians. Although he felt "irradiated by the Discoveries of Great Sir Isaac Newton," he returned most often to John Ray's *Wisdom of God Manifested in the Works of the Creation* and William Derham's *Physico-Theology*. To Cotton Mather, the "wondrous workmanship" of the eye and the purposive contrivance of a bird's wing provided irrefutable evidence of godly design while the universal force of gravity could have no other cause "but the Will and Work of the Glorious God."[41]

Not even the Mathers, however, were entirely sanguine about natural philosophy, and their treatises were neither exercises in disinterested observation nor confident assertions that science inevitably supported natural theology. They wanted to ensure that scientific explanation not preclude an awareness of the supernatural, and one ironic consequence of their embrace of science was an intensified supernaturalism. After the appearance of comets in 1680 and 1682, Increase Mather immersed himself in astronomical theory. As a result he published between 1681 and 1683 three essays on "the nature, place, motion of Comets, which only such as have some skill in Astronomy can understand." Citing the astronomers Johannes Kepler, Tycho Brahe, and Robert Hook, he sought to prove that comets served as portents of divine judgments. In his *Kometographia* (1683), he argued that comets caused fires and floods and altered the weather in order to call for repentance and faith. They signaled imminent divine judgment on the world.[42]

A similar aim motivated the publication in 1683 of his *Doctrine of Divine Providence*, which he followed up the next year with his *Essay for the Recording of Illustrious Providences*. In these essays Mather distinguished between ordinary providences, which occurred in accord with "the Law and Course of Nature," and extraordinary providences "above and beyond the Constituted order of nature." Both were "wondrous" means by which God's governance "extended to the least and most inconsiderable things that happen in the world." He had long collected instances of what he called "remarkable providences," "prodigious" and unusual happenings that illustrated God's intervention in human affairs. The *Essay* described "preternatural events" wrought by God, often through spirits and demons, which confuted the skeptics who wanted to attribute everything to "natural causes."[43]

The same era that witnessed the clerical enchantment with science could give birth, therefore, to a flurry of intense interest in a topic like the doctrine of angels. Willard's catechetical lectures in 1690 contained a protracted discussion of invisible angelic spirits. The Mathers showed a distinct fondness for angels, and two years after an evening discussion of the topic in the Cambridge Association of Ministers, Increase published his *Angelographia* (1696), a biblical proof that the "Ministry of Holy Angels" continued daily throughout the world even though "apparitions" by good angels had "in a great measure ceased." Cotton Mather, however, claimed that an angel appeared to him in

1693, and he continued thereafter not only to seek angelic communications but also to preach and write about the "thousands of thousands, myriads of myriads" of angels who dwelt in the heavens and visited the earth.[44]

Like the Anglican minister Joseph Glanvill in England, whom they both admired, the Mathers believed that skepticism about angels, spirits, demons, and witches cloaked a covert materialism. Increase Mather tried to confute unnamed English skeptics who thought that "meer natural Disease" could account for the extraordinary behavior of people claiming to be afflicted by demons and witches. The intensified supernaturalism — intensified because it now had to be consciously defended — colored the involvement of the Mathers in the witchcraft cases in New England during the 1680s and in the trials at Salem in 1691.[45]

The period produced, therefore, an extended discussion of the wondrous and miraculous. In England, the Platonist Henry More collected accounts of miracles, as did the Calvinist biblical exegete Matthew Poole. Willard explained the standard Reformed position: God's providence could be ordinary, manifest in secondary natural causes, or "extraordinary," skipping over or inverting the order of natural causes. The extraordinary in this sense was equivalent to the miraculous, for a miracle, precisely defined, was any divine work "above the power of Second Causes to produce." Men and women might, through prayer, be the moral causes of such works, but only God could produce them.[46]

No Christian theologian in the seventeenth century doubted the ability of God to work miracles, but the topic was sensitive among Protestants because of the Catholic claim that miracles continued within the Catholic Church as a means of confirming the truth of Catholic doctrine. The normal response in New England was the standard Protestant claim that the age of miracles had ceased at the end of the apostolic era, meaning that God no longer used miracles to confirm doctrine and no longer endowed ministers with miraculous gifts: "God works now by men and means," wrote the preacher John Richardson, "not by miracles."[47]

Increase Mather, like most other New Englanders, referred therefore more to "wonders" than to "miracles," and he explained that some wonders occurred through second causes, but Mather also displayed a greater willingness than some of his peers to affirm the continuing of miracles even in contemporary New England. He explained that some wonders were "of a miraculous nature . . . above and beyond the Constituted Order of Nature." The prime example was conversion, the only "standing miracle" remaining in the church, but Mather also saw signs of the miraculous in several instances of divine answers to prayer for healing and deliverance from death in recent New England history. He drew on the accounts of "miraculous cures" that he found in Poole's collections.[48]

Cotton Mather saw miracles everywhere and with typical intensity collected miracle stories, which he published in 1696 in his *Things for a Distress'd People to Think Upon,* describing military victories, foiled assassinations, spiritual conversions, and physical healings that demonstrated the continuing occurrence of miraculous events. He had no reluctance to call them miracles, and he thought that they offered the best evidence against the "Infidel Spirit, that (under the falsely assumed name of Deism) would turn all Revealed Religion, and indeed all Religion into Ridicule."[49]

The heightened supernaturalism found vivid expression among theologians preoccupied with "the world to come." By the end of the century, a select few in New England developed an intense interest in Christ's return and the millennial events that would surround it. For a time after the Restoration of 1660, millennial theology had a bad reputation as an excuse for the political radicalism of such groups as the English Fifth Monarchy Men. In the catechetical lectures in which Samuel Willard explained the second coming and the resurrection of the dead, he made no explicit reference to an earthly millennial kingdom, though in *The Fountain Opened* (1700) Willard cautiously alluded to the "happy times predicted for the church" at the time of the conversion of the Jews. By that time, other theologians had also seen the millennium approaching.[50]

No one saw it more vividly than Increase and Cotton Mather, whose views of the end time were strikingly different from those of Thomas Brightman or John Cotton earlier. In 1666 Increase Mather heard that the Turkish Jew Sabbatai Zevi in Syria had proclaimed himself the Messiah. The news prompted his interest in Romans 11:26 — "And so all Israel shall be saved" — and he launched a series of lectures on the relation between the conversion of Israel and the millennial age. His colleagues in Boston felt uneasy, but in 1669 he published the lectures as *The Mystery of Israel's Salvation Opened,* initiating half a century of millennial speculation in the Mather family.

He knew that some considered the notion of an earthly millennium to be heretical, so he persuaded other ministers to write prefatory recommendations, and he filled the book with references to other Reformed theologians who agreed with him. He begged his readers not to be "offended with the seeming Novelism which is in these notions," and he reminded them that the Bible "abundantly witnessed" to the imminent Chiliad, the thousand-year reign of Christ and the saints on earth. Mather argued that New Englanders were living in the time of the pouring out of the fifth of the seven apocalyptic vials mentioned in the book of Revelation. During this period, Rome would be destroyed. The sixth vial would then begin the conversion of the "Israelitish Nation." After Richard Baxter in England proposed that Romans 11 merely denoted the conversions among the Jews in the days of the apostles, Mather wrote, between 1692 and 1695, *A Dissertation Concerning the Future Conversion of the Jewish Nation* to show that the conversion of Israel was in the imminent future, not the distant past, and that it would issue in the "first resurrection" (Rev. 20:5–6) with which the millennial dispensation would begin.[51]

His millennialism was graphic and detailed. He described the first resurrection as an event in which the bodies of the departed righteous would rise to be reunited in a celestial form with their souls, which had ascended to heaven. The risen righteous and the living saints would then, in accord with 1 Thessalonians 4:17, be caught up in the air in a divine rapture while God destroyed the wicked through the fire in which the returning Christ appeared from heaven. Then the New Jerusalem would descend to the earth for a "dispensation" of at least a thousand years, during which the saints in heaven would return to this lower world, the church would flourish, and pain and death would cease. Mather expressed doubt that Christ would reign personally, but he thought that the saints of the New Jerusalem would rule the world. The drama would conclude on the last day with the second resurrection (Rev. 13) — the resurrection of the wicked — and the second, or ultimate, judgment, in which the wicked would be consigned to their punishment. Then the citizens of the New Jerusalem would return to heaven, Christ would give up his mediatorial kingdom to God, and God could be "all in all."[52]

Increase Mather could speak of the New Jerusalem as the "church triumphant" in the highest heaven, the "metropolis" of the new millennial world, and the "state of the church on earth" during the millennium. He never specified its location. He certainly never claimed that it would be established in Boston, New England, or America. He knew that the English theologian William Twisse had suggested to Joseph Mede, the dean of millennial wisdom, that America might be the place of the New Jerusalem, but all that Mather would say, in an exhortation in 1674, was that the Lord had "as it were" caused "New Jerusalem to come down from Heaven" by dwelling with the colonists, who could take comfort that though God would scourge them he would not destroy them. He added five years later that New England had once been "like unto the New Jerusalem," a "Type and emblem" of it. But this had nothing to do with the literal descent of the New Jerusalem, which remained for Mather an event in the future.[53]

He presumably knew that Joseph Mede had convinced Twisse of his error; he certainly knew that Mede had reached the conclusion that America, far from being the New Jerusalem, would likely become the kingdom of Satan and his minions Gog and Magog, who would rise up against the New Jerusalem toward the end of Christ's reign. If Mede was right, New England did not have a bright future. Mather felt obliged, therefore, to prove, not that America would be the New Jerusalem, but that the region would not be totally excluded from the benefits that the New Jerusalem would bring.[54]

The merchant Samuel Sewall did try to show, in his *Phaenomena quaedam Apocalyptica* (1697), that America might be "the place of the New Jerusalem." Arguing against Mede's dismissal of the continent, he contended that the New World "stands fair for becoming the seat of the Divine Metropolis." But he also never presumed that God would choose Boston. It was far more likely, he thought, that he would choose "the Mexican Continent." "Why may not New Spain be," he asked, "the place of New Jerusalem?" He answered the question by outlining the prophetical resemblances between Mexico and Peru and the apocalyptic verses of the book of Daniel.[55]

By the same token, neither Increase Mather nor any of his second-generation colleagues assumed that New England was the antitype of ancient Israel. They maintained the view of the first New England theologians: Israel's antitype was the true church, just as the antitype of Jerusalem was the New Jerusalem. And the true church was the company of the elect, who dwelled in all the earth. The New Englanders still called New England a New Israel; they still found countless analogues between themselves and the ancient Jews; but they did not think that their society fulfilled the biblical types.[56]

No one described the millennial kingdom more expansively than Cotton Mather, and the most he would say was that New England had reason to hope that it might "belong" to the future Holy City—that Mede was wrong to consign America to a hellish future—and that America might be where Christians would find shelter during the tribulation elsewhere. For much of his life, he accepted the scenario that his father had drawn, but eventually Cotton Mather became more venturesome, more willing to predict times and dates, even more detailed than his father in his descriptions. Beginning in 1691 he published more than forty sermons and essays on eschatology, and in his most minute investigations—the "Problema Theologicum" (1703), "Triparadisus" (1726), and the "Biblia Americana" (1728)—he described the New Heavens and New Earth in an outpouring of images that exceeded anything his father had ever attempted.[57]

He also decided that his father had been wrong. By 1726, he concluded that there would be no future national conversion of the Jews. He also concluded that the return of Christ—and the conflagration that would purify the earth—might happen much sooner than anyone thought. For years he speculated about possible dates, first 1697, then 1716, then 1736. Whatever the date, the return of Christ would inaugurate the millennium, resurrect the bodies of the departed saints destined to rule with him (these Mather called the Raised Saints), draw them into the air with the saints still living (these he called the Changed Saints), and destroy the earth by fire before transforming it. Then the New Jerusalem would descend as a material but ethereal city, hovering in the air above the restored earthly Jerusalem. There the Raised Saints would dwell while the Changed Saints returned to the New Earth and reigned throughout the Chiliad, guided not only by the Raised Saints, who would descend and ascend regularly from the New Jerusalem, but also by the triumphant Christ who would make an appearance whenever he thought it necessary. After the battle of Armageddon at the end of the millennial reign, the second resurrection would raise both the righteous and the unrighteous to receive their due sentence, and God would be all in all.[58]

The vivid millennialism of the Mathers was an expression of the heightened supernaturalism of New England theology in the late seventeenth century. What seems remarkable now is how easily it coexisted with confidence in reason, enthusiasm about natural philosophy, and an assurance that rational evidences could prove the truth of Christian revelation to any reasonable person. The supernaturalism was in part a defensive response to what theologians saw as misreadings of natural philosophy that could generate a latent threat of materialism and mechanism. Their way of countering the threat was to proclaim the mysteries of the invisible world at the same time that they drew the cosmology of the natural philosophers into their theology. Both the religious rationalism and the intense supernaturalism served conservative ends. Like the catechetical exercises in the churches, they functioned to preserve an older Calvinist vision during an era in which it was coming under increasing critical scrutiny.

4

Nature, the Supernatural, and Virtue

Calvinists believed that God governed the world through both natural causation and supernatural intervention. Most maintained a sense of balance between grace and nature, revelation and reason, and special providence and natural order. In their soteriology, they emphasized both special grace and the participation of the human will and understanding in the order of salvation. In their view of religious knowledge, they stressed the priority of scriptural revelation but left a considerable space for reason to operate. In their understanding of the cosmos, they found numberless signs of divine providence, but they also agreed that secondary natural causes displayed sufficient regularity to justify natural philosophy. Such a sense of balance was implicit in the Calvinist idea of divine accommodation. By the 1720s, however, even as the Mathers promoted their heightened supernaturalism, some were beginning to rethink the balance by expanding the scope of the natural, the volitional, the reasonable, and the ethical.

For the most part, the rethinking stayed within the boundaries of Calvinist theology. In the opening decades of the eighteenth century, a small group of "catholick" Calvinists, clustered in and around Boston, cautiously employed a language that shifted the tone of Calvinist doctrine even as they affirmed its content. By the 1730s, this impulse assumed slightly more daring expression, blending with a concern for virtue that led a few clergy beyond traditional

Calvinism. At the same time, the anti-Calvinist temper of post-Restoration Anglicanism left its mark both on Anglican theologians in the southern and middle colonies and on converts to Anglicanism in New England. On occasion, the resulting disputes reflected the two forms of reason that had distinguished the Cambridge Platonists from the physico-theologians, especially when the New England Anglican convert Samuel Johnson adopted the Neoplatonist epistemology to construct a philosophical idealism quite unlike the more empirical temper of the "catholick" Congregationalists. For the most part, however, the clergy differed about reason only insofar as a few of them spoke with slightly more appreciation of its powers than others did.

The more important dispute was about virtue, especially about the extent to which the virtuous life made salvation more likely. All Calvinists honored the virtuous life, but some sought ways to link the virtuous life more closely to salvation. Others gradually veered away from their Calvinist heritage because they came to believe that it could not accord proper weight to virtue. The revivals of the 1740s stimulated a reassertion of Calvinist thought and piety against such innovations, but by mid-century, a few colonial theologians, some Anglican and some Congregationalist, often reacting against the seeming excesses of the revivals, opened the way toward a theology that defined the virtuous life as a clearer sign of religious devotion than the experience of conversion itself. The ensuing debates revealed the extent to which many Calvinists adjusted their theology to accommodate a turn in eighteenth-century intellectual life toward ethics and the ideal of virtue.

"Catholick" Calvinists

In 1730 Thomas Foxcroft, the pastor of Boston's First Church, voiced a lament that in New England the old zeal had yielded to a "Catholick Spirit, as 'tis called." Across town, Benjamin Colman, the pastor of the Brattle Street Church, found nothing to lament: to him an "enlarged Catholick Spirit" was a badge of intellectual breadth and generosity, and he especially praised Harvard College for providing the "free Air" in which it could flourish. By expanding the reading lists, the Harvard faculty — John Leverett, William Brattle, and Ebenezer Pemberton — had encouraged Harvard students to read the Cambridge Platonists, English Latitudinarians, and natural philosophers. Increase Mather warned of "Pelagian and Arminian" principles, and Cotton Mather complained that students were reading "rank poison," but after Leverett's appointment as tutor in 1685, the "catholick" ideal reigned at Harvard.[1]

No precise meaning defined the "catholick spirit," but the heart of it theologically was a cautious shift of emphasis toward the natural. The shift was visible, for instance, in the growing interest in a discipline of ethics distinct from the exegesis of biblical commandments; the Harvard tutors introduced the *Enchiridion Ethicum* of the Cambridge Platonist Henry More to students during the 1680s. The college also founded a professorship of natural philosophy and encouraged students in philosophical studies. None of this brought any immediate challenge to Calvinist orthodoxy, but the catholick spirit implied a sensibility and a rhetoric that worried the conservatives.[2]

Benjamin Colman irritated conservatives when he returned in 1699 from a four-year sojourn in England to be the pastor of the new Brattle Street Church, which announced that it would admit members without a narrative of conversion. Traditionalists felt aggrieved, and it did not help that the congregation defined the duties of the pastor and his flock by appealing to "the dictates of the law of nature" or that Colman introduced to provincial Boston a "grand and polite" rhetorical style modeled after the prose of Joseph Addison in England. But Colman's theology illustrated the caution that marked the new spirit.[3]

He published ninety books and sermons, which included reflections on earthquakes and smallpox inoculation, and his admiration for natural philosophy was evident at every turn. He urged his readers to seek the divine majesty by reading "the vast Roll of Nature, written within and without" in the light of the "new philosophy," with its marvelous discoveries of motion, gravitation, and planetary attraction. The cosmos conveyed to him the immensity of God. Yet he never called Calvinist theology into question, and he combined his interest in natural philosophy with a conventional supernaturalism. While he thought that earthquakes resulted from secondary causes, he thought also that they signified the wrath of God. While he urged modesty in eschatological speculation, he felt that it was not immodest to say that Christ would make his physical return only after the fall of the Antichrist, the conversion of the Jews, and the church's period of peace and tranquility, just before the final battle with Satan. He insisted that his "favourite subject" was the covenant of salvation through Christ, and he was said to have never referred to natural theology without linking it to the revelation in Christ. Although he asserted that reason alone could discern God's existence, he thought "the book of nature" fully legible only to the mind illumined by biblical revelation.[4]

Nonetheless, Colman represented a clerical group who were drawn to the language of natural theology and natural law. Puritan moralists had always recognized a natural law, but by 1715 John Wise (1652–1725) of Ipswich defended congregational polity almost exclusively on the basis of "the Light of Reason as a Law and Rule of Right." Drawing on the continental natural law theorist Samuel Pufendorf, Wise argued that congregational "democracy" had its origin and justification in "the Light of Nature" that was innate in "the Original State and Liberty" of humankind. He thought the light of reason owed its existence and authority to the creative power of Christ, but having secured this point he built his argument entirely on the "Natural Libertie, Equitie, Equality, and Principles of Self-Preservation" mandated by the law of nature.[5]

One telling expression of the new spirit came in a reevaluation of natural religion. In 1730, John Bulkley of Connecticut contended in his treatise on *The Usefulness of Reveal'd Religion, to Preserve and Improve that which is Natural* that the "weightiest matters" — judgment, mercy, and faith — belonged to the realm of natural religion, the faith and obedience taught by "Nature, or Natural Light." Long before Christ this natural religion taught men and women to love God, hope for immortality, expect eternal reward and punishment, love themselves, and treat their neighbors with justice and charity. The purpose of the biblical revelation was not to replace but to preserve and improve this natural religion, partly by reaffirming its truths, partly by revealing additional ones. Bulkley expressed wonder that deists should criticize a revelation that was intended to confirm their own natural religion. He thought that the deists should recognize that both sides shared a common interest in the cultivation of virtue.[6]

New England Calvinists had always said that theology was practical, retaining the medieval sense of the distinction between the practical and the theoretical. In the eighteenth century, some of them began, without fully noticing, to define the practical as the ethical, a definition that narrowed the scope of the medieval usage. With increasing frequency, the catholicks spoke of the imperatives of virtue, including the virtue of self-love. But self-love was only one of the many duties that the catholick ministers pressed on their readers. They wrote on moral obligation, the imitation of Christ, and "obedience to the divine law." As John Barnard emphasized in 1738, living "according to the Christian scheme" meant for them not only believing "the Doctrines of Christ" but also fulfilling "the moral Duties which he requires."[7]

Yet the catholick theologians proposed no alteration of Calvinist doctrine. Although they drew their images from natural philosophy, fashioned a rhetoric attuned to natural theology, preached ethics and virtue from their pulpits, and said that rational creatures owed God a rational service, which included the gathering of rational evidence for the truth of Christianity, they were confident that such affirmations were consistent with total depravity, predestination, and invincible grace. They shared with their predecessors an interest in conversion, eschatology, and providential causation. In most ways, they were still conventional New England clergy, but they subtly modified and expanded the older vocabulary in order to make more room for natural causes and moral virtues.[8]

Arminianism and Virtue

In 1726 Cotton Mather could boast that among the ministers of the two hundred New England Congregational churches, he found not a single Arminian. By 1734, John White, pastor of the church in Gloucester, saw things differently. In his *New England's Lamentations* he charged that some of the "young men" now openly preached the "Arminian scheme." Jonathan Edwards also thought that 1734 marked the beginning of "the great noise that was in this part of the country, about Arminianism."[9]

By the eighteenth century, the label "Arminian" acquired an expanding range of meanings. When such English "Arminian" theologians as Daniel Whitby, Thomas Stackhouse, and John Taylor criticized Calvinism, they meant to reject not only predestination but also imputed guilt, imputed righteousness, and original sin. Whitby's *Discourse on the Five Points* in 1710 initiated a round of anti-Calvinist critiques founded in biblical exegesis. By 1740 John Taylor of Norwich argued in his *Scripture Doctrine of Original Sin, Proposed to Free and Candid Examination* that the doctrine of original sin was incompatible with biblical teachings about God's goodness, holiness, and justice. He thought that the idea of native depravity made God responsible for evil because it implied that he sent his creatures into the world with insuperably sinful inclinations. Taylor acknowledged the ubiquity of sin but denied its heritability; sin was, in his view, a personal act, not an inherited status.[10]

In the 1730s, New Englanders began to accuse one another of Arminianism, though the accuracy of the charge remains open to question. Some of the accused complained bitterly about "being branded with the opprobrious Name of an Arminian," and most of the celebrated cases were ambiguous. In 1733 in North Yarmouth, Maine, a church council brought the minister Ammi Cutter to trial for alleged Arminian views, but it cleared him. Robert Breck, who settled in 1735 in Springfield, Massachusetts, faced charges that he thought the heathen who obeyed the light of nature could be saved, but he subscribed, during the squabble, to the canons of the Synod of Dort. The trial of Benjamin Kent in Marlborough, Massachusetts, in 1735 posed a clear alternative. Kent's church dismissed him for denying the eternal decrees, describing election as conditional on good works, and rejecting original sin. But the next incident was more ambiguous. In 1738, the Second Parish in Eastham dismissed Samuel Osborn, who had preached that Christ's sufferings did not abate the obligation to obey the law, that men and women could "do that upon the doing of which they shall certainly be saved," and that obedience was a cause of justification. But Osborn did not deny that faith and obedience resulted from the special grace of election. Eleven other ministers declared him orthodox. He might have been no more than a catholick Calvinist linking theology more closely to moral virtue.[11]

During the 1740s, critics of Calvinist doctrine became bolder. In 1743 a group of Boston laymen decried "rigid Favourers of the Doctrines of Calvinism." In the same year, William Balch of Bradford, Massachusetts, said that the Apostle Paul had understood "faith" to include moral obedience. In the ensuing pamphlet battles, Balch argued that everyone received grace "sufficient" for salvation and that this grace could be resisted. His argument carried him outside Calvinist boundaries. In 1744 Experience Mayhew, the minister on Martha's Vineyard, published *Grace Defended,* in which he tried to revise Calvinism by arguing that Jesus died for everyone, that God offered grace to all, and that all had the liberty to accept or resist the offer. His revisions left in place little of traditional Calvinist doctrine.[12]

As a self-educated theologian, Mayhew had limited influence against the clergy from Harvard and Yale, but in 1749 Harvard graduate Lemuel Briant published a provocative sermon on *The Absurdity and Blasphemy of Depretiating Moral Virtue* in which he asserted that the "pure religion of Jesus" suspended "our whole Happiness upon our personal good Behaviour." Briant would always deny that he was Arminian, since he did not attribute justification to the merit of personal righteousness, but he inserted into his sermon a long paragraph that obliquely criticized the doctrines of unconditional election, original sin, irresistible grace, and the perseverance of the saints. A council of seven churches deplored his errors. Its moderator, the aged Samuel Niles at Braintree, charged that Briant had deprecated ministers of "Calvinistical Character and Perswasion" and made Christianity a "meer scheme of Morality." It was sometimes difficult to distinguish the "catholick" spirit from Arminian deviation.[13]

The Anglican Alternative

Calvinists who worried about Arminians worried also about Anglicans. The anti-Calvinist temper in the Church of England after the Restoration meant that Anglican missionaries to America would have little respect for Calvinist doctrine. The first Anglican commissary to Maryland, Thomas Bray (1656–1730) organized in 1698 a Society for Promoting Christian Knowledge, which sent to America books that prominently included alternatives to Calvinist thought. Three years later, Bray organized a Society for the Propagation of the Gospel in Foreign Parts, which sent missionaries whose instructions included admonitions to teach in the rational style prevalent in England. They were to begin "with the principles of natural Religion," appealing to reason and conscience, before proceeding to show the necessity of revelation and the proofs that validated the Christian scriptures. The tone was to be reasonable, moderate, and judicious, and these were not traits that Bray associated with Calvinism.[14]

Arriving in 1699, Bray remained in Maryland only three months, so he can hardly be called a colonial theologian, but he wrote treatises — such as *A Short Discourse Upon the Doctrine of our Baptismal Covenant* (1696) — designed to be read aloud in the American plantations, and he laid out a position that would continue to find adherents in later colonial Anglican thought. Bray was a covenant theologian who thought that to know the covenant of grace was to grasp "the whole tenor of Christianity," but his was no Calvinist covenant. Entry into it came through baptism, and every baptized church member who continued to profess true religion and obey the laws of the gospel remained within it. Bray thought, therefore, that justification required both faith and obedience; for him the doctrine of grace meant that God provided assistance, chiefly in the sacraments, through which Christians could conform to the Christian religion and obey its laws. What distinguished the covenant of grace from the covenant with Adam was that Christ's atonement ensured that God would accept "imperfect Righteousness" as fulfilling its conditions, and Bray also had no doubt that a moral life was a covenantal condition: to implant morality, he wrote, "was the great Design of our Saviour's Coming into the World."[15]

Among eighteenth-century Anglicans in the middle and southern colonies, Calvinist theology never prevailed against the theological temper that Bray represented. When the revivalist George Whitefield, who was both Anglican and Calvinist, toured South Carolina, his most vigorous critic was the Anglican commissary, Alexander Garden (1685–1756), who cast his criticism as a refutation of the whole "Calvinistical scheme." In his *Six Letters* to Whitefield, Garden argued that even the doctrine of justification by faith alone presupposed good works as a "condition" of justification, since the epistle of James described faith without works as dead. Garden observed in his *Doctrine of Justification* that he assigned no "merit" to either good works or faith. Only the mediation of Christ had saving merit, but since justifying faith preceded justification, and since justifying faith necessarily entailed good works, then good works also had to precede justification. Infants might be justified through baptism, but for adults justification was conditional on both faith and good works.[16]

Equally troubling to Garden was Whitefield's doctrine of regeneration as a sudden act of the Spirit upon a passive subject. For Garden, the new birth was a lifelong process, beginning at baptism and advancing by degrees of faith, repentance, and obedience by means of the "gradual co-operating Work of the Holy Spirit." The whole economy of grace, he thought, "is an Oeconomy of Co-operation" between the Spirit and sinful but reasonable human agents. Such a theology, he believed, represented the best insights of both "natural reason and the written Word of God."[17]

Within a decade of Garden's clash with Whitefield, Samuel Quincy, priest at St. Philips in Charlestown, South Carolina, espoused a full-blown Anglican theology of virtue. In his *Twenty Sermons* (1750) Quincy presented Christianity as a rational religion consisting "principally in moral Goodness." "The whole of Religion" comprised duties to God, self, and neighbor, and the saving work of Christ perfected only those who obeyed the laws of God as "absolutely necessary to Salvation." For Quincy, morality became the criterion of doctrine: a belief that failed to "promote every virtuous and good Disposition" was "false and counterfeit."[18]

Such views found wide acceptance among Anglican clergy in the southern colonies. When the Anglican revivalist Devereux Jarratt (1733–1801) became the rector of Bath Parish in Virginia in 1764, his preaching conveyed Calvinist views of sinfulness, free grace, and regeneration. Even though he rejected the doctrine of predestination, he found that these views brought opposition and reproach from the Anglican clergy of the colony, who called him a fanatic because of his revivalism and a Presbyterian because of his belief in the "utter inability" of men and women to "restore themselves to the favor and image of God, which were lost by the *fall*, by anything they could either do or suffer." Like the Congregationalist Arminians, most Anglican clergy worried that Calvinism hindered the nurturing of virtue.[19]

Anglicans in New England, especially, spoke for a minority who often felt aggrieved at Calvinist dominance. For them it was a signal victory when, in 1722, the seven-member faculty of Yale College converted from Congregationalism to the Church of England. Four had second thoughts, but three sailed to England to receive Anglican orders. Their conversions had more to do with church order than with the order of salvation, but Calvinist clergy found the root of the crisis in "Arminian books." One of the converts replied that "we hold no doctrines now but what were held and taught in our Church long before Arminius was heard of," but to New England Calvinists the Anglicans were Arminians, which meant that they were concerned more with ethics than with faith.[20]

The Yale converts included Samuel Johnson (1696–1772), who would become the most erudite colonial Anglican theologian of the eighteenth century. After his ordination, he spent his career as the rector in Stratford, Connecticut, and after 1754 as the first president of King's College in New York (later Columbia). As early as 1714 he had begun to seek an alternative to "rigid Calvinistical notions," and when English friends of Yale sent the college a library of new books, he and his friends read Francis Bacon, Isaac Newton, and Robert Boyle, the theologians Daniel Whitby and John Tillotson, the philosophers John Locke and John Norris, and other representatives of what Johnson called the "New Learning."[21]

When Johnson joined the Yale converts, he was concerned mainly about the order of the church, and he inaugurated a tradition of "high church" thought in Connecticut that endured into the mid-nineteenth century. Its defining themes included the arguments that a true church required episcopal authority; that the three orders of bishop, priest, and deacon were essential for its proper order; and that salvation normally required participation in the sacramental means of grace. An admirer of Archbishop William Laud in England, Johnson attempted to translate the high church theories associated with Laud and his followers to the American colonial setting. This entailed a sacramental piety in which church membership came through baptism (rather than through a prior covenant that the sacrament merely sealed) and the Eucharist offered a real, albeit spiritual, communion with the body and blood of Christ.[22]

In New England, however, Anglican loyalties also suggested disdain for Calvinist theology. The Anglican polemicist John Checkley had published in 1720 his *Choice Dialogues* against the doctrines of election and predestination, and in 1733, Johnson published his own criticism of "the Calvinistic doctrine of absolute predestination and reprobation." In three letters to the Congregationalists of his town, published between 1733 and 1737, he began more than a decade of anti-Calvinist polemics, culminating in 1745 in his *Letter from Aristocles to Authades Concerning the Sovereignty and the Promises of God*, which led to a long pamphlet debate with the Presbyterian revivalist Jonathan Dickinson. His critics labeled him an Arminian. He repudiated the label, but he could not escape it, since by now it served to connote almost any detour from Calvinist orthodoxy.[23]

After transferring his allegiance to the Church of England, Johnson still believed in original sin (though without imputed guilt), still affirmed Christ's atonement (though denying that it was only for the elect), still insisted on inward regeneration (though viewing it now as a gradual change), and still thought repentance impossible without grace. But he objected to the doctrine of "God's eternal, arbitrary and absolute determination of the everlasting fate of his creatures, from his own mere motion, and without any consideration of their good or ill behavior." It contradicted his understanding of God as a benevolent moral governor; it seemed to make sin necessary and so blameless; and it left no room "for either virtue or vice."[24]

He believed that God had issued one decree: the righteous would be happy and the wicked miserable. Their own free choices as "self-exerting and self-determining agents" determined their fate. Only through grace could there be sensibility of guilt and a striving for something better, but this was a common grace bestowed on all humankind, and only those who responded rightly could rely on "the promises of divine efficacious aid or special grace."[25]

To preserve his confidence in divine benevolence, Johnson abandoned the belief that salvation came only through conscious faith in Christ: "Is he the God of Christians only?" The issue had been raised by English deists, who thought it unjust that God would condemn the many souls who never heard of Jesus, and by 1747, when Johnson discussed the question in his letter to Dickinson, a number of theologians in England were responding to the deists by emphasizing the broader possibilities for salvation implicit even in the Christian revelation. Johnson found biblical warrant for his position in Romans 2: "the doers of the law" would be justified. "As they have only the light of nature to guide them," he wrote, "so God will expect only such a conformity to it as their abilities and circumstances will admit of."[26]

His understanding of divine mercy led Johnson to say that the true glory of God — and God's "great end" — was human happiness. The aim was that human beings might be happy as long as they obeyed the divine laws. The Calvinist view that God's end was the divine glory now struck him as implying a "selfish" God. For him, God created the world because of an "earnest desire" to extend happiness to others, as would befit an ethical God. Happiness had long been a guiding theme in Christian theology. Augustine assumed that men and women necessarily sought it; Thomas Aquinas thought of it as the proper good of every intelligent being; and Calvin believed that the highest happiness came through trust in God. Calvinists spoke often of happiness as one of the ends of creation, but they subordinated it to the supreme end of God's glory. It was this contrast between human happiness and divine glory that Johnson now rejected. The aim of a practical theology, he thought, was to point out the means to happiness.[27]

When Johnson spoke of theology as practical, he meant that its purpose was ethical. He sometimes defended his theology by arguing that his "amiable apprehensions" of God would serve better than Calvinist theology to encourage holiness. The "general drift" of the Bible was to excite the pursuit of virtue, and the defect of Calvinism was that its determinism undercut ethics. His preoccupation with virtue led him in 1746 to publish his *Ethices Elementa*, a text in moral philosophy defending a "rationalist" ethical theory that had been used to counter such moral "voluntarists" as Thomas Hobbes and René Descartes, who derived morality from either arbitrary divine commands or prudential social agreements. This ethical rationalism had emerged with the Cambridge Platonists, and Johnson admired the argument of John Norris and Ralph Cudworth that immutable moral truths, reflecting eternal essences within the divine nature, were accessible through an intellectual insight into "the truth and reality of things."[28]

He read also other ethical rationalists, especially Samuel Clarke and William Wollaston. Clarke's Boyle Lectures on *Natural Religion* in 1705 rooted morality in the necessary and eternal "relations" that different things bear to one another. To act rightly was to act in a "fitting" manner — a manner in accord with the true "nature of things." Against Hobbes, Clarke contended that no social compact or sovereign command could make an unfitting action right. The obligation to refrain from murder, for example, arose from the nature of human beings as creatures made in the image of God, created to live in community, sharing similar wants and desires, needing mutual help, and maintaining expectations of fair treatment. To murder was to contradict these truths about human beings. Such a contradiction would prevent the happiness that God had designed for the creation. Wollaston's *Religion of Nature Delineated* (1724) carried the rationalist ethic to its logical conclusion: to be virtuous, he thought, was to act according to the truth.[29]

The leading motif of Johnson's *Ethices Elementa* was the claim that moral good consisted in "freely choosing and acting conformable to the truth and natures of things," and he cited both Clarke and Wollaston throughout. On occasion he used the language of "moral sense" popularized by Francis Hutcheson in Glasgow, who wanted to ground morality not in reason, which Hutcheson viewed as merely sagacity in pursuing an end, but in moral feelings that provided a more reliable perception of the good. But Johnson thought that the primary ethical task was to discover the truth about ourselves, to consider ourselves "as we are" in our relations to God, self, and each other.[30]

He differed from his British predecessors in two ways. Far more than Clarke, he saw individual happiness as the overriding purpose of ethical propriety. "The great end of my being," he wrote, "is that my rational and immortal nature might be completely and endlessly happy." Far more than Wollaston, he circumscribed the reach of reason. He described ethics as "the religion of nature," but he insisted that its truths and duties would never have been "obvious to our weak reason, without revelation." When he argued that ethics was rational, therefore, he meant that its truths were "founded in the first principles of reason and nature," not that reason alone could have discovered them. Johnson assured Benjamin Colman, who urged him to state the point more clearly, that neither he nor Wollaston could have reached their conclusions "without the help of revelation." Nonetheless, the Calvinist Joseph Bellamy, a student of Jonathan Edwards, thought that Johnson failed to reconcile his grounding of ethics in reason and nature with his claim that moral obligations originated in the revealed command of God.[31]

In addition to his interest in ethics, he had, from his student years, been concerned about a broad range of theological and philosophical questions, and between 1714 and 1731 he drew up three encyclopedic outlines of the arts. They revealed a special fascination with the philosophy of George Berkeley (1685–1753). The dean of Derry in Ireland, Berkeley came to Rhode Island in 1729 and spent two years in Newport. Johnson read his *Treatise Concerning the Principles of Human Knowledge* (1710), and Berkeley's sojourn in America allowed the two men to talk and correspond. Johnson became a proponent of Berkeley's "immaterialist hypothesis," and in 1752 he published his *Elementa Philosophica,* in which he expounded a Berkeleyan theory of reality.[32]

During the same period he read widely in the antideist debates. Anthony Collins's *Grounds and Reasons of the Christian Religion* (1724) disturbed him, though he thought that both Samuel Clarke and the English Bishop Edward Chandler had written convincing refutations. He pondered Thomas Woolston's theory that the miracle stories were allegories, though he believed that Bishop Richard Smallbrooke had confuted it. He also read Matthew Tindal's *Christianity as Old as the Creation* (1730), along with Bishop John Conybeare's refutation of it. His conclusion was that "the mere light of nature uninstructed" could not have discovered even the truths of natural religion.[33]

What he found in Berkeley's thought, however, was a way to envision the divine presence in the cosmos depicted by eighteenth-century natural philosophy: "it not only gave new incontestable proofs of a deity, but moreover the most striking apprehensions of his constant presence with us and inspection over us, and of our entire dependence on him and infinite obligations to his most wise and almighty benevolence." For some, eighteenth-century natural philosophy suggested a contrary vision, a cosmos of material atoms related to each other in mechanistic relations of cause and effect. For some, in fact, John Locke's *Essay Concerning Human Understanding* (1690) appeared to support this mechanistic theory, for Locke described a world in which the "primary qualities" of matter were solidity, extension, figure, motion or rest, and number. The mind's ideas of solidity or extension, therefore, represented the world as it really was.[34]

Locke saw that we perceive more than solid, extended particles. We also have "ideas" (that is, perceptions) of colors, tastes, and other sensations. But he described these qualities as "secondary," partly because they varied in accord with the minds that perceived them and partly because they were not essential to a mechanical system. One way to read Locke was to view his epistemology as implying a world of matter and force. Locke thought, to be sure, that the mind also had "ideas of reflection" that allowed it to observe its own activity as spirit, and that it enjoyed intuitive evidence for an eternal, most-powerful, most-knowing God. He made room for spirits and Spirit. But Berkeley thought he failed to see that spirit was all in all.[35]

In Berkeley's view, Locke failed to make the case for his distinction between primary and secondary qualities. Since the supposedly primary qualities of solidity and extension, for instance, were accessible only through our ideas of them, why assume that they had a primacy over color or pain? In Berkeley's view, moreover, Locke's theory of knowledge led also to skepticism. If ideas merely represented their objects, the mind had no way to compare its ideas with the objects they supposedly represented. Maybe the ideas deceived. In his view, finally, Locke was not sufficiently empirical, for when Locke assumed that ideas of primary qualities represented material substances, he went beyond experience. By Locke's own theory, the mind had immediate access only to its ideas. Since we cannot think of anything as existing unperceived (for to think of it at all we have to perceive it at least mentally), why assume that anything exists apart from its being perceived? It made more sense to Berkeley to think that reality consisted of ideas and the spirits that perceived them.[36]

Berkeley assured Johnson that he accepted most of Newton's science. His point was that the Newtonian scheme required no material substances. It required only consistent natural phenomena and laws that described their activities. Berkeley's philosophy could explain both the phenomena and the laws. Since to be *(esse)* was to be perceived *(percipi)* or to be a perceiver, and since the world continued in being even when finite spirits did not perceive it, there had to be a Mind, omnipresent and ever active, whose perceptions maintained it. This world "would shrink to nothing, if not upheld and preserved in being by the same force that first created it."[37]

What attracted Johnson was the thought that "ideas" — the immediate objects of experience — depended on the incessant agency of God. He also liked Berkeley's contention that minds had, in addition to sensory ideas, "notions" of spiritual objects — conceptions of mathematical truths, or justice, or mental operations — for this also suggested to him "the universal presence and action of the Deity." Johnson explained these "notions" with a theory of "intellectual light" derived from the Cambridge Platonists, especially Ralph Cudworth, the French monk Nicolas Malebranche (1638–1715), and the Catholic Archbishop of Cambrai, François Fénelon (1651–1715).[38]

By "intellectual light" he seems to have in mind three distinct mental activities. It referred, first, to the mind's awareness of itself and of other minds, including its awareness of its own existence as the necessary condition of its thoughts. The light also denoted for Johnson the medium "by which" the mind could know "the objects of pure intellect," the first principles that did not come through sensory experience, including mathematical and logical truths. Such truths, being necessary and eternal, entailed for him "the necessary existence of an eternal mind" and the certainty of our communion with it. And the light meant, third, the standard "whereby" created minds could recognize a true statement as true, or a good act as good, or a beautiful object as beautiful — mental acts that presupposed the prior presence in the mind of a standard of truth, goodness, and beauty. This third point linked Johnson, through Fénelon and the Cambridge Platonists, with Augustine and with Neoplatonic thought.[39]

Johnson's discussion of the intellectual light revealed the theological motivation behind his philosophy. For Johnson the intellectual light revealed our "entire dependence" on the Mind that contained all the eternal and necessary truths, the Mind whose true ideas served as the standard of truth. Everything bespoke the divine presence. Nature was a language through which God communicated to the creatures without ceasing.[40]

Toward the end of his life, Johnson became entranced with the theology of John Hutchinson (1674–1737) in England, who taught that the Hebrew text of the Old Testament contained all the truths of science and philosophy and proved the inconsistency of Newton. Hutchinson's *Moses' Principia* (1724) persuaded him to expend his considerable energies on the study of the Hebrew language. But the core of his theology resided in his earlier reflections on the church, natural philosophy, metaphysics, and ethics, and these interests showed his similarities to the "catholick" Calvinists and Congregationalist Arminians. Especially in his handbook on ethics, he displayed the expanding interest in the place of virtue within the Christian life. To some ministers in New England, however, it seemed that careless talk about virtue threatened the integrity of Calvinist truth. Their fears found expression in their defense of New England revivalism.[41]

Theology and the Revival

In August 1737, an Irish-born Presbyterian minister named Gilbert Tennent (1703–64) complained to a congregation in New Brunswick, New Jersey, that too many people were so "curious in the Search of other Sciences" that they neglected "the Search and Study of their own Hearts." Like Solomon Stoddard,

Tennent believed that the purpose of theology was to promote an "experimental" knowledge — embracing the will and affections — and that every other kind of doctrinal and speculative knowledge merely prepared the way for this practical wisdom. Tennent was returning to the medieval conception that theology was practical not because it outlined the path of virtue in this world but because it provided a knowledge of God for the sake of salvation.[42]

A little over two years later, the English revivalist George Whitefield stepped ashore in Lewistown, Delaware, and began the first of two preaching tours that would generate religious excitement from Georgia to Maine. This was the start of what Jonathan Dickinson called "the great Revival of Religion," and it colored American theology for more than a decade by drawing theologians back to the study of their own hearts. The revivals to which Dickinson referred were a series of local religious awakenings, affecting mainly Congregational and Presbyterian churches in New England and the middle colonies, which aroused disputes over the nature of conversion, the practices of lay exhorters, the qualifications of ministers, the style of preaching, and the behavior of converts whose ecstasy struck some as extreme. The significance of the revivals for theology was that they further displayed — just as catholick Calvinism had displayed — the way in which minute differences could create serious divisions within Calvinism, and they illustrated the divided mind of Calvinist theologians about the relation between faith and virtue.[43]

The revivals divided the Congregational clergy into ranks of New Lights, who favored the revivals, Old Lights, who opposed them, and, to use a term suggested by Samuel Mather, Regular Lights, who took no firm position either way. Revivalism also divided Presbyterians into companies of New Side revivalists and Old Side critics of revivalist piety, who from 1741 to 1758 split into two churches. Such divisions also created stresses in the relationships between clergy and laity, sometimes emboldening lay exhorters to criticize the theology of their Old Side or Old Light ministers, sometimes provoking lay pamphleteers to ridicule New Lights and New Side preachers. Some of the lay criticism extended into eighteenth-century America the anticlerical traditions visible earlier in the ideal of the pious plowman and the preaching "mechanick."[44]

While the populist spirit would not emerge in full force until after the American Revolution, the early eighteenth-century revivals aroused unease among some of the educated about the audacity of uneducated self-proclaimed theologians. Charles Chauncy (1705–87), the pastor of First Church in Boston and a critic of the revival, felt dismay about lay exhorters, even including "female exhorters," who left their "proper station" to teach. He led other Boston critics in condemning the rash of "Private Persons of no Education, and but low Attainments in Knowledge, in the great Doctrines of the Gospel" who took it upon themselves to promote the revival and its theology. They were "babes in understanding," they were even illiterate, and yet they judged and censured able ministers, and their censorious spirit was spreading "among the Common people."[45]

For their part, the revivalists sometimes replied to such criticism by seeming to encourage a theological democracy. To complaints that "most of us are unlearned," the Presbyterian revivalist Samuel Finley (1715–66) noted that Jesus himself had been followed "by what we call the Mob, the Rabble, the common and meaner sort." Revivalists who defended the lay exhorters had to affirm that the unschooled could understand and teach the scriptures. To Chauncy it seemed that they were turning theology over to the "raw" and the "weak" and that they were exposing ministers to contempt.[46]

It might seem tempting to view the revivalist preachers as critics of the expanding efforts to demonstrate the reasonableness of Christianity, but Gilbert Tennent and other revival preachers could outline all the standard proofs for the existence of God and all the evidences for the authenticity of the biblical revelation. In matters of morals, the revivalists felt perfectly justified in appealing to natural law, the light of nature, and a "reasonable self-love." They wanted to ensure, however, that all the talk about rationality and virtue did not lead the New England churches away from the piety of rebirth.[47]

The rational side of the revivalist agenda was visible in the early thought of Jonathan Dickinson (1688–1747), a Yale graduate who settled at Elizabethtown, New Jersey, in 1708, became a Presbyterian minister by 1717, and published in 1732 his treatise on *The Reasonableness of Christianity*. Although he remained a Calvinist, Dickinson cited the Anglican Samuel Clarke, admired John Locke, adapted Christian apologetic to the new astronomy, and treated the credibility of Christian doctrine as a matter of converging "probabilities." He attained a considerable reputation in Britain, where the theologian John Erskine claimed that the British Isles had produced no theological thinkers in the eighteenth century to match America's two Jonathans—Edwards and Dickinson.[48]

Dickinson thought that he could find "rational evidence" for all the central Christian truths, ranging from the existence of God to the fall and redemption of humanity. He shared the evidentialist confidence that the biblical prophecies and miracles provided "public" evidence of "matters of fact" that confirmed Christian doctrine. He was equally confident in natural theology. He thought it irrational to suppose that a contingent world could have existed eternally and necessarily, or that "the prodigious magnitude and amazing extent of the Universe," let alone the "art and contrivance" manifest in everything from human bodies and souls to "the least pebble," could be explained without reference to a cause sufficient to the effect. He thought, moreover, that the doctrines of sin and reconciliation were fully "agreeable to the light of reason," and that reason could "demonstrate" the justice of divine punishment, the credibility of the incarnation, and the plausibility of the atonement. Reason could prove, by amassing probabilities, the truth of Calvinist orthodoxy. To John Locke, Christianity was credible because of its simplicity; to Dickinson, it was credible because a "throng of probabilities" converged as evidence for it. No catholick Calvinist, and no critic of the revival, had a higher estimation of the reasonableness of Christianity.[49]

They might agree about reason, but the opposing sides still accused each other of doctrinal error. Tennent looked around him and saw nothing but the "spread of Arminianism, Socinianism, Arianism, and Deism." Chauncy found just as many "Errors in Doctrine," including the recurrence of antinomian heresy. One striking feature of the dispute, however, at least among the Reformed theologians, was the subtlety of the theological differences between the revivalists and their opponents. The controversy was not, at its heart, a matter of conflicting theologies, but some of the issues did reveal differences in attitude toward the new emphasis on virtue.[50]

The revivalists saw themselves as the champions of the "great Reformation doctrine" of justification by faith alone. Jonathan Edwards made this the centerpiece of his sermons during the revival in Northampton, and the refrain of Whitefield's sermons was the "absolute necessity" for utter dependence on the justifying grace of God in Christ. When Tennent preached in 1740 on "The Danger of an Unconverted Ministry," he warned that unconverted clergy were likely to neglect "the doctrines of original sin, justification by faith alone, and the other Points of Calvinism." When the Irish-born Presbyterian minister in Londonderry, New Hampshire, David McGregore (1710–7?) defended the revival in 1741, he also saw the theological issue as the preservation of Calvinist truths about original sin, the new birth, and justification by faith alone.[51]

The revivalists accompanied this insistence on justification by faith alone with a reassertion of predestinarian doctrine. In 1740 William Cooper published his treatise on *The Doctrine of Predestination Unto Life*, with a preface by five ministers who said that the doctrine was essential. In 1742 the Irish immigrant Samuel Blair (1712–51) of Londonderry, Pennsylvania, published *The Doctrine of Predestination*, arguing that the fundamental Christian doctrines depended on this truth. At about the same time, Jonathan Dickinson published his *True Scripture-Doctrine Concerning Some Important Points of Christian Faith*, which Thomas Foxcroft ranked — with John Norton's *Orthodox Evangelist* and Samuel Willard's *Compleat Body of Divinity* — as one of the three outstanding American treatises that set the "great points of Gospel-Truth" together in "one View." Dickinson's aim was to vindicate the Calvinist doctrines of original sin, conversion, justification, and predestination.[52]

Arguing that God's Will was God's essence, Dickinson insisted that if the Will changed in response to conditions in the world, then the divine essence would change, which he saw as impossible. The language of divine election in Ephesians 1:4 therefore entailed the eternal predestination of the elect. Dickinson used a Lockean argument to show that this divine necessity was consistent with human freedom. Since every free agent must choose whatever the understanding, appetites, and affections represented as the fit object of choice, freedom could not be opposed to necessity. Agents were free when they could choose in accord with their understanding and affection and then act as they chose, even though their choices were determined. The unregenerate freely chose to turn away from true faith because their understandings, appetites, and affections prompted such a choice.[53]

The revivalists attributed salvation solely to the righteousness of Christ, and they preferred the traditional language of "imputation" — God imputed to all humanity the guilt of Adam's sin and to the elect the righteousness of Christ — to describe sinfulness and conversion. They had no doubt about the alternative against which this language of imputation should be directed. They were contrasting faith in Christ with reliance on human virtue. They compared their "preaching [of] Christ" with the preaching of "meer Morality," "natural religion," and "moral Duties" that they found when they read the sermons of their opponents.[54]

Andrew Croswell (1708–85), for instance, was the minister in Groton, Connecticut, and an itinerant revivalist known for invading Old Light parishes. When he defended Whitefield in 1741 against Anglican critics in South Carolina, he insisted that the issue was justification: the "followers of Mr. Calvin" knew that elect believers could receive it without doing "one Good Work." An admirer of the volatile itinerant James Davenport (1716–57), Croswell carried his denigration of "abominable good Works" to such an extreme that even other revivalists suspected him of antinomianism. He replied that "only a few" New England Congregationalists dared to "adhere to the Doctrines of the Reformation."[55]

Among the prominent critics of the revival, however, deviations from Calvinism on the doctrines of justification by faith and election are hard to locate. Chauncy's formulation of justification in his *Seasonable Thoughts on the State of Religion in New England* in 1743 shows how narrow the differences were. Chauncy believed that salvation came solely by grace, "antecedent to all other Causes and Considerations." He believed that justification resulted not from good works but from the "free, unmerited mercy of God," "the Righteousness of Christ," and the gift of faith. Like every other New England Calvinist, he believed that the law remained as a "Rule of Life" for the Christian, but he thought that the scriptures made it plain that "we are saved by Grace." What he wanted to add, however, was that faith included "a living, active, never-failing Principle of all holy Obedience to the Laws of God." Only on this point — whether the gift of justifying faith included a principle of obedience — did Chauncy differ from the revivalists about justification. The division, how-ever narrow, was about virtue.[56]

The second dispute, alongside the one over justification, was about rebirth and preparation for salvation. Eighteenth-century Calvinists interpreted the new birth, or regeneration, as the result of a new supernatural principle wrought by the Spirit in the soul, making possible faith and obedience. Dickin-son's *Nature and Necessity of Regeneration* (1743) argued, against Anglicans in England, that rebirth was essential and that it resulted from the "immedi-ate" influence of the Spirit on the will and understanding, bringing a new "View of divine things," a new volition, and a new obedience. Only through the new birth could faith arise in the soul. Faith was the "first grace" exercised by the reborn soul.[57]

Revivalists often suggested that regeneration proceeded in stages — that one could distinguish a variety of sequential graces. A similar argument appeared in continental Pietism and in reforming movements in Holland. The Dutch pastor Theodore Frelinghuysen (1691–ca. 1747), active in the Raritan Valley in New Jersey, might have encouraged Gilbert Tennent to emphasize it. But not everyone approved of it. Jonathan Edwards was cautious about the idea, and several opponents of the revival were even more wary. John Thomson, one of the ablest Old Side Presbyterian opponents, especially disliked any suggestion that regeneration occurred in a set manner, as if the Spirit always first worked faith, then repentance, then love. Thomson assumed an ordering of regeneration, but he saw it as more variable than some of the revivalists seemed willing to admit.[58]

The revivalist view of the order of salvation resurrected questions about preparation. No topic recurred more often in revivalist preaching and po-lemics. The New Light and New Side theologians believed it necessary that the Spirit "prepare" the heart for regeneration by bringing the sinful to discover "their Guilt and Misery." Dickinson wrote his *Display of God's Special Grace* (1742) to press this point, and Tennent argued that it was incumbent on every minister to proclaim "the great necessity of a Work of Humiliation, or Convic-tion, in order to [effect] a sound Conversion from Sin and Satan, to God and Holiness." The first act "in the Order of the Spirit's working" was to produce a conviction of guilt and misery. It became a New Light truism that conviction preceded regeneration.[59]

Old Light and Old Side ministers actually agreed with the revivalists that the Spirit normally convinced the heart of its sinfulness before infusing the grace of regeneration. Chauncy conceded that there was "ordinarily some Preparation" by which the Spirit brought "conviction" to sinners by opening to them a view of their guilt. Opponents of the revivals usually denied, however, that the preparatory convictions had to be so great "as to fill the heart with a fear and terror." Solomon Stoddard had urged the preaching of terror, and Whitefield was known for his ability to induce it. Revivalists regularly employed "the Terrors of the Law," and their opponents thought that they fell into excess. But even the tactic of terror denoted no clear theological distinction. Chauncy said that he had no objection in principle to the "Preaching of Terror," and neither did John Thomson, who insisted only that the terrors of the law remain "secondary" to the "inviting and encouraging doctrines" of the gospel. New Lights were not averse to including comfort and encouragement in their sermons. The antirevivalists merely denied that preparatory convictions were always necessary. The dispute was about a matter of emphasis, a question of strategy, not of bedrock doctrines.[60]

A third point of disagreement was about self-love. Tennent saw error in the tendency of Old Light and Old Side preachers to equate the glory of God with human happiness—a tendency that John Thomson defended as being in harmony with the Westminster Catechism. Tennent felt especially uncomfortable when Old Lights appealed to self-love as a motive for Christian belief and practice, but Thomson replied that self-love was so closely linked to the rational human constitution that it was impossible to renounce it. The issue seemed to create a clear party distinction. Yet revivalists like Benjamin Colman and Thomas Foxcroft also believed that self-love was part of human nature. This was again no dividing line between theological factions; it was a dispute over strategy in the pulpit.[61]

Chauncy thought that he found a fourth point of difference when he accused the revivalists of appealing to the passions alone. He thought religious faith precarious if it arose from the passions rather than the will and understanding, and he saw the revivals as outbreaks of passion. As a description of some revivalist practice, the criticism made sense. Extremists like Davenport and Croswell did play on the emotions of their congregations. But other revivalists denied that their theory differed from Chauncy's. Tennent said that revivals excited the passions only "after the information of the understanding," and he contended that the "first and principal work" of the Spirit in conversion was to give light to the understanding, which in turn established the heart and engaged the will. Dickinson believed that the renewing of the will and affections followed the renewal of the understanding. For at least some of the revivalists, the difference faded away.[62]

The revivals did produce a real dispute over a fifth matter: the meaning of Paul's claim in Romans 8:16 that the Spirit bears witness with the spirits of the faithful that they are children of God. From the beginning of the revivals, Whitefield maintained that Paul intended for Christians to have an immediate experience of the Spirit that assured them of their faith. This brought the accusation that the revivalists were "enthusiasts" who believed in immediate revelations from God, so when Dickinson preached his 1740 sermon on *The Witness of the Spirit,* he spoke cautiously. Sometimes, he said, the Spirit witnessed to the faithful by infusing the sanctifying influences that produced a holy life. But sometimes the Spirit's witness was more "immediate" and "extraordinary," with an influence "sensible" and "perceptible."[63]

Gilbert Tennent's insistence on the immediate witness was at the center of his debate with John Thomson, who believed it wrong to interpret Paul as meaning that all believers were "assuredly sensible" of their gracious state from the time of their first entrance into it. Tennent seemed to him to be saying that assurance was of the essence of faith, and this was not the doctrine of the Westminster Catechism. Assurance, as Thomson saw it, normally came through the fruits of holiness and humility, though he did not deny that some converts might also be "sensibly assured" of their estate. He also thought it ludicrous for some of the revivalists to claim that one converted person could surely recognize another.[64]

The disagreement contributed to the split of the Presbyterian Church in 1741, and after this division Tennent tried to state his view with more precision. He did not believe, he said, that all gracious people attained a full assurance in this life; he did not insist that everyone be able to recite the time and place of conversion; he did not believe that to lose the sense of assurance was to lose one's faith. But he did think that "ordinarily" most true Christians had "a lesser or greater Degree of comfortable Perswasion of their gracious state."[65]

This was not enough for more radical New Lights like Croswell, who disliked it when Jonathan Dickinson tried in 1742 to formulate a mediating position. Dickinson argued that true believers would never content themselves without assurance and that assurance could come from the sensible impressions of the Spirit, but he also denied that assurance was "essential to true faith," and he insisted that believers look to their "habitual course of vital and true Holiness" for evidence that their inner sense of assurance really came from the Spirit. This seemed to Croswell more dangerous than "the worst Arminian Performance that ever was written." Croswell told Dickinson that "persuasion of our justified estate" was essential to faith, that no one could trust Christ without being "sensible" of his or her trust, and that Dickinson was making assurance dependent on holiness without the joyful "Discoveries of Christ" that the direct witness of the Spirit made possible.[66]

Chauncy formulated the Old Light position. Citing the Westminster Confession, the Cambridge Platform of 1648, and the synod that condemned Anne Hutchinson, he declared it an error to say that assurance belonged to the essence of faith. The problem as he saw it was a recurrence of antinomian heresy. The new Hutchinsonians were decrying sanctification as evidence of justification and asserting wrongly that one believer could peer into the heart of another. Chauncy had no objection to a properly formulated doctrine of assurance, but he thought that assurance came when the faithful perceived God's sanctifying work within them through their new capacities for love and humility, not from "the immediate Witness of the Spirit." Claims of direct testimony from the Spirit struck Chauncy as "enthusiasm."[67]

When Dickinson replied to Croswell in 1743, he sounded almost like Chauncy. He never repudiated his belief in the direct witness of the Spirit, but he agreed that the danger now came from the new antinomians. Citing the Westminster Confession and the first-generation New England theologians, he denied that assurance was essential to faith. His reading of Ephesians 1:13, which seemed to imply a distinction between faith and the Spirit of promise, provided him a biblical warrant. He insisted that the New Testament assumed a holy life as the chief evidence of a faithful heart.[68]

Croswell had conceded from the beginning that the "work of sanctification" had some evidential value. Dickinson, therefore, could not understand Croswell's vehemence. He thought him simply inconsistent. But when Croswell published *What is Christ to Me, If He is Not Mine?* (1745), he showed that the revivalists disagreed about the witness of the Spirit. For Croswell, faith was "particular": when people were faithful they had a "particular faith" that they were forgiven, not simply a "general faith" that Jesus was the savior. Faith and assurance were the same thing: believers had "just so much Assurance" as they had faith. The faithful gained their assurance "directly, immediately," before they saw any good works in themselves.[69]

Croswell became increasingly disinclined to tolerate the "terms and conditions" of the covenant theology, and his theology of ecstatic experience drew him away from the other revivalists. When he said that justification came from faith, he meant that it came without preparatory convictions, without any requirement of repentance, without humiliation, and without any prior love to God. And assurance was no inference from sanctification, no accompaniment of the virtuous life. Christ gave the faithful the "personal confidence" —

immediate, not inferential — that salvation was theirs. Solomon Williams, the pastor in Lebanon, Connecticut, pronounced the majority verdict of the "calvinistical ministers." Croswell's faith, he said, was "refined self-love," and it was antinomian, as well. On the matter of the witness of the Spirit, the two sides had a real disagreement, but the dispute drove both Tennent and Dickinson to emphasize anew the correlative evidence of sanctification. In order to avoid the excesses of Croswell and his allies, the revivalists felt it necessary to display their own convictions about the importance of virtue.[70]

When the debates over the revival are set alongside the disputes over Arminianism and Anglican theology, they highlight the degree to which questions of ethics assumed increasing importance in eighteenth-century theology. In debating about how far to expand the scope of the natural and the volitional, theologians were asking partly about the significance of ethics in the definition of what it meant to be a Christian. But they were also asking what it meant to insist on the reasonableness of Christianity; they were trying to decide whether rationality lay in Samuel Johnson's intuitive illumination, in Jonathan Dickinson's cautious argument for converging historical, natural, and scriptural probabilities, or in the inductive explorations of "physico-theology." And they were attempting to define rationality in the midst of a revivalist piety that raised quite another set of issues about conversion, faith, and assurance of salvation. It was rare to find a theologian able to write thoughtfully about such a broad variety of questions, but these were the debates that produced the theological works of Jonathan Edwards, and no American theologian of the era matched Edwards in either the breadth of his undertakings or the subtlety of his arguments.

5

Jonathan Edwards

In typical New England Calvinist fashion, Jonathan Edwards (1703–58) defined theology as "the doctrine of living to God by Christ." In many other ways, Edwards was a typical New England theologian, a Calvinist concerned about piety in a local congregation. Yet no other theologian in America would equal him in intellectual depth or enduring influence on generations of successors. For a hundred years after his death, competing schools of theology either struggled for his mantle or strove to overcome his logic. He never lacked for critics: Arminians of every variety would continue to view him as a monumental defender of Calvinist error while some conservative Calvinists would long view his theology as a source of heresy. His admirers, however, formed an Edwardean theological culture that entrenched itself in the leading Reformed seminaries of the nation even as some of them crafted theological revisions that Edwards could never have accepted.[1]

Edwards drew the common distinction between the two kinds of theological knowledge, the first speculative, derived from the exercise of the understanding, and the second practical, consisting of the "sense of the heart," the gracious inclination of both the understanding and the will. The aim of theology was to nurture a "sense" of divine things that took one deeper into their nature than the speculative understanding alone could penetrate and to "guide and influence us in our practice." His favorite text in systematic theology was the *Theoretico-Practica Theologia* of the Reformed theologian Petrus van Mastricht (1630–1706) — a teacher at Utrecht in the Netherlands from 1677 until his death — who made a point of showing that every speculative truth in theology had a practical implication. Just as Edwards strove to overcome a sharp distinction between the will and the understanding, so he tried also to ensure a close linkage between the speculative and the practical. A "speculative knowledge" was of "infinite importance" for without it there could be no "practical knowledge."[2]

Edwards was the grandson of Solomon Stoddard, and he bore the weight of Stoddard's heritage. After graduating from Yale College in 1720, receiving the master's of arts degree there in 1723, preaching in Connecticut and New York for a year, and teaching two years as a tutor at Yale, he became in 1726 Stoddard's assistant in Northampton. In 1729, after Stoddard's death, he became the sole pastor. He shared Stoddard's revivalist inclinations. Although he deplored the excesses of the separatists, he defended the revivals against the Old Lights, and his *Treatise on Religious Affections* (1746) remains the best defense of revivalism published in colonial America. When he challenged Stoddard's theories about sacraments and church membership, however, his congregation dismissed him, and in 1750 he accepted an invitation to serve the Housatonic and Mohawk mission in Stockbridge, Massachusetts. He died in 1758 within three months of assuming the presidency of the College of New Jersey (Princeton).

Some feared that his support for revivals encouraged the theological populists, but Edwards joined Charles Chauncy in thinking it lamentable when uneducated exhorters presumed to preach and teach. He believed that theologians, learned in divinity, had the high calling "to spend themselves, in order to impart knowledge"; their congregations had the Christian duty "to apply themselves to receive it." When his Northampton congregation proved unwilling to apply themselves, Edwards told them that they had a covenant with him — and with God — to heed his teaching. He could sound like a religious populist when he assured pious but uneducated Christians that their knowledge of God's glory was worth more than "all the human knowledge that is taught in all the most famous colleges and universities in the world." But he belonged to New England's theological aristocracy, and he defended its prerogatives against usurpers.[3]

He entertained no doubts about either the value of rationality or the rationality of theology. Edwards wrote about moral philosophy, metaphysics, atomist theory, optics, the corpuscular theory of light, and the nature of gravity. In essays written when he was a student at Yale between 1716 and 1720, he displayed a knowledge of Newtonian science, and his reading of John Locke, probably when he was a tutor at the college, confirmed an interest in philosophy that went back to his undergraduate years. In 1729 he began to think about writing a "Rational Account" of all the "Main Doctrines of the Christian Religion," and in the mid-1740s he projected a book to "shew how all the arts and sciences, the more they are perfected, the more they issue in divinity, and coincide with it, and appear to be as parts of it." Theology for Edwards remained the highest expression of rationality, though he also thought that it offered the clearest insights into reason's limits.[4]

While some read him chiefly as a philosophical theologian, immersed in conversation with Locke, Malebranche, the Cambridge Platonists, or the British moralists, others, like his first biographer Samuel Hopkins, emphasized that he "studied the Bible more than all other books" and that his most frequent recourse as a theologian was to such works of biblical criticism as Matthew Poole's *Synopsis Criticorum* (1669–76) and Matthew Henry's *Exposition of the Old and New Testaments* (1708–10). In response especially to the deists, he occupied himself with the critical study of scripture, writing on inspiration; the scope of the canon; authorship of biblical texts, including the Mosaic authorship of the Pentateuch; and the historicity of biblical reports. He was, in fact, both a philosophical and a biblical theologian, and for him these two sides of theology coincided. Both as a philosopher and as an exegete, he sought to preserve Calvinist orthodoxy, including the standard Calvinist balance between reason and revelation. Nevertheless, he recast conventional categories, and his vision of divine "excellency" inspired a way of thinking that shaped his views of rationality, ethics, metaphysics, biblical interpretation, and the meaning of the practicality of theology.[5]

Excellency

The religious center for Edwards was his sense of the glory of God, a glory manifest especially in divine sovereignty, which Edwards learned to interpret by means of the idea of "excellency." As a young man he objected to the thought of a divine sovereignty exercised in decrees of election and reprobation. Gradually, however, this thought became "pleasant, bright, and sweet" to him because he gained a "new sense" of the "excellency" of a Being who united both "majesty and grace." Edwards initially analyzed the idea of "excellency" in his notes on "The Mind," which he probably began in 1723 after completing his theology degree at Yale. He opened the notes with the observation that he found himself "more concerned" with excellency than with any other theme: "yea, we are concerned," he said, "with nothing else."[6]

European scholastics, Puritan theologians, and British philosophers had long used the term "excellency," and Edwards was familiar with definitions of it as harmony, symmetry, or proportion. By associating excellency with mathematical relations like proportion and harmony, and by linking those concepts to the notion of beauty, he carried New England theology into the mainstream of seventeenth-century philosophy and eighteenth-century aesthetic and ethical theory. Concepts of harmony pervaded the thought of the Cambridge Platonists, whom Edwards read as a student at Yale. He found similar ideas in his reading of the Dutch philosophers Franco Burgersdyck (1590–1635) of Leiden University, who emphasized, in Platonic fashion, the harmony of the moral virtues, and Adrian Heerebord (1613–61), also of Leiden, who argued in his *Meletemata philosophica* (1654) that all goodness consisted in "fittingness." He further refined his understanding of excellency through his involvement in the eighteenth-century British debate over ethics. The great divide in British moral thought was between "sentimentalists" like Anthony Ashley Cooper, earl of Shaftesbury and Francis Hutcheson, who grounded ethics in a "moral sense" that approved the "beauty" of virtuous actions, and "intellectualists" like Ralph Cudworth and Samuel Clarke, who emphasized the capacity of reason to discern the "fitness" between human actions, on the one hand, and "the proportions" and "relations" of being, on the other. Edwards criticized both sides, but their debates helped him work out his own idea of excellency as a spiritual harmony mirrored in the order of the natural and social worlds.[7]

His attempts to explain this spiritual harmony drew him into metaphysics. The question was why the human mind found harmony or proportion so pleasing. His answer was that proportion defined being itself: "if we examine narrowly," he wrote, being is "nothing else but proportion." Reality consisted of relations, and the mind found disproportion and disharmony jarring because it found them contrary to being. Reality was a web of relations constituted by "the consent of being to being." Eventually, Edwards qualified his definition of being as proportion, but he never abandoned his understanding of excellency as the consent of being to being. Although he began early in the "The Mind" to limit the "proper" meaning of consent to agreements among spirits — minds and wills — he also continued, as he noted, to "borrow" the term to designate relations in the natural world. In either case, excellency had its grounding in the nature of being itself.[8]

Notions of excellency, consent, harmony, symmetry, proportion, and fitness affected the way Edwards thought about almost everything. And although they had their origins in the intellectual traditions that formed his reading, their prominence in his thought must also have reflected his sensitivity to the tensions of his own local society. Edwards was writing theology at a time when population growth in Northampton and other nearby towns produced increased competition for good land and resources close to the villages. He frequently deplored the divisions in Northampton and the "spirit of contention, disorder, and tumult" throughout the region. Part of his enthusiasm for the revivals came from their apparent success in resolving "old quarrels," and in 1742 he had his congregation subscribe to a covenant that they would seek harmony with each other and with God. He was, moreover, acutely sensitive to conflict with other people, and he often complained of it in his letters. Both his personality and his social location therefore drew him to the theme of harmony. Envisioned as "excellence," that theme shaped a style of thinking that made Edwards unique among the eighteenth-century colonial theologians.[9]

Reason and Revelation

Like the second-century Christian apologists, Edwards believed that all philosophical truth embodied remnants of divine revelation and that "the doctrines of revealed religion, are the foundation of all useful and excellent knowledge." He followed a tradition known as the *prisca theologia* (ancient theology), inaugurated by such fathers of the church as Clement of Alexandria (ca. 150–ca. 215), Origen (ca. 185–ca. 245), and Eusebius (ca. 260–ca. 340), who employed it to prove that the wisdom of Greek philosophy came from the revelation to the ancient Jews. Renaissance thinkers adopted and altered the tradition in the sixteenth century to prove the compatibility of Christian truth and Neoplatonic philosophy. Seventeenth- and eighteenth-century Protestants like Ralph Cudworth (1617–88) at Cambridge, Philip Skelton (1707–87) in Ireland, and Chevalier (Andrew Michael) Ramsay (1686–1743) in France used it to show that non-Christians could have knowledge of the Christian God. Edwards read these thinkers, and they convinced him that non-Christian religions could contain fragments of truth even about such Christian mysteries as redemption and the Trinity. For him, however, the chief implication in the idea of a *prisca theologia* was that all seemingly natural religion — and natural theology — rested on the foundation of the original revelation to Adam and the ancient Jews. The deists might have assumed that their theologies came from reason alone, but Edwards thought that they had unwittingly absorbed revealed truth transmitted through cultural traditions.[10]

He held conventional views about the harmony of reason and revelation. While revelation was above reason, right reason did not conflict with revealed truths. Edwards also believed, however, in accord with Calvinist tradition, that unassisted fallen reason, left to itself, could never avoid idolatry. In matters of religious truth, reason required the illumination of both the biblical revelation and the Spirit. Edwards therefore spoke of three levels of religious knowledge, the first drawn from natural theology, the second grounded in biblical knowledge, and the third constituted by the perception of divine excellency made possible when the Spirit opened the mind and will to the deepest level of biblical truth.[11]

At the first level, the "light of nature" could discover multiple truths about God. Edwards thought nothing was more demonstrable than the "Being of a God," and he used the standard rational arguments for God's existence. The order of the world suggested an orderer; the creation required a sufficient cause; the complex human soul could not have resulted from chance; and the yearnings and habits innate in the mind—as well as the mind's inclination toward excellence—required God for their fulfillment. The supposition of a self-moving first cause provided a better explanation for an ordered world than any alternative. Edwards employed the arguments that had long been standard in both the Catholic and the Reformed traditions.[12]

The most distinctive argument in his natural theology probably had its immediate source in his reading of the Cambridge Platonist Henry More. The argument first appeared in Edwards's essay "Of Being," which he began as a graduate student at Yale in 1721. He observed that it was impossible for the mind to conceive of "a state of perfect nothing," for to conceive of nothingness was implicitly to assign to it a form of being. In order to avoid self-contradiction, therefore, one must necessarily concede that "some being should eternally be." Eternal being was logically necessary. This was a scholastic style of argument, similar in form to the metaphysical dialectics of Heerebord and Burgersdyck, as well as the Spanish Catholic metaphysician Franciscus Suarez (1548–1617), but the closest parallels were in More. Edwards drew explicitly on an argument about space advanced earlier by More and by Sir Isaac Newton: one could not conceive of a place where pure nothing existed, for even empty space was a form of being: "So that we see this necessary, eternal being must be infinite and omnipresent."[13]

In yet other ways, Edwards spoke of reason as a channel of religious truth. Reason could demonstrate that human beings were imperfect and fallen, that they owed a duty to their Creator that they could not fulfill, and that some form of mediation between God and humanity was necessary. Reason could also show that it was plausible to expect a divine revelation making known the means of this mediation. Edwards could even say that a mediation "like that of Christ might be absolutely Proved to be necessary by pure naked demonstration," though logic alone could never show that Jesus Christ was the mediator to whom the argument pointed. He could assert, in a manner foreign to more conservative Reformed scholastics, that it was "within the Reach of naked

Reason to perceive Certainly that there are three distincts to God," though he added that reason could not know the full truth about the Christian Trinity. Edwards sounded frequently like a "catholick" Congregationalist entranced by the promise of natural theology.[14]

At the same time, he wrote far more often than the Congregational "catholicks" about the limits of reason. He reflected on the problem that reason alone, when it tried to consider truth about God, encountered paradoxes that it could not unravel. The notion of a being who was "self-existent and without any cause" struck him as "utterly inconceivable" to pure reason. The idea of an infinite spiritual being, which implied omnipresence without extension, was a mystery. The notion of eternity — whether conceived as an endless succession or as duration without succession — seemed to reason as either empty of meaning or contradictory. Injustice and suffering in a world overseen by an infinitely holy and good God baffled reason. Edwards confined these more skeptical thoughts to his private "Miscellanies," where they functioned mainly as a critique of the deists, but they reflected his belief that any adequate theology required a revelation above the capacity of reason.[15]

What fallen humanity needed was the knowledge of Christ as the second Person of the Trinity incarnate and as the mediator in the "gospel scheme," and Edwards was especially convinced that reason could never have discovered these "mysteries" apart from revelation. Whatever its capacities to discern religious truths, naked reason was also subject to "extreme and brutish Blindness in things of Religion." Like Calvin, Edwards contended that unaided reason invariably distorted the religious truth that it discovered. Like Calvin, he concluded that "Christian divinity, properly so called" was therefore not evident by "the light of nature." In a fallen world, the truths of salvation were matters "of pure revelation, above the light of natural reason."[16]

This revealed knowledge — the second level of religious knowledge — came through the Bible, which Edwards understood as "God's own words." He found the idea of revelation itself highly rational, since it was "fit and requisite" that a sovereign and gracious God would reveal something of his design in the world. Like his predecessors in the evidential tradition, Edwards found proof of the authenticity of scriptural revelation in the credibility of the miracle accounts and the fulfillment of the prophecies, especially those of Christ. He defended the biblical miracles against the derision of the English deist Thomas Woolston, and throughout his career he displayed an avid interest in supporting, against such deists as Anthony Collins, the argument that the biblical prophecies proved Jesus to be the Messiah.[17]

In 1757 he told the trustees of the College of New Jersey that he was writing a "great work, which I call *The Harmony of the Old and New Testaments*."

Since the mid-seventeenth century, Christian writers had shown an interest in reconciling the differences in the four gospels — John Eliot had written such a harmony in New England — but Edwards's project was more ambitious. Since the second century, one stream of Christian thought had emphasized the unity of the Old and New Testaments. This stream had flowed into the Reformed tradition through John Calvin, and Edwards followed Calvin in laying out the details of the unity by showing that the Old Testament prophecies of a coming Messiah found their fulfillment in Christ, that the Old Testament types pointed toward New Testament antitypes, and that the two testaments displayed a "harmony" in "doctrine and precept." His project, for which he wrote five hundred manuscript pages, countered deist attacks on the unity of the Bible, but the theme of harmony was of special interest to him even apart from polemical intentions because it illustrated the Bible's "excellency."[18]

So impressed was Edwards by biblical harmonies that he could account the "internal" evidence for revelation as far more important than "external evidences" like miracles and prophecies. The gospel carried its own "light and goodness with it," both in the grandeur of its contents and in its internal "harmony," its "consistency" and "concurrence." The Bible contained a "vast variety of parts," each with a "various and manifold respect to others," connected in "one grand system." Just as Edwards viewed the natural and spiritual realms as networks of relations, so also he read the Bible as a revelation marked by internal harmony, and the consistency of its interrelated parts manifested for him a proof of the book's divine origin.[19]

His admiration for these harmonies accounts for his immense interest in typology. Edwards prepared extensive commentaries on the biblical text, and the greater part of them explored types and antitypes. In 1724 he began his "Notes on Scripture," which by 1758 had become 507 numbered entries, with typology as the unifying theme. In 1730 he began his "Miscellaneous Observations on the Holy Scriptures," otherwise known as the "Blank Bible," which placed equally heavy emphasis on the deciphering of the types. Reading widely in biblical history, chronology, and geography, Edwards found in the places and figures of the Old Testament an extensive foreshadowing of New Testament truths that underscored the harmony of the Bible.[20]

He was so attracted to typology that he found types not only in scripture but also throughout the natural world. Edwards joined a number of other eighteenth-century theologians in expanding typology beyond scriptural boundaries. The whole of nature sparkled for him with types of spiritual truth. Nonetheless, he never elevated nature to a level of authority coequal with revelation. The listing of types that he began to assemble in his notebooks in 1728 as "Images of Divine Things" rather displayed nature filled with types of *biblical* truths. Scripture interpreted nature by explaining the spiritual mysteries typified in the natural world. This project, like much of his biblical interpretation, was about excellency: the images showed the "excellent agreement" between nature and the Bible.[21]

Edwards's main concern, however, was that the reader grasp the "spiritual sense" of the text, the third and deepest level of religious knowledge. This spiritual apprehension depended on the movement of the Spirit within the heart, allowing the reader to have "a true sense of the excellency of the things revealed" and to grasp their "truth and reality." Such a grasp of truth embodied a threefold apprehension of the "excellency" of God and Christ: it apprehended their intrinsic beauty; it imbued the heart with a "sense" of that beauty, more profound than any merely "notional" judgment; and it elicited a consent that the natural reason could never have given, since reason alone could never discover "the beauty and loveliness of spiritual things." It was a commonplace of Protestant thought to distinguish intellectual assent from a heartfelt consent made possible by the Spirit. Edwards linked the distinction to his idea of excellency.[22]

Like his Puritan predecessors, Edwards was interested mainly in a form of knowing that moved the will as well as the understanding. Only through this kind of ideal apprehension, which Edwards described as "sensible," could a person grasp the beauty of an object, or feel pleasure in it, or have longing for it. Some forms of sensible ideal apprehension grasped only natural objects, such as the beauty of a landscape, but to grasp the beauty of God required an ideal apprehension that was actual (consisting of more than assent to words), sensible (rather than speculative), and spiritual (created by the immediate activity of the Spirit). To know God in this way was to "have a sense" of God's excellency, or of the beauty of God as an end in itself. This intuitive perception of the divine excellency was the deepest form of divine knowledge available to human beings.[23]

The Excellency of God

Edwards believed that God knew the world by having "the actual ideas of things. . . . at once in His mind, and all in the highest possible perfection of clearness, and all perfectly and invariably there without any transitoriness or fading in any part." For him this was more than a description of the divine omniscience; it pointed, as well, toward the divine sovereignty and the dependence of everything on God. While a graduate student at Yale, Edwards found that he could express the glory and sovereignty of God by tracing the implications of a form of philosophical idealism. He inaugurated the project with "Of

Being," "Of the Prejudices of Imagination," and "Of Atoms and Perfectly Solid Bodies," essays that he began to write at Yale between 1720 and 1723 (though they remained unpublished until more than a century later). He continued it in his notes on "The Mind."[24]

In the essay on atoms, he took up themes that he probably discovered in his reading of Henry More's speculation about matter. Unlike More, however, Edwards defined an atom not as an ultimate unit of matter but as a body that infinitely resisted annihilation and therefore manifested the constant exercise of an infinite power. Its substance, rather than being a material substratum, could be no other than the infinite power that constituted it, so that "speaking most strictly" there was "no proper substance but God himself" in respect to the atoms that formed bodies. In "Of Being" he moved deeper into an idealist ontology by asserting that it was impossible to imagine that anything "has any existence . . . but either in created or uncreated consciousness" and that a universe devoid of "created intelligence" could exist only in "the divine consciousness." By the time he wrote #27 of "The Mind," he clarified the idea by noting that "every knowing philosopher" agreed that color was no more in the external world than pain was in a needle, and that figures and shapes were merely configurations of color. This left only resistance, or solidity, "out of the [created] mind." But resistance was nothing other than the "actual exertion of God's power" in accord with "a constant law or method" in God's mind: "And indeed the secret lies here: that which truly is the substance of all bodies is the infinitely exact and precise and perfectly stable idea in God's mind together with His stable will that the same shall gradually be communicated to us and to other minds according to certain fixed and exact established methods and laws." The visible and tangible world was "therefore an ideal one," absolutely dependent on the stability of God's idea and volition.[25]

Edwards's idealism had affinities with that of George Berkeley and Samuel Johnson, and since Johnson taught at Yale when Edwards was a student there, an earlier generation of scholars speculated about the links between their ideas. But Edwards diverged from the Berkeleyan style of argument that Johnson emulated. Berkeley denied that abstract ideas like "being" properly referred to anything; Edwards thought that they did. Berkeley argued mainly from sensory experience; Edwards argued more often from a priori definitions and conceptions. Berkeley denied the absoluteness of space, fearing that unless space was seen as a function of the relations of ideas, it might appear to be as infinite and eternal as God; Edwards said, in his early speculation, that space was God, precisely because there could be only one infinite and eternal being, though he later defined space as one of God's ideas. Berkeley believed that finite things unperceived by human minds continued to exist because God perceived them; Edwards could also say, both at the beginning and at the end of his career, that "all existence is perception," but he added his own distinctive note when he added that things also continued to exist because a divine "determination"—manifested in fixed laws through which God exercised a continual power of creation—maintained them in being. Berkeley's idealism supposed a divine Perceiver; Edwards agreed but placed much more emphasis than Berkeley on the divine Will. The two men read some of the same authors—Locke, Malebranche, the Cambridge Platonists—and worried over some of the same problems, but they proceeded in their own paths.[26]

Edwards shared with both Berkeley and Johnson, however, a desire to evoke a sense of divine presence by showing that the world depended, at each moment, on God's creative power. He therefore argued that no link of autonomous antecedent finite causes in the past could explain the present, for the moment an object vanished into the past it lost its causal efficacy: "No cause can produce effects in a time and place in which it is not." That the world continued from moment to moment was owing entirely to its "continued creation" by God "at each moment of its existence." In his "Miscellanies" he speculated that this continual creation also applied to finite spirits: "we are created anew every moment."[27]

The lawlike character of God's relation to the world did not preclude "God's immediate and arbitrary operation." It was God's arbitrary action that had established the natural laws in the first place, and although they continued to direct his "natural operation," God could disregard them at will. Most divine action was "mixed," combining both natural and arbitrary operations, but the higher one ascended on the scale of creation, "the more the manner of divine operation with respect to the creature approache[d] to arbitrary." It was especially "beautiful and every way fit [and] suitable," he argued, that the gift of grace to the elect saints, for instance, should be "arbitrary and sovereign," and that God's relationship to "the man Jesus Christ" should be "infinitely above the laws of nature."[28]

The idealist metaphysic meant for Edwards that God was "the sum of all being," the substance of all that was. By virtue of both the divine perceptions and the divine will, God "comprehended the entity of all His creatures; and their entity is not to be added to His, as not comprehended in it, for they are but communications from Him." The idealist metaphysic allowed him, as well, to conclude that "being in order is all that we call God, who is, and there is none else besides him." It underlay his assertions in 1755 that God was "Being in General" or "the Being of Beings," and that "His existence, being infinite, must be equivalent to universal existence."[29]

When Edwards wrote that he would admit of "none else" besides God, he sounded pantheistic, and some of the Neoplatonic language of his later writing intensified the seeming identity of God with the world of which God was the substance. In his *Dissertation Concerning the End for Which God Created the World* (1755), he spoke of creation as the communication of God's infinite fullness, an emanation from God, a diffusion of God's glory *ad extra*. The creation was an "enlarging" of the divine being through self-communication. But while Edwards thought that God "included" all things, he protected the distinction between God and the world. As utterly dependent on God, the world remained separate from God. The world of created spirits, especially, retained a separate identity, for even the elect saints, chosen for "an infinitely perfect union" with God in eternity, would never attain a perfect oneness. Even more, the reprobate in hell would eternally remain separate from the divine being.[30]

What most clearly marked the distinction between God and the world in Edwards's theology — and most clearly exemplified the force of the idea of excellency in his depiction of God — was his doctrine of the Trinity. Edwards began in 1723 to derive the Trinitarian character of God from God's reflection on and delight in his own excellency. Both in an unpublished essay on Trinitarian theology and in some of the longer "Miscellanies," he made it clear that the threefold unity of God served for him as the supreme instance of excellency and that the excellency of the created world could be only a dim reflection of the divine beauty in the timeless relations among the Father, the Son, and the Spirit.[31]

Edwards believed that "one alone cannot be excellent, inasmuch as, in such case, there can be no consent." Divine excellence therefore required a divine plurality. Though Edwards believed that Trinitarian theology consisted chiefly of deductions from biblical revelation, he thought that even "naked reason" could discover the divine tri-unity. It seemed rational that all knowledge, even God's knowledge, was "by idea." God must have an "idea of Himself," since otherwise God would lack self-awareness. But God's ideas were perfect, and "an absolutely perfect idea of a thing is the very thing," for it lacked nothing that was in the thing. It followed that God's idea of Himself was God. The divine self-reflection begot the "substantial image of God," the Son. And because the Father and the Son necessarily delighted in one another, the begetting of the Son issued in a perfect act of mutual love — or Spirit — which was distinct from both the Father and the Son. Edwards believed that his doctrine of an "exact equality" of the Spirit with the Father and Son improved on earlier Reformed theology that discussed the Spirit mainly as the agent who applied Christ's benefits.[32]

God created the world so that this divine excellency could be expressed, known, and admired. Here was the Calvinist conviction, expressed now in an aesthetic form, that the aim of creation was the glory of God. It was "fit, suitable, and amiable in itself" that the divine beauty should express and reveal itself. The ultimate end of creation was not human happiness but the diffusion of God's "excellent fulness" for its own sake. It was "good in itself" that supreme excellency should find expression in a manner that expanded the circle of consent to itself. In the diffusion of the divine beauty — an emanation — and in the creature's knowing and loving and delighting in that beauty — a "remanation" — God became his own end.[33]

Edwards found the definitive expression of the divine beauty in Christ. He still thought in terms of the traditional Reformed Christological *topics* — the person and work of Christ; his active and passive obedience; his three offices of prophet, priest, and king; his humiliation and exaltation — but he cast them in a form determined by his notions of excellency, fitness, and proportion. The second Person of the Trinity became incarnate in Jesus because only a divine-human mediator, united to both alienated parties, could suffer a punishment proportional to the offense of sin against God's infinite excellency. Both incarnation and atonement were "fit and proper."[34]

Edwards sometimes added that the atonement also maintained the divine law by providing a solution to human sinfulness "in proportion" to the seriousness of the legal offense. His disciples would develop this language into a distinctive "governmental" theory of atonement that they described as Edwardean, but unlike the later governmental theorists among his disciples, Edwards still thought of the atonement as an act of "satisfaction," not merely as an act that maintained the integrity of the divine moral government. For him, Christ's death satisfied God's wrath and paid the infinite debt that a sinful humanity owed. The "fitness" and "excellent congruity" of this act — its "suitableness" — provided evidence of the divine wisdom.[35]

The consequence of atonement was, as Calvinists had always argued, the imputation to the faithful of Christ's active and passive righteousness. Christ's active righteousness was his perfect obedience to the divine law; the passive was his perfect submission to death on the cross. By the time Edwards wrote his sermon on "Justification by Faith Alone" (1734), English Arminians had begun to ridicule the notion of imputation. Edwards defended its reasonableness by reverting to notions of symmetry and fittingness. It was agreeable to the "reason and nature of things" that God would impute the righteousness of Christ to the faithful since a relation of "union" between a patron and a client would make it "fit" to impute the entire merit of one to the other. Like Calvin, he argued that imputation was the consequence of the believer's "union" with Christ. This was the meaning of Edwards's aphorism that "what is real in the union between Christ and his people, is the foundation of what is legal." The union with Christ was the ground for God's willingness to acquit the offender for whom Christ had died.[36]

In dealing with Christological topics, Edwards returned often to the motif of excellence, expressed in images of fitness, harmony, and symmetry. Christ incarnated and revealed the divine beauty because he embodied "an admirable conjunction of diverse excellencies." He was both Lion and Lamb. He harmonized glory and humility, majesty and meekness, obedience and dominion, sovereignty and resignation, and justice and grace. The gospel accounts impressed Edwards as narratives about how Jesus had brought opposites into harmonious unity. He was born of a poor virgin but also born by the power of the Spirit. He lay in a base manger but drew the worship of the wise. He radiated holiness yet bore the charge of guilt. He lived for the divine justice and suffered from the divine justice. He suffered the "greatest degree of humiliation" and yet in those sufferings displayed his glory.[37]

The purpose of this "proportionable" manifestation of divine excellency in Christ was that the Christian might have a "proportioned" regard to God. The revelation in Jesus was designed both to humble and to encourage the faithful, to display God as both Judge and Redeemer. The harmony of opposites in Jesus ensured that Christians would have no "disproportionate" view of either the love or the majesty of God. It was the beauty of Christ that governed, therefore, the harmony of affections in the believer.[38]

The Excellency of Grace

Edwards cherished the Calvinist doctrine of the sovereignty of grace. He agreed that Christ died only for the elect and that they alone would experience the supernatural and sovereign "divine influence and operation, by which saving virtue is obtained." In his doctrine of the divine decrees, he held a supralapsarian view of election and a sublapsarian view of reprobation. In other words, the decree to redeem the elect logically preceded the decree to create them or to permit their fall, but the decree to damn the reprobate "supposed" their sinfulness in the sense that it presupposed a relation of "fitness" between sin and a damning decree. God created the elect in order to save them, but he did not create the reprobate in order to damn them. This was one of Edwards's few concessions to the eighteenth-century humanitarian temper.[39]

He conceded less on the embattled issue of original sin. In the last book he published during his lifetime, *The Great Christian Doctrine of Original Sin Defended* (1758), he took on the English Arminian John Taylor with the argument that Christianity had to presuppose the doctrine of innate sinfulness. Because Taylor had criticized the doctrine as unscriptural, Edwards spent more than half the book arguing with him over biblical passages. Because Edwards's other main opponent, the English philosopher George Turnbull, had called for "an experimental method of reasoning," Edwards also made a show of reasoning from "experience and facts" according to the rules of "experimental philosophy." But for the heart of his argument he returned to the idea of harmony and proportion.[40]

Although he appealed to biblical and secular history to show the human tendency to sin, he thought that the doctrine of original sin would stand even if innocent actions outnumbered crimes. To speak of original sin was to designate a "prevailing propensity" of the heart, a "prevailing liableness," that outweighed "all effects or consequences of any supposed good." The crucial point was that God deserved infinite love and the creature stood under an infinite debt to the Creator. Sin therefore bore an "infinite demerit"; any sinful propensity brought a guilt that outweighed all the good. Fallen human beings, moreover, never loved God in the proper "proportion," since this would require loving God for his own sake, as "infinitely excellent in himself," and not for any self-serving purpose. Edwards echoed the British moral rationalists by contending that the tendency of virtue was to "treat everything as it is, and according to its nature." True virtue required a love of God proportional to God's excellence, but without grace no one loved God merely because God was "infinitely excellent."[41]

In explaining how Adam's successors bore the guilt of original sin, Edwards diverged from Reformed orthodology. In his idealistic ontology, the continuing identity of anything depended on an "arbitrary divine constitution." The identity of humanity with Adam was merely one instance of this general truth; Adam and his posterity were one because God treated them as one. When Adam broke covenant with God, he lost the "supernatural" principle that enabled him to love God in proper proportion, leaving only "natural" principles, such as self-love. But because God constituted all humanity as one with Adam, all humanity shared in the sin and suffered the loss.[42]

The argument allowed Edwards to show the "reasonableness" of a doctrine that John Taylor found utterly unreasonable — the doctrine of the imputation of sin. Seventeenth-century Calvinist covenant theologians typically argued that God imputed Adam's guilt to his posterity because Adam was their legal representative. Taylor thought this unfair. In effect, Edwards conceded the point, but he still affirmed imputation. He proposed that God imputed the guilt of Adam's sin to men and women because they were truly guilty of it. This alternative resembled the doctrine of "mediate imputation" taught by the Amyrauldians at seventeenth-century Saumur and by the Swiss Reformed scholastic theologian Johann Friedrich Stapfer (1708–75), whose *Institutiones Theologicae, polemicae universae* (1743–47) Edwards read and admired, though Edwards's view also differed from theirs, since his metaphysical doctrine of identity entailed a view of sin as corporate in a distinctive manner. Nonetheless, conservative Calvinists in nineteenth-century America would never forgive him for this departure from the covenantal, or federal, tradition.[43]

The doctrine of original sin confirmed for Edwards that salvation required a "supernatural and sovereign operation of the Spirit of God." "Saving grace" had to be "infused." In saying this, Edwards positioned himself within a sixteenth-century debate that cut across the line dividing Protestants and Catholics. Jesuits and Arminians agreed that grace moved the will through "moral suasion" directed at the intellect. Thomists and Calvinists believed that grace moved the will "physically," that is, immediately, and they expressed this belief with the metaphor of "infusion." Petrus van Mastricht argued for infusion in his *Theoretico-Practica Theologia,* the book that Edwards once described as better than "any other Book in the world, excepting the Bible." In any event, Edwards used the word "infusion" to emphasize that the new "sense" of divine things came as the immediate, irresistible gift of the Spirit, not merely by the Spirit's assisting the natural principles of the mind but by its imparting a "new supernatural principle of life and action" that transformed the will and understanding.[44]

While Edwards usually drew philosophically from some variant of Christian Platonism, he explicated the idea of infused grace by building on the seventeenth-century Protestant recovery of Aristotle. The scholastic authors whom he read—Burgersdyck, Heerebord, Mastricht, William Ames, and Francis Turretin (1623–87)—employed and revised Aristotelian concepts of habit, disposition, and principle to describe the operation of grace. Edwards pushed such notions to the forefront of theology, not only in his descriptions of the laws by which God maintained and governed the created world but also in his explanations of religious conversion and its fruits. Like Thomas Shepard, whom Edwards often cited, he thought of saving grace as the indwelling and activity of the Holy Spirit in the soul, issuing in the formation of a new habit or disposition. This new disposition, an inherent "excellency," transformed the principle of human action even before it found public expression in "gracious exercises." Edwards sometimes spoke of the disposition as prior to conscious awareness, as when he speculated that some infants might have a "regenerated" disposition before their later conversion.[45]

The new disposition was the fountain of all Christian virtues, but for Edwards the prime virtue was love. He could speak of love as not only the "chief" affection but also as the "fountain" of all other Christian affections. In 1738,

Edwards delivered a series of sermons titled *Charity and Its Fruits.* Delivered two years after the ending of the first Northampton awakening, the sermons should be read as an expression of Edwards's efforts to evaluate the revivals and their consequences. This was evident in their central theme: "All that virtue which is saving, and distinguishing of true Christians from others, is summed up in Christian or divine love." Twenty years later, when he published his book on *Original Sin* shortly before his death, he made the same claim that religion "summarily consists in love." The prominence of this claim in his thought exemplified again the importance for him of harmony—he referred repeatedly to the "excellency" of love—but it also allied him with a wider impulse in the eighteenth century to pursue "the ethical transposition of doctrine" by moving the themes of love and Christian practice closer to the center of theology.[46]

This impulse found further expression in Edwards's insistence that "all grace leads to practice." During the revivals, Edwards produced a flurry of writings designed to state the criteria for discerning the "gracious operations of God's Spirit." They included not only *Charity and Its Fruits* but also *The Distinguishing Marks of a Work of the Spirit of God* (1741), *Some Thoughts Concerning the Present Revival of Religion in New England* (1742), and *A Treatise Concerning Religious Affections* (1746). Their main purpose was to defend the revivals while disassociating them from the New Light separatists who seemed to depreciate good works by resting assurance of salvation solely on the immediate witness of the Spirit. Particularly in his treatise on the affections, he amplified his notion of excellency, arguing that gracious affections enabled the Christian to love the "excellent and amiable nature of divine things, as they are in themselves" and to emulate God's "spiritual beauty" through holiness of life. He listed numerous signs of grace, but "the chief of all the signs" was Christian practice, or holiness of life as shown forth in the keeping of Christ's commandments and the doing of good works, whether through inward piety or public activity.[47]

Some of Edwards's disciples would later conclude that Edwards's views about the indwelling Spirit, infused grace, and the necessity for love in the regenerate heart implied that love must precede both faith and justification in the order of salvation. They were willing, on Edwardean grounds, to redefine what had been the cardinal Protestant doctrine: justification by grace through faith alone. Their reading of Edwards was at least plausible. He did suggest, more than once, that justification followed upon the conversion in which the Spirit infused the saving disposition of love for God. He argued explicitly, from time to time, that the Christian graces were so closely linked that they implied one another and that love was the "most essential ingredient in a saving faith," an argument suggesting that justification might require both faith and love. He avoided, however, the revisions that his disciples found necessary.[48]

One reason he could avoid them was that he became quite flexible about assuming any necessary sequence of stages in conversion. As a young man he worried that his own conversion had not followed the stages defined by earlier Puritan and Pietist theologians. He never relinquished the belief that God's "ordinary manner in working salvation" included a certain order of preparatory stages in which the Spirit convinced the soul of its distress, helplessness, and dependence as a prelude to conversion and sanctification. He observed such "legal convictions" during the revival at Northampton, and he urged revivalist preachers not to foreshorten them by offering premature comfort. But he moved away from the view that conversion could be assumed to follow "the steps of a particular established scheme." He found the "Spirit's proceeding" to be "often exceeding mysterious." As early as 1738 he decided that the various Christian graces — such as faith, love, repentance, and humility — were so closely "united and linked together" that rigid orderings of them missed the point.[49]

Yet he did distinguish faith from love, and he also continued — whether or not he was consistent in doing it — to insist on the Protestant doctrine of justification through faith. One of the sparks for the revival of 1734 in Northampton was his sermon on "Justification by Faith Alone," in which Edwards argued, on the basis of Romans 4:5, that God justified the "ungodly." In justification, God accepted the guilty as "free from the guilt of sin and its deserved punishment" and the unrighteous as having a "title to that glory which is the reward of righteousness." But what then did it mean to speak of faith, a mark of godliness, as a condition of justification? And how was this justifying faith related to the disposition of love infused by the Spirit?[50]

Edwards's solution was to revert once more to the theme of harmony and relation. He explained that faith did not produce justification but merely made it "fitting." God looked on it as "fit by a natural fitness" that a faithful relation to Christ should be "agreeable" to justification. It was not the excellency of either faith or love that justified. It was rather that faith, as a relation of union with Christ, rendered it "meet and suitable" that the believer should be justified. Christ initiated the relation, and the justification resulted from the excellency of the relation, not of the faith. And although no faith was genuine that was not united with love, Edwards could still say that the faith alone made justification suitable. He always opposed the view of the New England liberals and Anglicans that faith brought justification because it included moral obedience in its essence: "In truth, obedience has no concern in justification." As his followers would later recognize, the solution did not entirely resolve the tension, but Edwards found it satisfying.[51]

The concept of love continued to occupy him throughout his career, and after his expulsion from Northampton he pursued it while catechizing the Indians in Stockbridge. Around 1753 he began work on two treatises, designed to complement each other, in which he debated with the moral philosophers of the British enlightenment. He probably completed both works in 1755, though they were not published for a decade, by which time Edwards was dead. The first, the *Dissertation Concerning the End for Which God Created the World*, argued from both reason and scripture that God's ultimate end in creation was to "communicate his own infinite fulness of good" so that there might be knowledge and esteem of his glory. God's end in creation was therefore God's own glory; it was to glorify the highest excellency. The second treatise, *The Nature of True Virtue*, argued primarily on rational grounds that true virtue was born of a consent of the heart to this divine excellency. A consent to "Being in General" made possible a "general good will" directed toward both God and the neighbor. In both treatises, the highest good and the ground of virtue was regard for the excellency of God as the "Being of beings."[52]

Edwards believed that the British moralists — Francis Hutcheson, George Turnbull, Samuel Clarke, William Wollaston, and others — had accurately described some features of the natural conscience, or moral sense, but failed to see that it could never attain to this level of true virtue. It could affirm the secondary beauty found in the order, symmetry, and proportion of natural objects or social relations, but it could not discern and love the excellency of being in general. Apart from grace, the natural conscience would always adhere to one or another "private system," and the limited love that ensued would always be opposed to a truly virtuous consent to being in general. By implication, moral philosophy was misleading without theology. In this denial that ethics was an autonomous discipline, Edwards spoke as a conservative voice. He agreed with William Ames and Cotton Mather that ethics was a department of divinity and that it should not be detached from piety, either in conception or in practice.[53]

His interest in ethics was what moved Edwards to write the book that, above all the others, would evoke spirited rebuttals and revisions throughout the nineteenth century. In order to answer critics who believed that Calvinist theology made it impossible to assign moral blame and praise, he published in 1754 his *Enquiry into the Modern Prevailing Notions of that Freedom of the Will, Which is Supposed to be Essential to Moral Agency, Vertue and Vice, Reward and Punishment, Praise and Blame*. Written from the Stockbridge frontier, the book was designed to defend an understanding of human freedom compatible with Calvinist theology and yet also consistent with the language of moral praise and blame.

Edwards understood the critics of Calvinism—among whom he included especially the English writers Daniel Whitby, Samuel Clarke, and Thomas Chubb—to be insisting that the will had to be self-determining or else there could be no moral agency. His typical argument was to accuse the critics of contradiction: if the will were self-determining, every free act of the will, including its first free act, had to be freely chosen, and this led either to an infinite regress of free choices or to the self-contradictory notion of a free choice prior to the first free choice. Nor could willing be "indifferent," since willing was by its nature a preference or inclination. And it was also wrong to call the will "contingent," for this implied that it made its choices for no reason whatsoever.[54]

His opponents did not espouse precisely the views that Edwards criticized, but for Edwards the main point was to show that a Calvinist form of determinism remained compatible with praise and blame. His view was that the will responded always to the strongest motive—defined as the agent's perception of the greatest apparent good as determined by the nature of the object, the liveliness of the perception, the likelihood of attaining it, and the agent's state of mind. The motive operated as the cause of the volition in the sense that any act of the will was an inclination toward one motive or another. But human beings were still free moral agents, for they could do as they pleased, or act as they willed. "Let the person come by his volition or choice how he will," Edwards wrote, "yet, if he is able, and there is nothing in the way to hinder his pursuing and executing his will, the man is fully and perfectly free, according to the primary and common notion of freedom." They could not indifferently select their volitions or determine what they would will, but they were free if they could act as they were moved to act. They did what they wanted to do, and they did it willingly, regardless of how they came by their volition.[55]

In making the point, Edwards employed a distinction that had long been common in Reformed circles, among both traditionalists like Turretin in Geneva or Cotton Mather in New England and revisionists like Amyraut at Saumur. He distinguished between natural necessity and moral necessity. He conceded the absence of freedom, and of moral accountability, when a "natural necessity," a natural impediment external to the will, made it impossible for people to do what they willed. Moral necessity, however, meant only that the will could not defy its own inclination or disposition. Agents could not will, in a single act of volition, other than as they willed in that act. The will could not will two opposite things at the same time. But this moral necessity offered no impediment to freedom in its "plain and obvious" sense for it assumed the fact of choice and the natural ability to act.[56]

A distinction between natural and moral ability became one of the hallmarks of the Edwardean tradition. Other Calvinists often deplored it. Edwardean revivalists told the sinful that they had a natural ability to repent. They were therefore responsible if they failed to do it. While they lacked, apart from the assistance of special grace, the moral ability to repent, their failure to do it merely meant that they did not want to and could not choose against their predominant volition. They were naturally able but morally unwilling, and they were responsible for it. Edwards's followers made more of the distinction than he did, but he laid the groundwork, and it was one reason why some nineteenth-century Calvinists disliked his *Freedom of the Will*.

The Beauty of History

In addition to his passion for ethics, Edwards had a special interest in God's "moral government" of history, and his speculations on the course of history provided yet another occasion for him to display the "excellence" of God's works. He found in the Bible the clues to a "Grand design" that would bring all the world's diversity into a final unity. All history exhibited the "beauty" of Providence as God ordered all events toward a common end. This historical sense fed into Edwards's passionate interest in millennialism, and throughout his career he occupied himself with attempts to map the course of history toward the millennium and the creation of the "new heaven and new earth."[57]

In 1723 he began writing his "Notes on the Apocalypse," or exegetical comments on the book of Revelation, which he continued to expand until the end of his life. As an interpreter of the apocalyptic prophecies, Edwards carried forward a long-established project. He drew heavily from Whitby, the Cambridge don Joseph Mede, and Moses Lowman (1680–1752), a dissenting English pastor. Like them, Edwards found the clue to the course of history in the machinations of the Antichrist, which he assumed to be the Roman Papacy. Like numerous other Protestant predecessors, he correlated the prophetic forty-two months, or 1,260 days, of Revelation 11:2–3, each of which he assumed to be a year, with the events of western history. He decided that the forty-two-month period began in 606, when the Pope became the universal bishop, calculated that the year 1866 would bring the dethroning of the Papacy, and concluded, in agreement with Lowman, that the millennium would begin around the year 2000.[58]

Between his own time and the beginning of the millennium he anticipated years of struggle, marked by revivals and declensions, which he understood in accord with the "afflictive model of progress" that was common among eighteenth-century writers on eschatology. Progress would always alternate with adversity until the millennial era finally arrived. The revival in Northampton intensified his expectation, and his reading of Lowman's *Paraphrase and Notes on the Revelation* (1737) led Edwards to preach in 1739 a series of thirty sermons that were published long after his death as *A History of the Work of Redemption* (1774). He would later express an ambition to expand the sermons into a "body of divinity in an entire new method, being thrown into the form of history," but he died before he could complete the project. Nonetheless, the sermons traced the work of redemption through three periods of history — from the fall of Adam to the incarnation of Christ, from the incarnation to the resurrection, and from the resurrection to the end of the world — and showed that the pattern of adversity and deliverance had remained constant as the kingdom of Christ gradually prevailed. He interpreted the third period as a time of "the church's suffering state," but he felt that the world was now near the time of "the glorious work of God's Spirit" that would slowly begin to overthrow "Satan's kingdom" and end the reign of the Antichrist. Through revivals and the conversion of all the peoples of the world, this "glorious work" would eventually lead to "the prosperous state of the church," an era of peace and love that would last for a thousand years.[59]

In 1742, when he published *Some Thoughts Concerning the Present Revival of Religion in New England,* he even thought it "probable" that the "work of God's Spirit," which he seems to have associated with the long period preceding the millennium, might begin soon with events in America, a view that invited ridicule from Charles Chauncy and others, who reminded Edwards of Joseph Mede's prediction that America would become the kingdom of Satan. Edwards complained that his critics misread him, and indeed he typically assigned no special place to America in the events of the last times. In any case, he anticipated at least another two and a half centuries of struggle before the millennial era began. In 1743, he joined with ministers in Scotland to promote a concert of prayer for the advancement of God's kingdom, and in 1747 he contributed to the cause his *Humble Attempt to Promote Explicit Agreement and Visible Union of God's People in Extraordinary Prayer.* There he speculated that it might be plausible to expect 250 years of "commotions, tumults, and calamities" before the millennium.[60]

When he described the millennial era, Edwards employed the images of excellence, proportion, and beauty that pervaded the rest of his theology. Indeed, one thing that Edwards found most exciting about the prospect of the millennium was that it would display the unity hidden behind the diversity of history. When he wrote that "all the motions of the whole system of wheels and movements" in history tended toward one "appointed time," he was thinking of the consent of the many to the one, and in the millennial age "all the world" would be "as one church, one orderly, regular, beautiful society, one body, all the members in beautiful proportion." The church itself would be "beautiful," marked by "excellent order," and all the nations would unite in "sweet harmony." For a thousand years, the peoples of the world would live in prosperity, increasing knowledge, vital religion, and happiness. All would "agree in the sure, great and important doctrines of the gospel." It would be a time when "this whole great society shall appear in glorious beauty, in genuine amiable Christianity, and excellent order . . . , 'the perfection of beauty' [Ps. 50:2], 'an eternal excellency' [Is. 60:15]."[61]

Unlike Increase and Cotton Mather, Edwards thought that the millennial era would precede the final return of Christ, but he described the end times with a supernaturalism fully as intense as that of the Mathers. At the end of the millennium, Satan would be released from bondage, most of the world would fall into apostasy, and Christ would return "in flaming fire to take vengeance." He would judge the nations, descending with the angels as the dead arose, the living were transformed, and the souls of the departed were reunited with their bodies. The saints would ascend to the "new heaven and new earth," which would be located at some "glorious place" in the universe, at an immense distance from the solar system. The wicked would be cast into fire, and the saints would rejoice, for they would see only the glory of God, and God's glory would "in their esteem be of greater consequence, than the welfare of thousands and millions of souls." Edwards thought this final judgment was "entirely agreeable to reason" because it was "suitable" that God's righteousness be displayed, that injustice be rectified, and that the godly be honored. The final judgment would be one more instance of "due proportion." Even hell would be beautiful for those who had the eyes to see.[62]

Both Edwards's millennial vision and his descriptions of the last things could function as criticisms of Northampton's church and society, and by the mid-1740s he was becoming more critical. Anxious about the waning of revivalist zeal after 1742, irritated by a dispute over salary, embroiled in a quarrel over church discipline, rebuked by parishioners who refused to allow him to decide who could join the church, Edwards began, probably by the end of 1743, to rethink the criteria for church membership that he had happily inherited from Stoddard. The signs of change were present in his *Religious Affections* (1746), but it was not until 1749 that Edwards was ready to defend, in his *Humble Inquiry into the Rules of God Concerning the Qualifications*

*Requisite to a Compleat Standing and Full Communion in the Visible Chris-
tian Church,* the conclusion that adults must make a confession of "hearty
consent to the terms of the gospel covenant" before they could join the church,
receive the Lord's Supper, or present their children for baptism. Edwards was
turning his back on Stoddard's practice. He was also repudiating the halfway
covenant and the popular piety in which the laity linked their church membership with their desire to have their children baptized. He refused to accept the
separatist view that membership should require the public relation of a conversion experience, but he tightened the standards, and the congregation
would have none of it.[63]

The controversy over admission revealed Edwards's lingering attraction to
the covenant theology. Throughout his career, especially in his "Miscellanies,"
Edwards still wrote on the covenant of redemption between the Son and the
Father, the covenant of works between God and Adam, and the covenant of
grace between the believer and Christ. The covenant metaphor allowed him to
employ the familiar homiletic hyperbole declaring that salvation was an "absolute debt to the believer from God," though in other sermons he reversed
himself on this claim. Yet until 1749 the covenant was less prominent in his
thought than it had been in earlier Puritan theology. In the *Humble Inquiry* he
relied heavily on covenant thought, arguing that to own the covenant was to
profess "the consent of our hearts to it" and that covenant privileges required
such consent.[64]

His position required that he repudiate Stoddard's view of the Lord's Supper
as a converting ordinance. It required as well that he soft-pedal the efficacy of
baptism. Edwards defended infant baptism on familiar covenantal grounds —
the sacrament sealed the covenant — but he viewed adult baptism as a token of
regeneration, a position that aligned him more closely with Baptists than he
would have wanted to acknowledge. Although Edwards thought that God
used outward means of grace, he had always been cautious about saying that
the means functioned as causes of faith: "There are not truly any secondary
causes of it; but it is produced by God immediately." In fact, he taught that
when the unregenerate prayed, sang, and listened to sermons — and yet remained unregenerate — they intensified the guilt of their sin. A minor point in
Edwards's theology, this idea would later produce intense debate between his
followers and their opponents.[65]

Edwards's congregants persuaded Solomon Williams, the minister of Lebanon, Connecticut, to answer Edwards, and Williams charged him with "inde-
cent and injurious treatment of Mr. Stoddard." Edwards replied that his revisions of Stoddard's practice actually honored Stoddard's "real sentiments,"
and it was true that both he and Stoddard aimed at conversion as the goal of

their pastoral ministry. But both in his musings on the order of salvation and in his ideas about sacraments, the church, and membership, Edwards moved further and further away from Stoddard's theology. In part this was because the themes of excellence, proportion, and fittingness led him in new directions. In part it was because he was far more interested than Stoddard in the rational consistency of his theology. The irony, however, was that Edwards, the theologian of unity and harmony, split his congregation and that his ideas would help fracture Reformed theology in America for almost a century.[66]

6

Fragmentation in New England

In 1787 Jonathan Edwards, Jr., divided the clergy of Connecticut into three groups: Edwardeans, Arminians, and "moderate" Calvinists. "A considerable number," he added, failed to "think or study enough to have any distinct scheme at all." A similar alignment prevailed throughout New England. Before 1750, most New England theologians would have described themselves as Calvinist. By 1760, some claimed not to be Calvinist, and Calvinists no longer agreed about what Calvinism was. In particular, the disciples of Edwards pressed the logic of his theology so vigorously that critics complained of a "New Divinity," and by 1770 it had become the custom to distinguish the three parties described by the younger Edwards.[1]

The Arminians and moderate Calvinists, known as the Old Calvinists, sought a theology fitted for a settled religious establishment in which church membership was open to adults who professed Christian belief and led sober and decent lives and to their children. The Edwardeans were revivalists who sought pure churches filled with regenerate members able to testify to saving grace. Even at their most abstruse, the debates among the three groups were about the practical matter of who should be admitted to the church and how the church should propagate its message. The disputes were also about virtue. Arminians, expanding the earlier theology of virtue, repeated the complaint that Calvinism undermined ethics; Edwardeans saw the ethical theories of the

Arminians, however, as a disguised form of self-love, while the Old Calvinists worried that Edwardean rigor ignored ethical complexity and the gradations of virtue in both society and the church.

The disputants had no fundamental difference about reason and revelation, though they believed that they did. Old Calvinists and Edwardeans thought that Arminians placed too much confidence in reason; Arminians believed that their opponents failed to see the value of natural theology. Edwardeans thought that Old Calvinists veered in the same rationalist direction as the Arminians, but Old Calvinists prided themselves on their measured estimation of reason's capacities. William Hart (1713–84) spoke for them when he insisted that reason was "the Candle of the Lord" that enabled men and women to distinguish truth and falsehood, good and evil: "Its eminent Province," he added, "is in things of religion." He believed that the exaggerated Edwardean denigration of human nature led to the false conclusion that "we . . . cannot judge of Divine and Spiritual things by our Reason, because it is blind and carnal." Yet Old Calvinists also saw Edwardeans as captive to a misuse of reason. For both Arminians and Old Calvinists, it became a truism that the New Divinity was "metaphysic-mad." Its adherents discussed "the plainest evangelical subjects, in a deep, abstruse, metaphysical way." The New Divinity men reminded one another that they were "suspected of refining too far, and of suffering that thing called Metaphysics," and they constantly defended themselves against the charge that they were guilty of "meddling with metaphysical subjects, and dark, abstruse matters."[2]

In their view of reason, however, the parties shared more in common than they acknowledged. All of them believed that reason could support a natural theology that furnished truth about the existence of God. They agreed that revelation stood above reason. They agreed that the rational evidences of Christianity proved the authenticity of the biblical revelation. On these commonplaces of eighteenth-century Protestantism, no one veered off in eccentric directions. Yet their disputes were intense. The Old Calvinist Jedediah Mills complained of a "paper war" that "raised disputes to the greatest height, divided towns, broke societies and churches," and alienated affection among "dear brethren." Their perceptions of each other as rationalists and metaphysicians signaled the depth of their disagreements over other topics in theology.[3]

Arminians

The Arminians of the 1750s were more adventurous than the earlier theologians of virtue, more willing to break openly from Calvinism. Tracing a progression from Ebenezer Gay to Jonathan Mayhew to the mature Charles

Chauncy shows not only an increasing respect for reason, about which the New Divinity theologians complained, but also a movement from a cautious theology of virtue to an open attack on Calvinist orthodoxy. For the Arminians, confidence in the reasonableness of theology was closely tied to a changing estimate of human nature and its moral potential.

The minister for seventy years in First Parish of Hingham, Massachusetts, Ebenezer Gay (1696–1787) was a man of quick wit who gathered around him younger ministers of liberal temperament and made of himself a godfather of Arminian dissent. He befriended ministers known for their departures from orthodoxy, but he avoided trouble because he developed equivocation into a fine art. He represented a group who ceased to care about the fine points of the Arminian-Calvinist dispute but retained an emotional identification with the Calvinist past.

Following the example of the English Puritan Richard Baxter, whom he admired, Gay advised ministers to avoid partisan quarrels and to emphasize "the more mighty things in which we are all agreed." Of such agreements, the necessity for Christian virtue should be uppermost. When he delivered the Annual Convention sermon in 1746, he warned the ministry not to abuse the doctrines of grace by calling "Good works abominable." His strategy was to retain Calvinist language but reinterpret its meaning, so he affirmed the "doctrines of grace" while designating them as doctrines "designed to promote universal Holiness." Gay added that belief in justifying faith did not require the "substituting [of Christ's] obedience in the place of ours."[4]

Gay was treading on sensitive ground, but he was only reaffirming the Old Light claim that faith included obedience. Most New England Calvinists had never denied that grace issued in holiness or that the redeemed were to keep the commandments. Most had also said that the effectual calling empowered rather than overrode the faculties. Gay's address was not old-style Calvinism, but he avoided the crucial question of whether the grace that elicited faith might be resisted, and his address was amenable to either a Calvinist or an Arminian interpretation. Nonetheless, he thrust to the forefront what in an earlier era would have been concessions and qualifications. He shifted the emphasis from justification to sanctification, accented holiness more than forgiveness, and talked more about obedience than about the sacrifice of Christ.

Thirteen years later, in 1759, he delivered the Dudleian Lecture at the Harvard commencement. His *Natural Religion, as Distinguish'd from Revealed* was a manifesto of the theology of virtue, its subject being the "moral obligation induced by the existence of God," and it showed how much Gay had transformed Calvinism into a theology of morality. Without denying that evangelical obedience could result only from the grace of sanctification, or that natural religion remained insufficient for salvation, he instructed his hearers not to disdain obligations discovered by the light of reason alone. The essential differences between right and wrong were founded "in the Natures and Relations of things," and they imposed an obligation to goodness antecedent to any biblical law. They also revealed to reason the "God of Nature" who originated them.[5]

Gay always guarded himself against deism. He said that revealed religion stood higher than natural religion and that natural religion derived its authority from the assistance of a higher revelation. The closer the deists were to the truth, he said, the more dependent they were on the biblical revelation that they decried. Biblical revelation had—as Jonathan Edwards argued—illumined the reason of the Christian West and allowed it to discern what would have otherwise remained hidden. But Gay's main point was that revealed and natural religion should "subsist harmoniously together" and that no doctrine should be inconsistent "with the Perfections of God, and the Possibility of Things" as understood by the natural religion of reason. This meant that God's justice had to be compatible with a rational concept of justice and that God's holiness could not differ in kind from human holiness. It also meant that natural religion—grounded in reason and conscience—could show human nature to be "designed and framed for the Practice of Virtue."[6]

By 1759, a few Congregationalist ministers were ready to leave Gay's equivocations behind. The topic that revealed the new temper was original sin, or more precisely, the idea that God imputed to human beings the guilt of Adam's sin. The leading refutation of the idea came from Samuel Webster (1718–96), the minister in Salisbury, Massachusetts, whose *Winter Evening's Conversation Upon the Doctrine of Original Sin* (1757) drew on the ideas of John Taylor and Daniel Whitby. Webster wanted to show that imputation could not be reconciled with "the goodness, holiness, and justice of God" because it made God the author of sin. He conceded a universal human sinfulness, but he argued that guilt was personal, not inherited, and that the conception of Adam as representative of the race was unbiblical. In any event, he added, we are not responsible for sins of our representatives.[7]

For some Calvinists the doctrine of imputation had become a badge of loyalty. Samuel Niles (1674–1762) of South Braintree, known widely for his hounding of Lemuel Briant as well as his attacks on illiterate ministers during the awakening, explained that Adam was both the natural and the federal head of humanity, its natural progenitor and its legal representative. It was absurd to deny that humanity partook, in the "imputative sense," of the guilt of his disobedience. Peter Clark (1694–1768), the pastor in Danvers and a man of sufficient reputation to be invited as the Dudleian lecturer at Harvard, employed the same argument, adding that if there were no imputation of guilt, there would be no need to impute righteousness, in which case Christ died in vain.[8]

Clark was more willing than Niles to make concessions, and his amiability got him into some trouble. Webster had charged that imputation implied the damnation of children who died in infancy. Clark said it did no such thing, and he suggested that Calvinists no longer held to the damnation of dying infants. Clark's suggestion gave Charles Chauncy an opportunity to express his growing disenchantment with Calvinist theology, and he did it by showing that true Calvinists made no exception for infants. His remarks carried the message that he no longer included himself in the Calvinist camp.[9]

By that time, Chauncy had an ally in the person of Jonathan Mayhew (1720–66), who was ready not only to criticize specific Calvinist doctrines but also to be more explicit about his alternative. Mayhew benefited from the example of his father, Experience Mayhew, who had long been a skeptic about Calvinist orthodoxy. The son's congregation at West Church in Boston consisted, moreover, of wealthy merchants and their wives who would not be cowed by the orthodox. When their first try at ordaining Mayhew in 1747 fell flat because not enough ministers showed up, they invited ministers from outside the city. When other clergy excluded Mayhew from the Boston Thursday Lecture series, he inaugurated a West Church lecture series of his own, publishing the results in 1749 in a book — *Seven Sermons* — that earned him an honorary doctorate from the University of Aberdeen.[10]

His *Seven Sermons* promoted the theology of virtue: "A right faith," he wrote, "is an excellent and valuable thing; but it is advantageous no further than it purifies the heart, and works by love . . . and leads us to live an holy and godly life." He advised the clergy to avoid "metaphysical niceties" and preach holiness and good works. For Mayhew, Christian good works were identical with natural moral duties. He adopted Samuel Clarke's idea that both truth and moral rectitude had "their foundation in the nature of things," particularly in the "relations" that men and women had to God and to each other. Like Clarke, he believed that if something were speculatively true, there had to be some "corresponding fitness of actions." But he also believed in a moral sense that took pleasure in moral good, and he thought that reason and the moral sense worked together to discern the right.[11]

Mayhew sounded in 1749 like one more theologian of virtue, urging that the "weightier matters" of Christianity were the "doctrines of love" to God and neighbor, but he soon moved beyond his friend Ebenezer Gay. For one thing, he was more lyrical in his paeans to reason. He thought that since many religions claimed a revelation, reason alone, employing "probable evidence," could determine which was genuine and interpret its meaning. The fact that God had revealed himself through "human language" meant that he had accommodated revelation to rationality. Mayhew still taught that biblical revelation brought a truth beyond reason's capacity insofar as it showed the proper motives for morality, revealed Jesus as the mediator, and assured the repentant that God would pardon their sins. But Mayhew considered it "blasphemy" to reproach reason.[12]

He also surpassed the earlier theologians of virtue in his enthusiasm for happiness. For Mayhew, the criterion of moral goodness was the production of happiness: "Since happiness, in a large sense of the word, is the only good end, the only thing that is valuable for its own sake, it follows that an action is so far good, and no farther, than it produces happiness." He avoided a purely utilitarian position by insisting that piety required esteem for God without consideration of gain and that to serve God for the sake of "some consequent advantage" was "religious selfishness." But the two themes — happiness as the sole intrinsic good and piety as a disinterested esteem of God — blended together in his confidence that piety would always serve the "interest" of the faithful.[13]

In a world overseen by a "compassionate Parent" solicitous of human happiness, the notion of an imputation of original guilt to infants seemed to Mayhew both unjust and implausible. He conceded the universality of sinfulness but insisted that guilt resulted from personal transgression. By 1761 he began also to emphasize the need for the sinful "to work out their salvation." Without denying that salvation came "entirely of grace" and without claiming that God was "bound in justice" to reward the exertions of the unregenerate, Mayhew announced in his sermon on *Striving to Enter in at the Strait Gate* that God had established a "certain connexion" between the striving of awakened sinners and their obtaining salvation.[14]

Mayhew shared the eighteenth century's intense interest in theodicy, the justifying of God's goodness in the face of suffering. He tried to convince his readers that even barren deserts and noxious insects had their good ends, and that the suffering of animals was balanced by their "surplusage of pleasurable sensations." All the more, then, would the goodness of God reward the yearnings of human beings for eternal salvation, granting to all the grace to strive and ensuring a good result for all who yielded to that grace. This showed that benevolence was God's principal moral attribute and that God was the "infinitely good One who aims at making [others] happy without any selfish end."[15]

His sense of divine benevolence led Mayhew to adopt the governmental theory of the atonement proposed earlier by Hugo Grotius (1583–1645) in Holland. Christ died not to redeem a debt but to preserve the dignity of the divine government. Having promulgated a moral law, God could not permit its subversion without allowing the destruction of the moral order itself. When Christ died to vindicate the honor of the law, he made it possible for God to forgive sinful rebels without upsetting the moral order. For Mayhew, the doctrine meant that Christ died so that God could preserve a moral order for the sake of the creature.[16]

His view of Jesus led him even further outside Calvinist circles. Jesus remained, in Mayhew's theology, the mediator whose death renewed the relation between God and humanity. But from his earliest publications, Mayhew saw Jesus chiefly as a teacher who "preached his own gospel," and by 1755 he called into question the doctrine that Christ was the incarnation of the second Person of the Trinity. He would leave questions about the "metaphysical abstract nature" of God to fourth-century theologians, but he was certain that since Christ's mediation resulted from the grant of the Father, Christ had been subordinate to the Father. Mayhew would refer to Christ as the Son of God, but not as God the Son, for that would derogate from the honor due "the One Living and true God."[17]

Mayhew was following the lead of Samuel Clarke in England, who in 1712 in his *Scripture Doctrine of the Trinity* argued that the Athanasian Trinity had no scriptural warrant. Clarke proposed an eighteenth-century variation of Arianism, but he made his proposal for the typically Protestant reason that the Bible "no where at all" taught the Trinitarian doctrine that appeared in the creeds. By 1756 American colonists could also read other anti-Trinitarian polemics, ranging from the *Humble Enquiry into the Scripture Account of Jesus Christ* written around 1702 by the English cleric Thomas Emlyn to *Primitive Christianity Revived* (1711) by the onetime Cambridge professor William Whiston, but it was Mayhew who generated reactions from other colonial theologians.[18]

His convictions about divine goodness led Mayhew to the brink of still another break with theological convention. He became manifestly uncomfortable with the notion of eternal damnation. Mayhew speculated about the end times, and he looked forward, after a thousand-year period in which the church would increasingly flourish, to the physical return of Jesus to pass judgment. He believed that everlasting flames in which the sinful would be punished would then consume the earth. But by 1763, he balked at saying that the punishment lasted forever. Since reason could not decide the issue, he said, he had to accept what God had revealed, but he also had to interpret that revelation in the light of "the infinite goodness and mercy of God." Infinite mercy implied universal salvation.[19]

Charles Chauncy had also pondered the question of universal salvation secretly since 1752, when he undertook a study of the Bible with the design of rejecting every "human scheme" and rewriting theology from "the scheme of revelation alone." In 1782, he published the first of four books arguing for universalism. He broke his silence because of his dismay at the public response to John Murray, who came to New England from England in 1770 promoting the universalist teaching of James Relly of London. Relly and Murray taught that a universal atonement entailed universal salvation. Chauncy believed that their teaching ran the risk of licensing immoral behavior.[20]

In 1782 Chauncy and his assistant John Clarke issued a short preview of Chauncy's doctrine, with a preface that criticized Murray for encouraging "libertinism." Titled *Salvation for All Men,* it listed biblical passages asserting that God would have all to be saved (1 Tim. 2:3), that God's grace sufficed for the salvation of all (Titus 2:11), and that just as all died in Adam so all would be made alive in Christ (1 Cor. 15:22). Two years later, Chauncy published two longer books with more detailed argumentation. In *The Benevolence of the Deity* he contended that divine benevolence entailed the "communication of happiness" to the creation. Drawing on the Anglican theologian William King, he explained evil and suffering by pointing out that human beings were free agents and part of a vast chain of beings within a great whole that yielded happiness and good.[21]

His other book was Boston's theological sensation. In *The Mystery hid from Ages and Generations, made Manifest by the Gospel Revelation; Or, the Salvation of All Men,* he presented his version of universalist doctrine. He argued that the sinful would undergo terrible punishments. At the final judgment, they would be sentenced to penal sufferings in hell "for a long time" — perhaps as long as the biblical thousand years — until the torment changed their hearts, but eventually they would see their folly, repent, and join the saints for an eternal existence here in this world, which would be renewed by the final conflagration as an earthly paradise. No sinful creature could finally thwart the purpose of God to shower happiness on the entire creation. The books revealed Chauncy's attraction to a humanitarian ideal that made Reformed doctrines of eternal punishment suspect on moral grounds.[22]

Chauncy kept his views secret for so long because he and his allies believed that they were, as one minister pointed out, "too sublime for the soaring of vulgar imaginations." They were designed for "the wise and learned." Both Chauncy and Mayhew distrusted "the common people." Mayhew gained a reputation as a political radical because he criticized unlimited submission and passive obedience to tyrannical rulers, but neither he nor Chauncy favored popular democracy. All the more, they thought, should only men of learning judge theological wisdom. Mayhew was scathing in his contempt for what he saw as "unlettered" and "unstudied" criticisms of his views. To him and to other liberal Boston ministers, moreover, the Edwardean theologians of the New England backcountry, while not quite unlettered, seemed almost equally unsuited as qualified critics.[23]

The New Divinity

The strongholds of the Edwardeans were the small towns and rural areas of western Massachusetts and Connecticut. Seen from the elevated heights of Boston, they were unlikely candidates for theological stardom. Most came from obscure families in obscure places. Their critics derided them as "Farmer Metaphysicians" and described them as low, uncouth, and unsocial. But the Edwardeans themselves were not theological populists, and they were not willing to allow the unlearned to intrude on their precincts. They also had no liking for "ingenious, self-taught, self-sufficient novices in divinity." "It is one thing," said one of them, "to know the gospel as a Christian, and another to know it as a divine." They produced difficult and abstract theological reasoning that often left their hearers and their readers baffled.[24]

The Edwardeans had their main strength among Congregationalists in western New England, where one of the leading figures, Samuel Hopkins, could boast in 1796 of more than one hundred adherents to his views, but their influence extended into the Presbyterian churches of New York and Pennsylvania. Such clerical celebrities as James Wilson of Philadelphia, Jacob Green of North Hanover, New Jersey, and Gardiner Spring at New York City's Brick Church became outspoken Hopkinsians. Hopkins's influence even reached Virginia, where the Presbyterian revivalist Samuel Davies adopted Edwardean views after reading the works of Joseph Bellamy, and Tennessee, where after 1795 the Presbyterian Hezekiah Balch braved heresy trials to make Greenville College a New Divinity hothouse. The fiction of Harriet Beecher Stowe later introduced New Divinity ideas to readers who preferred novels to straight theology. Stowe had turned decisively away from New Divinity theology, but she still admired its consistency.[25]

The New Divinity theologians held to conventional views of the relation between reason and revelation. Though eager to show that their theology was "perfectly consistent with right reason and agreeable to its dictates," the Edwardeans espoused the familiar conviction that the "best and most sure guide" for the theologian was scriptural revelation. They assumed that reason could demonstrate some religious truths — such as the existence of an omnipotent God — but they continued to believe that revelation stood above reason, offering truths that reason alone could not attain. And they used the common "evidences" to prove that "the Scriptures are a revelation inspired of God." But what gave them their reputation as metaphysicians was their confidence in consistency. They would provide a "systematic knowledge of the Gospel." They would discern the "first principles" of biblical and rational truths, and then link them "in the form of systems."[26]

Despite the desire for consistency, the New Divinity theologians adhered to no monolithic philosophical system. Apart from a few references to the divine "constitution" of reality, they seemed uninterested in Edwards's idealism, and their theologies bore no pronounced idealist imprint. By the early nineteenth century, some Edwardeans accepted the new Scottish philosophy of Common Sense and appealed to "consciousness" as a source of evidence for certain of their theological arguments, but none of the New Divinity theologians formulated philosophical conclusions in the manner of Edwards.[27]

Their opponents accused the Edwardeans of preaching a "new divinity," and the name stuck, but they preferred to think of themselves as Consistent Calvinists. Their leading motif was their linking of a doctrine of divine sovereignty with the revivalist's demand that the sinner had the responsibility and the ability to repent now. They also shared with their mentor and with the liberals a pressing interest in true virtue and its expression through benevolence, both human and divine. Against critics who claimed that Calvinist views of divine sovereignty made it impossible to believe in a benevolent God, they insisted that "if we leave out the idea of Sovereignty, we shall have not only an imperfect but a wrong view of divine benevolence." Against critics who charged that Calvinism depreciated virtue, they replied that Calvinist theology described the only virtue worth having.[28]

Samuel Hopkins (1721–1803) read theology with Edwards after graduating from Yale and then spent twenty-five years in a backwoods community, Great Barrington, Massachusetts, before moving to a modest congregation of merchants and their families in Newport, Rhode Island. A melancholy man who remained doubtful of his own salvation, he regarded his sermons as "low and miserable," and observers agreed about his disagreeable delivery, but his writing achieved such influence that for many the New Divinity became synonymous with "Hopkinsianism." He was the editor of Edwards's unpublished manuscripts and the author of his biography. More important, he was the author of the two-volume *System of Doctrines* (1793), the first self-conscious attempt in America to formulate a theological system in which all the doctrines would be "connected and implied in each other." His admirer Nathanael Emmons later boasted that Hopkins "brought the whole system [of Calvinism] to a greater degree of consistency and perfection, than any who had gone before him."[29]

Joseph Bellamy (1719–90) served as pastor for fifty years in the small town of Bethlehem, Connecticut. After graduating from Yale, he ended up at Northampton as Edwards's first student. When he settled in Bethlehem he emulated his master, building a two-room log college — the first "school of the prophets" in New England — in which he trained close to sixty young ministers in the arts of revivalism and theological speculation. He was a large man with a strong voice and a forceful personality (his enemies called him domineering) who acquired a large house and farm and respectable wealth, along with enough local influence to be envied as the Pope of Litchfield County. A probationary period with an urban congregation in New York convinced him, however, that he was destined to remain "a minister out in the woods," not "fit for the city."[30]

The careers of Hopkins and Bellamy illustrate the importance for the movement of Edwards's treatise on virtue, but they also suggest that the preoccupation with virtue had additional sources: it came from the effort to refute the Arminian ethical critique of Calvinism; it represented the indignation of small-town ministers and their congregations about self-interest in a market economy; and it revealed lingering worries about the continuing appeal of antinomian theology at the fringes of the revival. For all these reasons, the Edwardeans trained their sights on virtue.[31]

The disdain for Arminianism, antinomianism, and the presumptions of commercial society appeared in the first major treatise of the New Divinity — Joseph Bellamy's *True Religion Delineated* (1750) — published with a commendatory preface by Edwards. Bellamy had gained a following as an itinerant preacher during the revivals, but their excesses persuaded him to return to his parish. There he pondered the antinomian doctrines of Andrew Croswell and Ebenezer Frothingham (1719–98), a Connecticut separatist. At the same time, he continued to preach that the moral philosophers and the New England Arminians were wrong about both Calvinism and true virtue. The title of his *True Religion Delineated* suggested an opposition to William Wollaston's *Religion of Nature Delineated*. The book was an effort to show that Calvinism promoted virtue in a way that philosophers, Arminians, and antinomians failed to appreciate.

Bellamy followed Edwards in believing that the heart of true religion and true virtue consisted in the love of God for God's own intrinsic excellence. The common failing of Arminians, antinomians, and corner-cutting merchants was that their religion contradicted this virtue. All three promoted a counterfeit virtue that disguised self-love. The Arminians urged people to do their duties in order to obtain heaven, but this was little more than refined self-regard. The antinomians preached that the faithful loved God because of their confidence that God would save them, but Bellamy thought that people who loved God because God loved them loved themselves more than they loved God. And no love was more counterfeit than that of the "ambitious" and "worldly" merchants who loved God out of gratitude that God had granted them prosperity.[32]

Bellamy thought that Christians should love God solely because they had a "Sense" of God's "own intrinsick Worth, Excellency, and Beauty." The excellence of the divine nature made such a love "infinitely Fit." From this claim, Bellamy could proceed to the point that Christians who loved God for God's intrinsic excellence would love God's law, which was "a transcript of his nature." True religion — this was the thesis of *True Religion Delineated* — therefore turned out to be a "conformity to the Law of God, and a compliance with the Gospel of Christ," and the gospel did not annul the law. Such a solicitude for law found repeated expression among the Edwardeans, who argued that divine law was founded in "the reason and nature of things" and that believers remained under "as great [an] obligation to a perfect conformity" to law as they ever were.[33]

Against Arminians who charged Calvinism with denigrating holiness, Bellamy said that Calvinists preached "doctrines according to holiness" that nurtured "universal Benevolence." Against antinomians who charged other Calvinists with denigrating grace, he said that a proper view of law kept the gospel from becoming an ideology of self-regard. Quarrels with antinomians occupied him throughout his career. During the 1750s, several extreme New Lights adopted the positions of James Hervey, William Cudworth, and Walter Marshall, English proponents of a solafideism who disparaged any human works, including repentance, prior to justifying belief, and denied that a virtuous life signaled a good estate. These New Lights found assurance of salvation only in an immediate witness of the Spirit, and they defined justifying faith as each person's Spirit-given assurance of God's "particular" love. To Bellamy they were as dangerous as the Arminians.[34]

Indeed, to Edwardeans, the extreme New Light insistence that faith required such a "particular" assurance — which amounted to a certainty of election — seemed unbiblical and excessively self-confident. When the Edwardean convert Sarah Osborn in Newport described to a friend the evidences of grace that God had wrought in her soul, she denied that she had "any desire to establish assurance as the essence of saving faith." Osborn led a women's prayer group for twenty years, and during periods of religious excitement in Newport she led broader religious conversations in her home, and she was knowledgeable in the finer points of Edwardean thought. She knew to guard against any doctrine associated with antinomian sentiments.[35]

During the 1760s, other New Lights adopted the ideas of the Scottish separatist Robert Sandeman (1717–81), who proposed that neither good works
nor a persuasion of being forgiven gave evidence of saving faith. For Sandeman, faith meant intellectual assent to Christian teaching about redemption
through Christ, and everyone who assented could be assured of salvation.
Several pastors and congregations adopted Sandemanian doctrines, but Edwardeans, Old Light Calvinists, and Arminians all united against Herveyites
and Sandemanians, and Bellamy's *Theron, Paulinas, and Aspasio* (1759), directed against Hervey, ignited a debate over antinomian doctrine that lasted
for four years and involved theologians on both sides of the Atlantic.[36]

In Bellamy's view, Hervey and Sandeman ignored the obligation of Christians to love God for God's intrinsic loveliness "antecedent to his being our
reconciled Father and Friend." "If I love God merely because he loves me," he
said, "I am the Object really beloved: And the act is properly an Act of self-
love." In literary dialogues and published sermons, he promoted the view that
faith was a trusting of Christ, not a confidence in subjective experience, that it
presupposed a repentance for sin induced by the law, and that it issued in a
sanctified life in accord with the law. In describing repentance as prior to faith,
Bellamy — and other Edwardeans — departed from the assumption of earlier
Calvinists that true repentance presupposed faith. Some New Divinity thinkers argued that both repentance and a true love of God preceded faith, for it
would be selfish of Christians to love God only after gaining the faith that God
loved them.[37]

So unrelenting were the Edwardeans in their demand for immediate repentance and selfless love for God that they revised the doctrine of justification by
faith in Christ. Edwards had sometimes seemed to suggest that justification
presupposed the indwelling of the Spirit, infused grace, and love in the regenerate heart. Bellamy added that love for God and the divine law normally
preceded justifying faith. Hopkins was even more explicit: a sinner must have
"a heart to love God and his law, antecedent to his pardon and justification,
and in order to it." Such a heart resulted from a divine act of regeneration. He
was no longer preaching the justification of the sinner as much as the justification of the reborn. Later New Divinity theologians exposed the tendency
implicit in Hopkins's theology. They said that sinners were justified only after
becoming saints, and they also referred to justification as a "partial" and
"provisional" forgiveness that required perseverance in faith and obedience.
In their own way, the theologians of the New Divinity valorized virtue as much
as the New England liberals.[38]

The most thorough definition of virtue came from Hopkins in his *Inquiry
into the Nature of True Holiness* (1773). Denying any claim to originality,

Hopkins represented himself as an interpreter of Edwards who wanted only to state "more particularly" the opposition of holiness and self-love. In fact, he departed from Edwards by linking love and law in the fashion of Bellamy and by defining all sin as selfishness. His argument was that both reason and revelation defined holiness as disinterested benevolence. This was what Jesus meant when he told his followers to love God with all their heart, mind, and strength (Matt. 22:37–40), and this law of love stood in absolute opposition to self-love.[39]

Hopkins emphasized the point by insisting that the real test of love would be a willingness to surrender even one's eternal interest for "the greater good of the whole." More than a century earlier, Hooker and Shepard had claimed that the truly humiliated sinner would will to be damned for God's glory. Hopkins was now saying that such a will was the mark of a true saint. It was a passing comment, but it aroused a furor, so Hopkins returned to it in his "Dialogue Between a Calvinist and a Semi-Calvinist," which remained unpublished when he died. If one could save millions by perishing, he asked, should one not do it? Would this not serve a greater good? But what good was higher than the glory of God? Anyone who loved God unselfishly could say only one thing: "let God be glorified, let what will become of me."[40]

The New Divinity allowed no middle ground between sinners and saints. One either loved God above self or one loved self above God. This is why Hopkins found it so distressing to read Jonathan Mayhew's 1761 sermon on *Striving to Enter in at the Strait Gate,* in which Mayhew encouraged the unregenerate to use the means of grace to strive toward holiness and suggested that their striving made them more acceptable to God. Bellamy also taught that the means of grace helped people overcome sin, but Hopkins saw in Mayhew's doctrine a gradualism that made no immediate demand for repentance. He replied to Mayhew four years later in his *Enquiry Concerning the Promises of the Gospel,* in which he argued that the Bible made no promises of salvation to "the exercises and doings of the unregenerate." In telling his followers to strive, Hopkins thought, Jesus was addressing true disciples. Hopkins acknowledged that the New Testament held out salvation to everyone who desired it. But in the New Testament, he said, to desire salvation was to desire "holiness for its own sake," and the unregenerate never wanted to be saved in this sense. In the background stood Edwards's conception of true virtue.[41]

The debate over the promises of salvation furnished the context in which Hopkins employed the New Divinity distinction between regeneration and conversion. Expanding on a point that Edwards had once made in reference to infants, Bellamy concluded in 1750 that regeneration preceded conversion, which he defined as an exercise of the heart that flowed from a new disposition. Hopkins used the same distinction to counter Mayhew. He argued that God regenerated the sinful by laying a foundation in their mind by which they could discern the excellence of Christian truth and embrace the gospel with their hearts. This regeneration was an "unpromised favor," a divine work, immediate, instantaneous, and imperceptible. The conditional promises of the New Testament — do this and you will be saved — were directed to men and women who were regenerate but not yet converted. They still had to turn to repentance, faith, and holiness. This turn constituted their conversion, and in it they were active. Mayhew was right to say that the promises implied a capacity for response, but he failed to see that only the regenerate could respond.[42]

In describing regeneration as immediate, Hopkins threw into question the old Puritan assumption that God normally produced regeneration through such "means of grace" as sermons and prayers. The initial change, he said, came from the Spirit — not from "any medium or means whatsoever." Means of grace were necessary. They accomplished a "preparatory work" — producing the knowledge, conviction, and humiliation that normally preceded regeneration. They ensured that the saint would be "prepared to act properly when regenerated." But as Edwards had also argued, the means could not bring about regeneration, which was an immediate act of the Spirit.[43]

Hopkins further disturbed the Old Calvinists when he added that the unregenerate became "more vicious and guilty in God's sight" the more knowledge they derived from the means of grace. This was the point that first caused opponents to accuse him of espousing a "New Divinity." Almost a century earlier, Samuel Willard had warned about the special danger of remaining unfruitful under a gospel ministry. Edwards made a similar observation. Bellamy taught that even the best religious performances of the unregenerate remained "sinful," because the sinner was interested in "only what he can get." But Hopkins emphasized the point in a way that drew spirited reactions. He insisted that resistance from the awakened brought greater blame than resistance from someone who knew nothing of the gospel. Instead of encouraging sinners to rely on the means of grace, ministers should encourage them "to repent and believe the gospel" now, without delay. The premise was again Edwards's theory of virtue, with its suggestion that the unregenerate would pursue only "Self-Ends."[44]

The New Divinity theologians therefore attacked the lax standards of membership permitted by the 1662 synod that expanded rights to baptism. Bellamy derided the synod's decision as a "halfway covenant" that discouraged conversions. He recognized only "one covenant," and it required "holy obedience, an obedience which proceeds from faith and love." The church covenant signified no less than compliance with this covenant of grace. Hopkins considered the unregenerate no more entitled than the openly scandalous to the privileges of church membership, for to oppose regeneration in one's heart was "wholly more scandalous and wicked" than drunkenness or prostitution.[45]

Their position exposed them again to the charge that Calvinism disparaged morality and called into question the goodness of God. Not only did they propose to expel decent halfway members from the churches, but they also seemed to say that true virtue was possible only for a chosen few. To Arminians, they appeared, like all Calvinists, to depict God as condemning men and women for failing to do what they could not do. This was serious because the New Divinity men were as eager as any English Arminian to affirm the benevolence of God. Hopkins said in his *System of Doctrines* that "benevolence, clothed with omnipotence" was the essence of God's moral perfection and that this benevolent God never condemned men and women for what they could not do.[46]

The principal reply on the issue of alleged human inability came from John Smalley (1734–1820), the New Divinity pastor in New Britain, Connecticut, who in 1769 published two sermons on *The Inability of the Sinner to Comply with the Gospel*. Smalley was a Yale graduate who learned his theology from Bellamy before serving for more than half a century as pastor of the Congregationalist Church in New Britain, Connecticut. He won the admiration of fellow Edwardeans for having "thoroughly digested Mr. Edwards' writings," and he was among the most successful pastor-theologians of the group. His congregation recalled him from retirement even though most of them disliked his opposition to the American Revolution. He was attracted to the New Divinity because it promised to put scriptural teachings "in a consistent light," but he produced no system and contented himself as an author with polemics against Arminians and Universalists.[47]

Smalley's aim was to convince his listeners of their entire dependence on divine grace but also to reconcile their helplessness — in a manner "consistent with reason" — both with the preacher's exhortation to immediate repentance and with "the goodness or the justice of God." Paul's claim in Romans 9:18 that God hardened the hearts of unbelievers and Jesus' admonition in John 6:44 that no one could come unto him without being drawn by the Father provided evidence for the Calvinist doctrine of inability. But Smalley distinguished, following Edwards, two forms of inability: (1) a natural inability that arose from a physical hindrance, a lack of physical strength, a want of opportunity, or an absence of understanding, and (2) a moral inability that consisted in the want of a will or disposition.[48]

Unlike most other Calvinists, the Edwardeans claimed that everyone had a natural ability to repent. Everyone who understood the law had a natural ability to obey, and everyone who understood the gospel had a natural ability to accept it. Earlier Calvinists had occasionally made a similar distinction, but the New Divinity theologians made it a centerpiece of their thought. As long as no one physically restrained the unregenerate, or took away their mental faculties, or prevented their hearing the gospel, they labored under no natural inability. Emmons even said that everyone had the "natural power to frustrate as well as to fulfill the decrees of God."[49]

Insofar as sinners languished in coils of inability, their entrapment had its source in their own wills. If they refused to love God, they wanted to refuse. They lacked the will to love, or to obey, or to accept the gospel. The Edwardeans had no wish to minimize this moral inability. It was as binding as any other invariable relation between a cause and its effect: "A man *must* act," Smalley said, "according to his own heart." But the want of a moral disposition rendered no man or woman excusable. Since the cause of their inability was their own willing, and the necessity arose from within them, they remained morally responsible. Smalley observed that we continually presuppose the distinction by excusing the want of a natural ability to do good but not the want of a will to do it.[50]

To show that the distinction between natural and moral inability was consistent with freedom, they returned to Edwards. They repeated his argument that freedom consisted in the ability to do what one willed, to act as one was moved to act. In this sense, freedom was simply natural ability. "If we have natural ability," wrote Emmons, "we always act freely," even in fulfilling inexorable divine decrees. Further, they argued that it was no infringement on freedom that people always had to act in accord with their own nature. An ability to act in accord with one's nature was what free agency meant. And finally, they observed that whenever one acted in the absence of external coercion, a will to act obviously accompanied the act. In that sense, as well, the act was voluntary. Liberty consisted in acting voluntarily, no matter what the cause of the volition.[51]

To press on sinners their responsibility for their sin, the New Divinity pastors took the view that sin consisted in sinning. By definition, sin for them became the free, voluntary exercise of the mind. All of them insisted on total depravity, and Bellamy emphasized that the divine constitution linking Adam to his posterity made original sin universal. In a reply in 1758 to Webster's *Winter Evening's Conversation,* he said that the mortality of infants made sense only if every soul came into the world "in a lost Perishing Condition by Nature." But Bellamy also taught, with a seeming lack of consistency, that all sin consisted in the "quality of the exercises" of a moral agent. Hopkins —

more consistently — eventually denied the distinction between original and actual sin, arguing that Adam's posterity shared in his sin and condemnation only by consenting to his sin.[52]

Most of Edwards's followers — Bellamy excepted — then took a step that had remained unstated in Edwards's own theology: like the liberals, they rejected the doctrine that God imputed the guilt of Adam's sin to humanity. They said that sinners became guilty of Adam's sin only by consenting to it. Because of the "divine constitution" between Adam and his posterity, it was certain that they would sin, but their sin was no other than their consent, and this consent alone made them guilty. The younger Jonathan Edwards objected even to this formulation, telling Hopkins that Adam's posterity no more consented to his sin than to any other.[53]

Because they viewed the understanding as a natural rather than a moral faculty, moreover, they refused to designate the understanding as a site of depravity. Hopkins said that "depravity or sin lies wholly in the heart, and not in the intellect, or faculty of understanding." Smalley thought it absurd to suggest that "ignorance and misapprehension" were "the primary cause of all our enmity and opposition to God." If they were, then mere knowledge would "produce a cordial reconciliation" with God, and the Edwardean preachers knew that such speculative knowledge was not enough. Total depravity, said Emmons, was of a "moral nature" — it indicated a corrupt heart — but it was entirely distinct from the "intellectual powers." If depravity arose from the reason or conscience, the sinner would be naturally incapable of right or wrong. That would undercut the responsibility to repent.[54]

Some New Divinity theologians were so intent on showing that both holiness and sin consisted in voluntary exercises that they redefined the "heart" — or the willing person morally regarded — as consisting entirely in its "exercises." As early as 1768, Hopkins noted that it was "difficult, and perhaps impossible" to form any distinct and clear idea of a passive "principle, taste, temper, disposition, [or] habit," though he still insisted that God shaped such a "good taste, temper, or disposition" as the "foundation" for "holy exercises of heart." John Smalley, Levi Hart, and Samuel Austin worried that Hopkins's concession had unwittingly subverted the idea of "spiritual substance," and their concerns caused Hopkins to worry about "divisions among themselves." And indeed the Edwardeans divided. By 1772, Stephen West, the successor of Edwards at the mission in Stockbridge and a disciple of Hopkins, was arguing in print that human "nature," or "disposition," was "no more than certain laws or methods of constant divine operation," adding that it was impossible for the mind to obtain any idea of a spiritual substance or power behind its voluntary acts and exertions. West feared that any notion of a passive disposition underlying exercises of the will would give the sinful a reason to define their sin as something other than a wrongful act of choice for which they were responsible.[55]

The issue would not disappear, and in 1783 Nathanael Emmons (1745–1840) thrust it once more into the forefront of debate. Emmons was another Yale graduate who studied with Smalley and preached for four years as an itinerant before becoming in 1773 the Congregationalist pastor in Wrentham (later Franklin), Massachusetts. He was a plump man with a squeaky voice who wore three-cornered hats and breeches long after they went out of style, but his congregation held on to him for fifty-five years. By his own assessment, he delivered sermons that were "doctrinal and argumentative" rather than "superficial and declamatory," and he aspired for a time to arrange them into a system, though it fell to his son-in-law after his death to collect them into *A System of Divinity*. Almost ninety students read theology under his tutelage, where they heard some of the boldest speculative theology written in eighteenth-century America. He became the foremost proponent of what came to be known as the "exercise scheme."[56]

Like West, Emmons feared that the idea of a sinful human nature underlying sinful actions — or of a new principle, power, or taste underlying gracious exercises — could serve as an excuse for sinners. It could allow them to think that they were unable to repent until they were given this new taste and that repentance was no immediate moral obligation for them. In order to prevent such an excuse, Emmons contended that "the heart consists in voluntary exercises." Like Edwards, he attributed to a "divine constitution" the identity of human nature from moment to moment, which implied, though he did not clearly say it, that the soul was no more than a chain of exercises constituted and unified by a divine law. But unlike either Edwards or Hopkins, he was ready to say outright that in a world maintained each moment by a sovereign God, every thought, word, and deed came from an immediate act of divine power. It followed that God produced all the "moral exercises" in which "moral depravity properly and essentially consists." In this sense, at least, God was the author of sin.[57]

Since Emmons advanced this argument in order to remove any excuse for failure to repent, he added that men and women acted freely under the divine agency. Universal divine causality extended to every thought and volition without interfering with human freedom; the will was fully free and active and fully passive at the same time. Nothing, including an act of volition, could exist for a moment without constant divine creativity; but an act of volition was also a free human act. Emmons found evidence for this in Paul's assertion that God works in us "both to will and to do," though he also thought that common sense taught men and women that they were free, while reason taught them that they were dependent.[58]

Hopkins feared that Emmons had allowed the exercise scheme to cloud his judgment. To him, it seemed wrongheaded to suggest that sinful acts might be "the immediate production of God." He continued to admire Emmons, but his own views remained closer to those of the faction later known as "tasters" because of their defense of the idea that a disposition or taste underlay both sinful and holy exercises of the heart. He thought that Emmons had made himself vulnerable to the Arminian charge that Calvinists subverted virtue and worshiped a God who was something other than just and benevolent.[59]

The defense of God's justice and benevolence — theodicy — had been on the New Divinity agenda since 1750, when Bellamy pointed out that an omnipotent God could have prevented sin and misery. It was obvious that "in his infinite Wisdom he did not think it best on the whole" to prevent either one. Five years later, Bellamy exchanged letters with the Scottish minister John Erskine, who told him how the German Reformed theologian Johann Friedrich Stapfer had used the theodicy of the philosophers Christian Wolff and Gottfried W. Leibniz to shore up Calvinist theology, especially their contention that since nothing happens without a sufficient reason there had to be a sufficient reason that justified the world's moral and natural evil. Bellamy did not adopt the scheme of Leibniz, who had argued that evil would necessarily accompany any finite system and that God could not prevent sin. But in 1758 he published his own theodicy in three sermons on *The Wisdom of God in the Permission of Sin.*[60]

Writing during the French and Indian wars, Bellamy aimed to console by showing that sin and evil did not impugn the justice, goodness, or sovereignty of God. Depicting God as a being of infinite wisdom who always did "what is most fitting," Bellamy argued that the "universal Plan" for the world, however imperfect our vision of it, must be "perfect in Wisdom, Glory and Beauty." Sin must have a reason, and Bellamy thought he had found it. By permitting sin, God made it possible to manifest himself as merciful and redemptive, to set "all his moral Perfections in the clearest and most striking Point of Light." Because the highest good was the fullest communication of divine goodness and glory — which were manifest in God's mercy to the sinner — then the sinner's sin (though evil in itself) occasioned the greatest possible good, advancing both God's glory and the "moral System." He cautioned that the highest good was not simply human good; it was irrational and unscriptural to believe that "the Welfare of Creatures is the only Thing of Worth." The highest good was the display of the fullness of God, and this was the best of "all possible systems" to realize it.[61]

Liberals like Samuel Moody (1726–95) found in Bellamy's doctrine the scandalous implication that God was the author of sin and Satan an agent of good. Within the year, Samuel Hopkins scandalized them further in three sermons published under the title *Sin, through the Divine Interposition, an Advantage to the Universe* (1759). The aim of the sermons was to show that God's permission of sin did not justify human sinfulness, but even the title, he conceded, was "so shocking to many that they would read no further." Hopkins stuck to the position that God had determined to permit sin knowing that "all things considered, there is more good in the universe than if sin had not entered." Sin displayed the holiness and mercy of God, and the revelation of God as a redeemer in Christ made sin the occasion of so much good that the sinful world was a better place than a sinless one would have been. In a later sermon, he made the point even more strongly than Bellamy by insisting that sin was "necessary" to promote "the greatest possible good of the universe" and the glory of God: "Every thing, circumstance, and event is right; and all conspire to promote the greatest good, and, all things considered, it is on the whole best that they should be just what they are, and take place exactly as they do."[62]

The doctrine of Bellamy and Hopkins became standard Edwardean fare. It convinced Stephen West that the world needed sinners so that God could display his hatred of sin, and it caused Emmons to describe the fallen world as "the best possible system of intelligent creatures." It appealed to one of the deepest Edwardean ambitions: to link divine sovereignty and benevolence in a way that undercut the ethical critique of Calvinist doctrine.[63]

To become the champions of God's benevolence, however, the Calvinists had to answer the Universalists. After 1770, Universalist preachers toured New England charging that the idea of eternal damnation besmirched the character of God. Some also argued that the doctrine of universal salvation followed logically the doctrine of universal atonement — the doctrine that Christ died for everyone. In formulating a reply, the Edwardeans turned to the same governmental theory of atonement that had attracted liberals like Mayhew. Both Bellamy and Hopkins retained older Calvinist views of atonement even as they said that Christ died to secure God's moral government. But their use of governmental metaphors and their rejection of a limited atonement opened the door for a more explicit governmental theory. In 1785, Jonathan Edwards, Jr. (1745–1801) stormed through the door with a governmental scheme.[64]

The younger Edwards had graduated from the College of New Jersey and studied theology with both Hopkins and Bellamy before becoming the pastor of the White Haven Church in New Haven. He remained there a quarter of a century before his strict membership standards reduced a congregation of 480 to a few dozen saints and ignited a rebellion that exiled him to the village of Coleridge, Connecticut. "Ordinary minds," it was said, found his sermons neither interesting nor intelligible. Like his father, he soon accepted a college presidency (at Union College in New York), and like his father he died shortly after assuming his duties. He was a reserved man, distant and unapproachable, but he attained a permanent influence on nineteenth-century theology through his adaptation of the governmental doctrine of atonement to the needs of Calvinist theology.[65]

He argued that Christ died for all, not by paying their debt to God but by accepting the punishment for their infinite infraction of the law, thus making it possible for God to forgive them without displaying disregard for moral government. He conceded to critics of Calvinism that a forgiveness resulting from the satisfaction of a debt would have been no free gift. It would have been an act of strict justice, imposing an obligation on God. But Christ's death merely honored and preserved the moral government. This obliged God to save no one and placed God under no debt. With the integrity of the system now preserved, God could save, by sheer grace, whomever God wished to save.[66]

This doctrine of atonement still required a mediator who was both fully human and fully divine. It was largely in defense of their views on atonement — which was, as they saw it, a practical doctrine — that Bellamy and Hopkins so vigorously censured the Christology of the liberals, which veered away from the affirmation of Christ's divinity. In preaching on "The Divinity of Jesus Christ," Bellamy explained that only the sacrifice of the eternal Son could expiate the infinite evil of sin. Suggesting that Mayhew and Chauncy preached "another gospel," Hopkins also argued that only Christ's dignity as fully God and fully human permitted him to atone for an infinite sin. Without the traditional Christology, neither atonement nor forgiveness appeared possible.[67]

The Edwardeans still had to answer Universalists who said that eternal punishment cast into doubt the benevolence of the Calvinist God. Hopkins wrote his *Inquiry Concerning the Future State of Those Who Die in their Sins* (1783) to show that eternal punishment promoted "the highest good of the whole" and displayed God's "infinite benevolence and goodness," because an infinitely good being must display an infinite hatred of the infinite evil of sin. Yet even the Edwardeans could no longer tolerate the thought that only a few might be saved. They agreed that divine benevolence ensured the salvation of "the greater part" of humanity. Their desire to expand the ranks of the saved helped stimulate their renewed interest in the millennium.[68]

In keeping with a resurgence of prophetic writing during the English wars with France after 1746, Bellamy and Hopkins wrote millennial treatises describing the glories of the coming era, when the church would flourish and all would accept the gospel. Using forms of prophetic numerology derived from Lowman, Whitby, and the elder Edwards, Hopkins concluded that the millennium might begin early in the twenty-first century, after a hundred years of war and pestilence. Christ would then reign in spirit for at least a thousand years before his bodily return for the last judgment — a period in which millions could be saved. Bellamy's calculations led him to conclude that the millennium might last longer than a thousand years and that during this period as many as seventeen thousand souls might be saved for every single one lost. The numbers added up to a benevolent God.[69]

The New Divinity theologians differed about millennial details, especially about the timing of the millennial onset. For the most part, however, the Edwardeans resisted the trend, strong during the wars with France between 1746 and 1763, to conflate religious eschatology and political ideology. Frequently during this period — and then later in the era of the Revolution — colonial clergy updated apocalyptic language by identifying the Antichrist with political foes and predicting that military victory might inaugurate the events of the end time. The Virginia Edwardean Samuel Davies, for instance, suggested that the wars with France signaled "the commencement of this grand decisive conflict between the Lamb and the beast," a coalescing of theological and political rhetoric that reappeared in colonial sermons for the next three decades. But Bellamy, Hopkins, and most other New Divinity theologians in New England kept their distance from this form of civil millennialism.[70]

Nonetheless, their millennial theory overflowed with lessons not only about the benevolence of the Redeemer but also about the ethics of the redeemed. Hopkins and Bellamy described the millennium as an age of justice, when peace would prevail and disinterested benevolence would promote general and cordial friendship, and Hopkins turned this millennial vision into a critique of his own era when he combined it with attacks on the slave trade in Newport. The Edwardean vocabulary — especially the Edwardean twist on the notion of disinterested benevolence — permeated nineteenth-century movements to abolish slavery, send out missionaries, form women's colleges, stimulate revivalism, establish seminaries, organize churches, and propagate theology. But the Edwardeans had to face continued criticism from other Calvinists, especially the Calvinists who considered themselves the guardians of an older tradition.[71]

Old Calvinism

The Calvinist opponents of the New Divinity never formed a unified movement, but because they presented themselves as the defenders of tradition, they became known as the Old Calvinists. They came mainly from the ranks of the Old Light opponents of revivalism, though they also included a few New Lights, and the first public attack on Hopkins for promoting a new divinity came from a New Light minister at Stratford, Connecticut, named Jedidiah Mills (1697–1776). What the critics of the New Divinity shared was a desire that the church retain its social influence, a concern for the underpinnings of morality, a preference for moral gradualism, and a sense that the Edwardeans had allowed a penchant for bad metaphysics to lead them into excess and error.

Mills opened the long, rancorous dispute in 1767 when he took exception to Hopkins's claim that the unregenerate grew worse the more they used the means of grace while remaining unconverted. Mills thought that the claim not only depreciated the value of sermons, prayers, and meditation but also threatened morality. For him, mandates to pray, meditate, and listen to sermons bore a moral quality, since they were commands of God. To encourage the neglect of these duties, moreover, implied a careless regard for other moral injunctions. If the unregenerate could not be encouraged to pray, how could they be commanded to exercise justice or refrain from moral evils? Hopkins's statement that the use of the means of grace made the sinner worse rather than better opened "a flood-gate to all manner of iniquity."[72]

The underlying issue was the nature of the church. This became clear in such treatises as Moses Hemmenway's *Discourse Concerning the Church* (1792), which represented the Old Calvinist conviction that the visible church should consist of everyone, the saved and the unsaved, willing to assent to the "common faith," along with their children. Hemmenway (1735–1811) was the pastor of a church in Wells, Maine, and a Harvard graduate who memorized passages from Virgil and loved to read the Greek and Roman classics. He saw membership in the church as both a duty and a blessing, and he denied that anyone had either the right or the ability to require more from applicants than an "external holiness" manifest in orthodox belief and a virtuous life. Old Calvinists tended to like the halfway covenant—some preferred a Stoddardean conception of the church—and they normally disregarded any requirement for a narration of conversion as a prelude to membership. For Moses Mather (1719–1806), the pastor in Middlesex, church membership signified access to the means of grace that God would employ to gather his elect. He cautioned that God had made only "indefinite" promises to the visible church, but he pointed out that every member enjoyed the means by which salvation normally came.[73]

The Old Calvinists thought that almost every Edwardean misunderstanding led to the dissolution of the one institution—the church—that could transform moral New Englanders into true Christians. And they were convinced that the errors grew out of the Edwardean betrayal of what Ezra Stiles (1727–95), the president of Yale, called "the Doctrines of Grace as held by the good Old Puritans and by our Ancestors." The Edwardeans' penchant for metaphysics had caused them to misunderstand both the church and the doctrines that sustained it.[74]

First, the Edwardeans had misunderstood virtue. William Hart, a pastor in the Connecticut village of Saybrook, claimed that the whole of the New Divinity must "stand or fall" with the conception of virtue as disinterested benevolence. He saw this as the "foundation" of Hopkinsian theology, and he also saw it as "new and strange" and destructive of morality. The problem, as Moses Hemmenway described it, was that the Edwardeans reduced the whole of duty to the love of being in general, which only the regenerate could express, and resolved all the other virtues into "self-love," which characterized everyone else. This required them to say that the unregenerate could perform no duty, that the natural conscience could do nothing that God required, that the "best actions" of the unregenerate — even when they were awakened, enlightened, and operating under the highest improvements of common grace — had no "really good" qualities. To the Old Calvinists it seemed that this scheme made it impossible to impress upon the unregenerate any moral obligation whatsoever.[75]

The Old Calvinists taught that virtue, or holiness, was "complex." It was more than simply love of God and the neighbor. True virtue included a variety of "good works." Hemmenway argued that even the Great Commandment of Mark 28 — according to which love was greater than all the other commandments — implied other binding commandments. Complexity meant also that actions manifested a gradation of moral qualities: only acts performed from a spirit of regard to God were virtuous in the highest sense, but other actions could have degrees of real virtue. And complexity meant, finally, that some moral actions — perhaps most — could be virtuous in some respects and vicious in others. Hemmenway liked the argument that a holy act required a holy principle and a holy end, and he conceded that no acts of the unregenerate could be holy in this sense, but he also thought that the "matter" of an action could be distinguished from its principle and end. A sinner who obeyed the divine command did something "materially good" and to that extent evidenced a choice materially good. The Old Calvinists wanted New England to be a moral society. This required that even the unregenerate be told that they bore a responsibility to do the good.[76]

The most detailed critique of the Edwardean ethics came in Hart's *Remarks on President Edwards's Dissertation Concerning the Nature of True Virtue* (1771). Hart thought that Edwards had fallen into "false metaphisicks." Edwards's notion of "love to Being in General" was a meaningless abstraction that elevated an ontological idol above God and made "virtue itself idolatrous." Edwards's "imaginary and arbitrary reasoning" had diminished the natural virtues and underestimated the power of the moral sense. The Old Calvinists depended heavily on theories of moral sense that had come to the colonies from the Scottish enlightenment. Hemmenway thought that the moral faculty made all men and women, however depraved, able to feel the force of their obligation to obey the divine commands. Hart equated it with the "enlightened conscience," which imposed on everyone a "natural obligation" to be virtuous. He thought that New England could be a moral society.[77]

From an Old Calvinist perspective, the New Divinity preachers misunderstood not only virtue but also sin. The Old Calvinists refused to accept the Edwardean equation of sin with sinful exercises. Most of them clung to the notion that the imputation of the guilt of Adam's sin caused all his posterity to come into the world with a sinful nature. The sinful nature preceded the sinful acts. "We hold ourselves bound to be humbled for the depravity of our natures," wrote Hemmenway, "besides our actual sins." They refused, as well, to accept the New Divinity contention that sinfulness had its source solely in the will. They held that the fall corrupted all the faculties. Depravity was universal; it pervaded body and mind. This was both biblical truth and a safeguard against liberal error.[78]

The Old Calvinists repudiated the Edwardean distinction between moral and natural inability. Hemmenway claimed that the impotency of the sinner was "natural as well as moral." The inability consisted not merely in the "want of a will" but in the absence of any "power" for holy exercises. Sinners were "unable to do holy duties," and their inability was different from merely being unwilling. It was "a want of power" resulting from the absence of a "principle" of holy action. Old Calvinists thought it was senseless for New Divinity preachers to tell the unregenerate that they had a natural ability to repent when they lacked the power to repent. Sinners labored under a "real inability," said Moses Mather, not a mere unwillingness. The Old Calvinists agreed that sinners bore the blame for their sinfulness. Adam fell because he abused his freedom; sinners continued to choose to sin, and their choices made them blamable even though the choices resulted from a corrupted human nature. The blameworthiness of an act resided in its nature, not in its cause. But the unregenerate still lacked the power not to sin.[79]

Old Calvinists saw only two alternatives—both unsatisfactory—to their doctrine. Either one went with the Arminians or one made God the immediate cause of sinful actions. They could tolerate neither alternative. The Old Calvinist critique of Edwards on the bondage of the will grew out of the worry that the Edwardean position made God the cause of moral evil. James Dana (1735–1812), the pastor in Wallingford, Connecticut, wrote his *Examination of the Late Revd. President Edwards's Enquiry on the Freedom of the Will* (1770) with a "single question" in mind: "Whether Mr. Edwards's doctrine makes God the efficient cause of all moral wickedness." Dana had to endure accusations that he was a closet Arminian, and the doctrinal squabbles in his Wallingford congregation attracted attention throughout New England, but he wrote his criticism of Edwards as a champion of "the Calvinistic divines," and his argument reflected the Old Calvinist uneasiness with the Edwardean treatment of the will. His cause, he said, was to "vindicate the moral character of the Deity."[80]

In Dana's view, Edwardean freedom — one's freedom to do as one willed — was no freedom at all. Edwards had made several mistakes. He brought confusion to the theory of motivation, arguing sometimes that motives and volitions were the same (thus undercutting any assertion that the one caused the other), but then also speaking of motives, rather than agents, as causes. He argued against the self-determination of the will when the real question was about the self-determination of the moral agent. But worst of all, he made God the cause of sin: if motives determined the will, and if motives came from without, then ultimately only God could have caused "the first and leading sinful volition, which determines the whole affair." Not all the Old Calvinists would have accepted all of Dana's views about the freedom of the agent, but they agreed in wanting to make a distinction that Dana's critique helped them make: sinners without grace lacked the power to choose the holy, but they had sufficient freedom to avoid morally corrupt actions, and Edwardeans implied that they did not.[81]

The Old Calvinists balked especially at New Divinity speculation that sin must be the necessary means of the greatest good. Such an argument, they feared, debased the divine character and sovereignty (making it sound as if God had no other way to meet the ends of his government) and also turned the moral universe topsy-turvy by implying that sin was good. Should we, asked Dana, praise God for moral evil? Should we, asked Joseph Huntington (1735–94) of Norwich, Connecticut, proclaim "the infinite excellency and utility of all sin in general, and every great sin in particular?" Moses Mather preferred to say that the world, as a place of testing for created beings, implied the "possibility," not the necessity, of sinfulness. New Divinity speculation had not solved the mystery of evil.[82]

Sin came from the sinful choices of creatures with sinful natures, creatures unable to choose the highest good without the gracious infusion of regenerating grace. This was an Old Calvinist consensus. But they did not believe that the doctrine of depravity led to the conclusion that every action of an unregenerate sinner was selfish. The Old Calvinists disliked the New Divinity's reduction of sinfulness to selfishness. They also wanted to distinguish between selfishness and self-love, because they thought self-love was a good thing.

Despite their conviction that sin pervaded the fallen creation, they believed that the "natural principle" of self-love—along with other natural principles such as reason and conscience—gave the sinner the ability to perform some "acts of religious obedience" and ethical fitness. They could not understand, therefore, the continual deprecation of self-love by New Divinity theologians. The Old Calvinists saw self-love as "an innocent, useful, and good principle." It was owing to a rational self-love, Hemmenway thought, that the "peace and good order of the world are preserved." Self-love had its proper place even in the Old Calvinist view of the order of salvation. Motivated by a healthy self-love (a "desire of happiness and dread of misery"), even sinners could recognize the benefits of going to church each Sabbath. The sinner's self-love would never issue in a selfless love for God, but it could move the sinner to take the first steps toward true piety.[83]

Insofar as reason, conscience, the moral sense, and self-love could draw the unregenerate into the New England churches, the unregenerate obviously had, as Hemmenway put it, "a natural power to do their duty." They were capable of "external obedience," and this was good as far as it went. Hemmenway entered the controversy after New Divinity attacks on his *Seven Sermons, On the Obligation and Encouragement of the Unregenerate, to labour for the Meat which endureth to everlasting Life* (1767). The point of the sermons was to argue that certain natural capacities in the unregenerate could serve as a "foundation" for "real desires to obtain further degrees of that common light and grace, which is ordinarily preparatory to conversion." But even Hemmenway and the Old Calvinists continued to believe that the unregenerate lacked all "power to convert themselves, or perform holy duties."[84]

Conversion required regenerating grace, and this truth too the New Divinity had misunderstood. First, the Edwardeans had insufficiently appreciated the "common work of the Spirit of God preparatory to a saving faith." Hart believed that Hopkins allowed for "no preparatory work of the Spirit," but Hemmenway saw that the problem lay in differing understandings of preparation. The difference was visible in the readiness of the Old Calvinists to talk of degrees of preparation, to claim that some of the unregenerate might be "more prepared than others." The New Divinity could tolerate no such idea of progress in the unregenerate state, no such gradualism in the religious life. The Old Calvinists also said that the same means of grace that prepared the heart also produced its regeneration; the New Divinity denied that means ever regenerated anybody.[85]

To the Old Calvinists, one of the worst errors of the Hopkinsians was their failure to recognize that regeneration occurred through the illumination of the mind by the means of grace. A recurring theme in Old Calvinist polemics was the assertion that "all judicious Calvinist divines" believed that "conversion or regeneration is wrought by light, by the moral power of divine truth." In the Old Calvinist order of salvation, the Spirit first illumined the mind with a "common doctrinal understanding and belief of truth." This truth brought a sense of guilt, a fear of punishment, and an affecting view of the holiness and mercy of God; and the assent to truth moved the will toward a heartfelt consent and faith. How, the Old Calvinists asked, could the will ever consent to anything without first understanding it? Only the conviction that faith came "through the truth" made such means of grace as sermons and meditations worth defending.[86]

They found yet another error in the New Divinity tendency to think of regeneration as a change in the "exercises of the heart" rather than in the "principle" that underlay them. Hemmenway argued that every human act presupposed a power — or principle, or habit, or virtue ("call it what you will") — in the agent. For him, regeneration brought a change not simply in the exercises of the heart but also in the "permanent principle from which all holy exercises are derived." The Spirit infused, as even Edwards had recognized, a new principle that served as a "foundation" for all "holy views and exercises." Hemmenway knew that Hopkins was ambivalent on this point, but he thought he saw the logical consequences of the New Divinity talk about "exercises," and it was his critique of Hopkins that helped push the New Divinity theologians into separate factions of exercisers and tasters.[87]

To the Old Calvinists, moreover, the new principle came into being as the Spirit convinced the sinner of God's mercy. It was inconceivable that the test of piety should be a willingness to be damned, even for the glory of God. The whole point of the Old Calvinist appeal to self-love was to show prudent sinners that their happiness came through surrender to an "amiable" God. All Christians knew that they deserved to be damned, said Ezra Stiles Ely (1786–1861), a New York Presbyterian, but their prayer was that "God [might] be merciful to me a sinner."[88]

Having rejected Edwardean innovations in the doctrine of regeneration, the Old Calvinists saw no need to accept the Edwardean alterations in the doctrines of justification and the atonement. They taught that God justified the sinner, not the obedient saint, and that justification resulted from the imputation of Christ's righteousness. A few Old Calvinists accepted a governmental theory of atonement, but most taught that Christ atoned for sin by becoming the substitute who bore the curse. God imputed the sinner's sin to Christ (who was therefore "legally guilty") and Christ's righteousness to the sinner. Only as he perfectly obeyed the law and bore the punishment did Christ make a full and proper satisfaction to God. And the Old Calvinists felt no hesitation in saying that after the atonement God owed salvation to the elect. God could not, consistently with his justice, punish those for whose sins Christ had atoned. They continued to believe, as well, that Christ died only for the elect.[89]

They disliked the social implications of New Divinity theology. Ebenezer Devotion (1714–71), a pastor in Windham, Connecticut, worried that Edwardean doctrines would vacate the obligations of morality, "burst the bonds of social life," and "strike at the foundations of civil government." Just as a renewed preoccupation with ethics and law stood behind both liberal Arminianism and the New Divinity, so also the Old Calvinists of the eighteenth century found in the doctrine of an "external covenant" a warrant for saying, with Thomas Clap (1703–67), the president of Yale, that "the moral part of all true Religion" was "the foundation of the Whole." Moses Mather could even write that "to preach morality is as really preaching Christ, as when we preach articles of faith." The New Divinity was a theology for a regenerated church and a revivalist piety; Old Calvinism was a theology of moral order in a moral society.[90]

The Old Calvinists thought that none of the debate would have been necessary if the New Divinity theologians had not been so enamored of consistency and so much attracted to "metaphysical" forms of argument. They saw the Hopkinsians as metaphysicians attempting to become "Oracles" rather than humble servants of scriptural truth. The result, wrote Ezra Stiles, was that "the new divinity scheme looks well indeed on Paper, but does not succeed so well as to Practice or when they come to act upon it." But even at more rarefied levels of abstraction, the eighteenth-century New England debates marked a new unease about how reason should function in theology. In criticizing the Edwardeans as "metaphysicians," the Old Calvinists and Arminians seized upon a term of opprobrium that would resonate with theologians for the next fifty years. It was disdain for the "metaphysical" that gave impetus to the cult of "common sense" in American theology, and after the great controversy over deism, common sense would begin to define the very meaning of theological rationality.[91]

PART II

The Baconian Style

7

The Deists

By 1795, when Thomas Paine published the second part of his *Age of Reason*, American theologians had a long history of contending with the deist critique of Christianity, but Paine touched a nerve. His book gave deism a new visibility. Neither in Europe nor in America did a unified deist movement espouse a common set of positive teachings, but the thinkers usually designated as deists shared a critical attitude toward traditional Christianity, and their critique is a pivotal part of the history of Christian theology.

They had an influence on Christian thought in America far out of proportion to their numbers, for their criticisms of Christianity, particularly their attacks on belief in biblical revelation, produced, by way of reaction, a renewal of interest in the Christian evidences. Their claim of superior rationality and practicality produced corresponding Christian counter-assertions. And their defense of a natural religion, independent of any particular revelation or tradition, prompted a Christian defense of a natural theology linked to the biblical revelation. One explanation for the later prominence of the Baconian style of theology in nineteenth-century America — a style calling for empirical, inductive, and nonspeculative modes of thought — was the perception on the part of theologians that ideas and methods widely associated with Sir Francis Bacon, an Elizabethan Englishman who valorized inductive investigation, might strengthen the Christian apologetic against the threat symbolized by the deists.

The Forms of English Deism

English writers produced one form of deism congenial to a selective approval of the biblical accounts and another form dismissive of the Christian Bible. The first group saw themselves as contributing to a reform of Christian thought in accord with eighteenth-century norms of reason; the second group believed that a natural religion should replace Christian superstition. The difference was one of mood and temperament as much as anything else, but it had conceptual consequences.

At one end of the spectrum were writers whose theories of religion allowed for a special revelation but denied that it was essential. This was the position of Edward, Lord Herbert of Cherbury (1583–1648), the English ambassador to Paris, who sought, in his *De Veritate* (1624), to display the universal common notions that were present in all true religion in all times and places. He believed that these common notions — such as God's existence and the propriety of worshiping God through moral conduct that would be subject to divine judgment — were accessible apart from any specific revelatory book or event. They were the core of all the particular religious traditions of the world, and after having viewed the early disasters of the Thirty-Years War (1618–48), when armies slaughtered each other under banners of religious particularity, Cherbury thought that the search for a common core made more sense than assertions of confessional superiority. But he also thought that the common notions found an added confirmation in the biblical revelation itself.[1]

John Locke (1632–1704) was no deist, but the publication of his *Reasonableness of Christianity* in 1695 had the effect of promoting the deist cause. Claiming to be a disciple of Locke, John Toland (1670–1722), a freelance writer and political pamphleteer, wrote in his *Christianity Not Mysterious* (1696) that he believed in a biblical revelation, but he insisted that nothing in the gospel was "contrary to reason, nor above it." This differed from Locke's position that some of the truths of revelation might be above reason, though never contrary to it, and Locke repudiated Toland's conclusion. To Toland, however, it made no sense to speak of a truth above reason, though he did not wish to deny that a biblical revelation might contain some rational truths.[2]

Some English authors widely associated with deism described themselves as intent on restoring primitive Christianity but claimed that biblical criticism had convinced them that the Bible could no longer be the authoritative source of religious truth. Anthony Collins (1679–1729), a Cambridge graduate and justice of the peace in Essex, as well as a friend of Locke, tried to show that the traditional Christian appeal to biblical authority had "no just foundation" by proving that the New Testament erred in viewing Jesus as the fulfillment of the Old Testament prophecies. Collins's *Discourse on the Grounds and Reason of the Christian Religion* (1724) argued that the prophecies plainly pointed "in their obvious and primary sense, to other matters" than those to which the New Testament writers made them refer. If the New Testament was unreliable on this point, then the prophetic proof no longer sufficed. Collins associated himself with the Church of England, but he called for "freethinking," and his moral form of nondogmatic Christianity had its grounding in the discoveries of the unaided intellect.[3]

Collins's contemporary, Thomas Woolston (1669–1733), launched a far more acerbic attack on the proof from miracles. Woolston was also a Cambridge graduate who attained a scholarly reputation by defending allegorical interpretation of the Old Testament. After his religious views led in 1721 to the loss of his appointment as a Cambridge fellow, he promoted the deist cause by contending that much of the New Testament, including the accounts of Jesus' virgin birth and resurrection, was also allegorical. Sentenced to prison for blasphemy, he responded that he was merely a Christian layman committed to religious toleration and the humbling of a persecuting priesthood, and that he exposed the "fable and forgery" of the New Testament's "absurdities" only in order to restore the ancient "mystical" way of reading the biblical text. He argued in his *Discourses on the Miracles of our Saviour* (1727–29) that the New Testament miracle stories could not attest to the truth of Christianity because the stories themselves were incoherent and incredible. Only by proving the historicity of the miracles, which Woolston thought an impossible task, could theologians continue to use them as evidence that the Bible contained a divine revelation.[4]

By 1730, Matthew Tindal (1655–1733), an Oxford graduate and a fellow of All Souls College, was ready to announce that the case against Christian orthodoxy had been satisfactorily made. Tindal associated himself with the "true Christian deists," but the House of Commons had one of his books burned and the magistrate hauled him before the courts for blasphemy. In his *Christianity as Old as the Creation* (1730), he contended that the purpose of the gospels was merely to restate the eternal law of reason. He thought that the immutability and universal benevolence of God precluded any new or particular revelation in history. Any religion fitted to serve an unchanging God had to rest on a natural religion that was itself, in its essential core, unchanging and universal. A benevolent God, moreover, would not give a special revelation to a chosen people while leaving out all the rest.[5]

Deist Diversity in America

American deism reflected the same ambiguities of definition and differences in style and temperament that could be found in England. One group of Americans sympathetic to the deist impulse tended to be sedate, aristocratic, prudent, and willing to identify themselves with a purified Christian theology. They took the moderate stance of Benjamin Franklin (1706–1790) and Thomas Jefferson (1743–1826), who criticized the theology of the churches but attended Anglican worship, excoriated dogma but admired Jesus, and spent more time promoting a natural religion of virtue than exposing errors in the Bible. The second group was aggressive, populist, polemical, disdainful of a Bible riddled with contradiction and immorality, eager to debunk the gospel stories, and hopeful that a religion of nature would altogether replace an effete Christianity. They espoused the radical deism of Thomas Paine (1737–1809), Ethan Allen (1738–89), and Elihu Palmer (1764–1806), and they tried to spread their religion to the masses.[6]

Ethan Allen, a former revolutionary war soldier who had discussed deistic ideas with French prisoners, published in 1784 — with ample help from the physician Thomas Young — the first American "system of natural religion" containing an extensive criticism of "supernatural revelation." He admitted his confusion about nomenclature: "As to being a Deist, I know not strictly speaking, whether I am one or not, for I have never read their writings." But Young had introduced Allen to the ideas of the Englishman Charles Blount, whose "Summary Account of the Deist's Religion" in his *Oracles of Reason* (1693) described the deist as one who admired one Supreme God and placed the morality of religion above the mystery in it. That definition captured the spirit of Allen's *Reason the Only Oracle of Man* (1784) as well as the self-understanding of other prominent American deists. Elihu Palmer defined deism, in contrast to "Christian superstition," as belief in one perfect God who is known by means of his immutable natural laws and honored through "the practice of a pure, natural, and uncorrupted virtue." Paine agreed in defining the "true Deist" as someone who found evidence in nature for one God and who reverenced that God by endeavoring to "imitate Him."[7]

In the eyes of the church theologians, all the deists and alleged deists, whether sedate or seditious, were interlopers, amateurs, meddling with matters beyond their grasp. The deists, on the other hand, connected their cause to populist impulses. A number of English deists and their sympathizers had long ridiculed learned theology and contended that "the setting men apart for the study of divinity does not exclude others from the study of divinity . . . nor from knowing as much divinity as any doctor of divinity." They had claimed that "the vulgar" were just as competent as the learned in judging "the true sense of things." In America, this populist spirit marked especially the deists who concentrated on exposing Christian superstition.[8]

One segment of American deists grew to maturity in laboring class families and saw themselves as representatives of the common people. Paine had made corsets in England before he immigrated to America in 1774 and gained fame for writing political tracts. Allen was a poor farmer's son who described himself as "deficient in education." Franklin served as a printer's apprentice rather than going to college. But some deists of more privileged backgrounds also announced their preferences for a democratic culture. Jefferson came from the Virginia planter elite, but his confidence in the common sense of the yeoman farmer was as intense as his dislike for most of the educated theologians of his era.[9]

Elihu Palmer could claim a background of theological learning, but he had no liking for theological elites. After graduating from Dartmouth he studied divinity under John Foster in Massachusetts, and he preached for a few months in Presbyterian churches before his doctrines led to his being driven from the pulpit. Impelled by the desire to make deism a popular movement, he encouraged anticlerical sentiment and expressed contempt for learned theologians.[10]

As heralds of a new theology for the people, the American deists were relentless simplifiers. To the radicals like Palmer and Paine, intent on debunking, this meant exposing the "absurdity and contradiction" in the complicated Christian scheme of theology and replacing it, in Paine's words, with a religion of nature "which every man can read." Paine wrote the first part of *The Age of Reason* while he was a political prisoner in France in 1793 after his return to Europe following the American Revolution. He hoped that the book would counter the militant atheism of the French Jacobins by showing another alternative to Christian theology. The moderates like Franklin and Jefferson, more interested in revising Christian teaching than in discarding it altogether, also admired simplicity. Franklin scorned metaphysics as a source of "endless Disputes" and thought that "the Essentials of every known Religion" could be reduced to a few simple beliefs: that God was the Creator of the Universe, that he governed it by his providence, that he ought to be worshiped, that the most acceptable worship was doing good to his other children, that the soul was immortal, and that it would be treated with justice in another life. Jefferson felt disdain for the "indistinct" conceptions and "incomprehensible jargon" of traditional theology and tried to define a form of Christianity that would rely almost solely on the ethical teachings of Jesus.[11]

The demand for simplicity and clarity had roots in some common epistemological preferences. Ethan Allen spoke in Lockean terms of simple and complex ideas derived from sensation and reflection and insisted that we could know little about a future existence after death because our "present organized sensations" were inadequate for such discoveries. Palmer claimed that it was Locke's description of sensation as the source of ideas that had happily subverted "the credit of divine Revelation" and prepared the way for a true philosophy of religion.[12]

Jefferson also staked everything on a sensationalist epistemology: "on the basis of sensation, of matter and motion, we may erect the fabric of all the certainties we can have or need." Abandon "the basis of sensation," he wrote John Adams, and "all is in the wind." Jefferson followed closely the French debate over Ideology, a philosophical movement named and nurtured by Destutt de Tracy, who between 1796 and 1803 tried to construe philosophy as a biological science rather than a metaphysical quest. Tracy's Ideology drew on Bacon and Locke to reduce all ideas to elemental feelings, activities, or sensations that could be directly experienced and verified. Jefferson found in Tracy the building blocks for a natural religion: the senses gave ample evidence for "design, consummate skill, and indefinite power" in every atom of the universe. They disclosed a natural world that manifested the unity and simplicity of the Creator.[13]

Confirmed empiricists, the deists located the corruption of religion partly in the superstitions of the ancient Jews and partly in the metaphysical vagaries of Greek philosophy. Palmer found the origins of Trinitarian doctrine in the "reveries of Plato"; Paine derived Christian doctrine from "ancient mythology," finding the basis of belief in Satan, for example, in the classical myth of the war of the giants against Jupiter. No one displayed greater hostility to Greek philosophy than Jefferson, who found evidence in Joseph Priestley's *History of the Corruptions of Christianity* (1782) that Platonic idealism lurked behind the nonsense of Christian dogmaticians.[14]

An English Unitarian minister who spent the last ten years of his life in America, Priestley (1733–1804) attributed to Hellenistic theologians the blame for "platonizing" and corrupting primitive Christianity. His *History of Early Opinions Concerning Jesus Christ* (1789) argued that even Jesus was subject to error, but he convinced Jefferson that it was the "artificial scaffolding" of Greek philosophy that bore the responsibility for such absurdities as the doctrine of the Trinity, the virgin birth, and the resurrection.[15]

Jefferson once told John Adams that he was "not fond of reading what is merely abstract, and unapplied immediately to some useful science." His comment exposed a thread that linked the deists to the American expectation that theology should be practical. Running through all the deist literature was the assumption that metaphysics blocked the progress of a practical religion. And like the New England liberals, the deists equated the practical with the moral. Religion, said Paine, was belief in God and "the practice of moral truth."[16]

"The practice of moral truth" — here was the constructive ideal of American deism. Allen concluded *Reason the Only Oracle of Man* with the declaration that "a conformity to moral rectitude, which is morality in the abstract, is the sum of all religion." The "principal design" of Palmer's *Principles of Nature* was "to give moral principle a basis as durable as time" by rendering the sentiment of virtue "independent of all the theological vagaries of antiquity." The book's prime constructive argument was that moral virtue had its basis in the "relations" — another allusion to Samuel Clarke — embedded in the eternal laws of nature. Blinded by yellow fever and scorned by polite society, Palmer maintained his difficult struggle against Christian theology because he believed that "a corrupt and vitiated theology has ever been the bane of morality."[17]

On the equation of religion with morality, both the moderate and the radical deists could agree. Benjamin Franklin, who had been baptized in Old South Church in Boston by Samuel Willard, was still a teenager when he "became a thorough Deist" after reading Charles Blount and Anthony Collins along with the arguments against deism. The hostility that greeted his revelation of his new ideas helped persuade him to leave Boston, going first to Philadelphia and then, briefly, to London. There he wrote his youthful *Dissertation on Liberty and Necessity, Pleasure and Pain,* in which he suggested that the omnipotence of God implied the moral equivalence of every action, since no act could occur without God's consent. He soon repented of this exercise in provocation, however, and in 1728 wrote some private "Articles of Belief and Acts of Religion" in which he resolved to serve God — and promote his own happiness — by being virtuous. He claimed later that he still admired Cotton Mather's *Bonifacius: Essays to Do Good.*[18]

He never surrendered the conviction that morality was the heart of religion. When a Presbyterian synod in Philadelphia brought to trial the minister Samuel Hemphill in 1735 for preaching morality instead of grace, Franklin, at that time a member of a Presbyterian congregation, printed a piece in his *Pennsylvania Gazette* describing Jesus as a teacher of morality, faith as a means of producing morality, and morality as the way of salvation. Unlike the Calvinism from which he sprang, Franklin's views gave little attention to purity of intention and inward renewal, but he saw religion as an aid in the formation of habits of virtue, and he worked for years on an ethical guide to be called *The Art of Virtue,* though he never completed it.[19]

In later life, Franklin modified his views by denying that a moral life "deserved" a reward of eternal happiness; he would rest his confidence on God's goodness rather than on his own merit. But it was his reinterpretation of

Christianity as a religion of morality — and his belief that Christian churches were socially useful — that prompted his continued association with a local Anglican congregation in the aftermath of the Hemphill affair. Without ever becoming a member (at least, no record exists), he supported Christ Church in Philadelphia and even wrote an abridged version of the *Book of Common Prayer* (which may have had a satirical intent). When the Old Calvinist Ezra Stiles questioned him three months before his death about his religious sentiments, particularly about his opinion of Jesus, Franklin made it clear that the value of the Christian religion lay mainly in the "System of Morals" that Jesus had taught before the theologians had a chance to corrupt it.[20]

The "universal philanthropy" in the ethics of Jesus also enabled Jefferson to call himself a Christian. "To the corruptions of Christianity I am indeed opposed," he said, "but not to the genuine precepts of Jesus himself. I am a Christian, in the only sense in which he wished anyone to be. . . ." Jefferson valued the ethical teachings of the New Testament because they seemed to confirm his belief in a moral sense within human nature — a belief that he probably acquired from reading the Scottish philosophy of Dugald Stewart in Edinburgh. Jefferson's motive for sweeping away the "gossamer factitious religion" of Christian orthodoxy was to recover the ability to "moralize for ourselves, follow the oracle of conscience." While he was in the White House he began work on an abridged New Testament, a book of forty-six pages titled "The Life and Morals of Jesus of Nazareth," which depicted Jesus as an ethical teacher who had presented "the most sublime edifice of morality which had ever been exhibited to man."[21]

American deists had diverse assessments of Jesus. When Franklin and Jefferson praised Jesus' ethical teachings, they frequently added that respect for his ethics did not imply belief in his divinity. Franklin told Stiles he had "some Doubts as to his Divinity; tho it is a question I do not dogmatize upon." Jefferson could ascribe to Jesus "every *human* excellence," but he denied that Jesus himself ever claimed more than human excellence. Even Paine praised Jesus as a "virtuous and amiable man" who preached and practiced the most benevolent kind of morality. Others ridiculed this idealized portrait of the human Jesus. For Palmer, Jesus was "an illegitimate Jew" who preached immoral doctrines — telling his followers, for example, to hate their families — and engaged in immoral behavior, as when he had his disciples steal a colt. The gospel of Jesus Christ, he wrote, was "calculated to annihilate every thing valuable in human existence."[22]

What united the radicals was the attention they devoted to the critical debunking of special revelation, particularly the Bible. Neither Franklin nor Jefferson accepted the notion of special revelation or the authority of the Bible, but neither of them—despite Franklin's revision of the Lord's Prayer and Jefferson's abridgment of the New Testament—devoted much energy to biblical criticism. For the radicals, however, the progress of natural religion required a demolition of the Christian pretension of possessing a special divine revelation.

The idea of a supernatural revelation above human reason they found illogical. A truth above reason would elude rational comprehension and so reveal nothing. It was morally objectionable, as well, to suppose that a benevolent God would have revealed himself so late in human history to a small nation on the margins of the civilized world if the salvation of humankind depended on access to the revelation. And they sounded the populist note when they criticized the idea that divine inspiration made the revelation trustworthy. Even if that idea were true, they said, it would mean nothing to ordinary readers of the Bible, who had to depend on translations. Without translators able to convey infallibly the original meaning, an infallible revelation would be of no use.[23]

Paine and Allen thought, in any case, that the defenders of revelation had never considered the relativity of language and meaning. How could the meaning of a revelation given in one language be preserved over centuries of linguistic change? Even within one language, meanings changed over time; so much the more did meanings vary with translations. Paine concluded that language, always local and changeable, could never preserve unchangeable and universal truths. He assumed that God was changeless; it followed, he said, that the word of God must be changeless, as well. But this meant that nature—the "everlasting original"—must be the divine word.[24]

In any case, the Bible could be no divine revelation. It held too many contradictions, displayed too many confusions. The radicals helped introduce the American laity to the methods and conclusions of biblical criticism that had circulated among the educated in Europe since the late seventeenth century. They offered no insights that had not already emerged among such of their English predecessors as Collins and Woolston, but they drew attention to unnoticed features of the biblical text—the multiple authorship, for instance, of the Pentateuch and Isaiah—that would later become commonplace among many biblical scholars.

Paine assumed that since the Bible consisted of books of testimony, its authority rested on certainty of authorship, so he devoted most of part two of the *Age of Reason* to showing that the traditional ascriptions of authorship could not be trusted. Moses never wrote the Pentateuch, for instance, for the book of Deuteronomy recorded his death. But authorship was not the sole problem. The Bible abounded in contradictions, chronological confusion, unscrupulous characters, and immoral teachings about a vengeful God who ordered slaughter and bloodshed.[25]

The standard evidences for the authenticity of the Bible seemed to deists utterly unreliable. To the claim that the fulfillment of prophecies proved divine inspiration, they responded with the argument that most of the prophecies were so vague and indefinite that they could be made to refer to numerous events. The more specific the prophecy — as when Jesus predicted the destruction of the temple and the return of the Son of Man within "this generation" (Matt. 24) — the more it was obvious that it was never fulfilled.[26]

As for the claim that the biblical miracles evidenced biblical inspiration, the deists replied that the miracles never occurred and that the argument from miracles degraded God to the status of a showman. Echoing David Hume's earlier critique, Palmer contrasted the "universal experience and general observation" of most men and women in the eighteenth century against "the testimony of a few" in the past. The argument against miracles reflected the deist commitment to the idea of divine immutability. To suggest that God intervened miraculously in history was to imply variability and inconsistency in the divine purpose — making God subject to temporality — and a changeable God was a finite God. This the deists would not accept.[27]

Though all deists rejected Christian Trinitarian theology, they agreed upon no single conception of God. Jefferson, ardently opposed to a metaphysic of Spirit, thought that the divine essence required some form of material embodiment, albeit a highly refined one. Franklin spoke of one supreme God, infinitely transcendent and indifferent to human affairs, and a number of lesser gods, one of whom ruled over the solar system and providentially intervened in history, though never in nature. His language about multiple gods might have been a form of subtle irony, or it might have referred to different cultural modes of attempting to describe the indescribable supreme God, but it is equally plausible that Franklin held to a literal polytheism. Ethan Allen thought of God as self-existent Activity — an eternal Providence who never intervened at discrete moments in space and time, for even to think of God as "first cause" was to subject God to categories of finite temporality. Allen's God rather upheld the laws of nature continually "by the infinite and immediate agency of his power." But Palmer, who agreed with Allen that the world was co-eternal with God, thought it sufficient to conceive of God as the distant Creator who set the laws of nature in motion.[28]

They agreed in their common dislike for Christian doctrines of sin and redemption. To most of them, the idea of original sin implied an unjust God, depravity a libeled human nature. The partial exception was Franklin, who in his more somber moods could sound as bleak as any Calvinist in his assessment of human selfishness, pride, avarice, and lust. But Franklin, like the others, found the idea of imputation absurd. By sin, or better, sins, the deists meant the antisocial acts of free men and women — violations of the laws of justice and utility. The notion of eternal punishment, moreover, seemed unfair; Allen and Palmer made a point of arguing that human sins were finite acts that should never deserve infinite punishment. (Allen influenced the theology of Christian Universalism.) None could make sense of the claim that God became incarnate as a man, and the doctrine of substitutionary atonement seemed to Palmer — and to some of the others — as nothing more than a tale of "murder, carnage, and injustice." Conceding, like Franklin, that some punishment might be necessary in a future life, Allen thought that God's "ultimate plan of doing good" would never allow any sinner to languish eternally in hell.[29]

It is impossible to know how successfully the crusading deists reached their audience. The poet Philip Freneau claimed that it was the clergy who publicized the deist arguments. Paine's *Age of Reason*, he said, "would never have been known in this country if the clergy had suffered it to rest, but they dragged it into publicity — let the text be what it would, animadversions on Paine made a part of the sermon. The clergy wrote — the people read." But deism had a popular following. Deist societies sprang up in New York City, Philadelphia, Baltimore, and Richmond and flourished awhile even in smaller cities such as Lexington, Kentucky, and Newburgh, New York. Palmer preached a deist theology for a year to a congregation in Augusta, Georgia, and he founded two deist newspapers — *The Temple of Reason* (1800) and *The Prospect* (1803). Clergy complained that some regions — Kentucky, for instance, or the region east of Chapel Hill in North Carolina — had "infidel" majorities, but the clergy sometimes confused infidelity and indifference. One important social setting for the diffusion of deist notions was the Masonic movement, which popularized a language about God that had an affinity with deist theology. The God of Masonic ritual was the Grand Architect, the Cosmic Orderer, and even Christian Masons learned to blur the distinctions between traditional and rationalist language about God. The Masonic movement came closer than any other to being the deist church.[30]

The theologians rarely had to deal with religious positions more unconventional than those of the radical deists. It was hard to find in America a sustained and explicit literary defense of atheism or thorough skepticism. Various forms of free thought found early expression in the lectures and publications of a handful of social reformers, but they had to endure popular abuse. None was more outspoken than Frances Wright (1795–1852), a native of Scotland who became an American citizen in 1825 and found in Robert Owen's communal settlement in New Harmony, Indiana, the inspiration for a plan to educate southern slaves for freedom. Her hopes for Nashoba, the community she built near Memphis, collapsed within two years of its founding, but in 1828 she began a lecture tour to support social reform and free inquiry.

Wright's view was that theology, even the theology of the deists, claimed a knowledge that it could never attain. Of "things unseen," she argued, the human mind could know nothing. Theology therefore consisted of "nonexistent knowledge, impossible knowledge, and knowledge which, even under the supposition of its possibility, could serve no conceivable purpose." If God exists, she thought, then nature will bear witness to it, and she did not deny this possibility; but even though the mayor of New York once disparaged her as a "female Tom Paine," she had less confidence than the deists that the mind could know for sure about anything outside the reach of the senses and the reasoning faculty built on them.[31]

The skepticism that she represented would become a vital issue for theology after the Civil War, but theologians in the early nineteenth century could rather safely ignore her views. For them, the more serious challenge came from the deists who presented the public an alternative form of theistic belief. Against the deists it was necessary to array the evidences.

Antideism

In 1759, Ezra Stiles, at that time a minister in Newport, Rhode Island, told President Thomas Clap of Yale that the time was ripe to launch a new attack against the deists: "Deism has got such Head in this Age of Licentious Liberty that it would be vain to try to stop it by hiding the Deistical Writings: and the only Way left to conquer & demolish it, is to come forth into the open Field & Dispute this matter of even footing—the evidences of Revelation in my opinion are nearly as demonstrative as Newton's Principia, & these are the Weapons he used." Several American writers would enter the field, but they employed familiar arguments, drawing heavily on earlier English apologists like Charles Leslie (1650–1722), an Anglican divine whose *Short and Easy Method with the Deists* (1697) tried to prove the credibility of the biblical accounts; Richard Watson (1737–1816), bishop of Llandaff, who had answered the deists with *An Apology for the Bible* in 1795; and especially Joseph Butler (1692–1752), whose *Analogy of Reason, Natural and Revealed, to the Constitution and Course of Nature* (1736) contended that the biblical revelation was so consistent with the manifestation of God in nature that the deist who accepted the one should therefore accept the other. The deist who criticized scripture for its darkness and ambiguities, Butler said, should face up as well to the ambiguities of nature. The British arguments persuaded most American theologians.[32]

The eighteenth-century American antideists were intent on disseminating this English critique to a popular audience. Uzal Ogden (1744–1822), the rector of Trinity Church in Newark, New Jersey, wrote the first American book-length reply to Thomas Paine—a two-volume *Antidote to Deism: The Deist Unmasked* (1795)—with the aim of competing with Paine for the allegiance of men and women of "common understanding." After hearing that Paine's *Age of Reason* was selling briskly for a cent and a half a copy in Philadelphia, the New Jersey lawyer and congressman Elias Boudinot (1740–1821) published *The Age of Revelation* (1801) because he was convinced that Richard Watson's austere arguments could not reach young people or the lower classes.[33]

Moses Hoge (1752–1820), president of Hampden-Sidney College in Virginia, heard a rumor that Americans had bought more than 100,000 copies of Paine's book: "We ought certainly to do something," he urged, so he published an American edition of treatises by Richard Watson and William Paley and then added his own effort, *The Sophist Unmasked* (1797). Andrew Broaddus (1770–1848) of Virginia, a self-taught theologian who sought rural isolation with small Baptist congregations, was equally hopeful of showing in his *Age of Reason and Revelation* (1795) that Christian doctrine, unlike that of the deists, was "adapted to the common apprehension" as well as to "the philosophic mind." Paine's *Age of Reason* drew more than thirty book-length replies in Britain and America, and most of the Americans joined Broaddus in trying to adapt the antideist argument to "the common apprehension."[34]

The controversy had two large consequences for the course of theology in America. First, it called forth a reassertion of the limits of reason and the practical functions of theology. The antideists contended that a true rationality would remain aware of its own limits. Broaddus argued that reason itself showed human beings to be creatures of passion and prejudice, sufficiently reasonable to recognize their dilemma but not to overcome it. From similar premises, the Presbyterian James Muir (1757–1820) of Alexandria, Virginia, argued that reason could never be granted an "absolute control" over every subject matter. Even apart from passion and prejudice, moreover, reason faced insuperable limits. Ogden observed that no one ever attained more than an "imperfect" knowledge of even the natural creation and that this limited apprehension could never support a "religious system." Most early antideists believed that reason could not demonstrate the certainty of immortality—a certainty that some deists took for granted—or explain the prevalence of evil and sinfulness. Some things essential to religion, said Broaddus, were "beyond the comprehension of human reason."[35]

In addition, the antideists reemphasized the practicality of theology. This could mean defending Christianity by urging its social utility. Like the deists, they sought a religion that promoted social morality. They simply thought that Christianity nurtured ethics and social reform in a way that deism had never been able to do. But the appeal to the practical could resurrect notions of practicality that had long been part of the Christian tradition, as when Broaddus argued, in acknowledging that the biblical cosmology could not be taken literally, that the primary purpose of scripture was not to "teach us philosophy" but to "guide our feet in the paths of immortal felicity." Without casting the slightest doubt on the truthfulness of Christian propositions, Broaddus still could defend Christian belief by describing it as a form of practical knowledge.[36]

At the same time, deism prompted a reassertion of Christian reasonableness. The antideists disclaimed any desire to "deprecate" reason. "Christians know something of philosophy too, as well as Deists," wrote Broaddus. One of his main contentions was that Paine's doctrine of the mutability of language would make rational interpretation of historical texts impossible, and he argued against Paine that "the substance" of what was conveyed in one time or language could be "faithfully conveyed" in another. But the prime example of the Christian claim for reasonableness was the renewed emphasis on natural theology. In the intellectual atmosphere of the late eighteenth century, to concede natural theology to the deists would have been tantamount to a confession that belief in God was irrational. After the deist debate, the arguments from design and the necessity of a first cause would attain increasing importance in American theology.[37]

The reassertion of reasonableness meant, above all, an unprecedented degree of interest in the Christian evidences. Agreeing with their opponents "that rational evidences are necessary," the antideists remained confident that reason could prove the genuineness of the biblical revelation, and much of their polemic consisted of "evidential" reasoning, including renewed appeals to the familiar internal and external arguments. What emerged was a stronger sense among theologians that Christianity had to prove itself as rational in the way that men and women of "common sense" understood rationality. In the early nineteenth century, the common sense test seemed to call for a Christianity grounded in evidence.[38]

8

Evidential Christianity

As the new century approached, Samuel Miller, a Presbyterian minister in New York City, assessed the intellectual achievements of the previous hundred years. His labors reached the public in 1803 as *A Brief Retrospect of the Eighteenth Century*, a two-volume, encyclopedic summary of progress in every intellectual discipline from anatomy to zoology, not only in the physical sciences but also in philosophy, historiography, linguistics, classical studies, poetry, and fiction. In assessing the status of religion, he concluded that the century had been, from one perspective, an age of infidelity. Never before had revealed religion suffered "so many deliberate and systematic attacks" from enemies prating about "the triumph of Reason." Yet Miller also thought that the eighteenth century could be viewed as an "age of Christian science," in which the "most authentic discoveries and the soundest principles of science" had led to "a complete and unprecedented triumph" of "the Religion of Christ." His expectation was that the nineteenth century would bring to full consummation the scientific and rational evidence of religious truth.[1]

When Leonard Woods (1774–1854) went to Andover seminary in 1808 as the school's first professor of systematic theology, he let it be known that he shared that yearning for rationality. Informing his students that "a doctrine proved by sufficient evidence, is not to be rejected on any account whatever," he began his lectures with discussions of right reason, natural theology, and the evidences of the Christian revelation. To understand reason he had the students read the Scottish philosophy of Common Sense. For natural theology, he immersed them in readings from the English theologian William Paley. On the evidences, he had them read the deists, from John Toland to Ethan Allen, and then the critics of deism, from Joseph Butler to John Leland to the Tübingen theologians G. C. Storr and C. C. Flatt. He assured them that "all religious truths must harmonize with the divine intelligence, which is the highest reason in the universe."[2]

Nothing that Woods told his students was new or surprising. Ever since the seventeenth century, theologians in America had affirmed the reasonableness of Christianity, produced treatises on natural theology, and countered deism with the evidences of revelation. But never had the issue of rationality assumed as much importance as it did in the early decades of the nineteenth century. The period saw the maturation of a style of theology devoted to the promotion of evidential Christianity and convinced that the methods of Baconian science could work for theology as well as they did for geology or chemistry.

Bacon and the Scottish Philosophy

The patron saint of evidential Christianity, at least in its American Protestant forms, was Francis Bacon, whose advocacy of inductive science in his *Novum Organum* furnished an ideal that sustained theologians in America for half a century. Samuel Miller (1769–1850) told his readers that the whole of eighteenth-century science had confirmed the advantages of "Lord Bacon's plan of pursuing knowledge by observation, experiment, analysis, and induction," and the admiration for Bacon spilled across theological boundaries. The Unitarian Edward Everett could say by 1823 that "the *Baconian* philosophy has become synonymous with true philosophy." The conservative Calvinist Samuel Tyler contended in 1844 that "the Baconian Philosophy is emphatically the philosophy of Protestantism." Noting that periodicals in both England and the United States teemed with expositions of Baconian method, Tyler asserted in his *Discourse on Baconian Philosophy* that Baconianism signified the most wondrous philosophical revolution "of any within the whole history of the world."[3]

Bacon was more a symbol than a carefully studied resource for theologians. What he symbolized for them was the conviction that theology should be a science grounded in the same inductive methods that marked the other sciences. They learned three lessons from him. The first was that progress came through the observation of particular facts as a prelude to generalization. Whether the facts were construed as descriptions of natural phenomena, delineations of mental states, or readings of discrete biblical passages, the careful thinker assembled them diligently before reaching a conclusion about general laws or higher truths. The second was that theology should avoid the meta-physical, or speculative, or theoretical. Theologians were to draw inferences from the facts of consciousness and biblical revelation and to go no further, es-pecially not to venture into the metaphysical regions of the German philoso-phers. The third was that the theologian, like the naturalist, should become an expert in taxonomy, the discipline of classifying the facts and ordering the clas-sifications. In theology the rage to classify made the new discipline of "mental science," which consisted of describing and classifying states, or "facts," of consciousness, a prolegomenon to theology. Few doubted that adherence to these three rules would make theology "a strictly inductive science."[4]

American Baconianism was an import from Scotland. The Americans ad-mired Bacon because the founders of Scottish Common Sense Realism — Thomas Reid (1710–96), a professor of moral philosophy at Aberdeen and Glasgow, and Dugald Stewart (1753–1828), a student of Reid who taught at Edinburgh — convinced them that Bacon was the inspiration for the Scottish effort to establish the authority and the limits of reason. Samuel Miller called Scottish philosophy "the most important accession which the philosophy of mind has received since the time of Locke," and for Miller that was the highest praise. No other single philosophical movement has ever exerted as much influence on theology in America as Scottish Realism exerted on the ante-bellum theologians.[5]

The honors of priority in the introduction of Scottish Realism to America have gone to the Presbyterian immigrant John Witherspoon (1723–94), who used Reid's ideas to overcome Edwardean idealism when he became the presi-dent the College of New Jersey (Princeton) in 1768. By the 1790s the Scottish philosophy had a secure place in the lectures of David Tappan at Harvard and Timothy Dwight at Yale. Leonard Woods made it part of the seminary training at Andover, and it became the reigning philosophy in every Protestant semi-nary of note. Even in the populist traditions scorned by the seminary elite, the Scottish philosophy took hold. In 1822 the Methodists issued a complete set of the works of Thomas Reid. By 1857 the *Quarterly Review* of the Methodists in the South could speak of Stewart as "the Prince of Scotch Metaphysicians" and of his Edinburgh successor William Hamilton as "the most illustrious philosopher of the age."[6]

Scottish Realism had its origins in Thomas Reid's attempt to correct the epistemology of John Locke and refute the skepticism of David Hume. In his *Essay on Human Understanding* (1690), Locke grounded knowledge in sen-sory experience and the mind's reflections on its own operations, and to this

Reid assented, but he thought that Locke had erred by speaking as though the mind's ideas merely "represented" objects in the external world. To perceive an object, Locke thought, was to have an "idea" of it. As Reid understood him, Locke was saying that "ideas in the mind are the only immediate objects of thought." But how could one be assured that the ideas accurately represented the objects to which they referred?[7]

In Reid's judgment, David Hume unearthed the skepticism hidden in Locke's "ideal theory." Hume concluded, first, that an empiricist should abandon any concept not supported by sensory experience. The concept of a substantial spiritual soul, for instance, could not be maintained; the introspective search for a soul or a self discovered only fleeting impressions, not a spiritual subject. The concept of causation was equally vulnerable, for sensory experience could discern precedence, contiguity, and change, but not a causal force. An observer could repeatedly watch one billiard ball hit another without ever knowing for sure that the ensuing movement evidenced a fixed principle of causality. But Hume's skepticism went even further. It seemed to him, second, that a mind with access only to its own impressions and ideas could never know whether they conveyed objective knowledge of the external world or not. Reid thought that Hume had left no reason "to believe any one thing rather than its contrary." He also thought that Hume's logic was faultless.[8]

The fault lay, rather, in Locke's theory. Rather than assume with Locke that ideas were mental objects, Reid proposed in his *Inquiry into the Human Mind on the Principles of Common Sense* (1764) to think of them as mental acts. To have an idea, he argued, was to perceive an object, not an image that mirrored the object. As evidence, he appealed to "consciousness," which he defined as the mind's ability to discern its own internal operations. Through an introspective survey of consciousness, the philosopher would discover in sensory experience a distinction between internal sensations and perceptions of the world. In touching a table, a thoughtful person would find the perception of dense material cohesion distinguishable from the sensation of resistance. In feeling a pinprick, the observer could recognize a sensation of pain different from the perception of figure and extension in the pin. Both the sensation and the perception were immediately present to consciousness; one could not be derived from the other. The sensation registered an inner state; the perception carried the knower into the world of real objects.[9]

A thorough analysis of consciousness would also reveal, Reid thought, that "natural and original judgments" accompanied these perceptions of the world. Every experience contained and presupposed implicit judgments about existence, causation, and other relations. No one could consistently reject these assumptions, which were present in every coherent experience, because their truth would have to be assumed even in the act of negating them. Every sensation implied a judgment that the sensing self existed; every impression presupposed a judgment that it had a cause sufficient to produce it; every perception contained a reference to both a subject and an object, and any claim that the object was inaccessible had no ground in experience. He spoke of these implicit judgments as the "first principles" of the mind.[10]

Reid was thinking along the same lines that Immanuel Kant would later explore with much greater sophistication, but unlike Kant he felt confident that the regulative principles of the mind ensured knowledge of things as they really were. Just as it made no sense to deny the rules of logic or the axioms of mathematics, so also it made no sense to deny the necessary truths implicit in metaphysics: the reality of self, causation, and the external world, as well as the mind's ability to know it. All experience presupposed axiomatic assumptions, or "beliefs," that could not be reasonably doubted, principles of thought that made coherent experience possible. These were the principles of "common sense."[11]

He recognized that he could not logically demonstrate the common-sense principles. As axiomatic, they would have to be presupposed in any attempted demonstration. He thought that he could confirm the evidence given in consciousness, however, by appeal to the principles of contradiction and universality. He could verify a "natural judgment" if it appeared to be universal in human experience, and he found evidence for universality not only in arguments from logical necessity but also in the fact that the principles lay embedded in the structure of all known languages. He also felt confident that he could reject any set of conclusions — like the skeptical conclusions of Hume — that were self-contradictory.[12]

In his *Essays on the Active Powers of the Human Mind,* Reid argued further that the same inductive method could also discover in consciousness the grounds for belief in freedom, duty, justice, and virtue. Like the other senses, the moral sense also implied judgments about a real world: "Every power to which the name of a sense has been given, is a power of judging of the objects of that sense, and has been accounted such in all ages; the moral sense, therefore, is the power of judging in morals. But Mr. Hume will have the moral sense to be only a power of feeling without judging: this I take to be an abuse of a word."[13]

Reid's philosophy seemed to ground the truths required for theology, but he was also useful for theologians because he cautioned against metaphysical speculation. The caution became even more pronounced in the philosophy of Dugald Stewart, who built upon Reid but emphasized in his *Elements of the Philosophy of the Human Mind* (1792) the dangers of trying to move beyond "facts for which we have the evidence of our own consciousness." The mind could know the qualities of things but not their essences. An honest philosophy would admit the existence of a region "into which philosophy is not permitted to enter." This warning coincided with the theologian's belief that the truths of revelation stood above reason.[14]

The limitations of reason became even more prominent in the philosophy of Sir William Hamilton (1788–1856), who taught logic and metaphysics at Edinburgh from 1836 until his death. Hamilton tried to synthesize the Scottish philosophy with Kantian thought, emphasizing that knowledge was always relative to the faculties of the knower and that a finite mind could never comprehend the Infinite. The speculative reason always encountered insuperable barriers whenever it sought the Absolute; reason would never preclude the need for faith: "A learned ignorance is . . . the end of philosophy, as it is the beginning of theology." The American theologians who read Hamilton usually found him too skeptical for their tastes, but his strictures on rational pretension served their cause.[15]

The Scottish philosophy pointed in two directions at the same time. It stayed largely within the boundaries of empiricism, arguing that knowledge began with "impressions made upon our senses by external objects." At the same time, the Scottish turn to the presuppositions implicit in experience opened the way to an exploration of the intuitive assumptions of reflective thought. This dimension of the Scottish philosophy would make it easier for later American critics of empiricism to affirm an intuitive knowledge deeper than the senses could reach, but most American theologians would emphasize the empirical side, especially since Reid and Stewart also taught that the signs of design in the visible world justified the inference of a divine designer.[16]

While most Americans agreed that Reid had corrected Locke's "ideal theory," most also agreed with Samuel Tyler that the Scots retained the core of Lockean empiricism. The arrival of the Scottish philosophers did not mean that Locke suddenly disappeared from American theology. Samuel Miller announced at the outset of the century that Locke's essay on understanding formed "an era in the history of metaphysical thought," and his assessment endured. From the aristocratic Unitarian Alexander H. Everett, who reassured readers of the *North American Review* that Locke's essay would always remain "the textbook," to the populist Alexander Campbell, who saw Locke as the trustworthy guide for a theology of the people, most American theologians continued to speak well of Locke. But most now read him from a Scottish angle of vision.[17]

Scottish philosophy seemed tailor-made for a theology that would show the rationality of faith while preserving the necessity for revelation. The critique of Hume's skepticism made natural theology possible; the recognition of reason's limits made revelation more plausible. The Scots also offered numerous other benefits. The appeal to consciousness — with both Lockean and Scottish authority behind it — became a recurring feature of theological debate, despite the drawback that advocates of conflicting views always found consciousness on their side. Scottish moral thought gave theologians a way to emphasize the authority of conscience. The Scottish praise of an inductive method supported both the logic of natural theologians, who would try to harmonize religion and science, and the rhetoric of biblical interpreters, who would claim merely to present the biblical facts. The Scottish defense of the freedom of the will would both generate arguments against Calvinism and help Calvinists refine their own interpretations of the meaning of free agency. Equally important, the Scottish philosophy helped to make "mental science" a prelude to revealed theology.

The first important American text in mental science appeared in 1827 when Thomas C. Upham, a professor at Bowdoin, published his *Elements of Intellectual Philosophy*. Within three years, the *Biblical Repertory* at Princeton Seminary was alerting its readers to the high importance of the subject, and before long Edwards Amasa Park (1808–1900) at Andover seminary could write that the philosophy of mind furnished the "animating prospect" for the future of theology: "Now it is to a clear unfolding of what are at once the first and last principles of mental science, that theology looks with her highest anticipations."[18]

Theologians produced scores of articles and textbooks on mental science, outlining the differences between sensation and perception, the dynamics of consciousness, abstraction, the association of ideas, memory, reasoning, imagination, language, emotions, desires, appetites, propensities, affections, volitions, and conscience. The Congregationalist Joseph Haven could contend by 1857, with some justice, that theology received "its shape and character from ... the philosophy we adopt of the human mind." Haven argued that not only arguments for God's existence but also the idea of God itself came from "our previous conception of the human mind." "Our philosophy," he said, "underlies our theology."[19]

Throughout the early nineteenth century, theologians battled on the terrain of mental science. It shaped not only conflicts over the freedom of the will but also disputes over the nature of sin, conversion, and sanctification. It formed the core of the debate between partisans of evidential rationality and intuitive reason. It left a mark on discussions of the person of Christ and the inner relations of the Trinity. It stood behind the era's disputes over the function of theological language. A striking new proposal in mental science — as occurred, for example, when Friedrich Rauch (1806–41) at Mercersburg seminary introduced to Americans the idealism of G. W. F. Hegel in his *Psychology, or a View of the Human Soul* (1840) — could support distinctive theories of salvation, sacraments, and the church. In his 1841 inaugural address at Union Seminary, moreover, the biblical scholar Edward Robinson assigned to "the science of mind" the duty of ratifying the principles of biblical and theological interpretation. It was not surprising that at Yale Divinity School the first year of instruction consisted of two series of lectures, one on the Bible, the other on mental philosophy, as the prerequisites for the study of a theological system in the second year. As the dominant influence on the rise of mental science in America, the Scottish philosophers helped redefine the meaning of theological rationality.[20]

Natural Theology

In 1815, the Virginia Presbyterian minister Samuel Stanhope Smith, successor to Witherspoon as president of the College of New Jersey, published *A Comprehensive View of the Leading and Most Important Principles of Natural and Revealed Religion*. As a student at Princeton, Smith had allowed Witherspoon to convert him from idealism to Scottish Realism, and the book exemplified a style of reasoning that was becoming characteristic of theology in the colleges and seminaries. Like Woods at Andover, Smith began with natural theology, proceeded to the evidences of the Christian religion, and discussed the principles of moral duty. Only after laying these foundations did he proceed to "the principles of revealed religion," from the Trinity to the covenants.[21]

In his natural theology Smith laid out the rational evidence for the existence of God, and his assessment of that evidence epitomized what became a Baconian consensus. He dismissed as "refined speculation" the various a priori — or ontological — arguments with which Anselm and Descartes had tried to show that the mind's idea of a perfect, or infinite, being entailed God's existence. It became a fixed conviction among Baconians across the theological spectrum that the ontological argument did not prove the reality of a personal God.[22]

Nor did the Americans respond favorably to the more abstruse presentations of the cosmological argument. At best, Samuel Clarke's deductive version of the argument — that the infinitude and necessity of space and time required an infinite self-existent substance — proved to them only, as the Unitarian Francis Bowen would note, that "something exists." Most would accept only a simpler, commonsense version of the argument: that the chain of causes entailed a first cause, an eternal, uncreated source from which all other things came. But it never became the favored argument because it too failed to provide sufficient evidence that the first cause was an intelligent, good, loving, forgiving personal God.[23]

Like most other Baconian theologians, Smith found the argument from universal consent more convincing. To a theologian wedded to Scottish philosophy, the very fact of almost universal popular belief in some divine being suggested that the belief was an "intuitive perception," entitled to the same implicit credit as other perceptions. In Smith's view, however, none of these arguments could even approach the force of another mode of reasoning "infinitely more simple and obvious": the argument from design.[24]

He found the exemplary model for this "teleological" argument in the *Natural Theology* (1802) of William Paley (1734–1805), the archdeacon of Carlisle in England, and his admiration for Paley mirrored the theological spirit of the age. At least fifteen American editions and several English editions of Paley's *Natural Theology* circulated in America before the mid-1840s, and some enjoyed multiple printings. Between 1829 and 1839 a single publisher in Boston reprinted the book seven times. Paley was a popularizer who was able to transform the earlier ideas of John Ray, William Derham, and the Dutch Bernard Nieuwentyt (1654–1718) into a clear exposition that defined the meaning of natural theology for more than half a century.[25]

Paley found evidence for design when he discovered distinct parts of a mechanism working toward a common end, and every instance of design indicated an intelligent designer. The argument was analogical. Just as the mechanical intricacy of a watch disclosed the intelligence of a human watchmaker, so the infinitely more complex contrivances of the natural world, from the marvels of the eye to the vastness of the cosmic harmony, required a benevolent intelligence beyond human capacity. By the middle of the nineteenth century, most American theologians, nurtured on Paley, agreed that "the central idea in natural theology" was that "design, apparent in the phenomena of creation, indicates an intelligent Designer."[26]

The bias in favor of the teleological argument ensured that the alliance between theology and science would continue. Despite wariness about materialism, most theologians believed that science would assume "a direct and active agency in the support of the Christian system." Some contended that modern science rested on a foundation of biblical truth. A. B. Van Zandt, an Old School Presbyterian in Virginia, told an audience at the state university in 1851 that science had an unspoken faith in the purpose and rationality of the cosmos, and the source of this faith was biblical: "The maxim that 'Jehovah has created nothing in vain,' we hold to have been the basis of all those minute investigations of the scientists." What bound the alliance together in the minds of theologians was the promise that science would confirm the argument from design.[27]

By 1846, E. A. Park could claim that every advance of philosophy and science was "adding to the materials of Natural Theology." Chemists, geologists, astronomers, and metaphysicians were providing "new data for that science which comprehends all others within itself." During the following decade, the theological journals carried articles alleging evidence for design in leaf appendages, coal formations, the orderliness of bee cells, and the fixed proportions of the chemical elements. They found nature filled with pattern and regularity and therefore with intelligence.[28]

No American produced a natural theology remotely as influential as Paley's. The Americans preferred, for the most part, to borrow their ideas from the British, whose ingenuity in natural theology found continuing expression in the Bridgewater Treatises (1833–40) written by eight prominent naturalists. The nearest American counterparts came out of the Dudleian Lectures, which had begun in Boston in 1755, and the Lowell Institute, which also sponsored a periodic lecture series on natural theology and Christian evidences in Boston after its founding in 1839. With the journal article and the lecture as the preferred genre for natural theology, the American contributions tended to be more narrow and circumscribed than the British.

The work that best represented this American style came from the collected lectures of the Amherst College naturalist Edward Hitchcock (1793–1864). A Congregationalist who studied theology under Nathaniel William Taylor and geology under Benjamin Silliman at Yale, Hitchcock set forth in his *Religion of Geology and Its Connected Sciences* (1851) the position of the "geological theist." Convinced, with Paley, that "contrivance, adaptation, and design" marked the natural world, he wrote as a geologist who worried that too many theologians knew too little about geology and that too many materialists had entrenched themselves within natural science.[29]

Geological theism, as he saw it, proved itself on both scientific and religious grounds. Geology supported the argument from design — including the unity of the divine plan — by showing that adaptation followed the same laws throughout geological history. It could not alone prove that the world had a beginning in time, but it could show that the creation of organisms required a creative divine intervention, since no known physical law could otherwise explain the transition from the inorganic to the organic. By describing the features of natural history that supported and enhanced human life, it provided evidence that "benevolence decidedly predominates" in the natural economy. And it showed that God had intervened miraculously, above or against natural law, in the distant past, since each new species would have required a separate divine intervention. Hitchcock was repeating familiar arguments, but originality was not the point, since he felt himself to be expressing the consensus among scientists who submitted to the limits of the Baconian method.[30]

Hitchcock had confidence in the alliance of scientists and theologians, but he had to engage three issues that threatened to fragment it. The first was development, a problem that became acute after the English journalist Robert Chambers published in 1844 his *Vestiges of the Natural History of Creation*. To counter Chambers's theory that an evolutionary process had produced the physical universe by moving inexorably from the simple to the complex, Hitchcock adduced evidence for regression in nature — evidence found, for example, in the fact that some species of mollusks had apparently taken a retrograde path from the complex to the simple. For Hitchcock, as for other antebellum theologians, the problem with evolutionary theories was not only that they seemed to contradict the Bible but also that they implied a materialist account of human origins.[31]

The second and larger problem was that geology itself seemed to contradict the Bible. As commonly interpreted, the book of Genesis implied that the creation of the earth had occurred about six thousand years ago. By the time the Scotsman James Hutton published his *Theory of the Earth* (1785), geologists had begun, however, to conceive of immense changes over a vast period. At the beginning of the century, Samuel Miller could assume that these theories would not endure, but by 1829, when the devout Benjamin Silliman (1779–1864) edited an English geology text for his classes at Yale College, he felt the need to add an appendix in which he reinterpreted Genesis to fit the new awareness that the creation of the earth in its present form had stretched over an almost inconceivable duration.[32]

Theologians lined up behind two competing interpretations of Genesis. Silliman's way of harmonizing the biblical and the scientific accounts was to argue that each of the six days of the Genesis story had been a geological period of indefinite length. Popular also in Germany, where the eighteenth-century Tübingen theologian Albert Knapp had adopted it, and in Britain, where it gained the favor of the naturalist Hugh Miller, this "long-day" theory commended itself because the Genesis story could be stretched to make a rough fit with the fossil record in the geological strata. The *Quarterly Review* of the southern Methodists asserted wide acceptance of the theory as late as 1857.[33]

In an 1835 article in the *American Biblical Repository*, Hitchcock supported the alternative solution. He suggested that Genesis could be read to mean that the first creation of a physical world long antedated the six days of creation described in the biblical story. The fossils came from the antecedent creation, which had been followed by a gap of time — "the chaotic state of the globe" — before the re-creation or renovation of all things in six literal days. This "gap theory" also had support among Christian scholars in Europe, and it carried the imprimatur of the Scottish theologian Thomas Chalmers (1780–1847), whose *Natural Theology* appealed to theologians in America.[34]

The search for harmony between Genesis and geology led, however, to years of conflict over biblical interpretation. The freethinking president of South Carolina College, Thomas Cooper, complained that Silliman's editorial comments in an American version of an *Introduction to Geology* by the English writer Robert Bakewell had undermined science in order to preserve a contradictory ancient text that was not worth saving. For Moses Stuart (1780–1852) at Andover, however, the complaint was rather that both Silliman and Hitchcock had naively tried to make nineteenth-century science determine the meaning of an ancient text.[35]

Hitchcock's reply to Stuart was that science had frequently guided biblical interpretation. It had once been customary, for example, to find in Genesis the view that the earth was stationary, but in a post-Copernican world such a reading no longer commanded assent. In 1837 he tried to show that the geological record also compelled a revisiting of the story of Noah and the flood. Since the geological remains showed no trace of a universal deluge, the biblical scholars needed to recognize that the flood must have been a local event that covered only the earth's populated regions.[36]

By 1847, the Methodist Thomas Ralston claimed that "the most intelligent Christians of the present day" accepted the need to revise the interpretation of Genesis in the light of modern science, but by no means did every theologian agree with him. The Presbyterian Tayler Lewis (1802–77) at Union College represented a small but vociferous company who shared Stuart's view that philology alone should determine the meaning of biblical words. In a rancorous dispute with the geologist James Dwight Dana (1813–95), an advocate of the long-day theory, Lewis argued that the biblical writers never intended to offer scientific explanations, though he too ended up by affirming a long-day theory on philological grounds. Neither Lewis nor Dana could have accepted the solution of the Unitarian Rufus Stebbins, who suggested in a review of Hitchcock that Genesis 1 might be simply a collection of "the opinions of the ancients" rather than scientific or historical truth in any modern sense.[37]

In addition to questions about evolutionary development and the interpretation of Genesis, a third point of tension between theology and science came from the question of the unity of the human race, which arose in the 1820s when the Philadelphia physician Samuel G. Morton argued that differences in the shape of human skulls proved the race to have had multiple origins. This polygenetic theory had some celebrated defenders, including the highly respected naturalist Louis Agassiz of Harvard, but theologians believed that it threatened the account of a unitary human creation in Genesis as well as Paul's assertion in Acts 17 that God created all humankind of "one blood." Hitchcock considered it a form of infidelity.[38]

Ever since Samuel Stanhope Smith wrote his *Essay on the Causes of the Variety of Complexion and Figure in the Human Species* (1787), few theologians had seen reason to question his contention that human difference resulted from adaptation to different environments. The Lutheran John Bachman (1790–1874) of Charleston, South Carolina, authored the principal theological refutation of polygenetic theory. An able naturalist who wrote the text for J. J. Audubon's illustrations in *Viviparous Quadrupeds of North America* (1845–49), Bachman labored to demonstrate the vast extent of variation within species as a way of showing that human difference need not signify diversity of origin or type. While Bachman employed scientific arguments, the Presbyterian Thomas Smyth (1808–73) tried to show that Agassiz's reading of Genesis as merely an account of one creation among many could not be reconciled with a comprehensive reading of biblical claims about the universal effects of the fall and the promise of salvation. Both good science and good exegesis, they thought, led to the same theological conclusion: that the Genesis account remained the most plausible story of human origins.[39]

The three controversies raised the possibility that science and theology might collide, but few theologians took that possibility seriously. Nathaniel William Taylor (1786–1858) at Yale expressed the majority view when he wrote that "the voice of nature, speaking through all her works, is but the voice of the same God who speaks to us in revelation," so that a contradiction could "never occur." The Baconians had an unflagging confidence in the unity of truth, and only a few explored the idea that religious and scientific truths might be of a different logical order.[40]

All the more, therefore, did they affirm the unity of natural and revealed theology. It was common for them to argue that the biblical revelation presupposed the truths of natural theology. The Bible, for example, assumed the existence of God; it did not try to prove it. For those proofs, the appeal "must be to reason." And all would have agreed with Van Zandt that any rational person could grasp the reality of "an invisible, almighty power, the disposer of events and the arbiter of destiny."[41]

This natural revelation, however, was fragmentary and incomplete. The biblical revelation had to fulfill and correct the natural apprehension. Scripture alone revealed the mercy of God to sinners and the economy of salvation in Christ. It alone provided assurance of grace and forgiveness. Natural theology pointed toward truths that natural theology alone could not comprehend. It prepared the way for the higher revelation of biblical truth.[42]

One way it accomplished this preparation was to discover the analogies between natural and revealed truth. The penchant for analogical reasoning in antebellum theology came partly from the enormous influence of Joseph Butler's antideist argument that there should be no greater difficulty in believing the religion of revelation than in believing the religion of nature. Both were congruent, in similar ways, with human moral experience in the world. Both presented the mind with similar enigmas and ambiguities. Deists who rejected the biblical revelation because of its mysteries should, in all consistency, face up to the mysteries of nature. Deists who accepted the one should accept the other. The Presbyterian Albert Barnes (1798–1870) said that Butler's *Analogy* needed "no revision."[43]

Butler's argument was risky, for it supposed far more ambiguity in the Christian revelation than some theologians wanted to acknowledge, but it embodied the Baconian sense of both the capacities and the limits of rationality. It granted that reason could discern religious truth; it insisted that reason alone could not grasp the highest religious truths. It protected the special status of the biblical revelation. It also suggested the massive stake of postenlightenment theology in the attempt to prove that biblical revelation was itself rational. For that enterprise, the theologians turned to the Christian evidences.

The Evidences of Revelation

When Mark Hopkins (1802–77) of Williams College delivered in 1844 his Lowell Institute lectures on the evidences of Christianity, he assured his listeners that "the Christian religion admits of a certain proof." It must have seemed sometimes that an entire generation of American theologians devoted themselves to providing it. "In no department of Theology," wrote a reviewer in the *Christian Spectator* in 1825, "have more talent and learning been displayed; and in none, perhaps, have the effects of thorough investigation been more apparent, or more useful" than in the department that came to be known simply as "the evidences."[44]

Theologians in America had produced essays on the evidences ever since the seventeenth century, but the flood of publications after the late eighteenth century marked an unprecedented shift in theological interests. The theologians themselves offered multiple explanations for their surge of interest in the evidential: the example of their British counterparts, the need to confute deism, their feeling that evangelical doctrine was under "furious assault," and a desire to teach "serious believers" how to convince the large numbers of un-churched Americans. Some said that the growing naturalism of science re-quired a reassertion of Christian proofs. Others thought that science itself was strengthening the evidences. The rising prestige of science encouraged theolo-gians to emulate the scientific demand for rational proof and evidence. The popularity of the evidences registered the authority of the Baconian spirit within the theological traditions.[45]

The first step in the presentation of the evidential arguments was usually the demonstration that natural theology established the antecedent probability of a special revelation. God created human beings with physical needs and made provision for their satisfaction; they also had intellectual and moral needs, so it seemed to follow that God would satisfy those necessities as well. It was "reasonable," wrote the Presbyterian William Plumer, that a God who had created human beings would reveal the necessary knowledge to make known his will and intentions for them. Since reason alone did not furnish that knowl-edge, a special revelation became plausible.[46]

By the beginning of the nineteenth century, the evidential arguments at-tained a formulaic character. Theologians still distinguished between the ex-ternal and the internal arguments. The external argument still consisted of the appeal to prophecy and miracle, including the miraculous diffusion of early Christianity. As new forms of biblical criticism became widely known, the argument required increasing attention to the "authenticity" of scripture — the question of whether the books of the New Testament were written by the authors whose names they bore. The internal arguments now included a wide range of proofs that could be summarized under the theme of consistency: the Bible was internally consistent as well as consistent with reason, with the deepest desires of the heart, with the highest human morality, with the needs of human nature, and with the requisites for social order and justice. The intent of all the arguments was to prove that the Christian Bible was the unique divine revelation toward which natural theology pointed.

The only point of dispute was over the relative authority of the internal and the external. The Scot Thomas Chalmers questioned the efficacy of the inter-nal arguments on the grounds that they could not convince the skeptic, and by the time the Harvard Unitarian John Gorham Palfrey delivered his two-volume Lowell Lectures on the evidences in 1843, he was ready to agree that the internal argument too often meant an appeal to feeling rather than to real evidence. Palfrey thought that the New Testament rather offered proofs de-signed "to be conveyed by the channel of external, historical testimony." But others, including the influential Archibald Alexander (1772–1851) at Princeton, thought the internal evidence superior because it appealed not merely to the understanding but also to the heart and conscience. Most evidential writers typically used both internal and external arguments.[47]

In an era given to the cultivation of religious subjectivity, whether in romantic or revivalist forms, the internal argument flourished. The vogue of Scottish philosophy made it tempting to argue that scriptural teaching commended itself to "the common sense" of humanity. But the argument was attractive in this setting for two additional reasons. It tapped into an ethos of revivalism and devotionalism in the churches. The Presbyterian Robert Jefferson Breckinridge (1800–71) unintentionally presented both an apologetic proof and a sociological commentary when he observed that "our religious experience" confirmed the authority of the Bible. In an era drawn to sentimental fiction and the depiction of character in the novel, moreover, the apologists gave new emphasis to "the character of Jesus Christ" as proof of the divine origin of Christianity. At its simplest level, this meant a new attention to a narrative recounting of the gospel stories, with emphasis on the human excellence and sacrificial suffering of Jesus as an apologetic strategy. The further claim was that such a character would have been "hard to invent." The New Testament story itself, and especially its main figure, stood beyond the reach of the merely narrative imagination.[48]

Some variant of the internal argument would find defenders even among the critics of Baconianism, but the special preserve of the Baconians was the external argument. Appeal to prophecy and miracle seemed to present facts — observable, public, verifiable. At the same time, the external proofs accented the supernaturalist claims of Christianity. They guarded against a rationalistic naturalism. The point of employing them was to show that a supernaturalist view of reality had the support of the same empirical reasoning that had succeeded in the sciences.

When Anthony Collins argued in his *Discourse on the Grounds and Reasons of the Christian Religion* that the biblical prophecies included a great many predictions that failed to come true, he set English apologists on the task of authenticating the predictive accuracy of the prophets. A century of apologetic historical argument, archaeological excavation, and antideist polemic stood available to the American Baconians. Reading the biblical material as accurate history and interpreting prophecy as prediction, they found ample evidence that the course of time had seen the fulfillment of prophecies about the destruction of ancient Israel, the fall of Egypt, the dynasties of Syria and Greece, and hundreds of similar historical events. What impressed them was the "vast extent" of biblical prophecies and the "wonderful minuteness" with which the Bible recorded their fulfillment. Even more remarkable, they thought, they could themselves search history — and look to the future — for more evidence of fulfilled prophecies.[49]

The prophetic argument gained additional credibility from the observation that Jesus seemed to prophesy future events that could be confirmed in ancient records, none more impressive than the destruction of Jerusalem. Unaware or dismissive of biblical scholarship suggesting that the gospels contained retrospective interpretations of Jerusalem's fall rather than anticipatory predictions of it, the theologians marveled at the accuracy of biblical details about the event. Since no human sagacity could so consistently predict future events with such unerring accuracy, the fulfillment of prophecies offered evidence that the authors and characters of biblical history spoke with a divine authority.[50]

In a similar way, the biblical miracles confirmed the divine origins of the biblical teachings. If theism was true, argued Palfrey, then miracles were credible. If miracles ran through the whole biblical history, they revealed a divine presence within it. They signified the divine commission accorded to the biblical actors and the divine verification of their teaching. "Without some miraculous token of the Divine sanction," wrote the Presbyterian Henry Ruffner, "no system of religion can present infallible evidence of its being a revelation." The biblical miracles provided such evidence for the system of the Christian Bible. Palfrey concluded that it was untenable to claim to believe in Christianity and not in the miracles.[51]

In order for the miracles to confirm the revelation, however, the theologians had to confirm the historicity of the biblical miracles. This, in turn, required rational proof that miracles were even possible. And this made it necessary once again to refute David Hume. In 1748 Hume had published his essay "On Miracles" as part of his *Philosophical Essays concerning Human Understanding,* arguing that testimonies to miraculous events were intrinsically dubious. Hume thought a miracle, as a violation of the laws of nature, was by definition an exception to uniform experience, which provided the only criterion for evaluating testimony. The uniformity of experience amounted to a presumptive proof against any testimonial on behalf of the miraculous.[52]

Hume repelled and fascinated the American Baconians. No critic of Christianity attracted more attention. Ralston in 1847 suggested the extent of the preoccupation with Hume: "Such has been the fame of Hume's arguments against miracles, that scarce a treatise has appeared on the evidences of Christianity, since the first enunciation of that gilded sophism, in which it has not been brought upon the arena for discussion. . . . [No] treatise on the question can ignore it entirely without being viewed by many as incomplete." The Americans offered, however, no original refutations. They borrowed freely from the long British discussion, especially from the *Dissertation on Miracles* of George Campbell, the principal of Marischal College in Aberdeen, who had discovered a certain equivocation in Hume's definition of experience. What the Americans offered the reader was usually a summary of the logical flaws that the British had found in Hume's reasoning.[53]

Mark Hopkins laid out the Humean equivocation: was Hume talking about the uniform experience of any given individual? If so, his argument proved nothing. No single person's failure to experience miracles warranted a general disbelief in all testimony to the miraculous. Was he then talking about general human experience? If so, he begged the question, for he assumed rather than demonstrated the uniformity of general human experience. His argument, moreover, would rule out any testimony to new or unusual facts.[54]

The more important question for the theologians was the competence and credibility of the witnesses. Convinced that the gospel writers had been eyewitnesses to the miracles of Jesus, they strove to confirm the trustworthiness of the authors. Written by honest men who had no motive to lie, who suffered for their convictions, who wrote while other eyewitnesses, most of them hostile, still lived, the gospels bore the mark of competent and credible testimony.[55]

Hume and the theologians had more in common than they would have wanted to acknowledge. They both assumed that the aims of the biblical writers were the same as those of modern historians. They both assumed a world governed by natural laws, with the only difference being that the theologians either admitted exceptions or redefined miracles as the results of laws yet to be discovered. They both valued knowledge grounded in sensory experience, and they both thought that religious and scientific statements should have, in principle, the same logical status. All of these assumptions would come under attack in America as early as the 1830s, but they continued to mark the Baconian style of theology.

American Biblical Criticism

The Baconian style left its mark on early American biblical scholarship, much of which consisted of efforts to carry forward the evidential project by demonstrating the authenticity and integrity of the separate biblical books. Even more of it consisted of attempts to implement an inductive hermeneutic that reached doctrinal conclusions by grouping together separate biblical passages, as if the text constituted a field of facts analogous to the terrain from which geologists collected rocks. It became a commonplace of Baconian theology that the Bible revealed facts and that Christian faith required assent to them. When a reviewer in the *Biblical Repertory and Princeton Review* insisted in 1845 that competent biblical scholars limited themselves to "the definite facts of revelation," he stated what had become a truism.[56]

Modern American critical biblical scholarship had its symbolic birth in 1812 when Joseph Stevens Buckminster died. A liberal Boston minister at the Brattle Street Congregational Church, Buckminster traveled to Europe in 1806–07, bought a three-thousand-volume library, and returned it to the United States. In Germany, he discovered the new critical methods. The scholarship of J. D. Michaelis (1717–91) made him aware of the history behind the biblical canon and allowed him to question the received canon; his reading of Johann Jakob Griesbach (1745–1812) introduced him to "textual criticism," the collating of the extant manuscripts in order to attain the most accurate text; and his purchase of Johann Gottfried Eichhorn's *Einleitung ins Alte Testament* (1780–83) made possible the first serious American encounter with "higher criticism," the interpretation of the biblical books in the light of their authorship, integrity, and historical setting. The sale of his library after his death launched a new kind of biblical study in America.[57]

Buckminster believed that biblical criticism would explode Calvinist theology, especially its belief in verbal inspiration, but he also believed that critical studies would support the logic of evidentialism, and most other biblical scholars also treated biblical investigation as an extension of the internal and external arguments. By confirming the authorship of the books, they would strengthen the Baconian case for eyewitness reliability and historical accuracy. But biblical criticism had its dangers: attention to the context of the biblical writings could challenge accepted methods of using the texts in theology, raising questions about evidentialist reasoning.[58]

The first two schools of biblical criticism, one linked to Andover seminary and the other to Harvard, shared a common loyalty to evidential logic. Moses Stuart at Andover had absorbed a moderate Edwardean theology under Timothy Dwight at Yale and preached in the Congregationalist Center Church in New Haven before accepting the call to Andover in 1810. In order to teach Sacred Literature, he had to learn the subject, and his serious study began with his purchase of Eichhorn's *Einleitung* at the Buckminster sale. His wide reading in German scholarship disturbed the trustees at Andover, but he defended the methods, if not the conclusions, of the German critics, and employed them against the New England liberals by showing that they confirmed biblical support for Calvinist doctrine. In 1822 he translated Johann August Ernesti's *Elements of Interpretation,* popularizing the "grammatical-historical method" that taught biblical students to read the text historically and to ground their interpretations in ancient philology rather than modern science or philosophy. The aim was to guard against reading present-day meanings into the biblical texts. Stuart thought that these rigorous methods would serve apologetic ends.[59]

He pursued evidential ends, but his methods also raised some questions about current evidential assumptions. On the one hand, he defended traditional views of authorship for both Old and New Testament books, including the Mosaic authorship of the Pentateuch and the unity of the book of Isaiah; he argued for the historicity of biblical miracles; and he held to the doctrine of plenary, though not verbal, inspiration. God inspired the writing of the entirety of the Bible, though without putting the exact words into the minds of the authors. On the other, he made a point of emphasizing that the Bible taught religion, not astronomy or geology, and he brought critical methods to bear against harmonizers like Hitchcock and Silliman. Reason and revelation coincided, but the harmonizers made them coincide too easily.[60]

Andrews Norton (1786–1853) at Harvard represented the Unitarian approach to biblical criticism, but he shared Stuart's confidence in evidential reasoning. By 1837, when he published his three-volume *Evidences of the Genuineness of the Gospels,* he was contending not only with the Calvinists but also with "the mystical and barbarous obscurity" of such German critics as Eichhorn, Ferdinand Christian Baur, and D. F. Strauss. Norton came to distrust the Germans so much that he forbade his son to learn the language. The Germans threatened the historicity of the biblical narrative, and Norton thought its historicity essential.[61]

What made the gospels genuine, he argued, was that they bore the names of their true authors; they had remained, despite a few later insertions, essentially unaltered through the centuries; and their reports, including the miracle accounts, were historically accurate. For evidence of genuineness he looked mainly outside the canon to second- and third-century writers who cited the New Testament, but he also tried to show the historical plausibility of the gospel accounts, especially the miracle stories, on the same rational grounds that had always been part of the evidential tradition. In his posthumous *Internal Evidences of the Genuineness of the Gospels* (1855), he expanded, with more than ordinary scholarly erudition, the familiar argument that the gospel writers could never have created a person with the character and majesty of Jesus. The four gospels were too consistent, too artless in their narrative form, and too reliable in their portrayal of contemporary history to permit any doubt that they conveyed historical truth. It seemed to follow that the biblical authors were rational men of "common sense" who wrote factually accurate history.[62]

Stuart wrote a largely favorable review of Norton's first three volumes, but Norton's scholarship offended conservative Baconians because he denied biblical infallibility, discarded the tradition that Moses wrote the Pentateuch, and asserted that most of the Old Testament was no "revelation from God." Much of it was inaccurate, much was myth, and much of it contradicted the teachings of Jesus. Intent on separating the eternal truths of the Bible from its time-bound forms of expression, he emphasized the ambiguity of language and found a few spurious passages in the gospels (including the first two chapters of Matthew). Norton redefined revelation, moreover, to include only "the few all important truths" proclaimed by Jesus. Intending to strengthen the evidential legacy, he also subjected it to criticism from within.[63]

The critical edge became even sharper in the New Testament studies of William Henry Furness, the pastor since 1825 of the Unitarian congregation in Philadelphia. Like Norton, he read the New Testament as a set of "true histories of real persons and real events," and his *Remarks on the Four Gospels* (1836), along with the subsequent *Jesus and His Biographers* (1838) and *A History of Jesus* (1850), tried to show the accuracy of the narratives. What made Furness different was his predilection for giving natural and psychological explanations for the New Testament miracle stories. The miracles had not been "departures from the established order of nature." The healing miracles demonstrated the power of faith; other miracles could be explained through an enlarged knowledge of natural law. When no such explanations seemed plausible, Furness was willing to question the miracle accounts, including the birth stories and the story of Jesus' transfiguration. Had his views been widely shared, the external argument from miracle would have lost much of its force.[64]

Even more disturbing to evidentialists were the studies of George Noyes, a scholarly local pastor until 1840, when he became the Dexter Lecturer at Harvard. Noyes brought critical scholarship to bear against the external argument from prophecy. The state attorney general threatened him with blasphemy charges when his essays in the *Christian Examiner* rebutted the doctrine that the Old Testament prophecies referred to Christ. In a critical review in 1834 of the Berlin Lutheran Ernst Hengstenberg, whose *Christology of the Old Testament* presented the prophecy-fulfillment scheme as proof of biblical infallibility, Noyes pointed out that the prophetic predictions of a messianic king who would subdue all the nations could hardly be reconciled with the history of Jesus. He read the New Testament as inspired and authoritative but found the Old Testament of doubtful value and detached its prophetic sayings from any association with the coming of Christ.[65]

Most Baconians, including most Unitarians, rejected or ignored conclusions like those of Furness and Noyes. The continuing strength of the evidential arguments could be seen in the vigorous reaction of Unitarians after the German Hegelian David Friedrich Strauss published his *Life of Jesus* (1835), in which he argued that the gospels expressed in mythic forms the religious consciousness of the early church, presenting religious ideas clothed in pictorial representations.

Reviews of Strauss's book appeared in the theological journals throughout the 1840s; almost uniformly the reviewers tried to refute him through recourse to arguments that had long been used against David Hume and the British deists. They defended the historicity of the miracles and the reliability of eyewitnesses, argued that Strauss played havoc with the rules of evidence, claimed that his methods would render impossible any historical account of the ancient world, and said that he had ignored the evidence in favor of the genuineness of the gospels. Andrews Norton added a refutation of Strauss to a new edition of his *Internal Evidences*.[66]

Only the Unitarian radical Theodore Parker (1810–60), who would soon cast aside the whole evidential tradition, found virtue in Strauss's scholarly ambition, though he too believed that Strauss had imposed a Hegelian philosophy on the biblical text. Still convinced in 1837 that the gospels depicted a true history, Parker thought that Strauss relied too heavily on the category of myth. By 1841, however, Parker had become the one prominent American theologian to incorporate many of Strauss's assumptions into his own thought. Parker went on to contribute to biblical scholarship by publishing in 1843 an annotated translation of W. M. L. DeWette's *Critical and Historical Introduction to the Old Testament,* but by then he stood so far outside the mainstream that few took him seriously.[67]

Outside the Unitarian community, radical German biblical scholarship received relatively little attention. The biblical criticism and translation of Francis Patrick Kenrick (1796–1863), who became the Catholic bishop of Philadelphia in 1842, inaugurated a tradition of Catholic biblical scholarship that remained distinct from either the Andover or Harvard streams. Kenrick had an interest in the methods and conclusions of Eichhorn and other German critics, and he introduced his readers to some of their conclusions, though he never accepted them. His primary aim as a scholar was to produce an American English translation and to defend the use of the Latin Vulgate—the text approved by the Council of Trent—as the best source of a vernacular rendering, though he eventually became so open to the use of the Greek and Hebrew manuscripts that his translations created displeasure among more conservative Catholics. His *Four Gospels* appeared in 1849, and he prepared critical translations of several of the Old Testament books.

Despite his resistance to the critical conclusions of the Germans, Kenrick revealed that Catholics had the same interest in the reasonableness of biblical teaching as their Protestant counterparts. When he published his translations of the Pentateuch in 1860, he conceded that the seven "days" of the creation accounts in Genesis might be indefinite periods, that the biblical records needed to be read in accord with modern astronomy, and that Moses, whom he assumed to be the author of the first five biblical books, did not necessarily have accurate knowledge about matters of science. Unlike either the Andover or the Harvard scholars, however, Kenrick strove to show that his conclusions were consistent with the tradition of the church. This respect for tradition would mark Catholic biblical scholarship throughout the early nineteenth century.[68]

In both academic and popular religious thought, and in both the Protestant and Catholic churches, theologians remained intent on showing, in the words of Princeton's Archibald Alexander, that "no doctrine can be a proper object of our faith which is not more reasonable to receive than to reject." Whether they were writing natural theology, promulgating Scottish philosophy, adducing the evidences of revelation, or interpreting scripture, they assumed that Christian theology was rational and that its rationality would commend it to the educated public. Before the mid-1830s, the evidential arguments and the confidence in natural theology commanded almost universal assent among theologians in America.[69]

Theologians also continued, however, to think of theology as practical, and the practical issues proved more troubling and divisive. By the early nineteenth century, the theologians were altering the meaning of theological practicality. Seventeenth-century theologians used the term "practical" to refer to all of theology, and some nineteenth-century theologians retained this habit of thought. In 1849, when Henry Boynton Smith lectured at Andover on "Faith and Philosophy," he repeated the familiar formula: "Systematic theology, by our ablest divines, is recognized as a science, both theoretical and practical." By this time, however, some theologians had lost the original meaning of the distinction. They began to distinguish between theoretical and practical doctrines. The "practical" no longer meant a way of appropriating all theological truth; it began to refer to doctrines about sin, conversion, regeneration, and holiness. The word "theoretical" no longer meant that the aim of theology was truth about God as an end in itself. It began to refer to conclusions that had no immediate and obvious application. For many it was an easy step to conclude further that the practical doctrines were the teachings that awakened the "passions and affections."[70]

On the truths of evidential Christianity, most theologians could, until the mid-1830s, agree. Only a few isolated voices — the transcendentalists, Horace Bushnell, the Mercersburg theologians, Orestes Brownson — would challenge the evidential consensus. Most of the theological debates were about the practical doctrines, whether the nature of the church, the requirements for salvation, the function of good works, or the definition of regeneration. Both debates — over the warrants for Christian truth claims and the meaning of the practical doctrines — became increasingly entangled, after the American Revolution, with class tensions that helped fuel populist movements in theology, but within both the populist and the academic traditions, the two sets of debates dominated the course of theology.

9

Unitarian Virtue

In 1821 William Ellery Channing (1780–1842), the minister of the Federal Street Church in Boston, delivered the Dudleian Lectures at Harvard on "The Evidences of Christianity." He employed the standard internal and external proofs, but he also related them to a distinctive understanding of the purpose of Christianity as "the moral perfection of the human soul." By incorporating the theme of moral virtue into a lecture on evidential Christianity, Channing expressed three of the defining notes of Unitarian theology: its appeal to the Bible, its respect for reason, and its honoring of virtue. The early Unitarians believed that they were returning to a pure biblical faith unmarred by the later corruption of Augustinian and Calvinist deviations. No other theological movement in nineteenth-century America expressed greater solicitude for the New Testament, devoted itself more fully to the defense of the rationality of Christianity, or contended more earnestly that a reasonable form of Christianity would define virtue as its end.[1]

The Unitarians stood in a straight line of continuity with the "catholick" Congregationalists and the Arminian liberals of the eighteenth century. They saw themselves as restoring the primitive Christianity of the New Testament churches, and occasionally they linked their movement to the Italian Socinians — Lelio Sozini (1525–62) and his nephew Fausto Sozzini (1539–1604) — who had promoted a unitarian theology in sixteenth-century Europe. The orthodox tried to associate them with more unconventional forms of English Unitarianism, but they had far more in common with Jonathan Mayhew and Charles Chauncy than with Socinians or with Unitarians in England. George Edward Ellis of the Harvard Divinity School rightly observed in 1857 that New England Unitarianism had emerged over the course of three generations in New England by "slow and scarcely perceptible degrees." Its emergence resulted from a gradual transfer of allegiance on the part of numerous ministers and congregations, especially in Massachusetts, from Calvinism to the eighteenth-century theology of virtue, a transfer that often occurred almost silently as ministers ceased to refer to distinctive Calvinist doctrines in their sermons and lectures. As a theological movement, Unitarianism was the attempt to defend this theology of virtue once it came under attack by Calvinists.[2]

The first historians of Unitarianism viewed it more as an "anti-doctrinal solvent" than as a theological movement. Impressed that no early leaders tried to produce a theological system — and convinced that such an effort would have contradicted the genius of the movement — they saw theology as a minor interest. Such a judgment bears a measure of truth, and antebellum Unitarians sometimes wondered about the reasons for their "want of a scientific theology." Ellis conceded that it seemed "almost impossible to define and identify" the movement theologically. Edward Hall explained in 1832 that the soul of the movement lay deeper than "doctrinal statements": "In our view, a Unitarian is not so much one who believes a particular doctrine or number of doctrines, as one who desires and strives to make his belief an incentive to a particular life and character, a religious, useful life, and a religious and forever improving character." Ellis thought that Unitarian preaching was therefore "less doctrinal and more practical, in the technical sense of those words." Its purpose was to guide the formation of a Christian character that would manifest the salutary results of redemption.[3]

Neither Hall nor Ellis, however, would acknowledge that Unitarians were indifferent to theology. Hall insisted that they affirmed "settled, clear . . . scriptural, rational" doctrines. Ellis thought that the "essential principles" of Unitarian theology were "well determined, so that it is at least as definite a system as that which goes by the name of orthodoxy." George Burnap tried to convince the movement that its mission was "theological reform," and Unitarians did publish some short but relatively systematic expositions. In 1844, Andrew Preston Peabody (1811–93), the pastor of the South Church in Portsmouth, New Hampshire, until he became in 1860 the Plummer Professor of Christian Morals and Preacher to the University at Harvard, published his *Lectures on Christian Doctrine,* and in 1857 William Greenleaf Eliot (1811–87), the pastor of the Church of the Messiah in St. Louis and the organizer of the Western Unitarian Conference, published his *Discourses on the Doctrines of Christianity,* both of which became standard works, at least to the extent that Unitarians would recognize any work as standard.[4]

Ellis believed that it was not difficult to state the four theological doctrines that commanded the widest assent in the movement: the unity and paternal character of God, the unity of Christ, the human potential for virtue as well as evil, and a view of the atonement as intended to alter the human heart rather than satisfy an abstract law or divine wrath. These four, properly defined, constituted, he thought, "a rational view of the Gospel," a series of principles that would come to the fore whenever the Bible was "thoroughly tested by reason" and read as a guide to the formation of Christian "character."[5]

The Controversy

Long before Channing rose to prominence the liberal clergy in New England had ceased to talk much about a Trinitarian God, and more than a few had ceased to believe in one. Rumors circulated about the heterodoxy of the liberal clergy as early as 1735, but not until Mayhew openly questioned the Trinity twenty years later and an anonymous dissenter in 1756 republished the *Humble Inquiry* of the English Unitarian Thomas Emlyn did the orthodox become alarmed. By 1768, Samuel Hopkins could claim that most of the ministers of Boston disbelieved the doctrine of the divinity of Christ. By 1785 James Freeman succeeded in leading the Episcopal congregation at King's Chapel in Boston to delete Trinitarian views from their liturgy.[6]

Channing once observed that the liberal clergy followed "the system of excluding controversy as much as possible from our pulpits," but the polemic against Calvinism shaped Unitarian theology from beginning to end. The struggle began around the turn of the century when Calvinist ministers began to exclude liberals from pulpit exchanges. It intensified in 1805 when the liberal Henry Ware, Sr. (1764–1845) won election as the Hollis Professor of Divinity at Harvard. It exploded again in 1815, when the Old Calvinist Jedidiah Morse (1761–1826), editor of an aggressive journal called *The Panoplist,* tried to embarrass the American liberals by linking them to the views of the English Unitarians.[7]

The more radical English Unitarianism did receive a hearing in America. In 1794 the English Unitarian minister Joseph Priestley migrated to Pennsylvania. English mobs had shown their dislike for Priestley's religion and his republican politics by plundering his house in Birmingham. After initially preaching in Elhanan Winchester's Universalist meetinghouse in Philadelphia, he helped organize in 1796 a small, short-lived Unitarian Society. His theology attracted a small community of English immigrants in Philadelphia, and it excited Thomas Jefferson and a few other American intellectuals.

Priestley agreed with the New Englanders in affirming the unity of God and rejecting the doctrines of Calvinism, including original sin, but he was a materialist who repudiated any notion of an immaterial soul. (He affirmed the physical resurrection of the body at the return of Jesus.) Unlike the early New Englanders, he taught that Jesus was merely a human teacher, and in his *History of the Corruptions of Christianity* (1782) and his *History of Early Opinions Concerning Jesus* (1789), Priestley denied that Jesus was sinless or that he possessed infallible knowledge. Unlike the New Englanders, moreover, he rejected any doctrine of atonement, believing that a benevolent God would forgive the penitent without requiring Jesus' death as a condition, and he eventually combined this belief with an argument for universal salvation. Unlike them, finally, he held a doctrine of divine providence that involved a determinist view of volition. Channing saw Priestley as striking a blow at "our most intimate and strongest moral convictions" and robbing human nature of all its "grandeur." When Morse tried to associate the Boston liberals with such English Unitarian views, Channing complained in an open letter of an "unchristian spirit."[8]

In 1819, at the ordination service of Jared Sparks in Baltimore, Channing preached the sermon on *Unitarian Christianity* that served as the manifesto of the movement. Interpret the Bible as one interprets any other book, he argued, and one must end up believing in the unity of God, the unity of Christ, the moral perfection of God, and the centrality of virtue in the Christian life. Channing employed the familiar principle of accommodation — the principle that God had adapted himself to human capacities — but for him it suggested that the truth of revelation was to be "decided at the bar of reason." All interpretation required the exercise of reason in accord with "the known truths of observation and experience." And a reasonable interpretation of the Bible revealed that the aim of the New Testament was "Christian virtue," which Channing defined as love for God manifested through rectitude of life, love for the Christ whose resurrection founded the hope of immortality, and the practice of benevolence. The sermon stimulated a round of written exchanges that came to be known as the "Unitarian Controversy."[9]

From Andover, Moses Stuart wrote a volume of *Letters to the Rev. Wm. E. Channing* (1819) in which he claimed that Channing had misread both the Bible and the orthodox position on the unity of God. For Stuart, the Trinitarian question was a matter of biblical facts. He pointed out that the New Testament assigned to Christ both divine and human attributes. The purpose of Trinitarian doctrine was to summarize these New Testament descriptions and relate them to other descriptions of the Father and the Spirit. Stuart conceded more than some of his allies wished. He said that the orthodox used the word "Person" in reference to the Trinity only because the "poverty of language" denied them a better word. He also rejected the "eternal Sonship" of the second Person on the grounds that "eternal generation" implied subordination. But he made known the orthodox determination to engage the issue on biblical terrain.[10]

The reply came from Andrews Norton, the only liberal who could match Stuart as a biblical critic. Convinced that "orthodoxy must be broken down," Norton had gained a reputation as a caustic critic of Calvinism's "barbarous jargon." He was, as one admirer noted, "not a man given to compromises." Channing looked askance at Norton's aggressiveness, but he had broad respect from the liberal clergy. In 1819, Norton wrote for the *Christian Disciple* an article that he later expanded into a book-length *Statement of Reasons for Not Believing the Doctrines of the Trinitarians* (1833). He argued that to posit three divine Persons while affirming one God was "essentially incredible." Efforts to explain Trinitarian doctrine, therefore, either resulted in tritheism or collapsed into a disguised unitarianism or a mere evasion. Stuart had chosen evasion by insisting that "Person" not be taken in its "usual sense" but refusing to specify the sense in which it should be taken. The related doctrine of the hypostatic union in Christ—the union of the human and divine in one Person —was even more incredible because it assumed that the same being could be finite and infinite at the same time.[11]

To Norton it was conclusive that no passage in the Bible "expressly taught" the doctrine of a threefold divine nature. In the gospels, rather, Christ spoke of himself as dependent and referred the divine power and inspiration manifest in his miracles and words to the Father who was greater than he. The orthodox case lacked biblical grounding. It consisted of absurdities imposed by the "later Platonists" of the fourth century on the biblical accounts. In addition, the orthodox overlooked the ambiguity of biblical language. They failed to recognize elementary distinctions between literal and figurative speech, or between cognitive and emotive discourse, or between ancient and modern linguistic conventions. Norton thought it self-evident that one should never interpret literally a sentence that "contradicts common sense" in its literal meaning. He took issue with Locke's belief that it was possible to express in human language truths that were "above reason." What could not be comprehended could not be revealed, and the Trinity was beyond comprehension.[12]

The Trinity, however, was not the main issue. When Norton concluded his book with the warning that the battle over the Trinity was also a battle about "happiness and virtue," he pointed toward the central question that troubled people on both sides. From a liberal perspective, Trinitarian thought was one part of a theological scheme that obscured the meaning of the New Testament by disparaging human nature, making it harder to recover the biblical ideal of virtue. The topic of human nature moved to the foreground when Leonard Woods, the Edwardean Calvinist colleague of Stuart at Andover, took on Henry Ware in an exchange that lasted for two years. Baconian assumptions governed the debate. Woods's *Letters to Unitarians* (1820) announced that the dispute about human nature came down to the question, "What is fact?" Theologians dealt with facts, not speculative theories, and the facts pointed, Woods thought, to "innate moral depravity."[13]

By "facts" Woods meant the objects of true propositions grounded in revelation and experience. Channing had said that moral depravity was inconsistent with the perfection of God. A morally perfect God would not allow infants to come into the world in a state of original sin. Woods thought that he missed the point. The book of Genesis described a universal wickedness, and Paul confirmed that everyone sinned, without exception (Rom. 5:12). These were propositions from an infallible revelation; they pointed therefore to real facts. The same infallible revelation declared it a fact that God was morally perfect. Theologians might not be able to discover by the "mere exercise of reason" the consistency of these two facts, but this did not prove them inconsistent. It proved only the limits of reason.[14]

Henry Ware had been the pastor for eighteen years in Hingham, Massachusetts, before he became the first theologian in Harvard's new divinity school. It fell to him to make the case against Woods. The principal argument in his *Letters Addressed to Trinitarians and Calvinists* (1820) was that if Woods's two claims could not be proved consistent, one of them had to be false. The truth, Ware argued, was that human nature was neither good nor bad in abstraction from human actions; men and women were "free from all moral corruption, as well as destitute of all positive holiness" until they actually formed, by their choices, a character either good or bad. Ware proposed, like Woods, to appeal to the facts. Nowhere, he claimed, did scripture expressly assert a doctrine of innate depravity. It taught only that everyone sinned, an assertion—a fact—that no Unitarian denied. Ware thought it more consistent with scripture and experience to attribute this sinfulness to the "voluntary" abuse of human nature.[15]

The debate between Woods and Ware covered everything from the psychology of motivation to the moral nature of children and the goodness of God. Both men agreed that the issues were "in the highest degree practical." Both kept returning, therefore, to the "moral tendency" of the two schemes. Woods thought that Unitarian theology would form a prideful and moralistic community; Ware thought that Calvinist theology led to the neglect of moral exertion and to spiritual lassitude. Jared Sparks (1789–1866), the first minister of the Baltimore Unitarian Church and later the president of Harvard, conducted in 1820 a similar debate with Samuel Miller of Princeton. Sparks found in the Calvinist suggestion that men and women "sin from necessity" an "immoral tendency" that discouraged hope for improvement. The Unitarian system would be far more likely to "fix the principles of religion in the soul, and to produce the fruits of piety, righteousness, and a good life."[16]

William Ellery Channing

The Unitarian view of theology as practical helps to explain the honor the liberals paid to Channing, a man who felt far more at home in the pulpit or on the lecture stand than he did in the study. He detested systems, and he could not be called a systematic theologian, but since he believed that all the doctrines of Christianity were "designed to teach the supreme worth of Christian virtue," he had a standard by which to provide a "practical" interpretation of all the traditional topics of theology. Unitarians would appeal to his example and his ideas for the remainder of the century.[17]

A native of Newport, Rhode Island, Channing had spent his first twelve years as the neighbor of Samuel Hopkins. He would later honor Hopkins for his willingness to reason about religion, his awareness that the human fault resided in the will rather than the understanding, his doctrine of unlimited atonement, and his treatment of impartial benevolence. Some have viewed Channing as an eccentric Hopkinsian Calvinist, but he saw Hopkins's theology as "appalling."[18]

It was his reading of British moral thought as a student at Harvard that set the direction of his thinking. He read works by Francis Hutcheson, Thomas Reid, Joseph Butler, and Richard Price. He found himself drawn especially to Price (1723–91), a Welsh dissenting minister who espoused a Unitarian theology and an ethical philosophy opposed to the moral sense theories of Anthony Ashley Cooper, earl of Shaftesbury, and Francis Hutcheson. Price introduced Channing to the Platonic view of ideas and convinced him that the intuitive understanding, as opposed to either a separate moral sense or the more discursive and calculating reason, could attain an immediate knowledge of eternal and immutable moral principles. Channing preferred to speak of reason where Price would have said understanding, but he thought that Price had saved him from a narrowly empirical form of Lockean epistemology.[19]

In Price he found a philosopher who criticized the excesses of empiricism. Price argued that the understanding stood in judgment over the senses and rose above them. Even to distinguish a stone from a tree was to use general categories of the understanding, like essence, number, identity, solidity, or causation, that were not given in the sensory experiences themselves. It was the understanding that gave rise to these "original ideas," which included the ideas of right and wrong. Such ideas were intuitions, or presuppositions of any coherent experience. Channing's appropriations from Price would endear him to the transcendentalists, who turned to similar ideas about intuitive reason, but Channing also held to the Baconian evidentialism that was anathema to Ralph Waldo Emerson and his transcendental friends.[20]

From one perspective, Channing founded his theology on his confidence in "the use of reason in interpreting Scripture." He pointed out that scripture was addressed to human reason, and he liked to remind his critics that any reading of scripture presupposed the operation of ideas, like causation, that had their origin in the processes of human understanding. Without denying that revelation stood above reason, providing access to truths that reason could not have discovered, Channing refused to accept any reading of scripture that seemed repugnant to reason. He explained in his sermon on "Christianity a Rational Religion" that reason meant universality and consistency; it comprehended universal truths and strove to unify them. Unlike more traditional evidentialists, who thought that reason authenticated the revelation but then had to submit to revealed truths that it could not validate, Channing believed that each scriptural truth should commend itself to rational inquiry.[21]

He never saw reasonableness, however, as an end in itself. The end of both reason and revelation was the perfecting of "the Moral power." For Channing, Christ's mediation had the "moral end" of engendering "a generous and divine virtue." It nurtured "the laws of our moral nature" and perfected "all the virtues." When he described theology as a "practical discourse," he meant, as the eighteenth-century theologians of virtue had meant, that it promoted the love of God and neighbor and strengthened character. Every doctrine was to be "urged simply and exclusively for this end." Christianity had one great principle: "This great principle can be briefly expressed. It is the doctrine that God purposes, in his unbounded fatherly love, to perfect the human soul; to purify it from all sin; to create it after his own image; to fill it with his own spirit; to unfold it forever; to raise it to life and immortality in heaven, — that is to communicate to it from himself a life of celestial power, virtue, and joy." Channing's nephew later published several of his sermons under the title *The Perfect Life* (1872). Their aim was to show that the perfecting of the soul was "the beginning and end of Christianity." This was a far cry from the divinizing perfectionism of seventeenth-century sectarians like Samuel Gorton or John Rogers, the Quakers' perfect conformity with the Inner Light, the discernible experience of entire sanctification as proclaimed by the Methodists, or the perfect obedience of the revivalist Charles Finney, but Channing, like them, was a perfectionist in theology.[22]

Like other Christian perfectionists, Channing sought perfection because Jesus called on his disciples to "be perfect" (Matt. 5:58), but his ideal of perfection blended New Testament Christianity, Stoicism, and Neoplatonic ethics. When he listed the virtues, he combined the New Testament ideals of love of God, love of neighbor, self-denial, forgiveness, and self-sacrifice, with the Stoic ideals of calmness, constancy, fortitude, and magnanimity. He thought that British moral philosophy and "Stoical morality" — not Hopkins's New Divinity — had predisposed him to the ideal of disinterested benevolence. During his brief career as a tutor in Virginia after college, he made so much of Stoicism that his brother finally told him that he was no Stoic. His brother was correct. Channing sought rather a Platonic ideal of perfection as a harmony of the soul in which "the whole nature of a being is unfolded in due proportion, so that the highest and worthiest powers will hold ascendancy, and all others, by acting in their true spheres, will fulfill the end for which they were given." Channing could sometimes sound like Jonathan Edwards discoursing on harmony and excellency.[23]

In revising theology in accord with the ideal of perfection, he discarded the doctrine of original sin. He denied both infant depravity and the idea of imputed sin. He conceded human sinfulness, but he traced it to "voluntary wrong-doing," the willful transgression of a command, and he rejected the idea that it left the soul helpless. When he spoke of "the divinity of human nature," however, he was referring not to its inherent or achieved goodness but to its capacity for transcendence, its ability to yield the new, to push in thought, imagination, and moral harmony beyond its current limits. To him this aspiration, even insatiability, of the soul showed that it partook of infinity and found its perfection only in the Infinite One.[24]

His ideal of perfection informed his criticisms of Trinitarian theology. On one level, Channing found the doctrine of the Trinity irrational; to say that three Persons constituted one substance seemed to him to utter words without meaning, and like Norton, he also found no evidence for the doctrine in scripture. But Trinitarian doctrine had for him dangerous religious and moral consequences. Its incarnational corollary entangled God in a material body — a fatal flaw for a theologian who linked spiritual perfection to a dualistic rendering of matter and spirit. It also diminished devotion to the Father, an equally serious error for a theologian who assumed that the perfecting of character occurred through devotion to the one perfect Paternal Being.[25]

Channing's favorite image for God was Father, and he thought that the recovery of that biblical image was a signal contribution of Unitarians to modern theology. God's fatherhood had implications for human moral perfection. Channing's essay on "Likeness to God" (1828) — in which he contended that true religion made men and women "more and more partakers of the Divinity" — argued that the metaphor of Father expressed a spiritual relation in which one mind educated another after its own likeness. Speaking of God as Father was another way of saying that God was "the perfection of our own spiritual nature," the ideal reality toward which all striving was to be directed.[26]

Describing God in accord with the theology of virtue, Channing emphasized God's immanence in the creation. With Neoplatonic imagery he contended that God delighted "to diffuse himself everywhere." Might the human intellect, he once asked, "not be God in a more direct sense than we can imagine?" Channing's God was an infinite Mind present within the world but not identifiable with it. He emphasized the affinity between this Mind and human minds, proposing that theologians speak of God by selecting "the qualities which they esteemed most highly" in human beings and enlarging them without bounds. The idea of God was "the idea of our own spiritual nature, purified and enlarged to infinity," and only when God was defined in this way could virtue have a solid grounding. If a growing likeness to God was the goal, it was unwise to posit a God whose perfection could have nothing in common with human perfection.[27]

Equally dangerous was a deified Christ. It made no sense to Channing to talk of two natures in one person, and he found the idea of Jesus' subordination to God throughout the New Testament. Uppermost among his reasons for rejecting the traditional doctrine was that it placed the emphasis on Christ's "rank" rather than on his "character." For Channing the "efficacy" of the Christian religion lay in the character of Jesus, who revealed through his virtues both God's perfection and the ideal of human striving. The calling of the Christian was to become one with Christ "in feeling, in power, in holiness." Anything that drew attention from the excellence of Jesus' character therefore diminished true religion.[28]

Channing's Jesus was always "more than a human being." He conceded that some of the liberals believed only in the "simple humanity" of Jesus, but he never himself stopped believing that Christ was the "divine Master," the "Son of God" in whom "the fullness of the divinity dwelt." Yet Channing never managed to escape ambiguity. He said in 1815 that Christ "existed before the world" and that "he literally came from heaven to save our race." He had been impressed by reading the English Independent Isaac Watts (1674–1748), who claimed biblical authority for affirming Christ's preexistence while denying him equality with God. But Channing later argued that Christ attained his unique status through his obedience and reverence for goodness. If the two different ideas revealed a change in Channing's thinking, he never acknowledged it.[29]

He did not accept older theories of the atonement, with their notions of substitution, imputation, and satisfaction, for they called God's love into question. Even governmental theories made God's reign one of terror and not paternal love. Such theories were "unfavorable to character." They suggested that Christ came to change God's mind rather than to communicate holiness and "form us to a sublime and heavenly virtue." Channing conceded that the liberals differed in their assessments of Christ's death; some thought that it procured forgiveness by evoking repentance; others, among whom Channing numbered himself, thought it had a "special influence in removing punishment," though he could not explain how. What was important was that it promoted virtue.[30]

Virtue implied the freedom of the will, and Channing ridiculed the Edwardean distinction between natural and moral ability as meaningless. He thought of salvation as the result of free choices and voluntary obedience. The value of faith was that it produced a freely willed "virtuous obedience" that pressed toward perfection. Channing equated faith with belief that Christ and his religion came from God, but for him such belief served the end of obedience. He had no intention of denying divine grace. He thought that God's grace presented itself in all God's acts of mercy, especially in the "influx of light and strength" that God granted to all who sought it, and that there could be no salvation without it. It was grace when the Spirit illumined and persuaded the moral faculties. But "grace" could never for Channing become a warrant for depreciating either freedom or the obedience that perfected the soul in virtue.[31]

In 1841, shortly before his death, Channing rued the rise of "Unitarian orthodoxy." His comment enabled some of his admirers to isolate Channing from the continuing Unitarian movement and to view his successors, in Emerson's phrase, as "corpse cold" rationalists, drab Lockeans intent on proofs and evidences and constrained by genteel norms of respectability. Such a judgment oversimplified a complicated history.[32]

The Unitarian Conservatives

From the outset, Unitarians retained the pietistic inwardness that had been part of the New England tradition since the seventeenth century. They departed from the older morphology of conversion and the introspective quest for signs of grace, and they spurned the "excitement of the feelings" generated by revivalism, but they thought of Christianity as "not merely a truth but a sentiment" and they described themselves as "friends to Experimental Religion." Their ideal was "constant and genial warmth" rather than heats of revivalist fever.[33]

The most prominent figure in the promotion of the more pietist, devotional side of Unitarianism was Henry Ware, Jr. (1798–1843), the pastor at the Second Church in Boston until 1830, when he joined the Harvard faculty as the professor of pastoral theology and pulpit eloquence. Apart from Channing's sermons, no Unitarian writing found greater favor with the public than Ware's short treatise *On the Formation of the Christian Character* (1831), which located the essence of religion in the moral sentiments and in the performance of Christian duties in accord with "the teachings and example of Jesus Christ." Ware cautioned against identifying true religion with a "cold judgment of the intellect." His contention was that "thought, reflection, inquiry, [and] argument" remained incomplete until they led to "devotion and duty." His book was a manual of piety showing how prayer, meditation, worship, and self-discipline might form a Christian character by governing the inner life so diligently that virtuous dispositions would become second nature.[34]

For a few Unitarians the emphasis on a religion of the heart was so pronounced that theology become a hindrance. This was the conclusion of Lydia Maria Francis Child (1802–80), who gained celebrity as an editor, an author of books on motherhood and family life, an abolitionist author, and a popular historian of women's experience. In her three-volume *Progress of Religious Ideas Through Successive Ages* (1855), she placed Christianity alongside other world religions, which she attempted to describe with sympathy, though she believed that the Christian religion contained within itself "a vital element of progress superior to any other spiritual influence." Convinced that religion was a state of feeling rather than of knowing — "sentiments of reverence toward God, and of justice and benevolence toward our fellow men" — she concluded that "religion diminishes in the same proportion that theology increases." She thought it "impossible to exaggerate the evil work" theology had done in the world, stifling the religious affections and obscuring the pure precepts of Jesus by identifying Christianity with transient formulations of doctrine.[35]

The main trend of Unitarian thought moved in another direction. The formation of an American Unitarian Association in 1825 created a need for positive doctrinal definition. Ezra Stiles Gannett (1801–71), the successor to Channing at the Federal Street Church and the driving force behind the new organization, recognized that the association needed "affirmative propositions." The push for clearer doctrinal definition intensified after Ralph Waldo Emerson's Divinity School Address in 1838, in which he scandalized most

Unitarians by elevating the intuitive reason over the Bible and ridiculing any "noxious" exaggeration of the person of Jesus. Three years later Theodore Parker intensified the scandal by arguing that Unitarians should abandon notions of special revelation and the authority of Christ. Over the next two decades, some Unitarians abandoned theology altogether. By far the larger majority, however, strove to reinforce lines of continuity between Unitarian theology and Christian tradition.[36]

In 1840 Gannett pointed out that almost all Unitarians affirmed a special biblical revelation, viewed Jesus as the "necessary" revealer of divine truth, and saw the gospel as a means for deliverance from sin. By that time some of them, like Nathaniel L. Frothingham (1793–1870) at Boston's First Church, urged that Unitarians formulate a creed. In his 1845 lectures on *Deism or Christianity?*, he contended that only a creed could let Unitarians know what they believed. Religion was "a doctrine as well as a sentiment." The creedal faction that Frothingham led did not succeed, but they reflected the trend toward more definite doctrinal self-understanding. Whether they were defending their empirical epistemology or restating their doctrine of Christ, the conservative Unitarians sought a theology that could be distinguished from both transcendentalism and orthodoxy.[37]

Conservative Unitarians defined themselves in part by their loyalty to the Baconian empirical philosophy. When Emerson and his friends valorized an intuitive reason that transcended the senses and the discursive understanding, more traditional Unitarians sensed danger. They could accept the idea of "spiritual perceptions" analogous to the perceptions of sense. James Walker (1794–1874), the Alford Professor of Natural Religion at Harvard and later the university's president, defended the reality of such perceptions in a celebrated sermon in 1834 on "The Philosophy of Man's Spiritual Nature in Regard to the Foundations of Faith." Nonetheless, Walker welcomed the limits on reason imposed by the Scottish philosophy. So also did Francis Bowen (1811–90), a tutor in philosophy at Harvard who would later hold a Harvard chair and the editorship of the *North American Review*. In 1837, in a review of Emerson's *Nature*, he sounded an alarm about any departure from the principles of Baconianism, insisting that sound theology required the evidentialist appeal to "facts." His *Critical Essays on a Few Subjects Connected with the History and Present Condition of Speculative Philosophy* (1842) distinguished him as the Unitarians' most adept critic of idealism, pantheism, and intuitionist epistemology. The conservatives shared his conviction that sound theology depended on a Baconian view of reason.[38]

One motive for this defense of empirical epistemology was to shore up the Paleyite natural theology that the transcendentalists had ridiculed. The conservatives could not accept the Emersonian claim that an intuitive insight could replace the patient accumulation of facts in support of design. They still admired Paley's *Natural Theology,* and in their more technical essays, like the senior Henry Ware's two-volume *Inquiry into the Foundation, Evidence, and Truths of Religion* (1842), they continued to lay out the rational evidence for the existence of God, especially the argument from design. They were determined to maintain the alliance between religion and science, and they thought that the transcendentalist disdain for empirical methods would sever it.[39]

Equally important as a motive for their attachment to empiricism was their investment in the evidential arguments, especially the argument that miracles confirmed the New Testament teachings. In 1836, Orville Dewey (1794–1882), an Andover graduate who had assisted Channing for two years and was beginning his pastorate at the Second Congregational Church in New York City, complained in his Dudleian Lecture at Harvard about the "presumption against miracles" in European liberal circles. Warning against natural explanations for the New Testament miracle narratives, he argued that Christianity was "founded on miracles." When Emerson, two years later, disparaged miracles as evidences, the conservatives rallied in their defense. In 1839, Andrews Norton attacked Emerson and German liberal theology in a *Discourse on the Latest Form of Infidelity* (1839) in which he argued that to deny the "miracles attesting the divine mission of Christ" was to strike at the root of Christian faith. Norton rehearsed the familiar arguments against David Hume, which he extended to counter David Friedrich Strauss and the German liberals. To defend empiricism was to rest Christianity on the testimony of eyewitnesses who had seen the miracles. To discard empiricism was to imply that their testimony was irrelevant.[40]

Appeals to the biblical miracles became a recurrent feature of conservative Unitarian thought, but some of the conservatives backed away from the prophetic proof. George Noyes's argument in 1834 that the prophetic predictions of a conquering messianic king could not have applied to Jesus convinced more than a few. Already in 1835 Andrew Preston Peabody acknowledged that the Old Testament prophecies could not prove Jesus' divine mission, though Peabody believed that some of them did refer to him as the Messiah. Eventually even Frothingham redefined the prophetic proof to mean only that Christ had satisfied "vague expectations" in ancient Israel.[41]

The concern for the miracle accounts was merely one expression of the weight that Unitarians placed on the New Testament. Though some questioned, with Norton, the divine authority of the Old Testament, no conservative doubted the claim of William Ware (1797–1852), the pastor of All Souls Church in New York City, that Unitarianism was nothing other than "the religion of the New Testament." Unitarians no longer believed in infallible inspiration, but most viewed the Bible as a vehicle for the communication of revealed truths, professed that the New Testament conveyed "unfailing knowledge" of the inspired doctrine of Christ, and contrasted their reliance on biblical revelation with deism and transcendentalism.[42]

Among the revealed truths in the New Testament, none was more important than the revelation of a personal God. One early Unitarian response to Emerson's 1838 address — at least, most took it to be such — came from Henry Ware, Jr., who was preaching at the time a series of sermons in the Harvard College chapel. Two months after Emerson spoke, Ware preached on "The Personality of the Deity," warning against the danger of reducing God to "a set of principles or a code of laws." "There is a personal God," Ware wrote, "or there is none." The order in the creation suggested an agent as orderer, worship required a Person as its object, and belief in a personal God preserved a sense of moral responsibility, but equally important, revelation presupposed a Person as revealer and the biblical God had personal attributes. After 1838, the Unitarians often identified themselves by contrasting their idea of a paternal and personal God both with the Calvinist sovereign and with the impersonal transcendentalist Law.[43]

When Emerson and Parker said that Christ was not essential to a pure Christianity, they also pushed the second-generation Unitarians to rethink Christology. Even though conservatives denied the deity of Christ, as it was understood by their opponents, they accepted the Christian consensus that Jesus revealed God, taught divine truth, performed miracles, died a redemptive death, and rose from the dead as a guaranty of eternal life. Their piety found expression in such works as the younger Henry Ware's *Discourses on the Offices and Character of Jesus Christ* (1825) and his more popular *Life of the Saviour* (1833), which depicted "a teacher and reformer, claiming to bear a special commission, from God, and confirming his pretensions by supernatural works."[44]

Samuel Gilman (1791–1858), who had the task of promoting the Unitarian gospel in Charleston, South Carolina, laid out in 1829 a position that would command wide assent among later Unitarians: Jesus was neither God nor a mere human being, but he had a "glory peculiarly his own" because God conferred on him an "unlimited exaltation," and he died to reconcile the sinful to God. By the 1840s most Unitarians agreed with Frothingham that Jesus was "the Son of God with power," even though they differed about what this meant. For some, it meant a doctrine of the eternal generation of the Son; for others, it defined a Christ who was preexistent yet subordinate to the Father; and for yet others, it referred to a miraculous divine endowment of power to a fully human

Jesus. Nonetheless, in 1853 the American Unitarian Association affirmed belief in Christ as a supernatural Messiah through whom God made a "special and miraculous interposition" into the world for the redemption of humanity. They also disagreed about the meaning of the atonement. Some accepted a governmental theory, but most interpreted atonement to mean that Christ's life and death had the power to transform human affections. As Gannett wrote, it was a case of "moral influence," not of "mystery." But after Emerson, conservative Unitarians reiterated their devotion to the atoning Christ.[45]

They still deplored the Calvinist insistence on original sin and dramatic conversion, but they became increasingly inclined to emphasize sinfulness and the need for regeneration. Ellis observed in 1857 that any idea of imputed guilt was still "infinitely" objectionable to Unitarians, who tended to equate sinfulness with selfish dispositions formed by sinful choices, but some, like Gannett could speak of "depravity," though not total depravity. Rebirth into a new disposition, a gradual and difficult journey, also required choices. A change of heart, Gannett explained, must be "effected by the sinner's own will in cooperation with God's spiritual influence." W. G. Eliot described it as a radical "change in motives and affections," occurring through a gradual alteration of the heart as Christians, assisted by grace, consistently chose the way of virtue.[46]

Their belief that the aim of the Christian life was virtue made Unitarians wary of sermons about justification by faith that did not append careful qualifications. They thought that Luther and other early Protestant reformers had erred in seeming to separate justification from moral goodness, for in their reading of the New Testament they found, as Dewey pointed out, that "the Bible everywhere demands repentance, sanctification, inward purity, as the means of favor with God." Francis William Pitt Greenwood, the preacher at King's Chapel in Boston, taught his congregation in 1847 the standard Unitarian view that the only faith that justified was a "faith producing good works abundantly." He was recapitulating the eighteenth-century theology of virtue.[47]

Because of how Unitarians understood regeneration and virtue, no doctrine drew more attention in Unitarian popular writing than the doctrine of "probation," the view of life as a period of preparation and trial for "the happiness of an eternal world." The purpose of mortal existence was to enable men and women to prepare themselves, by enduring difficulty, overcoming temptation, and building moral character, for "an eternity of conscious existence." Probation explained suffering in this world; it shored up ideas of freedom and responsibility; and it made sense of the doctrine of a future judgment. Probation even allowed for a Unitarian form of pulpit evangelism: since the forming of a character worthy of heaven required time, it had to be undertaken without delay.[48]

Unitarians found it difficult to reconcile their idea of God's paternal care with the notion of a judgment that would send anyone to an eternal hell, but most of them found it equally difficult to take an outright stand for universal salvation. Universalism seemed incongruent with their doctrine of probation and their solicitude for moral virtue. Most declined to think that "all alike, at the close of this preparatory state, should enter on a state of equal felicity." One popular solution was to speculate that the obdurately hardened sinner might resist God's love forever and therefore suffer forever a punitive pain, which Unitarian sermons depicted as fearful and horrifying, but the younger Ware discouraged speculation, and most followed his admonition. Yet hell still meant something, even if did not mean a literal place of fire and physical suffering. Sermons like James Walker's on "The Day of Judgment" warned that if this was a "world of probation," the next world would be one of "retribution," whatever its duration might be.[49]

Unitarianism was no otherworldly theology, for a host of social activists found in Unitarian theology the justification for service to the poor, moral reform, and opposition to slavery, but Unitarian preachers also dwelt, especially in their popular writings and sermons, on the promise of heavenly rewards. They stood among the many American theologians of every denomination who welcomed the momentous transition in depictions of heaven that had occurred since the eighteenth century. In earlier Christian history, theologians had described the heavenly state primarily as one in which the redeemed would praise and adore God. By the eighteenth century, they began to speak of heaven more as a continuation of earthly life, with its social relationships, family ties, and energetic activity. When Channing urged Unitarians to promote "a more definite conception of the future state," he was urging that they depict heaven as a place of loving relationships with kindred and friends, lively conversation, and energetic growth in knowledge and virtue. Unitarian clergy took up the idea with enthusiasm.[50]

Andrew Preston Peabody expressed in 1847 the theme that would define many a Unitarian consolation treatise: "I can hold no sympathy," he wrote, "with that stern, gloomy mood of theological teaching which tells us that our affection for our kindred and friends ought to be here, and will be in heaven, completely merged in our love for God and for man in general." Instead, he described heaven as a place of domestic joy, renewed friendships, and wholesome activity. He and his colleagues shied away from millennial speculation, and they ceased to draw graphic depictions of a literal day of judgment. James Walker explained that the biblical images referred not literally to a judgment day but figuratively to the judgment that each individual would face immediately after death, as lifetime habits and dispositions stood revealed before the ideal of virtue. But like other American Christians of the period, they had a remarkable confidence that they could describe a heavenly world with a wealth of detail.[51]

The Broad Church Unitarians

By the 1840s, the Unitarians, many of whom had resisted becoming a separate denomination, began to struggle with what it meant to be a church. Some of the impetus came from theologians sympathetic to some of the contentions of the transcendentalists but unwilling to affirm either their individualism or their contempt for tradition. At the same time, they were uneasy that the conservatives seemed so willing to define doctrine in ways that excluded one wing of the movement. They sought an inclusive church, open both to transcendentalists and to Unitarians desirous of greater respect for the historic creeds, liturgies, and communal sensibility of the worldwide church. Their leading spokesmen were James Freeman Clarke (1810–88) and Frederic Henry Hedge (1805–90). Hedge furnished the label with which they would be described when he published in 1860 an article on "The Broad Church." The label came from struggles within the Church of England, which Hedge followed closely. He edited in 1860 an American edition of the *Essays and Reviews* (1860) of seven authors often associated with an Anglican Broad Church group calling for free inquiry in religion. But the "broad" theology of Hedge and his allies was a response to issues in the American Unitarian movement.[52]

Clarke and Hedge would publish their most important works after the Civil War. Clarke's *Orthodoxy: Its Truths and Errors* (1866) attempted to find the true "substance" — the usable truth — in traditional doctrines that Unitarians had rejected. His *Ten Great Religions* (1871), the first extended American discussion of what was then called "comparative theology," expressed his hope that a purified Christianity could one day become the religion of humanity. Hedge's *Reason in Religion* (1865) distinguished between the truths of the "understanding," or scientific rationality, and the functions of "reason" as a critical principle making theological judgments possible, and differentiated both from the knowledge of faith. But even though both attained their reputations primarily after the war, they began their careers as theologians during the 1840s, and both shared in the long discussion that led to the creation in 1865 of the National Conference of Unitarian Churches — the event that most clearly marked the growing denominational consciousness of the movement.[53]

Both Clarke and Hedge graduated from Harvard College and from the Divinity School. Both joined in the transcendentalist movement, and the group was sometimes called the "Hedge Club," because it met whenever

Hedge was in town. Both believed that religion rested on intuitive knowledge as well as biblical truths. Both hoped for a Unitarian community that would include everyone who might "seek our fellowship in Christ's name." Both became local pastors and concluded that the Emersonians — and their successors in the Free Religion movement — failed to recognize the importance of the church. Hedge held a series of pastorates in Massachusetts, Maine, and Rhode Island before becoming in 1857 the professor of ecclesiastical history at Harvard. Clarke carried Unitarianism to Louisville, Kentucky, where he served a church and edited the movement's *Western Messenger* before returning to Boston in 1841, where he founded a reform-minded congregation known as the Church of the Disciples.[54]

Clarke envisioned the Church of the Disciples as a congregation preparing the way for a "church of the future" that would be open to all who professed their allegiance to Christ, whether they be orthodox, unitarian, or transcendentalist. In a brief treatise on *The Church* written in 1848 to explain the meaning of his venture, he called for a community with only the one article of "faith in Christ" as its creed. But he directed his criticisms most pointedly against the Emersonians who saw no need for a visible church. Clarke thought that the impulse for community was rooted in human nature, and that only through uniting with each other could Christians embody their faith in service to the world.[55]

Frederic Henry Hedge placed Unitarian thought about the church in the larger context of Christian history. Hedge studied four years in a German *gymnasium,* and for the rest of his life he transmitted German culture and literature to America, both through editorial work as in his *Prose Writers of Germany* (1848) and through such incisive essays as his 1833 article in the *Christian Examiner* on Samuel Taylor Coleridge, which was the first influential exposition of Kant, Johann Gottlieb Fichte, and Friedrich Wilhelm Joseph von Schelling by a native-born American. Just as Emerson's divinity school address of 1838 was the manifesto of transcendentalism, so also Hedge's divinity school address of 1849 was the most cogent statement of Broad Church Unitarianism. A critique both of transcendental individualism and of the creedalism of the conservatives, Hedge's address set forth his ideal of the church as the embodiment of the Spirit, able to contain diverse gifts and theologies, developing through history under providential oversight. Two years later he wrote that the "church question" was "the prominent question of the day," and he wanted to add a Unitarian voice to a debate that was raging across the country.[56]

Hedge found in the "theory of progressive development" the key to the history of the church and the clue to the movement of the Spirit. Theology for

Hedge was the effort to express in categories of the "understanding" the experience of a Spirit that revealed itself over centuries and providentially led the church to a progressive comprehension of truth. Each historic doctrine, including the doctrines of the Trinity and original sin, expressed a "legitimate form of Christianity" for a particular place and time, embodying the truth that "the time required." A comprehensive church, he wrote in 1860, would combine continuity and movement, experience and form. Certain ideas, like reconciliation and atonement in Christ, Hedge considered fixed and unchangeable; the expression of those ideas would vary over time. Such a church would always nurture a "consciousness of God," exemplified above all in the great mystics of the Christian tradition whom Hedge always honored; the same Spirit that generated such experience, however, would always become "articulate in forms and rites." Hedge edited a *Christian Liturgy for the Use of the Church* (1853) that included retrievals from ancient Greek liturgies. This theory of development in history allowed him to value a "true catholicism," including the contributions to Christendom of the Roman Catholic Church, in ways quite uncharacteristic of Protestants in antebellum America.[57]

Hedge and Clarke worked closely with Henry Whitney Bellows (1814–82), the pastor of the First Unitarian Church of New York City and the dominant Unitarian leader of mid-century. During the 1850s Bellows was more receptive than they to calls for a broad creedal statement, but the three shared disquiet about the absence in Unitarianism of a profound sense of the church. In an 1859 address at Harvard that he called "The Suspense of Faith," Bellows called for Unitarians to answer "the Church question" by recognizing that religion meant more than "human development and self-perfection" and that maturity as a Christian required "the organic, ritualized, impersonal, steady, patient work of the Church" as a "divine and specific institution." The address created a mild uproar, but it defined one of the issues that would engage Unitarians for the next half century.[58]

The Broad Church group did not abandon the Unitarian theology of virtue. Hedge still saw Christianity as a means to promote moral and spiritual growth. Their aim was to expand the conception of virtue to include issues of social injustice, and Hedge later concluded that the meaning of such a Christian doctrine as atonement, which he viewed as a power of at-one-ment, was to be found partially in its application to social relations. For him and for Clarke, a "practical Christianity" would address the questions of nineteenth-century society.[59]

From Channing to Hedge, Unitarian preachers had a social conscience. In Boston, they pioneered in new forms of ministry to the poor. But they recognized that they spoke for an educated middle class, and they pursued their theological program partly because they believed that Christian theology was losing the allegiance of the educated. Unitarians worried that Christian faith might suffer in America the fate of Christianity in parts of Europe where, wrote Andrews Norton, "scarcely an intelligent and well-informed Christian is left." They saw their movement as a reformation of theology designed for "enlightened minds." The elder Ware believed that liberal doctrines saved for Christianity men and women of "cultivated minds and enlarged views" who would otherwise reject "the popular creeds." Unitarian views, he claimed, attract "the most elevated, intelligent, and enlightened."[60]

Partly for this reason, most of the early Unitarians viewed populist forms of theology with suspicion. Even Channing, with his pronounced sympathy for the laboring classes, found it incredible that the untrained would presume "to decide on the most intricate points, and to pass sentence on men whose lives have been devoted to the study of the Scriptures." Contemptuous of "the rabble's smile, the rabble's nod," Andrews Norton numbered himself in "the party of the few" who transcended the "miserable love of popularity." To him it seemed that the "spirit of democracy" had created a "poisonous atmosphere" that corroded everything beautiful. Unitarians sometimes resisted the criticism that their reform was suited only for the "select and favored few" rather than the "common people," but they maintained their distance from populist movements, even movements that reached conclusions very much like their own. Some of the distinctions between academic and populist forms of American theology would surface especially in the contrast between the Unitarians and the Universalists.[61]

Universal Salvation

In 1829, Hosea Ballou, the pastor of the Second Universalist Society in Boston, issued to the public a series of commendations and reproofs directed at the Unitarians. He commended them for their affirmation of the unity and fatherly character of God, for their rejection of the doctrine of depravity, for their belief that regeneration occurred through gradual growth rather than a radical alteration of character, and for their confidence in the right of the individual to exercise reason in reading scripture. He reproved them for refusing to acknowledge that their principles led necessarily to the doctrine of universal salvation. He chided them, as well, for their lack of charity in refusing pulpit exchanges with Universalist clergy, whose theology did not "come exactly to their views." The "Unitarian doctors" failed to observe their own principles of liberality.[1]

Ballou rightly observed that Unitarians and Universalists brought to theology many of the same passions. Like the Unitarians, the Universalists repudiated Calvinism, appealed to a fresh reading of scripture, and advertised themselves as the architects of a rational theology. Both opposed an orthodoxy that they found "unreasonable, unscriptural, and heart-hardening." Both shared the American enthusiasm for evidential theology; the Universalists produced conventional treatises defending the evidential force of the prophecies and the biblical miracles. Even though they drew their inspiration from quite different forms of European thought, both engaged in a larger European conversation. For quite different reasons, both shared a concern with the moral dimensions of Christian faith. While the earliest Universalists remained Trinitarian, many of their successors shared with the Unitarians similar views of Christ, the atonement, and the unity of God.[2]

Despite the doctrinal similarities, however, the culture of the Universalists had little in common with the Unitarian ethos. It had a different leadership and appealed to a different social class. Universalism became an organized movement among those whom the Philadelphia physician Benjamin Rush described as "the second and lower classes of our citizens." Rush himself, who remained a nominal Presbyterian but greatly admired Elhanan Winchester and often attended his church, was an exception. The cultural centers of the movement were in the hill country of rural New England, the working-class neighborhoods of the northeastern cities, and the small towns of western New York among people far removed from the powerful and the educated. The New England Baptist Isaac Backus suspected that most of the educated ministers of late eighteenth-century Boston quietly accepted the universalism of Charles Chauncy, but New England liberal Congregationalists kept their distance from the Universalist preachers.[3]

The Unitarians spoke for a society of merchants and civic leaders, the Universalists for a society of mechanics, farmers, and shopkeepers. Most Unitarians supported the legal establishment of the Christian churches in New England; Universalists raged against religious establishments. Unitarians honored the biblical scholarship of the learned; Universalists affirmed the authority of common people to "read and study the scriptures for themselves." Unitarians cherished Harvard as a center of theological learning. The earliest Universalists disdained any "theological school of human establishment." They relied not on "the writings of great and learned men, who have been at the trouble of inventing schemes of their own" but on the Bible alone for their doctrine. Unitarians deplored populist theology; Universalists were inveterate populists.[4]

Critics of Universalist doctrines scored polemical points by ridiculing Universalists as vulgar. Universalists responded by decrying the "philosophical divinity" and "unintelligible jargon" of the learned. The Universalist John Murray announced his scorn for the "studied Elegance of Style" that he associated with the clerical elite. He claimed to write for his "plain, simple, honest, wayfaring Friends." Universalists eventually followed the path of other early populist groups and formed such colleges as Lombard in Illinois in 1852, Tufts in Boston in 1855, and St. Lawrence in New York in 1856, and the schools established theological departments, but many Universalists remained suspicious of theological seminaries.[5]

They did not, however, abandon the quest for rationality. The early Universalists reasoned and read scripture in ways that Unitarians considered crude and unsophisticated, for the Universalists had their origins in a sectarian culture that combined biblical literalism with allegorical and figurative readings of the Bible that educated Unitarians saw as sheer fancy. By the early nineteenth century, however, Universalist authors began to move away from "mystical interpretations" toward "a more rational exegesis," and by the middle of the century, a few were ready to cast their vote for reason alone. Most, however, continued to argue for a synthesis that combined philosophical and scientific arguments with the biblical texts that supported universal salvation. Like the Unitarians, most Universalists believed that theology could unite reason and revelation.[6]

John Murray: Biblical Allegory and Union with Christ

The core idea of Universalist theology — that the Bible promised eternal salvation to everyone — had defenders in America long before it became the motif of an organized religious movement. The sectarian turbulence of seventeenth-century England gave rise to speculation about universal salvation, which surfaced in early New England. In Rhode Island, Samuel Gorton (ca. 1592–1677) led a small community convinced that the incarnation had transformed and saved all humanity, and in Connecticut a group led by John Rogers (1648–1721) — the Rogerenes — claimed that the atonement brought saving pardon of all sin. Some of the German Baptists known as Dunkers who filtered into Pennsylvania after 1708 held universalist views, and when Conrad Beissel broke away from them in 1725 to form his Ephrata Society, he taught that after the wicked endured centuries of purgatorial fire, all would be saved.[7]

The arrival in Germantown of the physician George de Benneville (1703–93) in 1741 brought to Pennsylvania a form of universalism grounded in ecstatic mystical experience. A series of visions had ensured him of universal salvation through Jesus Christ, and he always combined his universalist teaching with the belief that it was possible to communicate with the spirits in the heavenly world. Benneville believed that his spirit guides had shown him the seven stages of the afterlife through which souls were gradually purified by suffering. First sentenced to execution and then, after a reprieve, driven from France because of his religious views, Benneville fled to Germany where he met the Dunkers, who encouraged his immigration to America.[8]

Benneville considered his mystical visions to be entirely compatible with scriptural teaching, and in 1753, he arranged for the publication of the *Ever-*

lasting Gospel of the seventeenth-century German mystic Georg Paul Siegvolck (a pseudonym for Georg Klein-Nicolai of Friessdorf). Siegvolck elaborated a biblical universalism grounded in the conviction that "God is love
essentially" (1 John 4:16) and that the absolute loving Sovereign had willed
that none should perish (2 Peter 3:9). Viewing Christ as the "propitiation for
the sins of the whole world," he believed that Christ was a "special savior" for
those who believed in him and who would at death ascend to his throne to
partake of his glories and reign with him during the coming millennium. But
even for those who did not believe, Christ was the savior whose power could
not be thwarted, and some of them would be saved after the millennium.
Those who continued to resist would undergo humbling in the fires of hell, but
even they would surrender to the divine love. Siegvolck pioneered in the exegetical studies with which Universalists attempted to show that "eternal"
punishment, as the biblical writers understood it, would someday end.[9]

The first flowering of Universalist thought came through reinterpretation of
the Calvinism that still dominated American theology in the eighteenth century. The earliest spokesman to obtain a wide hearing was John Murray
(1741–1815), the immigrant son of working-class Calvinist parents in Alton,
Hampshire, England. He had associated with Wesleyan Methodist revivalists
in Ireland, but his Calvinism made him feel awkward in Methodist circles until
he heard the Calvinist preaching of George Whitefield, whose chapel he later
attended. He learned of universalist theology in the modest meetinghouse of
the Independent Welsh revivalist James Relly (1720–78) in London.[10]

Relly's meetinghouse was a place with "a pulpit framed of a few rough
boards." When Murray came to America in 1770, a storm forced his boat to
land at Good-Luck Point on the coast of New Jersey, where he met a sailor
named Thomas Potter who had built an equally unassuming meetinghouse
and was waiting for someone to preach in it. Murray agreed to preach, but he
did not confine himself to Potter's meetinghouse. During a preaching tour in
New England in 1779 he organized a group of separatists in Gloucester, Massachusetts, into a Universalist congregation. In 1793 he became the minister of
the First Universalist Church in Boston.[11]

As a Calvinist, Murray had long accepted a theology in which "election and
final perseverance" were "fundamentals." By 1770 he rejected Calvinist theology, but he continued to embrace the doctrines of election and perseverance in
a version of Calvinism without damnation. Murray adopted James Relly's
doctrine that God had beheld humanity "in Christ" from the beginning of
creation. He took this to mean that Jesus was "from everlasting ordained to be
the savior of all, who were exposed to the Curse of the divine law." Since all
stood under the law's curse, this everlasting decree amounted to an eternal

election of all to salvation. According to Romans 11, Murray thought, God had included "all in Unbelief, that he might have mercy on all." Like the Calvinists, Relly and Murray taught that salvation resulted from an eternal decree, but unlike the Calvinists they universalized the decree.[12]

Murray linked this doctrine of universal election to a Christology in which the incarnate Christ so identified himself with humanity that he "contained within himself the fullness of the human, as well as of the divine nature." Such an incarnation was a universal "new birth" of human nature and the whole "human family" in the person of Christ, whose death on the cross was therefore an act of satisfaction for the sins of every person. United with Christ, everyone was justified by his vicarious atonement. Murray had reached his conclusions through close study of Relly's *Union: Or a Treatise on the Consanguinity and Affinity Between Christ and his Church* (1749), and union with Christ defined for him the heart of Universalist theology: "The comprehensive term *union* is the key by which we unlock this mystery, the head and members are united, and the iniquity of the members is visited on the Head." Election and union with Christ had long been essentials of Calvinist theology, but with Relly's help Murray cast them into a Universalist form that altered their meaning.[13]

One of the clearest expositions of the doctrine of union with Christ appeared in a catechism published in 1782 by Judith Sargent Stevens, who would later marry John Murray and would gain a regional reputation as a novelist, playwright, essayist, and defender of women's rights. Even though she recognized that as a woman writing on theological topics she appeared to be stepping outside the line that "custom hath circumscribed" and that her efforts would draw charges of "arrogance, heresy, [and] licentiousness," she published theology in the pages of the *Massachusetts Magazine* as well as in her catechetical exposition, *Some Deductions from the System Promulgated in the Page of Divine Revelation,* where she identified the "new birth" of humanity with the birth of Christ: "We were conceived pure in the womb of the virgin. . . . Christ is the head of every man, the human nature considered as 'individuals' are his members, we were born with him, and this is the new birth which constitutes us pure in the sight of the Father." Christ's sacrificial death could satisfy the debt for all human iniquities because the incarnation of Christ had incorporated all of humanity.[14]

In graphic depictions of the future life, both John Murray and Judith Sargent Murray interpreted the eschatological texts of the New Testament to mean that righteous believers would, in the "first resurrection," pass at death immediately to glory. Unbelievers and the sinful would remain after death in an intermediate state, fearful and miserable. Some would be delivered from the intermediate state; others would remain there until the day of judgment, when they would undergo the "second resurrection" and see that it was right for them to accept the condemnation of their sinful natures. The last judgment, conducted by the Redeemer flanked by the faithful who had risen in the first resurrection, would separate the unbelieving from their "body of sin and death." It would then issue in a glorious conclusion in which "every tongue would confess" Christ.[15]

The Murrays defended their theology by weaving together a web of biblical texts that they would interpret sometimes in literal, sometimes in figurative and allegorical ways. John Murray could be literal with a text like Romans 11:32 — "for God hath included them all in unbelief, that he might have mercy upon all" — but he never hesitated to allegorize the text when it served his purposes. He found cryptic allusions to Christ and to universal salvation throughout the Bible, especially in the New Testament. Jesus' command to render unto Caesar what was Caesar's and to God what was God's became for Murray a command to render back human sins to the devil and human souls to God (Luke 20:25). Judith Sargent Murray viewed the eschatological separation of the sheep from the goats at the last judgment (Matt. 25) as the separation of the soul from its sinful qualities.[16]

His critics believed that John Murray employed orthodox language in deceptive ways until he attracted the trust of his hearers; then he reinterpreted the words. They also accused him of teaching an antinomian doctrine that "turns the grace of God into lasciviousness," and it remained a primary complaint of the opposition that Universalist doctrine weakened moral restraints. Judith Sargent Murray tried to refute the charge by showing that Universalists believed in a "place of darkness" awaiting the sinful, who would suffer protracted, though not everlasting, punishment for their sins. She depicted Universalist doctrine as the purest morality: universal union with Christ meant that all were "members in the same body," so that each person was encouraged to minister to "the necessities of every son and daughter of Adam." But it remained a commonplace of critics that the Murrays' doctrines weakened moral restraint.[17]

The same critics ridiculed the Murrays' reading of the Bible. Andrew Croswell dismissed it as "irrational," a matter of "sport." The pastor of the Second Church in Ipswich, John Cleaveland (1722–99), charged that it was "too senseless to be maintained by any person." In his *Doctrine of Universal Salvation Examined and Refuted* (1782), the Separate Baptist Isaac Backus (1724–1806) in Middleborough, Massachusetts, contended that neither Relly nor John Murray ever proved that the New Testament viewed all men and women as "one in Christ." Allegorical exegesis did not convince him otherwise.[18]

Elhanan Winchester: Restorationist Literalism

One accomplishment of Elhanan Winchester (1751–97) was to show that the Universalist case did not need to rely on allegorical readings of the Bible. The son of a farmer and shoemaker in Brookline, Massachusetts, Winchester received only minimal schooling. Converted by New Light Calvinists in 1769, he became an itinerant Baptist preacher. His sermons followed the high Calvinist scheme of the English Baptist John Gill (1697–1771), who taught a doctrine of "eternal justification," which guarded against the slightest possibility that good works might be seen as conditions of salvation. While Winchester was preaching to a Baptist congregation in South Carolina, however, he read Siegvolck's *Everlasting Gospel,* and its arguments slowly persuaded him. He moved to Philadelphia in 1780 to preach in the First Baptist Church. There he developed a friendship with Benneville, and in 1781 he announced his belief in a Universalist theology. When his views split the congregation, Winchester moved to England for seven years, but in 1794 he returned to the Society of Universal Baptists in Philadelphia, where he remained as the pastor for the last three years of his life.[19]

Murray and Winchester formed a brief alliance in 1784, but they taught two different versions of Universalist doctrine, and the conflict created tension. In place of Murray's notion of universal election, Winchester taught a universal grace that would enable a free decision from every person. They differed also in their styles of biblical interpretation. Winchester believed that the Bible should be read in its "most plain and obvious sense" and that a "mystical" reading should never overwhelm the literal. Scriptural passages amounted to "a proof in themselves," and he often argued merely by listing the scores of passages with a universal reference. He thought that "the plain letter of the Scripture" infallibly proved that God would "gather together in Christ all things, both in heaven and on earth." To the next generation, his methods appeared mechanical. Hosea Ballou 2d (1796–1861), the pastor in Medford, Massachusetts, and the ablest historian in the movement, wrote in 1848 that Winchester relied too much on "verbal relations of particular texts" while ignoring their context. Ballou 2d also thought that he veered into "enthusiasm" by accepting as literal the prophetic and apocalyptic visions. Winchester was not entirely consistent in his interpretive methods, and he still made an occasional recourse to allegory, but later Universalists saw his "more rational" exegesis as progress.[20]

He answered critics by adducing biblical texts that became fixtures of Universalist polemic. Genesis promised that "all" the families of the earth would be blessed (Gen. 12:3); Isaiah prophesied that "every" knee would bow (Isa.

45:23). Jesus said that he came not to judge but to save the "world" (John 12:47); Paul taught that God desired for "all" to be saved (1 Tim. 2:4), that God would reconcile "all things" unto himself (Col. 1:20), and that God consigned all to unbelief "that he might have mercy upon all" (Rom. 11:32). As in Adam all died, so in Christ all would be made alive (1 Cor. 15:22). Winchester found more than two hundred biblical passages that taught the doctrine of universal salvation.[21]

He grounded his doctrine on five "foundation principles" that he considered either self-evident or fully demonstrable from scripture: (1) God was love, "essentially and communicatively"; (2) God's design in creation was to make his creatures happy in the knowledge of his perfection; (3) God's designs could not be frustrated; (4) Christ died for all; and (5) Christ came to destroy sin. It followed that everyone would accept the gift of salvation, either in this life or in the next. Winchester conceded that some would resist. Countless souls might undergo years of punishment in the next life. Winchester still believed in a terrifying, even an "everlasting," hell. Yet his reading of Siegvolck had convinced him that the Bible meant by "everlasting" not "endless" but only "of long duration," and so he could say that the torment would cease as it accomplished its redemptive effect. After he argued in *The Universal Restoration Exhibited in Four Dialogues Between a Minister and His Friend* (1788) that God's unchanging love would ultimately restore even the most resistant sinner, his doctrine came to be known as "restorationism."[22]

John Murray accused Winchester of teaching a doctrine of "purgatorial satisfaction" that detracted from the "finished redemption wrought out by the Redeemer of men." To him, Winchester's notion of salutary punishment implied that the sinful had to "obtain salvation by their own deeds and sufferings." He thought that Winchester taught salvation through obedience, not through the atoning act of Christ. Such a teaching would mean that Christ's atonement was "not sufficient," that the sinful had to "pay their own debt" rather than rely on "the Blood of Jesus Christ alone." In Murray's eyes, Winchester was an Arminian trying to insinuate notions of free will that diminished reliance on grace.[23]

In fact, Winchester's theology was a mixture of Arminian and Calvinist ideas. He published an *Elegy on the Death of John Wesley* (1792) in which he praised the English Methodists for recognizing "that all the world might taste redeeming love." The Wesleyan idea that grace restored freedom, however, required Methodists to say that the free will might resist divine love, with eternal consequences. Winchester thought that the will might be sufficiently free to resist God stubbornly for thousands of years but that "God's absolute, ultimate designs cannot be eternally frustrated." In *The Mystic's Plea* (1781) he said that God "predestined" all men and women to be "conformed to the image of his Son," and he never backed away from the idea that "Christ died for all, and died not in vain." Winchester and Murray understood grace differently, but both of them held to the Calvinist assertion that grace was sovereign.[24]

In his theory of the atonement, Winchester diverged from Calvinism. While Murray retained the Calvinist idea that Christ died to satisfy God's justice by paying the infinite debt owed by humanity, Winchester denied that the atonement satisfied the justice of a wrathful God. Occasionally he argued that Christ died to display God's love, but he also proposed a more complicated idea of atonement. He argued that Christ, by the shedding of his blood, broke "the Power of Death" and overcame "the Wrath of fallen nature" in principle, making it possible for his followers to "stand complete in that divine nature which we derive from him." The atonement was a cosmic event for Winchester, but it altered the possibilities of human nature rather than the mind of God.[25]

He dismissed the notion that sin incurred an infinite debt. Infinitude was solely a divine property. Deists sometimes also contended that sins were finite acts that did not deserve infinite punishment, but Winchester probably derived this idea from his reading of Siegvolck and the *Philosophical Principles of Natural and Revealed Religion* of Andrew Michael Ramsay (1686–1743), a Scottish exile to France who tried to combine Christian theology and ancient mystery religions. All of them agreed, as did Winchester, that it was absurd to say that "creatures" could commit "infinite sins."[26]

He linked his universalism to millennialism. Winchester pursued millennial exegesis so relentlessly that Benjamin Rush, having read his two-volume *Lectures on the Prophecies that Remain to be Fulfilled* (1789), described him as "our Theological Newton." His English lectures on the prophecies in 1789 laid out an elaborate scenario in which God would make a "new covenant" with Israel, ensuring the Jewish return to Jerusalem and the final catastrophe of history. Jesus would then return, resurrect the saints, and reign over the earth for a thousand years before the general resurrection and final judgment. The judgment would inaugurate the descent of the New Jerusalem to a renewed earth on which all would eventually abide forever. In his *Two Lectures on the Prophecies* (1792), Winchester showed that the same prophecies that described the end times also predicted "the restoration of all."[27]

Neither Murray nor Winchester could accept an eschatological future without suffering for the sinful. Murray placed it in the interval between death and the day of judgment, Winchester in the extended duration — possibly fifty thousand years — after that day. Murray thought of the suffering as merely punitive, Winchester gave it redemptive meaning. But both emphasized future punishment partly because their critics accused them of teaching a doctrine that undermined moral order. In an era when theologians especially emphasized the moral corollary of Christian faith, Murray and Winchester had to offer continual reassurance that they were proposing no "licentious doctrine." Universalists tried to show that their theology encouraged a moral life as much as any other. Lucy Barns, author of *The Female Christian* (1809), continued the tradition of the Murrays when she said that Universalist morality was the purest because it unified all of humankind in a bond of love.[28]

Universalists resisted formal organization, believing, like the Unitarians, that they represented a movement rather than a denomination. Eventually, however, political pressures, including the refusal of the state to recognize marriages performed by Universalist clergy or to exempt Universalists from religious taxation, made cooperation necessary. By 1785, Universalists met in conventions that evolved into a permanent organization. When Universalists drew up their first confessional statement—which they called the Winchester Profession because it was adopted at an 1803 gathering in Winchester, New Hampshire—they emphasized that holiness and happiness were inseparably connected and that believers ought to practice good works. The creed revealed how much they worried about the accusation that they encouraged immorality. The remainder of the Winchester Profession was sufficiently broad to encompass the disciples of both Murray and Winchester. It affirmed Universalist reliance on the scriptures, confidence that Christ revealed a God "whose nature is Love," and a conviction that the "Spirit of Grace" would finally restore holiness and happiness to all humanity. By 1803, however, Hosea Ballou was attempting to lead Universalists in new directions. His theology would generate controversy within the movement for almost half a century.[29]

Hosea Ballou and Ultra-Universalism

Hosea Ballou (1771–1852) was the son of a Calvinistic Baptist farmer-preacher in New Hampshire. Denied a formal education by the poverty of his parents, he gravitated toward Universalism through reading the Bible, listening to the Universalist preacher Caleb Rich, and immersing himself in the deism of Ethan Allen. In 1790, at age twenty, he began to preach on a Baptist circuit that extended from New Hampshire and Vermont to Massachusetts, but when his Universalist ideas became known, the Baptists excommunicated him. He then sought ordination from Winchester and became the pastor of Universalist churches in New Hampshire and Massachusetts. In 1817 he began a ministry that would last thirty-five years at a working-class congregation called the Second Universalist Society in Boston. He became the best-known American Universalist theologian of the nineteenth century.[30]

Some of Ballou's earliest writings suggested the influence of Relly, of whom he learned directly from John Murray, and he also read the works of Charles Chauncy and Elhanan Winchester. Nonetheless, he diverged from all his predecessors. His reading of the deist Ethan Allen convinced him that it was "utterly impossible to maintain Christianity as it had been generally believed in the church," and he felt a certain admiration for the deists' confidence in reason. Ballou insisted that "our own reason must determine what is true," and he contended for a figurative rather than a literal interpretation of biblical material that seemed unreasonable. Universalist theology had been preeminently biblicist. Ballou added a new emphasis on reasonableness.[31]

He remained wed to the Bible and to the maxims of evidential Christianity. Ballou admired William Paley and recommended his treatise on the evidences to anyone with doubts about the truth of revelation. In 1820 he published his own *Series of Letters in Defence of Divine Revelation* in which he laid out both the prophetic proofs and the evidence from the miracles. He employed both the internal and the external proofs, but he found miracles and prophecies the most convincing because they were facts available through the medium of the senses. The evidences of revelation had the same honored place in Universalism that they had throughout antebellum Christianity, but Ballou insisted, like the Unitarians, that each biblical truth still had to stand the test of reason. "All the truth which is necessary for our belief, is not only reasonable," he wrote, "but reducible to our understandings."[32]

Ballou combined his rationalism with an eighteenth-century liberal sense of divine benevolence, an insistence on divine sovereignty that recalled his Calvinist background, and a philosophical determinism drawn from the Swiss minister Ferdinand Olivier Petitpierre, but he took scripture as his primary guide. His first important publication was his *Notes on the Parables of the New Testament* (1804), which found universalist meanings in the parables of Jesus. The book that pushed him to the forefront of Universalist theology, however, was his *Treatise on Atonement* (1805), in which he also claimed that the gospel would have been better understood "had the Bible been the only book ever read on the subject." But Ballou's treatise on the atonement was distant in spirit from Winchester's collections of biblical texts, and it led to different conclusions.[33]

The treatise charted new directions in Universalist theology. It set aside the Trinitarian thought of the earlier movement and coupled universalism with unitarian views of God. It defined Christ as a "created, dependent being" to whom God had given the "power to be mediator." It blurred the distinction between the human and the divine by contending that human beings embodied a divine principle, having been created from the "fullness" of God rather than from nothing. It also elevated the importance of the argument that since sin was finite, no infinite atonement was needed. Ballou defined sin as a transgression of the sinner's understanding of the law of love. Because the understanding was finite, the sin could be no more than a finite flaw, for otherwise it would share a divine property and would have infinite consequences, requiring all creatures to suffer endlessly by it.[34]

At the heart of the treatise, however, was the argument that no atonement was necessary to reconcile God to humanity. God loved unchangeably. The purpose of the atonement was to display that love and so renew the love of the creature to the Creator. Ballou had no liking for either substitutionary or governmental views of the atonement; he thought it immoral to suggest that God would require an innocent man to suffer for the guilty, and irreligious to conceive of God as the unreconciled party in a cosmic dispute. The purpose of the cross was to reveal the character of the Father in a way that would sway the heart.[35]

Ballou believed that God had "no interest to serve but our own happiness." He had no liking for the austere piety of the Edwardean New Divinity theologians who claimed "that we have to love God for what he is, and not for what we receive from him." To the Hopkinsian argument that the highest happiness of the universe was consistent with the endless misery of the damned, Ballou replied that the highest happiness of the universe required the eternal happiness of each individual. Yet he shared the cosmic optimism of the New Divinity, even to the point of agreeing that sin was the will of God, an idea he took not from Hopkins, however, but from Petitpierre. Everything happened in accord with "God's design," and therefore sin and evil had to be means of realizing the divine purpose.[36]

To support his notion of divine sovereignty he appended a philosophical argument for determinism that he also learned from Petitpierre's *On the Divine Goodness*. Since the will always followed the dictates of the understanding, all agents remained, in all their actions, dependent on their perceptions. Ballou rejected the Edwardean argument that inability resulted merely from unwillingness. The bondage of the will was natural as well as moral, rooted in the fact that the objects of perception exercise a binding allure both on the judgment and on the choice. Ultimately, this meant that every action was the result of God's will. Ballou liked the idea of divine determinism because it guaranteed a happy outcome.[37]

For Ballou, the outcome was happier even than earlier Universalists had supposed it to be. By the third edition of the *Treatise on Atonement* in 1812, Ballou was suggesting that there might be "no future punishment." In 1817 he arranged a discussion of the point, which he published in "The Gospel Visitant." By then, he was convinced of a position that his detractors castigated as "ultra-universalism," or "death and glory" theology. Every person entered into immediate bliss at the moment of death. Unlike Murray and Winchester, he saw no reason to assume any future punishment. For the rest of his career Ballou defended this position, which he expanded, especially in his *Examination of the Doctrine of Future Retribution* (1834), with the contention that sin always brought its own punishment in this life.[38]

To critics who saw portents of moral license in his doctrine, Ballou responded with the observation that doctrines of eternal punishment had never deterred moral corruption. They had resulted only in a shallow morality of external reward. The defenders of endless punishment had failed to see that righteousness was its own reward and that love for God could never be induced by threats and warnings. Men and women would act morally, he thought, when they recognized that the moral course would always serve their own higher interests in this world. But Ballou and other Universalists also sought, like the New Divinity theologians, an "unselfish" faith that encouraged the faithful to link their own interests with the whole of humanity. They argued that their theology promoted a higher morality than that of the Calvinists by emphasizing each person's common bond with everyone else.[39]

Ballou's theology, however, offended not only John Murray, who called him a deist and Socinian, but also the restorationists who followed Winchester. They attacked by appropriating a point from their own critics: Ballou's doctrine would discourage morality in this life by removing any fear of punishment in the next. The minister of the Universalist congregation in Westminster, Massachusetts, Charles Hudson, criticized Ballou's doctrines for their adverse "moral influence." If every sin were its own punishment, he said, even earthly laws and punishments would be needless.[40]

The reply to Ballou's restorationist critics came from Walter Balfour, a Scottish immigrant to Massachusetts, who came into prominence in Universalist circles in 1824 with an exegetical treatise designed to prove that the Bible made no reference to any "place" of future punishment. In a revision in 1826, he added that the Bible also justified neither belief in a literal devil nor fear of an endless punishment. Answering Hudson two years later in *Three Essays on the Intermediate State of the Dead,* Balfour taught that the spirits of all the departed, now resting in Christ, would awake at the resurrection on the last day and enter immediately into endless felicity. As for Hudson's charge that such a doctrine undermined morality, Balfour observed only that fear of eternal punishment had not produced "good morals among all nations in past ages." In the 1820s, probably a majority of Universalists accepted the "ultra" position.[41]

Opponents of Universalism took delight not only in the disagreements within the movement but also in the public career of Abner Kneeland, a sometime Universalist minister whose intellectual odyssey led him eventually to deny an afterlife, identify God with nature, and debunk the story of Jesus as "a fable and a fiction." Kneeland's conviction for blasphemy by the Commonwealth of Massachusetts in 1834 proved embarrassing, since he still described himself as a Universalist "in some respects." By the 1850s, however, the Universalists had distanced themselves from Kneeland, moved away from Ballou, and reached a rough consensus around the restorationist theology of Winchester.[42]

By that time, they had also begun to defend Universalist theology by means other than the assembling of the familiar biblical texts. In 1829, Hosea Ballou 2[d], a grandnephew of the more celebrated Ballou, made the point that the early church had little to say about eternal damnation. The church fathers assumed some "future state of suffering," but they had little interest in trying to discover its duration. In his *Ancient History of Universalism*, Ballou 2[d] claimed for Universalists in America the authority of the great Origen of Alexandria (ca. 185–ca. 254), who had also argued in his *De Principiis* that all creatures, even the devil, would be saved. Ballou 2[d] found it impressive that Origen's doctrine of universal salvation attracted so little negative attention in the early church. He concluded that the great authority of Augustine in the late fourth century had lured the church into its fascination with eternal punishment.[43]

Within a year, Thomas Whittemore, one of Hosea Ballou's converts, supplemented this historical work with his own *Modern History of Universalism from the Era of the Reformation to the Present Time* (1830), which found additional precedents for Universalist belief in the sixteenth-century Reformation. The historical argument took still another form when Thomas Baldwin Thayer (1812–86), a pastor and editor in Massachusetts and New York, traced the doctrine of endless punishment to non-Christian sources, chiefly in Egypt.[44]

By the late 1840s, several groups within the denomination began to downplay the biblicism of the movement and elevate reason as the source of Universalist truth. For some, this turn toward reason took the form of an argument that science alone could confirm religious teaching. In particular, they sought rational evidence for the immortality of the soul and the working of God in history. As a result, a small company of Universalist thinkers discovered proofs of religious truths in Mesmerism, the view of the eighteenth-century Viennese physician Franz Anton Mesmer, who promoted belief in a universal electrical force with therapeutic powers. Others believed that phrenology, a system that attempted to localize the source of human traits in the brain and to reveal those traits through examination of the skull, could provide evidence for divine determinism. Still others sought to defend Universalist theology by exploiting the popular interest in spiritualism, the belief that it was possible to communicate directly with the spirits of the departed. A few Universalists concluded that a rational religion could dispense with the notion of a supernatural God.[45]

Most, however, continued to seek a synthesis between reason and revelation. In 1847, a New York Universalist convention, reacting against the New England transcendentalists, declared that all Universalist ministers must believe that the Bible contains "a special and sufficient revelation from God, which is the rule of faith and practice." When Universalists in Massachusetts adopted a similar statement, some dissenters withdrew rather than be compelled to assent to belief in biblical miracles and the necessity for special revelation. The majority, however, rejected what Hosea Ballou 2[d] called "rationalistic and transcendental tendencies." In their frequent oral debates with antebellum Methodists, Universalist preachers still made their case mainly by quoting biblical passages.[46]

At the same time, Universalist theologians divided over the extent to which the movement should recover the traces of Calvinist piety that marked the early theologies of Murray and Ballou. In 1854, Obadiah Tillotson argued in his *Divine Efficiency and Moral Harmony of the Universe* that only the principle of universal divine causation could ensure the universality of salvation, but by that time most Universalist leaders had cast their lot with the defenders of free will and repudiated Ballou's theology as a hindrance. Hosea Ballou 2[d] could argue in 1858 that the common sense of the Scottish philosophers offered ample arguments against any form of determinism.[47]

The divisions formed the background for the publication in 1862 of Thomas Baldwin Thayer's *Theology of Universalism*. Thayer would become the premier Universalist theologian of the later nineteenth century, and he tried to maintain a balance between the competing parties. He accorded authority to scripture but attempted to show that Universalists relied not merely on biblical exegesis but also on a coherent and rational "system" of thought grounded in the premise that a benevolent God would always adapt punishment to "the condition and needs of the offender." He defended the freedom of the will and saw the voluntary formation of character as the purpose of the Christian life, but he recovered something of the Calvinist sensibility in his insistence that in a world created by a benevolent and omnipotent God, evil would always have a purpose. For Thayer, an understanding of evil as purposive clarified the aim of the Christian life as the formation of character and the mission of Jesus as the model of Christian character. He praised Jonathan Edwards for having seen that divine omnipotence, not human freedom, ultimately ensured the well-being of humankind, but he also continued the quest for a theology of virtue.[48]

From the beginning of the movement, John Murray had claimed that universal salvation was the doctrine of "Reason as well as divine revelation." Hosea Ballou then elevated the norm of rationality higher than Murray could have ever imagined. Ballou's rationalism never replaced the force of biblical argument in the movement, but it made clear that the Universalists, like the Unitarians, were searching for a way of reading biblical texts that would be congruent with right reason. Thomas Whittemore declared Universalism to be "the only consistent System of religious doctrine I have ever known," and he found in the consistency a sign of superior Universalist rationality. Yet the reason of the Universalists was, for the most part, still the reason of evidential Christianity, devoted to the defense of biblical revelation and convinced that reason could show the Bible to be the sole word of God.[49]

Episcopal Theology and Tradition

The American Episcopalians inherited an Anglican theological tradition that had been divided into party alignments ever since the seventeenth century, and like their English predecessors, the Americans fell into groupings of latitudinarians, evangelicals, and high-church theologians. The latitudinarians sought a reasonable faith that dispensed with doctrinal strictness. The evangelicals espoused views of scripture and religious experience that led them into a closer alliance with other American Protestants. The high-church theologians maintained a veneration of tradition that shaped a distinctive Episcopal agenda. These alignments found expression in Episcopal attitudes toward rationality. Latitudinarians defined themselves by their reasonable approach to religious faith; the high-church theologians found in the communal decisions of the church through the centuries a check on the "private judgment" of the rational individual; the evangelicals were both more appreciative of private judgment and more convinced of the value of the evidentialist apologetic. In the Anglican traditions, however, an enduring interest in the doctrines of the church and its ministry gave Episcopal theology and Episcopal rationality a distinctive coloration.

A respect for the authority of tradition — and for the learning necessary to recover it — made Episcopal theologians wary of theological populists. Like the New England Unitarians, the Episcopal Church attracted more than its share of the economic and political elite, and its image as the church of the affluent and educated classes made it a primary target of populist rhetoric. In response, the Episcopalians insisted all the more on an educated clergy. Although Episcopal theologians could insist that Christianity always remained accessible "to common understandings," the denomination expected its clerical leaders and theologians to be men "chastened by habits of study and reflection" and marked by "attainments of theological literature." The powerful bishop of New York John Henry Hobart expressed the consensus of the church leadership when he insisted that the Episcopalians seek a "learned as well as a pious ministry." Sensitive to what the bishop of North Carolina, John Stark Ravenscroft (1772–1830), referred to as the "contempt" for the Christian ministry "manifested by the wealthier and better informed classes of society," the Episcopalians began early to encourage the creation of an educated clerical leadership.[1]

The denomination built a series of institutions for theological training, beginning with the General Theological Seminary in New York City in 1821 and the Protestant Episcopal Theological Seminary in Virginia in 1823. Within the next thirty years it added Nashotah in Wisconsin, Berkeley in Connecticut, and Kenyon in Ohio. The schools not only provided a setting for theological scholarship but also educated a clergy who mixed pastoral and theological vocations within their parishes. Respect for the academic training of the clergy registered the interest in a rational theology, even though Episcopalians disagreed about what theological rationality should mean.

William White and the Episcopal Parties

The chief influence on the course of American Episcopal thought in the early nineteenth century came from William White (1748–1836), a graduate of the College of Philadelphia who in 1779 became the rector of that city's United Parishes of Christ Church and St. Peter's Church. White was wealthy, well-educated, and well-connected, by the marriage of his sister, to the Robert Morris family that helped to finance the revolutionary government. He also had the diplomatic skills to induce antagonists to cooperate. His *Case of the Episcopal Churches Considered* (1782) guided much of the thinking that led to the formation of the Protestant Episcopal Church in 1789, and his two-volume *Comparative Views of the Controversy Between the Calvinists and the Arminians* (1817) was the premier theological work produced by an antebellum American Episcopalian.

White's leverage over early Episcopal theology came, however, not only from his publications but also from two of his institutional accomplishments after his consecration as the bishop of Pennsylvania in 1787. First, he persuaded the denomination to recognize the authority of the Thirty-Nine Articles, the summary of doctrine adopted by the Church of England in 1563, which became the standard to which all factions of Episcopal theologians in America would appeal. Second, he almost certainly compiled in 1804 the Bishops' Course of Study, a list of preferred readings for clerical candidates. Consisting of fifty texts in apologetics, scriptural studies, church history, and divinity, the list recommended mainly Anglican authors of the seventeenth and eighteenth centuries. Its titles would appear repeatedly as authorities in the publications of American Episcopalians.[2]

White served as a tutor to a generation of Episcopal theologians who studied under him in Philadelphia. His most noted students, however, shared little of his latitudinarian temper, and by the end of the first decade of the nineteenth century they were dividing into the high-church and evangelical factions that would define the issues of Episcopal theology throughout the antebellum era.

The high-church group turned for leadership to John Henry Hobart (1775–1830), a graduate of Princeton College who studied under White before serving churches in Pennsylvania and New Jersey. At Princeton, he had learned to defend Episcopal doctrine against the Presbyterian majority among the students, and when he became in 1801 the assistant at Trinity Church in New York City, he was well-prepared, both by training and by temperament, for polemical as well as pastoral duties. The city was not known for its welcoming embrace of the Episcopal Church, which some still associated with disloyalty during the Revolution. Polemicists could flourish there, and Hobart earned his reputation when he published *An Apology for Apostolic Order and Its Advocates* (1807), a defense of Episcopal polity against the criticisms of John M. Mason (1770–1829) of the Associate Reformed Church.[3]

By 1811, when Hobart became the assistant bishop of the diocese of New York, he held the view that the episcopacy belonged to the essence *(esse)* of a true church, and his theology helped define the high-church movement. Leery of revivalist piety, the adherents of Hobartian theology honored the forms and ceremonies of Anglican tradition, and they adopted positions on church order, sacraments, the ministry, and salvation that would distinguish them not only from other Protestants but also from the evangelical party within the denomination.[4]

The evangelical party has its geographical and spiritual center among a circle of clergy in and near Washington, D.C. All of them had undergone an intense religious experience; all hoped that the Episcopal Church would become more open to a moderate form of revivalism. They carried on the tradition of Devereux Jarratt (1733–1801), whose reaction against the eighteenth-century Episcopal theology of virtue drew him into cooperation with Methodist evangelists and prompted him to accentuate the doctrines of depravity and free grace. Like Jarratt, the nineteenth-century evangelicals defined themselves theologically by their emphasis on original sin, the experience of rebirth and renewal, the doctrine of justification by faith alone, and the sole authority of scripture as a source of theological truth. Eager to cooperate with other Protestants, they downplayed ideas of Episcopal exclusiveness and sought alliances with evangelicals of similar views in other denominations.[5]

Two prominent evangelicals took the lead in drafting their theological platforms. William H. Wilmer (1782–1827), a native of Maryland and a graduate of Washington College, became in 1812 the rector of St. Paul's parish in Alexandria, Virginia. Forming a close friendship with William Meade (1789–1862), a young clergyman in Frederick and Fairfax parishes who had chosen to receive his schooling at Princeton in order to escape the aura of deism at William and Mary, Wilmer labored to make the diocese of Virginia a stronghold of evangelical piety. Wilmer's *Episcopal Manual* (1815) summarized the evangelical doctrines; his essays in the *Washington Theological Repertory*, which he helped to found in 1819, popularized them; and his lectures as a professor of systematic theology from 1823 to 1826 made the Theological Seminary in Virginia at Alexandria a center of evangelical thought.[6]

Charles P. McIlvaine (1799–1873), the son of a U.S. senator, was a graduate of Princeton College who studied theology at Princeton Seminary before becoming rector in 1820 at Christ Church in Washington, D.C. He spent several years teaching at West Point, where he sparked a revival among the cadets, before moving to New York City, where he served at St. Ann's Church in Brooklyn while occupying the professorship of Christian evidences at the University of the City of New York. In 1832 he published his lectures as *The Evidences of Christianity*, but he left the university in that year to become the bishop of Ohio and the president of Kenyon College and its theological seminary. McIlvaine became known in the 1830s as the ablest evangelical opponent of the English Oxford Movement, and his *Oxford Divinity Compared With That of the Romish and Anglican Churches* (1839) was the most forceful American criticism of the theology of John Henry Newman (1801–90).[7]

The American disciples of Newman and the English Oxford Movement began to coalesce after 1840 into a fourth force within the church, distinct from earlier latitudinarians, from the evangelicals, and from the older high-church group. After 1838, American Episcopalians followed closely the debate in England over the ideas of Newman, a fellow at Oxford University and a vicar at St. Mary's Church in Oxford. Newman led a movement of reaction against the intrusion of the English parliament into sacred matters. He and his allies — especially Edward B. Pusey and Richard H. Froude — reasserted the independence of the church and reaffirmed the Anglican linkage to the Catholic tradition. They considered the Protestant Reformation a mistake and called into question the Protestant character of the Church of England. Because they advanced their views in a series known as the *Tracts for the Times,* they became known as the Tractarians.

The Americans published their own edition of the tracts in 1839, and a number of influential Episcopal clergy who had associated with Hobart's tradition — including Bishop George W. Doane (1799–1859) of New Jersey, Bishop Benjamin T. Onderdonk (1791–1861) of New York, and Samuel Seabury III, editor of *The Churchman* — began to promote some of their ideas. A few of them, including the bishop of North Carolina, Levi Sullivan Ives (1797–1867), eventually entered the Catholic Church.

The evangelical and high-church parties debated each other during the 1820s and 1830s, but they had enough in common to maintain the unity of the church. During the early nineteenth century, Hobart's high-church group set the tone for Episcopal thought. By 1826 even William White was referring to himself as a high churchman, and in 1840 fourteen of the nineteen bishops of the denomination were high church in theological sympathies. By the 1840s, however, as some of the high churchmen gravitated toward the Oxford Movement, the disagreements became harsher, and the secession of more than thirty Episcopal clergy to Roman Catholicism had the effect of strengthening the evangelical party. After 1840, an increasing number of evangelicals became bishops, but high-church sympathies remained strong in New York, Wisconsin, and North Carolina. By the 1850s, Episcopalians could foresee a possible institutional division, and after the Civil War, a group of evangelicals broke away to create the Reformed Episcopal Church. What held most Episcopalians together throughout the period was a shared appreciation for the liturgy, authority, and tradition of the church.[8]

The Question of Calvinism

What Episcopalians did not share was a consensus about Calvinist piety. In the sixteenth and seventeenth centuries, Calvinism had a substantial place in the spectrum of Anglican theological positions, but after the Restoration of Charles II in 1660, Anglican Calvinists found themselves stigmatized by the memory of an unpopular revolution. In colonial America as well, Anglicanism usually signified an alternative to Calvinism. Yet Calvinist theology created problems for Episcopalians. Although they organized the denomination in 1789, it took them until 1801 to adopt the Thirty-Nine Articles, partly because both latitudinarian clergy like William Walter of Massachusetts and high-church conservatives like the elder Samuel Seabury of Connecticut found them too Calvinist. One mark of William White's ability was his success in leading the denomination beyond what might have become an impasse over Calvinist theology.[9]

White followed a precedent set in the seventeenth century by Gilbert Burnet, the bishop of Salisbury, whose *Exposition of the Thirty-Nine Articles of the Church of England* (1699) promoted the view that the articles remained open to both Calvinist and Arminian interpretations and that since theologians had no way to arbitrate between the two, the Church of England had to allow both. White believed with Burnet that interpretive freedom was the proper institutional solution to theological differences, and he persuaded the General Convention to adopt the articles almost unchanged, with the understanding that no one interpretation of them would be forced upon the church.[10]

White's own preferences became clear in the reading list he prepared for clergy, which consisted exclusively of anti-Calvinist or non-Calvinist authors. They became even clearer when he published in 1817 his *Comparative Views*, a two-volume treatise in biblical theology that made the case against Calvinism through exegesis of Romans, citations from the early church, appeals to the standards of the Anglican reformation, and excurses on necessitarian philosophy from Hobbes to Edwards.

White was one of the first American theologians to decide that the contest between Calvinists and Arminians during the previous two centuries had rested on a misreading of Paul by both parties. He reached his conclusions gradually. In 1785 he thought that Paul's doctrine of election in Romans 9 referred not to elect individuals but to elect nations, chosen to hear the gospel and respond to it. By 1801 he had moved away from this view, conceding, with Burnet, that the articles allowed but did not mandate a Calvinist doctrine. But he found further clues in John Locke's commentary on Romans and in the 1805 Bampton Lecture delivered by the archbishop of Cashel, Richard Laurence, who presented evidence that the theologians of the early Greek church had understood the language of Romans and Ephesians to refer to God's choice of individuals for membership in the church, not for eternal salvation.[11]

While acknowledging that he preferred the Arminian rather than the Calvinist position, he observed that Paul's letter to the Romans provided no evidence "of there having crossed his mind . . . a single thought on either side of any one of the points comprehended in the controversy." He believed that Paul's chief purpose in writing Romans was to say that the gentiles had the benefit of the Christian covenant even though they did not adhere to the Jewish law. By "election," White thought, Paul had meant merely the "election of the Gentiles, to be in the same state of visible covenant with those of the Jews, who should embrace the faith of Christ." Paul had no "doctrine of predestination relative to the future condition of individuals." His message was that every member of the church could be counted among the elect, though as White read Paul, membership in the church by no means assured salvation.[12]

The high-church theologians agreed, and before long even some of the evangelicals accepted White's exegesis, but the two parties still had different attitudes toward Calvinist thought. The high churchmen were among the fiercest critics of Calvin within the denomination. Hobart was the son-in-law of Thomas Bradbury Chandler (1726–90), the distinguished New York clergyman who had once schemed with Samuel Seabury in Connecticut to publish a historical essay showing that the Anglican Church had never been Calvinist. Hobart shared the same attitude, and his followers agreed that Calvinist theology was both "repugnant to Scripture" and contrary to "the common sense and feelings of mankind." All of them found "the peculiarities of Calvinism" to be reprehensible, and all of them saw in the Episcopal tradition a theology entirely independent of the Calvinist lineage.[13]

The evangelicals found more to respect in Calvinist thought. Several of their prominent leaders had attended Andover Seminary, and others had close ties to Leonard Woods there. William Wilmer spoke for them when he suggested that Calvin and the Calvinists had "received a measure of severity not due them." Eager to cooperate with evangelical and revivalist Calvinists, they drew from their reading of White and Burnet the lesson that the Thirty-Nine Articles set forth no "regular system either of Arminianism or of Calvinism," and they refused to undertake what Wilmer called the "voyage of speculation" that a full-blown Calvinist theology required, but they could at least agree with the Calvinists about depravity and the need for regeneration.[14]

When the high-church party in 1821 accused the evangelicals of crypto-Calvinism, the editors of the *Theological Repertory* replied with a defense of their position: "If by Calvinism be meant the doctrines of original sin, sanctification by the Holy Spirit, and justification by the sole merits of our Lord Jesus Christ, we plead guilty to the charge." They simply thought that such views should not be labeled "Calvinist"; they saw them as the doctrines of primitive Christianity. Stephen Tyng (1800–85), the rector of St. John's Church in Georgetown, joined with two other of the Washington evangelicals the following year in a letter to the bishop of Maryland in which they disclaimed "the doctrines of particular redemption and unconditional reprobation" and therefore disavowed the suggestion that they were Calvinists, but they conceded that some of their views might plausibly be read as reflecting some Calvinist insights. It all depended, they said, "upon the definition you give."[15]

A few evangelicals found outright Calvinism convincing, but they failed to make an impression on the denomination. Uzal Ogden, the rector of Trinity Church in Newark, New Jersey, was Calvinist in theology, but the Episcopal Church proved to be so uncongenial for him that he became a Presbyterian. More important was the Calvinism of Reuel Keith (1792–1842), the first full-time professor at the theological seminary in Virginia. A graduate of Andover, Keith argued that Calvinist theology was both the historical standard of the Episcopal Church and the only faithful interpretation of scripture. His *Lectures on those Doctrines in Theology Usually Called Calvinistic,* delivered to his classes in Virginia, found in Ephesians and Romans ample evidence that the New Testament viewed faith and good works as the effects of an eternal act of divine election. His was a moderate version of Calvinist doctrine, influenced by Edwardean teaching at Andover. He denied, for example, that God predestined the reprobate to unbelief. But even though some at the seminary agreed with him, his moderate Calvinism failed to gain much of a hearing within the denomination, and when he fell into depression in 1840 and took his own life, the rumor circulated that his doctrine was to blame.[16]

The evangelical party therefore had its Calvinist sympathizers, but historic Calvinism, even in the revised forms that it was assuming at such places as Andover and Yale, never found a solid footing among them. Most of them agreed with the high-church party at least to the extent of remaining aloof from the Calvinist doctrines of election and of special grace for the elect. In accord with the Thirty-Nine Articles they affirmed a doctrine of preventing grace — in White's words, "the grace of God going before us in all good and disposing to it" — but most agreed that this was a "persuasive" grace that enabled the will to accept the gospel but allowed it to resist. It empowered assent but did not make it certain, a qualification that allied most Episcopal theologians with their poorer Methodist cousins and also distinguished them from the Calvinism not only of Princeton but also of Andover and Yale. Yet differing Episcopal attitudes toward other Calvinist emphases — including the Calvinist insistence on the sole authority of scripture — still marked lines of division within the church.[17]

Revelation, Reason, and Tradition

Anglicans had long argued that scripture alone could not be the sole guide to theological truth. In the sixteenth century, Richard Hooker (ca. 1554–1600) explained in his *Treatise on the Laws of Ecclesiastical Polity*

(1594–97) that Christians had to read scripture in the light of a law of reason that reflected the eternal law of God. At the same time, Anglicans since the sixteenth century had also looked to the Christian authors of the first three to five centuries — the church "fathers" or "patristic" writers — as having a special importance as guides to the interpretation of scripture. Far more than most other American Protestants, the American Episcopalians also strove to balance scripture, reason, and tradition as sources of theological authority, though they themselves differed about the proper weighting.[18]

A high assessment of church tradition had not always characterized Anglican thought in America. A latitudinarian mood lingered throughout the eighteenth century, supplemented by the new confidence in rationality that defined the post-Newtonian intellectual culture. Especially in the early South, some Episcopalians viewed their church as a "temple of reason" besieged by sectarian irrationality. Bishop James Madison (1749–1812) of Virginia and Bishop Samuel Provoost (1742–1815) of New York cultivated such an image of intellectual tolerance that their critics suspected them of deist sympathies. The lofty regard for reason and natural theology in latitudinarian circles found full expression in the pedagogy of Scottish-born William Smith (1727–1803), a graduate of the University of Aberdeen and the first provost of the College of Philadelphia, who laced his theological reasoning with Scottish Common Sense philosophy and the "physico-theology" of John Ray.[19]

Smith exemplified the casual attitude toward church tradition in the latitudinarian strain. He led the effort during the 1780s to omit from the proposed prayer book of the post-Revolutionary Episcopal Church two of the ancient creeds (the Nicene and the Athanasian), to drop from the Apostles' Creed any reference to Christ's descent into hell, and to remove any reference to baptismal regeneration. William White, who also wanted to make it clear that his church did not espouse a "magical" view of baptism or an unreasonable reading of scripture, supported the revisions, but the two men failed to gain the assent of the majority, who in 1789 reinserted the omissions into the *Book of Common Prayer*.[20]

As a result of this experience, William White became far more cautious about doctrinal innovation. Throughout the church, the latitudinarian temper gradually faded into the background, and its proponents had no real voice in the nineteenth-century debates. By 1820, White was emphasizing the limits of reason in theology. Convinced now that the threat to the church came from popular deism, he began to point out that the deists had overlooked the extent of their dependence on ideas revealed in the Jewish and Christian scriptures. He insisted that "no effort of reason" could "ascend from the creature to the creator" unless reason had first been instructed by revelation, either through remnants of the primordial communication with Adam or through the Jewish and Christian scriptures. This was again the idea of the *prisca theologia* (ancient theology), and it caught on with both high-church and evangelical clergy, who used it against deism. It enabled them to reclaim natural theology even as they reasserted the centrality of scripture and church tradition.[21]

Like most other American theologians, Episcopal thinkers opposed rationalism with evidentialism. White's reading list urged a familiarity with the arguments of Paley, Butler, Edward Stillingfleet, and Charles Leslie — leading English masters of evidential reasoning — and both high-church and evangelical Episcopal writers rehearsed the arguments from miracles, fulfilled prophecy, and intrinsic consistency. Such prominent clergy as William Meade in Virginia and Leonidas Polk (1806–64), the first bishop of Louisiana, testified that their first serious understanding of Christian doctrine came through their reading of treatises on the evidences, and such testimonies encouraged the denomination to cultivate evidential literature. Prominent clergy sponsored lectureships and published evidential treatises throughout the antebellum era.[22]

They combined their defense of scripture with a distinctively Episcopal emphasis on the authority of the church "fathers." Even William White was arguing by 1823 that "the history of the early ages of the church," especially the first three centuries, had a normative importance that was "next to Scripture." Ever since the sixteenth century, Anglicans had elevated the patristic era to a position of normative importance. In his *Apologie of the Church of England* (1562), John Jewel (1522–71), the bishop of Salisbury during the Reformation, stressed Anglican conformity to "the fathers and councils of old times" as a way of countering Catholic claims that the reformers were guilty of innovation. Jewel's allies used the same strategy to oppose the Puritan claim that the only permissible practices in the church were those explicitly warranted by scripture. Against the Presbyterian Thomas Cartwright (1535–1603), for example, the Elizabethan bishop John Whitgift (ca. 1530–1604) insisted that the first five hundred years of Christian history — not only the era described in the New Testament — retained a normative authority for later Christian thought and practice. This historical way of arguing became a permanent feature of Anglican thought, and in America it distinguished Episcopal theologians from other Protestants.[23]

Invoking the example of the early church could mean different things, however, to different parties in the denomination. When John Henry Hobart said that "the apostolic and primitive church" guided the interpretation of scripture, he usually referred to the texts and practices of the first three centuries. He thought that St. Jerome (342–420), for example, had lived too far after the founding events to bear the same authority as earlier writers. In a similar fashion, John Henry Hopkins (1792–1868), the high-church bishop of Vermont after 1832, defined "the period of the primitive Church" as the era "before the Nicene Council" of 325. In *The Primitive Church* (1835), he argued that scripture as it was read during this period demonstrated the necessity for bishops, the authority of the Anglican liturgy, the propriety of the Episcopal sacraments, and the proper view of the church. Closer in time to the church of the first century, the Christians of the primitive era had the clearest understanding of what the biblical writers meant.[24]

The Tractarians also turned to the early church for norms, but as they became more convinced of the values of later medieval practice, they expanded the rule of faith to include the united witness of the church throughout its history, a move that opened the way to a more Catholic sense of tradition. William Ingraham Kip, the rector of St. Paul's in Albany, New York, and later the first bishop of California, published in 1849 his *Double Witness of the Church,* in which he argued that both scripture and tradition served as authoritative witnesses. He did not accept the Catholic doctrine that scripture and tradition were parallel authorities; the value of tradition for him was that it ensured the correct interpretation of scripture. Although convinced that the most trustworthy reading of the Bible came from the primitive church, Kip also felt free to appeal to "the recorded wisdom and opinions of eighteen centuries," to the voice of the church "through all ages," as the norm of interpretation. He looked to "Scripture as it always has been interpreted by the Church" as an alternative both to Roman Catholic doctrine and to Protestant private judgment.[25]

So also did George Washington Doane, a graduate of General Theological Seminary who began his ministry as Hobart's assistant and became the bishop of New Jersey in 1832. By 1834 he supported the Tractarians and published the first American edition of the *Christian Year* by Newman's friend John Keble. Impressed by the Catholic argument that the apostles conveyed a tradition that predated the written scriptures, Doane told a convocation of his clergy in 1840 that the proper response to the extravagant biblical interpretations of the Protestant sects was to follow the guidance of the church throughout the ages: "Together with the sacred records, there has come down, in Christ's own Church, a parallel stream of testimony, unbroken, undivided, and unwavering." Denying the Protestant claim that the scripture interpreted itself and ridiculing — as Hobart had also ridiculed — the Protestant refrain about the virtues of private judgment, Doane taught that church tradition alone could ensure "the true reception of the doctrine of the Gospel."[26]

The Tractarian position went beyond what most of the Hobartian high-church clergy would accept. John Henry Hopkins, sympathetic in many ways to Tractarian ideals, defended the older Episcopal reliance on the early church. The evangelicals found the Tractarian argument even more appalling. To them it appeared that the Tractarians had defined the tradition not merely as an aid to understanding scripture but as a "part of the authoritative rule itself." When the evangelical John S. Stone moved from Boston to the diocese of New York, he was dismayed by Bishop Benjamin Onderdonk's Tractarian sympathies, and he published a series of rejoinders — *The Mysteries Opened* (1844), *The Church Universal* (1846), and *The Contrast* (1853) — that defended the evangelical position that the Bible was the "sole, ultimately authoritative rule of faith."[27]

Like the high-church theologians, the evangelicals recognized the distinctive authority of the early church as a source for norms of biblical interpretation. Charles McIlvaine agreed that the early fathers clarified the scriptures. But the evangelicals depended finally on "the single authority and entire sufficiency of Scripture as a rule in matters of faith," and McIlvaine warned that the early church could never have "final authority." Stone revealed one possible implication of that warning when he resurrected the familiar American Protestant endorsement of "the duty of private judgment." By the mid-1840s, the evangelicals were trying to counter what they saw as an excessive veneration of ecclesiastical authority — and an unfortunate doctrine of the church — in both the older high-church and the more recent Tractarian circles.[28]

The Church Question

Hobart's *Companion for the Festivals and Fasts of the Protestant Episcopal Church* (1804), which set forth the theological underpinnings of high-church liturgical practice, represented the church as the sole visible divine society that mediated the grace of salvation. This position irritated other Protestants because the high-church party wanted also to say that only the Church of England, the Episcopal Church, and some of the Eastern Orthodox churches met the criteria for a proper visible divine society. They alone had maintained orthodox doctrine, the required sacramental practice, and the proper ordering of the church through episcopal governance and the succession of bishops.[29]

For Hobart, a proper ecclesiology required the threefold order of bishop, priest, and deacon in the church's ministry. The strong emphasis on the threefold ministry had its origins in the English struggles of the 1590s when Anglican apologists reacted against the Presbyterian challenge to the episcopal office. The popular reaction against the disorder of the English civil wars of the 1640s strengthened the hand of theologians who argued that the traditional episcopacy and the threefold order of ministry were of divine right, a doctrine that governed the expulsion of clergy with Presbyterian ordination after 1662. Hobart read widely in the high-church authors of the seventeenth century. He followed familiar patterns of argument when he found a foreshadowing of the threefold order in the Old Testament, with its high priests, priests, and Levites. He viewed these three Old Testament orders as types prefiguring Christ, the apostles, and the Seventy in the church of the first century. In turn, the first-century example set the precedent for apostles, elders, and deacons in the early Christian mission, and that precedent found continued expression in the offices of bishops, elders, and deacons in the first-century New Testament churches.[30]

To Hobart and the high-church party, the threefold order was so much "the institution of Christ and his apostles" that no true church could exist without it. And the threefold order required the episcopal succession. Without an unbroken line of bishops extending from the apostles, bearing the authority to ordain elders and deacons, the "power to be derived from the Head of the Church" would have been broken. Churches that separated from that episcopal succession were no true churches. Hobart's view was more stringent than that of seventeenth-century Anglicans. Most high-church theologians in England after the Glorious Revolution of 1688 conceded that churches without bishops could be true churches. But one group of eighteenth-century high-church theologians had a position similar to that which Hobart would defend. Influenced by the Anglican "non-jurors," who refused to give an oath of allegiance to William and Mary after 1688 because they had pledged allegiance to the Stuart king James II and his successors, the eighteenth-century high churchmen launched a more exclusive defense of the succession and the threefold order. Hobart stood in continuity with them.[31]

The evangelicals thought that Hobart considerably overstated the argument for the Anglican ministry. They followed William White in seeing the three orders as necessary not to the church's being *(esse)* but only to its well-being *(bene esse)*. By the 1830s, such evangelicals as McIlvaine and Alexander Viets Griswold (1766–1843), the bishop in upper New England, defended the divine origin of the threefold order and the apostolic succession. McIlvaine insisted that both would be "continued in the Church, by the will of its divine Head, to the end of the world." But while these external ordinances were essential to the perfection of the church, they were not essential to its validity, and so most of them refused to pass judgment on the authority of ministers in other denominations without episcopal ordination. They could not accept the high-church formulation of apostolic succession. They could view themselves as standing within an unbroken apostolic succession, but they refused to draw the conclusion that such a succession alone constituted true ministers and sacraments. The evangelical William Sparrow at Virginia Theological Seminary thought that no one could hold the apostolic succession as "essential" to a true church and still maintain "true Protestant principles."[32]

The issue was of pressing importance because the high-church party thought that a church governed by bishops was "the only appointed road to heaven." To the evangelicals this implied that baptism and conversion were invalid, and salvation inaccessible, in churches without bishops, and they found it embarrassing when critics like the Presbyterian Samuel Miller charged the Episcopalians with uncharitable dogmatism for suggesting such an idea.[33]

The high-church response was that the members of non-episcopal churches could rest their hopes on the "uncovenanted mercies" of God. In his reply to Miller, the high-church theologian Thomas Yardley How denied that Episcopal theology had no place for Presbyterians: Christians outside the Anglican covenant, he said, could place their hope in "the *general mercy* of God, with whom sincerity of heart is of great price, who can dispense with his own institutions." The answer failed to satisfy Miller, who recognized that How had placed Presbyterians in the same position as non-Christians.[34]

In fact, the doctrine of uncovenanted mercies placed erring Protestants and all Catholics in greater peril than Hindus and Muslims. It afforded non-Christians ample grounds for hope. All men and women, Hobart said, were "in the hands of an infinitely merciful and righteous God, who will judge them according to their works." How added that non-Christians would be judged "not by the law of the Gospel, but by the law which they are placed under," the law of their "reasonable nature." God would accept everyone who tried to obey the divine will as revealed to reason and conscience. In the high-church reading of Pauline theology, this was the teaching of Romans 2:14–16, in which Paul taught that gentiles "not having the law" could yet do the things "contained in the law." But everyone who "willfully and knowingly" rejected the "duly authorized ministry of the church" risked a special guilt. The only hope of the Presbyterians and other groups outside the succession, therefore, lay in their ignorance. God would not cast away Christians with "imperfect information."[35]

To bolster the doctrine of uncovenanted mercies, the high-church theologians appealed to the doctrine of atonement that they held in common with other non-Calvinist evangelicals: Christ died for all. William Adams, high-church professor of divinity at Nashotah House in Wisconsin, pointed out in 1847 that advocates for a limited atonement remained a "miserable minority" in the Episcopal Church. For the high-church writers, this doctrine of general atonement, or universal redemption, meant that the effects of Christ's death extended even "where the name of Christ is not proclaimed." Non-Christians could do what was required because they shared in the benefits of a universal atonement. Samuel Seabury III, editor of the *Churchman* and a professor at the high-church General Theological Seminary, argued in a provocative 1838 essay on the "Salvability of the Heathen" that everyone could share in the benefits of the atonement even without being aware of them. Christ remained necessary for salvation, but Christian profession did not. Seabury's blunt clarity created a stir, and the trustees of General Seminary discreetly distanced themselves from his views.[36]

Some evangelicals also held to the doctrine of uncovenanted mercies. In his *Episcopal Manual*, William Wilmer interpreted Paul to mean in Romans 2:14 that non-Christians could be saved on the basis of sincere hearts and good works because Christ had died for the sins of all. But while the point was important for the high-church party, it was a mere footnote for the evangelicals, who wanted to press the necessity for explicit faith. To everyone who heard the message of Christ, they thought, the way of salvation came solely through the instrumentality of faith, and they did not want to emphasize the theoretical possibility of salvation for non-Christians when the pressing necessity was for the hearers of the gospel to accept and trust it. Most of all, they did not want to suggest that evangelical Christians outside the Episcopal Church had to depend on uncovenanted mercies.[37]

The question had special implications for Episcopal views of the sacraments, especially baptism. A long line of Anglican theologians, extending back into the seventeenth century, had interpreted baptism as the rite of admission to the visible church and the entry into a covenant relation with God. This was the doctrine that William White taught in his *Lectures on the Catechism* (1813), in which he designated the baptismal covenant as the source of assurance for Christians who had never undergone a specifiable experience of conversion. The covenant metaphor appealed to both evangelicals and high-church clergy; Wilmer and Hobart could both describe baptism as a means for entering into covenant.[38]

For Episcopal theologians, however, baptism was also a sacrament of regeneration. In addition to defining it as a covenant rite, William White also described it, on the basis of the New Testament (John 3:5, Titus 3:6) and the *Book of Common Prayer*, as the means of regeneration. He meant that baptism, by introducing the baptized into Christ's church, brought them into a new "state" in which they could be assured of receiving all "the aids of the Holy Spirit." This baptismal grace would, if improved by repentance and faith, be "sufficient for the exigencies of future life" even into eternity. Baptism for White conveyed no immediate "moral change." Like Gilbert Burnet and John Tillotson in England, he said only that it placed its recipients into a new "state of grace." But for him this still meant that to be baptized was to be "born again."[39]

He tried to maintain a balance between the regeneration in baptism and the renewal through which the baptismal covenant found its fulfillment. Among later Episcopal theologians, the balance proved hard to maintain. The evangelicals underscored the renewal, and the doctrine of adult renewal or renovation became for some of them, like McIlvaine and James Milnor (1773–1845), a lawyer and former congressman who became rector of St. George's Church in New York in 1816, the Anglican counterpart to the revivalist's doctrine of conversion. Wilmer demanded a change of heart in which the baptized adult moved from spiritual immaturity to repentance, faith, and holiness. For him, as for William Meade, the head of the powerful evangelical faction in Virginia, the sacrament was no substitute for a "recovery from sinful dispositions to holiness of heart." Their position distanced them from White, who had disliked revivalist piety and construed renewal as a lifelong process manifest not in intense feeling but in moral obedience. It also separated them from almost all high-church theologians.[40]

High-church theologians accepted the need for adult renewal, but they did not want it to overshadow sacramental regeneration. Hobart had no problem in saying that the final title to the spiritual privileges of baptism would depend on renewal, which he understood as the culmination of repentance, faith, and obedience. But he wanted to protect a belief in baptism as the means and pledge of spiritual grace, the rite that translated the baptized into the "holy Church of which Christ is the head, where we become members of Christ, children of God, and heirs of the kingdom of heaven." Drawing on the sacramental thought of Daniel Waterland (1683–1740), who had been a revered master of Magdalene College in Cambridge, he taught that baptismal "regeneration" was normally the necessary condition of the later adult "renovation."[41]

In tone and nuance the evangelicals and high churchmen were worlds apart. The difference came to the fore most clearly in the desire of the evangelicals to use the term "regeneration" to refer not only to the results of baptism but also to a "renovation" or "renewal" that was similar to the revivalist Protestant understanding of conversion. Wilmer wanted to say that baptismal regeneration had no inseparable connection with a true "spiritual regeneration," which he equated with renewal. McIlvaine also preferred to define regeneration as referring only to the spiritual renovation, and he argued as well that it had no invariable connection with baptism. Hobart and his followers, however, found such an extension of the meaning of regeneration wrongheaded. Ravenscroft taught that regeneration in its proper sense occurred "in baptism," and he made every effort to ensure that the clergy of his North Carolina diocese understood that the sacrament brought regeneration "absolutely and virtually flowing from the promise" that it ratified, as long as the baptized did not abuse the grace given to them. During the mid-1820s the high-church group tried to persuade the General Convention to codify a clear distinction between the two terms, restricting "regeneration" to a sacramental usage.[42]

The convention refused and left the matter to the theologians, some of whom sought compromise. The high-church Henry U. Onderdonk (1759–1858), the bishop of Pennsylvania, wrote an *Essay on Regeneration* (1835) in which he distinguished two types of regeneration, one baptismal, the other moral, gradual, and progressive, and insisted that each remained incomplete without the other. His effort, like others, failed to gain a consensus. After 1839 the dispute became even sharper when some of the Tractarians claimed that baptismal regeneration made a subsequent "renewal" unnecessary. By 1849, Levi Sullivan Ives, the bishop of North Carolina, was making the case in America for the Tractarian doctrine of baptismal rebirth. In *The Obedience of Faith* (1849), he contended that infants came out of the baptismal waters with "a new and heavenly nature." This doctrine was quite different from the evangelical and older high-church consensus that baptismal regeneration denoted a change not of nature but of "state," or entry into a covenantal relationship to which belonged the conditional promises of salvation. For Ives, the unbaptized remained in a state of condemnation, regardless of their seeming faith; the faith that purified the heart presupposed baptism as its necessary condition.[43]

Both the Hobartians and the evangelicals believed that Ives had left Episcopal theology behind, and most thought it good riddance when he converted to Rome. The evangelicals especially distrusted the high-church theology of sacramental rebirth, and it was even more objectionable to them that a minority among the high-church group linked their sacramental views to the argument that only bishops could convey the authority to baptize.

In the 1840s the Eucharist became an additional subject of contention, especially after the Oxford tracts persuaded a few to affirm what Newman called a "substantial" presence of Christ in the elements of bread and wine. For the most part, even the high-church group rejected Newman's view of the sacramental presence. The young Hobart felt the lure of a doctrine of real presence and Eucharistic sacrifice, but White persuaded him to reject it, and in his later theology he accepted neither the corporeal presence of the Lutherans nor the transubstantiation of the Catholics. He also rejected the doctrine of the Eucharist as a sacrifice. He spoke only of the sacrament's "becoming" the "spiritual body and blood of Christ" to those who received it faithfully. Evangelicals also wrote of it as a sign of Christ's body and blood or as a vehicle of his "virtual" presence to the faith of the communicant.[44]

To the American Tractarians, however, neither the evangelical nor the older high-church doctrine of the Eucharist adequately conveyed the truth of the real presence of Christ in the ritual. They felt it necessary to emphasize the "reality" of the presence even though they saw no need to define precisely what they meant. Both evangelicals and the older high-church group worried about Catholic doctrines creeping into the Episcopal Church. The evangelicals tried in 1843 to stop the ordination of a student at General Seminary when he affirmed, among other seemingly Catholic views, the real presence, even though he disavowed belief in transubstantiation. Even the high-church John Henry Hopkins, enthusiastic about some of the Tractarian directions, charged that Tractarian views of the real presence veered too near the edge of Catholic thought. Evangelicals especially disliked the Tractarian tendency to speak of the Eucharist as a sacrifice, and McIlvaine once refused to consecrate a church until a table replaced the stone "altar."[45]

Sin and Justification

The various Episcopal parties shared the conviction that the atonement did not preclude the necessity of good works. Most continued to speak of the atonement as a sacrifice that propitiated a wrathful God and satisfied a debt that human beings could not repay, though a few, especially among the Tractarian sympathizers, felt uneasy with a satisfaction theory. Before 1838, however, most agreed that good works were also necessary. Justification had conditions affixed to it, and most agreed also that the conditions included repentance, faith, and holiness of life. No one argued that either faith or works of holiness merited justification; Hobart spoke for most when he said that no qualifications whatever in the creature, even the faith wrought by the Holy Spirit, had any merit whatsoever. The only merit resided in the righteousness of Christ, who was the sole meritorious cause of justification. But both Hobart and Wilmer could speak of obedience and holiness as conditions of acceptance, Hobart arguing that obedience was always the fruit of a lively faith, Wilmer affirming the different argument that true faith included obedience within it.[46]

After 1838, some of the evangelicals began to fear that such formulations played into the hands of the Oxford Movement. Newman published in that year his *Lectures on Justification,* in which he argued that justification required both faith and obedience and that the justified were both accounted and made righteous by the indwelling of Christ's righteousness. To McIlvaine, a lifelong friend and college classmate of the Princeton Calvinist theologian Charles Hodge, it appeared that the Tractarians had once again capitulated to

Rome, and in his episcopal charge of 1839, *Justification by Faith,* he rejected even the view—common among eighteenth-century Anglicans—that repentance, love, and obedience could be considered as "included in the faith that justifies."[47]

Conceding that good works sprang necessarily from faith, McIlvaine hammered the point that faith never derived "any of its justifying virtue from these fruits." He returned to the doctrine that justification occurred only through the imputing of Christ's righteousness to the faithful. He tried to show that both Paul, especially in Romans, and the most authoritative theologians of Anglican tradition, especially Richard Hooker and Bishop William Beveridge (1637–1708), considered imputed righteousness to be the heart of justification. In 1841 McIlvaine expanded this anti-Tractarian argument in his *Oxford Divinity,* in which he set out to resist the "zealous efforts" that "have been made to commend the peculiarities of Oxford Divinity." To McIlvaine, Oxford had become Rome, and the task of the hour was to reassert that the righteousness that justified was the righteousness of Christ, imputed to the sinner, received by faith alone, and that there was no justifying efficacy in love, holiness, or any of the other fruits that sprang from the justified life.[48]

The American Tractarians replied that McIlvaine's doctrine made salvation depend on "a mere act of the mind called faith." Levi Sullivan Ives thought that the evangelicals misunderstood faith, which he considered "a moral perception, and not a mere mental exercise," a power that worked by love and purified the heart. He thought, as well, that they misconstrued justification, which he saw as having nothing to do with any legal imputation but rather occurring through a gradual transition in which, through sacramental grace and faithful obedience, the righteousness of Christ was "wrought into the very texture" of the regenerate life. He denied that his position was "Romanizing," but his denial failed to convince his critics.[49]

To McIlvaine, imputed righteousness implied imputed guilt, but even McIlvaine discarded the Calvinist understanding of original sin as the result of the imputation to humankind of the guilt of Adam. William White had argued that it made no sense to adjudge men and women guilty of sin prior to their exercise of volition, and most Episcopal theologians, both high-church and evangelical, followed him. While they continued to speak of the imputation of guilt, they meant only that God imputed to the sinful—but did not impute to the faithful—the guilt of their own sins. On this point Episcopal theologians agreed with Wesleyans, the later Edwardeans, the New Haven and Oberlin theologians, and New School Presbyterians.[50]

In no way did this caution about imputation imply reservations about original sin. Across the spectrum—evangelical, high-church, and Tractarian—

everyone assumed original sin. Their different ways of defining it, however, suggested some of the hidden theological fault lines in the denomination. For William White, claims about a natural "hatred" for God seemed extreme, and he preferred to speak of original sin as a "liability to sin, originating in the first transgression." The high-church party took a similar position. We are not "wholly defiled," added Hobart, even though we are, as the Thirty-Nine Articles asserted, "very far gone" from original righteousness and utterly lacking any power to do the good without divine grace. A few Tractarians found even that position extreme; Levi Sullivan Ives preferred the Catholic view that original sin meant merely the absence of the superadded preternatural gifts — the "divine nature" — that Adam had lost in the fall, which left the unregenerate will with "no prompting but to sin" but did not obliterate the freedom not to sin. For an evangelical like McIlvaine, however, original sin meant a depravity of heart so pervading the moral nature as to leave the sinner in a condition of unremitting enmity to God.[51]

The Eschatological Peculiarity

On one issue, the Episcopal theologians stood virtually alone. Unlike most other American Protestants, they insisted on the doctrine of what they called the "intermediate state." This doctrine had originated among sixteenth-century reformers trying to define the Anglican alternative to the Catholic doctrine of purgatory and to deal with the ambiguities of the biblical accounts of an afterlife. John Pearson (1613–86), the bishop of Chester, gave it authoritative expression in his *Exposition of the Creed* (1659), a book prominent on William White's list of books for clerical candidates.[52]

The New Testament allowed for varying views of an afterlife. In 1 Thessalonians 4 and 1 Corinthians 15, Paul seemed to suggest that the dead would sleep until the day of Christ's return, when they would receive spiritual bodies. Jesus' parable of Lazarus and the rich man in Luke 16, however, and his words to the thief on the cross in Luke 23 suggested a conscious continuation of life immediately after death. The scenario became even more complex in the book of Revelation, which described an elevation of the souls of the martyrs in the "first resurrection" to a heavenly altar before the beginning of the millennium. They were to join Christ in his thousand-year reign, whereas "the rest of the dead" would not come to life again until after the millennium, when they would be judged (Rev. 6:9–11 and 20:4–15).

In an attempt to harmonize the accounts, theologians offered various depictions of the end times. The Calvinist consensus in the Westminster Confession was that the souls of the departed proceeded immediately to God — and thence to heaven and hell—where they awaited the final judgment that would send them, reunited with their celestial bodies, either to bliss or torment. Most Anglicans had a different view. In 1789, one of the notes in the American version of the *Book of Common Prayer* announced that the dead proceeded immediately to Hades, or "hell." According to this doctrine, however, hell was not the place of the damned (which was rather "Gehenna") but an intermediate state in which the souls of the departed awaited a judgment before their going on to bliss or punishment.[53]

William White knew that American Protestants had some difficulty with this depiction because it suggested a Catholic doctrine of purgatory. White found the depiction plausible, partly for exegetical reasons and partly because of its roots in Anglican tradition. He taught, with the mainstream of that tradition, that departed spirits waited in hell—the "lower parts of the earth" into which, according to Ephesians 4, Jesus had also descended—in the interval between their death and their resurrection for judgment. This "hell" was not the place of eternal punishment but an intermediate state.[54]

To his chagrin, his student John Henry Hobart chose to explore the topic at an ecumenical gathering of clerical dignitaries assembled in 1816 to memorialize the life of Bishop Benjamin Moore of New York. Hobart's funeral sermon disturbed the harmony by arguing that the souls of the righteous departed would enter heaven only after the last judgment, when they would be reunited with their bodies. In a longer published version of the sermon he offered further detail about the intermediate state in which the souls now waited. To some of his readers it seemed that Hobart had returned to a Catholic doctrine of purgatory. The sermon, however, tried to make it clear that this was not what he had in mind, since he did not teach that the soul could become better in the intermediate state.[55]

The high-church party defended the doctrine. Hobart insisted that it came directly from scriptural revelation. For the most part, the evangelicals accepted it too, though they did not agree that it could be called a necessary doctrine of faith. Both sides found it attractive for similar reasons. It not only solved exegetical puzzles but it accentuated the importance of renewal and the sanctified life. The entry into heaven would await the judgment, and as Matthew 25 made clear, one criterion for judgment would be the deeds of goodness that issued from the sanctified heart. Other Protestants, however, worried that the Episcopal doctrine was dangerously close to Catholic teaching. Almost a quarter century after the sermon, the *Princeton Review* still consigned this "meager" offering of Hobart to "the field of fiction and romance."[56]

Episcopal theologians had more to say about the intermediate state than about the earthly millennium, but they had millennial interests. White left an unpublished manuscript in which he followed the general outline of Thomas Newton, the bishop of Bristol, who agreed with Joseph Mede that the millennium would begin 1,260 years after the rise of the Papacy. By White's reckoning, that put the date at roughly 2000. But for the most part the Episcopalians were wary of setting dates, and they reached no consensus about the millennium. Some, like Hobart, rejected the idea of a specific millennial period; others, like Hopkins, thought that Christ would appear before the millennium; others envisioned a millennium before the return of Christ.[57]

For all the Episcopal groups, however, the important themes of the Christian life were the doctrines of the church, sacramental grace, and moral renewal. Like the Unitarians, with whom they had almost nothing else in common, they believed that the moral life counted heavily in the divine scheme, and most of them agreed that Calvinist theology wrongly placed more stress on "theoretical opinions" than on "practical points on which professing Christians generally agree." The point of doctrine, said William Wilmer, was to illustrate and enforce piety. White agreed that the aim of Christianity was to influence "conduct," and Anglican theologians like Jasper Adams (1739–1841), a graduate of Andover who served for twelve years as president of Charleston College, occasionally wrote manuals in moral philosophy as guides to the cultivation of the sense of duty. They were far from reducing theology to ethics, for practicality in their lexicon referred not merely to moral conduct but also to all the dispositions of piety relevant to "acceptance with God." But they strove to avoid "the voyage of speculation," eschewed the aim of "system," and, from their own point of view, left the "theoretical" issues to the Calvinists.[58]

Methodist Perfection

As theologians, the early American Methodists traveled light. They thought of themselves as an evangelical wing of the Church of England, and their self-understanding came initially from the Anglican theology of their founder John Wesley as it was filtered through the English Methodist revival. They got their start in America between 1764 and 1766 when Irish lay preachers formed local communities in Maryland and New York, and they remained for almost two decades a lay movement that ignored theological intricacies. Only in 1784 did they become a separate denomination, and even then some Methodist leaders sought reunion with the Church of England. As the Methodists expanded, however, they presented themselves as a church for the common people, disdainful of Episcopal formality and any dependence on an educated clergy. The characteristic figure was the revivalist and circuit rider, traveling on horseback from one isolated spot to another, not the theologian. Within half a century of the founding, the Illinois preacher Peter Cartwright could boast of Methodist indifference to theological learning. "Literary gentlemen" might disdain the Methodists as "ignorant babblers," he wrote, but the Methodists "set the world on fire" while the gentlemen were still lighting their matches.[1]

As the Methodists multiplied, they encouraged their converts to ignore the "dogmas" of the educated elite. "Are divines and philosophers the only men," asked one Methodist writer, "to whom God has given the right to think and judge for themselves?" Richard Allen, who emerged from slavery to found in 1816 the African Methodist Episcopal Church, explained that the "plain and simple gospel" of the Methodists could reach everyone: "for the unlearned can understand, and the learned are sure to understand." But the learned, in fact, usually dismissed the early Methodist preachers as "enemies to learning," and the Methodist blending of Christian doctrine with popular folk beliefs earned them a reputation in some quarters as enthusiasts who "disgusted all men of correct taste and wise discernment."[2]

In the circles of the educated, it was easy to treat them, as Nathan Bangs (1778–1862) complained, with "silent contempt." Bangs was a self-educated Methodist minister who preached in Canada and New York before becoming head of the Methodist Book Concern in New York City, where he strove to transform Methodism into a piety that could appeal to the educated as well as the illiterate. By 1810 he thought he saw signs of progress—a "new sort of warfare" between Methodists and their competitors—as the Methodists began to produce theologians and the fashionable denominations began to pay attention to them.[3]

Embarrassed by what Bangs called the "ill-digested effusions" of unlearned exhorters, a faction within the denomination began as early as in 1784 to promote colleges to train "rational, Scriptural Christians." Wesleyans eventually created a network of colleges stretching from New England to the far West. They introduced in 1789 a short-lived journal, which they revived in 1818 as the *Methodist Magazine,* devoted to drawing Methodists away from credulous acceptance of "curious tales" and miracle stories toward a faith "grounded in evidence." By 1841, the *Methodist Quarterly Review* could compete with the best of the denominational quarterlies. By that time, Methodists had fully joined in the pursuit of a rational theology.[4]

They sought also a "practical" theology. This was Bangs's message when he published in 1838–40 his four-volume history of American Methodism. The Methodists, he said, proclaimed the deity of Christ, the depravity of human beings, a universal atonement, and the need for repentance and faith, and they "pressed upon their hearers with the greatest earnestness" three doctrines of "practical" piety—the necessity of a new birth, the inner assuring witness of the Spirit, and "holiness of heart and life." But the new breed of Methodist theologians also became apostles of evidential Christianity to the common people.[5]

Popular Rationality

For decades the Methodists depended on theology imported from England. They considered Wesley's sermons to be "the most comprehensive, the deepest, the most experimental and practical body of divinity to be found in the English language." They admired the *Checks to Antinomianism* by John Fletcher, the vicar of Madeley, whose arguments against Calvinists in England persuaded Wesley to recruit him as his successor, and they published an American edition of Fletcher's work as early as 1791. They also required their clergy to read the *Theological Institutes* (1823–29) of Richard Watson, a second-generation English Methodist whose two-volume treatise, packed with evidences for Christianity and contentions against Calvinism, became a model for what it meant to write a Methodist theology.[6]

Eventually the American Methodists published their own theology. When Asa Shinn (1781–1853), a self-educated preacher from West Virginia, published *An Essay on the Plan of Salvation* (1812), he began a tradition of theological writing designed to stay in touch with the common people. He apologized for any passages "abstruse and metaphysical." Thomas Neely Ralston (1806–91), a Kentucky educator and pastor, continued the tradition when he published in 1847 his *Elements of Divinity*, the first American Methodist systematic theology. Though he enjoyed his reputation as the scholar of Kentucky Methodism, Ralston described his work as "theology made easy," simple in style, and devoid of "the technicalities of the schoolmen," a book that would please both young readers and "ministers of all grades." A similar effort to reach the laity marked the *Elements of Theology* (1853) of Luther Lee (1800–89), an antislavery Methodist who helped form the Wesleyan Methodist Church in protest against denominational waffling on slavery. When the Ohio preacher Asbury Lowrey published his *Positive Theology* (1853), he boasted "a style direct and practical" that would reach young members and young ministers, and when in the same year A. A. Jimeson printed a similar summary of Methodist doctrine, he assured the public and the church that he was writing for "the people," the "common reader."[7]

In 1862, Samuel Wakefield (1799–1895), a pastor in Pennsylvania who had not yet gained a reputation as a theologian, published *A Complete System of Christian Theology*. Its aim was to attain "a new and strictly systematic form" of Wesleyan thought, and the *Methodist Quarterly Review* found it impressive: "the completeness of his success, attested by the more than ordinary routine compliments of the press, has taken some of us by surprise." But like his predecessors, Wakefield was not writing only for other theologians; his ambition was to reach "all classes of readers, from the aged theologian to the Sabbath-school scholar." Many of the early Methodist theological essays came directly from oral debates against Calvinists and Universalists, conducted before lay audiences who encouraged their champions to publish. Even more of them grew out of polemical sermons.[8]

In 1865, William F. Warren, a Massachusetts pastor who had been appointed to a Methodist seminary in Bremen, Germany, and would become the first dean of Boston University's School of Theology, published in German an introduction to a new kind of Methodist systematic theology. Convinced that theologians had to adjust to the movement from a mechanical to an organic and dynamic picture of the physical world, he wanted to produce a system attuned to European ventures in the philosophy of religion. He addressed his *Systematische Theologie* not to the common people but to the "theological public." The phrase foreshadowed a transition in Methodist theology.[9]

Even the theologians who addressed "the people," however, assumed that the people wanted a rational theology, and to provide it they turned to the same philosophical sources that attracted the academic elites. The *Methodist Quarterly Review* printed regular essays on English, French, and German philosophy and theology, but like the theologians at Harvard, Yale, Andover, and Princeton, the Methodist theologians especially admired Scottish philosophy. Shinn set the course in 1812 with a long excursus on Thomas Reid, and for the next half-century, Methodist theological texts repeated Scottish Common Sense axioms and definitions and appealed in Scottish fashion to "consciousness" as a source of philosophical truth. In 1822 Nathan Bangs recommended the Scottish philosophy as an antidote to "the errors of Locke," and as book agent he issued a complete set of Reid's works, insisting that Reid stood "at the head of those metaphysical philosophers who adorned the last century."[10]

The Scottish philosophy allowed the Methodist elite to say that they were as mindful of reason as the professors at Yale and Andover. They claimed that no part of true religion could be "incompatible with reason," rightly understood, and they found encouragement in the maxim of John Wesley that to renounce reason was to renounce religion. Richard Watson promoted the idea of the *prisca theologia* — the doctrine that reason could attain religious truth because it bore residues of a primal revelation — and some American Wesleyans liked it because it allowed them to deploy a natural theology without conceding a purely natural religion. Only because "the light of nature" included "a degree of supernatural instruction traditionally preserved," wrote Wakefield, could it discover religious truths. The doctrine justified both natural and evidential theology.[11]

With or without allusions to a *prisca theologia*, educated Methodists joined in the chorus of confidence in natural theology. Henry Bidleman Bascom (1796–1850), a Methodist pastor in Kentucky before he became a professor at Augusta College and later the president of Transylvania University in Lexington, tried in 1837 to present to urban southern audiences an argument for the truth of Christianity "based exclusively upon the facts and principles of Natural theology." By the time of the Civil War, one author in the *Methodist*

Quarterly Review could announce that any prejudice against natural theology resulted from an outmoded Lockean philosophy. In educated Methodist circles, the Scottish philosophy made natural theology respectable.[12]

Even for the natural theologians, however, the Bible held dominion in Methodist thought. It was an inspired, infallible text, "without error or mistake." It was the word of God, produced through the inspiration of the Spirit. Its inspiration was plenary, extending to every book, even to every word. Wesley had believed the Bible to be inspired, though he never went into detail about what this meant; Watson had even less to say. But by 1862 Samuel Wakefield thought it necessary to devote a full chapter of his systematic theology to a defense of plenary and verbal inspiration. The Methodists now felt that they had to defend the authority of scripture by insisting on its infallibility.[13]

They defended their biblicism with the rational "evidences." Their theological textbooks began with the familiar demonstrations that the biblical miracles had really happened, that the prophecies had been fulfilled, and that the church had survived against all odds in the ancient world. They uniformly applauded the internal evidences showing revelation to be consistent with itself, with reason, with the highest morality, and with the yearnings of the heart. In 1837 William McKendrie Bangs worried that evidential reasoning concealed an implicit rationalism that displaced trust in the Bible itself, but most Wesleyan writers ignored such cautionary advice, and the evidences became permanent fixtures in the Methodist journals and theological textbooks.[14]

Against Universalism and Calvinism

Questions about reason and revelation hardly represented the heart of antebellum Methodist theology. What the Wesleyan writers thought they understood better than anyone else was the order of salvation, and they wrote mainly about sin, repentance, the new birth, and holiness. They refined this "practical" theology through conflict with Universalists and Calvinists, and it was this conflict, almost as much as the Anglican heritage, that defined antebellum Methodist theology. The Americans largely ignored Wesley's Anglican admiration for patristic sources, his sacramentalism, and his liturgical piety; they appropriated his anti-Calvinism, his revivalism, and his perfectionism, and they reshaped even that by filtering it through the lens of Scottish philosophy, mental science, and the freewheeling denominational polemics of American popular Christianity.

They did debate the Anglicans about church government, attempting to refute Episcopal theologians in America on questions of apostolic succession and the legitimacy of Methodist ordination. Nathan Bangs's *Vindication of*

Methodist Episcopacy (1820) typified a substantial literature defending Methodist church order against Episcopal and other theologians who questioned its legitimacy either on traditional or biblical grounds. The Methodists themselves divided over questions of church order in 1830, forming a Methodist Episcopal Church with bishops and a Methodist Protestant Church without them. The disputes over that division produced a further outpouring of works on church polity in which some Methodists, like the reformer Alexander M'Caine (ca. 1768–1856), raised objections to the power of bishops, and others, like the bishop of Maryland, John Emory (1789–1835), replied with defenses of episcopal authority. Disputes over church order did not, however, shape Methodist theology in the same way as the debates with Calvinists and Universalists.[15]

In the Northeast and West, the Methodists and Universalists competed for converts among the same laboring people, apprentices, shopkeepers, and small farmers. It was incumbent on the Wesleyans to distinguish themselves from Universalist competitors, and the Methodists therefore emphasized that Wesleyan doctrines of general atonement and universal grace did not imply belief in universal salvation. Oral debates between Methodist and Universalist preachers became regular events after the turn of the century, and the Methodists often published the results in such popular theological manuals as Timothy Merritt's *Discussion of Universal Salvation* (1846). Methodist preachers drove home the point that Universalist doctrine encouraged sin and threatened to "dispossess religion . . . of most of its motive influence with which it addresses itself to the better interests of mankind." If the Universalists were right, the wicked would have nothing to fear.[16]

The Methodists became notorious in more fashionable circles for their willingness to induce fear. The New England transcendentalist Orestes Brownson recalled that the Methodist preachers he heard when he was young "gave the most vivid pictures of hell-fire and the tortures of the damned." More refined Methodists also complained on occasion about the stereotype of Wesleyan preaching as a constant refrain about the dangers of damnation. When William Capers, whose degree from South Carolina College distinguished him from most of the Wesleyan preachers, arrived in 1813 at his new appointment to a congregation in Wilmington, North Carolina, he took note of the attitudes that greeted him: "It seemed to be admitted on all hands that the Methodists were, on the whole, a good sort of enthusiasts, and their religion very well suited to the lower classes, who needed to be kept constantly in terror of hell-fire." Capers was not happy with the image.[17]

The Universalists charged that the Methodists disdained God's mercy; the Methodists replied that Universalist doctrine impeached God's justice. Since the sinful prospered and the righteous suffered in this life, a universal salvation would recompense no wrongs. Timothy Merritt found no evidence for Hosea Ballou's confidence that the wicked received their punishment in this world. And since Ballou defended a deterministic view of volition, Wilbur Fisk added, his God still punished people for what they could not help. A just world required a future punishment, and since sin carried an infinite weight of guilt, it could be punished only by an unending punishment. But the main Methodist arguments were biblical. The New Testament announced a day of judgment when the heavens and earth would cease to be and Christ would return to cast the sinful into "the eternal fire prepared for the devil and his angels" (Matt. 25:41). No little amount of Methodist polemic against the Universalists consisted of extended word studies showing that the term *aionios*, eternal or everlasting, did in fact mean unending.[18]

In their disputes with the Universalists, the Wesleyans held to an unremitting literalism. Arguing that the figurative interpretations of which the Universalists were fond made the scriptures "mean anything, or nothing, as suits their system," Wesleyans claimed that the "proper sense" was always the literal one. This insistence on the literal led some Methodists into long exegetical proofs that the devil was a personal agent, that the world was filled with demons and fallen spirits, and that hell was a lake of fire. More liberal Methodists said that readers did not have to interpret scriptural language about hell "in a strictly literal sense." Even so, they hesitated to understate the "cup of woe which is prepared for the finally impenitent."[19]

Methodists entered the debates about the millennial age, but they enjoyed no consensus. Wesley had accepted the German Pietist Johann Bengel's conclusion that the church would prosper on the earth for a thousand years, followed by another thousand-year reign of Christ and his saints before the final judgment, but he had also admonished Christians who were "inordinately fond of knowing future things." Methodists were prone to accept the view that an impending millennial age would precede the final judgment, but a number of Methodist clergy agreed with the Baptist William Miller that an imminent return of Christ would inaugurate the millennium. In their theological textbooks, Methodist theologians devoted more attention to arguments for the immortality of the soul, the resurrection of the body, the final judgment, and the eternal blessedness of the saints than to millennial speculation.[20]

If the Universalists were the upstart competitors, the Calvinists were longtime foes, but as Thomas Ralston explained in 1847, earlier Methodist polemics, like Watson's *Institutes*, had not anticipated "the modern phases of Calvinism" represented by the New Divinity of Samuel Hopkins and the New School of Calvinist thought at Yale. Modern Methodists, Ralston contended, had to produce a theology "adapted to the state of religious controversy in the United States at the present crisis," which meant a theology that countered not only Calvinist traditionalists but also the "modern" New England Calvinists.[21]

Methodists criticized Calvinists of every variety for their doctrines of predestination. Nathan Bangs, serving as a young minister in Durham, New York, established a place for the Methodists in the theological landscape of the region in 1815 when he published *The Errors of Hopkinsianism,* a book that sold three thousand copies in six months. Twenty years later, the way to make a theological reputation in Methodism was still to refute Calvinist doctrine. Wilbur Fisk (1792–1839), whose degree from Brown distinguished him as one of the few Methodist clergy with a college degree, made his name as a theologian by publishing his *Calvinistic Controversy* (1835) while serving as the president of Wesleyan University in Connecticut. Both books coincided in their depiction of Calvinism as a speculative system with dangerous practical consequences.[22]

The whole array of Wesleyan anti-Calvinist arguments — filling a multitude of books, journals, and sermons — could be reduced finally to three points. Methodists thought that predestination impugned divine love and justice by making God responsible for the sin of the reprobate; it implied that God was like a judge who caused the crime and then punished the criminal. They thought also that it subverted confidence in free human agency — "one of the most undeniable truths of philosophy and religion" — and therefore threatened the idea that human beings were morally responsible. And they thought that it was unbiblical. The New Testament's promises of salvation on condition of faith — promises addressed to all men and women — made no sense if only an elect few could perform the condition.[23]

Like William White earlier, Wilbur Fisk said that both Calvinists and their opponents had imposed on the biblical language a meaning alien to the logic of the text. He thought that the Pauline texts to which both sides referred, especially Romans and Ephesians, said nothing about the election of individuals to salvation; Paul wrote about election only to assert the admission of gentiles as well as Jews to the privileges of the covenant. More frequently, however, the Wesleyans tried to outdo the Calvinists in the adducing of biblical texts that supported their doctrine.[24]

To their Calvinist opponents it seemed that the Wesleyan critique of predestination implied softness on original sin. If everyone could meet the conditions of salvation, the ravages of sin were not as deep as the Pauline letters claimed. Yet no one emphasized depravity more than the Methodists, who preached that Adam was the federal head of all human beings and that when he fell, all fell. Some Wesleyans claimed that God imputed Adam's guilt to everyone. Most said that the imputation of guilt awaited the onset of moral agency. They agreed that every man and woman was "by nature so depraved as to be totally destitute of spiritual good, and inclined only to evil continually."[25]

Methodists argued that it was the New Divinity and New School Calvinists who had grown soft on original sin. They had softened it when they said that men and women had a natural ability to choose the good; when they located sin in the moral exercise of the will rather than in a fallen human nature lying behind all our exercises; and when they attributed depravity to the will but not to the understanding. In refuting these "modern" Calvinist views, the Wesleyans returned to favorite biblical texts: all had fallen, all were conceived in iniquity, all had sinned, every heart was deceitful, and all were "born with an unholy or sinful nature" (Rom. 3:10–18, Gen. 8:21, Ps. 51:5). No one had a natural ability to repent and trust.[26]

Yet the Wesleyans also taught that everyone had the "gracious" ability and the power to repent and trust. Wesley had retrieved from the post-Augustinian Catholic tradition the doctrine of prevenient grace: every human being received a gift of grace, alluring though not compelling, that enabled the soul "to make that choice which is the turning point, conditionally, of the soul's salvation." By nature, all were impotently sinful (hence the Methodist criticism of the New Divinity's "natural ability"); through prevenient grace, however, all had the power (not merely the formal ability) to repent, even though some might resist the gift. The Methodists called this — in a phrase popularized by Wilbur Fisk — "gracious ability."[27]

As Fisk observed, the idea of prevenient grace was Augustinian, though he thought that Augustine had wrongly linked it to predestination. The idea became a commonplace in the scholastic theology of the twelfth century, and the Catholic Council of Trent (1545–63) later affirmed prevenient grace as an aid to a weakened though not extinguished free will. Debates about it persisted through the seventeenth century, especially after Arminius employed it in his "Declaration of Sentiments" (1608) and his allies used it in their "Articuli Arminiani" (1610). The concept also appeared in the Anglican Thirty-Nine Articles, which gave it authority for Wesley. The Wesleyans occupied a position midway between Augustine and Trent. Unlike Trent, they taught that prevenient grace alone freed the will; unlike Augustine, they taught that prevenient grace could be resisted.[28]

It became a matter of the deepest importance for Methodist writers to show that adults were free moral agents, and it was not enough merely to assert that prevenient grace restored freedom. Methodist theologians argued for freedom on philosophical grounds, and always the opponents of choice were Jonathan

Edwards, the later Edwardeans, and the Calvinist revisionists at Yale. John Wesley had briefly engaged Edwards in his "Thoughts Upon Necessity" (1774) by asserting that liberty was an essential faculty of spirit, and the American Methodists began as early as 1817 to produce philosophical arguments against the Edwardean position. Nathan Bangs's *Examination of the Doctrine of Predestination* (1817) used Reid's mental philosophy to contend that Edwards's insistence on the determining force of motives rested on a false analogy between matter and mind. The Scottish vindication of introspection allowed Bangs to say that consciousness of freedom was the best evidence for freedom. Wilbur Fisk also drew support from the "philosophy of mind" for the Methodist position.[29]

In 1840 John M'Clintock, a teacher at Dickinson College in Pennsylvania, wrote that "Edwards's metaphysics are the basis of the dogmatic theology of Calvinism." Refute Edwards on the will, he said, and you stand on the threshold of Methodist doctrine. M'Clintock's only contribution to the cause was a brief review in 1844, but the next year Albert Taylor Bledsoe (1809–77) published the treatise for which M'Clintock was hoping. The *Methodist Quarterly Review* described it as the "incontrovertible refutation" of Edwards.[30]

Bledsoe had been a teacher at Miami University in Ohio, an Episcopal priest, and a lawyer whose hopes of becoming a Methodist minister met with resistance, but he associated himself with the Methodists, especially when he taught mathematics at the state universities of Mississippi and Virginia, and they treated his *Examination of President Edwards' Inquiry Into the Freedom of the Will* (1845) as a denominational victory. After the Civil War, Bledsoe, who supported the South and touted slavery as a benefit to humanity, founded a journal — the *Southern Review* — that the southern Methodists regarded virtually as their voice in the region.

Bledsoe's book was one of the strongest of the nineteenth-century attempts to refute Edwards. He believed that he could demonstrate circularity in the Edwardean claim that the strongest motive determines the will, which Bledsoe saw as a tautology that could be reduced to the statement that men and women choose what they choose. He thought also that Edwards had assumed that every act of volition was an effect of an efficient cause. But if this were true, Bledsoe argued, Edwards fell into an infinite regress. If volitions are the direct effects of motives, then motives, as alterations of the will, have to be the effects of prior motives, ad infinitum. In fact, Bledsoe argued, volitions were not the effects of antecedent efficient causes. The evidence for this could be found, as the Scottish philosophers had shown, through introspection. Men and women experienced volitions not as passive effects but as instances of active effort, however much they might recognize that forces external to their wills occasioned their choices. In an era captivated by Baconian induction and Scottish philosophy, this appeal to "consciousness" and "observation" could seem plausible.[31]

Bledsoe drew especially on the move in American intellectual discussion away from a bipartite view of the mind as consisting of will and understanding toward a tripartite distinction of will, understanding, and sensibility. By the time he wrote, the tripartite view had become, as he noted, "well-known" through the writings of the Scottish philosophers, Victor Cousin in France, and Samuel Taylor Coleridge in England. Edwards had thought that to be pleased with something was the same as to will it and that the mind could not choose what would not please it. Bledsoe argued that the will should not be confused with the sensibility—the mind's desires, affections, feelings, and emotions. To desire rain was not an act of volition. And the will could—often did, in fact—resist the desires and passions of the sensibility, as any virtuous person could attest.[32]

Bledsoe displayed some of the theological implications of his essay when he published his *Theodicy* (1854), which traced the history of the problem of evil from Lucretius and the early Greeks to nineteenth-century Calvinists. Repeating many of his arguments against Edwards but also expanding his criticism to encompass such figures as Calvin, Kant, Locke, and the New Divinity theologians, he argued that the existence of sin and evil could be reconciled with the power and goodness of God only if the design of God's moral government was the production of the greatest amount of moral good among free agents. Such a design presupposed the freedom to sin and the possibility of misery as conditions for the attainment of virtue. The argument drew rebuttals even from some Methodists, but its main target was Calvinism. The *Southern Presbyterian Review* accused Bledsoe of deifying reason.[33]

Even better known than Bledsoe as a defender of free will in Methodist theology was Daniel D. Whedon (1808–85), considered by some as the premier theologian of the denomination. A native of New York, Whedon graduated from Hamilton College and studied law before falling under the spell in 1830 of the revivalist Charles Finney. By 1833 he was teaching at Wesleyan University, where he became a close friend of Wilbur Fisk, who encouraged him to study Edwards. Whedon moved back and forth between teaching stints at Wesleyan and the University of Michigan and appointments to local churches in New York and Massachusetts. In 1856 he became the editor of the *Methodist Quarterly Review*. For twenty years, in the midst of all this activity, he labored on the question of freedom, and in 1864 he published his *Freedom of the Will*.

Whedon assumed the validity of the "moral intuitions." If people were as morally responsible as they intuitively sensed themselves to be, then they had to have moral freedom. But they had moral freedom only if they had a "power to the contrary" such that even the strongest of motives did not inexorably determine the will's choice. What we call the strongest motive, he argued, is merely whatever the will chose. We can isolate it only in retrospect. In fact, the word "causality" refers only to the interplay of probabilities, and any volition can always accord with a lesser probability. This is what we mean when we say that freedom is "a power of choosing either of several ways." In Whedon's eyes, the captain who went down with his ship resisted the strongest motive the mind could entertain — the motive of self-preservation. To such arguments he added the familiar Scottish refrain that the mind's conscious awareness of its freedom had to count for something.[34]

Whedon added that any meaningful freedom — the freedom to perform an act pleasing to God — presupposed the atonement of Christ, which conferred on every human being the gracious ability requisite for the fitting act. For other Methodists, as well, everything went back to the atonement. Methodist theologians were wont to say that "the substance of the entire controversy" among themselves, the Calvinists, and the Universalists turned on the atonement. After Hosea Ballou's treatise on the topic became popular, Universalists often denied a vicarious atonement, saying that Jesus died to win hearts by exhibiting divine love. Most Calvinists limited the efficacy of the atonement to the elect. The Wesleyans argued for a vicarious general atonement that made salvation possible for every human being. New Divinity and New School Calvinists conceded that the atonement was general, but they combined this concession with a doctrine of particular election. Wesleyans found them inconsistent: if Christ died for everyone, then everyone should be able to benefit.[35]

In their own theories of atonement, Methodists in America went in every direction. Some used the older theory of satisfaction as the payment of a debt; some referred to a "satisfaction" but declined to define it as the payment of a debt; most gravitated toward governmental theories. Even at the end of the nineteenth century, a knowledgeable Methodist could write that most Wesleyans still accepted "some form of governmental theory." Governmental images pleased many Methodists because the idea of Christ's having died to preserve moral government suggested a universal effect for Christ's death. Their overriding aim was to argue that he died for all, not for the elect alone.[36]

Calvinists thought that Methodist views of the atonement led the Methodists to minimize the doctrine of justification by faith alone. John Wesley had, in fact, speculated long about justification and good works. After 1738, he always affirmed justification by faith, but his wariness of Calvinism led him continually to redefine what he meant. In 1745 he cautioned that though faith was the sole condition of justification, a justifying faith implied repentance and good works. By 1770 he spoke more explicitly of good works as a "condition" of justification, and he found himself tempted by John Fletcher's elaborate doctrine of "double justification," a justification first by faith at the time of conversion but then by the works of the faithful believer. He sought for a way to contend that justification came by grace through faith but that nonetheless without holiness no one would "see the Lord."[37]

The Americans shared the ambivalence of their founder. Some taught that "nothing else" but faith could be a condition of justification; these theologians refused to describe justification as God's response to faith and works together because they believed that this view, held by Wesley himself at some stages in his career, failed to recognize that to justify was to forgive, not to reward. Others shared Wesley's wariness of a justification without good works: one had to "cease from evil, and learn to do well," they argued, as a condition "in order" to be justified.[38]

One common Methodist solution — reminiscent of Wesley after 1745 — was to insist on faith and repentance alone as the conditions of justification — and thus of a "salvation . . . received by faith" — but to add that obedience to the law of Christ was necessary for receiving "future, everlasting salvation." This distinction, in which the term "salvation" had two meanings, permitted Timothy Merritt, for example, to make holiness, of which faith was only a part, the "grand condition of future salvation." The distinction was implied when John Ffirth argued that sinners were justified by grace, without works of the law, but that good works, though never meritorious, remained necessary to salvation. For Calvinists, justification ensured salvation; for Wesleyans, it made salvation possible.[39]

In the Methodist vocabulary, justification was not the imputation of Christ's obedience or active righteousness to the sinner; this Calvinist doctrine implied to them that sinners could be credited with having obeyed the moral law when they had not. It was also not the imputation of the passive righteousness that Christ earned through suffering on the cross; this version of Calvinist doctrine still seemed to assume that God considered the acts and sufferings of one person as belonging to another. The Methodists used the language of "imputation" only to mean that God looked upon faith as righteous, which meant simply that God pardoned the faithful and restored them to divine favor.[40]

Conversion and Perfection

Wesleyans thought that Calvinist theology distorted the entire "order of salvation," especially the moment of regeneration or new birth that formed the conversion experience in the Methodist revivals. In the doctrine of regeneration, wrote Thomas Ralston, "all the important doctrines of the gospel meet." Regeneration was the subjective correlate of justification. It was the inner event that accompanied the divine pardon, the inward change from the love of sin to the love of God, the supernatural bestowing of a new heart. The Calvinists thought of it as the first effect of saving grace in the heart, a "passive work" of the Spirit prior to both repentance and faith. While Methodists agreed that it resulted from the "direct and efficient operation of the Holy Spirit on the heart," they thought that it always followed "preparatory" works, such as repentance, that were both divine gifts and "acts of the creature." The "agency of the creature" was always a condition for the experience of rebirth.[41]

On this matter, the Wesleyans also took issue with Anglican and Catholic ideas of regeneration through the sacrament of baptism. Wesley himself had thought of the sacrament as the "ordinary means" of regeneration, a means to infuse a principle of grace and wash away the guilt of original sin. The Americans either denied that Wesley had ever believed in sacramental rebirth or claimed that he had renounced the dogma as his insight deepened. Their alternative was to define the sacrament as a seal to a universal but conditional covenant. Since Christ had died for all, every new infant came into the world as a beneficiary of the conditional covenant of grace established by his death. Baptism recognized their status and gave them title to the salutary influences of the church, and in this sense the Wesleyans could describe it as "a saving ordinance." But since the covenant was conditional, the efficacy of baptism was also conditional. The benefits that it signified could be realized only by repentance and faith.[42]

The result of regeneration was "adoption," a topic that preoccupied Methodists because they related it to their doctrine of the witness of the Spirit. Paul's letter to the Romans, as Wesleyans read it, stipulated that the evidence of adoption was "the direct witness of the Holy Spirit in the heart of the Christian." Methodists understood this to mean an immediate and inward testimony of the Spirit, providing assurance of forgiveness. This was the doctrine with which they interpreted the ecstatic emotional experiences of the revivals. It earned them their reputation as "enthusiasts." As Calvinists and Anglicans read Paul, he meant to say only that the Spirit witnessed to the faithful that their faith was genuine when it issued in good works. For most Methodists, the witness of the Spirit meant that the assurance of salvation was immediate, palpable, and emotional.[43]

In Methodist theology, moreover, the Spirit witnessed not only to conversion but also to an experience of perfection. One distinguishing feature of Methodist thought was the deep interest in sanctification, or the increasing holiness that was supposed to follow the new birth. It became the slogan of the

Methodists that their duty in America was to "spread scriptural holiness," to proclaim that sinners could be cleansed from the "power, and pollution of sin." The Wesleyan formula was that justification produced a relative change — a change in the relation to God — but sanctification produced a real change, an inward transforming of the affections. Justification removed the guilt of sin; sanctification removed the power of sin by producing an increasing capacity to love God and neighbor.[44]

This cleansing reached its apex in Christian perfection. Wesley's followers looked on him as God's instrument to revive "the apostolic doctrine of Christian perfection," and during the Methodist revivals the preachers reported not only conversions but also experiences of "entire sanctification," or Christian perfection. Wesleyans found the Bible filled with admonitions to be perfect (Matt. 5:48, 2 Cor. 7:1) and to love God with the whole heart (Mark 12:30). They also discovered in the reports of their converts evidence of both a gradual movement toward perfection and a sudden, instantaneous experience in which the heart was filled with perfect love.[45]

Wesley's views about perfection reached Americans through his preachers, through the reprinting in 1789 of his perfectionist writings in the Methodist book of discipline, and through the *Collection of Interesting Tracts* that the denomination published in 1814. A year later, Nathan Bangs defended Methodist perfectionism in his attack on Hopkinsian Calvinism. The Methodist version of the doctrine had little in common with the Platonic harmony about which Channing preached or the divinizing perfectionism of Samuel Gorton and John Rogers in early New England. It differed also from the perfectionist doctrine preached by the revivalist Charles Grandison Finney and taught at Oberlin College. Unlike others, the Methodists talked single-mindedly about perfect love, and they connected the experience of perfection to the witness of the Spirit.[46]

In 1825 Timothy Merritt (1775–1845), who spent most of his career in local parishes in Maine, published *The Christian's Manual: A Treatise on Christian Perfection*. After 1839, he would, as the editor of *The Guide to Christian Perfection*, generate enthusiasm for what became a twenty-five-year holiness revival in Methodism. Merritt told his readers that entire sanctification was both a progressive and an instantaneous work of the Spirit, and they should expect it "now." In a sermon in 1821, he had already, like John Fletcher, linked it to the "baptism of the Spirit" — an association that became increasingly important in Wesleyan (and later holiness) circles. His manual reassured readers that both the ethical fruits of the Spirit (love, joy, and peace) and the immediate witness of the Spirit would provide the evidence for entire sanctification. Perfect Christians should have no serious doubt that they had been perfected.[47]

Such views, common within the movement, could create problems for earnest seekers after perfection, and they proved especially troubling for Phoebe Palmer (1807–74), who with her sister Sarah Lankford founded in 1836 the Tuesday Meeting for the Promotion of Holiness, a group that met in Palmer's home in New York City. Sarah Lankford admired Timothy Merritt, but Palmer found it unsatisfying to think that the witness of the Spirit should have to provide immediate, sensible, emotional evidence that the gift of perfect love had been received.

Palmer found a guide to holiness in *The Life of Hester Ann Rogers,* an autobiography of an eighteenth-century English Methodist, which helped convince her that she need not wait upon any strong feeling of emotion before she accounted herself dead to sin, and in 1837 she resolved to accept the biblical promise that God would sanctify all Christians who consecrated their lives to Christ and that she could rely on "naked faith in a naked promise," regardless of her feelings. She believed that she had discovered the three "simple and rational" steps to the attainment of entire sanctification: the surrender and consecration of her life on the "altar" of Christ, faith that the altar sanctified the gift (Matt. 23:19), and a willingness to confess publicly to having received this sanctifying grace. In *The Way of Holiness* (1843) she described this "shorter route" to entire sanctification. Neither arduous self-examination nor inward feelings were necessary to confirm the gift. She would still speak of "the witness of the Spirit," though she now meant not a direct experience of the Spirit but simple faith in the biblical promises.[48]

Palmer disdained "theological hair-splitting" and vowed to avoid "theological technicalities." She drew instead on her reading in Methodist devotional classics. Eighteenth-century English Methodists had prepared the way for her doctrine: Adam Clarke had emphasized the instantaneous nature of entire sanctification and linked holiness with power; John Fletcher had defined faith as belief in the written promises, described perfection (to Wesley's discomfort) as a baptism of the Holy Spirit, and insisted on the importance of testifying to the gift; Hester Ann Roe Rogers had used the "altar" terminology; and William Carvosso had employed the image of "naked faith" in the promises. Palmer connected the themes in a way that coincided with the demand of Methodist revivalists for an immediate decision.[49]

In 1842, a year before the appearance of Palmer's book, the New York Methodist pastor George Peck (1797–1876) published *The Scripture Doctrine of Christian Perfection,* a series of lectures stimulated by the recent discussions of sanctification among Congregationalists and Presbyterians at Oberlin. Like Phoebe Palmer and John Fletcher, Peck described holiness as a "baptism of the Spirit," but he adhered to the view that the witness of the Spirit confirming Christian perfection was a matter of "personal consciousness," a "sensible" impression that could be discovered in "the feelings." One of his targets was Finney and the Oberlin perfectionists; another was probably Phoebe Palmer.[50]

As Palmer's views gained adherents, her critics fastened on Peck's point. Randolph Sinks Foster (1820–1903), a pastor in New York City who would later become the president of Drew University, charged that she was encouraging her followers to claim entire sanctification without the witness of the Spirit. Hiram Mattison (1811–68), another New York pastor, issued the same criticism, adding that her view of the immediate efficacy of faith, her altar theology, and her insistence on testimony diverged from Wesley. Eventually Nathan Bangs arose at one of her Tuesday meetings and criticized her altar theology, her description of faith as a "holy violence" that inevitably attained the promises, and her revisions in the Wesleyan doctrine of the witness of the Spirit. Bangs told her that the assurance of entire sanctification had to be felt in emotions of joy and peace.[51]

In the wake of such criticisms, Palmer increasingly spoke of holiness as a baptism of the Spirit that brought an "enduement with power," and it is likely that the Spirit language served in part to counter critics who charged that she had reduced entire sanctification to an act of assent. Her theology continued to attract some support among Methodist leaders, and in some circles of the church she was a revered figure. In North Carolina, for example, the editor of *The Weekly Message,* Frances Bumpass, looked to Palmer both as the model theologian of holiness and as an example of women's power within the denomination. But her opponents contended that her views divided churches and created conflicts. By the 1850s, the Methodist bishops were warning against new watchwords employed by holiness advocates. After the Civil War, her distinctive language appeared most often in the holiness circles that separated from mainline Methodism.[52]

Defining themselves as much in contrast to Universalists and Calvinists as in continuity with their Anglican heritage, Methodist writers came to be associated with a brief list of doctrines — regeneration, perfection, and the witness of the Spirit — that they used to interpret their revivalist piety. The revivalists gave Methodist theology its distinctive character. But even the theologians of a revivalist and populist group like the Methodists insisted on the rationality of faith, and when they defended their doctrines they employed the ideas of the Scottish philosophers, the discoveries of mental science, the confirmation of natural theology, and the Christian evidences. In the Baconian era, the Methodists, like almost everyone else, appealed to "the rules of evidence by which alone the human mind can be successful in the search for truth."[53]

13

The Baptists and Calvinist Diversity

Writing in 1860, the Baptist historian David Benedict recalled that at the turn of the nineteenth century the Baptists in America had been a "poor and despised people," regularly "denounced as the dregs of Christendom." The early Baptist movement took hold mainly among the uneducated, and many saw little need for educated theologians to guide them. They shared the view of New England's Isaac Backus that "divine enlightenment" was preferable to "human learning." John Leland, a native of Massachusetts who spent much of his time in the South campaigning for religious liberty, ridiculed the "learned clergy" and proclaimed that theology belonged to the people: "Is not a simple man, who makes nature and reason his study, a competent judge of things? Is the Bible written (like Caligula's laws) so intricate and high, that none but the better learned (according to common phrase) can read it?" His sentiments connected him with deep impulses of Baptist life.[1]

Within the Baptist movement, however, as in the Methodist, the populist impulse also ran up against opposition. As early as 1746 the Baptists founded the College of Rhode Island — later Brown — which became a stronghold of Edwardean divinity. The career of Richard Furman (1755–1825) in Charleston, South Carolina, exemplified the ambivalence about theological democracies. Converted by Baptist revivalists in 1771, Furman began preaching when he was sixteen without any formal education. By the time he became the pastor at the First Baptist Church in Charleston in 1787, he had risen into the ranks of affluent slaveholders and denominational leaders, and he made it his mission to promote an educated ministry. Conceding that "human learning" could never be the "principal" qualification for ministry and denying that he "idolized" learning, Furman nonetheless argued in a circular letter of 1797 that ministers needed deeper exposure to knowledge about "the nature and evidence of religion," including "the laws and powers of nature." Baptists needed theologians who could recite the evidences of Christianity, follow the logic of natural theology, and, as one of Furman's allies argued, reach "the reflecting men of the world."[2]

Writing in 1857, the president of Brown, Francis Wayland (1772–1849), showed that the populist ethos could endure even in unlikely places. By that time the northern Baptists had founded Newton Theological Seminary (1825) and more than a dozen colleges. But even while overseeing the best of those schools, Wayland still thought it important to say that Christian truth was not mainly for "the learned or the philosophically wise." He noted that the Baptists had not produced "profound philosophers, learned philologists, acute logicians," but he found the deficiency salutary: "we have arrived at a clearer knowledge of divine truth, for the very reason that we have had no such guides to follow." Wayland was a graduate of Union College with a year of study at the Andover seminary, and he supported an educated clergy, but he thought the educated had no monopoly on religious truth and should not presume to retail it "by the pennyworth to the people," who had an "absolute right of private judgment in all matters of religion."[3]

The suspicion of elites did not lead to any rejection of Baconian rational orthodoxy. While insisting on the limits of reason, Baptist theologians affirmed natural theology along with the standard internal and external proofs from the evidential tradition. Instead of merely affirming biblical authority, they attempted, like almost everyone else, to ground it by appeal to rational evidence. At the same time, most Baptist theologians adhered to some variety of Calvinist theology. The Baptists provided a demonstration that the populist impulse did not invariably assume anti-Calvinist forms. Indeed, some of the most decidedly populist factions of the Baptist movement attached themselves to a predestinarian doctrine so extreme that other Calvinists found it strange. Devoted almost single-mindedly to the authority of the Bible, the Baptist movement nonetheless read the Bible through lenses provided by both the Baconian impulse and the Calvinist traditions.

Reason

When the self-educated Virginia Baptist preacher Andrew Broaddus answered Thomas Paine in his *Age of Reason and Revelation* (1795), he observed that "Christians know something of philosophy too, as well as Deists," and he assumed that "rational evidences are necessary" to support belief in the Christian revelation. When the self-taught Georgia theologian John Leadley Dagg (1794–1884), the president of Mercer University, published in 1857 his *Manual of Theology*, the first comprehensive theological text in the American Baptist traditions, he still assumed that natural theology taught "the fundamental truths on which all religion is based" — the "voice of Nature is the voice of God" — and he still laid out the standard internal and external evidences of revelation. Wayland worried by 1857 that the frequent appeal by Baptist theologians to "natural religion" as a proof for revealed religion ran the risk of suggesting that reason was "a higher authority than the word of God." Yet neither Wayland nor any other antebellum Baptist thinker would dismiss the force of the rational proofs. By the time Dagg published his manual of theology, the axioms of Scottish philosophy had assumed a prominent place in Baptist thought.[4]

Baptist rationalism, like that of the Methodists, supported rather than supplanted the assumption of biblical authority. Wayland noted that "the essential principle of Baptist belief, is that in all matters relating to religion, we know no authority but the Bible." Most thought of the Bible as an inspired and infallible rule of saving faith, though John Leland took the unconventional view that it was better to speak of it simply as "authentic." The more troubling issue was the balance between biblical and confessional authority. In 1742 the Philadelphia Baptist Association adopted the Second London Confession (1677) of English Calvinistic Baptists — a document derived from the Westminster Confession — and this Philadelphia Confession remained authoritative in Baptist churches for more than a century.[5]

One strand of Baptists in the eighteenth-century South — the Separates, who moved southward after breaking from New England Congregationalism during the revivals of the 1740s — had reservations about confessional statements. In Virginia and the Carolinas they refused to subscribe to the Philadelphia Confession, a refusal that created tensions with the so-called Regular Baptists who favored subscription. The Separates feared that subscribing to a creed would suggest that something other than the Bible guided their faith. By 1787, however, Separates and Regulars in Virginia reached compromises that permitted both groups to subscribe "in substance." By that time, confessions of faith, the "substance" of which was Calvinist, regularly furnished guidelines for interpreting the Bible. Wayland would claim later that Baptists believed in an "absolute right of private judgment in all matters of religion," and that "no standards" other than the Bible had authority over Baptist belief and practice, but other Baptists challenged him. He acknowledged that the Westminster Confession probably expressed Baptist thinking on "the plan of salvation."[6]

The Church

A main part of the Baptist plan of salvation was a vision of the church as a congregation of faithful adult baptized believers. "Hereditary membership," Wayland contended, "has been the great curse of the Christian church." The symbol of church purity was baptism, and Baptists produced countless tracts and sermons supporting a view of baptism as the immersion of adult believers who submitted to the ordinance as a sign of their faith. They considered it decisive that the New Testament contained no explicit command or example of infant baptism, but the debates almost always pursued covenantal themes. It became a commonplace by the nineteenth century that the doctrine of the covenant was "the hinge on which the whole argument turns."[7]

Protestant groups that practiced infant baptism contended that the biblical covenant with Abraham, sealed by circumcision, was identical in substance with the Christian covenant of grace, which required baptism as an analogous seal. Baptists drove a wedge between the two covenants, accusing their opponents of confusing a national promise to ancient Jews with the promise of salvation. In their view of the church, they maintained the essentials of seventeenth-century covenantalism, but without its sacramental implications. In the middle of the nineteenth century they were still debating with pedobaptists using exactly the same arguments that Baptists had used in the seventeenth century.[8]

Baptists enjoyed no consensus, however, even about the church. The spectrum ranged from theologians who saw the local congregation as little more than a voluntary association, to others who emphasized its divine mandate but limited its authority, to those who saw it as a divinely ordained institution that defined the meaning of the kingdom of God. At the voluntarist end, Francis Wayland taught that religion was a matter of individual piety and that churches were voluntary societies of the pious designed to promote mutual holiness and pursue the conversion of souls. Wayland's individualism advanced themes present earlier in the writings of Backus and Leland, who valorized individual consent and conscience as a safeguard against state religious establishments. For all three, the important ecclesiological concern was membership in the invisible church of the elect rather than the visible institution.[9]

In the middle of the spectrum stood the Baptists who honored the Philadelphia Confession, affirming a universal church of the elect but emphasizing that Christ commanded visible churches for all who, in the "judgment of charity," had been effectually called by regenerating grace. Apart from their rejection of infant baptism, their criteria for membership followed the pattern set by the seventeenth-century Puritans. Yet they were willing to cooperate through organizations above the congregational level. They accorded all "church power" to local congregations, but they found in the idea that Christ alone was the head of the church, and hence of every congregation, a warrant for according a limited power to supralocal institutions.[10]

At the other end of the spectrum, far removed from Backus, Leland, and Wayland, stood the mid-nineteenth century southern Landmarkists, who asserted the sole validity of local Baptist congregations as the only true churches of Christ and the "only authorized exponents of Christ's revelation." The Landmarkists combined their pronounced localism with an uncompromising assertion of what came to be called "successionism." Seventeenth-century Baptists had never asserted an unbroken succession of visible churches. They wrote of a succession of true believers since the time of Christ, but not of institutional continuity. In 1738, an English Baptist historian, Thomas Crosby, advanced the slightly different argument that Baptists could prove an unbroken succession of Baptist "principles," a view that became popular among American apologists. He did not claim a succession of churches.[11]

By the early nineteenth century, however, some Baptists began to assert a continuous succession of Baptist churches. In 1838 the English Baptist historian G. H. Orchard argued in his *Concise History of Foreign Baptists* that the evidence proved such a succession of Baptist congregations, hidden under sectarian labels, from the time of John the Baptist to the present. This argument altered the texture of Baptist life in the South after James Robinson Graves (1820–93), a self-educated pastor and editor in Nashville, began in 1851 the movement known as Landmarkism. The name was derived from the publication of *An Old Landmark Reset* (1854) by a Kentucky pastor named James Madison Pendleton (1811–91), who argued that pedobaptist assemblies were not true New Testament churches and their ministers were not true ministers.[12]

Graves shared with Pendleton a desire to separate the Baptists from other Protestants. A native of Vermont who had overseen academies in Ohio and Kentucky before moving to Nashville in 1845 to lead the Second Baptist Church, he entered a congregation divided by the ideas of Alexander Campbell, who was attracting Baptists to his efforts to restore primitive Christianity. The experience prompted Graves to embellish and popularize successionist doctrines as a way of countering Campbell's appeal. He argued that local Baptist churches had existed since the time of John the Baptist, that they were the only true churches, and that together they constituted the kingdom of God. To worship outside such a church was to worship outside the kingdom, though Graves did not therefore conclude that salvation belonged only to Baptists. He did conclude that adult baptism by immersion was essential to the validity of a church and that the only valid baptism came from an immersed believer acting under the authority of a local congregation.[13]

The movement divided southern Baptists for decades because it had implications for Baptist practice. Graves thought that members of one congregation should not receive the Lord's Supper in another, that Baptist churches should baptize again any applicants who had been immersed by unauthorized ministers, and that Baptists should never invite into their pulpits ministers from other denominations. When his opponents, who included John Leadley Dagg, Robert B. C. Howell (1801–68) of Nashville, and Jeremiah Jeter (1802–80) of Richmond, insisted that the New Testament described the church as both local and universal, they were also contending for practices like intercommunion among Baptists, the acceptance of "alien immersion," and interdenominational cooperation. But the Landmarkists also intensified sectarian debate, with polemical pieces such as Graves's *Great Iron Wheel; or Republicanism Backwards and Christianity Reversed* (1855), directed against the Methodists, and his *Trilemma; or, Death by Three Horns,* against the Presbyterians, claiming that neither of these denominations could presume to be true churches.[14]

Calvinist Diversity

In the background of these disputes over the church stood assumptions about Calvinist theology, and it would be no exaggeration to say that Baptist theology in America was, for the most part, an extended discussion — and usually a defense — of Calvinist doctrine. Divided in the seventeenth century between Calvinist and non-Calvinist factions, and always compelled to contend with a strong undercurrent of internal Arminian protest, the Baptists gravitated after the mid-eighteenth century toward the Calvinism of the Westminster and Philadelphia confessions or toward Edwardean variations of it.

The earliest Baptists turned away from Calvinist theology. In 1608, the English separatist John Smyth (ca. 1544–1612) inaugurated one strand of Baptist tradition when he led a migration to Holland in search of the freedom to form a true church. Having decided that the Church of England was no church, he and his congregation from Gainsborough concluded that Anglican baptism was also no true baptism, and Smyth's reading of scripture convinced him further that the New Testament had no warrant for the baptizing of infants. In conversation with Dutch Mennonites, Smyth's group disavowed Calvinism. Smyth assured the Mennonites that his party believed that all sin was actual and voluntary (thus denying original sin) and that Christ died for all, not for an elect few. While asserting that the preventing grace of the Spirit gave every adult the ability to believe, he said that the will could resist the Spirit's prompting. While arguing that justification resulted from the imputation of Christ's righteousness, he acknowledged that it also resulted from the

Spirit's creating in the faithful an inherent righteousness. As negotiations continued, the group affirmed a "free power to the choice of good" even in sinful humanity. When some of Smyth's group returned to England in 1612, their conviction that the atonement had a general or universal, not a limited, scope earned them the name of General Baptists. Not all of them would affirm the freedom of the will or deny the doctrine of election, but they believed that Christ died for everyone.[15]

By 1652 this General Baptist theology had a foothold in Rhode Island, and by the end of the century it spread to the southern colonies. It remained a minority voice, but similar anti-Calvinist impulses eventually flowed alongside it. In New England, Benjamin Randall, a sailor, sail-maker, and tailor who became a lay exhorter — first as a Congregationalist and then as a Baptist separatist — began to preach in 1778 in Durham, New Hampshire, that God offered "assisting grace" freely to everyone. His conflicts with Baptist Calvinists led to the founding shortly after 1800 of a Free Will Baptist Church.[16]

The group found a source of theological inspiration in the writings of a New Light farmer-evangelist from Nova Scotia named Henry Alline (1748–84) who came to Maine with an anti-Calvinist treatise titled *Two Mites Cast Into the Offering of God, for the Benefit of Mankind* (1781). Randall found the book so compelling that in 1804 he added "amendments" to it and had it reprinted. An eclectic mixture of themes from the English Methodist John Fletcher, the Anglican William Law, and the poet John Milton, it promoted a speculative Protestant mysticism combined with esoteric ideas popular in English occult circles. Alline envisioned the original creation as a spiritual "Outbirth," or emanation, of an androgynous God. The exercise of free choice led to a fall into materiality, but a "spark of the divine nature" remained intact within every human being, and Christ's atonement enabled the "inmost soul" to follow the law of love and embrace the God who existed in an "eternal now" that transcended time. Alline's penchant for spiritualizing doctrine, for viewing heaven and hell, for example, as spiritual conditions of the soul, never made headway in the denomination. But by 1830 his vision of a God who redeemed "all that possibly can be redeemed" by restoring free agency was shared by around three hundred congregations of largely rural, working-class Baptists.[17]

Nonetheless, Calvinism became the predominant Baptist dialect — a dialect also with seventeenth-century roots. Withdrawing in 1638 from an independent congregation in London, a group of separatist Puritans formed the first of several congregations that assumed the name of Particular Baptists. The name proclaimed their belief that Christ died only for the particular souls whom God had chosen from eternity as the elect. In 1644 the seven Particular Baptist churches in London joined in a "London Confession," in which they affirmed original sin, divine election, a limited atonement, and entire reliance on special saving grace. The writings of John Clarke (1609–76) and Roger Williams (during his brief Baptist phase) in Rhode Island secured a place for this Particular tradition in the colonies.[18]

This English Calvinistic Baptist tradition continued for three centuries to form the backdrop for most American Baptist theology. The Americans especially felt the ripples of what became known in eighteenth-century England as "the Modern Question." In 1737, Matthias Maurice, a Congregational pastor in Northamptonshire, published a book titled *A modern question modestly answered*. The modern question was whether any but the elect had the power and therefore the duty to believe the gospel. Maurice argued that although only the elect would finally believe, all of the unconverted had a duty to accept God's offer of grace. The argument set him against certain forms of high or hyper-Calvinism in which it was thought heretical to suggest that God "offered" grace — since grace was a sovereign power and not an invitation — or that the preacher should "offer" Christ to the sinful. Among some of the English hyper-Calvinists it became customary to preach the "gospel" only to those showing signs of election while preaching the "kingdom" alone to broader audiences (who were assumed to live under Christ's kingship but not his priesthood). In this high Calvinist tradition, theologians would not speak of faith as a "duty" or approve the efforts of preachers to persuade the unregenerate.[19]

For Americans the modern question became formative through the writings of England's two most prominent eighteenth-century Baptist theologians. The first, John Gill, the pastor of the Horsleydown Baptist Church in metropolitan London, came to the defense of the hyper-Calvinists, even though he did not defend their more extreme positions. His *Body of Doctrinal Divinity* (1769) became a standard of Calvinist orthodoxy. Gill did not share the hyper-Calvinists' wariness about preaching about the moral law or their refusal to preach the gospel to the sinful and exhort them. He even affirmed a duty to believe. But he defended the more extreme Calvinists against some of their critics; he agreed that it made no sense for a Calvinist to speak of God's merely offering grace to the sinful; he promoted the high Calvinist doctrine of an "immanent" and eternal justification (the view that the elect were not only chosen but also justified by an eternal act); and he emphasized the imputation of guilt and righteousness, a limited atonement, and the "everlasting covenant" that sealed the salvation of the elect. Both his critics and some of his admirers associated him with the hyper-Calvinist party.[20]

The second, Andrew Fuller (1754–1815), the pastor at Kettering, began his ministry in 1775 as a high Calvinist but in 1781 reversed himself with the publication of *The Gospel Worthy of All Acceptation,* a book that became the manual of Baptist foreign missions. Fuller advocated an evangelical Calvinism anchored by the conviction that the church had the duty to proclaim the gospel to every person and that every sinner had an obligation to repent and accept it. He called himself a "strict Calvinist" and defended total depravity, sovereign and unconditional election, and the inability of the will to change the prevailing inclinations of the heart. He affirmed that the only true believers were men and women "chosen of God from eternity." But he sought, like the Edwardeans, a rationale for revivalist appeals, and he found resources in the theology of both Edwards and Hopkins to support the demand for "immediate repentance." He liked the Edwardean insistence on the harmony between the law and the gospel, the obligation to love God unselfishly, and the duty of ministers to call for repentance. He communicated with Hopkins and made ample use of the crucial Edwardean distinction between natural and moral ability.[21]

The pivotal doctrine in Fuller's theology was his description of Christ's atonement as sufficient for all even though it was "efficient only for the elect." He could affirm the older theory of the atonement as a substitutionary act of satisfaction, but in *The Gospel Worthy of All Acceptation* he denied that it had to be understood as the literal payment of a debt and argued that its primary function was to render the exercise of mercy consistent with righteousness. The important point was that Christ's sacrifice sufficed for all, even though God "applied" it "to the salvation of some . . . and not of others." Its all-sufficiency established the duty of all to exercise faith. Combined with his criticisms of hyper-Calvinism, these doctrines created a stir in Baptist circles in both England and America.[22]

David Benedict claimed that by 1810 "large bodies of our people were in a state of ferment and agitation" over the struggle between "Gillites" and "Fullerites." "The Fuller system, which makes it consistent for all the heralds of the gospel to call upon men everywhere to repent," he wrote, "was well received by one class of our ministers, but not by the staunch defenders of the old theory of limited atonement. According to their views, all for whom Christ suffered and died would certainly be effectually called and saved." Francis Wayland also described the history of Baptist theology in America as the story of a transition from a period in which "Gill's *Divinity* was a sort of standard" to another in which Fuller's theology became the "almost universal" authority, at least in the Northeast. Wayland's comment blurred the subtle differences between Fullerites and Edwardeans. Fuller did not adopt the Edwardean emphasis on the love of God as supremely beautiful, the accent on disinterested benevolence, or the concern about self-love. He emphasized faith more than love and stressed that God justified the ungodly. Nevertheless, Wayland grasped the importance of the shift away from Gill.[23]

Calvinistic Baptists, in short, proclaimed different kinds of Calvinism. By the mid-nineteenth century at least four varieties had emerged: (1) Baptist Edwardeanism, (2) a Fullerite Calvinism that was closely related to the Edwardean strand but not identical with it, (3) the Calvinism of the Philadelphia Confession, and (4) an eclectic populist Calvinism, influenced by the hyper-Calvinists but receptive also to other Baptist impulses, as well as to older esoteric and mystical continental traditions.

Traces of Edwardean influence could be found among New England Baptists as early as the 1740s, when Isaac Backus of Norwich, Connecticut, began to produce the forty-two books and tracts on theology and church-state relations that formed the first large body of Baptist thought in America. Backus had joined the Congregational Church in Norwich during a revival in 1741 and switched to a separatist congregation five years later. In 1748, he became a Separate Congregationalist pastor in Titticut Parish, Massachusetts, adopting Baptist views at the same time. In 1756, unable any longer to remain in communion with Separatists who baptized their infants, he formed a Separate Baptist congregation in nearby Middleborough. Although "a person of very little note in the learned world" — disdained by "learned gentlemen" — he determined to expose the corruption of state-supported religious establishments and promote evangelical Calvinist theology.[24]

Backus defended the customary Baptist alteration of covenant theology, which defined the covenant with Abraham as a covenant of works, not of grace. For Baptists this meant that God's command to Abraham to circumcise his offspring as a seal of the covenant provided no warrant for Christians to baptize their infants. In his *Short Description of the Difference Between the Bondwoman and the Free* (1756), Backus argued that Abraham typified Christ and that Abraham's offspring typified the spiritual children of Christ. Their circumcision therefore typified not baptism but rather the regeneration in which Christians were separated from their sins. Proponents of infant baptism who appealed to the covenant with Abraham as a precedent — as almost all pedobaptists did — misunderstood what the covenant with Abraham meant.[25]

Backus admired John Gill, but he admired Edwards more, and his theology represented more a conservative Baptist appropriation of Edwardean themes than an allegiance to Gill's high Calvinism. Backus felt hesitant to advance a theology, like that of Gill, that exalted the atonement "in such a manner as to pay little or no regard to a divine work within us, of conviction by the law, and relief by the Gospel." He saw in Gill — and distrusted — an antinomian impulse to disregard the law. He much preferred the appreciation for law that he found in Edwards, and he employed the Edwardean distinction between moral and natural ability as a weapon against Arminians and as a basis for evangelistic appeals. In his essay on *The Sovereign Decrees of God* (1773), Backus repeated Edwardean arguments about the determining efficacy of motives and the absurdity of self-determination. He never accepted, however, the governmental theory of atonement of the later Edwardeans, insisting instead on a limited atonement.[26]

Even more representative of Edwardeanism among New England Baptists was Jonathan Maxcy (1768–1820), the president of Rhode Island College, whose 1796 "Discourse Designed to Explain the Doctrine of Atonement" became a standard essay in the Edwardean tradition. Maxcy made the normal New Divinity distinctions, defending a general rather than limited atonement, saying that it satisfied public rather than distributive justice, and distinguishing natural ability and moral inability. In 1809 he became the first president of the University of South Carolina, where he promoted his Edwardean theology among Baptists in the South. He was a mentor to William Bullein Johnson (1782–1862), an advocate of Baptist missions who led the organization of the first national Baptist organization, the Triennial Convention (1814) and later of the Southern Baptist Convention (1845). In 1848, Johnson wrote that South Carolina Baptists widely accepted "moderate" Calvinism. Three years later he praised the influence of Furman University's theological professor, James S. Mims, whom he described as "imbued with the Spirit of New England Theology." John Mason Peck (1789–1858), who became an agent for the Triennial Convention and promoted Baptist theology in the West through a forty-one-year mission to settlers in Missouri and Illinois, also employed Edwardean ideas. The New Divinity's alteration of theology to encourage evangelistic appeals for immediate conversion perfectly suited the temper of early Baptist home missions. In 1847, the educator James L. Reynolds, who taught at Furman and Mercer, accused Mims and Johnson of heresy for denying the imputation of sin, and a battle raged for three years, but he could not extirpate the New England ideas, which had advocates from North Carolina to Arkansas.[27]

In 1857, Wayland claimed that among Baptist theologians in New England the doctrine of general atonement prevailed "almost universally," and he described New England Baptists as holding to New Divinity views of depravity and regeneration. On the doctrine of regeneration — understood as the renovation of character "in consequence of a change in the affections" — the views of most northeastern Baptists approached "very nearly to those of the first President Edwards, and the writers of that class." Wayland recognized that a substantial number of Baptist writers shared in an Edwardean theological culture that cut across denominational and regional boundaries.[28]

The second form of Baptist Calvinism — the Fullerite tradition — also transcended regional boundaries, but Baptists could not agree about how Fuller should be interpreted, and their disagreements had a regional shading. One group, numerous in the Northeast but with representatives in the South, read Fuller as saying that the atonement was "general" in nature even though it was "particular" in application, a reading that emphasized the generality and drew Fuller closer to the New Divinity tradition. Another group, numerous in the South though not exclusively southern, read him as arguing merely that the atonement, although "sufficient" for all, was not "efficient" for all, a reading that emphasized the particularity and drew him closer to Gill.[29]

In 1830 Jesse Mercer (1769–1841) of Georgia published his *Letters on Atonement* to counter mistaken readings of Fuller. A farmer-preacher in Oglethorpe, Hancock, and Wilkes counties and a founder of Mercer University, Mercer insisted that Fuller was "not so opposed to Dr. Gill as many have thought." Concerned that another Georgia Baptist had used Fuller both to abandon Calvinism and to encourage missions, Mercer wanted to make it clear that support for missions should not rest on a misreading of Fuller's thought. While the atonement was "sufficient to have saved all the world," Mercer wrote, God had not made it "effectual" to that end, and he noted that Fuller accepted doctrines of imputation, depravity, and substitutionary atonement that distanced him from both White's doctrines and the New Divinity. Yet Mercer himself accepted the Fullerite and Edwardean distinction between natural and moral ability, thus defending a Calvinism slightly different from that of the Philadelphia tradition.[30]

Baptists who adhered strictly to the Calvinism of the Philadelphia Confession accepted none of the innovations with which Edwardeans and Fullerites tried to refine Calvinist doctrine. Patrick Hues Mell (1814–88), a Georgian who taught at Mercer and reigned for years as president of the state's Baptist convention, spoke for them when he said in 1858 that Samuel Hopkins was not to be "acknowledged as a Calvinist at all." Mell could recommend Edwards on certain topics — God's end in creation, for example — but in *Predestination and the Saints' Perseverance Stated and Defended* (1858), he revealed his preference for the seventeenth-century scholastic theologian Girolamo Zanchius. In Mell's form of Calvinism, God determined from eternity to permit Adam's fall, impute the guilt of it to all humanity, save some, and leave others to perish. Christ bore, by imputation, the guilt of this sin and died vicariously for the elect — and for them alone — as a substitute to satisfy the divine wrath and pay the debt they owed. The Spirit regenerated the elect — to whom Christ's righteousness was imputed — to secure their repentance and faith, ensuring that they would persevere forever. As Mell saw it, God reigned as sovereignly "in the moral as in the physical world," and God's providence controlled every circumstance and event, "however minute," though "in perfect consistency with the free agency of the creature." This was the Calvinism of seventeenth-century scholasticism, enshrined in the Westminster and Philadelphia Confessions.[31]

Southern authors in the Philadelphia tradition produced a small library of Calvinist treatises, like Robert B. C. Howell's *The Covenants* (1855) or Nathaniel M. Crawford's *Christian Paradoxes* (1858), that promoted scholastic Calvinism. Howell, a pastor in Nashville and Richmond, quoted from both Fuller and Gill but repeated the themes of the seventeenth-century federal or covenant theology. Crawford, who served as president of Mercer, emphasized the particularity of the atonement and the inability of the sinful to perceive spiritual things. James P. Boyce (1827–88) of Charleston studied under Wayland at Brown, where he learned about the New Divinity innovations, and under Charles Hodge at Princeton Seminary, where he learned that those innovations were dangerous. He returned to the South to preach at Columbia, South Carolina, and to teach, first at Furman and then in 1859 at the Southern Baptist Seminary, where he taught the Calvinism of the Swiss scholastic Francis Turretin, which he had absorbed through Hodge. Boyce drafted an "Abstract of Principles" for the school that was grounded on the Philadelphia Confession.[32]

The most influential Baptist exposition of the Calvinism of the Philadelphia tradition was the *Manual of Theology* (1857) written by John Leadley Dagg, a largely self-taught pastor in Virginia and Philadelphia whose health problems forced him to turn his energies to writing and teaching. From 1844 to 1854 he was the president and professor of theology at Mercer University, where he wrote a series of works on close communion, believer's baptism, and biblical authority. After his retirement he produced not only the first American Baptist theological system but also three volumes on church order, moral science, and the evidences of Christianity. In addition to his promotion of Scottish philosophy and the evidential tradition, he represented the doctrines of Westminster (and Philadelphia) federal Calvinism.

Dagg taught all the doctrines that the Edwardean theologians had hoped to replace. He defended the federal union of Adam with all his posterity, an original sin propagated from parents to children, the imputation of Adam's sin and Christ's righteousness, and a limited substitutionary atonement designed to secure "distributive" justice to the elect rather than "public justice" in the Edwardean sense. Some glimmer of Fuller's interests might be visible in Dagg's insistence that everyone had the duty to obey God even with no assurance of election, but Dagg did not adopt the crucial Fullerite and Edwardean distinction between moral and natural ability. He distinguished rather between moral and physical inability, with the purpose of showing that even physical inability could not excuse a corrupt heart, a distinction quite unlike that of Fuller and the Edwardeans. Dagg could sound like Edwards when he described freedom of action as "doing what we please" even when our volitions are determined by our ruling principles of action, but that was a position held in various Calvinist circles. Dagg's theology avoided John Gill's formulations and he had no sympathy with hyper-Calvinist denigration of appeals to the unconverted, but he found Gill instructive. His theology exemplified the continuing force of seventeenth-century Calvinist thought in the nineteenth-century South.[33]

Populist Calvinism

The final form of Baptist Calvinism pressed the Calvinist tradition to its limits and showed the power of the democratizing ethos, especially on the western frontier. The populist impulse had always been strong among Baptists, who wandered throughout the seventeenth and eighteenth centuries on the far borderlands of religious respectability in the eyes of the learned. By the early nineteenth century, however, they moved closer to the mainstream, erecting fine churches, building colleges and seminaries, and cooperating with broader Protestant efforts to expand the faith and reform the society. Those efforts often included the formation of voluntary societies designed to reform the republic or carry the Christian gospel to the unchurched. The leaders of the voluntary societies came from the urban Northeast, and they sometimes displayed a condescension that unsettled rural Baptists who still remembered earlier indignities. These populists resented educated easterners who seemed to look down on them while asking them for money to support missions. The founding of voluntary societies also troubled Baptists who were wedded to the primitivist assumption that the Bible alone set the blueprint for Christian organization. They saw no biblical blueprint for extralocal organizations. Ever since the eighteenth century, moreover, some Baptists, especially in the South, had interpreted John Gill's hyper-Calvinism to prohibit all human efforts to win converts for Christ. By 1815, however, northern Baptists had formed more than sixty small mission societies, and after 1832 a Baptist Home Mission Society sent more than seven hundred missionaries to the West and the South. The cultural resentment and the theological heritage combined to produce an antimission sentiment that coalesced into the Primitive Baptist movement.[34]

The antimission movement was not restricted to one region or one denomination. The Baptist opposition to missions was part of a larger resistance to mission societies, Sabbatarian legislation, and reforming crusades that took their cues from rabble-rousing editors of religious newspapers in the Northeast. In Philadelphia, Elias Smith formed *The Herald of Gospel Liberty* (1808) — the first American religious newspaper — to excoriate voluntary societies, seminaries, and mission agencies. Theophilus Ransom Gates, who communicated with God through dreams and visions, took up the same cause in the same city through his antimission periodical *The Reformer* (1820). Anne Royall published a newspaper in Washington, D.C., that promoted Democratic Party politics and states' rights, and in her *Black Book* (1829) she exposed the "rapacity" of the missionary movement. The Baptist John Leland wrote for antimission newspapers throughout the country, and by the end of the 1820s a score of such popular periodicals, from *Priestcraft Exposed* to *Priestcraft Unmasked* and *Cry from the Four Winds*, rallied antimission and anti-Sabbatarian forces.[35]

John Leland (1754–1841), a native of Massachusetts, was a self-educated theologian who spent fourteen years after 1777 itinerating through Virginia. Battling against an Anglican establishment that fined and imprisoned Baptist activists and against mobs that stormed Baptist churches, he stood in the line of New England "Separates" who resisted any religious authority for the state. Leland contended for a view of religion as a matter between God and the individual conscience, and he envisioned churches as "little republics" in which "liberty and equality, the boast of democracy," exalted the poor and brought low the rich. He was a political supporter of Jefferson, working alongside him for separation of church and state in Virginia, and his conviction that the American Revolution represented the "world's best hope" spilled over into his theology. The true church, he thought, would always manifest the "democratical genius" of Christ's kingdom.[36]

Leland illustrates the point that the antimission cause did not always presuppose a hyper-Calvinist theology. His writing also exhibits the eclectic character of popular Calvinism, which blurred the fine distinctions of the confessions. Leland once claimed that the most profitable preaching assumed "a doctrine of sovereign grace in the salvation of souls, mixed with a little of what is called Arminianism." This casual attitude separated him from the Philadelphia traditionalists. He also found the Edwardeans unappealing. He criticized them for their hesitancy to affirm original sin, for their distinction between moral and natural ability, for their belief that saints could be willing to be damned for God's glory, and for their claim that sinners could come to Christ if they would. Leland thought of sinners as laboring under a natural, not merely a moral, necessity to sin and as lacking both the desire and the power to repent.[37]

Such matters were finally for him of secondary interest, for he doubted that differences over "theoretic principles" had much effect on piety. Leland was a simplifier, and he urged his fellow Baptists to "preach the gospel to every creature" without worrying about "abstruse questions or metaphysical niceties." He preached about the covenant of works and the covenant of grace, but he brought to these doctrines none of the subtle refinements that had appeared in seventeenth-century Puritanism. "When I hear a long harangue of metaphysical reasoning on abstruse questions," he wrote in 1830 after he had returned to Massachusetts, "I feel more like calling for my night-cap than anything else." On the matter of creeds and confessions, he stood with the earliest Separates rather than with their successors who became more receptive to written "articles" and "principles" of faith. He would subscribe to the Bible but not to "systems or creeds."[38]

Leland embodied the spirit of an eclectic Calvinism that followed no predictable path, and in the antimission movement of the South and West, self-taught Baptists created their own theology out of an unstable mix of hyper-Calvinist tradition, immediate revelation, and cultural resentment. John Taylor (1752–1835), a native of Virginia who became a Baptist pastor in Clear Creek, Kentucky, in 1785, launched the antimission attack in that region with his *Thoughts on Missions* (1820). He accused the missionaries of greed, corruption, and tyranny and deplored "theologians" who tried to "take our Bible from us" by requiring knowledge of the original languages. Believing that regeneration resulted exclusively from the operation of the Spirit on the elect chosen in accord with the "everlasting covenant," he contended that Baptists should use only the methods of Paul and the first apostles and trust in God to convert whomever God would. Yet Taylor was no consistent hyper-Calvinist, for when he published later his *History of Ten Baptist Churches* (1823), he approved a confessional statement that urged the preaching of repentance and issuing of invitations to all men and women and refused to bar communion with believers in a general atonement.[39]

An even more complex mixture of traditions appeared in the writing of Daniel Parker (1781–1844), a Virginian constantly on the move through Georgia, Tennessee, Kentucky, Illinois, and Texas and always in conflict with religious error, whether expressed by Methodists and Universalists or Baptist missionaries. His *Public Address to the Baptist Society* (1820) opposed seminaries and mission societies on the grounds that only God can summon ministers. He demanded biblical precedent, but he also preached a doctrine of the Spirit that verged on an assumption of immediate revelation as the source of his ideas.[40]

Parker wrote two tracts — *Views on the Two Seeds* (1826) and *The Second*

Dose of Doctrine on the Two Seeds (1826) — in which he promoted, on the basis of Genesis 3:15, a "two seed in the spirit" predestinarian doctrine. According to this doctrine, an inherited "seed of Satan" (or of Cain) doomed most men and women to damnation while a gracious "seed of Christ" (or of Seth) preserved a handful of elect souls. Salvation he viewed as unconditionally predestined for the seed of Seth, but he left open the possibility that the seed of Cain could, in theory, repent.[41]

Parker might have been retailing ideas that had their source in English high Calvinism, but he also might have been transmitting themes that had been part of religious folk culture in seventeenth-century England, possibly with ancient roots. Radical sectarians during the English civil wars had taught similar "two-seed" doctrines. The leader of the utopian Diggers, Gerrard Winstanley, had divided the world into heirs of the serpent seed and heirs of the righteous seed and speculated that God would destroy the serpent seed and bring the chosen to perfection. Ludowicke Muggleton (1609–98) and John Reeve (1608–58), the founders of the seventeenth-century Muggletonians, claimed to have received a revelation that the good seed of the blessed Israelites and the bad seed of the cursed Canaanites were now intermixed in all the children of Eve. Parker's metaphors might have had their sole source in his isolated reading of Genesis 3:15, in which God decrees enmity between the seed of Eve and the seed of the serpent, but speculation about the two seeds had long been a feature of popular religious culture. In any case, he demonstrated the eclectic ambiguity of populist Calvinism.[42]

By the 1850s, the antimission theology that Taylor and Parker helped to popularize assumed more consistent and precise formulation in the creeds of "Primitive" or "Old School" Baptists, and the hyper-Calvinism came more to the fore. By the time the Primitive Baptists formed themselves into an alliance at the Black Rock Convention in Maryland in 1832, writers like Gilbert Beebe of western New York and Samuel Trott of Virginia had formulated a popular hyper-Calvinist theology around the theme of the absolute predestination of all things. Their doctrine of "eternal and unconditional election," limited atonement, and the sovereign and irresistible effectual work of the Holy Spirit became now the consistent foundation for their opposition to mission societies, seminaries, and social reform.[43]

Baptist Calvinists were thus divided into schools and factions, but all of them could unite against one common enemy: the reform movement of Alexander Campbell. A substantial portion of Baptist theology in the South and Midwest consisted of polemical forays against Campbell, who attacked both Calvinism and revivalism at every turn and who built his movement partly by persuading Baptist congregations to accept his views. Jeremiah Bell Jeter, the long-time pastor of the First Baptist Church in Richmond, represented a host of Baptist authors who tried to counter Campbell's attack. His *Campbellism Examined* (1855) defended revivalistic Calvinist views of inherited depravity, the bound will, the efficacy of the Spirit, the need for an experience of conversion, and an insistence that repentance and the remission of sin had to precede baptism. His book was part of a widespread effort to stem defections from Baptist churches.[44]

Campbell's movement made inroads into Baptist strength partly because he presented it under the banner of theological democracy. This touched vital chords in Baptist life, and it also revealed that not all Baptists felt at ease with the Calvinist theologies that had formed their piety. Campbell could link his reform to ideals they already held: their localism, their biblicism, their ambivalence about creeds and confessions, and their suspicion of elites. He claimed to be more democratic in spirit; he also claimed a more rational theology, a more reasonable way of reading the Bible, in harmony with both enlightenment philosophy and the message of scripture itself. For many Baptists, Campbell's combination of commonsense rationalism and biblical literalism proved more attractive than any of the Calvinist traditions in the Baptist past.

14

Restoration

The restorationist theologians who called themselves "Christians" or "Disciples" came partly out of Presbyterian traditions and partly from a background in Baptist populism. Like both the early Presbyterians and the Baptists, they desired to restore the Christianity of the first century. They linked this restoration to confidence in the authority of ordinary people. They would reform Christian theology by ridding it of all "human invention," including formal creeds and confessions, and they would ground their reform in a rational, commonsense reading of the Bible by ordinary Christians untainted by the erudition of a clerical elite. This would return the Church to its primitive purity, return theology to the people, and return reason to theology.

Restorationist theology appeared on the scene with renewed force as part of the cultural commotion that followed the American Revolution. In 1801 a one-time Baptist preacher named Abner Jones founded a "Christian" congregation in Lyndon, Vermont. He was determined to escape sectarian error — and he viewed all the existing denominations as erring sects — by recovering the beliefs and practices of primitive Christianity and identifying himself and his followers simply as "Christians." He joined with another former Baptist, Elias Smith, who in 1802 created a similar congregation in Portsmouth, New Hampshire, and they drew others into a loose alliance that they called the Christian Connection. After 1803 these eastern Christians cooperated with like-minded groups in the South and West, especially with Barton W. Stone's Christian movement and with the followers of Thomas Campbell and his son Alexander Campbell, who in 1809 created a Christian Association in Pennsylvania. In 1832 Stone merged his followers with those of the Campbells to form the Disciples of Christ or Christian Church. They hoped to overcome Christian division by restoring first-century truth.

Populist Themes and European Sources

From the beginning, they believed that Christian unity would come as the people threw off the bonds of elite theologians, their creeds, and their "aristocratic spirit," and three of them — Smith, Stone, and Alexander Campbell — took the lead in writing a theology for the people. Elias Smith (1769–1846), the son of Connecticut farmers, made his name as an editor who opposed every innovation of the early nineteenth-century churches. Restlessly moving through Vermont, New Hampshire, and Pennsylvania, he condemned mission agencies, Sabbath societies, colleges, seminaries, and every hint of an alliance between the church and the state. He used his *Herald of Gospel Liberty* to expose the clergy of New England as political Tories, secret monarchists, and apologists for the rich.[1]

Barton Warren Stone (1772–1844), a native of Maryland, briefly taught school in Georgia before becoming a Presbyterian minister. Despite reservations about Calvinist theology, he sought ordination in 1798 and accepted the leadership of Presbyterian congregations in Cane Ridge and Concord in Bourbon County, Kentucky. In 1800 he was swept up in the emotion of the camp meetings. Resisting efforts by the Synod of Kentucky to impose doctrinal discipline, he joined others in 1803 in writing the "Last Will and Testament of the Springfield Presbytery," left the denomination, and gathered a movement of people determined to be called "Christians only." Ridiculing the Presbyterian ministers who lived in "parlors" and "fine houses" and wore "costly apparel," he attracted a following in the upper South and Midwest.[2]

Alexander Campbell (1788–1866), a native of Ballymena, County Antrim, Ireland, migrated to Pennsylvania in 1809, withdrew from the Presbyterians, formed a Baptist congregation, and then decided that the Baptists had failed to restore the true church. He and his father, Thomas Campbell (1763–1854), launched a movement to overcome denominational divisions by restoring primitive Christianity. He also announced in his *Christian Baptist* newspaper that he would eternally oppose clerical power and expose the viciousness of the distinction between clergy and laity. The chief vice of the clergy was theological. They had misled the people into believing that they alone could "expound the New Testament — [and] that without them, people are either almost or altogether destitute of the means of grace."[3]

Campbell thought that the seminary-educated theologians were out of touch with ordinary people: "A religion requiring much mental abstraction or exquisite refinement of thought . . . is a religion not suited to mankind in their present circumstances." Smith saw the New England ministers as the architects of an arcane "scholastic Divinity" that owed more to Plato than to the New Testament, " which was a plain book, written for common people." The aim of restorationist theologians was to write for "readers of the most common capacity and most superficial education." They thought of theology as "a subject which ought to be leveled to the apprehension of all."[4]

Underlying these criticisms was a vision of the church as a fellowship with no hierarchy or elevation of one class above another — no patricians, said Campbell, no feudal barons or serfs: "All are one in rank and privilege in Christ's kingdom." The movement imported the rhetoric of the Revolution into its ecclesiology. Its leaders began to think of the church as a "school of equal rights," a "cradle of human liberty," which commanded its citizens to "think, speak, and act for themselves." Elias Smith grew to believe that even the notion of a church covenant was "contrary to the perfect law of liberty."[5]

It was not that the reformers disdained education. They merely disliked any claims to deference for the educated. Smith and Jones lacked any formal education, but Thomas Campbell graduated from the University of Glasgow. Alexander Campbell spent a year there after his father tutored him in Latin, Greek, and John Locke's philosophy. The chief ally of the Campbells, Walter Scott (1796–1861), a Scottish immigrant who learned his primitivism in a small Baptist congregation in Pittsburgh, probably graduated from the University of Edinburgh. Stone studied at David Caldwell's Guilford Academy in North Carolina. In 1840, Alexander Campbell founded Bethany College in Virginia (now West Virginia) to provide a more learned ministry, and he served as its president for twenty years. But the call for "freedom of thought" for all, including the uneducated, continued to color the rhetoric of the movement.[6]

It was once customary to view the restorationists as the products of a frontier American mentality. They did flourish in western counties, rural areas, and small towns that had relatively egalitarian social relations among whites coupled with resentments against distant elites, but the movement also had philosophical and religious roots in Britain and Europe. Alexander Campbell brought with him to America not only the ideas of Locke and the Scottish philosophers but also a serious acquaintance with the thought of two Scottish

Independents, Robert and James Haldane, and of the Scottish theologian Robert Sandeman. His ideas about sacramental practice and his views of creeds closely resembled those of the Haldanes, about which he learned at Glasgow, and his understanding of faith resembled that of Sandeman, to which also he had been exposed before coming to America.[7]

Walter Scott had a similar immersion in Lockean and Scottish philosophy and even closer links than Campbell to Sandeman and the Haldanes. Barton W. Stone studied Scottish moral philosophy at Caldwell's academy, and even Elias Smith, who had almost no formal education, claimed that he had practically memorized the *Compendium of Christian Theology* (1739) of the Swiss Calvinist Jean-Frédéric Ostervald (1663–1747), who conceived of theology as a "science totally practical," both "simple and perspicacious," accessible not only to "the learned . . . but to all men indiscriminately, the rude, and plebeans" — themes repeated endlessly in the American restoration movements.[8]

Eager to reach "the rude, and plebeans," the restorationists published most of their theology in newspapers and popular journals. Some of them wrote longer theological treatises; Alexander Campbell's *Christian System* (1835, 1839) and Walter Scott's *The Gospel Restored* (1836) were influential texts, and Elias Smith's *New Testament Dictionary* (1812) attempted to discuss "every subject in the New Testament." But for most of their readers, they were editor-theologians, and the main vehicles for their ideas were newspapers and journals like Smith's *Herald of Gospel Liberty* (1808–17), Campbell's *Christian Baptist* (1823–30) and *Millennial Harbinger* (1830–70), Stone's *Christian Messenger* (1826–45), and Joseph Badger's *Christian Palladium* (1832–59). Campbell made special use of public oral debate as a means of spreading his ideas. Five of his most substantial theological works were the published transcripts of his debates with the Catholic Bishop J. B. Purcell, the skeptic Robert Owen, the Presbyterians N. L. Rice and W. L. McCalla, and the Scottish Seceder Presbyterian John A. Walker.[9]

Theological differences among the restorationists thwarted Stone's efforts to merge the eastern and western branches, and Campbell remained suspicious of Stone even after their two groups united. No one theologian can stand as the representative of a unified restorationist theology. Here the emphasis will fall on Alexander Campbell because as a theologian he was both more prolific and more widely known than the others, but the eastern Christians disliked some of his ideas as much as he deplored some of theirs. All agreed on the two goals of restoring primitive Christianity and attaining the unity of the church, and all thought that their restoration was not only more biblical but also more rational than the current theologies, but they were not men prone to compromise and agreement.

Restoration, Reason, and Revelation

Thomas Campbell and his friends expressed the watchword of the movement when they and Alexander formed in 1809 their Christian Association: "Where the holy Scriptures speak, we speak; and where they are silent, we are silent." Before 1830, the Campbells called for an express command, example, or clear deduction from the New Testament for every church practice. As a result, they rejected Christian sponsorship of creeds, presbyteries, synods, conferences, Sunday schools, moral societies, mission societies, education societies, Bible societies, colleges, seminaries, instrumental music, and hymns with printed musical notes, since none of these had biblical precedents or commands.[10]

It was hard to be a consistent primitivist when the ideal of unity also beckoned. Stone believed that Alexander Campbell was so rigid that he lost opportunities for unity with like-minded groups. Campbell believed that Stone was too willing to compromise the restorationist ideal. Critics accused Campbell of inconsistency. Sidney Rigdon, later a Mormon, told him that he should accept the primitive communism of Acts 4, and others chided him for not adopting such New Testament rites as the kiss of charity. By 1830 Campbell was conceding that while the Bible instituted certain mandatory "statutes" — a weekly celebration of the Lord's Supper (which he understood as a symbolic commemoration of Jesus' death), a weekly Lord's Day gathering, singing, prayer — it guided the church more by principle than by precedents. By the 1850s, as his movement grew, he changed his mind about colleges and mission societies. But he never abandoned the ideal of restoring "primitive Christianity" by uniting and building "upon the Bible alone."[11]

Campbell turned to the Bible alone, but not quite the whole Bible. Earlier primitivists, like the seventeenth-century New England Calvinists, found binding precedents in the Old Testament as well as the New. In 1816 Campbell preached to a Baptist association in Virginia a "Sermon on the Law" in which he contended that the gospel replaced the Old Testament dispensation, including not only its ceremonial but also its judicial and moral laws. This meant that the Calvinist custom of preaching the Mosaic law to prepare sinners for the gospel had no place in the pulpit. It meant also that the New Testament command to love God and neighbor replaced the Old Testament laws, including the ten commandments. And it meant that no ancient Jewish practice — from circumcision of infants to tithes and from holy days to national covenants — could bind adherents of the kingdom of Christ. The sermon created a storm of protest and led to attacks on Campbell as an antinomian, but its principle defined the interpretation of scripture among the Disciples.[12]

He elaborated the principle by describing biblical history as a series of periods or "dispensations" culminating in the establishment of Christ's kingdom. This idea came from the covenant theology that he encountered in his Irish Calvinist heritage and in his reading of seventeenth-century Calvinist scholastics like Johannes Cocceius (1603–69) and Herman Witsius. Campbell expanded the two dispensations of the covenant theologians into three—the patriarchal, the Jewish, and the Christian—each with a separate revelation appropriate "to the different ages of the world and stages of human improvement." The distinction supported his view that only the Christian dispensation could furnish statutes and precedents for the church.[13]

According to Campbell's reading of scripture, the Christian dispensation began after Christ's resurrection and the bestowing of the Spirit recorded in the book of Acts. When Campbell's followers sought biblical precedents, they looked almost exclusively to Acts and the New Testament epistles, with a special place for the letter to the Hebrews. The events of the four gospels occurred, as they saw it, in the Jewish dispensation, so the gospels provided no statutes for the church. Early Disciples could not agree even on the propriety of repeating the Lord's Prayer in public worship. They found a genuine revelation of God in the Old Testament and the gospels, but they looked elsewhere in organizing their congregations.[14]

"The Bible, the whole Bible, and nothing but the Bible is the religion of Protestants," Campbell wrote, echoing the seventeenth-century English latitudinarian theologian William Chillingworth. Theologians were therefore to propound no doctrine that lacked biblical warrant, and they were to restrict themselves to the language of scripture: "We choose to speak of Bible things by Bible words because we are always suspicious that if the word is not in the Bible, the idea which it represents is not there."[15]

Campbell's dispensational formula allowed for flexibility in his view of the Bible. It permitted him to argue, like the New England Unitarians, that the writers of the Old Testament had an incomplete knowledge of God. He contended for the inspiration and infallibility of the Bible—the "narratives and episodes" were "infallibly correct"—but he denied that a "plenary and verbal" inspiration extended to "every jot and tittle" and claimed only that "the ideas and leading terms" were infallibly inspired. He denied, moreover, that the entire Bible could be considered a revelation, for he defined revelation as divine communication about spiritual matters beyond "the exercise of . . . reason upon material and sensible objects." The center of the Bible was its testimony "concerning the person and mission of Jesus Christ."[16]

A competent student of textual criticism, he admired Moses Stuart at Andover. When he published a translation of the New Testament known as *The Living Oracles* (1826), copied mainly from British translators but filled with his own emendations, he conceded that the received Greek text underlying the King James Version had spurious passages resulting from additions to later manuscripts. Nonetheless, he held, like the other restorationists, to a biblical literalism that assumed the historical and scientific accuracy of the text. While he recognized its figures and metaphors, he read it mainly as a source of univocal propositions. In his lectures on the Pentateuch delivered to classes at Bethany College in 1859–60, he made no concessions to geology or to the poetic imagination, insisting on a six-day creation and asserting that God spoke audibly to Adam and Eve in the garden.[17]

Above all, he read the Bible as a simple and clear book. Both he and Elias Smith outlined rules of interpretation that would encourage ordinary people to read the Bible for themselves. Among Campbell's followers, the tendency was to valorize the "inductive" study of the text, which in practice meant collecting all the passages on a given topic and drawing conclusions from them. This was the method popularized by James S. Lamar, a pastor in Augusta, Georgia, in *The Organon of Scripture: Or, the Inductive Method of Biblical Interpretation* (1859), but some Disciples objected even to the idea that the Bible had to be interpreted. To Walter Scott, the Baconian inductive method made interpretation unnecessary; it simply laid out the facts for anyone of clear mind to see.[18]

For Campbell, what counted were the facts. He grounded his understanding of the Bible on his assumption that it was "a book of facts, not of opinions, theories, abstract generalities, nor of verbal definitions." His understanding of "fact" came from Francis Bacon, who had defined it as "something said" or "something done," and Campbell might have learned it from his teacher at Glasgow, George Jardine, who made similar claims about the Bible. The leading facts on which Christianity rested could be reduced to three: Jesus was crucified and buried and he rose from the dead.[19]

Since theology was a set of inferences from the Bible, theologians had no business grounding their claims in natural theology. To make this point, Campbell drew on John Locke, but he pushed Locke's empiricism further than any other American theologian. He argued that Locke had been insufficiently empirical when he asserted that reason could prove the existence of God. When Campbell debated Robert Owen in Cincinnati, he pressed the Lockean point that all the mind's ideas came either from sensations or from reflections on its own operations. Unaided reason therefore had no way of conceiving an uncaused Creator able to produce the world *ex nihilo*. Nothing in sensory experience or self-reflection remotely suggested such an idea. Even the argument from design, the favorite of the natural theologians, merely assumed, rather than proved, he said, that the physical world was an effect.[20]

Campbell countered the deists by arguing that their own professed empiricism subverted their theology. His main contention against Owen was that since reason could not have originated the idea of God, the mind must have received it from a source external to itself. Campbell accepted the familiar idea of the *prisca theologia:* every conception of the divine must have had its origin either in dim traditions that began with God's audible speech to Adam and Eve or in the written biblical revelations.[21]

Theologians also had no business with creeds. The restorationists uniformly believed that creeds had done nothing but create discords and parties. Creeds prevented unity and usurped the authority of the Bible. Stone called them competitors of the Bible; Elias Smith classed them among the "fables" used to deceive the people. Both Stone and Campbell accepted the Apostles' Creed as a fair statement of Christian belief, but neither would allow it to exercise authority. Campbell once described his movement as a "campaign against creeds."[22]

The attack on natural theology, creeds, and speculation, however, did not lead to the conclusion that the Christian faith was unreasonable. Campbell thought that "the verity of Christianity" was "exclusively a question of fact, to be tried by all the rules of evidence which govern our decision upon any question of historical fact." Restorationists deprecated philosophy in the abstract, but Campbell acknowledged his debt to Locke, Bacon, and the Scots. From Locke came his conviction that knowledge of the external world came only through the senses. From Bacon, "the great teacher," he took not only his understanding of "facts" but also his confidence that "inductive philosophy" provided a counterweight against speculation. From Reid and Stewart he learned both the limits of speculative thought and the method of appeal to "consciousness" to clarify issues of human nature, including theological questions about sin, conversion, and freedom. When Campbell founded Bethany College, he served not only as president but also as professor of mental philosophy, and in his inaugural lecture he valorized both Bacon and the Scottish philosophers.[23]

It was not surprising, then, that he reintroduced a chastened natural theology. While he denied that the mind could originate the idea of God, he said that the natural world sparkled with confirmations of the divine reality for a mind enlightened by revelation. The argument from design made sense by clarifying a truth already known. It became a commonplace of the movement, moreover, that rational arguments could prove Christianity true and that to preach the gospel meant simply presenting it along with the evidence. Campbell employed the traditional evidences, drawing heavily on such British apologists as Soame Jenyns, Nathaniel Lardner, George Campbell, and Thomas Chalmers. Like them, he believed that miracles and fulfilled prophecies proved the authority of scripture, that the Bible's consistency demonstrated its truth, that the martyrdom of the apostles confirmed their trustworthiness, and that ancient history and ancient traditions confirmed biblical accounts. He also deployed the standard arguments against Hume's rejection of miracles, claiming that Hume had appealed to uniform human experience without knowing what human beings experienced uniformly. By Campbell's criteria, the gospel accounts stood confirmed by rational evidence.[24]

The restorationists incorporated this evidential tradition into their understanding of faith. Smith taught that to believe was merely to "give credit to the report of another." Both Stone and Campbell taught that faith was assent to testimony that was confirmed by evidence. "Faith," Campbell said, "is neither more nor less than the belief of some testimony." For him, as for John Locke, faith meant assent to the testimony of the apostles that Jesus was the Messiah who rose from the dead. He thought that the evidence for this testimony was so strong that anyone hearing it with an unbiased mind had no alternative but to believe it. Campbell and Stone also spoke of faith as trust—heartfelt consent as well as the assent of the mind—but it was a trust grounded in rational assent.[25]

Campbell saw this rational faith as the alternative to the "headless" piety of revivalism. He disliked the idea that faith was a matter of feeling, that it required a period of terror and despair, or that it came through an emotional experience of conversion. He disliked the methods of revivalists who sought to induce belief by threatening people or arousing their emotions. He found no biblical requirement for a rehearsal of a conversion experience as a prelude to baptism or church membership. He rejected the assumption that conversion depended on a mysterious change wrought by the Spirit. If faith meant rational assent to well-grounded testimony, it made no sense to think of it in Calvinist terms as an immediate gift of the Spirit. He rejected as well the common distinction between historical and saving faith. If faith meant assent to a historical testimony, then historical faith was saving.[26]

Campbell's antirevivalism drew conflicting responses from other restorationists. Walter Scott fully concurred with Campbell and introduced an alternative form of evangelism: the evangelist laid out the evidence; the seeker responded with faith, repentance, and baptism, which issued in the remission of sins and the gift of the Spirit. He first proposed the formula in 1827 and later claimed that it represented the restoration of the "ancient gospel," corresponding to Campbell's restoration of the "ancient order." Campbell thought it a pretentious claim, but by 1839 he had accepted the formula as a helpful summary of what conversion meant.[27]

In the East, however, the Christian movement flourished in a revivalist ethos, and the leaders of the Christian Connection berated Campbell for rationalistic betrayals of "experimental religion." For them, it was the Spirit who awakened the sinful. Stone stood somewhere in the middle, advocating revivals and reassuring the easterners that the Spirit was active in conversion but also defending the position that faith was a response to testimony, not to a special illumination by the Spirit.[28]

This struggle over revivalism influenced the debate within the movement over the relation between the Spirit and the written scriptural word. As early as 1824 Campbell wrote in the *Christian Baptist* that "the Holy Spirit now operates upon the minds of men only by the word." By 1827, Stone agreed, and by the 1830s the Disciples had forged a consensus that it was misleading to "separate the Spirit and word of God." This teaching further divided them from the Christian Connection, whose leaders saw it as one more attack on their revivalism. They accused Campbell of limiting the work of the Spirit exclusively to the written word. There was some truth to the accusation. Campbell sometimes spoke as if word and Spirit were identical—a tendency that worried Stone—though it seemed clear by the late 1830s that he did not intend to identify the one as the other. Nonetheless, he did emphasize that the appeal of the Spirit was to the mind, through the words, testimonies, and evidence of scripture. The Spirit, too, was reasonable.[29]

Millennial Hopes

The early restorationists shared an intense eschatological expectation. From the outset of his career, Campbell anticipated that restoration and unity would usher in the millennial era described in Revelation 20, a new order of peace, prosperity, and justice, with massive conversions to the faith on the part of both gentiles and Jews. During the 1830s and 1840s, he believed that it would begin "sometime soon, perhaps in the present century." The object of his *Millennial Harbinger* was to announce the conditions for its beginning, though by the mid-1850s he was postponing its arrival to around the year 2000. He never ceased to believe that an earthly millennial era would precede the return of Christ, the resurrection of the dead, the final judgment, and God's creation of the new heavens and new earth. Other restorationists were more confident than he about predicting dates, but they were of different minds about the sequence of events.[30]

Though he rejected the term "millennium" as unbiblical, Elias Smith began his career with a millennial theology similar to Campbell's, but by 1808 he concluded that Christ would physically return and rule on earth throughout the thousand years. In 1812 he defined the coming kingdom as the time when all would "live in love and peace, and honor him as the one Lord and king over all the earth." He combined his eschatology with republican politics and speculated that the French Revolution and the election of his beloved Thomas Jefferson both might signify that the reign of the Antichrist was ending. Barton W. Stone also started out as a postmillennialist, but by 1833 he began to argue that Christ would imminently return to condemn and destroy the wicked, resurrect the saintly dead, and rule with the saints on earth for a thousand years. Unlike Smith, he concluded that Christians should withdraw from politics. Walter Scott, on the other hand, started out with premillennial views and shared with Stone a fascination during the early 1840s with the end-time speculation of William Miller, the Vermont farmer-preacher whose predictions of a literal return of Christ in 1843 or 1844 generated wide interest. But Campbell thought too many prophecies remained unfulfilled to permit belief in an imminent end. After Miller's predictions proved wrong, Scott, greatly disappointed, turned back, in his *Messiahship or Great Demonstration* (1859), to a postmillennial theology.[31]

In yet other ways the leaders of the movement changed their minds — and reached differing conclusions — about eschatological matters. At the outset, Campbell believed that the millennium would bring the destruction of nation states — including America — and that national entities could contribute nothing to its inception. In 1832 he attacked patriotism as collective selfishness. By the 1850s he had come to think that the growing unity of Americans might mean that this Protestant nation could lead the world toward the millennial era, but by 1860 such national — and nationalist — hopes faded. The millennium would come only through the preaching of the gospel.[32]

He taught that the millennium would progress as Christ reigned over it through his earthly kingdom, the church. The main theological interest of all the restorationists was the doctrine of the church, and Campbell, Stone, and Scott identified the church with the kingdom, just as Graves and the Landmarkists were doing. Campbell believed that the kingdom began with the revelation to Moses but that now Christ was its sole monarch and that his subjects were the members of the church. "There is but one real Kingdom of Christ in the world," Campbell wrote in 1853, "and that is equivalent to affirming that there is but one Church of Christ in the world." All conceded that the kingdom would come in its fullness only at the end of time, but they thought that to join the true restored church meant becoming fully a "constitutional citizen" of the kingdom.[33]

Calvinism Opposed

The doctrine of the church was a practical doctrine. This was, as the restorationists saw it, the appropriate kind of question for theologians to answer. Above all, theologians had no business with "speculation," a term that the restorationists used mainly to disparage the Calvinism in which most of them had been nurtured. The Campbells had been members of a strict Presbyterian group in Ireland — the Old Light, Anti-Burgher Secession Presbyterian Church, a denomination of Scottish origin that got its name from its rejection of any patronage system for choosing pastors and of any oath to support the state church — and both of them were deposed in America after they strayed from the orthodox way. The Presbyterian Synod of Kentucky had expelled Stone for theological errors. Smith had been a Calvinistic Baptist who then allied himself with Benjamin Randall and the Freewill Baptists.[34]

When Stone preached for a time in a Presbyterian congregation in Kentucky, he managed to survive with his integrity intact by ignoring predestination and reprobation as "speculative divinity." As a young man, Campbell felt as if he were "tossed on the waves of speculative divinity," taught by Calvinists who had "renewed the speculative theology of Saint Augustine." The tendency across the movement was to view any departure from biblical language — and any hint of Calvinistic doctrine — as a speculative evil.[35]

The debates with Calvinists were about the order of salvation. Campbell agreed with the Calvinists, against the Wesleyans, that faith preceded repentance, but he otherwise had little positive to say about Calvinism. The Christians disliked the Calvinist notion that regeneration preceded faith; this notion implied predestination, which seemed to them unfair. The only predestination Campbell would accept as scriptural was God's predestination of all true Christians to be conformed to God's image. Elias Smith argued that predestination, biblically understood, meant no more than the calling of Christ's original apostles. Campbell also disliked the Calvinist — and Wesleyan — introspective quest for assurance of salvation. He thought that assurance came solely from testimony of the word. Anyone who accepted the testimony that Jesus was the Messiah could be assured of living within a state of salvation.[36]

The restorationists rejected the Calvinist understanding of original sin, especially the doctrine of imputation. Campbell even preferred not to use the word "depravity," because it implied that all were equally sinful. Neither Campbell nor Stone wanted to deny that sin was universal or that Adam's sin altered human nature in a way that created a proneness to do evil, but they deplored the idea of any "invincible necessity to sin." Elias Smith said that the notion of original sin was an incredible fable. All repudiated, therefore, the Calvinist doctrine of the bondage of the will.[37]

Campbell challenged the prevailing Calvinist understanding of the doctrine of justification by faith alone. He believed that scriptural teaching was more complex than the Calvinists recognized. The sinner was justified through faith, and good works were not meritorious and could never earn salvation, but they were necessary for continuing in a justified state. Moreover, Campbell taught that forgiveness required not simply faith but an "act" of faith. It required a "change of state," a new relation, as well as a change of mind and heart. The required "act" was baptism.[38]

What especially distinguished Campbell from evangelical revivalists — Calvinists, Wesleyans, and the eastern branch of the Christian movement — was his doctrine that baptism conveyed the remission of sins. As early as 1812 he declared infant baptism unscriptural; after 1812 he declared immersion the only proper mode of baptism; by the time of his debate with W. L. McCalla in 1823, he was announcing that the purpose of baptism by immersion was the forgiveness of sins. He appealed especially to three New Testament passages — Ephesians 5:26, Titus 3:5, and John 3:5 — that seemed to connect baptism with regeneration. But the doctrine also served a more immediate religious motive by offering a warrant for assurance of forgiveness. The baptized need not indulge in anxious introspection. The ordinance itself brought assurance of favor with God.[39]

He qualified the doctrine with a distinction between real and formal remission. Faith and repentance brought real remission; baptism changed the "state" of the sinful by introducing them into the church and therefore into a new relation to God and the kingdom. His critics denounced him as "Catholic," but Campbell replied that he attached no efficacy to baptism itself. Even more of his critics denounced the seeming implication that only the immersed could be forgiven. This question divided the Christian movement, further alienating the eastern Christian Connection and troubling Stone, as well, for while Stone could accept the connection between baptism and the remission of sins, he could not agree that the unimmersed remained unforgiven. The doctrine also had practical consequences that troubled Stone, since most of Campbell's followers took it to require the exclusion of the unimmersed from religious fellowship.[40]

In 1837, Campbell softened the doctrine. The change might have been a result of his preparations for his 1837 debate with the Catholic bishop of Cincinnati, John B. Purcell, in which Campbell cast himself as "a Protestant," standing in defense of "the great cardinal principles of Protestantism." This was hardly a position consonant with a belief that most Protestants remained unforgiven, and in his "Lunenberg Letter," he conceded that the unimmersed could be forgiven unless they opposed the scriptural truth that immersion was normally necessary for forgiveness. Reacting to followers who said that even

Baptist immersion was invalid because it was not performed for remission of sins, he wrote that immersion was not "essential" to forgiveness. What counted most was faith and love. But he continued to insist on baptism as the normal "act" required for justification, and several in his movement regretted his 1837 concession.[41]

Campbell's reading of the New Testament convinced him, as well, that "the most prominent object" of Christian worship was the celebration of the Lord's Supper, which he preferred to call "the breaking of the loaf," since the phrase seemed a closer description of what the biblical narrative accentuated. His understanding of the rite reflected his Reformed heritage; he understood it as a commemoration of Jesus' death and of the divine love that reconciled Christians with God. The elements were "emblematic" of Christ's body and blood. But Campbell departed from Reformed tradition in his insistence that the New Testament required a weekly celebration of the rite. Both Campbell and Stone viewed the ritual as the sign of the Christian unity they sought.[42]

The restorationist quest for unity, however, led repeatedly to charges of heresy as the leaders of the movement criticized traditional doctrines. Elias Smith felt the attraction of universalism. He decided in 1805 that at the day of judgment the sinful would be destroyed, not punished eternally. By 1816 he was agreeing with Universalists that the sinful would not be destroyed on the judgment day but gradually purified through suffering. His universalism created a tumult in the eastern movement, and he eventually left the Universalists and rejoined the Christian Connection, but he wavered on the issue throughout his life.[43]

Smith and Stone agreed, moreover, in denying any understanding of the atonement as an act of satisfaction that altered the divine will. For Smith, atonement meant only that Jesus turned the faithless from their iniquities and reconciled them to God. For Stone it meant that Jesus' death displayed "the love of God to sinners" and confirmed the abolition of death for believers. He argued in his *Atonement* (1805) that Christ died to display God's "love, grace, and mercy." He found substitution and satisfaction incompatible with grace: "If my surety or substitute has fully discharged my debt, . . . can it be grace in my creditor to forgive me?" The same question drew Edwardeans to governmental theories, but to Stone the Edwardean option was as objectionable as the theories it replaced. Stone also clashed with Campbell on the issue, for while Campbell wanted to argue that Christ's sacrifice was not the cause of God's benevolence, he insisted that without the sacrifice God could not be propitious.[44]

The movement further divided over the Trinity. Smith saw Christ as unique but only as a mediator upon whom God had conferred religious authority, and many in the Christian Connection referred to themselves as unitarian in sentiment. They were sometimes called "Evangelical Unitarians," and one of their editors, Joseph Badger, sought negotiations with William Ellery Channing in hopes that the Christians could join with the Unitarian Association. Channing, however, thought that they were too emotional and too content with an uneducated ministry. They also talked too much about sin.[45]

Barton Stone also referred favorably to Channing, though he regretted the decision of eastern Christians to describe themselves as unitarian. Stone rejected Trinitarian belief on the grounds that the language was not biblical; he also thought it unreasonable that a substantial being could beget itself or be begotten by itself. Kentucky Presbyterians placed him in the Unitarian camp, and the Presbyterian minister in New Providence and Harrodsburg, Thomas Cleland, charged that he had reverted to the language of German infidels. Drawing on Isaac Watts, Stone tried to counter such charges by arguing that the Son was "the first begotten of every creature," who became, in the fullness of time, incarnate in Jesus Christ, but that he was not an eternal Person consubstantial with God the Father. "My reason shall ever bow to revelation," he wrote, "but it shall never be prostrated to human contradictions and inventions."[46]

On this issue, Stone and Campbell differed. Like Stone, Campbell wanted to discard nonbiblical language, and he criticized the "metaphysical technicalities, and unintelligible jargon" of Trinitarian theology. But he believed that scripture displayed a "society in God himself, a plurality as well as unity in the Divine nature," and he thought it rational to believe that God was never without his word. On the meaning of the Spirit, he remained ambivalent; addressing God as Father, Son, and Spirit, he nevertheless cautioned against prayer or hymns to the Spirit on the grounds that the Spirit remained under the dispensation of the incarnate word. He thought that he affirmed divine plurality and unity as scripture taught it, even though he disliked the word "Trinity." Stone thought that Campbell sounded like a Calvinist.[47]

For the most part, the restorationists saw Trinitarian doctrine as "speculation." They preferred to talk about the "practical part" of Christian truth. Doctrines, wrote Elias Smith, were principles of action, "something to be believed and reduced to practice." The purpose of revelation was to "produce purity of heart," Campbell said, so as to enable Christians to enjoy both "present and future happiness." When Christianity became a "science, a fit subject of speculation," it fell into corruption. The restorationist Christians saw it as more rational and more biblical to restore its practical intent.[48]

15

Roots of Black Theology

To identify a distinct black theological tradition in the early nineteenth century is to move outside the self-understanding of the era's African-American religious authors. The small company of African-American writers who gained access to printing presses had no conception of themselves as creating a theological tradition outside the boundaries of denominational allegiance. The notion of a specifically black theology during the era is the result of the emergence during the twentieth century of a black theology movement that looked to the past for anticipations of its interests. Yet all traditions are, in part, constructions of successive generations who identify themselves with earlier figures whose activity or authority enhances present interests. Religious communities reconstruct traditions by virtue of their own changing self-understanding. Historians construct traditions as heuristic aids that help identify patterns that may not have always been apparent to actors in the past. More than one of the traditions defined for closer examination in this book, from the eighteenth-century theology of virtue to the "New England theology," are, in varying degrees, constructions of either theological partisans or historical observers. From this perspective, it is useful to set apart the antebellum black theologians as a distinguishable group.[1]

In one sense, black writers and orators stood within the circle of theological populism. Most lacked any formal theological training, and more than a few voiced the populist rhetoric that defined the antiacademic style. The Methodist exhorter John Jasper ridiculed educated preachers as "educated fools." The African Methodist Jarena Lee claimed that God called preachers "by inspiration only," and she justified her own desire to preach by recalling that Jesus had chosen "unlearned fishermen" as his disciples. Other opponents of clerical education in the African Methodist Episcopal (AME) Church erupted into "open conflict" in 1843 with reform-minded advocates for an educated ministry. They charged that the reformers had branded the denomination's largely self-taught clergy "with infamy." Bishop Daniel Alexander Payne (1811–93), the leading advocate of theological learning for AME ministers, reported that the issue "convulsed" the denomination "from center to circumference" for two full years. In 1854, the AME newspaper, the *Christian Recorder,* still carried articles praising "the mechanic" preacher who, "fearing not the sneers and scorn of the great and the learned," held audiences spellbound with "earnest pleadings and awful threatenings."[2]

African-Americans voiced, however, no uniformly populist sentiment. Payne, who studied at Lutheran Theological Seminary in Gettysburg, Pennsylvania, for two years, was not an isolated voice when he urged that African-American clergy should be adept in "natural and revealed theology." The New England Congregationalist Lemuel Haynes (1753–1833) learned Latin and Greek under clerical tutelage, admired learned theologians, and educated himself theologically by reading Calvinist authors. The Episcopalian Alexander Crummell (1819–98) graduated from Oneida Institute in Whitesboro, New York, in 1837 and sought admission to General Theological Seminary, which refused him because of his color. He later received a degree, though not in theological studies, from Queen's College, Cambridge. While some black preachers displayed a populist distrust of academic theology, others admired learned theologians and yearned for higher theological learning themselves.[3]

Black authors produced theological texts — sermons, essays, public addresses, and catechisms — that fell into two genres. The first consisted of expositions that mirrored the standard themes of the denominational traditions. The second consisted of a protest literature cast in theological forms. In addresses at commemorative events, National Negro Conventions, and church assemblies, black writers made claims and raised issues that stood outside the interests of most white theologians. Theological interests in the black churches — and in other public settings — assumed multiple forms; black theologians could be detached from social conditions or they could convey radical social protest; they could be Calvinist or Arminian, or they could be indifferent to such distinctions; they could promote the sophisticated qualifications of the Edwardean tradition or they could adopt the narrative style of the slave preacher. They could also display both the practical impulse and the interest in the evidences of Christianity that prevailed in the broader theological culture.

The Theological Traditions

Blacks remained largely outside the Christian traditions until after the middle of the eighteenth century. When they began to convert to Christianity, they moved in disproportionate numbers into populist traditions that did not require an educated ministry or value a sermonic style that favored close theological distinctions. In joining the popular churches, they retained features of older African religions, but many of them adopted the theological positions that had long defined the Baptist and Methodist traditions, and when they gave expression to theological ideas, they spoke most often as Calvinists or evangelical Arminians. Among the few surviving theological essays written by black authors, statements of Calvinist thought remain prominent.

The Long Island slave preacher Jupiter Hammon (1711–1806), for example, published essays and addresses that promoted an evangelical Anglican theology with pronounced Calvinist overtones. His owners were the wealthy and powerful Lloyd family, who were Anglican in heritage, but he attended a Congregational church with them until the Anglicans erected a building in the vicinity. When Hammon learned to read, the Lloyds permitted him to use their substantial library of religious authors, from the moderate Anglican Calvinist William Beveridge to the Connecticut Congregationalist Solomon Stoddard. Sometime after the revivals of the 1740s, Hammon became a part-time preacher to the slaves, and he eventually wrote and published both poetry and theological essays.[4]

His two essays — *A Winter Piece* (1779?) and *An Evening's Improvement* (1790) — and his *Address to the Negroes in the State of New York* (1787) incorporated themes from both revivalist Calvinism and an Anglican heritage that combined a moderate Calvinism with an emphasis on "holy living." One side of his thought resembled Stoddard's revivalist piety. Hammon found in Stoddard's *Safety of Appearing at the Day of Judgment in the Righteousness of Christ* the idea that the unregenerate must confess their sinfulness, desire a "saving change" in their hearts, and cast themselves entirely on "the merits of Jesus." He declined to follow Stoddard's admonition to "drive" the sinful to Christ "by the terrors of the law," thinking it better to "allure" by "the invitation of the gospel," but he described Stoddard as a "great divine." Like Stoddard, he taught a doctrine of particular election — God designed to "save some of mankind" — along with a Calvinist insistence that the true saint would "continue to believe," but he enclosed these doctrines, as Stoddard had done, within a revivalist appeal for "spiritual regeneration."[5]

The other side of Hammon's thought, drawn partly from the Anglican authors William Beveridge and William Burkitt, an eighteenth-century biblical commentator, drew him to insist on the necessity of a "holy life" for salvation. Explaining that God rewarded every man and woman "according to" their works, he urged his hearers to "work out" their salvation and "behold the Lamb of God by a holy life." He drew frequent attention to the sacraments. Cautioning his readers not to "depend on the use of means alone," he urged them not to neglect "baptism and the sacrament," since salvation came "in the use of means."[6]

Hammon preached these themes to "encourage" his "dear fellow servants and brethren, Africans, in the knowledge of the Christian religion." He was, on the surface, socially conservative, even about slavery. His address to the slaves of New York questioned any assumption that it was "right and lawful in God's sight" for white Americans to enslave Africans, but he told his listeners that he had no desire to be free, that they were obliged to obey their masters, and that enslavement had served the purpose of Christianization. Yet his address had a subversive undertone in its Pauline message that God had "chosen the weak things of the world, and things which are not, to confound the things that are," and Hammon combined an otherworldly piety with a recognition that liberty in this world was also "a great thing." Both his essays and his address revealed his awareness that his public teaching aroused the distrust of some owners and planters.[7]

A Calvinist theology was more pronounced in the sermons and polemical writings of Hammon's younger contemporary, Lemuel Haynes, a freeborn native of Connecticut who served as the pastor for more than thirty years of mostly white Congregational churches in Connecticut, Vermont, and New York. Haynes's formal education consisted of tutoring by Connecticut clergy, who supported his inclinations toward a New Light piety and an Edwardean theology. Connecticut Separates gave him his first pulpit, from which he preached the doctrines of Edwards and Whitefield.[8]

Most of Haynes's writings concerned themselves with the standard themes of the New Divinity. His earliest effort at theology, a sermon on John 3:3, insisted on the necessity for regeneration, and he developed the point in accord with the Edwardean notion that "the very essence of religion consists in love to God" and that the regenerate would love holiness "for what it is in itself," which included a love for "the law of God." In a later sermon, preached soon after his ordination, he expanded on the Edwardean point that sinfulness consisted "in the voluntary exercises of the heart" and that human inability was entirely a moral inability consisting in the enmity of the heart to God.[9]

He did not accept every New Divinity tenet. In one of his first published theological pieces, "Divine Decrees, an Encouragement to the Use of Means," he argued that God could not "execute his designs" except through the intervention of "means" and other "second causes." Entirely absent from the sermon was the Hopkinsian reserve about the efficacy of the means to effect regeneration, though Haynes did defend the argument, widely associated with Hopkins, that "even the wickedness of men is effected or brought about by the agency or providence of God."[10]

His best-known production was his sermon on universal salvation, published in 1805 after Haynes heard a lecture by Hosea Ballou. The sermon went through more than seventy editions, and he and Ballou then engaged in an extended debate in which Haynes defended the point that God must have an "infinite hatred toward sin" and that it would be "less than the crime deserves" for God to threaten and execute anything other than an "eternal" punishment. He noted that a close reading of Hopkins's *System of Theology* would illustrate the point "largely and clearly."[11]

Calvinist theology in the black community had its broadest influence among the Baptists. It is plausible to speak of an "Afro-Baptist Sacred Cosmos," with both African and Christian features, but the form of Christian thought that most often surfaced in black Baptist writing was Calvinist. The Georgia preacher George Liele (b.1750) helped establish at Silver Bluff, South Carolina, between 1773 and 1775 one of the first independent black Baptist congregations. In 1791, after emigrating to Jamaica, Liele described the Calvinist theology that he promoted in his mission: "I agree to election, redemption, the fall of Adam, regeneration, and perseverance, knowing the promise is that all who endure, in grace, faith, and good works to the end shall be saved."[12]

Liele preached briefly in Savannah, where he baptized Andrew Bryan, who founded a Baptist congregation that became a center for Calvinist teaching. Bryan's successor, Andrew Marshall (d. 1856), taught in accord with "the old Calvinistic order," drawing the praise of a Presbyterian minister for giving "so clear and decided a testimony to the precious though unpopular [Calvinistic] doctrines of Grace." Marshall admired the biblical commentaries of the English Calvinist John Gill. For a while, he became a follower of Alexander Campbell, creating disruption in the congregation, but by 1837 he returned to Calvinism, which became so fixed a feature of some Baptist churches that the appearance of a preacher who advocated a doctrine of "free will" in one Virginia congregation created an "excitement" that proved utterly disruptive. When black Baptists in the South formed associations and missionary conventions after the war, they often adopted Calvinist confessions of faith.[13]

In a similar way, Black Methodists remained loyal to the evangelical Arminian theology of the Wesleyan tradition. A year after Richard Allen took the lead in forming a new denomination in 1816, he and his ministerial colleague Jacob Tapsico published *The Doctrines and Disciplines of the African Methodist Episcopal Church,* containing the Twenty-Five Articles of the English Methodists along with the 1744–47 doctrinal Minutes of the English Methodist Conferences, which Allen and Tapsico cast in the form of a catechism. The catechism taught the standard Wesleyan views on prevenient grace, justification, sanctification, the witness of the Spirit, and Christian perfection. The longest surviving sermon from Allen — "A Short Address to the Friends of Him Who Hath No Helper" — was a plea for charity to the needy, and it conveyed the typically Wesleyan theme that "works of mercy" could help to ensure "an inheritance in the kingdom of heaven." Echoing Wesley's claim that no one could "see the Lord" without holiness, Allen taught that the Christian "virtues" were "the condition of our right to Heaven."[14]

Similar themes appeared consistently in other sermons and essays of the Wesleyan black clergy. The grace of God was "all-sufficient," and it issued in a universal atonement that made possible a saving "change of heart." This change of heart required "the influences of divine grace," but it also required "constant exertions." The practice of obedience could "make faith easier." The regenerate Christian might expect not only the witness of the Spirit but also a sanctifying grace that could issue in "perfect love." True sanctification resulted in a "charity" that was "truly sublime." Daniel Payne regularly taught that "the pure in heart" — men and women of "unspotted holiness" — would see God. When he delivered his *Welcome to the Ransomed* for former slaves in Washington, D. C., he commended moral and mental self-improvement, but he also issued, in effect, a brief Wesleyan exhortation to Christian perfection, emancipation "from sin without, and from sin within you."[15]

In 1833, Noah Calwell W. Cannon (d. 1850) produced the earliest extended theological work in the black Methodist movement. A native of Delaware, Cannon served AME congregations in Zanesville, Ohio; Washington, D.C.; Baltimore; Philadelphia; New York; and Boston. His *Rock of Wisdom* consisted of exhortations to prayer and piety, meditations on the historical books of the Old Testament, and encomiums to virtue, and although he defended the AME separation, he said nothing distinctively Wesleyan. His Wesleyan heritage appeared prominently, however, in his *History of the African Methodist Episcopal Church* (1842), in which he again defended African Methodism from its critics while calling for a "vital piety" rooted in an "experimental knowledge" of holiness. Claiming that the "exercise of obedience," empowered by "the love of God in us," made believers into heirs of salvation, he also taught that the "improvement of Christian graces" would deepen the "life of holiness." This was familiar Methodist theology.[16]

The same pattern of adherence to denominational theology could be found among black Episcopal clergy. In 1787, Absalom Jones (1746–1818), a Methodist lay preacher who had once been a slave in Delaware, joined Richard Allen in leaving St. George's Methodist Episcopal Church in Philadelphia after whites there tried to force black members into segregated seats. In 1794, Jones organized the St. Thomas African Episcopal Church. He became the first black Episcopal priest in 1804, and St. Thomas became the center of black Episcopal piety in Philadelphia, vowing in its constitution to uphold the "general doctrines" of the Protestant Episcopal Church.[17]

In 1854, the fifth rector of the congregation, William Douglass, published his *Sermons Preached in the African Protestant Episcopal Church*. Douglass, who took satisfaction in "sober, rational" worship, with canonical readings from "the Lessons, Epistles, and Gospels," also had an Anglican sacramental sensibility and a strong conviction of the "divine origin" of the church. He delivered the twelve sermons with the aim of nurturing hope, peace, forgiveness, and piety, and the Episcopal heritage pervaded the theology. He reminded his hearers that the life-giving influence of the Spirit would "abide with the church forever," that the "persevering use of all the means of grace" provided a way of "co-operating with God," and that human beings were both "sinners before God" and creatures capable of "progressive improvement in moral and intellectual worth."[18]

Several assumptions in black preaching and writing, however, cut across denominational boundaries. The first was the common insistence on the close relationship between theology and ethics. When Samuel Cornish (1795–1858), a Presbyterian minister in New York and Philadelphia, founded *The Colored American* in 1837, he used the newspaper for two years to promote an evangelical version of a theology of virtue, inserting essays on religion and the virtuous life in almost every issue. "Virtue, in the strict sense of the word," he wrote, "implies true religion." Cornish added that no person could be "strictly virtuous," since no heart was free from sinfulness, but his newspaper still taught that to practice the virtuous life was to soar "into a higher region." Even after he resigned his position, the paper continued to insist on a necessary linkage between moral character and "pure religion."[19]

Adopting another theme that transcended denominational boundaries, a few black authors displayed an interest in evidentialism. Jupiter Hammon observed that the miracles of Jesus confirmed his authority. Richard Allen emphasized that Jesus fulfilled the Old Testament prophecies. By 1844, AME conferences were asking their clergy to study William Paley's *Evidences of Divine Revelation* and *Natural Theology*, along with Joseph Butler's *Analogy*. Daniel Payne took natural theology for granted, sometimes reminding worshipers that nature showed forth "the power, wisdom, and goodness of God." William Douglass taught his Episcopal congregation that reason alone could prove "the non-existence of the Deity" to be "impossible."[20]

Most African-American sermons assumed a form quite different from Douglass's reflections on piety and the religious capacities of reason. Especially among the slave preachers in the South, the sermon took shape as biblical narration in a form reminiscent of West African storytelling practices. Some of these sermons earned regional reputations for their narrators. The Virginia slave preacher John Jasper entertained numerous requests to repeat his sermon "The Sun Do Move," a rendering of the story of Joshua. The former slave preacher known as Brother Carper in Missouri began one of his most popular sermons by explaining to his audience that the Bible consisted of both literal and figurative language, and that he was about to introduce them to Christ figured as "a Great Rock in a Weary Land." Such sermons often employed the devices of narrative, typology, and figuration. Yet southern slave preachers sometimes associated themselves more explicitly with European and American doctrinal traditions. A Virginia exhorter impressed the Princeton theologian Archibald Alexander because the "favorite themes" of his preaching were the doctrines of "total depravity," the "absolute sovereignty of God in electing [men and women] to salvation through the imputed righteousness of Christ, [and] the necessity of regeneration by the Spirit, through the truth." Just as other features of black plantation culture stood in complex relationships with the surrounding white culture, the exhortations of the slave preachers could sometimes ignore, sometimes exploit, and sometimes represent mainstream theological movements.[21]

Theology and Protest

The other side of black religious thought was a persistent attention to the bearing of theology on the question of slavery. Lectures and addresses on slavery constituted a great part of the published writings of black authors, not only among ministers but also among lay writers and orators, especially in the northern cities. The same clergy who carried forward the denominational theologies in the black churches also addressed a larger public in the slavery debate. In his essay "Liberty Further Extended" (1776), written nine years before his ordination, Lemuel Haynes interpreted slaveholding as the bitter fruit of Adam's fall and urged that disinterested benevolence ought to banish slavery as well as every other unjust disparity in society. Richard Allen reminded slaveholders "how hateful slavery is in the sight of that God who hath destroyed kings and princes for their oppression of the poor slaves." The AME minister Daniel Coker (1780–1846) published one of the earliest Methodist attacks on slavery in his *Dialogue Between a Virginian and an African Minister* (1810), which made it clear that a former slave knew how to interpret, in the interest of emancipation, every one of the biblical passages commonly used to defend black enslavement.[22]

Much of the black polemic against slavery employed the narrative forms of the black preaching tradition, interpreting the biblical stories to coincide with the yearning for slavery's overthrow. The Episcopal priest Absalom Jones illustrated in his thanksgiving sermon in 1808 a common mode of biblical interpretation in which blacks identified their experience with narratives of deliverance, especially the freeing of Israel from bondage in Egypt. His rendition of the Exodus story depicted a God who appeared "in behalf of oppressed and distressed nations, as the deliverer of the innocent, and of those who call upon his name." Black orators reiterated the themes of Acts and the Pauline epistles, especially Paul's assurance that God made all nations of "one blood" (Acts 17:26), and they highlighted the assertion of the Psalmist that princes of Ethiopia would stretch their hands once again unto God (Ps. 68:31). But antislavery lecturers relied heavily on allusions to biblical narratives, especially the Exodus account. When the activist Maria W. Stewart (1803–79), a Baptist laywoman and social activist speaking at Boston's African Masonic Hall in 1833, assured her audience that God was "still as able to subdue the lofty pride of these white Americans, as He was the heart of that ancient rebel," the Pharaoh of Egypt, she was employing a standard sermonic metaphor for the freeing of the American slaves.[23]

More often than not, black activists read the biblical narratives through the ideas and images of the American revolutionary tradition. The Philadelphia reformer William Whipper (1804–76) never joined a denomination, and he criticized the churches, black and white, for their timid positions on slavery, but he believed that the divine law of the Jewish and Christian scriptures fully accorded with reason. Speaking to the American Moral Reform Society in 1837, Whipper argued that the Declaration of Independence, especially its assertion that all are born equal and endowed with inalienable rights, contained the same truths found in "the book of Divine Revelation." The Freewill Baptist preacher in Providence, Rhode Island, John W. Lewis, explained in 1852 that Paul's claim in Acts 17 that God made all nations of "one blood" corresponded to the doctrine of the Declaration of Independence that all people were created free and equal. The doctrine of natural rights enabled black — as well as some white — preachers to find in the Bible the teaching that all men and women were moral and rational beings, created equal and endowed with the same rights, and to teach that the enlightenment's "Supreme Being," the

"Great Governor of the Universe," was the biblical God who would rectify the disorder that slavery introduced into the creation.[24]

Samuel Cornish's *Colored American* regularly argued that the "Supreme Ruler of the Universe" had determined that "human rights" were inalienable. The "God of Benevolence" supported "life, liberty, and the pursuit of happiness." Cornish and Whipper disagreed strongly about strategy in the fight for emancipation, with Cornish calling for a racially conscious politics and Whipper rejecting racial language and exclusively black institutions, but they both read the Bible in the light of the natural rights rhetoric of the American Revolution.[25]

In a similar way, black clergy took the theme of divine moral government from post-seventeenth century theologies and adapted it to the fight against slavery. Daniel Payne told the Lutherans' Franckean Synod that American slavery was sinful because it destroyed moral agency and so subverted "the moral government of God." Insofar as the black clergy employed the concepts of inalienable human rights, human equality, and republican liberty, their gospel of antislavery was as indebted to the enlightenment as it was to Paul and the book of Exodus.[26]

Like other post-enlightenment religious authors, black clergy worried about the problem of evil, but theodicy could assume a distinctive form when they talked about it in relation to slavery. Payne informed a Lutheran clerical audience that slavery had posed for him the decisive theological question: "I began to question the existence of the Almighty, and to say, if indeed there is a God, does he deal justly? Is he a just God? Is he a holy Being? If so, why does he permit a handful of dying men thus to oppress us?" The New York Baptist preacher Nathaniel Paul (1793–1839), speaking in 1827 to commemorate emancipation in the state, ventured a "bold inquiry" to God: "why was it that thou didst look on with the calm indifference of an unconcerned spectator, when thy holy law was violated, thy divine authority despised and a portion of thine own creatures reduced to a state of mere vassalage and misery?" Unlike the Edwardeans, who could not conceive that evil stood outside the directives of the divine will, Paul concluded that enslavement was a mystery but that God would bring good out of the evil.[27]

The Presbyterian minister James W. C. Pennington (1807–70) accepted a variant of Nathaniel Paul's solution, but it troubled him. Pennington escaped from slavery in Maryland as a young man and made his way to New York and then Pennsylvania, where he avidly pursued an education. In 1829, he joined a Presbyterian church and by 1838 he began a pastorate to Presbyterian and Congregationalist churches on Long Island, in Connecticut, and in New York City, where he served at the Shiloh Presbyterian Church. Several trips to Europe, where he preached and lectured against slavery, opened the door for an honorary doctorate of divinity from the University of Heidelberg. Eventually he wavered in his Calvinist convictions, temporarily joining the AME Church in 1864 before returning to the Presbyterians, but he was a Calvinist when he privately wrestled most intensely with slavery as a theological issue.

Pennington conceded, like Nathaniel Paul, that God must have "permitted" Africans to be enslaved "with intention to bring good out of evil," though he could not escape the haunting idea that God "could have brought about that very good in some other way," giving the gospel to Africans without making them slaves and enriching America "without making its riches to consist in our blood, bones, and souls." Pennington was aware that "the question, whether the Bible sanctions slavery," had "distinctly divided this nation in sentiment," but he thought that the Christian revelation, "rightly understood," was as antislavery as it was antisin. He believed that God's permission of slavery did not imply divine approval, but enslavement remained for him, as for Paul, a mystery, defying human understanding.[28]

The reasoning of Paul and Pennington remained within boundaries acceptable to most American theologians. In 1828, however, David Walker (1796–ca. 1830) departed from theological convention in his *Appeal to the Colored Citizens of the World,* in which he mounted what was in part a religious argument for violent slave resistance. Walker was the owner of a small second-hand clothing store, an agent for the black newspaper *Freedom's Journal,* and a member of the AME congregation on May Street in Boston. He admired Richard Allen, but he did not share Allen's confidence that conversion and persuasion could touch the heart of the slaveholder. In his appeal, he wrote of a God of justice and vengeance who would wreak destruction on an America that had created a form of slavery harsher even than the slavery of the ancient Egyptians. Walker's Jesus was the commander of armies, the kingly figure who would lead the black rebellion. He charged that the refusal of white preachers to speak out against slavery had "carried their country to the brink of a precipice," and he called for violent resistance from the slaves. Southern states banned his pamphlet.[29]

Fifteen years later, Henry Highland Garnet's address to the 1843 Negro Convention in Buffalo, New York, assumed a similar stance, which struck some as so inflammatory that the delegates voted narrowly not to endorse its views. Garnet (1815–82) had been born into slavery in Maryland, but his family escaped to New York City, where they barely evaded recapture. Educated under the sponsorship of African-American Presbyterian clergy, he became a Presbyterian minister in 1842, serving churches in New York and Washington, D.C., and becoming active in the antislavery movement. In his "Address to the Slaves of the United States of America," he employed a theological rationale for slave revolt. Insisting that the southern masters prevented slaves from fulfilling the divine commandments — keeping the Sabbath, reading the scripture, serving "no other God" — he warned the slaves that they could not be "certain of heaven" if they allowed themselves to remain enslaved. It was sinful to make "voluntary submission" to a system that did not allow them to fulfill their "obligation to God." He called for resistance by "every means," moral and physical. In a later address to the U.S. Congress, Garnet charged that slavery obliterated "the image of God" in the enslaved.[30]

For a few black activists, the battle against slavery led to an ideal of black nationalism, defined so as to encourage a return to Africa, and theology provided the idiom in which they described their hope. Martin R. Delany (1812– 85), a physician and journalist who devoted most of his energies to the fight against racial subordination, derived from Garnet's biblical interpretation a realization that the promise of Psalm 68:31 — "Princes shall come out of Egypt; Ethiopia shall soon stretch out her hands unto God" — pointed to the imminent regeneration of the people of Africa by the black Christian churches and the creation of a great African civilization to which American blacks could emigrate. The Episcopal priest Alexander Crummell, influenced by a friendship with Garnet that extended back into childhood, acted on this vision by spending the two decades after 1853 as a missionary in Liberia and Sierra Leone. On his return to America, Crummell became the theological interpreter of the black mission to Africa.[31]

Before leaving for England and then Liberia, Crummell preached in small Episcopal churches in Rhode Island and New York City. His early sermons promoted morality, the exertion of will, and the "personal responsibility" of every man and woman to "achieve salvation" by appropriating the gift of grace through "constant labors." His sermon on "The Day of Doom" (1854) used a graphic depiction of Christ's second coming to emphasize that the final judgment would call men and women to account "for the deeds done in the flesh" and grant "full rewards" for a moral and pious life. As early as 1851, he transposed this call for individual duty into a broader demand for the evangelization of Africa, and after the Civil War, he would develop the theme that God was training the African-American people for a grand destiny as a chosen community. This destiny required a missionary enterprise that would awaken Africa's greatness.[32]

Enslavement in the South and harsh prejudice in the North largely pushed blacks into separate enclaves of antebellum religious life and thought. In their worship, they developed distinctive forms of dance, patterned rhythms of speech, preaching punctuated by call and response, and ritual practices that had roots both in the African past and in revivalist piety. When they wrote about theology, they drew most often on denominational traditions. They received little encouragement to write, but a few black activists and clergy, whether they saw themselves through the lenses of denominational allegiance or in the mirror of prophetic social protest, insisted on being heard as Christian theologians.[33]

16

The Immediacy of Revelation

The populist principle in theology — the claim that the unlearned, even more than the learned, could discern theological truth — often countered traditional theologies. It could sometimes blend with the quite different idea that God continued to provide new truth through immediate revelation to faithful believers or to chosen prophets. From an assertion of private revelation it was easy to argue that the canon of scripture was not closed and that new truths required new canons. In America, this logic of private revelation produced more than one new claim to theological truth. This chapter examines three prominent examples of radical departure from assumptions that most theologians accepted. The Hicksite Friends of the early nineteenth century recovered an older Quaker confidence in the revelatory power of an Inner Light within every person. The Shakers — the United Society of Believers in Christ's Second Appearing — produced a theology grounded in a reading of the Bible filtered through revelations received by their founder Ann Lee. The Mormons — the Church of Jesus Christ of Latter-day Saints — discovered through revelations to Joseph Smith a source of new truths that carried them beyond biblical boundaries. Each of these movements employed the rhetoric of the theological populists. Each of them linked that rhetoric to a theology that redefined Christian truth as other American Christians understood it.

The Hicksite Quakers

The sermons, essays, and letters of Elias Hicks (1748–1830) dealt with theological issues that divided the Society of Friends in America for more than a century. A farmer from Rhode Island, Hicks became, after a religious experience in 1774, an itinerant Quaker minister who traveled from Virginia to Canada. His aim was to restore a primitive Quaker piety to a movement that was changing because of the economic success of its members and the allure of Protestant evangelicalism. He was a theological populist who, like Daniel Parker among the Primitive Baptists and Elias Smith in the Christian Connection, opposed missionary agencies and educated clergy. He strove to return to the Quaker past, with its simple message of an Inner Light within each person. But the Quaker past was, in fact, complex. The early Quakers, subject to constant attack from state churches, had cultivated theological ambiguity, and Hicks's critics could also appeal to the Quaker heritage. The "Hicksite schism" signaled social and cultural discord among Quakers as well as the appeal of theologies grounded in immediate and inward revelation.[1]

Hicks appealed to the authority of the Inner Light within each person. The same appeal had defined the early Quaker movement in seventeenth-century England. George Fox (1624–91) — the best known of several founding figures in the movement — attracted his first adherents largely from circles of seekers, mystics, and separatists who had turned their backs on the Church of England to seek an immediate encounter with the Spirit. An apprentice shoemaker, Fox left his home in 1643 in quest of religious truth. Four years later he felt the call to proclaim "the everlasting gospel" — the insistence that each person had a measure of what the gospel of John called "the true light that lighteth every man that cometh into the world" (John 1:9). For Fox, this was the light that had shone forth in Jesus. It was an eternal creative power that called each person to live in dependence on God and obedience to the divine will, and to practice love and humility. The Light was also a source of religious insight, and it provided the criterion by which scripture was to be interpreted. Fox referred to it as the "Seed of God," or the "Spirit," or the "Christ Within."[2]

Opposed to all existing churches, Fox's followers saw themselves not as one more church but as a movement of Friends, Children of Light, banded together against the world in order to restore primitive Christianity. Unlike other primitivists, however, their aim was not to reinstitute the order of the New Testament churches but to recapitulate the experience of the same Spirit who had moved the first Christians. Their worship — which alternated between devout silence and ecstatic outcry — gave them the name Quaker. Their defiance of polite convention, displayed in their egalitarian refusal to doff their hats and their use of familiar forms of address to people of high rank, made them objects of scorn. Their refusal to swear oaths in court left them vulnerable to exploitation. Their resistance to ecclesiastical and state establishments brought imprisonment, mistreatment, and sometimes execution.[3]

From the outset, they were theological populists, ridiculing an educated clergy and proclaiming that every Christian, men and women, could preach as the Spirit moved. Yet the Quakers proved to be prolific authors, and their fervor attracted a few university-educated converts who wrote theological treatises. In the first fifty years, Friends produced more than three thousand publications, from published journals, testimonies, and exhortations to books of theology. Among the more important Quaker theologians were William Penn (1644–1718), George Keith (1638–1716), and Robert Barclay (1648–90), all three of whom had studied in English or Scottish universities. Penn spent four years in his Pennsylvania colony, and Keith sojourned in New Jersey and Pennsylvania for eight. He visited New England, where he had literary debates with Samuel Willard and Cotton Mather. Barclay never visited America, but he served as the absentee governor of East Jersey, and his *Apology for the True Christian Religion* (1687) was the theological standard of the American Friends until the mid-nineteenth century.[4]

The relations of the three men illustrate, however, the diversity in early Quaker doctrine. Keith was disowned in 1692 by the Philadelphia Yearly Meeting for seeming to proclaim salvation by the historical death of Christ rather than by the Christ within, and his book on *The Deism of William Penn* (1699) alienated him from Penn. In 1700, Keith conformed to the Church of England and wrote a polemic against Barclay. Penn and Barclay remained close, but Penn's thought had a rationalist tinge that distinguished it from Barclay's efforts to emphasize that Quaker teaching did not contradict the "outward testimony of the Scriptures." Early Quaker thought contained tensions and ambiguities that enabled nineteenth-century American Friends to interpret it in contrasting ways.[5]

In dealing with the relationship between the Inner Light and scripture, for example, early Quakers could both cite the Bible as an authority and insist that it remained subordinate to the Spirit within. Margaret Fell, the wife of Fox after 1669 and the owner of the Swarthmore Hall estate that served as the English Quaker headquarters, argued in her *Womens Speaking Justified* (1666) for the validity of women's preaching by amassing scriptural texts. But Samuel Fisher (1605–65), an Oxford-trained vicar before his conversion to Quakerism, emphasized in his *Rusticos ad Academicos* (1659) the variants in the biblical manuscripts that undermined any theory of infallible inspiration. Fisher could seem to deprecate the "outward letter." Since the Inner Light was universal — and brought saving knowledge — Quakers like Penn relied on an inner revelation of Christ that could enlighten all men and women even if they had never read the scripture. They thought of the Bible as the inspired product of the Spirit, but they thought also that the Spirit revealed the truth apart from the external letter.[6]

Just as they cautioned against reliance on the letter of scripture, the Quakers warned against reliance on external evidences of revelation, though they left an opening for evidentialism. Penn, for example, subordinated proofs from external miracles and the fulfillment of prophecy to "the Evidence" within. He thought that the faithful should not need miracles as an external prop for faith. They should look instead to "the truth, equity, holiness, and recompense of the Christian religion, which miracles can never render more or less intrinsically so." Yet on occasion Penn referred to the biblical miracles to validate scriptural authority. More generally, the Quakers believed that a flowering of miracles had accompanied the "breaking forth of truth" in their movement, and Fox kept a "Book of Miracles." He minimized their evidential importance, but others saw them as signs of continuing revelation. Some Quakers claimed that their movement fulfilled biblical prophecies; others, like Penn, treated prophetic fulfillment in a conventional way as evidence for the authenticity of scripture. But Quaker writings also asserted that the only sure evidence of spiritual truth came through the inward apprehension of the Spirit.[7]

A similar ambivalence marked their judgments about the Christ within and the Christ of history. Their emphasis fell on the eternal Christ dwelling within the faithful, and Fox thought of him as a savior even outside his manifestation in Jesus. Early Quakers preached the inward Christ so single-mindedly that their enemies accused them of "denying Christ's humanity." They taught that the blood of Christ shed inwardly in the heart, not the outward blood shed on the cross, brought salvation. Yet Quakers also identified the eternal Christ with the Christ of the New Testament narratives, and in response to their critics they tended, in the manner of the London Friend George Whitehead, to insist that the Christ within and the Christ without were "one and the same Lord Jesus Christ." The "Christian Quaker" movement led by George Keith emphasized that salvation required a belief in the saving effect of Christ's death on the cross. Though Quakers remained opposed to Calvinist doctrines of election and satisfaction, they were underscoring by the 1670s the continuity of their belief with earlier Christian teachings.[8]

A certain ambiguity appeared, finally, in Quaker views of salvation. On the one hand, Quakers dwelt on human sinfulness and attributed salvation to the grace made available through the Inner Light. No group spoke more about the depravity of human nature and the passivity of regeneration. On the other hand, they made salvation contingent on the sinner's acceptance of the Light within, and they repudiated the Protestant tendency to separate justification and sanctification. Quakers could see no possibility of salvation apart from a sanctification of the heart that occurred gradually through spiritual discipline. They thought that the idea of imputed righteousness produced religious hypocrisy. Convinced of the power of the Light, they became teachers of Christian perfection.[9]

In Pennsylvania, Quaker thought found expression in the writing of the German lawyer and theologian Francis Daniel Pastorius (1651–ca. 1720), an immigrant who led Pietists and Mennonites in 1683 from Crefeld and Frankfurt to what would become Germantown. The son of Lutheran parents, Pastorius had studied law and languages for seven years in German and Swiss universities before he came to America. He was a friend of the Lutheran Pietist Philipp Jakob Spener. In Pennsylvania, however, he attended a Quaker meetinghouse, and he defended Quakers against their opponents. When Keithian critics in 1696 entered the yearly meeting at Burlington and slandered Quaker doctrines, Pastorius responded in *Four Boasting Disputers of this World Briefly Rebuked* (1697), claiming that Quakers believed that Jesus Christ was "true God and perfect man."[10]

By that time, Pastorius had broken away, for the most part, from his Lutheran heritage. He said that Christ, "the true unchangeable God," had taken upon himself "the nature of man" in order to sacrifice himself for the redemption of his followers, but he added that it was Christ as God, "manifest in the flesh," not Christ as he had "come in the flesh," who did this. In Quaker fashion, he drove a wedge between Christ's divine and human natures, insisting that Mary was the mother of Christ only in respect of his humanity, not of his divinity. Unlike Lutherans, moreover, he denied that Christ united himself with water, bread, wine, or "the like outward creatures." Under the dispensation of the law, the Jews had worshiped with "meat, drink, and divers Baptisms," but such "corruptible" instruments vanished at "the time of Reformation." Pastorius believed that the dawning of "the Day of the Lord's Redemption" had eclipsed all "figures, types, and shadows," leaving the way open for a religion of the Spirit.[11]

Within the next hundred years, however, English and American Friends moved toward the traditional side of Quaker theology. Visits to America by English evangelical Quakers such as Joseph John Gurney during the 1820s helped solidify a tendency for Quakers to affirm the authority of scripture, the divinity of the historical Christ, and the efficacy of Christ's propitiatory sacrifice on the cross. A countermovement formed in the late eighteenth century, but when nonevangelical Quakers supported dissenters like Hannah Jenkins of New York, who questioned the authority of scripture because the Old Testament approved of holy war, or Job Scott of Rhode Island, who said that he expected "no final benefit from the death of Jesus, in any other way than through fellowship in his sufferings," the evangelicals tried to impose discipline. In 1817, the Philadelphia Yearly Meeting proposed a uniform discipline that would oversee Quaker life in America.[12]

Elias Hicks was a member of the New York Yearly Meeting and was not subject to restraint from Philadelphia. His opposition to the Philadelphia elders, whom he considered men of wealth and fashion, compromisers of the original Quaker message, produced counterattacks from Philadelphia, where the elders published "Extracts from the Writings of Primitive Friends" in 1823 to defend their evangelical interpretation of the Quaker past. When the English evangelical Quaker Anna Braithwaite toured America in 1823, she debated privately with Hicks and then published a defense of the Philadelphia position. By 1825, pamphleteers on both sides claimed loyalty to primitive Quakerism and charged their opponents with apostasy.[13]

In 1825, Hicks, now seventy-seven years old, permitted his admirers to publish transcripts of sermons he delivered during a tour through Pennsylvania and New Jersey. This *Series of Extemporaneous Discourses* (1825) became, along with the *Letters of Elias Hicks Including Also a Few Short Essays Written on Several Occasions* (1834), the guiding documents of a movement that drew the allegiance of more than a fourth of the Friends in America. Opposed to centralized power, suspicious of urban wealth, heavily located in rural areas, the Hicksite Quakers carried a message of social and theological protest.[14]

Hicks constructed his thought around the themes of internality and externality. The letter of scripture was external, but the Spirit that underlay the letter was internal. The covenants of the Old Testament were Jewish and external; the Christian covenant was internal. External sacraments and ceremonies had no meaning; inward worship honored the Light within. The natural senses could know nothing of God unless they were animated by "immediate divine revelation" within. "Books of religion and morality" taught only the letter; the true teaching came from the Inner Light. The bodily acts of Christ — including his miracles and his death — had effect only in an earlier dispensation; Christians in the new dispensation relied solely on the Christ within. Hicks disturbed the evangelical Quakers most of all when he admonished his hearers that they should permit no "dependence on external things; even upon Jesus Christ in his outward manifestation."[15]

It followed that true revelation came through the "immediate impression" of the Spirit and not the external letter of scripture. Hicks thought it idolatry to "esteem and hold the Scriptures as the only rule of faith and practice." The Bible gave evidence of a revealing Spirit, but the "inspired teacher in the present day," open to the promptings of that same Spirit, could teach with more authority than teachers who lived in the ancient world. Hicks believed that the scriptures had caused "four-fold more harm than good to Christendom," because differences of interpretation had created conflict and schism. If the scriptures had been "absolutely necessary," God would have communicated them to all the nations of the earth. Hicks argued, against evangelical Quakers, that George Fox had presented the "light and spirit of truth in the hearts and consciences of men and women, as the only sure rule of faith and practice."[16]

When he drew on the authority of scripture, therefore, Hicks felt free to demythologize. He read the story of creation, the garden, and the fall as "allegory." He viewed the apocalyptic visions in the gospel of John as "allegorical similes." The garden of Eden was a figure of the soul in communion with God; Satan was a symbol of the human disposition to self-will. The story of Jesus' temptation in the wilderness was a reference to his facing the "spiritual wilderness" in his own mind. The true heaven was a state of inward felicity, not a local place. Hicks did not altogether reject the historical truth of the scriptural narratives, and he did not even deny the occurrence of the biblical miracles, but he saw the external events as significant only for the inward truths they suggested.[17]

Hicks also assumed that any true revelation would be consistent with reason, and he believed that it degraded the scriptures to "insist upon their being taken and believed literally just as they are, whether consonant with reason, yea or nay." He always insisted that "right reason" was a divine gift, and on occasion he wrote that reason should "bring to the test" the revelations of the Inner Light: "If it will not accord with right reason, we must cast it off as the work of antichrist." He believed, moreover, that every rational mind could know "every truth necessary to be known in the way of its salvation," if it only listened to the promptings of the Spirit within.[18]

Hicks's "reason," however, was not the reason of the Baconians, empirical and inductive. It was more akin to the intuitive reason of the American transcendentalists. During the period of the Hicksite controversy, a small number of Quakers in New England celebrated the affinity between transcendentalism and Quaker tradition, and Emerson thought that Quakers came "nearer" to "the sublime history and genius of Christ than any other of the sects." Elias Hicks was no transcendentalist, but he joined Emerson in defining revelation as inward, individual, and consonant with a reason that transcended the senses.[19]

Hicks had no sympathy for the evidentialism of the Baconians. No "external evidence," he argued, could "reveal the things of God, which are known only by the Spirit of God." Conveyed through the "medium of the animal senses," external evidences lacked the power either to persuade or to edify. Hicks believed that the New Testament contained historically accurate accounts of miracles, but he thought that external miracles, even of Christ, "sink into nothing" in comparison with the confirming presence of the Spirit in the soul. The miracles of Jesus belonged to an earlier dispensation. In the Christian dispensation, they served only as types of the inner miracle of the Spirit.[20]

In the Christian dispensation, the indwelling of the "spiritual Messiah" entirely superseded the actions and sufferings of the historical Jesus. Hicks considered the doctrine of the Trinity to be a "weak and vulgar error," and he defined the doctrine of Christ's divinity to mean that Jesus gradually received the divine Spirit, remained so obedient to it that he fulfilled the righteousness of the outward covenant, and became the Son of God fully at his baptism, when the Spirit attained fullness in his life. Because every man and women received the same Spirit—"the same divine light"—Hicks saw Jesus as an example and teacher whose ministry pointed the way toward "the inward, the law written in the heart." But Jesus told his disciples that he must leave them and that they must "turn inward to the Comforter within." The death of Jesus on the cross ended the old dispensation and inaugurated the reign of the Spirit.[21]

Hicks returned to an older Quaker vision of salvation. The crucifixion of Jesus was for him an atonement only for the "legal" sins of the Jews, an outward sacrifice for outward sins. The "outward Christ" was "limited" in his ministry and his saving power to "that particular people." For Christians, the crucifixion merely brought the era of Jewish ritual to an end and typified the inward sacrifice "that every sinner must make, in giving up that sinful life of his own will." Hicks saw salvation as a universal human possibility, contingent only on obedience to the Inner Light. Like the earliest Quakers, he rejected any distinction between justification and sanctification. God justified the soul who followed the "inward law of the Spirit of God" so faithfully as to come up to the righteousness of Christ. Only by partaking "completely" of the divine nature—by attaining "perfection"—did the faithful experience reconciliation with God. Hicks saw this spiritual union with God as fully the consequence of divine grace, requiring "passivity" and a recognition of "inability," but the grace was available to every human being through the indwelling of the Spirit.[22]

Hicks battled the Quaker evangelicals by associating them with Calvinism. He condemned the Calvinist doctrines of original sin, atonement, and election as "an outrage." Convinced that every human being had free agency, he insisted that the "elect" were constituted simply of all who elected God. The Calvinist doctrine of justification he regarded as a means of avoiding the spiritual discipline through which the faithful waited on the prompting of the Light, struggled to overcome self-will, and attained a state of submission and obedience. Hicks stood closer to the original impulse of the early Quaker movement than did his evangelical opponents. His notion of inward revelation led him far outside the Protestant circles into which the Quaker evangelicals were moving.[23]

Shaker Theology

In his polemic against special revelation, the deist Ethan Allen cited the "delusions" of an "Elect Lady" — a "pretended holy woman" — who claimed immediate revelations from God and acted as if she could "talk in seventy-two unknown languages." He was referring to Ann Lee (1736–84), who in 1781 began a missionary journey through eastern New York and central New England announcing that the millennial second appearing of Christ had occurred. Her converts called themselves the United Society of Believers in Christ's Second Appearing. Like the early Quakers, they grounded their faith in the immediate experience of the Spirit. Even more than the Quakers, they derived a theology not only from scripture but also from immediate revelation.[24]

When asked for the evidence of their faith, they pointed, like any evidentialist, to miracles and fulfilled prophecies, but they pointed to miracles in their own movement to validate continuing revelations of the Spirit, and they found the fulfillment of prophecy in their own experience. Elder John Lyon declared in 1844 that God's testimony had always been "accompanied by miracles, signs and wonders," and he pointed to such "manifestations" to confirm the testimony of Ann Lee. It was plain to them, furthermore, that they and Ann Lee fulfilled biblical prophecies. Like the Quakers, they transformed evidentialism into a validation of their experience.[25]

The sources of Ann Lee's revelations went back to the 1760s in Manchester, England, where James and Jane Wardley, both tailors in the textile industry, inspired a group of visionaries whose ecstatic worship earned them the name Shaking Quakers or Shakers. The group transformed the life of Ann Lee, who probably worked in the textile shops, and in 1774 she left England with her blacksmith husband and a few fellow Shakers and sailed to America. They lived inconspicuously before Ann Lee separated from her husband and led a small group to Niskeyuna, New York, where they bought land and in 1780 began to attract converts from the revivalist New Lights in nearby New Lebanon.[26]

Six years after Ann Lee died, Joseph Meacham, formerly a New Light Baptist in New Lebanon, published *A Concise Statement of the Principles of the Only True Church According to the Gospel of the Present Appearance of Christ* (1790). In 1808, three elders at Turtle Creek, Ohio, published a *Testimony of Christ's Second Appearing*, which became the standard work of Shaker theology. Its authors were John Meacham, a former Baptist who joined the movement in 1780; Benjamin Seth Youngs, a member of the society since 1794; and David Darrow, the leader of the society in the West. Lucy Wright, head of the eastern movement, assigned two eastern members, Seth Wells and Calvin Green, to help with a new edition in 1810, the first of several such revisions. But the West became the creative region of Shaker thought when John Dunlavy, a former Presbyterian minister drawn into Shaker preaching at Pleasant Hill, Kentucky, published *The Manifesto, or a Declaration of the Doctrine and Practice of the Church of Christ* (1818). Dunlavy recast Shaker thought into forms characteristic of Protestant theology.[27]

These Shaker authors peppered their treatises with populist asides. The authors of the *Testimony* expressed a dislike for "subtle arguments," and they prided themselves on their indifference to "refined taste" in style and "obscure erudition" in thought. "Where is the scribe?" they asked. "Where is the disputer of this world? hath not God made foolish the wisdom of this world?" In their view, the gospel had not been intended for "learned doctors" but for the "common people." Even as they cited learned authorities like the church historian Johann Lorenz von Mosheim of Göttingen, the Anglican evangelical Joseph Milner, and the English Independent Nathaniel Lardner, they identified themselves with the illiterate apostles.[28]

They began by following the teachings of Ann Lee; soon they formulated doctrines about her. Since she never wrote anything, it remains hard to know what she taught. In 1816, older Shakers recorded their recollections of her revelations and teachings, but by then the oral tradition had undergone thirty-two years of change since her death. Supplemented by reports from early observers, these testimonies hint at her teaching. She seems to have taught that she was the Woman in the Wilderness of Revelation 12. She received revelations from God, including one about the sinfulness of sexual intercourse. She appears to have told her followers that Christ made a second appearing in the Shaker society, inaugurating the millennial dispensation. Every person had the freedom to follow the revealed way. She asked her followers to confess their sins to her and assured them that they could attain perfection through celibacy and obedience, which formed them in the character of Jesus Christ.[29]

Meacham's *Concise Statement* of 1790 never mentioned Ann Lee. Meacham's aim was to outline the four "dispensations of God's Grace." In the patriarchal dispensation, Abraham worshiped Christ through types and shadows and attained the covenant relation "by promise." In the Mosaic dispensation, God accepted as just the Jews who obeyed the law, though they never attained the new birth. In the time of "Christ's first appearance, in the flesh," Christians who believed and denied worldly lust found salvation. But the year 1747, according to Meacham's calculation, inaugurated the fourth and final dispensation, the "second appearance of Christ," which came "to a number, in the manifestation of great light." In this final dispensation, all who believed, obeyed, confessed, forsook all sin, denied themselves, and bore the cross would be saved.[30]

The 1810 edition of the *Testimony of Christ's Second Appearing* accorded greater prominence to teachings about Ann Lee. Like Meacham, the authors organized their theology as a salvation history, proceeding through various dispensations to the era of Christ's first appearing in Jesus (followed by the reign of the Antichrist) and Christ's second appearing "in his body, the true Church." But they depicted Ann Lee as the "chosen agent" who commenced the second appearing, a woman anointed by the Spirit as Jesus had been. They did not place Jesus and Ann Lee on the same level. Only by her relation to the spiritual man, Christ Jesus, did she receive the "attribute of spiritual woman." But they described her as "the fit tabernacle and the abode of the 'only begotten' Daughter of the Most High," by which they meant that she "manifested" the eternal motherly attribute of God as Jesus had manifested God's fatherly attribute. Only if Christ could appear in both a man and a woman, Green wrote later, could both men and women be saved.[31]

Early Shakers reached no consensus about Ann Lee's status. Some described her as their savior, and during a decade of spiritualist revivals that began in 1837, a few came to think of her as having equality with Jesus. Others, in reaction, cautioned that the savior was only "in" her, or contended that she was "simply a woman anointed whereas Jesus Christ is the Godman anointed." The Shaker theologians—especially Youngs, Green, and Dunlavy—emphasized that Christ dwelt in the church, not in one person, and that no one member of the church received the same full anointing as Jesus. Calvin Green preserved the ambiguity when he described Ann Lee as the "vessel" who received "the true spirit of Christ" that also abided in "every member of the Church."[32]

In Shaker theology, "Christ" was the "anointing Spirit" with which both Jesus and Ann Lee were anointed. The church was the Body of Christ, his continuing abode, and the church was "as really anointed, as the man Jesus was, while visible on the earth." The revelation in Ann Lee increased the power of the church, enabling it to restore the gifts of the Spirit, such as healing, prophecy, miracles, and the ability to speak in tongues. The Shaker

Society held the key of heaven, for there was no salvation outside the true church they had restored.[33]

The Shakers dismissed the doctrine that Jesus was the divine-human Mediator. They believed only that he had received "anointing" in its "fullness." They rejected the doctrine of the Trinity and discarded the teaching that Jesus united two natures in one Person, preferring to say that the Christ was divine while Jesus was a "complete natural man," anointed by the Spirit as the Christ's vessel. They denied that he died on the cross as a sacrifice to God or a substitute for humanity, or that his death reconciled God to the world. The atonement rather helped reconcile the world to God. They denied also that his body underwent a physical resurrection. The resurrection was his dying to self and living to God only, his being "quickened by the Spirit."[34]

They thought, therefore, that salvation resulted not from any imputation of Christ's righteousness but from obedience. The idea of an imputation of sin and righteousness, along with the ideas of election, reprobation, and salvation by mere grace, they traced to the errors of Augustine — errors that had "darkened the earth." Salvation as they viewed it was rather the reward for belief and an obedience that would be manifest in the confession of sin, the love of the neighbor, and celibacy. They taught that the truly faithful could, by meeting all the requirements of God, be "perfectly justified." They conceded, however, that many souls would move toward perfection only during a period of probation after death. The Shakers were not universalists, for they thought that some would resist God's offer of salvation even in the next life, but everyone would have a further chance to believe and obey.[35]

Youngs and Green and their coauthors recognized that their views aligned them with those whom the fallen churches — the Catholics and Protestants — had excluded as heretics. Their list of heroes extended from the second-century Gnostic Christian Marcion of Sinope to the Quaker George Fox. They claimed that they stood in a "direct line" with the Gnostics, who also relied on the direct revelation of a special "gnosis" (knowledge) that brought salvation. The Shakers shared with the Gnostics a distrust of the "fleshly" or "material" as a source of evil and a penchant for figurative interpretation of scripture. They believed that Gnostic teachers had handed down "the primitive faith of the Church."[36]

It was Benjamin Youngs in Ohio who, in the *Testimony*, began to identify Shaker theology with the doctrine of the dual character of God as Father and Mother. Calvin Green claimed that Joseph Meacham "had an inspired view of the order of Father and Mother in the nature of God," but Youngs was the first to expand on the idea. The doctrine had its roots in the Shaker belief that the Christ had been manifested in both a male and a female, but Youngs gave other reasons to justify it. He found it in Genesis 1:26–27 — "let us make man in our image, after our likeness . . . male and female" — and in the identification of Wisdom as feminine in Proverbs. He also found grounds for it in the philosophical principle of cause and effect. The visible order of male and female in the natural world, he thought, required a sufficient cause, and if God were masculine only, then the effect — the created order with its duality of masculine and feminine — would be "superior to its cause" in that one respect. The feminine, moreover, would have issued from where the feminine was not. The doctrine assumed a special place in Shaker thought during a period of ecstatic revival that began in 1837.[37]

The Shakers found biblical warrants for their views, but they refused to identify the Bible as the word of God. They believed that the Old and New Testaments gave a "true account of the will and purposes of God," written by "holy men" who were "moved by the Holy Spirit." But Youngs explained that the scriptures were "a record of the operation of the Word in different ages," and what was revealed for one era might not be "equally fitting" for "every succeeding age and nation." The Bible was "composed of letters, and letters are no more than signs, marks, or shadows of things, and not the very substance of the things which they signify."[38]

Shakers refused, therefore, to accept the scriptures as the sole rule of faith and practice. They thought that "natural wisdom" provided no saving knowledge, but they denied that inspired revelation had ceased with the canon of scripture. The Bible itself spoke of an "influx" of revelations to the true church "in the last days." Although Shakers filled their writings with biblical interpretation, Dunlavy expressed a consensus when he asserted that "the pillar and ground" of the truth were not the scripture but the church, where Christ was manifest.[39]

The Mormon Revelation

In 1831, Joseph Smith, Jr. (1805–44) sent Sidney Rigdon, who had recently accepted Smith's version of Christian restoration, to visit the Shaker communities of the West and announce to them "my gospel, which you have received, even as ye have received it." Smith revealed to the Shakers that marriage was lawful, that the "Son of Man" came not in the form of a woman, and that they should repent, seek baptism for the remission of sins, and receive the Holy Ghost by the laying on of hands. Rigdon's conversion and his mission tour exemplify the close connections that often bound the leaders of populist Christianity.[40]

Sidney Rigdon (1793–1876) was a former Baptist preacher from Pennsylvania who joined Alexander Campbell's reform movement in 1821. He broke with Campbell in 1830 after failing to convince him that the restoration of the true church required the recovery of supernatural gifts and miracles as well as the primitive communism of the book of Acts. Rigdon had agreed with the Shakers that a restored Christianity would institute the communal economy of the first-century Christians in Jerusalem. The gospel of Joseph Smith seemed to Rigdon in 1830 to combine restorationist primitivism, Christian economic communalism, and the certitude derived from direct revelation.[41]

A native of Sharon, Vermont, whose family moved in 1816 to Palmyra, New York, Joseph Smith came from the social class that resonated to the message of the Universalists, the Methodists, and the restorationists. His own revelations were filled with condemnations of the "rich and proud," and he told his followers that the "learned men" were "unlearned in the things of God" because they lacked the gift of the Spirit. Apologists for Mormonism took pride in the fact that he was unlearned: God chose him in order to "cause the wisdom of the wise to perish." In the church that he organized in 1830, every worthy male member served as a priest, and the Mormons thought that priests and teachers should labor with their hands for their support. The Mormons carried the populist spirit.[42]

Like the Shakers, they formed a religious movement grounded in immediate revelation. Joseph Smith had his first revelation in 1820, when "two glorious personages" informed him that "all religious denominations" held incorrect doctrines. Three years later a heavenly messenger named Moroni told him that "the preparatory work for the second coming of the Messiah was speedily to commence" and that he was to ready a people for the millennial reign. Moroni delivered to him in 1827 the golden plates from which he translated the *Book of Mormon,* which told the story of the Jaredites, who came to America after the fall of the tower of Babel, and of the family of Lehi, who arrived from Israel about six hundred years before Christ. Lehi sired a race of people who divided into warring branches, the Nephites and the nomadic, dark-skinned Lamanites, ancestors of the American Indians. When the Lamanites destroyed the Nephite civilization, the Nephite prophet Mormon wrote on golden plates the greater part of the book that bore his name. His son Moroni buried the plates on Hill Cumorah in New York, where they remained until they were shown to Joseph Smith.[43]

In early Mormon thought, the aim of this revelation was to signal the imminent beginning of the millennium and to explain the origins and enable the conversion of the American Indians. The book explained that its teachings would restore the Indians to the knowledge of Christ, making them "white and delightsome," as part of the events of the last days. Alexander Campbell pointed out that the new scripture contained teachings on the fall, the atonement, repentance, regeneration, transubstantiation, the Trinity, church government, ordination, and infant baptism — "every error and almost every truth discussed in New York for the last ten years." Smith's critics dismissed it as a forgery or as plagiarism, but his followers formed a church in 1830 that they later called the Church of Jesus Christ of Latter-day Saints.[44]

The core of Mormon doctrine came from continued revelations to Smith, and in their defense of those revelations the Mormons exhibited the reach of the evidential spirit. They appealed to the evidential force of miracles and prophecies, but they pointed not merely to the biblical narratives but to miracles occurring now and to prophecies fulfilled by Joseph Smith. In the *Book of Mormon,* Nephi condemned the people for unbelief "notwithstanding so many evidences which ye have received," and the new religious movement provided ample evidence to potential believers. Parley Pratt, a former follower of Alexander Campbell, wrote in his *Voice of Warning* (1836), the most widely read Mormon apologia of the nineteenth century, that the *Book of Mormon* had "as positive testimony as has ever been found in the other Scriptures, concerning any truth which God has revealed," with the added confirmation of testimony from witnesses still living. By the time the Mormon preacher Charles Thompson in New York published his *Evidences in Proof of the Book of Mormon Being a Divinely Inspired Record* (1841), the Mormons had appropriated the evidential logic. Thompson attempted to "prove by the prophets" that the Bible foresaw the *Book of Mormon* and that Mormon believers, baptized and confirmed by the priesthood of the church, demonstrated the truth of their faith by "the working of miracles."[45]

Mormons used the miracles and prophecies not primarily to persuade the skeptical but to confirm the faithful. In a revelation of 1830, Smith instructed Oliver Cowdery not to attract converts with miracles without Smith's command "except it be required of you by those who desire it, that the scriptures might be fulfilled." When antagonists taunted Rigdon by claiming that miracles would accompany any true revelation, Rigdon denied the claim. Yet the Mormon leaders had every confidence that miracles confirmed their beliefs. In 1831, Smith taught that "signs follow those that believe" — miracles confirmed the faith of the believer. He taught also that the faithful could work miracles. The *Book of Mormon* had predicted a day when apostates would preach that the time of miracles had ceased: "But behold, I will show unto you a God of miracles." As early as 1830, Smith began to heal and exorcise evil spirits, and an 1831 revelation declared that he had been authorized to restore a priesthood able to perform "wonderful works."[46]

The early movement drew many of its adherents from a culture in which the miraculous and the magical were part of the texture of daily life. Smith used seer stones to aid him in treasure digging, a frequent practice in rural New York and New England. The earliest Mormon converts — people who lived on the margins of evangelical Protestant culture — were already accustomed to the use of seer stones, divining rods, amulets, astrology, healing objects, revelatory dreams and visions, and occult numerology. Despite the scorn of the learned, many of them lived in an enchanted world of esoteric rituals, magical symbols, and occult parchments. This was a folk culture they shared with other populist religious groups, but while some Methodist, Baptist, and Universalist clergy criticized the practices of enchantment, Smith and other Mormon leaders shared the magical worldview. In such a setting, reports of miraculous powers and events had extraordinary evidential force.[47]

The Mormons appropriated the prophetic proof in distinctive ways. Instead of merely contending that fulfilled prophecy proved the truth of scripture, they argued that the Old Testament prophets predicted the appearance of Joseph Smith and the *Book of Mormon*. Parley Pratt, for example, found in a verse of Psalm 85 — "truth shall spring out of the earth" — a prediction of Smith's discovery of the golden plates hidden beneath the ground in New York. Charles Thompson believed that the Mormon movement fulfilled prophecies that Zion would be rebuilt. Smith produced inspired translations of Old Testament books, and his *Book of Moses* (1833), correcting and supplementing Genesis, contained a prophecy that a "choice seer" would arise from the offspring of the biblical Joseph — a prophecy that Mormons applied to Smith. They found in the *Book of Mormon* predictions of current events and of a "prophet and seer" named Joseph.[48]

Unlike other evidentialists, the Mormons defended multiple scriptures. Smith's revelations and translations resulted in an expanded body of writings alongside the Bible and the *Book of Mormon*. The Mormons believed the Bible to be the word of God as far as it was translated correctly. They believed the *Book of Mormon* to be also the word of God, and they felt assured that it was translated correctly, because its translation came by direct revelation to Smith. By 1833, they collected in a *Book of Commandments* several of the revelations granted to Smith and his close counselors. Two years later they printed the first edition of *The Book of Doctrine and Covenants,* a further compilation of revelations. In 1835, Smith purchased some Egyptian papyri, which he translated as *The Book of Abraham* (1842), claiming it to be an extrabiblical revelation about the Hebrew patriarch (though later scholars determined that the papyri contained funerary inscriptions). The translations, some additional revelations, thirteen "Articles of Faith," and certain other writings by Smith were collected into *The Pearl of Great Price* (1851), which

Mormons eventually designated as canonical scripture. When they employed the evidences, they sought to prove the validity of this whole corpus of canonical writings.

In the early movement, Smith's oral reports of his revelations formed the main body of Mormon doctrine. On the day of the organization of the church, he received a revelation that he would be the "seer," and although other Mormons also reported revelations, the movement determined that only the prophet could bind the whole church. Believing that God would "yet reveal many great and important things pertaining to the Kingdom," they looked to Smith as the prophet. His revelations led them into realms of doctrine unimagined in traditional Christian theology.[49]

Before 1832, most of the important revelations to Smith cast Mormonism as a millennial movement. In September 1831, he announced that Christ would return before the millennium and that the immediate task was to convert the Native Americans, whom he considered descendants of the Jews, and gather them, with gentile converts, in the New Jerusalem that Mormons were commanded to build. Only in that earthly Zion and in the ancient Jerusalem, where the Jews of Palestine would gather, could anyone hope to escape the tribulations that would cleanse the earth before Christ returned to begin the millennial age.[50]

Smith laid down three teachings that would guide the movement. In the doctrine of "gathering," he called for latter-day saints to congregate in special locations where they would escape the impending wrath of God. A revelation in 1830 declared that Smith was "to bring to pass the gathering" of the faithful "in one place" to "prepare their hearts." In the doctrine of "Zion," he called for the construction of the city that would become the New Jerusalem. The Mormons interpreted Isaiah 24:23, which mentioned both Zion and Jerusalem in the same passage, to mean that Zion was distinct from the old Jerusalem. The *Book of Mormon* declared that Zion would be built in America, where it would furnish refuge for the Jews of the new world (the Native Americans) and the "Gentile" converts who were "adopted" into Israel through conversion to God's latter-day work. An 1831 revelation taught Smith, who had gathered his followers in Kirtland, Ohio, that the New Jerusalem would be built in Missouri, near Independence. The Jews of the old world, including the ten lost tribes who disappeared when Assyria destroyed the kingdom of Israel in 722 B.C.E., would gather in the old Jerusalem. Finally, in his doctrine of "consecration and stewardship," he attempted to persuade the saints to consecrate their property to the church (or kingdom of God), which would make them stewards of it and encourage them to share their surplus with the poor. This economic plan, which he called the United Order of Enoch, met resistance, but Smith's warnings about the premillennial destruction of the faithless and the urgency of founding the new Zion maintained a high degree of tension and expectation.[51]

The millennialism captured the Mormon imagination. Even before he became a Mormon, Sidney Rigdon had been drawn to the premillennial doctrines of the restorationist Elias Smith, and in 1833 he began the first of fourteen essays predicting the gathering of those who wished to escape the impending tribulation. In 1836 Parley Pratt's *Voice of Warning* described the destruction of all nonbelievers and the return of Christ to reign for a thousand years on a planet utterly renewed by cataclysms that leveled the mountains and exalted the valleys. In 1837 Orson Hyde, a former follower of Campbell and a missionary to England and Palestine, wrote *A Prophetic Warning to the People of England* in which he also described the imminent return of Jesus.[52]

The Mormons expected the end within their own lifetimes; they hoped that it might come when they constructed their new Zion. By 1840, however, they were extending their timetables. Smith and Rigdon opposed William Miller when he calculated that Jesus would return in 1843 or 1844. By then, the Mormons believed, as Alexander Campbell had believed, that too many of the prophecies remained unfulfilled to accommodate Miller's dating, especially prophecies predicting the return of the Jews to Jerusalem. But even after Mormon pioneers moved in 1838 from Ohio to Missouri, and in 1839 from Missouri to Illinois, they maintained their millennial fervor.[53]

They tied their millennialism to their conviction that they were restoring the primitive church. In June 1829, Smith and others learned by revelation that twelve apostles should carry the gospel into the world under the name of Jesus Christ, calling for repentance and baptism in his name, just as the original twelve apostles had done. The articles of faith in the new church specified that Mormons believed "in the same organization that existed in the primitive Church," apostles, prophets, teachers, and evangelists. Revelations in 1830 taught that church membership required faith, repentance, baptism by immersion for the remission of sins, and the receiving of "the Holy Ghost by the laying on of hands, even as the apostles of old." When Mormons spoke in tongues, healed the sick, washed each other's feet, prophesied, and received the bread and wine of communion, they considered themselves to be reenacting practices of the early church.[54]

As early as 1829, however, it started to become clear that Smith envisioned a restoration unlike that of other Christian restorationist groups. He and Oliver Cowdery reported that John the Baptist had given them the authority to baptize by conferring on them the Aaronite priesthood of ancient Jerusalem. Shortly thereafter, three apostles conferred on them the higher priesthood of Melchizedek, the king-priest of Genesis 14. The priestly genealogies that

Smith outlined in revelations of the early 1830s had parallels in astrology and the literature of magic, but the overriding impulse was to restore the institutions of ancient Israel. In 1831, Smith ordered the church to reinstate the ancient priesthood and build temples for priestly ceremonies, symbolic rituals of sacrifice, and the reenactment of patriarchal blessings through the laying on of hands and announcement of the convert's lineage in one of the twelve tribes of Israel. As Smith prepared the *Book of Moses* in 1831, he began to consider the restoration of patriarchal polygamy. At first, Mormons believed that through their new belief they were "adopted" into Israel. By 1832, some thought of themselves as literal descendants of ancient Israelites.[55]

During Smith's sojourn in Kirtland, Ohio, from 1831 to 1838, however, he led the Mormons beyond the boundaries of primitivism, whether Christian or Jewish. Without abandoning previous revelations, Smith announced new ones that also pulled the group away from traditional Christian doctrine. In an 1832 vision received while he and Rigdon retranslated the gospel of John, they learned of three celestial kingdoms that would receive the bodies and spirits of the dead. In the lowest, the "telestial," the wicked and faithless would dwell after they spent a millennium in hell expiating their sins. In the "terrestrial" would live people who failed to recognize the truth during their mortal existence but accepted it after their death. In the highest kingdom, the "celestial," would dwell the priests after the order of Melchizedek and their families. The revelation involved a doctrine of virtually universal salvation, and it produced contention. Smith's successor as prophet, Brigham Young, reported that the new doctrine was "a great trial to many," who resisted the idea of "degrees of glory" in "a place prepared for all, according to the light they had received."[56]

In the ecstatic ceremonies that dedicated the temple in Kirtland in 1836, Smith received a further revelation that led to the doctrine of baptism for the dead. Mormons could help their deceased loved ones inhabit the highest heaven by undergoing a proxy baptism for them in the temples. Smith might have known that Pennsylvania Germans in the Ephrata community had practiced baptism for the dead since 1738, relying on the Apostle Paul's reference to the practice in 1 Corinthians 15:29, but he authorized it on the basis of immediate revelation. In 1841 the church codified this "temple work" as a revealed commandment.[57]

The Kirtland revelations introduced a new cosmology into Mormon thought. In 1833, Smith announced a revelation that "the elements are eternal." Instead of speaking of a God who created the world from nothing, he began to speak of a God who organized eternal matter. Human souls shared this property of eternal existence: "Man was also in the beginning with God, Intelligence, or the light of truth, was not created or made, neither can be." By

1844, Smith revealed a detailed narrative of heavenly councils that followed the plan of Jesus to allow human beings to grow by assuming material bodies and undergoing a probationary period on earth. Although Adam failed the probation, the atonement of Jesus restored the innocence of Adam and of every soul at birth. Smith rejected any doctrine of original sin and contended that although Adam's fall made his progeny capable of sinning — and although all sinned — none would suffer punishment for Adam's sin. In the American Eden, individual responsibility was the rule.[58]

Around the same time, Smith began to explain that Jesus had become the Son of God gradually, as the Father "gave" his "fulness" to him. The Mormon saints could share that same fullness of divinity. In fact, the 1832 Kirtland vision revealed to Smith and Rigdon that the saints could become as God. In subsequent lectures on theology, Smith expounded the message that the saints could partake of "the same fulness" as the Son of God, who "partakes of the fulness of the Father." The new idea spread slowly, but for Smith it became important, and he returned to it at a moment of extreme crisis.[59]

After 1838, Mormons endured a series of harsh setbacks. The community in Kirtland fell apart because of a banking fiasco. Smith fled to the settlement in Missouri, where anxieties about Mormon political power led to a brutal "Mormon War." In 1839, enemies drove the Mormons to Illinois, where they purchased a small town that Smith named Nauvoo. In 1844, as Nauvoo Mormons split into factions and outside threats loomed, Smith proclaimed, in an emotional funeral sermon for a Mormon martyr, the full implications of the Kirtland revelation.

He announced that God was once "as we are now," that God possessed a body as Mormons possessed bodies, and that the Mormons had to "learn how to be Gods." The aim of the Mormon gospel was not salvation alone but godhood, attained through faith, belief in the prophet's revelations, and obedience to the precepts of the church. While every man and woman could be saved except for apostates from the church — and in the crisis of 1844 apostasy was a problem — only the Mormon faithful would enjoy the full benefit of eternal life. In the celestial heaven, the Mormon priesthood would reign over kingdoms as gods, each man with his families in a vast community stretching over endless worlds.[60]

By 1844, a new Mormon ideal of the family stood behind this depiction of heavenly domestic power. The highest heaven was reserved to men and their wives who entered "the new and everlasting covenant" of plural marriage. Smith's interest in plural marriage probably began in 1831 as he revised Genesis, and he probably began the practice himself five years later. In 1843 he recorded the revelation of the new covenant, teaching that no marriage could endure after death without "eternal sealing" in the temple. Faithful Mormons who practiced polygamy, however, would retain their families; inherit "thrones, principalities, and powers"; and ascend in the heavenly hierarchy: "They shall be as gods, because they have no end." The unmarried could attain celestial glory, but only as angels who ministered to others; a man with only one wife would occupy, with her, a lower heaven. The new order decisively separated the Mormon faithful from the surrounding culture.[61]

The church divided after the murder of Joseph Smith in a Missouri jail in 1844. The prophet's family formed a reorganized church that repudiated polygamy and gradually moved closer to Protestant tradition. Smaller divisions created more than two dozen Mormon communions. The Mormons who followed Brigham Young to Utah engaged in a flurry of theological speculation that threatened to divide the movement even further.

In 1855, Parley Pratt published a *Key to the Science of Theology*. The book explicated Smith's revelation of a Supreme God with "flesh and bones and sinews," of a Christ who differed "in nothing from His Father, except in age and authority," and of a panoply of lesser gods who had once been human beings, or spirits united with bodies. But the idea of God as possessing "flesh and bones" made it difficult to talk about divine omnipresence, so Pratt also depicted the Supreme God as possessing "Spirit," a refined and subtle fluidlike substance circulating through all the particles of matter and mind in the universe. He also argued that the Mormon miracles — which he thought confirmed the authority of the church — should be understood as "fully in accordance with the laws of nature." He held to the essentials of Smith's revelations — including the doctrine of the three heavens and the "everlasting covenants" of marriage — but he was also trying to adapt Mormon theology to "the progressive principles of the age." Brigham Young, a former Methodist minister who assumed the presidency of the church after Smith's death, disapproved, but Young engaged in his own speculations, arguing that the primary Mormon God was none other than Adam. As the church imposed discipline on its theologians, however, both Pratt and Young agreed not to publish further speculation, and by 1860 Mormons began to accentuate a Protestant language of repentance and atonement. The later-nineteenth century witnessed a halting but discernible reappropriation of traditional Protestant themes, but Mormons held on to the distinctive doctrines that made them a new religious tradition.[62]

The Hicksite Quakers, the Shakers, and the Mormons showed how the populist impulse could lead in unpredictable and unconventional directions, creating a theology that claimed Christian roots while expanding the boundaries of Christianity so broadly that the linkage to Christian tradition often seemed to break. Elias Hicks, Ann Lee, and Joseph Smith taught that new revelation, which came more often to the unlearned than to the educated, provided the criteria by which the old scripture was to be reinterpreted. They retained the evidential style, finding in miracle and prophecy the evidence to support their claims, but their miracles occurred in their own era, and when they turned to the prophecies, they discovered that the prophetic predictions referred above all to themselves.

17

Calvinism Revised

In 1901 the Yale historian Williston Walker took a retrospective glance at theology in New England and concluded that after 1800, if "all shades of Edwardeanism" were taken into view, the Edwardeans took control of the theological conversation among the Calvinists. The result was a flourishing of theological debate in New England, upper New York, and the Ohio Valley. The admirers of Edwards divided into competing factions, but they created an "Edwardean culture" that furnished the dominant vocabulary in Congregational circles, gained a following within Presbyterianism, and attracted support among Baptists. It was a culture of revivalism. Nineteenth-century Edwardeans thought of themselves as practical thinkers formulating a theology that made sense of the evangelist's call for immediate repentance and conversion. Edwards Amasa Park, who occupied Andover's chair in theology for forty-four years, spoke of the Edwardean "system" as "the scientific refutation of all excuses for prolonged impenitence. . . . We can say of it, as of few other systems, that it is fit to be preached."[1]

Its best-known proponents occupied chairs in the theological seminaries and published in seminary journals. For philosophical reasons, the Edwardean theologians appealed to the common sense of ordinary people, but they were no theological populists. Edwards's grandson, Timothy Dwight, told the faculty at Andover in 1808 that their seminary should be a citadel against the "ignorance and vulgarity, enthusiasm and vociferation" of popular theologians who presented themselves as "teachers of religion," people whose coarseness and arrogance threatened to "entail upon Theology . . . a character, derived . . . from the men themselves." In Andover classrooms, Park taught that the laity were not "competent to pronounce a decision" on theological matters; one should not "invite the mechanic or the ploughman to pass a dogmatical decision."[2]

The seminary professionals tried to preserve Calvinism by revising it. They saw themselves as meeting three challenges: to defend Calvinism from Unitarian, Universalist, and Arminian critics, a project that required proving its reasonableness; to formulate a Calvinist theology of revivalism; and to maintain a Calvinist piety, which involved, at a minimum, the sense of divine sovereignty, with its correlates of human sinfulness, election, and a grace that overwhelmed without coercing.

The tensions and transitions within Edwardeanism displayed themselves in the diverse ways the theologians talked about reasonableness. All stayed within the boundaries of rational orthodoxy, but their rhetoric about reason intensified in accord with the degree of their willingness to restate Calvinist doctrine. In the differences between the "New England theology" as taught at Andover, Bangor, and East Windsor (Hartford) seminaries; the "New Haven theology" at Yale Divinity School; and the "Oberlin theology" that dramatically revised the New England theology while transplanting it to the western states, one finds an increasing effort to make Edwardean Calvinism more revivalist by making it more reasonable.

The New England Theology

The first group to import Edwardeanism into the nineteenth century described themselves as the architects of the "New England Theology." The label became current after the founding of Andover seminary in 1808 as a joint venture of New Divinity and Old Calvinist theologians who opposed the spread of Unitarian liberalism. From the beginning, the two sides of the Andover faculty eyed each other warily, and they had to assent to two creeds, one Edwardean and the other protective of the Westminster standards. The school needed a theological self-designation that minimized older disagreements. The solution was to say that Andover represented "the theology of New England." Nonetheless, the phrase became linked especially to the New Divinity side of the Andover union. By 1832 Lyman Beecher could take it as accepted that "New England Divinity" meant the "Edwardean school."[3]

The New England theology was a system designed to retain the Calvinist doctrine of divine sovereignty and the predestination of the elect while consistently supporting a revivalist evangelistic strategy in which the preacher exhorted every sinful soul to undergo conversion. It was also designed to answer the Unitarian charge that the Calvinist God, who saved only the elect, was unfair, and to counter the evangelical Arminian charge that Calvinists were inconsistent when they exhorted everyone to repent. Park captured the spirit of the New England theology when he observed that it united a "high, but not an ultra Calvinism, on the decrees and agency of God, with a philosophical, but not an Arminian theory, on the freedom and worth of the human soul."[4]

The New England theologians built their system around five assertions that, at first glance, seemed contradictory. (1) Theologians had to accept the truths of the Bible even if they seemed to be paradoxes that defied reason, but they had to read the Bible with "common sense." (2) God was a benevolent moral governor of free and responsible creatures, but God was also a sovereign whose will determined both the destiny of every person and the course of history. (3) The guilt of sin resided in the sinful choice and not in an imputation of Adam's guilt to his posterity, but sin was inevitable as a result of the fall. (4) Every sinful person had the natural ability to repent, but the nonelect would be damned because they would not make use of this ability. (5) Spiritual rebirth was the irresistible result of the immediate power of the Spirit, but the Spirit exerted that power in ways consistent with human freedom. The goal of the New England theology was to show that the contradictions were merely apparent.

Around mid-century, three theologians employed the term "New England theology" so forcefully that it found a permanent lodging in the history books, but their definitions, taken together, highlight the ambiguities of the movement. In 1851 Leonard Woods, the first occupant of the Andover chair in theology, described the New England theology as an unbroken tradition extending into the seventeenth century, inclusive of the Westminster Confession, John Cotton, and Samuel Willard but invigorated with "new power" by Jonathan Edwards. Woods wrote to prove that the "orthodox Congregational clergy" had always been of the same mind, a mind unlike that of innovators at Yale. Woods's definition included earlier Calvinists who would not have accepted Edwardean conclusions, but it excluded the Yale theological faculty.[5]

In 1852 Edwards Amasa Park offered a different perspective. Having been accused by Charles Hodge of departing from Edwards, whom Hodge was claiming for Princeton, Park defined the New England theology as the product of the eminent New England theologians "during and since the time of Edwards." For Park, its quintessential marks were the doctrines that "sin consists in choice" and that human beings had no duties that exceeded their "natural power." Park had studied with Nathaniel William Taylor at Yale, and his definition could be read to include the New Haven theologians. It excluded, however, the older New England Calvinists whom Woods tried to include.[6]

Enoch Pond (1791–1882) of Bangor seminary in Maine, an outpost of Andover, proposed that the phrase designated Calvinism as modified by the influence of Edwards and his followers. A student of Nathanael Emmons, Pond joined Woods in claiming that the New England theology embraced features of an older Calvinism, though he moved closer to Park when he added that it did not "state, explain, or apply some of them precisely as did our fathers two hundred years ago." It was therefore neither "old Calvinism" nor "high Hopkinsianism," though it retained the best elements of both. Pond was clearer than Park in his insistence that it had no kinship with the "speculations" at Yale.[7]

All three — Woods, Park, and Pond — added that the essentials of the New England theology could be distinguished from eccentric themes in the earlier New Divinity, even from some eccentricities of Edwards. It became customary for New England theologians to disavow Edwards's idealistic metaphysics, including his explanation of human solidarity with Adam, to discard Emmons's extreme views of divine efficiency (which made God the author of sin), and to reject Hopkins's view that the saint should accept damnation for God's glory. Park wrote intellectual biographies of Emmons and Hopkins in which he applied his considerable exegetical skills to the end of blurring the sharpest edges of New Divinity piety and metaphysics. The New Englanders wanted to "improve" their mentors for a new era.[8]

The initial strategy was to seek a common language in the scriptures. Park could say in 1852 that the New England theology was, above all else, "a comprehensive system of Biblical science," which elevated the Bible above the creeds. This had also been the judgment of his predecessor Leonard Woods. A graduate of Harvard who had flirted as a student with the materialism of Joseph Priestley, Woods had turned to a moderate Edwardeanism after reading theology with the New Divinity theologians Charles Backus and Nathanial Emmons. As the minister at the Second Church in West Newbury, Massachusetts, he persuaded the congregation to adopt an Edwardean confession of faith, but his moderation made him the natural choice for Andover's chair.[9]

At Andover, Woods told the students to turn away from speculation and recognize that "the simple fact, that God declares" a truth in scripture was the "highest possible evidence" for it. He argued for the infallible plenary inspiration of scripture and the inerrancy of the original autographs (the manuscripts written by the biblical authors). Woods lamented that his opponents often accorded scripture "less influence than the arguments suggested by human reason."[10]

It strengthened the Andover strategy when Moses Stuart joined the faculty. When Stuart debated Channing in 1819, he employed the same tactic as Woods. The function of reason in theology, he said, was to interpret, not to legislate: "It is the highest office of reason to believe doctrines and facts, which God has asserted to be true, and to submit to his precepts; although many things, in regard to the manner in which those facts and doctrines can be explained, or those precepts vindicated, may be beyond her reach." Stuart thought that the Unitarians dismissed revealed truths that reason had no authority to judge. Like Woods, he defended the plenary inspiration of the autographs. He worried Woods when he failed to affirm "verbal infallibility," but he would acknowledge no substantial error in the biblical text. For the first generation at Andover, belief in an errorless biblical text would resolve conceptual issues and keep the faculty united.[11]

At the same time, the New England theologians shared with the Unitarians an admiration for reasonableness. Stuart told Channing that he was ready to "admit as fully you as you do or can do, the proper office of reason, in the whole matter of religion." The New Englanders believed that reason could generate a trustworthy natural theology, that revelation would never be contrary to reason, that reason could prove the authenticity of the revelation, and that the revelation required reasonable interpretation. Even Woods conceded that "the philosophy of mind" could illustrate and vindicate biblical truth. Scripture used language that had to be deciphered by "common sense."[12]

By the time Park assumed Woods's chair in 1847, he thought of common sense as indispensable. The son of an Edwardean professor at Brown, Park had been nurtured since childhood in the rational theology of the British enlightenment, especially the writings of Samuel Clarke, William Paley, and Joseph Butler. He had read Scottish philosophy as a student at Brown and then studied theology under Woods at Andover. After teaching Scottish thought at Amherst College, he went to Andover in 1836 as the Bartlett Professor of Sacred Rhetoric, convinced that Scottish mental science had brought theology to new levels of maturity. Because the ancient church fathers had written "before the rational processes of induction and the fundamental laws of belief had been distinctly explained" by Bacon and the Scots, Park preferred to think of them as the "Church babies."[13]

All the prominent figures in the New England theology subscribed to Scottish Common Sense philosophy, though Park was the most expansive in his praise. Weary of hearing "so much of the weakness of human reason," he cast aside Woods's admonitions. He urged that natural theology be accorded an "enlarged part" in theological science; contended that reason could demonstrate monotheism, divine moral government, and human immortality; and argued that confidence in scripture presupposed a prior rational demonstration of God's existence and benevolence. Park viewed the Bible as inspired, but he dropped the insistence that infallibility extended to each word, and he accepted Stuart's suggestion that the Bible be read as a religious, not a scientific, book. He intended to show that the Calvinist approach to the Bible was more rational than that of the Unitarians.[14]

His reflections on reason in theology cast him into the middle of one of the era's most important theological debates. The Connecticut pastor Horace Bushnell argued in an 1839 Andover address on "Revelation" that theological language was poetic and metaphorical, not scientific and literal. Bushnell repeated similar ideas in his 1848 Andover lecture on "Dogma and Spirit." The following year, the Amherst professor Henry Boynton Smith announced in another Andover address that Bushnell was wrong, that language was the express image of spirit and that it could convey thought and feeling with sufficient adequacy to make theological systems possible. In 1850, Park entered the fray with a lecture in Boston on "The Theology of the Intellect and that of the Feelings." Like Smith, he spoke out for intellect, philosophy, and reason in theology; but he conceded that religion often spoke a language of feeling and imagination, fitted to move the affections rather than to inform the scientific intellect.[15]

Park's intent was to preclude misguided polemics by establishing two points. First, the metaphorical and poetic language of scripture should not be taken literally. Thus far he agreed with Bushnell. But he thought that for the sake of writing a consistent system, the Bible's metaphors should be translated into rational propositions. It was an error to treat the images and metaphors as themselves propositions for the intellect. This error had led to unreasonable conclusions—for example, that God imputed Adam's guilt to others, that Christ died to pay a debt, that the faithful received his physical body and blood in communion, and that sinners were blamable even before they chose to do wrong. That such conclusions offended Christian sensibility was evidence of their inadequacy. A theology of the intellect would show them to be a misreading of the Bible's poetic language, and it would translate the biblical images into rational propositions that were consistent with overall scriptural truth.[16]

The essay drew fire from every side. Bushnell pointed out that Park's attempts to translate metaphors into propositions merely substituted one set of metaphors for another. He read Park's essay as an example of the excesses of orthodox rationalism. Charles Hodge, on the other hand, faulted Park for failing to see that metaphorical language could convey propositional truth just as easily as abstract language could. Hodge felt aggrieved that Park dismissed doctrines that Hodge considered reasonable and true. The issue led to years of debate in the journals, though Park was not saying anything new. Even Leonard Woods had said in 1820 that "common sense" had to determine when scriptural language was metaphorical rather than literal, and he had ruled out the same "hurtful" doctrines that Park was dismissing. Their "common sense" interpretation enabled the New England theologians to believe that they honored the claims of both reason and scripture.[17]

The ambiguity could be seen when Moses Stuart wrote his manifesto against Unitarians. His *Letters to the Rev. Wm. E. Channing* (1819) defended the Trinity "simply on the credit of divine revelation." Yet Stuart made his case as consistent with "common sense" as he could by contending that the language about "three persons" and "one substance" had no positive meaning beyond the simple affirmation of "distinction" within the Godhead, the insistence that God was internally differentiated "in some respect." Stuart's allies worried about his minimalism, but he would not go beyond a "common sense" reading of scripture.[18]

All of the New England theologians wanted to avoid "speculation" about the Trinity. Woods told his students that the doctrine was "practical," intended to move the religious affections and to shape the language of worship. He saw even the explanations of Augustine as "speculation." Stuart made a similar point: the Trinity was not "a mere subject of speculation." It was about the duties, hopes, and consolations of the faithful, not about philosophy. Given the commitments to a commonsense reading of scripture, it would have been difficult to say more.[19]

In any case, their central interest in speaking about God was not the Trinity but rather God's sovereignty and benevolence. "The sentiment, which forms the basis of our system," wrote Leonard Woods, "is, that God is Love," which meant that God's object was "to promote the highest degree of happiness." To counter the criticism that the Calvinist God unfairly condemned the sinful for an inherited sin, New England Calvinists reaffirmed divine benevolence. Yet they resisted any compromise of divine sovereignty. When Taylor at Yale said that God perhaps could not prevent all sin, the Andover theologians charged him with grave error. Woods's *Letters to Rev. Nathaniel W. Taylor, D.D.* (1830) repeated Hopkins's argument that sin was the "necessary means of the greatest good," that it was "on the whole for the best." Otherwise the believer could never be sure that the suffering caused by moral evil served a benevolent divine purpose.[20]

Edward Dorr Griffin (1770–1837), a student of the younger Edwards who achieved renown as a revivalist preacher before accepting in 1821 the presidency of Williams College in Massachusetts, made the point more strongly in his *Doctrine of Divine Efficiency Defended* (1833). If God could not prevent sin, then he was "liable to be defeated in all his designs, and to be as miserable as he is benevolent. This is infinitely the gloomiest idea that ever was thrown upon the world." Only if God were both benevolent and sovereign could the theologian provide an adequate explanation of suffering and sin.[21]

In the New England theology, therefore, God was both the moral governor of responsible creatures and the sovereign efficient cause of every event. Edwards, Bellamy, and Hopkins had sometimes referred to God as a moral governor. In the nineteenth century, the idea became an organizing principle for New England theologians, virtually replacing covenantal language. For Edward Dorr Griffin, the term "moral governor" designated the benevolent God who administered divine law and guided free agents by presenting motives to their minds: "It forms," he said, "the subject matter of nine-tenths, perhaps of ninety-nine hundredths of the Bible." In speaking of the divine government, he said, Calvinists and Arminians sounded the same. What made Calvinists different was their willingness also to designate God as the sovereign efficient cause, who dealt with the elect and the reprobate as beings "acted upon" rather than "acting." Dorr conceded that it was a mystery that God could be both the moral governor of free agents and the sovereign efficient cause who saved the elect, but he thought that the paradox was biblical. Theologians had to accept it.[22]

The emphasis on moral governance inclined Edwardeans toward a governmental atonement theory. In 1859 Park collected seven New England essays and published them as examples of "the Edwardean theory of the atonement." He found hints of governmental theory in the writing of the elder Edwards, Bellamy, and Hopkins, but his book featured the "Three Sermons" of the younger Edwards, who had recognized, in debates with Universalists, that it no longer sufficed to say that the death of Christ satisfied a debt owed to God. The nineteenth-century Edwardeans conceded that such a doctrine made salvation a divine obligation rather than a gracious gift. They accepted the alternative of the New Divinity theologians: Christ died to preserve the integrity of the cosmic moral government.[23]

Moral government implied a capacity for agency on the part of the governed. The New England theologians retrieved from Edwards and the New Divinity the distinction between natural and moral ability, though they stressed the natural ability more than Edwards had. Intent on encouraging revivalism and countering anti-Calvinist critics, they underscored the natural ability to repent. The pastor in Portland, Maine, Bennet Tyler (1783–1858), wrote that only a doctrine of natural ability could make sense of biblical commands, God's moral governance, and evangelical preaching. Non-Edwardean Calvinists complained that "not one word or intimation of natural ability" was found in the scriptures, but the Edwardeans continued to teach that sinners "have no inability to repent except their own unwillingness."[24]

Eighteenth-century Edwardeans had always been willing to defend free will as long as they could define the terms. Nineteenth-century Edwardeans continued to argue that freedom meant only that the will was active (regardless of what caused it to be), or that men and women were free to do as they chose (even without being able to choose their choice). A few departed from Edwards's language and logic. He had insisted on a strict causal connection between motives and choices; the will always *was* as the greatest apparent good. Park tried to soften the determinism; the will, he argued, could in principle choose the least apparent good, even though it never would. Park's "freedom" was theoretically freer than that of Edwards, but it was still bound in moral inability.[25]

Even more than their New Divinity predecessors, the early nineteenth-century New England theologians divided into parties of tasters and exercisers. In 1824, Asa Burton, a Congregational minister in Thetford, Vermont, defended the position of the tasters in his *Essays on Some First Principles of Metaphysicks, Ethicks, and Theology*. He argued for a tripartite division of the mind into the faculties of intellect, will, and "taste" (which he also called the "feelings," or "affections," or "heart"). Scottish philosophers made the same division, though Burton claimed originality. He found that the spring of moral action was feeling or "taste." His evidence was that the will could not control the feelings but that feelings did determine willing. Furthermore, the mind could desire what it did not will. No one confused a desire for companionship with a choice to visit the neighbor, even though the desire prompted the choice. A taste or inclination stood behind the voluntary exercise as the source of agency, determining the will. But people were free when their exercise of will expressed their inclinations and they could act as they willed. With this argument, Burton became an authority for the tasters.[26]

The division between the two groups expressed itself in debates over sin and regeneration. Although all the Edwardeans agreed that guilt was personal, one group of them, influenced by the exercise language, insisted with Emmons and Park that "all sin consists in sinning." Enoch Pond represented the Edwardeans who continued to deny any sinful nature "back of, and distinct from, sinful affections." Neither Park nor Pond accepted Emmons's view of God as the author of sinful exercises, though both conceded that God was the author of a "tendency" to sin, or a "foundation" or "occasion" for sin, which was not itself sinful. Their intention was to emphasize the voluntary character of sin.[27]

Other Edwardeans, wedded to the taste scheme, would not abandon the idea of a "sinful nature" prior to any exercises. Leonard Woods said that the "propensity to sin" was "itself sinful." Joseph Harvey argued that the sinful act was "the fruit and evidence of a sinful heart" and that actual sin had to result from "a cause which is sinful" — a position supported also by the Edwardean revivalist Asahel Nettleton. The tasters thought that the exercise scheme threatened the belief that human beings were depraved "by nature." Both sides appealed to Edwards, though the exercisers had to engage in some creative reinterpretation, for Edwards had thought that a sinful disposition underlay every sinful exercise of the will.[28]

The division led also to different ways of talking about regeneration. The tasters saw it as a change in the "taste," the "nature," something "back of, and furnishing the ground of, all holy affections." The exercisers saw it as an immediate "change in the affections themselves." They worried that talk about a change in "nature" would again provide the unconverted with an excuse not to repent. The tasters thought that the exercise scheme failed to recognize that regeneration required a change in the permanent disposition of the soul, not merely in volitional exercises abstracted from the whole person. They also thought, with some justification, that the exercisers departed too radically from the theology of Edwards and that the exercise doctrine threatened the idea of a permanent human nature.[29]

Woods lamented that the theologians were so quick to line up on either side — "some were for forming themselves into two armies, Exercise Men and Taste Men" — but by 1832 he thought that "more diligent study of the Bible" promised to unify once-divided hearts. By the 1830s compromise was in the air. Woods, a taste man, conceded that the disposition — or taste — "develops itself" in exercises. Park, an exerciser, announced himself willing to acknowledge a "taste" if it meant only a "foundation" for exercises and not a passive principle that determined choice.[30]

The two sides found other points of agreement. They agreed in rejecting the doctrine that God imputed the guilt of Adam's sin to the race. The standard Edwardean view came to be that God had established a "connection" between Adam's sin and the sinfulness of humanity but that no human being could be deemed guilty merely because Adam sinned. "None of them," Woods said, "suffer penal evil as a consequence of his sin, without being sinful themselves."[31]

The great debate over imputation — a debate chiefly between the Edwardeans and the Princetonians — began in 1830 when Moses Stuart and Archibald Alexander at Princeton squared off over original sin. Two years later, Stuart published his *Commentary on the Epistle to the Romans*, contending that Paul never taught imputation and that the crucial text in Romans 5:12–19 meant only that all became sinners "because" of Adam's sin, not that all became sinners "in" Adam or that God imputed Adam's guilt to all. The distinction permitted him to interpret Paul as meaning that all sinned as a consequence of Adam's sin—that was the "connection" with Adam—but that they sinned voluntarily. The publication led to further conflict with Charles Hodge, who thought that Paul did teach imputation, and the Princetonians always believed that the denial of the doctrine was one of the worst errors of the New England theologians.[32]

The New Englanders agreed also that regeneration was a divine act, the immediate inflowing of the Spirit. Whether it operated on human "nature" or human "affections," the Spirit transformed sinners from outside themselves. This was a rallying cry against the theologians in New Haven who seemed to suggest that regeneration was "an act of the will or heart." Moses Stuart had some discreetly held Taylorite sympathies on the issue, but most of the New Englanders thought that the New Haven view, as they understood it, surrendered the Calvinist insight that the new birth was the gift of the Spirit. The New Englanders agreed, as well, that regeneration was an instantaneous change. It occurred in a moment, even when it was not immediately recognized. It was no gradual process.[33]

They remained reluctant, therefore, to talk about the gradual efficacy of the means of grace. The imperative was to repent now. Bennet Tyler argued that sinners, properly speaking, never "used" the means of grace because they always misused them for selfish purposes. Enoch Pond told his students at Bangor not to encourage the unconverted to "use means and persevere." Tell them, he said, to repent and believe, so that when they used the means they would use them rightly.[34]

Finally, the New England theologians agreed that Congregational churches should require regenerate membership and not adopt the halfway covenant. When they served local parishes, they battled against the practice of allowing baptized but unconverted parents to present their children for baptism or receive the Lord's Supper. They called for pure churches, consisting of the regenerate and their children, and the aim of their evangelical theology was to evoke the repentance that would make pure churches possible.[35]

Because the Edwardeans agreed on so much, most of them could accept the admonition of Leonard Woods to bind themselves together even if they did not "think exactly alike on minor points." After 1828, Woods thought it increasingly necessary for right-thinking New England theologians to unite against innovators in their midst who claimed to be both Edwardean and Calvinist but promoted distressing revisions. He called for unity especially against the innovations of Nathaniel William Taylor at Yale, who he thought had abandoned the Edwardean standard. Another way of viewing Taylor and the New Haven school, however, is to see them as expanding the boundaries of the Edwardean culture. This was the way they viewed themselves, and their self-perception said much about the tenacity of an Edwardean way of thinking even among the revisionists.[36]

The New Haven Theology

When Andover seminary opened its doors, the inaugural address came from Yale's president, Timothy Dwight (1752–1817). Dwight was a graduate of Yale, where he taught classics and poetry before becoming in 1785 the pastor of the Congregational Church in Greenfield, Connecticut. He was well-known as a poet when he returned to Yale as president in 1795. At Yale he encouraged religious revival and supported the Federalists who resisted the disestablishing of the Congregational churches in the state. Worried by Unitarian successes and Calvinist factionalism, Dwight supported the union of Old Calvinists and Hopkinsians. In an era of infidelity and Republican politics, he thought, theological compromise could lead to good ends.

No one could agree about where he fit in the theological alignments. An early antagonist opposed his elevation to the Yale presidency in 1795 for fear that he would "establish the Edwardean system of doctrines and disciplines." The *Princeton Review* later praised him for rejecting New Divinity extravagance. Even though his five-volume *Theology Explained and Defended* (1818–19) became a standard authority, historians have also differed in their assessments of his theological lineage. The question remains of interest partly because he was the teacher for four years of Nathaniel William Taylor.[37]

The balance of the evidence suggests that Dwight was an Edwardean revivalist, though not a strict adherent of the New Divinity. He supported the Edwardean demand for immediate repentance; he employed the distinction between natural and moral ability, insisting that nothing prevented our being saved but "our own inclinations"; and he promoted the ideal of the pure church and rejected the halfway covenant. He thought that Edwards was "completely" right in his proof that freedom did not require self-determination or the indifference of the will. He defended the governmental theory of the atonement, and he expressed millennial views like those of eighteenth-century Hopkinsians.[38]

Like other theologians of the New England school, he rejected the idea of the imputation of Adam's guilt, saying only that all sinned "in consequence" of Adam's sin and that their guilt came from their action. His view of sin was that of the tasters, as he argued that a "controlling disposition" or "heart" or "temper" — metaphysically a mystery — caused the exercises of the will. Like the tasters, he believed that infants came into the world "contaminated in their moral nature." Though he did not emphasize the point, he shared the view of Hopkins and Bellamy that depravity corrupted the will, not the understanding or any other "natural" extravolitional faculty. Dwight had once been tempted by Emmons's "exercise" scheme, but by the time he wrote his theology he concluded that it verged on pantheism to attribute every volition to the immediate efficiency of God. He thought it perverse to think of God as the author of sin "by immediate agency," although God had obviously permitted sin to occur.[39]

Like the Edwardeans, moreover, he thought of regeneration as an instantaneous change, not a gradual transition. It was, as Hopkins had said, normally imperceptible; it occurred, as the tasters argued, when God created a "relish" for spiritual objects, a change in the disposition or heart, rather than through the immediate creation of virtuous volitions, as the exercisers had claimed. He believed that the result of regeneration was disinterested benevolence. But he did not share the view of Hopkins that the regenerate would be willing to be damned for the glory of God, and he refused to call himself a Hopkinsian.[40]

So far Dwight appears to be a conventional Edwardean theologian. What made him different was his confidence in the means of grace. Although he pressed sinners for "immediate repentance," he thought that preaching, prayer, and meditation could gradually "apply" the gospel to the understanding and affections and so promote salvation. When confronted with the Hopkinsian argument that the use of the means made selfish sinners worse since they used them selfishly, he dismissed it as "idle and vain." Dwight also struck an unusual note among Edwardeans when he emphasized that the "religious education" and nurture of children would "check" their propensities to wrong.[41]

Dwight was an early proponent of the Scottish philosophy. He made no extended comment on Reid and Stewart, but he read Hugh Blair, George Campbell, and James Beattie—all British representatives of the Scottish school—and he appealed to common sense throughout his writings. Like the Scots, he appealed to the authority of "consciousness" and referred often to assumptions implicit in ordinary language. He "proved," for instance, that faith was "a voluntary, or moral exercise" by appealing to the "universal judgment" and language of ordinary people. He accepted the Scottish epistemology and employed the Baconian appeal to "fact."[42]

He was reserved about the virtues of philosophy, but he accepted the premises of rational orthodoxy. He often contrasted the confusion and disagreements of the secular philosophers with the certainty of believers, and his trump card was usually the argument that infidel philosophy had dangerous moral and social consequences. But Dwight approved of the British texts on the evidences of Christianity, and his common strategy in *Theology Explained and Defended* was to expound the verdict of "reason" before he turned to the pronouncement of "revelation." Whatever his reservations about the unaided powers of reason, he also conveyed a robust confidence that Christianity was rational.[43]

None of his students took that confidence more to heart than Nathaniel William Taylor (1786–1858). The successor of Moses Stuart as pastor at New Haven's First Church, Taylor instituted strict discipline and oversaw four revivals before the theological department at Yale asked him to become the Dwight Professor of Didactic Theology. He worked there alongside Chauncy Allen Goodrich, who had come to Yale from the Congregational church in Middletown to teach sacred rhetoric; Eleazar T. Fitch, who had taught earlier at Andover; and Josiah Willard Gibbs, the professor of biblical literature. The faculty reached a consensus early and promoted it through the *Christian Spectator,* a journal that Goodrich purchased as a vehicle for the New Haven theology.[44]

Although more than a few of his theological ideas have made it seem that Taylor represented either a resurgence of Old Calvinism or an abandonment of any Calvinism, he identified himself as an Edwardean. His theology was aimed at converting "the multitude of the ungodly" — including the ungodly in "orthodox congregations" — by telling them that their obligation was to repent now, without delay, and love God above any other good. The challenge, as he saw it, was to hold in tension the "two great facts" of Edwardean Calvinism: "complete moral agency" as the basis of guilt and obligation, along with "dependence on the sovereign grace of God." He saw his theology as an attempt to show "the consistency of exhortation to immediate duty, with the doctrine of the sinner's dependence."[45]

If his emphasis seemed to fall on the moral agency, he explained, this was because Calvinists had exaggerated human dependence to the detriment of awakening and conversion. The "prevailing state of public opinion" required now an emphasis on agency and obligation, though Taylor conceded that this theme too could be overdone, in which case it would be necessary to emphasize again the dependence.[46]

It was an important part of the strategy that the theology be reasonable. One distinction between a New Haven Edwardean and the Edwardean conservatives like Woods and Harvey was to be found in their rhetoric about reasonableness. Taylor combined a serene confidence in Scottish Common Sense Realism with the view of the New Divinity theologians that depravity corrupted the heart but left the intellect still capable of "unperverted use." The result could be arresting: "the clear, unperverted deductions of reason are as binding in their authority, and not less truly to be relied on, than the word of God; and . . . the former can never contradict the latter." This meant that natural theology had logical priority over revealed theology, for the Bible assumed rather than proved the existence of God, and it was the task of reason to prove as well that God had issued a revelation.[47]

Woods accused him of assigning philosophy "too high a place," and Harvey condemned his excessive dependence on the testimony of common sense. But Taylor thought that any disparagement of reason would remove the stigma of guilt from sinners who needed to be told that their infidelity contradicted their right reason. He denied that he was exalting reason above revelation, and he gladly conceded that reason should not step outside its competency. But he thought that a revealed doctrine could not be a mystery, for to speak of a revealed mystery was absurd.[48]

Taylor drew on the Scottish philosophers, especially Dugald Stewart, and he admired Francis Bacon. He drew with equal enthusiasm from eighteenth-century British Christian rationalists like Paley, Clarke, and especially Butler, his favorite theologian. The New Haven theologians saw themselves as rigorously empirical, loyal to the facts of both scripture and consciousness. The final authority for Taylor was the Bible, but he could not imagine any contradiction between biblical revelation and impartial human reason.[49]

Much of his emphasis on reason resulted from his dismay at the success of the Unitarians. He thought that Leonard Woods's debate with Channing had "set back the controversy with Unitarians fifty years." In Taylor's debate in 1822–23 with Andrews Norton, he charged that Unitarians misrepresented the Calvinist view of depravity and free agency. Rather than believing that God creates human beings with a sinful nature, as Norton had charged, Calvinists believed only that all would certainly sin despite their power to the contrary. He also thought that Stuart's debate with Channing over the Trinity had failed to advance the orthodox cause. Toward the end of his life he argued that the three Persons of the Trinity were not merely "general distinctions," as Stuart seemed to say, but rather distinctions best described with personal pronouns. He added that no Unitarian had proved it impossible for God to be three in one sense and one in another.[50]

Another early target was Methodism. From the high atmosphere of New Haven, Methodists seemed "vulgar" and "coarse." The *Christian Spectator* saw some hope in the emergence of Methodist seminaries, but its writers still thought of Methodism as a worrisome movement notorious for its "fervid declaration against human learning" and its promotion of "wild and tumultuous" religious excitement. One of Taylor's first published essays, before he went to Yale, was a polemic against Wesleyan Arminianism in 1818, and during the early years at New Haven, the *Spectator* published numerous criticisms of Wilbur Fisk and other Methodist theologians. As New Haven saw it, the Methodist notion that prevenient grace empowered every soul implied that the soul had no natural ability — and so no obligation — to repent, while it also implied, illogically, an ability to make use — or not make use — of the grace itself. In any case, Methodist prevenient grace did nothing more than restore freedom; it furnished no certainty that any would use it rightly, and to that extent it was no grace. Calvinist opponents of Taylor charged him with Arminianism, but he saw his theology as a safeguard against the Arminian threat.[51]

The third barrier to a reasonable revival — in addition to the Unitarians and the Methodists — came from other Calvinists, not only of the Princeton variety but also other Edwardeans and New England theologians, even Edwards himself insofar as he misconstrued sinfulness and moral agency. Taylor thought that the Princetonians and Edwardean conservatives undercut revivalism and made Calvinism vulnerable to Unitarian and Methodist caricature by clinging, in different ways, to the theory of a sinful nature that determined sinful choices and an act of the Spirit that dominated the soul rather than drawing it into the circle of the reborn through the power of truth.

The New Haven option was a theology of moral government anchored by the conception of a benevolent God who ruled moral agents through law and the "influence of authority." Taylor found sources of inspiration in the work of Edwards, early Edwardeans, and Joseph Butler, but he told his students that "no writer in theology" had made moral government the central theme as he had. His *Lectures on the Moral Government of God* depicted God's aim as "the highest conceivable well-being" of his subjects, attained through the medium of the divine law, which guided free moral agents away from selfishness toward benevolence and happiness. He depicted human life as "a state of moral discipline" designed, as Butler had also argued, "to improve and ultimately to confirm men in virtue and happiness in a future world."[52]

Like the New Divinity theologians, Taylor shifted attention to law, virtue, and obligation. Like the younger Edwards, he said that the atonement did not set aside the demand of the law for obedience. Christ died rather to sustain the authority of the law while making pardon possible for the lawgiver. Taylor's governmental theory of atonement functioned as a spur to "right moral action," including the moral obligation of supreme love for God. Like other Edwardeans, he thought that certain formulations of Calvinism had denied the ability necessary for moral responsibility. Such a denial, he thought, subverted God's authority as a lawgiver, since a system of law presupposed obligation and an ability to obey. Calvinism, properly defined, confirmed that ability and obligation.[53]

The first New Haven controversy — over sin and depravity — began in 1821 when it became known that Chauncy Goodrich had told his students that sin was voluntary, not an innate property of human nature that rendered us sinful before we sinned. To some students it seemed that the Unitarians had infiltrated Yale. Five years later, Eleazar Fitch published two essays that originated as lectures to Yale students, arguing that "sin, in every form and instance, is reducible to the act of a moral agent in which he violates a known rule of duty," and suggesting that moral agents had the power not to sin. To conservative Edwardeans, the essays were disturbing.[54]

In 1828 Taylor delivered the "Concio ad Clerum," or "advice to the clergy" who had gathered at the Yale College chapel. The sermon had the ostensible purpose of reaffirming that "the entire moral depravity of mankind is by nature," but his main point was that depravity was "man's own act, consisting in a free choice of some object rather than God, as his chief good." To say that the depravity was "by nature" meant merely to say that men and women would uniformly "sin and only sin" in every relevant circumstance. Only this view of sin, he urged, could reach the conscience "with its charge of guilt and obligations to duty."[55]

He concluded by criticizing the Hopkinsian conception of sin as a necessary means to the greatest good. Perhaps even God, he said, could not prevent sin in a genuine moral system in which human agency had to be respected in order that the highest good might be attained. New England theologians expressed alarm at the suggestion that God could not prevent sin. Joseph Harvey found it "appalling." Most Edwardeans still thought of sin as the necessary means to the highest good of knowing God as redeemer. Taylor thought that nobody could prove this idea true and that it was repellent because it meant that God punished his creatures for doing what he made it necessary for them to do. Taylor met with the Andover faculty to resolve the question. No resolution could be found.[56]

In saying that sin was voluntary, Taylor was referring to a "permanent principle of action," a continuing elective preference for the world rather than God. He rejected the view that a sinful propensity could be the cause of sin. He thought it circular logic to say that sin caused sin, even though he did think that it was the "nature of the human mind" after the fall to "occasion" universal sin. He insisted that sin was not "physical," an inheritance from Adam altering the natural constitution of the soul. He also rejected imputation, but he did not disengage human sinfulness from the sin of Adam. He rather postulated, in familiar Edwardean fashion, a "constitution" of God by which men and women became sinners by their own act in consequence of Adam's sin. Most other Edwardeans, though, believed that he had jettisoned the doctrine of depravity that he was supposed to have been defending.[57]

The debate over the sinfulness of infants showed how Taylor and his opponents could be a hair's-breadth close and yet miles apart. Taylor said that infants sinned as soon as they became moral agents; they sinned as soon as they could. Tyler and Woods saw unfortunate implications. Were infants born innocent, as Unitarians thought? How could one explain the universality of sin that Taylor himself affirmed? Were infants moral agents at their birth? If not, they were mere animals, outside the economy of salvation. If they were moral agents, they had to be either innocent or guilty, and the only way to preserve the Pauline assertion that all sinned was to say that infants were "sinners from their birth." The questions forced Taylor to clarify. He would neither affirm nor deny that infants were sinful at the instant of their birth, but he conceded by 1833 that they sinned "so early that the interval, if there is an interval, between birth and sin, needs in popular language and ordinary cases, no particular notice." For Taylor's critics, even imperceptible intervals were too long.[58]

The issue lurking beneath the surface was freedom. To say that sin was voluntary meant, for Taylor, that it was chosen and that it was worthy of blame. To remain a Calvinist he had to say that sin was certain; to be an effective revivalist, he had to say that the sinner had the freedom to break from sin. He tried to hold the tension with a formula that became the slogan of the New Haven theology: "certainty with power to the contrary." It was certain that all would sin even though they had the power not to sin. The distinction sounded much like the Edwardean distinction between natural ability and moral inability, which on occasion Taylor seemed to reject. If Edwards defined moral inability as the inability to will opposites at the same time—as Taylor thought he defined it—then not even God, Taylor said, could remove moral inability, and the natural ability to obey God was an "essential nothing." But at other times in his career, early and late, Taylor made full use of the Edwardean distinction, and one can plausibly read the New Haven slogan as an effort to translate it into a more convincing form.[59]

Taylor did want a stronger concept of freedom than Edwards gave him. In 1819 he confided to Lyman Beecher that Edwards had left too many unsolved problems. It was not enough to say, as Edwards had said, that free will was "a power to do as we please or as we will." One could concede a connection between motives and volition and still allow for more freedom than Edwards had granted. In saying that the will was *as* the greatest apparent good, Edwards had not solved the underlying issue: What makes an object appear good to the will? The answer had to lie in the realm of motivation, but here Edwards had stopped short. He argued for a necessary connection between motives and volition—the will was always motivated—but he did not prove that motives necessitated the will.[60]

Taylor wanted to say that in every act the will retained the power to choose the opposite. He accorded to the will a power that Edwards would not have accepted. But Taylor ridiculed, with Edwards, the "notorious absurdities" of a "self-determining power of the will." He rather saw willing as an interaction between the will, other constitutional powers and propensities of the mind, external circumstances, and the moral governance of God. Taylor agreed that the will responded to motives, but the power of the response lay in the will, not in the motive. Moral agents had the power to do even what they did not want to do. Edwards could never have said this.[61]

The second phase of the controversy began in 1829 with Taylor's long review of Gardiner Spring's *Dissertation on the Means of Regeneration*. The pastor of the Presbyterian Brick Church in New York City, Spring was a Hopkinsian who issued the usual Edwardean admonition: since the sinful use the means of grace selfishly, they should not rely on them but rather repent now. Taylor's review of Spring is the main evidence for interpreters who place him among the Old Calvinists. He argued that the means of grace — reflection, prayer, preaching — could lead the sinner to eternal life. Like the Old Calvinists, Taylor said that the change occurred as the Spirit operated on the mind by presenting the motive of divine truth. Like them, he believed that the preacher brought the truth to bear on the sinner's self-love, or desire for happiness, which he and the Old Calvinists distinguished from selfishness.[62]

Taylor's retrieval of the idea of self-love struck his critics as one of his worst ideas. He took it from Dugald Stewart and Joseph Butler, though Edwards's comments on self-love in the sermons on *Charity and its Fruits* also helped convince him that there was a self-love different from selfishness, and his teacher Dwight had described a desire for happiness "inseparable from the rational nature." Taylor argued that the means of grace appealed to this natural desire for happiness. He then said that the use of the means could result in "the suspension of the selfish principle" even before regeneration, in the strictest sense, occurred. As the selfishness faded through the force of the Spirit-driven truth, the mind fell increasingly under "the control of that constitutional desire for happiness which is an original part of our nature." Such a mind was ripe for conversion.[63]

Bennet Tyler told Taylor that self-love was selfish no matter how one might try to redefine it, though he weakened his point by acknowledging that it was not selfish to love oneself "as part of the whole," which was the only opening Taylor needed. But Tyler went on: If the selfish principle faded away before the moment of rebirth, why was it even "necessary that the sinner should be renewed by the power of the Holy Ghost"?[64]

To the frustration of his Edwardean critics, however, Taylor claimed the authority of Edwards. Asahel Nettleton told Samuel Miller at Princeton that

Taylor was merely claiming Edwards on behalf of doctrines that Edwards deplored. But Taylor attempted to enclose his innovations within Edwardean Calvinist boundaries. He continued to teach that God "foreordains whatsoever comes to pass." God's eternal purposes extended to "all actual events, sin not excepted," and free moral agents would "sin in every instance, till their obstinacy in sin is subdued by divine grace." Their sin was not necessary but it was certain. Edwards had occasionally made the same distinction. In defining regeneration as "an act of the will or heart," moreover, Taylor used the language of the exercise scheme while quietly dropping its view of divine efficiency. In thinking of regeneration as the transcending of selfishness, he assumed Edwardean conceptions of sin as selfishness. In defending the use of means, he rejected the Old Calvinist doctrine that sinners had a "duty" to use the means; for Taylor, their only duty was repentance and love for God.[65]

According to his critics, he denied that regeneration was an act of the Spirit, but he replied that he never intended to deny "an immediate or direct agency of the Spirit, on the soul in regeneration." Regeneration was no mere matter of moral suasion, even though the most important part of the Spirit's activity was presenting truth and other motives to the mind: "The raising of the dead *by a word* displays the power of God no less than the same event without this preliminary summons." Taylor would not speak of the Spirit's influence as "irresistible," but he described it, with Dwight, as "unresisted," and then added that this meant "infallibly efficacious." Only through the Spirit would the means of grace be effective, and while Taylor urged the sinful to trust that they would be effective for them, he offered no guarantees. They would be effective for the elect alone: "all who are renewed by the Holy Ghost are elected or chosen of God from eternity, that they should be holy, not on account of foreseen faith or good works, but according to the good pleasure of his will." The saved would "persevere in holiness to the end, and obtain eternal life." It was no wonder that Arminians could not understand why other Edwardeans found Arminianism in Taylor's theology.[66]

Taylor reveled in paradox, and his opponents fumed that it was impossible to pin him down. "Indeed, I am completely nonplussed to see what Dr. Taylor could be at," wrote one of them. "What can be done with a man who will turn upon you at every corner with 'you mistake my meaning.'" He confused people, and the confusion could be seen even within the family to which he was most closely tied by bonds of friendship: the Beechers. Lyman Beecher, who sadly estimated that only about 10 percent of the clergy in Connecticut sympathized with Taylor's views, defended him as a Calvinist. Catharine Beecher, Lyman's daughter, eventually decided that Taylor was no Calvinist at all.[67]

In addition to her interests in education and reform, Catharine Beecher (1800–78) became a theological author as early as 1836, when she published her *Letters on the Difficulties of Religion,* in which she proposed to interpret the Bible in the light of "reason and common sense." Her views at that time were close to Taylor's. Her assessment of reason, her theodicy, her views of happiness and self-love, her admiration for self-denying benevolence, her views of character as the "governing purpose" of the mind, and her critiques of Unitarianism all revealed her affinities with Taylorite theology. The *Quarterly Christian Spectator* accorded the book its praise. By 1857, however, when she published *Common Sense Applied to Religion,* Beecher had left Calvinism behind.[68]

She claimed, however, that her new views of human ability, which she defiantly labeled as Pelagian, represented the position of both the Unitarians and the New Haven theologians. She had become disillusioned with Taylor as a person, believing that he had unjustly defended a former male student who had wronged a young woman in a romantic relationship. She could not have been unaware that she was twisting the knife when she asserted that her Pelagianism came with a New Haven imprimatur. Taylor, close to death, protested that she had misconstrued his theology.[69]

Taylor's opponents thought that Beecher had only brought to public view the heterodoxy that they had long suspected. She was not the only theologian who interpreted Taylor as a closet Pelagian. Long before she wrote *Common Sense Applied to Religion,* the Tylerites and Princetonians had decided that Taylor was a dangerous theologian. His views seemed all the more dangerous to them because they thought they could discern his errors in the raucous revivalism of Charles Grandison Finney. If Finney represented the results of Taylor's attempt at a reasonable Calvinism, the conservatives wanted another style of reason.

The Oberlin Theology

Charles Grandison Finney was an unlikely theologian. A lawyer in Adams, New York, he underwent a religious conversion in 1821, received Presbyterian ordination in 1823, and began to preach the next year as a revivalist for a women's mission society. His reputation initially rested on his "new measures," which included such devices as protracted meetings, the use of a separate "anxious bench" to seat sinners on the verge of conversion, and prayer for the sinful by name. A successful revival in Rochester, New York, in 1825 spread his name throughout the country, but the notoriety of his new measures distanced him from such Edwardean revivalists as Asahel Nettleton and Lyman Beecher, who met with him in 1827 in New Lebanon, New York, in a failed attempt to rein him in. Finney went on to become the best-known revivalist preacher of his day, traveling through the Northeast as well as England and Scotland and serving as the pastor for two large congregations in New York City, first as a Presbyterian, then as a Congregationalist. In 1835 he became the first professor of theology at Oberlin College in Ohio, even though he had never studied at either a college or a seminary.

Finney sympathized with theological populists. In his later career, he associated himself with people of wealth and education, but when he published his *Lectures on Revivals of Religion* (1835), he scorned the "theological trumpery" of the seminaries and praised the "unlearned" Methodist and Baptist ministers who remained ignorant of the sciences but wise in the ways of soul-winning. Throughout his career he accused the seminaries of isolating students from "the common mind" and filling their minds with irrelevant matters, an accusation to which the *Princeton Review* responded by reminding its readers that Finney was a theological amateur lacking in knowledge, grammatical ability, and good taste. Yet when the chance came to teach theology, he welcomed it, and his courses at Oberlin resulted in the publication in 1840 of his *Skeletons of a Course of Theological Lectures* and in 1846–47 of his much enlarged *Lectures on Systematic Theology,* the centerpiece of what became known as the Oberlin theology.[70]

He rarely discussed the sources of his theological ideas. He preferred to think of them as resulting from his study of the Bible and the "workings of my own mind as they were revealed in consciousness." By the time he began to publish theology, however, he was waist-deep in a theological vocabulary drawn from the Edwardeans and the Taylorites. From the inception of his brief theological study with his Princeton-trained pastor, George Gale, he rejected the Calvinism of the Westminster Confession, but in 1827 he read Edwards on revivals and religious affections and by 1828 he had access to the ideas of Taylor, with whom he had private conversations in the early 1830s, though Taylor distanced himself from Finney as early as 1833.[71]

More than one interpreter of Finney has contended that his theology was "no offshoot of New England" but "an independent development from its own root." His contemporaries, however, read him as an Edwardean, whether of the early New England or the New Haven variety. One Edwardean ally of Finney argued in 1832 that he followed in the path of Edwards, Hopkins, and Woods; critics at Princeton saw him as teaching unadorned New Haven doctrines.[72]

When he went to Oberlin, he joined colleagues steeped in the New England traditions. The president, Asa Mahan, had studied at Andover; John Morgan in New Testament had studied under Edward Dorr Griffin at Williams College and Lyman Beecher at Lane; Henry Cowles in Old Testament had worked with Taylor at Yale, as had his brother John. It was not surprising that the New England traditions provided Finney a language to express what might have been his own independent conclusions. He rejected a great many of the New Divinity ideas. He denied Hopkins's idea that saints should be resigned to damnation, Emmons's suggestion that God was the only proper agent in the universe, and Edwards's depiction of the moral bondage of the will. But New Divinity ideas of virtue, moral governance, and the obligation of immediate repentance permeated his theology, which also had several parallels with Taylor's thought. When Finney and the Oberlin theologians commended Christian perfection, they stepped decisively outside the New England Calvinist traditions, but even this departure carried traces of New England influence. The Oberlin theologians still lived within the Edwardean culture even though they stretched it to the breaking point.[73]

Finney also stretched the rational side of rational orthodoxy as far as it would go. While he viewed the Bible as his ultimate authority — inspired and infallible — he stood in the evidential tradition, confirming biblical authority through the force of reason. He had high confidence in natural theology, insisting that reason could prove not only the existence of God as a benevolent personal moral governor but also the reasonableness of atonement, moral obligation, freedom, repentance, and divine election. Devoted to the Scottish philosophy, he argued that most nineteenth-century theology hid the truths of the gospel "under a false philosophy" of the mind, and he urged clergy interested in either reading scripture properly or converting sinners efficiently to "study well the laws of mind" as the Scots described them. He would not "believe when revelation seemed to conflict with the affirmations of reason."[74]

Like Taylor, Finney thought that a rational theology would take its cue from a proper theory of moral government: "I could not but perceive that the true idea of moral government had no place in the theology of the church; and, on the contrary, that underlying the whole system were assumptions that all government was physical, as opposed to moral, and that sin and holiness are rather natural attributes than moral, voluntary acts." He said that the "key" to his system was his view of moral law and moral obligation. The moral law, founded in the divine reason, guided the right actions of both human beings and God. The ground of the obligation to obey it was "the intrinsic value of the well-being of God and the universe." Adopting the Edwardean theory of virtue, Finney saw moral law as demanding that every moral agent promote well-being through disinterested benevolence. True religion was obedience to the moral law, and the moral law demanded love. This was a truth of revelation and reason.[75]

More than any other theologian of his generation, Finney translated theology into the vocabulary of moral science. His theology of moral government consisted of a series of maneuvers to uphold the obligation of immediate and persisting obedience to moral law. Rather than contrast the law and the gospel, he urged that the design of the gospel was to establish the law and enforce obedience to it. Throughout his career he criticized Universalists because their doctrine removed a motive to obedience. He adopted the governmental theory of the atonement because it precluded the Universalist claim that Christ had satisfied the demands of the law for all. Employing the language of the younger Edwards, Finney said that the atonement simply satisfied "public justice" by making it possible for God to pardon the repentant without undermining moral government and obedience to moral law.[76]

The main opponent for Finney was Old School Calvinism. Like the Edwardean exercisers and like Taylor, he rejected any notion that moral depravity referred to a sinful nature derived from the imputation of Adam's sin or the inheritance of Adam's nature. The taste scheme, as Finney found it in Leonard Woods, was equally unacceptable. The idea of an inherited sinful nature, even a sinful taste, invited the charge that Calvinist theology condemned people for sin they did not commit. Equally important, the idea made it impossible to blame the sinful for their refusal to obey the moral law. Finney rather took the position, with Taylor and the exercisers, that moral depravity was a "voluntary attitude of the mind." It was the choice of self as the ultimate end.[77]

This meant agreement with Emmons and Taylor on the depravity of infants. Finney said that infants had no moral character until they transgressed, and he had no idea when this might occur, though he thought it "much earlier than is generally supposed." He conceded that a depravation of body and mind after the fall gave the sensibility, or "desire," a disproportionate influence over the will and intellect — a concession that Taylor too had made — but he, also like Taylor, refused to assign this weakness a moral character until the moment of voluntary disobedience to moral law. Sin consisted in choice.[78]

So also did regeneration. Finney's views about rebirth evoked opposition after 1831, when he preached in Boston a sermon titled "Sinners Bound to Change Their Own Hearts." Describing sin as a voluntary act, he told the sinful that they had the obligation, and so the ability, to change their ultimate choice from selfishness to benevolence. His sermon erased, as Taylor had also erased, the Hopkinsian distinction between regeneration and conversion. When the Edwardean Asa Rand charged that he had reduced regeneration to a mere act of the will and made it sound as if the sinner could "put off [depravity] as easily as persons change their plans of business," Finney responded with the Taylorite argument that the idea of the Spirit's "physical" agency undercut the demand for immediate obedience.[79]

Like Emmons and Taylor, but with more pronounced emphasis, he qualified the doctrine of justification by making it conditional on obedience to the law. God could not "justify one who does not yield a present and full obedience to the moral law." As a moral governor, God had no right to justify the sinful; God could justify only the obedient. Any suggestion to the contrary was "sheer antinomianism." Finney disliked the doctrine of justification through faith alone; for him, sanctification was not merely evidence of justification but a condition of it. God justified only the sanctified, the obedient, who were consecrated fully to God through their disinterested love.[80]

He repeated themes common to Taylor and the Old Calvinists, including the definition of self-love as an involuntary and hence sinless desire for happiness to which the revivalist could appeal, the insistence that regeneration occurred when the Spirit presented truth to the mind as a motive for decision, and the promotion of the means of grace. He became notorious in orthodox circles for the way in which he defined a revival as "the result of the right use of the appropriate means." Like Taylor, however, he refused to tell sinners that by using the means they did their duty. Their duty was to repent, to submit instantly. Finney did not exactly say, with Hopkins, that the sinner became worse in using the means, but he did say that sinners who used the means of grace risked a "hardened heart."[81]

On the question of the freedom of the will, Finney resisted Edwards and the Edwardeans. The dogma of the "necessitated will," he said, had distorted Christian teaching. He criticized Edwards for confusing volition and desire and for denying moral agency by subjecting the will to "the objective motive." Granted, the will always acted in view of motives; but the motives did not necessitate the will. Finney found his evidence for freedom in the appeal to consciousness, which showed that moral agents had the power to originate and decide their own choices and exercise their own "sovereignty" in every instance of choice, including moral decisions. In addressing questions about the will, Edwards had made "distinctions without a difference."[82]

One such meaningless distinction was the Edwardean description of moral and natural inability. As early as 1831 Finney emphasized, with the New Divinity theologians, the sinner's full natural ability to repent. He described the "cannot" of inability as no more than a "will not." By 1837 he was talking even of "a natural ability to be perfect." Sharing Taylor's dislike of the Wesleyan notion of "gracious ability," he insisted that the ability had to be "natural" if the failure to exercise it was to be blameworthy. But never in the early writings did Finney say that he understood natural ability in the same way Edwards did, and by 1846 he decided that "the natural ability of the Edwardean school is no ability at all." A true definition of natural ability had to include "the power to will," indeed, the power to obey or oppose the moral law. Edwards's distinction was "nothing but an empty name, a metaphysico-theological fiction."[83]

Yet for all this, Finney did not abandon everything Calvinist. While he said that the will had, in principle, the power to choose the good, he also said that sinners never, in fact, obeyed "without the gracious influence of the Holy Spirit." This sounded faintly like Edwardean moral inability, for even if the Spirit only lured and persuaded, Finney conceded that the will would not move forward without the lure, and unlike the Wesleyans, he added that only the elect would obey.[84]

He tried to remove some of the scandal of election by speaking of God's choosing the elect "upon condition" of divine foreknowledge—a typical Arminian move—but then he added that God "eternally designed or intended" the sanctification and salvation of "certain persons." What God foreknew was that "he could secure" their faith, repentance, and perseverance and that their salvation would serve the interest of the kingdom. Election logically preceded foreknowledge in the sense that God's knowledge of who would be saved had to follow his determination to save them. Finney spoke of both election and reprobation as "certain" from all eternity. And although in 1831 he questioned the doctrine of perseverance, by 1846 he was writing that the true saints of God "certainly" would persevere. This was not traditional Calvinism, but it was also not Arminian doctrine in the Methodist sense.[85]

At one decisive point, though, Finney and the Oberlin theologians left the Calvinist tradition, even if they did it partly by amplifying Edwardean premises. What identified the Oberlin theology in the Protestant religious world was its allegiance to perfectionist doctrine. Finney became interested in perfectionism as early as 1833, and he was soon reading not only the writings of Wesley but also the essays of John Humphrey Noyes, who would later establish the perfectionist Oneida community. He talked with Noyes in New York, though he later exerted great effort to distinguish his perfectionist teaching from the "antinomian" variety that legitimated Oneida's sexual experimentation. His move to Oberlin in 1835 brought him into the midst of an intense discussion of entire sanctification with Asa Mahan, Henry Cowles, and other faculty and students. Preaching at the Broadway Tabernacle in the winter of 1836–37, Finney announced that Christian perfection was attainable.[86]

Initially the Oberlin theologians sounded like Methodists, and Mahan acknowledged that the earliest formulations were cast in Methodist terms: perfection was a matter of intention, a "second blessing." Some of the Oberlin faculty wrote of it as a "baptism of the Spirit," a phrase characteristic of Methodist writers who adopted the language of John Fletcher. Mahan felt drawn to Wesleyan terminology, and his *Scripture Doctrine of Christian Per-*

fection (1839) used Wesley, though the book also employed New Divinity ideas about benevolence, natural ability, and obedience to moral law. As he became fonder of Wesleyan ideas, he and Finney moved apart. The Wesleyans criticized Finney's perfectionism as legalistic and tainted with ideas of natural ability; Finney described the Methodist doctrine as a theory about "states of the sensibility" rather than the will, and he disliked the ideas of original sin and gracious ability in Wesleyan doctrine. Because perfection for the Oberlin theologians meant entire obedience to the moral law, it also had little in common with the perfectionism of Noyes, who felt that perfection elevated the Christian above the obligations of law.[87]

By Christian perfection Finney meant "perfect obedience to the law of God," or "perfect, disinterested, impartial benevolence." Every sinner had the natural ability to be perfect—it required no more than the right use of the natural powers. The only hindrance was unwillingness, and since natural ability for Finney included moral ability, the sinner—and the Christian—had no excuse. In principle, perfect obedience was "possible on the ground of natural ability." In fact, the imperfect were wholly indisposed to use their natural powers rightly "without the grace of God." It was therefore always Christ who secured the entire sanctification of the Christian. But perfection was "attainable in this life."[88]

Finney appealed to biblical texts to make the case, though he also appealed to mental philosophy, especially after an Oberlin graduate named William Cochran introduced the doctrine of "the simplicity of moral action." Finney distinguished this teaching from the doctrine of entire sanctification, but the two ideas supported one another. Since the will could not at the same time make opposite choices, it followed that "in the choice of one ultimate end," the will was fully conformed to that end and no other. A supreme preference for the good of "being in general" precluded the contrary preference. This was an idea fully in accord with the conviction of Emmons that sin and holiness were opposite affections that could not inhabit one and the same volition, so that the will was either wholly virtuous or wholly sinful. It bore the either/or mentality of the Edwardean revivalist.[89]

Finney linked his perfectionism with his millennialism, suggesting once that the church must embrace right views of perfection before the millennium would come. During the millennial excitements of the early 1840s he tried to convince William Miller that his premillennial predictions were wrong, but Finney's millennialism rarely appeared in his theological works, and it paled in comparison with his interest in Christian perfection and disinterested benevolence. The idea of benevolence helped make Oberlin a center for the reforming movements of the early nineteenth century.[90]

Although the perfectionist preoccupations faded at Oberlin, they lived on in the later nineteenth-century holiness movements, which had not only Wesleyan but also Oberlin roots — and thus a connection to antebellum Edwardeanism. The Presbyterian William E. Boardman (1810–86) would read Finney and Mahan and lead a movement in quest of the "Higher Christian Life," which Boardman promoted in 1858 with a book of that title. Asa Mahan would take part in the "Keswick Movement" that propagated holiness ideas in England and influenced holiness movements in the United States. Somewhere in the deep background of even the holiness movements stood the unlikely figure of Jonathan Edwards.

A Waning Tradition

When Henry Boynton Smith (1815–77) lectured at Andover in 1849, he signaled some of the changes that would soon push the Edwardean questions to the margins of theological interest: "We are compelled to meet questions to which our theories about sovereignty, virtue, and free agency can give no definite response. Men are asking, What is Christianity as distinct from an ethical system? Who and what is Christ? . . . The questions of our time, in short, do not bear upon the point, whether the doctrines of the Christian system are in harmony with the truths of ethics and mental philosophy; but rather upon the point, what is the real nature of Christianity, what are its essential characteristics?" Questions of virtue and will, he told his audience, "have chiefly determined the character of our theological systems and parties." It was time to move in other directions.[91]

Smith represented a new generation. A student of Leonard Woods at Andover and Enoch Pond at Bangor, he also traveled in 1837 to Europe and studied with F. G. A. Tholuck in Halle and August Neander in Berlin. Even before he left America he decided that theologians should "make Christ the central point," and in Germany he learned to think of Christianity as "an organic, diffusive, plastic and triumphant force in human history," with "the Person of Jesus Christ" at its center.[92]

After teaching moral and mental philosophy at Amherst, Smith moved in 1850 to the chair of church history at Union Theological Seminary in New York, the seminary of the New School Presbyterians. Four years later he ascended to the chair of theology. But neither Woods nor Taylor would have understood the mental world that shaped Smith's theology. For him, history rather than mental science became the ancillary discipline; Christology rather than anthropology became the substantial center. Organic rather than mechanistic metaphors guided his thought. Smith turned his attention to the "history of the progress of the kingdom of God" rather than to the morphology of salvation. Although he rejected German idealism, he studied it closely and learned much from its view of history as a theater of conflicts moving toward higher forms of unity, not a mere background for static truths. Smith came to believe that each era had to state things in its own way, and in his era, this meant attention to historical and developmental ways of thinking.[93]

Yet Smith, who remained in many ways a traditional Calvinist, illustrated the ways in which Edwardean residues continued to linger even within the changing theologies of mid-century America. Smith retained an interest in the New England theologians and wrote a subtle essay on Emmons. He continued to think of Edwards as "our greatest American divine," though for him the seminal work was no longer *Freedom of the Will* but the *History of the Work of Redemption,* which he saw as anticipating the new historical consciousness. Although he no longer made theology turn on mental science, he continued to defend an Edwardean conception of the will and the distinction between natural and moral ability. He maintained a governmental theory of atonement, a focus on divine benevolence, and a conception of virtue as love.[94]

Elsewhere one finds the same blending of isolated Edwardean ideas and the new historical consciousness. The only pure holdout was Edwards Amasa Park, who stayed on at Andover until 1880, though he felt increasingly marginal with each passing year. At Yale, George Park Fisher, a student of both Park and Taylor, continued after the Civil War to praise Taylor's theology as "an important contribution to theological science," though he could no longer accept all the New Haven solutions. Edwardean ideas continued to appear even in the work of Samuel Harris (1814–99), who remained on the Yale faculty until 1895. Both Fisher and Harris, however, shared Smith's interest in historical development to such an extent that the Edwardean themes faded away. By the time they taught at Yale, one could no longer speak of an Edwardean culture.[95]

What did remain was the sense that theology was both rational and practical. Henry Boynton Smith's 1849 essay on "The Relations of Faith and Philosophy" still urged the utility of natural theology, assumed that external and internal evidences proved the authenticity of the biblical revelation, and accorded to reason the authority to test revelation but not to determine its substance. Faith, he said, was "perfectly rational," and faith and philosophy were "inherently at one." Defining theology as "a science both theoretical and practical," he still saw the great task of systematic theology as the "reconciliation between faith and philosophy." On this point, the Edwardeans — and almost everyone else — fully agreed.[96]

18

"True Calvinism" Defended

The Old School Calvinists of the Presbyterian churches positioned themselves as the defenders of the true Calvinist tradition against critics and revisionists on every side. Appealing to the authority of the Bible, the Westminster Confession, and the seventeenth-century Reformed scholastics, they expounded a theology that set them against innovation. But Old School Calvinism was more than merely a repristination of scholastic ideas; it bore the marks of institutional and regional rivalries, social attitudes, party alignments, and changing philosophical assumptions, and as a result it not only differed from the Old Calvinism of eighteenth-century New England but also never itself coalesced into a unified movement.

Because Old School Calvinists prided themselves on their allegiance to the seventeenth-century confessional standards, their thought illustrates how the quest for reasonableness could permeate even the most conservative of theological movements. Schooled in the subtleties of Scottish Realism, they used its tenets to subvert what they saw as the more insidious rationalism of European and American innovators. Archibald Alexander of Princeton made explicit a common presupposition of the group when he argued that the basis of theological error was almost always metaphysical. They had every confidence that the epistemology and mental science of the Scottish school confirmed the truths of the Westminster Confession.[1]

The Old School theologians began in the 1820s to recognize themselves as a party arrayed against an innovative New School. Within the next thirty years, they divided into three factions. The most influential, led by Archibald Alexander, Samuel Miller, and Charles Hodge at Princeton Seminary, formulated a distinctive "Princeton theology" designed to recover the best of the scholastic tradition. Conservative in both thought and temperament, they nonetheless found that their efforts to maintain harmony within the denomination drew from more zealous partisans the charge that they were "moderates," "compromisers," and "trembling brethren."[2]

The second faction, allies but also critics of Princeton, formed a group that Hodge called the "ultras" or "the Philadelphia Junto." Led by Ashbel Green, the pastor of Philadelphia's Second Presbyterian Church, they had few theological differences with Princeton but distrusted its spirit of moderation. They sometimes formed alliances with the third group, the southern conservatives, who took their cues from James Henley Thornwell (1812–62), at Columbia Theological Seminary in South Carolina, Robert J. Breckinridge at Danville Seminary in Kentucky, and Robert Lewis Dabney (1820–98), of Union Seminary in Virginia. The southerners disagreed on important points with Princeton, but they also disagreed with each other.[3]

In a land where, as they saw it, "public sentiment" swayed the scepter, all three parties of Old School Calvinists set themselves against theological populists. Alexander bemoaned the emergence of preachers "destitute of literary . . . qualifications," and Hodge decried the "flood of uneducated, undisciplined men" pretending to be theological teachers. Hodge could insist as much as any theological populist that "the gospel was intended for plain people." He worried that the Presbyterians seemed unable to reach the poor and uneducated, and he denied forcefully that the illiterate had to depend on the learned for saving truth. But he also believed that the truth was always "repulsive to the majority," that "the mass of the people" were "incompetent to judge in doctrinal matters," and that when uneducated amateurs ventured into deep theology, the "consequences were disastrous." Miller reminded his students that they would serve men and women "who, according to popular language, are your *inferiors*," and though he urged them to serve without condescension, his comment showed the gulf that separated the Princeton ethos from the populist cultures.[4]

Presbyterians, both Old School and New, assumed leadership in the professionalizing of theology. As a full-time theologian who never held a position outside the academy, Hodge joined the ranks of a new kind of American religious leadership. And as theology moved from the parishes to the seminaries, rivalries among the schools intensified theological disagreements. Princeton saw Andover, for instance, as dedicated to making "Old-School doctrines appear ridiculous and odious," and it viewed Yale as an enemy of orthodoxy. Old School seminaries competed also among themselves; the southerners at Union, Danville, and Columbia tried to "break the charm" of Princeton's "ascendancy," and northern ultraconservatives kept Princeton on the defensive by threatening to create new schools whenever the Princeton faculty strayed. Other seminaries, including Auburn in New York, Lane in Ohio, and Union in New York City, became centers of New School thought arrayed against the Old School institutions.[5]

Hopkinsians, New Schoolers, and Ultras

The Old School party formed its identity in reaction against the innovations of New England, but it was selective in its attitudes toward Edwardeans. As a young theologian, Alexander toured New England, preached for the aging Samuel Hopkins, and met with Nathanael Emmons and Stephen West, whom he continued to describe as "eminently pious men." Hodge made a similar tour and had long conversations with Nathaniel William Taylor and Moses Stuart. He admired Stuart despite the theological gap between them. Thornwell planned to study languages at Andover, visited the school briefly, disliked it, and moved for a year to Harvard, where he hated Unitarian theology but immersed himself in German and Hebrew. Ashbel Green's visit to the region led to a lifelong distaste for New England's theological diversity.[6]

With some reservations, the Old School nonetheless tried to claim Jonathan Edwards. The young Alexander considered himself a follower, employed the distinction between natural and moral ability, and conceded later that Edwards had done more than anyone else to give "complexion" to Calvinist theology in America. As he grew older, however, he gradually discarded his Edwardeanism. Hodge praised Edwards's *Religious Affections* and *Original Sin* because they distinguished moral dispositions from moral acts — a distinction important to the Old School because it countered New Haven doctrines — and he insisted that Edwards would have stood with Princeton against most of the principles of the Edwardean movements. But Hodge could never have been mistaken for an Edwardean. Although the Old Schoolers usually proved reluctant to criticize the great Edwards too harshly, they remained suspicious.[7]

Most of them would have cheered Hodge's criticisms. Hodge disliked Edwards's metaphysical idealism and his doctrine of continual creation. He thought that Edwards's doctrine of God veered toward pantheism. Unlike the young Alexander, he dismissed the distinction between natural and moral ability, insisting that the unregenerate had no ability whatever to change their hearts. Hodge thought that Edwards's treatise on the *Freedom of the Will* failed to make necessary distinctions — between willing and desiring, for example — and that Edwards used the term "necessity" too loosely. He distrusted the assertion, characteristic of Edwards, that religion consisted in holy affections, and he never agreed with Edwards's definition of true virtue as disinterested benevolence. He also thought that Edwards had been careless in writing about imputation.[8]

The Old School had even greater reservations about Hopkinsians. Presbyterians had struggled since 1798, when Hezekiah Balch of Greenville College in Tennessee drew the ire of both the Synod of the Carolinas and the General Assembly by disseminating Hopkinsian ideas. The issue returned after 1811, when Ezra Stiles Ely, a hospital chaplain in New York, published his *Contrast Between Calvinism and Hopkinsianism*, charging that every distinctive idea of Hopkins supplanted a Calvinist truth. Five years later, as a pastor in Philadelphia, Ely issued a letter against Hopkinsian error. In 1817 the General Assembly refused to issue the blanket condemnation that Ely desired, but spirits were so high that in 1818 Hopkinsians and their opponents in New York founded rival education societies. In 1824, John H. Rice in Virginia complained that the "mighty ado made in Princeton and New York about Hopkinsianism" refused to go away. It created disturbances elsewhere as well. At Columbia Seminary in South Carolina, the new professor of biblical languages, George Howe, tried in 1830 to teach from Leonard Woods's *Theological Lectures*, and it took a decision of the Board of Visitors to confirm Howe's orthodoxy.[9]

It was hard to know what to do about Edwardeans. The southern conservatives and the Philadelphia ultras did not want to tolerate Edwardean error. Thornwell could describe Edwards as a "great man," but he lamented his fuzziness on imputation, and he thought that Hopkinsian "excesses" had "departed widely from the simplicity of the Bible." But Princeton counseled moderation. Alexander wrote a reserved but approving review of Woods's book on depravity, and he tried to distinguish various forms of Hopkinsianism, some acceptable, others not. Samuel Miller sanctioned Ely's critique, but he angered ultras by saying later that he would not hesitate to ordain the right kind of Hopkinsian.[10]

By 1835, Hodge thought the better course was to recognize but minimize the Hopkinsian danger. He had little sympathy for the theology, and he enumerated its multiple errors: that the sinful shared in Adam's sin only by consent to it, that God imputed guilt to sinners only because they sinned, that depravity resided in the will but not the understanding, and that the unregenerate would not profit by means of grace. He disliked Hopkins's claim that repentance came before faith and the love of God before justification; and he censured the Hopkinsian insistence that the faithful would accept their own damnation if it served God's glory. He thought it wrong to say that disinterested benevolence was the highest moral good, and he considered the governmental theory of atonement unbiblical. He used Emmons as an example of speculation run wild. But he saw Hopkinsianism as a spent force: "Where are the Hopkinsians and Emmonites of former days?" he asked in 1835. Their doctrines, he answered, were "fast sinking." Their errors were not serious enough to split the church.[11]

By that time, the denomination was falling apart. As early as 1824 a letter in *The Christian Advocate* characterized the conflicting sides as the Old School and the New School, and the labels came to designate two theological parties. In 1837 the church divided, and one reason was the quarrel over theology. It was not the sole reason. Presbyterians also fought about slavery, interdenominational voluntary societies, social reform, and the Plan of Union by which they had agreed in 1801 to ally themselves with the Congregationalists in the West. Yet the theological differences inflamed others. Part of the Presbyterian dilemma, however, was that the Old School could not agree about exactly what New School theology was.[12]

Princeton's position was that the truly objectionable New School theology came from New Haven and the classrooms of Nathaniel William Taylor. The Princetonians also thought that this Taylorite theology had only a few advocates in the denomination and that the ultras were mistaken in going after all Edwardeans and Hopkinsians as if they were guilty of New Haven's more serious errors. The more extreme Old Schoolers, however, thought that almost all New School theology was a heretical jumble of Hopkinsian and Taylorite ideas, and that it had no place within the denomination.

The problem was that New Schoolers cultivated ambiguity. The New School theologians sought, like the New Englanders, to craft a version of Calvinism that would encourage evangelistic appeals to the unconverted. They shared the Edwardean tendency to use the distinction between moral and natural ability as a guide by which to revise doctrines that seemed incompatible with this end. They claimed to stand within the Calvinist tradition, even to represent it more faithfully than their Old School antagonists, but to protect themselves from accusations of heresy they avoided precision. Lyman Beecher, himself numbered among the New School partisans, observed that the term "new school" was "like fog," a label floating about "in a sort of palpable obscure."[13]

For the most part, the New School theologians were simply Presbyterian Edwardeans. Nathan S. S. Beman (1785–1871), a graduate of Middlebury

College in Vermont and a pastor in Troy, New York, came to be regarded by many as the New School leader. His chief theological work, *Four Sermons on the Doctrine of the Atonement* (1825), expounded the governmental theory, declared the distinction between natural ability and moral inability to be "all-important in preaching the gospel," defined sin as "voluntary bondage," and defended the early Edwardean view that the means of grace were beneficial only when they were used rightly. He wanted to ensure that the views of Edwards, Stephen West, and Edward Dorr Griffin reached a popular audience within the denomination.[14]

Albert Barnes, who became for the Old School a symbol of New School deviance, also remained within Edwardean boundaries. His sermon on "The Way of Salvation" raised no eyebrows when he first preached it in Morristown, New Jersey, in 1829, but it provoked heresy charges when he moved into Old School territory in 1830 as the pastor of Philadelphia's First Presbyterian Church. The Old School ultras, led by William Engles (1797–1867) of Philadelphia, editor of *The Presbyterian,* and George Junkin (1790–1868), the president of Lafayette College in Pennsylvania, charged him with multiple errors. In their view his sermon denied original sin, human inability, a vicarious atonement, and the imputation of Christ's righteousness to the elect. A series of trials made it clear, however, that Barnes simply denied that sinfulness resulted from imputation, defined inability as an "indisposition" (a moral inability) rather than a natural incapacity, taught the governmental theory of atonement, and questioned the idea that Christ had suffered the penalty of the law. His quarrel was with the "philosophical views" of the seventeenth-century federal theology, and he claimed the authority of Edwards in making his points. In 1831 the General Assembly merely admonished him for a few unguarded expressions, and in 1836 it acquitted him of heresy charges against his *Notes on Romans,* an acquittal that helped split the church.[15]

Lyman Beecher (1775–1863) was even harder to pin down. Moving back and forth between Congregational and Presbyterian churches, he had been a close friend and theological ally of Nathaniel William Taylor before moving from New England to Cincinnati in 1832 to become the president of Lane Seminary and the pastor of the Second Presbyterian Church. Having served earlier as the pastor of the Hanover Street Church in Boston, where he tried to defend Calvinism against its cultured Unitarian despisers, he decided that "the progress of mental philosophy" justified theological revision, and his Boston sermon on "The Faith Once Delivered to the Saints" advanced the familiar New England theses: natural ability, moral inability, the voluntary nature of sin, and governmental atonement. Like Taylor, he promoted "the use of means" by which the Spirit could apply truth to the sinful mind. The revivalist

Asahel Nettleton confided to Beecher that "we do preach moral obligation and dependence different from many of our old divines — that in some things the Calvinism of Connecticut or New England has undergone an important change." But Nettleton was a critic of Taylor, so he was not suggesting that either he or Beecher was a Taylorite, and even Ashbel Green in Philadelphia conceded at the time that the sermon could still be called Calvinist.[16]

When he published his *Views in Theology* in 1836 to defend himself against the heresy charges of another Cincinnati pastor, Beecher stuck to his Edwardeanism, though with Taylorite nuances, but rather than accenting its differences from Westminster Calvinism he now emphasized the similarities. He still insisted on natural ability and moral inability; affirmed original sin as a "bias or tendency" to actual sin while insisting that depravity was voluntary; denied that sin resulted from imputation; and described regeneration as a turn from love of self to love of God, effected by the supernatural agency of the Spirit, though not by direct omnipotent power without the agency of the word. One could find traces of Taylor's innovations, as when Beecher claimed that free choice implied the possibility of a choice to the contrary or when he insisted on the instrumentality of truth and the means of grace in regeneration. But he also affirmed, like Taylor in his more conservative moods, the divine decrees, particular election, effectual calling, and perseverance. He claimed Edwards, Bellamy, John Witherspoon, Dwight, and Andrew Fuller as the authors who had formed his theology, and though he should have added Taylor to the list, his self-assessment otherwise sounds plausible. More than anything else, he was a product of the Edwardean culture.[17]

The fourth prominent New School theologian was George Duffield (1794–1868), a graduate of the University of Pennsylvania who preached at the Presbyterian Church in Carlisle, Pennsylvania, before moving in 1838 to Detroit, where he led the First Presbyterian Church for thirty years. The Old Schoolers saw his *Spiritual Life, or Regeneration* (1832) as a channel for Taylorite ideas, and the Presbytery of Carlisle condemned the book. When Duffield cited authorities, however, he cited not Taylor but Timothy Dwight and Andrew Fuller. Like Taylor, he criticized the idea of "physical depravity," preferring to define depravity as "morally certain" but voluntary exercises of selfishness on the part of everyone "capable of moral action." Like Taylor he criticized Edwards and the conservative Edwardeans for defining regeneration as the creation of a "new principle" in the soul; Duffield thought of it as "an act or exercise." Like Taylor, moreover, he made much of the soul's instinctive desire for happiness. But he did not use Taylor's other catchphrases; he criticized the Taylorite theodicy; he took an older Edwardean rather than a Taylorite view of the means of grace, emphasizing the futility of using them with a sinful heart; and unlike Taylor he grounded his revisions on an explicit defense of the distinction between natural ability and moral inability. Like both Taylor and the Edwardeans, his chief goal was to confront the sinful with the demand for immediate repentance.[18]

With such ambiguity characteristic of New School theology, it was no surprise that the Old School found it hard to specify the origins of the problem, but by the time the denomination split it was clear that the ultras wanted to rid the Presbyterians of all Edwardean influence, not merely of Taylorite theology. They condemned the Edwardean distinction between natural and moral ability, the Edwardean dismissal of imputation, and the Edwardean theory of atonement. George Junkin thought that imputation was "fundamental," and William Engles tried to save it by implying that the race literally sinned in Adam, a view dismissed by Princeton but later defended by the Old Schooler Samuel J. Baird, a pastor in Woodbury, New Jersey, who wrote the history of the New School from the Old School perspective. Baird was open about the ultraconservatives' distaste for Edwards and his followers. The split occurred, he wrote, because "the teachings of Edwards were, in their consequences, fatal to the gospel."[19]

The Princeton Theology

Archibald Alexander spoke for the Princetonians when he explained that they followed the "old moderate plan, teaching the old doctrines of Calvinism, but not disposed to consider every man a heretic who differs in some few points with us." It was slightly ironic, therefore, that the Princeton theology came to epitomize for many the forces of archconservatism in antebellum theology. The Princetonians did pride themselves on their conservatism. Looking back at the end of his career, Charles Hodge took satisfaction in saying that no new idea ever originated at Princeton Seminary. But they also viewed themselves as using the tools of modern philosophy to show that conservative Calvinism was the most reasonable option available.[20]

Three theologians set the tone of the Princeton theology. Archibald Alexander became in 1812 the school's first professor after having presided over Hampden-Sydney College in Virginia and served churches in Virginia and Philadelphia. Educated at Liberty Hall Academy in Virginia under William Graham, a Witherspoon student who nonetheless encouraged the reading of Edwards, Alexander combined Reformed revivalism with an interest in the logic of the seventeenth-century scholastics and a yearning to face down the enlightenment. He distanced himself from his early Edwardean views after his New England tour in 1801 and his association with Ashbel Green in Philadelphia, but he continued to admire Edwards's piety, especially when contrasted with the speculative refinements of the later Edwardeans. He wrote extensively on the evidences of Christianity and the authenticity of the scripture as well as on moral science and biblical criticism, but his early attraction to revivalist piety also found expression in his *Thoughts on Religious Experience* (1841), in which he analyzed the experience of conversion.[21]

Samuel Miller graduated from the University of Pennsylvania and served churches in New York City before joining Alexander at the seminary in 1813 as the professor of church history. He had made a name for himself in 1804 with his *Brief Retrospect of the Eighteenth Century*. His defense of Presbyterian polity against the Episcopalian John Henry Hobart gave him a further reputation as a controversialist. He stayed in close touch with the ultraconservatives, and his associations helped draw Princeton closer to the conservative theological currents in the denomination.

Charles Hodge (1797–1878), the leading Princetonian, was a graduate of both the college and the seminary. As a child he had learned the catechism under Ashbel Green, but his dearest friend and mentor was Archibald Alexander, who served as a guide in both theology and piety. He shared Alexander's love for the seventeenth-century scholastics. But Hodge also stood in an eighteenth-century American tradition. His *Constitutional History of the Presbyterian Church* (1839–40) made it clear that he found his chief American precursors among the eighteenth-century Presbyterian Old Side theologians who had resisted Hopkinsian errors, opposed the excesses of revivalism, and battled for the authority of Reformed confessions. In their struggles he found a resonance with his own.[22]

Hodge was among the handful of American theologians with graduate-level training at European universities. After accepting a position as a tutor at Princeton Seminary in 1820 and moving into the professorship of oriental and biblical literature in 1822, he traveled in 1826 to Paris, then to Germany, where he studied almost two years at Halle and Berlin, working closely with Heinrich Gesenius on ancient languages and forming a close bond with F. G. A. Tholuck, one of the "mediating" theologians who tried to harmonize traditional doctrine with modern critical thought and who confirmed for Hodge the lesson he had learned from Alexander: that "truth and piety are intimately related."[23]

He returned in 1828 to Princeton, where, as an editor, he turned the *Biblical Repertory and Princeton Review* into one of the most learned journals of the era, contributing 142 essays of his own that covered almost all the topics of academic theological debate. As a lecturer, he produced not only exegetical commentaries but also crafted a theological system. His lectures as professor of exegetical and didactic theology—a chair he assumed in 1840—would, at the end of his career, form the chapters of his *Systematic Theology* (1871–72), which he did not publish earlier only because the trustees of the seminary convinced him that students would not come to Princeton if they had access to his theology elsewhere.[24]

The Princetonians saw themselves as the architects of a biblical theology pitted against two extreme positions that Alexander called "rationalism" and "fanaticism" and Hodge called "rationalism" and "mysticism." Theologians of the extremes, who in Hodge's view dwelt especially in Germany, turned away from an infallibly inspired Bible to reason and experience as their norms. In contrast, the Princeton theology affirmed a doctrine of biblical infallibility, "plenary" in the sense that it extended to every book and every word, not merely to the conceptual substance. The Princetonians rested their doctrine on three distinctions. Hodge distinguished between revelation, which imparted knowledge, and inspiration, which ensured its infallibility. He also distinguished the autographs written by the biblical authors from the later manuscript copies, in which he acknowledged variations and trivial errors. Only the autographs—no longer available—could claim infallibility. Finally, he distinguished the secular and scientific "opinions" of the biblical writers, which they shared with their age, from their "official" or inspired "teaching." This meant for him, as for Alexander, that the biblical authors, whatever their opinions might have been, "taught" no error on secular and scientific matters, even though their writings might have reflected an erroneous science. He never formulated the criteria for distinguishing their opinions from their teachings. The task of the theologian, in any case, was simply to arrange systematically "the facts revealed in the word of God."[25]

Such views about biblical inspiration have often defined the Princeton theology, but the Princetonians were only repeating commonplace distinctions. Seventeenth-century scholastics had distinguished between the copies and the *apographa* (the earliest accessible Greek and Hebrew texts), and antebellum theologians had long been accustomed to asserting the distinction between errorless autographs and later manuscripts. Moreover, the Princetonians also accepted the common distinction between the infallible scripture and its fallible interpreters. No interpretation could ever claim infallibility, so the doctrine of inerrancy had a purely formal force. And finally, the Princetonians, like almost everyone else, subscribed to a pious rationalism that accorded more authority to reason than appeared on the surface.[26]

On the one hand, they pointed out the limits of reason. It could not attain the highest spiritual truths; it could not rightly discard any biblical truth. On the other, they affirmed the rationality of revelation. They admired William

Paley, affirmed natural theology, and believed that arguments from design and causation proved the existence of God. They also thought that the internal and external evidences confirmed biblical belief. Alexander's discovery of the English evidentialist Soame Jenyns brought "bright and overwhelming evidence" to him as a young man, and in his *Brief Outline of the Evidence of the Christian Religion* (1825) and his *Evidences of the Authenticity, Inspiration, and Canonical Authority of the Holy Scriptures* (1826), based partly on antideist lectures to undergraduates, he advanced the usual evidential arguments. Hodge found the highest evidence in the witness of the Spirit, but he, too, subscribed to the evidentialist appeal to miracle, prophecy, and internal consistency.[27]

Their confidence in reason reflected their approbation of Scottish Common Sense Realism. Alexander had read the Scots under William Graham at Liberty Hall, and he thought of himself as a disciple of Reid and Stewart. Hodge felt certain that the Scots had discovered the "laws of belief" that confirmed both the limits and the reliability of rational knowledge. In typical Scottish fashion, he appealed to "consciousness" as evidence for conclusions ranging from human inability to the reality of spirit. He admired the Scottish recovery of Baconian induction and argued that theology itself was an inductive science in which the theologian gathered facts from the Bible and organized them into laws, much in the manner of the geologist in the field. Hodge was less happy with the later Realist Sir William Hamilton, who combined Reid with Kant in a way that cast doubt on the ability of the mind to know the Infinite. He believed that Hamilton had set rationality against itself, and Hodge's rationalist side could not abide that paradox.[28]

Hodge's views on science illustrated his attitudes toward reason. He worried about scientific overreaching but saw science and theology as partners. He thought that science, for instance, would confute the speculations of Josiah Nott, Louis Agassiz, and other ethnographers who denied that humanity was a single species with a common origin. He thought also that biblical interpretation would change in accord with changing scientific knowledge, and he adopted familiar solutions for reconciling texts like the creation narrative in Genesis with the findings of modern geology, speculating that either the day-age or the gap theories might explain the seeming conflict. Whatever the scientist discovered — if it were truly a discovery — would prove consistent with the Bible, properly interpreted, even if this meant that a scientific discovery could alter generations of interpretation. In this sense, reason and science carried authority for Hodge.[29]

It is true that at the end of his career Hodge concluded in his *What is Darwinism?* (1874) that Darwinian evolution was atheistic, but even his critique of Darwin reflected his admiration for science. Hodge referred far more to scientific than to religious critics of Darwin, and he conceded that some forms of evolutionary theory might be consistent with theism. His objection was that Darwin permitted no reference to teleology, and he thought that the denial of teleology amounted to an atheistic position. The theologian, he said, could not dispute any "scientific fact," but scientific explanations were another matter, and he thought that Darwin's explanation crossed the line into the realm of metaphysics.[30]

If the Princetonians read scripture through Scottish Realist eyes, however, they read it even more through lenses provided by seventeenth-century theologians and confessions. They drew from a variety of older theologians, from Augustine to Calvin, but they had a special fondness for the Reformed scholastics, who had "pushed theological investigation to its greatest length," and especially for Francis Turretin of Geneva, whose *Institutes* Hodge regarded as "incomparably the best book as a whole on systematic theology." Both Alexander and Hodge taught their classes with Turretin as the text. They assumed, as well, that no Calvinist theologian could reject "the constituent doctrines of the Calvinistic system" contained in the Westminster Confession.[31]

From the early 1830s, however, Princeton sought a policy of subscription to the Westminster Confession that could include the moderate Edwardeans while excluding the Taylorites. Both Hodge and Miller distinguished essential doctrines from modes of explanation, angering the ultras, who pointed out that New Haven made the same distinction. A quarter of a century later, in 1858, when Robert J. Breckinridge pushed the General Assembly to sanction a biblical commentary written according to Westminster standards, Hodge responded that no Presbyterian theologian accepted every one of the confession's propositions and that it should not, in any case, become an inflexible rule for interpreting scripture. When Old School newspapers attacked him for taking the position of New Schoolers who wanted to subscribe only for "substance of doctrines," Hodge explained that he preferred rather that clergy vow to accept the confession's "system of doctrines," which he believed to be "easily ascertainable."[32]

The Westminster doctrines were sufficiently ascertainable that they enabled the Princetonians to take a position on almost every disputed issue in antebellum theology. As a full-time professional theologian and an editor, Charles Hodge especially had the ability to define the Princeton theology by contrasting it to what he called the three great destructive principles of the nineteenth century—rationalism, mysticism, and ritualism—which he contrasted to what he called the evangelical principle.

At the center of Hodge's evangelical principle was the concept of "representation," which he saw as pervading "the whole Scriptures" and defining "the dispensations of God from the beginning of the world." The concept had a prominent place in his thinking by 1830, and in his lectures he described it as one of the pillars of the covenant theology. It meant that one person — whether Adam or Christ — could properly represent others in a legal relationship. It became one of the leading motifs in Princeton's debates with the New Englanders.[33]

For Princeton, representation required imputation. It was because Adam was a representative figure that God could impute his sin to his posterity. After reading an essay by Moses Stuart in the 1830 *Christian Spectator,* Archibald Alexander attacked the New Haven and Edwardean critics: "If the doctrine of imputation be given up, the whole doctrine of original sin must be abandoned. And if this doctrine be relinquished, then the whole doctrine of redemption must fall." Hodge also insisted on the analogy between imputed sin and imputed righteousness: just as Adam's disobedience as a federal representative resulted in the imputation of guilt, so also Christ's obedience resulted in the imputation of righteousness. In scripture, especially in Romans 5, the two belonged together. To discard one was to discard the other, which meant no redemption. Princeton was willing to tolerate Hopkinsians who omitted the doctrine, and they disagreed with the ultras who wanted to make it the test of orthodoxy, but they agreed that a true covenant theology entailed it.[34]

They described imputation as immediate. This meant a difference with John Calvin. "There is much in Calvin which we do not believe and never have," Hodge wrote. To define it as immediate meant saying that it preceded inherent depravity. They joined Turretin in opposing the theologians at seventeenth-century Saumur, who tried to rationalize Reformed theology with a doctrine of "mediate" imputation that defined it as subsequent to depravity. They disagreed with Edwards's occasional references to a mediate imputation grounded in the identity of Adam with his posterity. Later they would disagree with Old Schoolers like Samuel J. Baird, who linked imputation to the notion that human nature literally sinned in Adam. Against Moses Stuart and every other critic of imputation, Hodge insisted in 1830 that imputation did not mean a transfer of Adam's moral character to the race, and he greeted Stuart's commentary on Romans with his own extended exegesis of Romans, arguing that Paul had defined imputation as a judicial or forensic judgment, grounded in the representative character of Adam. For Hodge and Princeton, original sin meant both imputation and inherent depravity, but the imputation had priority.[35]

To take representation seriously meant rejecting the views circulating at Yale, Andover, and Harvard. Hodge found much to deplore in the New Haven theology: its dismissal of imputation, its definition of sin and regeneration as voluntary exercises, and its notion that the will had the power to choose the contrary of what it actually chose. Hodge wanted to speak not only of sin as original and imputed but also of regeneration as the immediate work of the Spirit, transforming the disposition that lay behind voluntary exercises, and of freedom as merely the power of men and women to act in accord with their dispositions even though they had not the slightest power to change their dispositions by willing it.[36]

Their commitment to representation prompted their criticisms of governmental views of the atonement. In 1824 Alexander argued that the governmental view violated the divine justice. If God did not impute sin to Christ and righteousness to the elect, then God pardoned sin without a vicarious punishment. Hodge would later criticize Beman's version of governmental theory as an empty effort to "make the atonement . . . perfectly intelligible" to an individualistic and utilitarian society that could not grasp either representative agency or divine justice. He saw the atonement as an act of satisfaction performed by a representative who bore the sins of the elect and accepted the punishment for them. Finally, Hodge disliked Yale's theodicy — Taylor's suggestion that God could not prevent sin in a genuine moral system. Hodge saw sin and suffering as penal afflictions resulting from Adam's fall as the representative of the race. All of Yale's errors he interpreted as a failure to understand representation.[37]

Princeton saw the alarming outcome of Yale's theology in the revivalism of Finney. Hodge linked Finney's techniques to Taylor in 1835, but his more extended critique came in 1847 when he reviewed Finney's *Lectures on Systematic Theology*. He saw the book as philosophy rather than theology, a production of the "speculative understanding," and he found in it two pivotal errors: that obligation was limited by ability and that happiness was the ultimate good. Hodge offered two alternatives: that the sinner could be both obliged and unable to obey the moral law and that religion consisted more in "loving God for his divine excellence" than in "the happiness of moral agents."[38]

The critique of Finney and Taylor signified an alternative reading of Scottish mental philosophy. Hodge made a portion of his case against Finney, for instance, by arguing that direct acts of volition lacked the power to govern emotions and affections. The argument against New Haven depended not only on biblical exegesis but also on an appeal to "consciousness," through which the Princetonians tried to ground a distinction between acts and dispositions, and between liberty and ability. When Hodge found "moral propensities, dispositions, or tendencies, prior to all acts of choice," or when he contended that the will was always determined by "the preceding state of mind," he was offering a particular reading of the Scottish philosophy. The philosophical views suffused the theological judgments.[39]

Yet the Princeton critique was more than simply the result of a philosophical difference. It also represented a reassertion of an older Calvinist piety. Countering powerful tendencies in American theology—tendencies shaped by a sense of freedom, individualism, personal responsibility, and the attainability of happiness—Princeton set itself against the view that happiness was the highest good. A proper happiness was good, but it was not the end for which God created the world. By the time Hodge clashed with Park over sin and free agency in the early 1850s, he had decided that the theological revisionists sought a "human-centered" rather than a God-centered theology. The end of creation for Hodge was "not the happiness of the creatures, but the infinitely higher end of divine glory."[40]

The stakes were equally high in a second round of disputes about "mystical" interpretations of religion, which for Hodge included any systems teaching the identity of God and humanity (or God and the world), the possibility of an "immediate intuition of the infinite," or the theory that the feelings rather than the intellect were the source of religious knowledge. He associated mysticism with Hegel and Friedrich Daniel Ernst Schleiermacher in Germany, Victor Cousin in France, Quakers in England, and transcendentalists in America, but he also saw mystical tendencies in American seminaries and pulpits, and it was the seminary disputes that led to his most extensive discussions.[41]

The first came in 1839 in an essay he coauthored on "Transcendentalism," directed against German Kantians, French Eclectics, and Ralph Waldo Emerson. The essay gave Princeton's response to Emerson's Divinity School Address at Harvard, which the Princetonians dismissed as "nonsense." They thought that Emerson had taught pantheism, immediate revelation, and trust in "sentiment" rather than intellect, not with reasoned arguments but by "endless assertion." The following year Hodge reviewed Andrews Norton's critique of Emerson and found himself agreeing with Harvard Unitarians, at least to the extent of defending the historical truth of the New Testament and the necessity for belief in miracles. But the essay also turned the question back to the Calvinist seminaries: the real danger was "the treason of friends" who used the language of a faithless philosophy in treating of the mysteries of God.[42]

Hodge would return to the transcendentalists in a mordant review of the French philosopher Victor Cousin, but his more important critiques of the mystical principle came in his remarks on other seminary theologians and of Horace Bushnell's lectures at Yale, Harvard, and Andover. In 1845 he turned his attention to the German Reformed seminary in Mercersburg, where Friedrich Rauch, Philip Schaff, and John Williamson Nevin had introduced German idealism. For the most part he liked Schaff's controversial inaugural address of 1844 — *The Principle of Protestantism* — but he complained of its Germanic "indefiniteness of language," and he fretted about Nevin, whose subsequent essay on sacramental theology, *The Mystical Presence* (1846), would alarm him. Nevin had been an Old School ally, but Hodge now saw him as a captive of "the mystical system."[43]

Nevin claimed that the divine-human Christ was present in the Lord's Supper in such a manner that believers could unite there with the whole of his "theanthropic life." He linked this sacramental doctrine with a larger claim that the divine-human life manifest in the incarnation had redeemed humanity in principle and created the church as a living organism through which the faithful were saved by being drawn into union with Christ's continuing life. Hodge thought that the whole idea rested on a psychology permeated by the mystical idea of identity; Nevin had lost sight of the difference between the divine and the human.[44]

For the next twenty-eight years, Hodge kept up the criticisms of Nevin, deeply alienating both Nevin, who resented the implication that he taught pantheism, and Schaff, who once quipped that Princeton would be the "one dry place to flee to at the next deluge." Hodge disavowed any intention to mislead, and Schaff eventually spoke well of him, but Hodge continued to complain that Nevin's theology left no place for imputation, atonement, justification by faith, or any real distinction between the human and the divine.[45]

He distrusted, moreover, the way Nevin and Schaff talked about history, especially historical development in the church. Hodge could concede a growing knowledge of Christianity, but he denied that the essential doctrines had undergone development. For Hodge, conceptions of historical development overemphasized tradition, intimated relativism, and suggested German notions of the self-evolution of the Absolute. He defended a conception of Christianity not as a developing "life" but as a system of truth recorded in scripture "in a definite and complete form for all ages."[46]

To think of Christianity as a developing "life" seemed to him to coincide with the theory that "feeling" trumped doctrinal truth, and the elevation of feeling suggested a theory of language as metaphorical or poetic. Hodge's criticisms of the mystical principle led him into the debates over religious language, and when he read Horace Bushnell's three addresses to the students and faculty of Harvard, Yale, and Andover, published in 1849 as *God in Christ*, he concluded that the book's preface on language reduced Christianity to poetic feeling.

He read Bushnell as a "mystic" who made the feelings the subjects of immediate divine impression and rendered the intellect, along with clear doctrine, unimportant. Bushnell believed that all abstract language had roots in sensory experience and therefore carried always a metaphorical, figurative quality. Hodge agreed that conceptual language was usually symbolic and in certain ways inadequate, but he refused to abandon the claim for the rational truth of religious propositions. If there were no doctrinal propositions — cognitive statements conveying to the intellect ideas that could be true or false — religious truth claims did no more than express emotion.[47]

The previous year Hodge had given a more favorable verdict about Bushnell's *Christian Nurture.* He approved of its sense of Christian piety as organic, communal, and covenantal, and he liked its emphasis on parental nurture and its wariness of revivalism. But he worried about its implicit rationalism and naturalism, and after the publication of *God in Christ* he adjudged Bushnell an incompetent theologian who had dissolved the atonement into subjective feeling, misunderstood Christology, and defined the Trinity away. When Bushnell tried to restate his views in 1866, Hodge pronounced that effort also a failure. Bushnell's views of language had convinced Hodge that he was "a poet, and neither a philosopher nor theologian."[48]

The question of language surfaced again in the debate with Edwards Amasa Park, who in 1850, responding partly to Bushnell, suggested that some religious language expressed and addressed the feelings and should not be taken literally, but that the theologian could translate such language of the feeling into precise doctrines of the intellect. Prominent among the emotive expressions, in Park's view, were Princeton's doctrines about inability, imputation, and atonement. Hodge charged him with mysticism. He believed that figurative language could be as definite in meaning as any other, that the feelings demanded a truth that satisfied the intellect, and that figures had their own cognitive meanings that could not be explained away or construed as expressions of feeling. He resisted any theological position that seemed to rob theology of its cognitive content.[49]

Hodge's third set of debates — over the principle of ritualism — embroiled him in the incessant disputes over "the Church question." This was a struggle that included debates over polity, clerical office, liturgical ritual, and soteriology, and it preoccupied theologians throughout the century. Of his many articles in the *Biblical Repertory and Princeton Review,* at least thirty-two, almost a fourth, dealt entirely or in part with questions about the church, its order, its ministry, or its sacraments, always in opposition to what he called "the church system" or "high churchism."[50]

Hodge defined the visible church as an organized society professing the true religion, united for worship and discipline, and subject to the same form of government and tribunal. The invisible church consisted of all the elect, wherever they might be. These definitions placed him in opposition not only to high-church movements but also to other traditions of Reformed piety. It distinguished him, for example, from the old Puritan idea that the visible church should consist, as far as possible, of the regenerate. Hodge would admit new members, along with their children, whenever they made a credible profession of true religion and promised obedience to Christ. The visible church could not "read the heart" and treat applicants according to their state in the sight of God.[51]

He worried that the "Puritan view," which he associated with Edwards and Edwardeans, had "gained ascendancy" among evangelical Protestants, "even, to a great extent, among Presbyterians." He found a greater threat, however, in "high-church" movements, by which he meant different things, depending on the opponent of the moment.[52]

When he was opposing the American Episcopal proponents of the English Oxford Movement, "high-church" referred to any theology that defined the church as the "storehouse and direct channel of grace" or made the sacraments the principal means of saving grace. Hodge condemned the Oxford Movement in 1838 and then again in 1841 in a polemic against the "church system" of the New Jersey Bishop George Washington Doane, arguing that this form of high-church thought substituted the church for Christ and sacramental piety for justification by faith. When he opposed the other American Episcopal high-church movement, linked to Bishop Hobart, the term referred to any theology that made a "particular form," such as the apostolic succession of the clergy, essential to the definition of the church. To Hodge, the Hobartians confused the church as the body of Christ, the company of believers, with "an external society" and its practices. He even criticized his evangelical Episcopal friend and ally Charles Pettit McIlvaine, bishop of Ohio, president of the seminary at Kenyon College, and foe of both forms of Episcopal high-church theology, when McIlvaine contended that bishops perpetuated the authority of the apostles. All three forms of Episcopal teaching were, for Hodge, "too close to Rome."[53]

The archetype of high-church doctrine for Hodge was Roman Catholic ecclesiology. He had no direct debates with American Catholic theologians, though he did favorably review Thornwell's arguments against Bishop Patrick Lynch of Charleston on the authority of the church and the Apocrypha. He more often argued with classical authors like Cardinal Robert Bellarmine or with confessions like the canons and decrees of Trent. In his mind, the Catholics had defined the church as essentially an external organization, formed by outward profession and ritual, subject to Papacy and priesthood, and claiming to possess exclusive sacramental channels of saving grace. He thought that such doctrines of grace usurped the place of justification by faith, that the elevation of priestly power contradicted biblical principles, that history disproved the Church's claim to infallibility, that Catholic devotion to Mary and the saints was idolatry, and that Catholic appeals to tradition denigrated the sole authority of scripture. For all these reasons, he deemed "Romanism immeasurably more dangerous than infidelity."[54]

Yet he resisted powerful currents of anti-Catholic teaching in his own denomination. When the General Assembly in 1845 denied the validity of Catholic baptism and pronounced Catholics "outside the visible Church of Christ," Hodge opposed the majority. He argued that the Roman communion included professing believers and that it taught enough about God, Christ, and the Spirit to convey saving truth; while the Papacy was outside the visible church, many ordinary Catholics were within it. The ultraconservatives, led by Thornwell and Breckinridge, pronounced Hodge's conclusions a disaster and launched another campaign to check the influence of Princeton, but Hodge refused to relent.[55]

Questions about sacraments surfaced not only in his writings on Rome but also in his disputes with the Mercersburg theologians, Episcopalians, Lutherans, and Baptists. Hodge viewed the sacraments in conventional Reformed terms as seals of the covenant of grace. This meant that baptism confirmed a child's status within the parental covenant while the Lord's Supper sealed the covenant by offering believers a means of grace in which the Spirit conveyed the "virtue and efficacy" of Christ's saving work. He opposed the doctrine of baptismal regeneration, the belief in either a corporeal or "mystical" presence of Christ's body and blood in the Lord's Supper, and the notion that the sacraments conveyed a grace not obtainable elsewhere.[56]

Sacramental issues provoked some of Hodge's relatively infrequent criticisms of Lutheran theology. He saw the Lutherans and the Reformed as "the two great branches of the Protestant church," and he maintained friendly relationships with such Lutheran traditionalists as Charles Porterfield Krauth at the Lutheran seminary in Philadelphia. In return, Krauth praised Hodge's *Systematic Theology.* He also noted Hodge's view that all who died in infancy were probably saved, and he approved his movement away from the "horrors" of a Calvinism that consigned many dying infants to damnation. On sacramental matters, though, Hodge and Krauth continued ancient Lutheran and Reformed disputes, with Krauth holding baptism ordinarily necessary for salvation and Hodge denying it. Hodge had maintained earlier that "no doctrine can be more radically opposed to the spirit and teaching of the New Testament than the doctrine of baptismal regeneration," and the doctrine remained for him a prime symbol of "ritualism."[57]

The Princeton theology was therefore much more than a set of beliefs about biblical infallibility. It was also more than simply a return to the seventeenth century. It was an effort to defend Westminster Calvinism against innovators and critics by showing that seventeenth-century doctrines met the standards of nineteenth-century philosophy, properly understood, and that the Calvinist piety nurtured by those doctrines embodied the truths of Christianity more effectively than rationalist, mystical, and ritualist alternatives.

The Southern Old School

Even Presbyterians, as Hodge saw it, could fall into a false "high churchism," and he especially bemoaned the fall of the southern Old Schoolers Robert Jefferson Breckinridge, John Bailey Adger (1810–99), and James Henley Thornwell. Those three, along with Robert Lewis Dabney, formulated the southern version of Old School theology, and in their views of the church they would diverge from the Princeton orthodoxy. But the southerners were themselves divided. They disagreed, for one thing, about slavery. Breckinridge hated the institution; Thornwell and Dabney defended it. Dabney disliked Breckinridge and accused him of plagiarism. Adger thought that Dabney misunderstood Calvinist sacramental thought. Thornwell thought that Breckinridge was too much drawn to millennialist notions. And even on theological points about which some Old Schoolers assumed unanimity, such as imputation, the southern differences could display the tensions within the Old School alliance.[58]

In the South, the New School had only a token presence. The *Calvinistic Magazine* of Frederick Ross in east Tennessee defended New School theology, and conservatives like W. L. Breckinridge and Nathan L. Rice in Kentucky issued warnings against "the leaven of New Schoolism," but others thought that the quarrels were baffling if not meaningless. After the 1837 split, Thornwell presented a paper to the Synod of South Carolina and Georgia in which he defined the meaning of Old School theology for a conservative southerner. It meant belief in the imputation of Adam's guilt, a substitutionary atonement that satisfied divine justice, an entire inability to comply with the demands of the law, and regeneration by the immediate agency of the Spirit, coupled with a willingness to say that both Hopkinsianism and Taylorism were "inconsistent with Presbyterian standards." Thornwell thought that "the New England theologians" had "broken their necks" because they had made the Bible merely an appendix to their "shallow and sophistical psychology."[59]

Thornwell was the dominant figure, a man who had overcome early poverty to become recognized, in the words of the nineteenth-century historian

George Bancroft as "the most learned of the learned." In 1831 he graduated from South Carolina College, two years later made his brief excursion to New England, and returned in 1834 to a pastorate in Lancaster, South Carolina. For the next seventeen years he moved back and forth between pastorates and teaching assignments in his alma mater, where he served first as professor of logic and belles lettres and then as professor of sacred literature and the evidences of Christianity. In 1851 he became the president, but in 1855 he moved into a professorship of the new theological seminary at Columbia, from where he wrote in 1861 the "Address to All the Churches of Jesus Christ throughout the Earth," justifying the southern separation from the northern church.[60]

Breckinridge attained some celebrity as a lawyer and legislator in his native Kentucky before deciding to study briefly at Princeton Seminary and assume the pulpit of the Second Church in Baltimore. He eventually returned as pastor of the First Church in Lexington and state superintendent of public instruction until he founded Danville Seminary, where he remained from 1853 until his death sixteen years later. He instigated in 1834 the Act and Testimony in which the Old School condemned the New School doctrines as heretical, and as the editor of the *Baltimore Literary and Religious Magazine* and the *Spirit of the XIX Century,* he earned a reputation as a fierce polemicist. His two-volume systematic theology, *The Knowledge of God Objectively Considered* (1858) and *The Knowledge of God Subjectively Considered* (1859), elicited, however, widely disparate responses from his Old School colleagues.

Adger entered the fray late. A native of Charleston who graduated from Princeton Seminary after study with Hodge, whom he considered a "great theologian," he worked from 1834 to 1847 as a missionary among the Armenians in Constantinople before returning to Charleston as a planter and missionary to African-Americans. After becoming professor of church history and polity at Columbia in 1857, however, he developed views of the sacraments, Christology, and salvation that separated him not only from Hodge but from most other southern Old Schoolers.[61]

Dabney was another latecomer. A graduate of the University of Virginia and Union Seminary in Virginia, he served as a pastor and headmaster before returning to Union, first in 1853 as an historian, then in 1859 as the professor of theology. His books belong to a period beyond the scope of this study, but he began his *Systematic and Polemic Theology* (1871) earlier as lectures at Union, and he not only published actively in the antebellum journals but also engaged himself in the theological maneuvering of the 1850s.[62]

All of them joined Princeton in defending Westminster. Thornwell claimed that it was the intellectual sublimity of the confession that drew him into the Presbyterian Church. All of them shared Princeton's admiration for the Reformed scholastics, and Turretin's *Institutes* served as the textbook of instruction at every seminary where they taught. For most this meant an unflinching doctrine of particular election and limited atonement, though Dabney softened these doctrines somewhat by arguing that the atoning acts had a "general design" even though they were intended to effect a "particular redemption."[63]

They shared Princeton's pious rationalism and its antagonism to the impious rationalism of the European idealists. Thornwell, for instance, tried to weave a way between Locke's empiricism, which led to Hume, and Hegel's idealism, which issued in the conception of an Absolute that was quite unlike the personal God of Christian belief. He appreciated Immanuel Kant's demolition of any "ontology of pure reason," but he thought that Kant had been excessively skeptical. The alternative he found in the Scottish philosophy, but he was far more open than Princeton to the more Kantian form of Scottish thought found in the philosophy of William Hamilton. Conceding with Hamilton that all knowledge was relative to the cognitive faculties of the knower, Thornwell also accepted Hamilton's argument that the mind necessarily believed in a ground or substance behind appearances. Hamilton, he thought, had shown both the possibilities and the limits of reason, and this was the philosophical conclusion that the theologian was seeking.[64]

Thornwell spent far more time than the Princetonians struggling against post-Kantian forms of theological revision. He admired the Germans — "they do not rave but reason" — but he thought that their refusal to recognize the limits of knowledge led to impersonal notions of God. He wrote essays on "The Personality of the Holy Ghost" (1843), "Miracles" (1857), and "The Personality of God" (1861) to show that only a conception of God as a supernatural person could pose the proper Christian alternative to naturalism. And though Thornwell thought that both reason and conscience could establish good grounds for such a conception of God, he believed that it had to rest finally on the authority of God's own self-revelation.[65]

"The true method," he said, was to "accept the facts of revelation as we accept the facts of nature." Like Princeton, the southerners called for a humble Baconian inductive reading of God's revelation in both nature and scripture. Like Princeton, they argued for the Bible's infallibility. Thornwell defended the theory of verbal dictation as the only theory that made the Bible "what it professes to be, the Word of God." But they took their doctrine of biblical authority in directions that Princeton refused to follow.[66]

Thornwell spoke for most of them when he insisted that "the Bible is our only rule, and that where it is silent we have no right to speak." On this ground, Thornwell's allies refused to admit that the church could establish or support either voluntary societies or denominational boards. In 1837 Hodge began a dispute when he defended the right of the denomination to create boards to oversee missions. Thornwell took the position that such boards lacked scriptural warrant. By 1860, when Hodge and Thornwell had their great debate at the General Assembly, Hodge had decided that Thornwell was guilty of "superlative high churchism" by virtue of having claimed that scripture prescribed the details of Presbyterian order, that every form required scriptural warrant, and that prescribed forms were essentials. Hodge believed that scripture laid down principles of Presbyterian order—the parity of the clergy, the right of the people to help govern, and the unity of the church—but that the church had discretion to alter its forms, for its prerogatives came from the indwelling Spirit, not from a biblical blueprint. Even *de jure* principles could not be considered essential to the being of the church if they were not essential to salvation.[67]

The dispute with Princeton deepened after 1845 when Thornwell persuaded the Old School General Assembly to deny the validity of Roman Catholic baptism. He had long been a critic of Catholic theology, gaining a wide reading with his debate against Bishop Patrick Lynch on the genuineness of the apocryphal books of the Bible, which he denied on the ground that they were not found in the Jewish canon supposedly approved by Jesus. But the issue of Catholic baptism had more far-reaching implications. Because the Roman Catholic Church denied that justification was by faith alone, because it taught that the believer had an inherent rather than an imputed righteousness, and because its sacramental teachings were false, he argued, the Church of Rome was no true church and its baptism was no true baptism. Hodge demurred, criticizing both Thornwell and the General Assembly. One result was the creation in 1846 of the *Southern Presbyterian Review,* which Thornwell envisioned as a challenge to Princeton's recalcitrance.[68]

Thornwell clashed with Princeton again when he defined his doctrine of the spirituality of the church. Driven by the crisis over slavery, he tried to remove the church from the debate by defining it as a "spiritual body," having as its only aim "the gathering and perfecting of the saints." Devoted solely to matters of the spirit, it had no mandate to league itself with any secular institution or involve itself in any secular cause. The purpose of the doctrine was to "restrain the Church within her own proper sphere." Thornwell did not invent the idea, but his defense of it left a mark on southern Protestant piety. Hodge was no abolitionist and no friend of radical reform, but he thought that Thornwell was proposing a "new doctrine," which removed any possibility for the church to oppose any social evil.[69]

On imputation, Hodge and Thornwell agreed. Thornwell differed from Hodge only in the way in which he tried to ensure a central place for the doctrine within his theological system. Thornwell's "Lectures in Theology," begun in 1856 for his classes at Columbia, argued that the unifying principle of theology was the doctrine of justification. How could a fallen moral creature be made just or righteous? In answering the question, Thornwell joined the New Englanders in turning to the metaphor of moral government, though he used it in ways quite foreign to them. He organized the lectures around three principles: moral government, or the essential relatedness of God and humanity; its modification by the legal covenant revealed in natural law; and its further modification by the covenant of grace revealed in scripture. His covenantal language reflected broad reading in seventeenth-century English and European theologians, especially Johannes Cocceius, Herman Witsius, Francis Turretin, and John Owen. His interest in moral government came from his reading of such eighteenth-century theologians as Samuel Clarke and Joseph Butler, whom he admired even though he found them deficient.[70]

For Thornwell, justification presupposed the imputation both of Adam's sin and of Christ's righteousness. Both Adam and Christ were representative figures, acting on behalf of the race. The doctrine of imputation therefore was "perhaps the distinguishing law of God's dealings" with human beings. It was, without doubt for Thornwell, "the very keystone which supports the arch of the Christian system." And he joined Hodge in claiming that imputation had to be immediate rather than mediate; it proceeded from the federal tie with Adam, not any natural kinship of the race with him. For Thornwell, this was the heart of Old School theology.[71]

His colleagues saw it differently. On the question of sin, Breckinridge taught a doctrine of mediate imputation, arguing that inherent depravity was the formal ground of the imputation of guilt. Thornwell conceded that one could interpret the Westminster Confession in this way, but he argued that the Westminster Catechism made it clear that Breckinridge was straying. On the question of salvation, Adger emphasized that the heart of the matter was not imputation but the believer's communion with the "life" of Christ. Dabney would eventually argue that the distinction between mediate and immediate imputation was "a novelty and an over-refinement," which merely aggravated difficulties. If imputation were immediate in the Princeton sense, he argued, then the innocent would be punished, without their consent, for the guilty. Dabney tried to argue, rather, that because of our federal union with Adam we enter existence both guilty and depraved, so that it made no sense to say that imputation preceded depravity. This was, he said, the "old Calvinistic doctrine," and he preferred it to "the new one at Princeton" and Columbia.[72]

Adger differed on other topics as well. Impressed by the sacramental theology of Nevin at Mercersburg, he began to teach students at Columbia Seminary in 1857 that the central point of theology was the incarnation, not simply the atonement; that Jesus was the fully human embodiment of a fully divine life; and that the sacrament provided a real union with not only the "spirit" but also the "flesh" of Christ. He was not arguing for a corporeal presence in the sacrament, but his eucharistic views and his doctrine of Christ both worried Dabney, who felt it important to retain the Reformed scholastic accent on the distinction between Christ's divine and human natures and to deny any special union with Christ through the sacrament. To Dabney, both Adger and Nevin had succumbed to speculation.[73]

The charge of speculation carried weight because by mid-century it was a commonplace that theology had to be practical. The southerners reflected at length on the relation between the practical and the speculative. Breckinridge tried to clarify it in his theological system by writing one practical and one speculative volume, but Thornwell thought the separation arbitrary. He argued that theology was "not a science of speculative cognition at all," even though it presupposed and employed "speculative knowledge" of divine truth. It was, to be sure, a science, a coherent system of truths mutually connected and dependent, but Thornwell acknowledged that there could be no "science of God" in any direct sense. Theology was rather "the science of a true and loving faith," a knowledge whose end was piety, a "form of knowledge that produces love, reverence, trust, and fear." Thornwell hesitated to say that theology was solely practical, but he clearly denied that its end was simple cognition or convincing metaphysics: "The knowledge of God which theology has in mind is the knowledge of God as the supreme good—the knowledge of God as the full and perfect and everlasting portion of the soul."[74]

Yet this was not to say that the end of theology was human happiness. Thornwell adored Aristotle, whose philosophy he considered "the nearest approximation which has been made by unassisted reason" to the doctrine of the scriptures, and he agreed with the Aristotelian dictum that happiness was the chief good of human beings. He also believed that the highest human happiness came through the glorifying of God. But he did not think that human happiness was the goal of the creation itself. "It is in no sense true," he wrote, "that the design of government in reference to God is to secure the happiness of His subjects." The design of God's moral government was rather the glory of God. And to Thornwell, as to Princeton, this was what Old School Calvinism was about.[75]

PART III

Alternatives to Baconian Reason

Lutherans: Reason, Revival, and Confession

When Philip Schaff described the status of Lutheran thought in America in 1855, he had to admit that "the multifarious differences of opinions and schools" within the tradition made it "no easy matter" to define a uniform Lutheran theology. Lutherans were on the verge of division over the normative status of the historic Lutheran confessions. One group hoped to restore the authority of the Augsburg Confession of 1530, in which the European reformers had presented their articles of belief before the Imperial Diet, and of the Book of Concord of 1580, which resolved theological disputes among second-generation Lutherans in Germany. Their "American Lutheran" opponents claimed to honor the confessions but wanted to abandon "non-essential doctrines." They also wanted to bring Lutheran theology into closer conformity with a more rational form of orthodoxy. The differences helped to split American Lutheran theologians into battling factions.[1]

The debate over confessions, or "symbols," drew the Lutherans into dispute about evidential logic. The most prominent American Lutheran theologian of the early nineteenth century, Samuel Simon Schmucker (1799–1873) of Gettysburg Seminary in Pennsylvania, the architect of the "American Lutheran" theology, not only followed the evidential model but also called for "liberty of thought" and regard for "the full influence of evidence" in any assent to the confessions. The confessionalists, their numbers strengthened by new immigrants from Europe, charged that Schmucker's position concealed a crypto-rationalism that lost sight of distinctive Lutheran truth.[2]

Reason Denied and Affirmed

The place of reason in theology had often been a source of tension within the Lutheran tradition. Martin Luther (1483–1546) disparaged natural reason as a foe to faith. His sense of faith's paradoxes produced a characteristic Lutheran style of theology, which emphasized that Christ was fully God and fully human at the same time, that believers were totally sinful and totally righteous at the same time, and that the grounding of the gospel was the paradoxical revelation of God in the suffering and dying of Jesus on the cross. In Luther's theology, the cross was the foundation for the doctrine that the justification of the sinful was a sheer gift of grace to be gratefully accepted in faith, not a reward for spiritual or moral achievement.[3]

For Luther, the cross also stood as a permanent "no" to the pretension of reason. Luther defended theological positions — such as the corporeal presence of Christ's body and blood in the sacramental bread and wine, or the doctrine that the baptismal water contained and conveyed a saving spiritual grace — that his critics derided as irrational. In turn, he saw his critics as more devoted to Aristotle than to a gospel that was "foolishness to the wise." His position led some of his later followers, like Matthias Flacius and Daniel Hoffmann, to conclude that any presumed natural knowledge of God was "fallacious and deceptive" and that what was true in philosophy was false in theology. Luther's humanist ally Philip Melanchthon, however, spoke more optimistically of reason in theology, and by the late sixteenth century, Lutherans were forming a scholastic orthodox tradition marked by the confidence that although natural philosophy could not discern saving truth it could correctly identify the evidence in nature for God's existence.[4]

The overriding aim of scholastic orthodox theologians like Abraham Calov (1612–86) and John Andrew Quenstedt (1617–88) at Wittenberg or John Gerhard (1582–1637) at Jena was to defend the truths of the Lutheran confessions, many of which they saw as standing above reason. But they thought that truths above reason did not need to be contrary to reason. They sought rational proof and confirmation when it was available, and they joined the Calvinist scholastics in restoring the importance for Protestant theology of the internal and external evidences of revelation.[5]

By the late seventeenth century, however, the orthodox theologians faced a Lutheran Pietist movement that turned attention to religious experience rather than doctrinal correctness and shared many of Luther's misgivings about reason in theology. The founders of Pietism, Philipp Jakob Spener (1635–1705) and his disciple August Hermann Francke (1663–1727), viewed reliance on reason as a sign of pride. In his *Pia Desideria,* Spener denied that reason was "capable of divine wisdom," and he contrasted its arrogant allure to the "simplicity of Christ and his teaching." Francke thought that "a hundred sacks full" of rational learning were nothing compared to the knowledge of Christ conveyed by the Spirit. It was important for the Moravian Nicholas Ludwig von Zinzendorf (1700–60), whose thought drew heavily on Spener and Francke, that true religion could be "grasped without the conclusions of reason," which he saw as hindrance both to religious experience and to the reception of revelation.[6]

The Lutheran Pietist movement accentuated the authority of scripture, the emotional experience of rebirth, the importance of sanctification as a corollary to justification, and the fellowship of disciplined Christian laity in small groups devoted to mutual encouragement and oversight. Pietist scholars also stimulated interest in millennial theologies that promised a partial realization of God's kingdom on earth. These Pietist attitudes would filter into America especially through the mission established by Francke at the University of Halle.[7]

Pietist inclinations found theological expression in print in the colonies as early as 1708, when colonial Lutherans recruited Justus Falckner (1672–1723), a Halle graduate who was living alone in the wilds of Pennsylvania, to serve churches in New York and New Jersey. Falckner published his *Fundamental Instruction (Grondlyche Onderricht)* chiefly to teach his congregants how to prepare for communion and to distinguish their faith from that of the Reformed majority. Its simple question-and-answer format reaffirmed the Pietist contentions that scripture alone taught the truths necessary for salvation — truths hidden from the "natural understanding" — and that rebirth and good works always accompanied justification by faith in Christ.[8]

The arrival in 1742 of Henry Melchior Muhlenberg (1711–87) — and his success as an organizer of Lutheran churches — would set the Pietist tone for colonial Lutheranism. Muhlenberg was a Halle graduate whose sole theological publication was a defense of Pietism against its orthodox critics, published in 1741 before leaving for America. While agreeing that justification by faith was the prime doctrine of Luther's reform, Muhlenberg declared his admiration for "the sainted Spener" and defended the Pietist emphasis on conviction of sin, repentance, and good works as the "necessary fruits of faith." He approved of the small Pietist conventicles, the *collegia pietatis,* as nurseries of faith, and he agreed with Francke about the importance of an experience of rebirth, especially about the need for Christian teachers to have undergone conversion.[9]

Unlike some radical eighteenth-century Pietists, Muhlenberg always accepted the authority of the Lutheran confessions — he has been described as a "confessional Pietist" — and he opposed Zinzendorf, who tried to unite German immigrants to America in a communion that would transcend confessional differences. Nonetheless, more rigorously orthodox Lutherans in the colonies, such as William Berkmeyer and Peter Sommer in New York, suspected the missionaries from Halle of indifference to purity of doctrine. Berkmeyer wanted the New York churches to accept as ministers only "orthodox Lutherans" from "orthodox Academies." Muhlenberg valued sound doctrine, but he was of a different spirit.[10]

For one thing, he disliked the rationalist tone that he discerned in some of the orthodox theologians. He thought that Christian truths should be presented simply and "practically," and he saw some of the orthodox critics of Pietism as theologians fettered by Aristotle, academics whose "philosophical notions" obscured the Bible. He praised Spener and Francke for having returned biblical truth to "illiterate and simple-minded people." And although he affirmed the Lutheran symbols, he did not have the same sense of their importance that had defined seventeenth-century orthodoxy and would define the nineteenth-century confessionalists.[11]

Pietism of the sort that Muhlenberg represented would flow into American Lutheran thought partly through a catechetical theology designed to instruct children and adults. Working closely with Muhlenberg, the Philadelphia and Germantown pastor Peter Brunnholtz prepared in 1749 an edition of Luther's *Small Catechism,* to which he affixed an "order of salvation," a typical Pietist summary of doctrine outlining the successive stages of saving experience, from conviction of sin to sanctification. Other Lutheran pastors, such as John C. Kuntze (1744–1807) of Philadelphia, would add to their editions of Luther's book detailed analyses that treated the whole of the catechism as if it were an order of salvation, moving from knowledge of the law to faith in the gospel. Before the 1820s, extended commentaries on catechisms formed the most important genre of Lutheran theology in America, and most of them showed traces of Pietist theology.[12]

Pietists trained and nurtured Pietists, partly through formal institutions, like the theological course taught by the Philadelphia pastor and professor of oriental languages at the University of Pennsylvania, Justus C. H. Helmuth, partly through more informal associations. Helmuth, for instance, trained John George Schmucker (1771–1854), the Pennsylvania pastor whose two-volume *Prophetic History of the Christian Religion* (1817, 1821) was the main conduit of Pietist millennial themes into antebellum American Lutheranism. Schmucker, in turn, became the "teacher for the instruction of young preachers" for the Pennsylvania Ministerium. Among his students was his son Samuel Simon Schmucker.[13]

By the early nineteenth century, the serious challenge to this moderate Pietist theology in America came not from orthodoxy but from theologians influenced by the theological rationalists of the German universities. Johann Salomo Semler (1725–91) at the University of Halle typified one form of this theological rationalism when he called for "free investigation" of the "so-called canon of Jews and Christians" as a product of an alien and antique culture.[14]

No American Lutheran theologian brought quite this critical spirit to theology, but one of Semler's students, Frederick Henry Quitman (1760–1832), a pastor in Rhinebeck, New York, rose in 1807 to the presidency of the New York Ministerium, and his *Evangelical Catechism* (1814) exemplified the milder form of rational theology that could attract American adherents. It earned him a reputation as the most prominent American Lutheran theologian of the generation between Muhlenberg and Samuel Simon Schmucker.

Quitman thought that "all unwarranted belief" was superstition, and his catechism tried to provide warrants from "reason, history, and experience" as well as from revelation. It was the coinciding of revelation and reason — of the life and teachings of Jesus with the evidence of design and order in nature — that provided reliable knowledge of God. Jesus' prophecies and miracles, as well as his character and life, offered rational proof that Jesus was "the high personage, whom he professed to be." The testimony of reason to the unity and benevolence of God and of conscience to the demands of morality confirmed the rationality of the gospel, as well as its "liberal and catholic spirit." The evidence for the authenticity of the gospel accounts provided added assurance.[15]

He believed that Luther's principle of *sola scriptura* justified a dissent from Luther's theology on such doctrines as entire moral depravity, absolute divine decrees, and an atonement meant to satisfy the divine wrath. In Quitman's theology, God was the "intelligent Author" of creation. Jesus was the messianic Son whose Lordship rested on his obedience to his Father and his sufferings for the benefit of humanity, which guaranteed the truth of the doctrines that he had preached. Human beings were fallen but free agents who, with the aid of the universal grace of the Spirit, could attain to faith, defined as a belief in the authority, the doctrines, and the promises of Jesus.[16]

Quitman had no problem with supernaturalism; he thought that Jesus was born of a virgin, rose from the dead, and would appear again visibly on earth. But he had no interest in Lutheran paradoxes. He thought that sinners attained justification as a "reward for belief," infants underwent baptism simply as a form of initiation into the church, and Christians received the Lord's Supper merely as a remembrance of Christ that strengthened their attachment to him and to each other. On each point, he departed from Luther and the earlier Lutheran tradition.[17]

He was disappointed when his catechism did not sell widely, but Quitman had supporters. When Samuel Schmucker toured New York in 1825 he decided that the ministers there were "rank socinians." The more typical theological stance, however, was an irenic biblical evangelicalism whose adherents sought to downplay confessional particularity in hopes of closer cooperation with other Christian groups. This spirit of irenicism was present when the Pennsylvania pastor John George Lochmann (1773–1826) published his *Brief Summary of Christian Doctrine* (1804) and his more substantial *History, Doctrine, and Discipline of the Evangelical Lutheran Church* (1816), in which he expressed the wish that Lutherans would designate themselves simply as an "Evangelical Church." Lochmann presented scripture as the normative source for theology and said that other formularies of the church had "no authority beyond what they derive from the scriptures, whose sense and meaning they are designed to convey." With that he proceeded to define away older Lutheran doctrines of original sin, imputation, the bondage of the will, predestination, baptismal regeneration, and the corporeal presence of Christ in the Lord's Supper.[18]

Even more intent on chipping away a distinctive Lutheran heritage, the Pennsylvania pastor Johann August Probst published in 1826 his *Reunion of Lutherans and Reformed* in which he complained that the historic differences enshrined in the confessions were of interest only to "scholars" and "the few learned" and claimed that doctrinal differences among Protestants were vanishing. Much in the old confessions, or "symbols," he dismissed as "obsolete." Johann Conrad Jaeger's introduction to the work declared that a "lifeless, formal theology" constructed from "symbols upon symbols" appealed only to the narrow-minded and "the haters of reason." Probst and Jaeger spoke for the Lutherans who hoped that the 1817 union between the Lutheran and Reformed churches in Prussia would stimulate a similar union in America. It could happen, they thought, if Americans grew into "more reasonable and scriptural opinions."[19]

Samuel Simon Schmucker

Samuel Simon Schmucker was the most influential American Lutheran theologian of the era because he was able to formulate a theology that gave expression to all three strands of belief—Pietist, confessional, and rationalist

—that had guided the tradition. By 1860 the ablest young Lutheran theologians decided that such a balancing act compromised the integrity of a distinctive Lutheran theology, and Schmucker ended his career with a sense of defeat, but throughout his life as a pastor, a professor, a theologian, an advocate of ecumenism, and a president of the General Synod of the Evangelical Lutheran Church, he defined the issues of Lutheran theology in antebellum America.

Mentored by his father in the Pietist tradition, Schmucker spent two years of study with Justus Helmuth at the University of Pennsylvania before undergoing an emotional religious experience at a revival meeting. In 1818 he entered Princeton Theological Seminary, where he studied for an additional two years alongside Charles Hodge under Archibald Alexander and Samuel Miller. Within five years after leaving Princeton, Schmucker realized his dream of founding in Gettysburg a Lutheran seminary — "a Franckean Seminary" like Halle — where in 1826 he became the professor of theology.[20]

Two years earlier he had lectured the synod on the history of the Lutheran Church in Germany "where Spener sowed the seed of truth, — where Arndt wrote and preached and lived his 'true Christianity,' where Francke wrought his works of love." He would continue to praise the "practical piety" of Spener and Francke as the model for American Lutherans and to link his vision with that of Muhlenberg, whom he viewed as a spiritual heir of Francke. Just as Muhlenberg's mission had been to "convert sinners and edify saints," Schmucker sought for a theology that would inform an "eminently practical" form of preaching faithful to the Pietist heritage.[21]

Yet Schmucker became convinced early in his career that confessions could be helpful in defining an American Lutheranism. His tour of New York as a young man taught him that "the Augsburg Confession should again be brought up out of the dust" and that the clergy should be required to subscribe to its fundamental doctrines, and he drafted a constitution for Gettysburg Seminary that would require professors to teach "the doctrines of the Holy Scriptures, as they are fundamentally taught in the Augsburg Confession." When Schmucker published his *Elements of Popular Theology* in 1826, he described the Augsburg Confession as the "authorized summary" of Lutheran belief, though he insisted that Lutheran clergy were obliged to affirm only its "fundamental doctrines" insofar as they conveyed, in a "manner substantially correct," the teachings of the Old and New Testaments, the "only infallible rule of faith and practice." Schmucker agreed that confessions should have authority; the dispute was about the nature and extent of their authority.[22]

Schmucker saw himself, therefore, as an opponent of rationalism in the church. He called upon the denomination's theologians to emulate Spener and Francke, who "stood up, not as philosophers to publish the speculations of

Plato or Aristotle, or their own far-famed Leibnitz or of Locke, but as ministers of the New Testament, to preach Christ crucified." Yet he subscribed to the tenets of rational orthodoxy and displayed throughout his life the American attachment to Baconianism. He studied Scottish Realism at Princeton, and in 1842 he published his own *Psychology, or, Elements of a New System of Mental Philosophy, on the Basis of Consciousness and Common Sense,* in which he contended that mental philosophy, as the "basis of all science," would "shed abundant light on some of the practical doctrines of Revelation."[23]

As a mental philosopher, Schmucker aspired to combine the insights of the Scots and the Germans, and he drew modestly on Immanuel Kant and Johann Gottlieb Fichte as well as Reid, Stewart, and Brown, even though the British empiricism took precedence over the traces of German thought. Like other American theologians, he admired the Scots because their ideas seemed compatible with a rational and biblical supernaturalism. Yet when Schmucker turned from mental philosophy to theology, he drew on Kantian thought in ways not common in antebellum America.[24]

For insight on reason and revelation, he read the German Lutherans Gottlob Christian Storr (1746–1805) and Carl Christian Flatt (1772–1843), whose *Lehrbuch der Christlichen Dogmatik* (1793) could be considered a German counterpart to American rational orthodoxy. In need of a textbook at Gettysburg, Schmucker prepared a translation of Storr and Flatt in 1826 that he titled *An Elementary Course of Biblical Theology,* which he presented to his students as a refutation of "metaphysical and speculative and infidel systems of pretended Christianity" and of "liberalist" biblical critics. He told them that its arguments exemplified a system of theology built "exclusively on the word of God."[25]

As central figures in the "old Tübingen theology," a movement that aimed to refute on both philosophical and biblical grounds the rationalism of the German "Neologians," Storr and Flatt selectively used Kantian critical philosophy to assert the limits of pure reason. They employed also the Kantian notion that moral experience, or practical reason, not pure rationality, made it possible to postulate God's existence. Unlike Kant, however, they thought that natural theology, especially the argument from design, could prove that God was more than a postulate of moral experience. They thought that the combination of the moral proof and the argument from design "compelled" reason to affirm, as a matter of knowledge, "a rational Being as the first great cause." In the manner of the American evidentialists, they then marshaled the internal and external evidences, with emphasis on the prophecies and miracles, to confirm the authenticity and credibility of the biblical revelation.[26]

When Storr and Flatt proved too technical and difficult for the seminary students, Schmucker published his own *Elements of Popular Theology*. Like the volume by Storr and Flatt, it expressed a decided ambivalence about reason. On the one hand, Schmucker doubted that unaided reason could have deduced from nature the existence of God, established that one God created the universe, clarified the course of conduct pleasing to God, or attained satisfactory evidence of life after death. He reverted to the notion of a primordial divine revelation, distorted by sinfulness, to explain the seeming universality of theistic belief — the idea of the *prisca theologia* (ancient theology) that was popular among both American Protestants and European Catholic traditionalists.[27]

On the other hand, Schmucker thought that reason, enabled by these revelatory remnants, could find ample evidence to confirm the reality of God through the standard arguments. Reason could also establish the plausibility of a divine revelation. And rational evidences, internal and external, could convince the unprejudiced mind that the revelation occurred in the Christian sacred writings. The human mind, he argued, had a "duty" to give its "sincere and uniform obedience to the strongest evidence," and he devoted a good portion of his systematic theology to laying out the evidences, demonstrating the plausibility of the biblical miracles, listing fulfilled prophecies, praising the internal harmonies of the Bible, and celebrating the Bible's salutary effect on the inner life of the believer.[28]

Since truth was harmonious, moreover, the divine revelation could not contain any truth "contrary to the plain and indisputable dictates of reason." Schmucker tried to prove, for instance, that the doctrine of the Trinity, though above reason, was nonetheless intelligible and comprehensible. Were it not, no Christian would have been obligated to believe it. Indeed, as a truth above reason, the Trinity could never be proved contrary to reason, and since the comprehensible doctrines of the biblical revelation could be shown to be rational, it was plausible that the incomprehensible doctrines were rational as well, even though they stood beyond the possibility of rational proof.[29]

Like the Reformed theological revisionists at New Haven, Oberlin, and Andover, Schmucker sought to reinterpret his tradition to make it more compatible with both reason and revivalist piety. A rational theology for him required a number of departures from the Lutheran thought of the sixteenth century. He abandoned Luther's doctrine of the bondage of the will and argued for freedom of the will by appealing to "consciousness" and feelings of moral responsibility. Accusing Luther of undue attachment to Augustine, he abandoned predestinarian teaching and described election as conditional on God's foreknowledge of "the voluntary conduct of each individual." The election that Paul discussed in Romans, he contended, was no more than a call to external membership in the visible church.[30]

Schmucker still held to total depravity, but he disagreed with the doctrine that God imputed Adam's guilt to his fallen offspring. For him, original sin became an occasion of condemnation only to those who voluntarily indulged their sinful propensities. Despite his theological training under Charles Hodge, he taught that all "real" sin consisted in "voluntary actions and their consequences." He also redefined older views of atonement. While he saw the death of Christ as vicarious, he denied that it should be viewed as "the literal payment of a debt," since this would give the sinner an unconditional claim to salvation. Schmucker defined the atonement, vaguely, as a "purchase" of a universal offer of salvation on the condition of faith. He criticized the governmental theory of the Hopkinsians because he thought that they still linked atonement too closely to a Calvinist view of election, but his conceptions of both atonement and sin drew him closer to revisionist Calvinism than to Lutheran traditions.[31]

The alterations that drew the special scorn of the confessionalists were sacramental. Schmucker argued that no Lutheran had to believe that the body and blood of Christ were corporeally present in the bread and wine of the Lord's Supper. He preferred to define the presence as "virtual" rather than "substantial," by which he meant that Christ "influenced" the faithful with unusual power through the sacrament. The idea of a corporeal presence, he thought, contradicted the teaching of the senses as well as the "universal observation" of human consciousness. Schmucker recognized that Luther had insisted on a "substantial" presence, but he argued that Melanchthon and others, including Calvin, had agreed on the "influence" theory, and he saw their view as an option for Lutherans of his own day, whom he wanted to leave "free to follow the dictates of their own conscience." In a similar manner he redefined baptism not as a means of regenerating grace but as a symbolic initiation into the church and the covenant. He had no sympathy with high-church and sacramentalist movements in the German Reformed, Episcopal, and immigrant Lutheran churches.[32]

What most clearly defined Schmucker's theology was a variant of Pietism that closely resembled the Reformed revivalism of the Edwardeans and the New Haven theologians. Like them, he emphasized conversion, insisted that repentance was a duty, and called on the sinful to repent "immediately." He recognized that Luther had described justification as the "article with which the church must stand or fall," and he affirmed it as a judicial act of divine forgiveness, but his emphasis fell, in Pietist fashion, on the "evidences" of justification in "good works and a life of evangelical obedience." Like the Edwardeans, he defined sanctification as a "progressive conformity to divine law" that issued in disinterested benevolence.[33]

Like many other American evangelicals, moreover, he looked forward to a millennium that would spread the gospel "over the whole earth, prior to the close of the present economy." Schmucker even speculated about the date of its commencement, exploring various possibilities, from 1859 (the date his father had determined) to 1882. As well as linking him to interests common among American Protestants, these views highlighted his affinity with traditional Pietism.[34]

Schmucker would have considered it no rebuke to hear that his theology would draw the Lutherans closer to other Protestant traditions. An active ecumenist, he distributed in 1838 a *Fraternal Appeal to the American Churches* in which he called for a Protestant confederation that would accept a common creed selectively pieced together from the existing formularies. In writing the creed, he sought to retain only the essential doctrines on which most Protestants could agree. It would have excluded the Unitarians, the Universalists, and the Catholics. Schmucker shared the typical evangelical bias against Catholicism and wrote three anti-Catholic treatises excoriating the "papal beast." Otherwise he thought that his "Apostolic, Protestant Confession" would enable all "orthodox Christian denominations" to share sacramental and ministerial communion. He thought that an "edifying, practical" theology could simply dispense with "everything to which Christians of any religious denomination could with propriety object."[35]

The growing confessionalist antipathy to this ecumenical spirit led Schmucker during the 1840s and 1850s to publish a series of essays defending his dream of an American Lutheran Church adapted to the revivalist ethos and reformist spirit of the broader American Protestantism. He supported the reforming voluntary societies of his era, from temperance to the abolition of slavery, and his outspoken abolitionism probably intensified the opposition to his "Americanism." Published together in 1851 as *The American Lutheran Church,* these essays contained his best work on the Pietist origins of American Lutheranism, the sacramental issues, and the vocation of American Lutheranism as a witness to the infallible authority of the Bible rather than a servant to the binding obligation of extended creeds.[36]

Four years later, Schmucker made the strategic mistake that accelerated the demise of his movement. Attempting to counter the growing strength of the confessionalists, he distributed, without signing, a *Definite Platform* (1855), of which he was the primary author. In it he called for Lutheran unity grounded on the scriptures as the only rule for faith and practice, the Apostles' and Nicene creeds as witnesses to scriptural truth, and an Augsburg Confession shorn of its errors. His "American Recension" of Augsburg would correct the sixteenth-century formulary by omitting its acceptance of the ceremonies of the mass, its approval of private confession and absolution, its doctrine of baptismal regeneration, and its views of the real presence in the Eucharist. The reaction to the document ripped the church apart.[37]

Although critics accused him and his allies of rationalism, the American party believed itself to be much closer in spirit to the seventeenth-century Pietists than to the eighteenth-century rationalists. Benjamin Kurtz (1795–1865), the editor of the *Lutheran Observer* in Philadelphia, defended the American revivals because they captured the spirit of the *collegia pietatis* of Spener and Francke, and the *Theological Sketch-Book* in which Kurtz formulated his theology consisted entirely of sermons with a revivalist tone. Simeon W. Harkey (1811–89) in Maryland gained his literary reputation for a brief treatise that called for "constant revivals of religion," defined the grand design of the church as the "conversion and sanctification of souls," and outlined the Pietist order of salvation as a guide for the revivalist. Schmucker's close friend Samuel Sprecher (1810–1906), the president of Wittenberg College in Ohio, said that he preferred "the immortal Spener" to any theologian who forgot that "the affections are a power stronger than the mightiest intellect." Their aim was a modern Pietism allied with revivalism and unshackled by what Sprecher called "bigoted attachment to doctrinal peculiarities."[38]

Confessional Lutheranism

In 1817, the Emperor Friedrich Wilhelm III united the Lutheran and Reformed churches in Prussia into one Evangelical Church. His action led the German theologian Claus Harms to publish "Ninety-Five Theses" (1817) in opposition to the union and in support of renewed Lutheran confessional integrity. When other smaller German territories followed Prussia's lead, the result was a reaction — and a persecution — that would alter the course of Lutheran theology in both Europe and America. By 1830, a variety of Lutheran theologians in Germany were defining a theology that returned to the sixteenth-century confessions for its grounding. Gottlieb Christoph Adolph von Harless in Erlangen, Johann G. Scheibel in Breslau, Wilhelm Loehe in Neuendettelsau, and August Vilmar in Marburg led a confessional movement intent on defining a true Lutheranism over against rationalism, Catholicism, and Calvinism. The university of Erlangen in Bavaria became a center of this confessional theology, which also had proponents in Denmark, Norway, and Sweden. As Lutheran immigrants from these regions traveled to America in the 1830s, they brought the confessional spirit with them.[39]

Much of the support for the confessionalism of the 1840s in America came from these immigrants and missionaries, who detested the Prussian Union, vowed to maintain their identity as Lutherans in their new home, and looked with scorn at the revivalist forms of piety and the unionist predispositions that they discovered among Lutheran churches in America. The missionary Friedrich Conrad Dieterich Wyneken spoke for them when he published in 1844 his *Distress of the German Lutherans in America,* a plea for help that encouraged confessional groups in Germany to lend their aid in countering the "Methodistic spirit."[40]

Confessionalism in America also had sources closer to home. As early as 1820, the Henkel family of New Market, Virginia, sparked a confessional resurgence in the South that would have a bearing on the northern disputes. The southern movement began after 1806, when the native-born Lutheran pastor Paul Henkel (1754–1825) opened a printing press in order to help preserve the German language and encourage the growth of Lutheranism in his region. At the outset, Henkel's theological publications, including his catechism and his treatise on *Baptism and the Lord's Supper* (1809), promoted a nonconfessional form of Lutheranism that sidestepped the differences between the Lutheran and Reformed traditions, but his sons moved toward a more confessional stance that persuaded him to join their reassertion of distinctive Lutheran doctrine.[41]

Henkel tutored four of his brothers and five of his sons in Lutheran theology, and in 1820 one of those sons, David Henkel (1795–1831), led a southern reaction against the General Synod because of its seeming indifference to the Augsburg Confession. After seceding from his own synod and helping form the confessional Tennessee Synod, David Henkel published a series of books in which he defended the doctrines of baptismal regeneration, the physical presence of Christ in the bread and wine of the Eucharist, the imputation of Adam's guilt to all human beings, and the imputation of Christ's righteousness to the faithful. He reaffirmed the Lutheran paradoxes that the human and divine natures of Christ exchanged properties (the *communicatio idiomatum*), enabling the human Christ to be omnipresent in the sacrament as both human and divine, and that the Christian was both fully righteous and fully sinful at the same time.[42]

The Henkels were self-trained theologians. Southern supporters of Schmucker, such as the Charleston pastor and naturalist John Bachman, criticized David Henkel as "crude, visionary, and inflammatory." Bachman thought Henkel wrong about both baptism and the Lord's Supper. The Henkels, however, were by the 1850s gaining support from the northern confessionalists. The main reason for that support was their publication of translations from the works of Luther and from the sixteenth-century confessions, especially the *Book of Concord,* for which they provided the first English translation in *The Christian Book of Concord* (1851). The confessional leader Charles Porterfield Krauth described its publication as "the most important contribution to the *Lutheran* theological literature of this country, which has yet appeared," and when they published a revised version three years later, some of Schmucker's northern opponents collaborated on the refining of the translations.[43]

The activities of the Henkels revealed some of the social dynamics in the dispute. Fond of the German language, they turned to English only with reluctance, and their sympathy for the language found an echo among northern immigrants who thought that the American Lutherans were too closely aligned with the English-speaking culture. The early confessionalists, like Charles Philip Krauth (1797–1867), were inclined to believe that German was "almost indispensable to the learned theologian and the intelligent Lutheran," and they also found in the Americanist dismissal of their views as "European" the suggestion that American culture was superior to the culture of the immigrants.[44]

The Henkels exhibited the populist ethos that marked the southern branch of the confessional movement. Their criticisms of the General Synod singled out its reliance on "patrons who are wealthy," while they claimed to speak for the "farmers and mechanics" who could not afford to pay for bureaucracies. David Henkel insisted that "the unlearned man has the same rational faculty as the learned," and he scorned the assumption that "literary accomplishments" ensured correct views of theology. In fact, a native-born educated elite joined the confessional movement, but both the Henkels and their Americanist opponents identified confessionalism with the cause of common people against elites. The Americanist reformers, on the other hand, thought that they were not only more American but also more learned and more closely tied to the colleges and seminaries than the confessionalists were. These social tensions, as well as the unspoken association of the American party with social reforms like abolitionism, formed an undercurrent of the dispute.[45]

One goal of the "Old Lutherans" who opposed Schmucker was to require clerical assent to the unaltered sixteenth-century confessions. Their cause gained an important ally in 1849 when Charles Philip Krauth, the professor of biblical literature at Gettysburg Seminary, published in the *Evangelical Review* a review of Heinrich Schmid's *Dogmatik of the Lutheran Church*, a compilation drawn from early modern Lutheran theologians. Krauth concluded that Americans needed a similar devotion to "pure, unadulterated Lutheranism." Within a year he was commending the whole range of sixteenth-century symbols—the Augsburg Confession, its *Apology*, the Smalcald Articles, Luther's catechism, and the Formula of Concord—and supporting the demand for required subscription to Augsburg. Krauth had been a pastor in Virginia and Maryland and the president of the Lutheran college in Gettysburg. In 1850 he joined the seminary faculty and became an editor of the new review, which was designed as a voice for the confessional party. To have someone of his stature on the confessional side gave it additional authority, even though the stricter Old Lutherans complained about his moderation.[46]

What especially disturbed confessionalists about Schmucker's *Definite Platform* was the claim that the Augsburg Confession contained doctrinal errors. One of the first confessionalist responses to Schmucker came from William Julius Mann (1819–93), who had studied at Tübingen before coming to America in 1845 with hopes of joining Philip Schaff on the faculty at the German Reformed seminary in Mercersburg. Gravitating toward the Lutherans, he became by 1854 the senior pastor at the St. Michael's and Zion's Congregation in Philadelphia. His *Plea for the Augsburg Confession* (1856) denied that it erred on any point of doctrine: "if Luther mixed truth with error, who can we trust?" In his subsequent *Lutheranism in America* (1857), he argued that it made no sense for the church to honor a confession and yet reject some of its doctrines.[47]

In 1850, Charles Porterfield Krauth (1823–83), the son of Charles Philip Krauth, entered the fray with an article in the *Evangelical Review* extolling the Augsburg Confession. A learned pastor in Virginia and Pennsylvania who had graduated from Gettysburg College and Seminary, Krauth would later publish the most erudite book to emerge from the controversy, *The Conservative Reformation and its Theology* (1871), which contained solid historical studies of the primary confessions and extended defenses of their doctrines. His overriding theme was that reformation always required a balancing of progress and conservation and that—in contrast to the other more radical sixteenth-century reforming traditions—the "reformatory conservatism" of the Lutheran movement moved closer to "the most perfect form of Christianity." The same theme had appeared in his writing in 1850: "Must Lutheranism be shorn of its glory to adapt it to our times or our land? . . . I am first a Lutheran and then an American."[48]

For the substance of doctrine, therefore, the Old Lutherans repeated the sixteenth-century Lutheran formulas on original sin, the imputation of guilt, justification by faith alone, the imputation of Christ's righteousness, the two natures of Christ, the sacramental presence, and baptismal regeneration. They saw in the American Lutheran attraction to Charles G. Finney's revivalism a threat to all of these truths, so they also defended more liturgical, catechetical, and traditional forms of worship and instruction. A pastor in Reading, Pennsylvania, J. A. Brown (1821–82), who would eventually replace Schmucker as the theologian at Gettysburg, charged in his *New Theology* (1857) that

Schmucker's ideas threatened essential Lutheran truth, but Schmucker was able to show in response that Brown's own position was often more Calvinist than classically Lutheran.[49]

The constant refrain was that Schmucker had succumbed to rationalism. John Hoffman's *Broken Platform* (1856) charged that Schmucker argued from "unaided reason"; J. A. Brown asserted that his arguments relied on mental science rather than biblical revelation; Julius Mann pointed out that one of Schmucker's arguments against the real presence — that it contradicted the testimony of the senses — would also count against the doctrine of the Trinity. Eager to show that the "light of revelation" could not be "made brighter by the taper of human reason," the Old Lutherans believed that Schmucker's rational orthodoxy was more rationalist than orthodox.[50]

Yet the confessionalists found it impossible to agree among themselves, and in the immigrant groups in the West the theological infighting became intense. The course of the western debates can be encapsulated in the career of Carl Ferdinand Wilhelm Walther (1811–87), an immigrant pastor who arrived in 1839 with several boatloads of refugees from Saxony and settled in Missouri where in 1847 he led in the formation of the Lutheran Church–Missouri Synod. Walther's influence in the West paralleled that of Schmucker and Charles Porterfield Krauth in the East.

Walther attained his reputation as a theologian when — in the Altenburg Debate of 1841 — he turned back challengers who believed that the Saxon immigrants, by leaving the state church of Saxony, had lost their churchly status and become sectarians, without proper ministers or rites. Walther argued, like Luther, that the true church existed wherever the word was purely taught and the sacraments administered according to Christ's institution. After he became a pastor in St. Louis and then the professor and president of Concordia Seminary there, he made his newspaper and journal — *Der Lutheraner* and *Lehre und Wehre (Doctrine and Defense)* — the rallying points for western confessionalism.[51]

His theology had little in common with Schmucker's rational orthodoxy. Drawn to Luther's suspicions of Aristotle, he refused to practice a rational apologetic: "A person who has been won for Christianity through the demonstration that Christianity can bear the closest scrutiny of science has not yet been won, and his faith is not yet faith." Belief in the infallibility of scripture could not rest on rational proofs. Reason could add nothing to biblical truth, provide no rational proof of the articles of faith, demonstrate no harmony between science and theology, and effect no accommodation between the church and "this scientific age." While granting reason a formal function in the presentation of biblical truth, he worried that efforts to explain and prove the mysteries of faith altered and destroyed them "in their substance." He was gladly willing to concede that the Lutheran confessions contained truths that conflicted with the world's fallen "reason."[52]

What he would not concede was that the Lutheran confessions contained any assertions that conflicted with scripture, "even in the smallest letter," or that any Lutheran could rightly enter the ministry of the church without subscribing unconditionally to "every one of the teachings" in the Augsburg Confession and the *Book of Concord*. His insistence on unconditional subscription set him against the missionaries of Wilhelm Loehe, who had once hoped to unite with his movement. While affirming the binding authority of the confessions, Sigmund Fritschl (1833–1900), a Bavarian who had studied with Loehe before assuming a teaching post at Dubuque Seminary, tried to persuade Walther to accept a distinction between essential and nonessential articles, to interpret the articles by locating them in their historical setting, and to recognize that doctrinal development did not end with the Reformation. Fritschl spoke for the Iowa Synod, which broke away from the Missourians in 1854 when Loehe disagreed with Walther's attempt to link the status of the ministerial office to the authority of the local congregation, but the dispute over "open questions" intensified the hostility. The Iowans, led by Fritschl and his brothers, insisted that some doctrines not clearly decided in scripture — including millennialism, Luther's belief that the Pope was the Antichrist, and the mandatory character of the Sabbath day — could remain as open questions on which disagreement should be tolerated within the church. Walther thought that Christian unity required consensus.[53]

The struggles among Lutheran confessionalists would continue after the Civil War, and Walther would remain close to the center of most of the disputes. Along with theologians from the Norwegian Synod, he would argue that the absolution pronounced by the minister imparted forgiveness to all who heard it, regardless of their faith, while Swedish-American theologians (and some Norwegians) would spurn this view as "romanizing." The Norwegians went on to argue that the justification wrought by the atonement extended to the whole world, including the faithless, though only the faithful would benefit by it; the Swedish theologians of the Augustana Synod would reply that although the atonement reconciled the world objectively to God, justification had to await a subjective acceptance of forgiveness through faith.[54]

Walther would carry his views to their logical conclusion by affirming a doctrine of unconditional predestination, a doctrine criticized even by some of the other Missouri theologians. He would make his deepest mark through his defense of congregational authority and his thirty-nine Friday lectures on *The*

Proper Distinction Between the Law and the Gospel, which remained in a stenographic manuscript form until almost the end of the century. The lectures, especially, became the classic statement in the American confessional tradition of Luther's distinction between the divine law, which set a standard no fallen human being could meet, and the gospel that nonetheless offered forgiveness to all who confessed their inability and their reliance on Christ as their justification.[55]

Walther relied so heavily on the confessions and on the orthodox theologians of the sixteenth and seventeenth centuries that his critics dismissed him as a *Zitatentheologe,* a "quotation theologian." His fondness for the confessions, however, gave his theology a family resemblance to similar theologies among high-church Episcopalians, the Princeton theologians, and even the Reformed theologians at Mercersburg Seminary — John Williamson Nevin and Philip Schaff — with whom he otherwise had little in common. More broadly, the Lutheran confessional movement represented a departure from American rational orthodoxy. Far more intent on fidelity to traditional witnesses to scriptural truth than on stating proofs for the compatibility of reason and faith, the confessionalists represented a conservative turn away from Baconianism. Even more than the American Catholic tradition — which still valued the evidences for Catholicity — the confessional Lutherans minimized the importance of evidential reasoning. More than any other widespread American theological movement, they drew an irreducible contrast between faith and a fallen reason.[56]

20

Catholics: Reason and the Church

John Joseph Hughes (1797–1864), who would attain national recognition as the bishop of New York, expressed in 1840 a Catholic judgment about the Protestant quest for reasonableness: "They proclaim that theirs is a Christianity of reason; of this they boast, and let them glory. Ours is a Christianity of faith; ours descends by the teaching of the Church." Hughes contended that reason was "not competent to decide anything," whether the mysteries of revelation or even the puzzles of the material world. Yet this was only one side of the complicated Catholic conception of theology and its rationality. Hughes could also acknowledge that reason had "its own invaluable sphere," and he joined in the broader Catholic effort to assimilate the evidential tradition in a distinctively Catholic manner. From the late eighteenth through the mid-nineteenth century, most Catholic theologians shared a consensus both about the substance of Catholic truth and about the efficacy of evidential reasoning.[1]

The Catholic missionaries to New France and New Spain produced an extensive literature describing and promoting their mission, but no substantial corpus of theology emerged in the Catholic mission until the Jesuits of eighteenth-century Maryland began to preserve their sermon manuscripts, most of which still remain unpublished, in which they exhibited both the rhetorical practices and the theology of the French tradition in which most of them were educated. This meant that the Jesuit sermons avoided the predestinarian theology of the

French Jansenists and the mystical piety of the French Quietists, promoting instead a humanistic tradition, associated with such figures as Francis de Sales and Jacques Bossuet in France, which saw virtuous living as the best exemplification of piety.[2]

The Jesuit sermons and manuals often provided practical instruction about the proper way to confess sin to a priest or to perform such popular observances as the Devotion of the Sacred Heart of Jesus. They sometimes drew instruction from the lives of pious Catholics such as Ignatius of Loyola, the founder of the Society of Jesus. But some of the sermons attempted to define complex theological doctrines in ways that illumined Catholic practice. Peter Attwood (1682–1734), who became the superior of the Jesuit mission in 1720, preached on the incarnation of Christ as the "foundation" of Christian faith, explaining that God became incarnate to redeem men and women from sin, transform them into the image of Christ, and exemplify the virtues of humility, and that the Virgin Mary, who had produced the divine word "in time, as the Eternal Father produced it in Eternity," was the "mediatrix" whose intercessions aided the faithful in their efforts to imitate Jesus. In a similar fashion, Joseph Greaton, who would found in Philadelphia the first urban American Catholic congregation, described in emotional detail the passion of Christ as an example of humility, meekness, and patience amid suffering. Since the sermons remained unpublished, they did not become part of a broader theological conversation, but they gave evidence of the concern to defend a distinctively Catholic doctrine that would, by the late eighteenth century, draw Catholic theologians into a wider exchange with others.[3]

The greater part of this American Catholic theology came from thirteen theologians, nine of whom became bishops. The bishops have been remembered more as managers than as theologians, but they included such figures as Hughes, whose theological production as a polemicist was voluminous; Francis Patrick Kenrick, whose four-volume *Theologiae Dogmaticae* (1834–40) and three-volume *Theologia Moralis* (1841–43) established him as the most accomplished American Catholic theologian of the era; and John England (1786–1842), whose theological writings in his *United States Catholic Miscellany* filled three volumes of his five-volume collected works. Most of the thirteen were immigrants: nine were born abroad (four in Ireland, three in France, one in The Hague, one in Alsace), but they quickly found their voice in the American debates.[4]

They included some of the best-educated theologians in America. Martin John Spalding (1810–72) graduated from St. Mary's College and St. Thomas Seminary in Bardstown, Kentucky, before earning a doctorate in theology at the Urban College of the Propaganda in Rome. Kenrick also studied six years at the Urban College, and John Carroll (1735–1815) spent two years in a Jesuit novitiate before moving on to three years of training in language and philosophy at Liège. Four of them—John Baptist Mary David (1761–1841), John Baptist Purcell (1800–83), Stephen Theodore Badin (1768–1853), and Benedict Joseph Flaget (1763–1850)—completed their studies in Sulpician seminaries in France. The American converts Orestes Augustus Brownson (1803–76) and Isaac Thomas Hecker (1819–88) were the only self-educated theologians in the group, though no one exceeded Brownson in the breadth of his learning.

In 1786 Catholics founded their first college, Georgetown in Washington, D.C., and in 1791 they founded the first American seminary, St. Mary's in Baltimore. By 1856 they owned thirty-seven seminaries and twenty-four colleges. The academy, however, was not the seedbed for their theology. Purcell briefly taught moral philosophy at Mount St. Mary's College and Seminary in Emmitsburg, Maryland, but he gained his reputation as a defender of Catholic doctrine after he became a bishop in Cincinnati, mainly through the publication in 1837 of the transcript of his oral debate with Alexander Campbell. Kenrick spent several years on the faculty of St. Thomas Seminary in Bardstown, Kentucky, but he published his systematic theology and his *Vindication of the Catholic Church* (1855), along with treatises on baptism, justification, and the Papacy and several biblical commentaries, while he was the bishop of Philadelphia and the archbishop of Baltimore. David taught theology in Angers and philosophy at Georgetown College, and he established the Seminary of St. Thomas and the College of St. Joseph in Bardstown, but his *Catechism of Christian Doctrine* (1825) appeared after he became the coadjutor bishop of Bardstown.[5]

Rare was the Catholic theologian without experience in a parish or administrative post. Spalding taught at the Bardstown seminary during the 1830s, but only after he became the vicar general and then the bishop of Louisville did he publish his *General Evidences of Catholicity* (1847) and the apologetic essays in his *Miscellanea* (1855). Demetrius Augustine Gallitzin (1770–1840), the son of a Russian ambassador and a Prussian countess, founded in 1799 the Catholic colony of Loretto in Pennsylvania, which he served as a priest while he wrote his *Defence of Catholic Principles* (1816) along with other theological tracts aimed at lay readers who would never have access to "the learned and frequently expensive and voluminous works" of England, Purcell, Hughes, and Brownson. The Swiss-educated Jesuit Anthony Kohlmann (1771–1836) was more of an academician, and his *Unitarianism Philosophically and Theologically*

Examined (1821), written while he was teaching at Georgetown, helped him secure a call to the chair of theology at the Gregoriana in Rome, but even he spent a decade in parishes and administrative work before he began his teaching.[6]

In addition to their books, they published extensively in Catholic journals and newspapers, often with serial articles that extended over months. They filled with Catholic apologetics such periodicals as England's *United States Catholic Miscellany,* Hughes's *Catholic Herald,* Spalding's *Catholic Advocate,* and *Brownson's Quarterly Review,* which became under Orestes Brownson's editorship one of the stellar intellectual journals of the period. The journals enabled the Catholic theologians to debate Protestants of every stripe: high- and low-church Episcopalians, Old and New School Presbyterians, the Mercersburg theologians, Baptists, Campbell's restorationists, Quakers, Unitarians, and transcendentalists. Through their polemical pieces in diocesan newspapers — and through oral debates with Protestants on theological topics — they also reached a popular audience.

They saw themselves as theologians of the people, defenders of popular faith against the elitism and fashion of Protestant culture. One of the enduring themes of antebellum Catholic apologetics was that Protestants catered to the wealthy and fashionable while the poor were "the favorites of Christ, and the favorites of the Catholic Church." They were sometimes critics of capitalist inequalities, which they saw as solvents of the culture's social ties. Kohlmann argued in 1821 that private property was no more than a concession to human fallenness and "the baleful cause of almost all the evils which afflict" humanity. John England also suggested that the common people were more trustworthy on "subjects of religion" than the "learned philosophers." But they felt no sympathy for theological populists.[7]

They had more than one reason to harbor suspicions of the populist trends. For one thing, they opposed the Protestant rhetoric about the right of "private judgment," which in theory accorded equal authority to every reader of scripture. In 1784 John Carroll observed that "the generality of mankind are neither by education, or abilities, or leisure, qualified to enter upon the inquiries necessary to judge for themselves." He considered it unlikely that laborers and mechanics could ever "acquire the knowledge in languages, and the critical discernment" necessary to master the theological sources. Carroll's objection became a frequent refrain. The scriptures were hard to understand. That is why, said John England, we have teachers and seminaries.[8]

More important, they added a theological argument against the populist impulse. It was not simply that the unlearned could not unravel the mysteries. Even "the most learned," wrote Spalding, were often "sadly puzzled" when they read scripture. For Catholics, the main problem with the populist spirit in theology was its individualism, its assumption that the isolated individual could arrive at truth without the guidance of an authoritative tradition. Spalding argued that Christ had divided his church into two departments, the teachers and the taught. But he did not mean that the learned theologians were necessarily the authoritative teachers; it was rather the great company of bishops, the successors of the apostles, who could define the doctrines of the church. No American theologian had more theological training than Spalding, but in his judgment, and in the judgment of the church, it was only when he became the bishop of Louisville in 1848 that he stepped into the circle of theologians authorized to discern and define collectively the church's theological truth.[9]

It was not irrelevant that Catholics often encountered the irrationality of the Protestant majority. Hovering around the edges of civilized theological debate in America were lawmakers who restricted Catholic immigrants, school committees who protected the Protestant Bible in the public schools, publishers who printed lurid anti-Catholic accusations, nativist political parties that stirred up public fears of papal domination, orators who warned of Roman invasions, church resolutions condemning the Catholic menace, and mobs who rioted and burned Catholic churches, homes, and convents. Catholics found in American religious fragmentation, moreover, the scandalous evidence that "the judgment of reason" led in conflicting directions. Yet the evidential tradition, confirmed by theological trends in Rome, was too strong to support any blanket condemnation of reason. Evidentialism and the quest for reasonableness flourished in Catholic as well as Protestant theology.[10]

Reason, Revelation, and Tradition

Historians have debated whether John Carroll and John England should be designated as "enlightenment" Catholic thinkers. The answer to the question hinges largely on conflicting views of what such a designation means. It is true that they opposed the anti-Christian enlightenment. It is equally true that they emphasized the rationality of Catholicism and strove to adapt the church to the values of republicanism, religious liberty, freedom of conscience, and church-state separation. Subsequent Catholic thinkers would hold many of the same values, though England's allies never shared his enthusiasm for representative democracy within the church. Like their Protestant counterparts, Carroll and England opposed certain features of the eighteenth-century enlightenment while appropriating others.[11]

John Carroll was a native of Maryland who spent more than a quarter of a century in Europe and England before returning to America, where he became in 1789 the first American Catholic bishop. In 1784 he published a reply to a former Jesuit named Charles Wharton whose *Letter to the Roman Catholics of Worcester* (1784) had contended that Catholics were too biased to conduct an impartial rational investigation of either their own faith or that of their Protestant antagonists. In his *Address to the Roman Catholics of the United States of America,* Carroll tried to prove that "rational investigation is as open to catholics, as to any other set of men on the face of the earth." While granting that Catholic faith rested on the authority of the church, he argued that Catholics always insisted that obedience to that authority "must be reasonable."[12]

In 1825 Joseph Blanco White, a Spanish priest of Irish descent who had left the Catholic Church, migrated to England, and joined the Anglicans, published a similar attack — *The Practical and Internal Evidences Against Catholicism* — in which he claimed that Catholics could not be tolerant and should not be relieved from punitive legal restrictions. The American edition in 1826 brought a reply from John England, who had long fought for religious liberty in Ireland before becoming in 1820 the first bishop of Charleston, South Carolina. An admirer of American culture, England created in 1823 a diocesan constitution modeled after the federal constitution, allowing both clerical and lay delegates to exercise legislative authority over temporal matters within the church. He felt that Catholicism flourished best in societies that nurtured republican values, practiced religious freedom, and respected rationality.

In 1826 he began to publish in his diocesan newspaper a series of "Letters on the Calumnies of J. Blanco White Against the Catholic Religion" (1826–28) in which he affirmed religious liberty, freedom of conscience, and the rationality of Catholic faith. In his subsequent publications he would argue, like Carroll, that the church never required its members to "believe without evidence," that faith could never contradict reason, and that revealed religion would never clash with natural religion.[13]

Their devotion to church-state separation and religious liberty marked Carroll and England as citizens of the enlightenment era, but they had no simple conception of the rationality of faith. Carroll conceded that Christian truth included "mysteries and unsearchable doctrines," and England added that unaided reason could neither discover nor comprehend them. By 1828 England could say that if he tested truth solely at the tribunal of his own reason, he would believe neither in the resurrection of Christ nor the existence of God. He sometimes asserted the position of the European traditionalists that reason could discover religious truth only because it benefited from the revelation given to Adam and transmitted to his posterity, and he never failed to insist that the mysteries of faith were above reason.[14]

In their precarious balancing of reason and faith, the two men expressed what would remain a consensus, determined in part by papal authority. The Vatican theologians in the early nineteenth century condemned both the rationalizing theology of the Germans Georg Hermes and Anton Guenther, who held that reason could arrive at all the Christian truths, and the fideism of the French traditionalist theologians Louis Bautain and Louis de Bonald, who held that unaided reason could discover no Christian truths, even no philosophical truths. By the 1830s the neo-Thomist theology of Giovanne Perrone in Rome, who tried to balance the claims of reason and revelation, was becoming the approved standard in Rome. Against this background, it made eminent sense for the Americans to affirm natural theology and the rational proofs for God's existence.[15]

Something about the claim of American Protestants that reason was on their side, however, drew from Catholic theologians a sustained attack on reason's pretensions. They contrasted Catholic faith with the Protestant attempt to measure the mysteries by a rational standard, and they delighted in displaying the ambiguities of Common Sense Realism. While John Hughes, for example, could employ Realist language about the primary truths presupposed in rational judgments, his point was that such truths, as the foundation of rational thought, could not themselves be demonstrated, so that even philosophy rested on faith assumptions. He ridiculed the enlightenment faith in a "universal human reason," citing the diversity of human thought as evidence against it. In his "Six Letters" (1857) in reply to the Episcopal theologian Nicholas Murray, he argued that the "common sense" to which Protestants so frequently appealed was always culturally determined, taking one form in one part of the world and another in others. To make common sense a criterion for discarding Catholic mysteries, moreover, ran the risk of subverting Protestant certitudes as well.[16]

Hughes's antirationalist polemics found echoes in Catholic thought throughout the period. In his reply to Unitarians, Anthony Kohlmann emphasized that reason could not comprehend even the empirical world. It was even more powerless when it tried to grasp spiritual realities. Spalding said that Christianity was what Christ made it, not what reason would have it to be. Gallitzin charged that the "blind reason" of Protestant theology was both limited and corrupt. By rejecting the Catholic mysteries, doctrines like transubstantiation and baptismal regeneration, Spalding said, Protestants were lurching toward an "empty rationalism."[17]

Yet the Catholic theologians found a crucial function for reason that drew them closer to the Protestants than they wanted to acknowledge. They fully accepted the logic of the evidential tradition and used it as a means to say that

Catholic faith was rational. Their strategy was to show that the "rational evidences" that Protestants used to confirm the scriptural revelation, when properly understood, confirmed the authority of the Catholic Church and made it reasonable to accept its testimony to Christian mysteries. As Spalding expressed it: "the Evidences which sustain Catholicity are substantially identical with those which establish Christianity itself."[18]

Catholics argued that it was reasonable to accept the church's testimony about truths that exceeded the grasp of reason, because reason could demonstrate the trustworthiness of the church. The logic found expression in Spalding's *General Evidences of Catholicity*. He wrote the book after delivering in the winter of 1844–45 a series of Sunday evening lectures in Louisville's cathedral to counter the anti-Catholic lectures of six Protestant ministers who had formed a "league" against "popery." It took him an additional two years to turn the lectures into the book. The arguments were familiar, drawn partly from the lectures of Nicholas Wiseman in England, but Spalding would not have seen originality as a virtue. The argument was simply that the Catholic Church represented the fulfillment of earlier prophecies, that miracles had continued to confirm its authority, that its success and its moral effects sustained its claims, and that its marks of catholicity, unity, and holiness proved it to be the only institution that conformed to the mandates of the New Testament. Only the Catholic Church could trace a visible link to the apostles, and only it had fulfilled the commission of Jesus that his apostles evangelize throughout the whole world (Matt. 18:18–20), proving it to be the church to which he had promised the guidance of the Spirit. The question was one of historical facts, amenable to the rational assessment of evidence.[19]

The argument invested heavily in the claim that reports of continuing miracles in the church confirmed the church's teaching authority. Defining a miracle as an extraordinary event beyond or contrary to the usual course of nature, Spalding argued that the reports of believable eyewitnesses, reports that the church normally examined with great care, had a credibility that made them plausible. Catholic theologians employed the standard argument against David Hume's denial of miracles: in saying that ordinary experience made it implausible to accept testimonies to the miraculous, Hume had elevated a limited experience to the status of a universal norm. Against the usual Protestant assertion that the age of miracles had ceased, they argued that the continuing ecclesiastical miracles had the same evidentiary support as the biblical miracles that Protestants accepted. Miracles could be shown to be factual, and the miracles verified the authority of the teaching.[20]

Their unceasing appeal to "fact" revealed the Catholic theologians as thinkers who inhabited the same Baconian world as Protestants. "Let us look for

facts," wrote England, "instead of hazarding conjectures, or maintaining opinions." That the Catholic Church had existed since the time of Christ was a fact;
so also was it a fact, recorded in Matthew 28:19–20, that Christ established the
church to teach his doctrines, promising that it would be guided by the Spirit of
truth. The church then testified to further facts — that Jesus rose from the dead,
for example, or that he remained present in the Eucharist — which could rationally be believed because the witness could be proved credible.[21]

The argument rested on a definition of the church as a "visible society" of
believers united by the same faith and sacraments and submissive to the same
legitimate pastors. Catholic theologians identified the visible church with the
kingdom of Christ and countered the Protestant contention that the true
church remained invisible. To speak of a church that gave no visible signs of its
existence seemed to Hughes both contrary to the Pauline image of the body of
Christ and beyond any rational proof. The Catholic theologians differed
about some matters. They differed, for example, about the extent to which the
institutions of the church should be republican, or representative, in their
decision making. Most rejected England's enthusiasm for republicanism
within the institution. But they agreed about its essential visibility.[22]

The same arguments that established the authority of the visible church
established also its infallibility, which issued from the promises of Christ that
he would teach his disciples all truth and that the Spirit would abide with them
forever, teaching them all things (Matt. 28:19–20, John 14:15–16, 26). He
promised, as well, that the gates of hell would never prevail against the church.
"If this Church can teach erroneous doctrines instead of God's truth," England
concluded, "it will be a prevailing of the gates of hell, manifestly." While no
individual pastor could be deemed infallible, the body of bishops in conjunction with the Pope could not err on matters of faith and morals, simply because Christ had promised to guard the apostles and their successors from
error. For Catholic theologians the promise of Christ was the vital fact that
proved the case.[23]

About the infallibility of the Pope, acting alone, however, the Americans
disagreed. All agreed that the Papacy was the sole supreme head of the church
on earth. All grounded the primacy of the Papacy in the assertion of Christ
that Peter would be the rock on which the church would be built (Matt.
16:15–20) and in the historical argument that the popes were the successors of
Peter. Francis Patrick Kenrick's study of *The Primacy of the Apostolic See
Vindicated* (1837) presented evidence that Peter's primacy had been the constant confession of the church throughout its history. But did primacy mean
papal infallibility?[24]

Kenrick taught in his *Theologiae Dogmaticae* that it did, attributing his conviction to the arguments he had heard as a student in Rome, but Catholic theologians shared no consensus. In 1837, when John Purcell debated Alexander Campbell in Cincinnati on the truth of Catholicism, Purcell disclaimed the doctrine of papal infallibility: "No enlightened Catholic holds the pope's infallibility to be an act of faith. I do not; and none of my brethren, that I know of, do." The Pope, he said, is "liable to error," infallible only when all the bishops acquiesced in his judgment about matters of faith and morals. For the most part, the theologians did not deny papal infallibility; they insisted rather that it was no article of faith but a matter of opinion, "every one being at liberty," in Carroll's words, "to adopt or reject it, as the reasons for or against may affect him." Spalding felt "inclined strongly" to affirm it, England to deny it. In his *Defence of Catholic Principles,* the Pennsylvania parish theologian Demetrius Gallitzin listed it among the "pretended principles" that malice and ill will falsely attributed to Catholics. Only after Vatican I defined the doctrine in 1870 would an American consensus emerge.[25]

To affirm the church's infallibility was to elevate the church's tradition, which the Council of Trent had made coequal in authority with scripture. In America, Catholic theologians emphasized that scripture confirmed the authority of tradition: the book of Acts related that Jesus gave forty days of instruction to the apostles (Acts 1:3); John taught that the whole world could not contain all that Christ spoke (John 18:21, 25); Paul told the Thessalonians to hold the traditions they had learned (2 Thess. 14:5). The church therefore looked to tradition as well as scripture to justify both doctrines and practices, from infant baptism to purgatory, auricular confession, absolution, and worship on Sunday. "We go for the Bible and tradition — the whole word of God, written and unwritten," said Purcell.[26]

When Protestants responded to the Catholic view of tradition by insisting on scripture alone as the norm of faith, the Catholic answer was to point out that scripture itself was the product of tradition. For decades after the resurrection of Christ, Catholics argued, the church had no authoritative epistles and gospels, and for centuries it debated the canonicity of the various New Testament books. Only in the fourth century did the church establish a canon of biblical writings, using church teaching as a criterion for selection, so that even in their use of scripture the Protestants depended on the tradition of the church. "The testimony therefore of the catholic church," Carroll wrote, "certified in the tradition of all ages, is the ground upon which we and others admit the divine authority of holy writ." Without trust in the tradition, Protestants had no certainty that they even had the word of God.[27]

In England, France, and Germany, Catholic theologians were interpreting tradition through lenses of historical development and change, and John

Henry Newman's *Essay on the Development of Doctrine* (1845) argued that truths only implicitly present in the original revelation had emerged later in the church's history. The Americans, however, emphasized the immutability of the church's truth and looked upon variation as a sign of apostasy. "We contend," said Hughes, "that no new doctrine is true." Hughes believed that the church knew all the doctrines of Christ "from the beginning." It had received a "deposit of doctrines" and transmitted them from one generation to another. The Americans would acknowledge a modest form of development. Hughes conceded that the church had defined the original doctrines "more clearly" in its general councils and that the "form" of doctrines had changed even while their substance remained immutable. Kenrick admired the *Symbolik* (1832) of the German theologian Johann Adam Moehler, who had spoken of an organic evolution of doctrine, though even Moehler had taught that it was the form, not the substance, of truth that changed. Kenrick also liked the notion of the Mercersburg theologian John Williamson Nevin that tradition was a "living stream," and he sometimes quoted Newman, though he insisted that development added no more than clarity to the original deposit of faith. For the Americans, immutability was the mark of truth.[28]

It was not that tradition gave the Bible its authority. England explained that biblical authority came from the sacred origin of the writings. Like most Protestants, Catholics argued for the Bible's inspiration and inerrancy. Unlike Protestant theologians, however, they did not treat the doctrine of inspiration as primarily a theory about how the books were written. What they emphasized was that only the testimony of the church could ground belief in biblical inspiration. They did not find convincing the Protestant view that the Bible testified to its own infallibility; they saw that as a circular argument. The important point was the church's acceptance of the books as inspired.[29]

A similar argument marked the debate over exactly what constituted the Bible. Protestants would accept as canonical in the Old Testament only the books contained in the Jewish canon of the Hebrew scriptures. This omitted fifteen books that ever since the fourth century had been designated as "apocryphal," meaning that they were set apart because of their absence from the Jewish canon. They were contained, however, in the Septuagint, the Greek version of the Hebrew scriptures derived from Alexandrian Judaism, and early Greek-speaking Christians had adopted them as part of their first Bible. Although Jerome had labeled them as apocryphal when in the fourth century he translated the scripture into Latin, they gradually assumed a quasi-canonical authority within the medieval church, and the Council of Trent accorded them canonical status, a decision rejected by the Protestant reformers. The argument of the Catholic theologians was that centuries of tradition had prepared the way for that conciliar decision, which assumed the standing of a doctrinal truth once defined by a council. Since Protestants, whether they recognized it or not, also received scripture on the authority of a church council, it seemed illogical and perverse of them to depart from a decision honored for centuries. The Protestant logic would lead, Kenrick said, to "one man adding, and another taking away" at will.[30]

The most frequent way in which tradition functioned as the rule of faith for Catholic theologians, however, was in biblical interpretation. The Protestant principle of "private interpretation" — the principle that each reader could be a competent judge of the meaning of the text — seemed to them to contain multiple errors. It made individual reason the criterion for doctrine and reduced truth to "private opinion." It led, therefore, to both rationalism and relativism, as evidenced in the sectarian chaos of American Christianity. It was also an empty principle, because in fact Protestants read the Bible through confessional lenses and communal assumptions as much as Catholics did. But since Protestants lacked an infallible interpretive authority, they sank into subjectivity and uncertainty.[31]

With the tradition of the church as their rule of faith, Catholics could look to centuries of interpretation to discern a consensus. Our rule, said Hughes, means that "Scripture . . . has but one sense and one meaning, through all the ages of the church, and all the nations of the earth." This unanimity still allowed for multiple meanings within the text. Interpreters like Gallitzin defended the medieval fourfold exegesis, in which a single text could have various meanings: "Jerusalem" could mean, literally, a city; allegorically, the church; anagogically, the kingdom of heaven; and tropologically, the faithful soul. But that kind of variety remained compatible with Hughes's claim for unanimity; the consensus of the church was still the norm. Catholic theologians stood for communal reason rather than private rationality.[32]

Instead of looking primarily to the early church theologians, however, the Americans usually elevated the authority of a medieval scholastic theology that was transmitted through manuals designed to state authoritative teachings in a form that lent itself to memorization. The early Catholic schools in America relied heavily on the *Theologia dogmatica et moralis* (1789) of the French theologian Louis Bailly. By 1846, they were turning to Giovanne Perrone's five-volume *Compendium*. One observer of the Catholic scene in America informed John Henry Newman in 1846 that "the scholastic form of doctrine is that which is in vogue here, and nothing but that." The respect of American Catholic thinkers for the scholastic theologians of the twelfth through the seventeenth centuries was so great, he noted, that many of the American clergy knew little of "the early Fathers." Kenrick's *Theologiae Dog-*

maticae relied more on the early church fathers than on scholastic authors, but his text never attained the influence for which he had hoped. The French and Roman manuals remained the vehicles for theological teaching in most American seminaries until after the Civil War.[33]

In any case, most Catholics claimed that only the testimony of an infallible authority could secure the central Christian mysteries of the Trinity and the incarnation. Most recognized that neither could be considered a doctrine of reason. The exception was Anthony Kohlmann, a native of Alsace who joined the Jesuit order in 1803 and sailed to America in 1806, serving as a priest to scattered German congregations in Pennsylvania before becoming first the administrator of the New York diocese and then the master of novices at Georgetown College. His 1821 critique of Unitarian theology ventured the judgment that reason alone could show at least the possibility and reasonableness of Trinitarian doctrine. Since natural theology confirmed the creativity of God, it suggested that productivity was an essential divine attribute, which had to exist from all eternity. Biblical evidence and the testimony of tradition then confirmed, through manifold references to the Father, Son, and Holy Ghost, that the productivity had taken Trinitarian forms. Others contended only that rational argument could protect Trinitarian doctrine from rationalistic criticisms. Catholic theologians not only confuted Unitarians but also joined in criticizing Moses Stuart and Albert Barnes, who had questioned the eternal generation of the Son.[34]

They shared Kohlmann's confidence that even the most exalted mysteries were far more than "mere metaphysical speculations." They were practical doctrines. Kohlmann believed that the doctrine of the Trinity displayed the pattern of harmony and love that ought to unite humanity; the incarnation taught how to despise riches, pleasure, and honor for the sake of others; the atonement brought consolation. Catholic theologians in America avoided the older sense of the "speculative" as knowledge of God for its own sake. Like other American theologians, they disparaged the term and said that Christian theology was "practical in its very nature."[35]

Christ and the Order of Salvation

No doctrine was more practical, from this perspective, than incarnation. The central mystery that Jesus Christ was both human and divine, God from eternity and a man born in time, permeated Catholic theology. Though most of the Americans did not argue, as some European Catholic theologians were arguing, that the church was itself the extension of the incarnation, they did see it as basis for affirming the "perpetual presence" of Christ in the church. Hughes contrasted Catholic doctrine, which taught that the benefits of the incarnation embraced the whole human race, with the Calvinist doctrine of limited atonement. He believed that the incarnation had elevated human nature and inaugurated a ceaseless reformation that altered the course of civilization.[36]

The doctrine of incarnation provided a defense against Protestant attacks on Catholic devotion to Mary and a rationale for affirming Pius IX's definition in 1854 of her immaculate conception. Denying that Marian devotion elevated the mother above the son, they argued that it rather signified "homage to the mystery of His incarnation." Both Hughes and Kenrick saw it as the inevitable consequence of an incarnational theology. To deny that Mary was the "mother of God incarnate" was to fall into ancient heresy, and to affirm it was to support a devotion that addressed her as a suppliant and intercessor at the throne of Christ. They agreed, as well, that the logic of the incarnation suggested the immaculate conception of Mary — the belief that she was free from any taint of original as well as actual sin. When Pius IX called in 1849 for episcopal comment, the Americans supported a papal definition of the doctrine, but Kenrick and Michael O'Connor, the bishop of Pittsburgh, both labored to excise language that claimed too much, language suggesting that redemption seemed to require Mary's consent, that the book of Genesis provided textual support, or that the tradition had always been clear in the church. Kenrick preferred to emphasize that it was implicit in the mystery of the incarnation.[37]

On the doctrine of original sin itself, Catholics emphasized their differences both with Westminster Calvinists and with the New England revisionists. Kenrick disputed the New England conception of sinfulness as voluntary, arguing against Albert Barnes that Romans 5 depicted every human being as "conceived and born in sin" as a result of Adam's "representative" sinfulness. But he also disputed the older Calvinist view that Adamic sin resulted in the utter corruption of human nature. In Catholic theology, Adam lost rather the "supernatural graces," given freely by God, which enabled him to know his Creator and freed him from "concupiscence," or disproportionate desire. The loss of that gift in the fall "weakened and despoiled" human nature, but it did not wholly corrupt it.[38]

Catholics therefore defended "the liberty of the will." They saw the will as sufficiently free to receive or refuse divine offers of grace, and they believed that Lutheran and Calvinist doctrines of bondage degraded human beings from their status as "moral and responsible" agents. For them salvation depended on "the exercise of . . . liberty in corresponding with grace." To counter charges of Pelagianism they always insisted that the Spirit prepared the will through "illumination and inspiration," but the will had to cooperate. The persistence of human freedom became for them both the explanation for evil in the world and the guarantee that salvation remained a possibility for all. Kenrick explained predestination merely as a divine judgment grounded in foreknowledge of a free response.[39]

Their view of a salutary response differed considerably from the standard Protestant view. They agreed that the response required faith, but they disputed the Protestant view that faith meant a confidence or persuasion of acceptance, the trust that one had been forgiven. Such confidence and trust rested on faith, they said, but it could not be identified with faith, which was rather "belief of what God has revealed." Such belief always produced "affections of the heart," and it was never "naked assent," but the essence of faith was "the belief of revealed truth, on the authority of God." When John England explained that faith was a "sincere disposition" to believe, John Baptist David wrote him discreetly from Kentucky and informed him that he was "theologically inaccurate." England conceded the point and agreed that "actual faith is positive belief upon the testimony of God" of all that had been revealed. Catholic theologians believed that the Protestant view of faith had fed indifference about doctrinal truth, and England wanted to avoid opening any door to this error.[40]

Since their doctrine assumed belief in specific Catholic doctrines, they had to fend off the charge that they denied the possibility of salvation for anyone outside the Catholic Church. They replied with a distinction between "communion" and "membership." Christians united in the church's profession of faith, sacraments, and ministry stood in communion. But the "members" of the church included all who "with a sincere heart seek true religion, and are in an unfeigned disposition to embrace the truth, whenever they find it." John Carroll was the first American to explain the distinction, and it became a standard reply. England distinguished between "external" communicants and others who abided anonymously within the "soul" of the church while remaining outside the institution; Hughes, between "professing" and "implicit" members. The implicit members included all who remained "invincibly ignorant" of Catholic truth but had such upright and sincere hearts toward God that they would embrace that truth if they rightly knew it. England included in their number both non-Christians and uninformed Protestants.[41]

In the normal order of salvation, faith was a condition of justification, but Catholics differed from Protestants not only about faith but also about justification itself. American Catholic theologians remained scrupulously true to the Council of Trent. The standard exposition came in Francis Patrick Kenrick's *Catholic Doctrine of Justification Explained and Vindicated* (1841), in which he accentuated the differences with Protestants. Catholics joined Protestants in viewing justification as an action of divine grace through which the believer became acceptable to God, but there the agreement ended.[42]

Unlike most Protestants, the Catholic theologians argued that justification required not faith alone but also repentance, hope, and love. Unlike the Calvinists, they denied that it resulted from a forensic act of imputation. They would speak of the imputation of Christ's merits and of the imputation of the believer's faith for righteousness (that is how they understood Romans 5), but not of any imputation of Christ's righteousness. Rather than viewing justice as merely imputed, moreover, they taught that through justification the believer became inherently righteous, a person changed from within. Therefore they denied the Protestant distinction between justification and sanctification, and described a single process in which the faithful became both more just and more holy at the same time. Unlike Protestants, they spoke of degrees of justification, of an increase of inherent righteousness, and unlike Calvinists, they also taught that the justified could fall back into a sinful state. They denied that the justified could be assured of their good estate. Such a presumed certainty, Kenrick thought, would be hard to distinguish from "illusions of self-love." It was sufficient that the faithful could "entertain the hope" that they were acceptable.[43]

Unlike most Protestants, moreover, Catholic theologians insisted on good works as a condition. As they read Paul, he had ruled out a righteousness derived solely from good works but had also warned in Romans 2 that only the "doers of the law" would be justified. They found salutary virtue in works done before justification, occasionally drawing on the medieval doctrine that such works exerted a "claim of congruity" upon God's further aid, making possible works that were "condignly" meritorious and deserving of divine favor. They also required good works on the part of those walking in the justified way. But they denied the Protestant charge of "works-righteousness." They insisted that they saw justification as "solely and exclusively from the merits of Christ." Even the first good work required the aid of God's prevenient grace; no subsequent work was possible without gracious assistance. It was, moreover, through sheer grace that God bestowed on good works "a merit which He will recompense with eternal rewards."[44]

The Catholic emphasis on good works found its practical corollary in the textbooks on casuistry and moral theology. Kenrick's *Theologia Moralis* (1841–43) seemed more important to some of his episcopal colleagues than his treatise on doctrine, because it offered guidance for the priest who had to give instructions on matters of morality and practice. His volumes followed a pattern set in 1586 in the "Ratio Studiorum" of the Society of Jesus, treating the topics of human action, conscience, sin, and law as a preface to the study of particular cases. The Jesuit Juan Izor had first followed this outline in his *Institutiones morales* (1600), and it became a fixture of Catholic moral writing. Kenrick merely applied it to the American setting. Weaving his way between an older Jesuit tradition that seemed too lax and a French Augustinian tradition that seemed too rigorous, he followed the mediating position of the Italian Alphonsus Ligouri (1697–1787), known as equiprobabilism, that taught priestly guides and confessors, when assessing a decision between two courses of action, to advise the stricter course when the law was clear but allow more laxity if no clear law existed. The issue was important in Catholic seminaries because equiprobabilism allowed the priest greater latitude in deciding whom to exclude and include in holy communion at the Eucharist and how to administer the sacrament of penance. Most of the seminaries taught from manuals—like the *Compendium Theologiae moralis* (1850) of the French Jesuit Jean Pierre Gury—that followed in the tradition of Ligouri.[45]

The Catholic bishops wanted their priests well-schooled in moral theology. Archbishop Samuel Eccleston told one seminary president that he would not ordain a priest without "a good course of Moral Theology," even if it meant neglecting instruction in "Dogmatic Theology." Moral theology provided the practical and ethical instruction that guided priestly decisions from day to day, especially in their work of hearing confessions. Catholic theologians believed that the Protestant doctrine of justification through faith alone wrongly minimized the need for careful moral reflection.[46]

Unlike most Protestants, finally, the Catholics linked justification and baptism. Kenrick again took the lead in defending the Catholic view, publishing a *Treatise of Baptism* (1843) designed not only to counter Baptist practice but also to oppose the Quaker disparagement of external forms that he found when he moved to Philadelphia. The Catholic view was that baptism canceled original sin and served as an instrumental cause of justification for both infants and properly disposed faithful adults. It conferred this grace *ex opere operato,* from the power wrought by God, rather than from the power of the baptizer or the baptized. When the New Testament called baptism a "laver of regeneration" (Titus 3:5) or spoke of rebirth by "water and the Holy Spirit" (John 3:5), Kenrick argued, it could mean only that the sacrament conveyed "the pardon of sins and grace of the Holy Ghost." He taught, with Trent, that it was "necessary for salvation," an "absolute necessity."[47]

Catholics viewed their sacramental doctrine as the prime example of their insistence on the continual need for grace. By insisting on seven sacraments—baptism, Eucharist, confirmation, marriage, ordination, penance, and extreme unction—rather than two, they not only adhered to the mandates of scripture and tradition but also, as Hughes argued, appropriately recognized both the believer's dependence on divine grace and the goodness of the corporeal creation. Countering Protestant claims that their sacramental doctrines made salvation mechanical and external, they emphasized the need for right intention and disposition, but they viewed Protestant criticisms as one more symptom of a rationalistic dismissal of mystery.[48]

They found that symptom even more pronounced in Protestant ridicule of their eucharistic doctrine, especially their doctrine of transubstantiation. The unrelenting Protestant charge in that Baconian era was that the Catholic doctrine defied reason and the evidence of the senses. Most Catholics replied that their doctrine was "above reason but not contradictory to it," and occasionally they offered analogies to explain it, as when Purcell reminded Campbell that it was something of a mystery even how food changed into flesh, but the more frequent reply was Kenrick's: "in supernatural and mysterious works the senses must not be wholly and absolutely relied on." In a series of defenses such as Kenrick's *Letters of Omega and Omicron* (1828) and England's "Letters on the Catholic Doctrine of Transubstantiation" (1838), Catholics argued that their doctrine took seriously the words of Jesus at his last supper: "This is my body" (Luke 22:19) meant what it said.[49]

Similar themes appeared when they defended their doctrine of the Mass as a sacrifice. Turning to scripture and tradition, they argued that Malachi 1:2 prophesied a perpetual sacrifice, that the priest-king Melchizedek (Gen. 14:18) typified with his bread and wine the priestly oblation of Christ, that Hebrews 9:24 confirmed the priestly and sacrificial character of the rite, and that Paul commanded the death of Christ to be shown forth until he came again. Rather than diminishing the one sacrifice of Christ on the cross, the Mass honored and perpetuated it. But the doctrine of the Mass also stood as a constant rebuke to "all the arguments of human reason" on which Protestants were wont to rely. Protestant skepticism, wrote Gallitzin, was "the natural consequence of making limited reason the arbiter of faith." The Protestant rejection of the Mass was the telling sign of that error.[50]

Much of the debate between Catholics and Protestants resurrected the sixteenth-century disputes over indulgences, purgatory, penance, and private confession. They were debates about practices that reflected theological presuppositions. Charles Constantine Pise (1801–66) was a graduate of Georgetown College and Mount St. Mary's Seminary who taught in several seminaries before moving into parishes in Baltimore, Washington, and New York. When he wrote his *Lectures on the Invocation of Saints, Veneration of Sacred Images, and Purgatory* (1845), one of scores of such tracts produced by Catholic clergy, he wrote as a parish priest interested in practical issues that required excurses on the canon, the rule of faith, and Catholic views of salvation. These disagreements about practice often raised the issues of reason, revelation, tradition, and the *ordo salutis* that occupied Catholic theologians throughout the period.[51]

By the 1840s, Spalding and Hughes were producing, in addition to their doctrinal treatises, a new kind of American Catholic apologia. They began writing and lecturing on history and publishing long reviews of historical works, hoping to show that the Catholic Church had led the way toward the civilizing of western society. In his "Influence of Christianity Upon Civilization" (1843), for example, Hughes argued that Catholic Christian principles stood behind western progress toward justice and truth. In his "Influence of Christianity on Social Servitude" (1843), he contended that the church had promoted principles that reduced the extent of slavery and uplifted the poor. In such accounts, the Reformation signified a rupture in the progress of civilization, exacerbating problems of poverty, greed, and political tyranny.[52]

The turn to history, similar to the turn made by Protestant theologians like Henry Boynton Smith at Union Seminary and John Williamson Nevin and Philip Schaff at Mercersburg, signaled an awareness of a European romantic temper that stimulated a renewed interest in the past, in tradition, in organic images of historical development, and in corporate institutions. Martin Spalding appealed to the romantic philosopher Friedrich von Schlegel to argue that Catholic Christianity discerned and abetted the providential movement of history. Like some of the Episcopal high-church theologians who followed the lead provided by John Henry Newman, he depicted the Middle Ages as a period of creativity and invention, beauty and learning, and both he and Hughes described medieval society as an organic unity to which the church had contributed especially by its concern for the poor and the weak. The essays displayed a willingness to explore patterns of thought that moved theology away from the Baconian spirit.[53]

Similar patterns could be found elsewhere, often combined with conceptions of rationality that countered the Baconian epistemology. In the transcendentalism of New England, the romantic theology of Horace Bushnell, the historical theology of Nevin and Schaff at Mercersburg, and the romantic conservative Catholicism of Orestes Brownson, Americans could find an alternative understanding of both faith and reason. These were the leading proponents of "intuitive rationality" as the ally of faith. They had little else in common. Brownson and the Mercersburg theologians took the conservative turn; Bushnell moved away from traditional New England theology; the transcendental thinkers often stepped outside the circle of Christian theology altogether. They shared only a single conviction: that theological evidentialism and American denominationalism had both failed.

The Transcendentalists: Intuition

The transcendentalist controversy began as a dispute over evidential Christianity, pitting defenders of the external evidences against proponents of the internal. When Ralph Waldo Emerson proclaimed in his Harvard Divinity School Address of 1838 that the word "miracle" had become a "monster," and that "to aim to convert a man by miracles is a profanation of the soul," he exposed the depths of feeling that had arisen among some Unitarian intellectuals about the evidences of Christianity. By the time the dispute ended, it had become a debate about the truth and meaning of Christianity itself, but questions about the evidences continued to inform the discussion throughout the controversy.[1]

Prominent among the founders of the movement were a group of liberal clergy in New England who believed that Unitarian theology had promoted a Lockean rationalism that privileged the senses over the spiritual faculties. A number of them hoped that a reform in theology would issue in a reformation of the church. Of the twenty-six New Englanders who became closely associated with the transcendentalist club that began to meet in 1836 at the home of George Ripley, seventeen were Unitarian ministers. The scope of the movement soon embraced literature, literary criticism, and social reform, but the aim at the outset was a different way of thinking about the rationality of theology.[2]

Margaret Fuller, editor of the *Dial,* the chief transcendentalist journal, recognized what was at stake when she told her friend William Henry Channing in 1844 that the leaders of the movement wanted to "work from within outwards" rather than continue to depend on a rationality that remained at the level of external proofs and evidences. "Disgusted with the materialistic working of 'rational' religion," she explained, "they become mystics. They quarrel with all that is, because it is not spiritual enough." Fuller suspected that literature and the arts would be more effective media of cultural reform than a purified theology, but she agreed that Christianity had suffered because its adherents "received it on external grounds." She sympathized with the revolt against externals, whether rituals or evidences, and cheered the turn inward to "the fountains of holiness in the soul."[3]

Transcendentalists had little agreement about what such an inward turn should mean, and they had little interest in defining their aims with any great precision. Emerson described the movement in 1842 simply as "Idealism as it appears in 1842." He associated it with the critical philosophy of Immanuel Kant, who he thought had discovered "a very important class of ideas or imperative forms, which did not come by experience, but through which experience was acquired, . . . intuitions of the mind itself." But none of the transcendentalists were Kantians in any strict sense of the term; their confidence in the reach of intuition had little resemblance to Kant's sober sense of the limits of reason. They also contradicted each other at every turn. James Freeman Clarke conceded that "no two of us thought alike."[4]

Yet most of the transcendentalists did share an excitement about the possibility that their rediscovery of intuitive rationality would correct the errors of a theology too intimately aligned with Lockean empiricism. Insofar as they retained a Christian identity, which some did more than others, they continued to rely on the internal evidences and to that extent embraced the evidential tradition, but they launched the first sustained effort to replace Lockean reason with an intuition that no longer relied on external proofs.

Reason

Convers Francis (1795–1863), an early sympathizer who later would become a critic of transcendentalism, observed in 1836 that the Unitarians were breaking into "two schools — the old one, or English school, belonging to the sensuous and empirical philosophy, and the new one, or the German School (perhaps it may be called), belonging to the spiritual philosophy." The main body of transcendentalists constituted the Unitarian new school. By 1836, they had concluded that Lockean empiricism was not only superficial and false but also irreligious. By founding knowledge on sensory experience and grounding religious truth on inferences and testimony, they argued, the Lockeans had denied the mind "the power of perceiving spiritual truth" directly. One reason the transcendentalists looked so favorably on William Ellery Channing, even though he gently distanced himself from their ambitions, was that he too had criticized Locke and praised intuition as a more reliable support for Christian knowledge.[5]

Some even among the moderate Unitarians had doubts about Locke, and some of these moderates turned also to intuitionist solutions, but they could rest content with the intuitionism of the Scottish philosophers. The editor of *The Christian Examiner* during the height of the controversy, James Walker, believed that confidence in the Scottish first principles should be enough to enable the theologian to talk about an intuitive knowledge of spiritual truth. After 1829, however, the men and women who found transcendentalism exciting began to find the Scots boring.[6]

After 1829, a small band of theologians in New England and New York began a long, earnest, and fruitful engagement with Samuel Taylor Coleridge (1772–1834), the English romantic poet and theologian whose *Aids to Reflection* would shake more than one set of theological foundations in America. In that year, the young president of the University of Vermont, James Marsh (1794–1842), a graduate of Andover who remained both Calvinist and Trinitarian in theology, published an American edition of the book. His introduction explained that both "Locke and the Scotch metaphysicians" had failed to establish the essential distinction between the natural and the spiritual. The principal ground of their error was their inability to distinguish between the understanding and the reason.[7]

The distinction between reason and understanding went all the way back to Plato, but it was Immanuel Kant's discussion of it that prompted a resurgence of interest among nineteenth-century romantics like Coleridge. Kant employed it to argue that the "understanding" never escaped entanglement with the sensory but that "pure reason" yearned to attain super-sensory truths, though its efforts inevitably ran up against logical conundrums that doomed it to failure. He was impressed by reason's limits. For Coleridge, however, the distinction suggested a confidence that reason, unlike the understanding, could lead the mind beyond the sensory world into a realm of eternal truth.

In the Coleridgian vocabulary, the understanding was the faculty of making judgments that depended on the senses. It was the capacity to draw inferences from empirical evidence, to abstract and quantify, to compare particulars and generalize from them. It designated capacities that human beings shared with even the lower animals. The reason, on the other hand, was the intuitive faculty by which the mind possessed the nonempirical ideas of geometry, the universal and necessary truths presupposed in empirical thinking, the feeling of ethical responsibility that underlay moral decision making, and the ideas of the soul, freedom, immortality, and God that constituted the core of religion.[8]

Transcendentalists found Coleridge congenial when he taught that Christianity was a "life" rather than a theory or speculation, when he found nature filled with symbols of spirit, and when he defended the moral freedom of the will, but it was the distinction between the understanding and the reason that especially suggested new ways to think about the rationality of faith. James Freeman Clarke, who carried transcendental thought to Cincinnati as editor of *The Western Messenger,* recalled that his reading of Coleridge as a student at Harvard confirmed his "longing for a higher philosophy than that of John Locke and David Hartley, the metaphysicians most in vogue with the earlier Unitarians down to the time of Channing." What he learned from Coleridge was that "though knowledge begins with experience it does not come *from* experience." Coleridge lured his American followers into the exciting possibilities of a priori reasoning, the discovery that certain universal and necessary ideas had to be present to the mind before any possible experience of the world as ordered and lawlike. He held out before them the heady prospect that reason's employment of those ideas was a form of participation in the eternal divine mind.[9]

The religious implications of a priori cognition became for some of the New Englanders even clearer as they read the eclectic philosophy of the French metaphysician Victor Cousin (1792–1867), a philosophical idealist who tried to synthesize the ideas of Reid, Kant, Hegel, and Schelling as a way of proving that the mind stood in an immediate relation to the Infinite. Like Coleridge, Cousin distinguished two operations of thought, the first spontaneous and involuntary, the second reflective and voluntary. In analyzing this secondary reflection, he discovered that it employed "the notions of cause, of substance, of time, of space, of unity, and the like." Since it required these notions for all of its operations, it could not have produced them or discovered them in the empirical world. It could only have derived them from the deeper, prereflective awareness that Cousin called the spontaneous reason. Since these notions were universal and necessary, they suggested a supra-individual reason in which all thinking participated.[10]

Convinced that Lockean sensationalism led to religious skepticism, Cousin also proposed that a true psychological method would prove that all thinking presupposed the Infinite. In distinguishing one thing from another, for instance, the mind recognized finitude. But to recognize the finite was to grasp implicitly and immediately the infinite as its corollary. The concept of the finite made no sense without the parallel concept of infinity. For Cousin this was no deduction of the one from the other; the two concepts were both equally original data for the mind, each implying the other, just as the idea of imperfection implied a standard of perfection. But "the infinite and the perfect," Cousin argued, "is God himself." The idea of God was therefore implicit in all thinking, and just as the idea of finitude produced the conviction of a reality corresponding to it, so also the idea of the infinite and perfect produced a similar conviction.[11]

The Episcopal theologian Caleb Sprague Henry (1804–84), who translated Cousin's *Elements of Psychology* for American readers in 1834, thought that its conclusions overthrew the principal positions of Lockean philosophy. During his tenure as professor of mental and moral philosophy at New York University from 1838 to 1852, Henry taught a practical Christianity defined by the ideal of unselfish devotion to the good of other people. For him, Cousin's philosophy made conviction of God's existence a "positive cognition" rather than merely a belief. Trained at Andover and Yale, Henry was proof that the new intuitionism could attract doctrinally conservative as well as liberal theologians, but an attack on Cousin as a pantheist by the *Princeton Review* in 1839 diminished his appeal to the conservatives.[12]

Cousin's American champion in the mid-1830s was Orestes Brownson, a self-educated native of Vermont whose transcendental phase was a stage in a spiritual pilgrimage that would eventually lead him into the Catholic Church. Brownson's journey began with a youthful conversion in a Presbyterian church in 1822, but within two years he became convinced that Presbyterian orthodoxy required too great a surrender of his reason, and in 1824 he transferred his loyalties to the Universalists, who allowed him to adopt reason as his criterion of truth. He became a Universalist preacher in New Hampshire and the editor of the Universalists' *Gospel Advocate*. Attempting to still his religious doubts, he read William Paley, but the inadequacy of Paleyan evidentialism pushed him toward skepticism, and by 1829 he decided to devote his life to reform in this world, joining the Workingman's Party and promoting the socialism of Robert Owen and Frances Wright.[13]

Brownson's religious yearnings eventually pulled him back into the pulpit as the preacher of a "religion of humanity" in which the incarnation symbolized the divinity of the human and Christ modeled social reform. His reading of Channing's essay on "Likeness to God" persuaded him in 1831 to join the Unitarians, and his further reading during two Unitarian pastorates resulted in his *New Views of Christianity, Society, and the Church* (1836), which used the symbol of Christ as God-Man to promote a religion of socialism and democracy. His aim, informed partly by the French socialist Claude Henri, Count de

Saint-Simon, was to lay the foundation for a Church of the Future, neither Catholic nor Protestant, that would unite the spiritual and the material and seek the common good of humanity.[14]

As editor of the *Boston Quarterly Review,* Brownson became a formidable presence among the transcendentalists. From Friedrich Daniel Ernst Schleiermacher (1768–1834), the dean of the theological faculty in Berlin, and from Benjamin Constant (1767–1830), the Swiss-born philosopher who had helped introduce Scottish ideas to the French, Brownson derived the idea that a "religious sentiment" produced a natural piety in all men and women, and he shared also Constant's belief that forms and institutions needed constantly to change in order to express the sentiment in categories that fit the spirit of the times. But he thought that Constant had failed to show that the religious sentiment was more than subjective feeling. Believing that Constant, like Kant, had been too willing to rest content with "the subjectivity of the reason," he turned to Cousin as a philosopher who guided the mind outside itself, moving from psychology to ontology.[15]

As Brownson read him, Cousin solved the problem of subjectivity by showing that individual personalities participated in a reason that remained independent of them, not subject to their wishes. Since this reason revealed the Infinite, it revealed God. Since it could reveal only what was within itself, it manifested God as "thought, reason, intelligence in itself," and since this objective reason could contradict individual desires and fantasies, it subjected the self to a criterion beyond itself.[16]

Through this revelation, Brownson could see the divinity within humanity: "The reason is God; it appears in us, therefore God appears in us." This insight also enabled him "to see God in nature, in a new and striking sense." As a manifestation of "the universal Reason," nature seemed now filled with thought, no longer a mechanism but a living intelligence, a "shining out of the Infinite and the Perfect." Brownson thus moved from intuitive rationality to a confidence in the intelligibility of nature as an expression of the divine Mind. This vision of divine immanence became a permanent feature of the transcendentalist temper.[17]

Ralph Waldo Emerson

Ralph Waldo Emerson (1803–82) issued toward the end of his career more than one searing criticism of "the corpse-cold Unitarianism of Brattle Street": "Luther would cut his hand off sooner than write theses against the pope if he suspected that he was bringing on with all his might the pale negations of Boston Unitarianism." The aphorisms capture the tone of Emerson's revolt against his past, but they disguise the extent to which he and other transcendentalists held on to themes that stood near the core of the Unitarian theology of virtue.[18]

From the beginnings of his tenure as a Unitarian minister to the final years of his career as a poet, lecturer, and essayist, Emerson remained in steady pursuit of the ideal of virtue. Throughout all the transitions in his thinking, he never veered from his conviction that "the main, central prominent power of the soul, is the moral sentiment"; that Christianity, properly understood, was the disciplining of moral character; and that the end of all proper religion was obedience to the sublime moral law that suffused the whole order of being. Even after Emerson began to doubt that the telos of nature was the moral growth of the individual, he still looked to the natural world as a moral guide.[19]

Like several other liberal ministers, he hesitated to call himself a Unitarian because he thought that labels connoted a spirit of faction and party, but Emerson grew up the son of a liberal Boston minister, read theology with William Ellery Channing, and served from 1829 to 1832 as the pastor of Boston's Second Church. He left the ministry when the congregation would not dispense with its customary celebration of the Lord's Supper, which Emerson had begun to view as an empty form subversive of a religion of the spirit. The deeper motive for his departure was his disdain for any religious authority, whether scripture or ceremony, that dimmed the authority of the moral sentiment. His convictions slowly drove him outside the bounds of historic Christianity, and he eventually interpreted theology as no more than "the rhetoric of morals." His discovery of the "God within" altered his early moralism, but he never fully abandoned his belief that the aim of religion, like that of nature, required conformity to a morally demanding Law.[20]

When he read the Scottish philosophy as a student at Harvard, the young Emerson concluded that the most valuable insight of Reid and Stewart was their recognition of a moral sentiment that differed from both the physical senses and the logical faculties. Within a year of his graduation in 1821 he was writing of the moral sentiment as a perception of a universal law grounded in the divine Mind. Emerson admired Reid's refutation of Hume's skepticism, but his chief debt to the Scottish philosophy was the theory of the moral sense.[21]

Emerson taught his Boston congregation that the "sum and substance" of religion was obedience to the moral law. "Our religion has one command, one aim, one end; and that is Duty." He presented Jesus to them as a figure who had "identified himself with the moral law" to such an extent that he could be the "channel through which the moral law flowed." To do the right, therefore, was "to be a Christian." By 1831 he would acknowledge the authority of Jesus' teachings only insofar as they confirmed the moral sentiment. He would accept the New Testament only insofar as it conformed to "the original edition" of it in the heart. And he would include within the circle of anonymous Christians everyone who followed "the sternest morality."[22]

This moral impulse provided the signposts that guided Emerson's discovery of the deeper meanings of nature. He sought the moral meanings of nature as early as 1821, when he heard the young Sampson Reid speak at Harvard on the thought of Emmanuel Swedenborg (1688–1772), the Swedish scientist whose visits to the celestial world of spirits and angels taught him the spiritual meanings of both biblical events and natural facts. Within five years he was saying that Reed's *Reflections on the Growth of Mind* (1826) was "the best thing since Plato." He would later conclude that Swedenborg allowed his "theological bias" to narrow fatally his reading of the natural world by fastening each natural object to a discrete theological notion rather than seeing nature's "slippery" symbols as shifting intimations of "the moral sentiment," but the Swedenborgian "correspondences" between the natural and the spiritual furnished Emerson with a way of viewing nature as mentor in the truths of the moral sense.[23]

During a European tour after leaving his pastorate, Emerson contemplated a scientific vocation, but by the close of his scientific lectures of 1833–34 he conceded that the empirical temper of the naturalist failed to grasp the true value of nature as a teacher of moral truth. He much preferred to follow the vocation of Johann Wolfgang von Goethe, who could read the factual within its larger context of moral truth, even though, as Emerson later conceded, Goethe seemed incapable of a real "self-surrender to the moral sentiment."[24]

In 1834, Emerson rediscovered Coleridge. He had read excerpts earlier and studied Marsh's edition of the *Aids to Reflection* soon after its publication, but not until after the European tour did he designate the distinction between the reason and the understanding as "a philosophy itself." "A clear perception of it," he later wrote in his journal, "is the key to all theology, and a theory of human life." For Emerson, as for Coleridge, the understanding dealt with the external world through the senses; the reason grasped the true, the good, and the beautiful through an immediate intuition that had to be prior to any empirical recognition of true facts, good deeds, or beautiful objects, since such a recognition implied an antecedent standard of judgment that was not derivable from the empirical itself. For Emerson, this meant that reason recognized the analogies and resemblances by which "all things" in the natural world preached to us "of the moral law."[25]

The quest for the moral significance of nature stood behind Emerson's growing fascination with philosophical idealism. Ever since his college years he had read in the idealism of the Platonic tradition, and in his essays on *Representative Men* he declared that "Plato is philosophy, and philosophy, Plato," partly because Plato had seen that "law determines all phenomena," partly because he had seen further that "all things are for the sake of the good." By the late 1820s Emerson was also plunging into Neoplatonism, reading Proclus and Plotinus on the unity of all things, the sovereignty of the Good, and the transcendence of the One. He was also drawing occasional insights from Bishop Berkeley. As he moved away from any notion of a specific Christian revelation, the idealism provided the reassurance that nature still manifested Mind. The natural world was not a mere regularity devoid of moral purpose.[26]

One way of reading *Nature* (1836), the book that enshrined Emerson in the American literary pantheon, is to view it as his announcement that the natural world, interpreted from an idealist angle of vision, served a moral end. He began it with a question — "To what end is nature?" — to which he gave later an ethical response: "This ethical character so penetrates the bone and marrow of nature, as to seem the end for which it was made." By serving as a source of commodity, beauty, language, and discipline, nature spoke to Emerson of the ineffable Spirit that acted through both the phenomenal world and human spirits to nurture the boundless possibilities of the soul, including the possibility of its overcoming its "mean egotism" and seeing itself as "part or parcel of God."[27]

By the time he wrote *Nature,* Emerson believed that he had found the "the greatest truth" of the religious life: "God is within us." Early in his ministry he had emphasized, largely in the manner of the earlier English devotional writer Henry Scougall, the life of God within the soul. By 1830 he was arguing that God was "in us" in the sense that conscience and the love of truth registered a "degree of participation (I speak it with reverence) in the attributes of God." The finite mind's grasp of eternal ideas, and particularly its embodiment of virtue, signified a union with God, though Emerson emphasized that the self always had a "double consciousness," one drawn to the senses, the finite, the selfish, the other to an "inner infinitude," a "supreme, calm, immortal mind" that stood in judgment over the lesser self. The self devoted to justice and truth was "in some degree" divine because it identified itself with divine realities, and at certain moments, which might as well be described as mystical, it could so fully identify itself with them that it partook of the universal Mind that united it to God, other selves, and the laws that governed nature.[28]

Emerson could speak of self-denial and self-reliance in almost the same breath because he was thinking of two different modalities of the self. Emersonian self-reliance was a reliance on the self that was one with God, the self that was formed by its devotion to eternal truth and goodness. Despite his reputation for unrealistic optimism, he never lost his awareness that the self's duality always meant an interjection of finite self-interest into human plans and projects. In an early sermon he praised as "generous and sublime" the self-abnegation of the Hopkinsians, who saw the true saint as willing to be damned for the glory of God, though he judged the sentiment finally an "absurdity." He preached an ethic of self-realization, but his aim was the realization of the moral self, at one with the law within, the inner God.[29]

When he wrote *Nature,* Emerson no longer believed in the transcendent and personal God of Christian tradition. Even early in his career he had insisted that what seemed to be natural laws bespoke the "present and immediate agency of God," and gradually he began to think of God not as an agent governing through law but rather as Law itself, as Absolute Goodness and Absolute Truth, or better, as the Neoplatonic One, beyond being, essence, and life, though partially manifest as Law. Emerson's "universal soul" or "Oversoul" could not be personal, for persons were bounded and finite. A personal deity would be a particular being rather than the unifying force and principle of the Whole. Emerson's God by 1836 was rather the Highest Law, the law of laws, the "dread universal essence" that remained ineffable, resistant to both language and thought. His reading in Buddhism moved him even further away from his earlier belief in a personal God.[30]

For all its impersonality, to be sure, the Emersonian God still bore faint traces of the Unitarian personal Father. His earlier Unitarian teleology found muted expression, for instance, in the early 1840s in his discussion of the law of Compensation that brought justice out of injustice, allowed no offense to go unchastened, and rewarded every pure act. As a Unitarian minister, Emerson had preached often of Providence, and although he dropped the idea of particular providences, he held on to the idea that the world had a general providential direction, that the self-existent law pushed toward the realization of the good. There were signs in 1841 that he was beginning to place his hope in the thought that nature might offer only moments of illumination rather than steady support for the moral self-culture of the individual, but even in the sober essays of his later career, when he confessed that "the way of Providence is a little rude," he still found in nature a deity that secured "universal benefit" and offered moral guidance.[31]

Nonetheless, Emerson came to see the "god of tradition" as the product of the "understanding," which tried to depict the truths of the "reason" as if they were "pictures from the senses." By 1836 he was advocating the demythologizing of Christian theology, viewing the incarnation as a symbol of the infinite reason incarnate in humanity, affirming Jesus only as one among many teachers of the moral law, and redefining heaven and hell as inward states of mind: "And so in the Scriptures generally what is said to be above is to be understood as that which is within."[32]

It was more than Coleridgian distinctions, however, that led Emerson away from Christian tradition. For all his distrust of empirical science, he also thought that post-Copernican science conveyed a sense of infinitude that rendered the older theological scheme incredible. Toward the end of his career he reflected that "Modern Science, beginning with Copernicus" had shown that "our sacred as our profane history had been written in gross ignorance of the laws, which were far grander than we knew." For Emerson the consequence was an inward turn that redefined Christian doctrines as symbols of "Conscience, Duty, and Love."[33]

In his Divinity School Address at Harvard in 1838, Emerson announced that his transcendental gospel could not be reconciled with the Christian gospel as it had been understood. He said little at Harvard that he had not said earlier, but he said it from a Unitarian platform at a time when Lyman Beecher and the evangelicals of Boston were intent on exposing the Unitarians as enemies to the historic faith. The address touched off a fury because it so clearly revealed Emerson's discomfort with "historical Christianity." By ridiculing evidential theology, belittling trust in a revelation "given long ago," and criticizing any "noxious exaggeration about the person of Jesus," Emerson revealed that his "sentiment of virtue" was something other than faith as understood by both the Unitarians and their evangelical opponents.[34]

Miracles

Emerson's Divinity School Address brought to a climax a dispute that had begun two years earlier over the Christian evidences. In saying that the word "miracle" had "become a monster," he linked his manifesto to that earlier dispute. His message in 1838 was that the proof of religious truth came not from logical inferences but from an intuition that could not be "received at second hand." The attempt to provide empirical verification was no more than an attempt to replace the truths of the intuitive Reason with the calculations of the understanding: "But there is no doctrine of the Reason which will bear to be taught by the understanding."[35]

His intellectual development displayed the distrust of evidentialism that blossomed in the initial transcendentalist disputes. As a young preacher in 1826 he criticized "German scholars" who attacked "the foundations of external evidence." It seemed obvious to him then, as it did to Channing, that miracles confirmed the authority of biblical teachers and teaching. As late as 1828 he observed that Jesus did "wonderful works" as proof that he came from God. Within two years, however, he began to preach that Jesus had appealed not to miracles but to the heart, and that the believer accepted the miracles only because the word moved the heart. By 1831 he thought that the miracles probably occurred—since the character of Jesus suggested that he would have avoided any pious fraud—but he began to speak of all events as miraculous illustrations of the uniform operation of Spirit and to dismiss miracle as "a lower species of evidence."[36]

The truth of the New Testament was convincing, he told his congregation, "whether the miracle was wrought, as is pretended, or not." He taught that "internal evidence far outweighs all miracles to the soul. A reasoning Christian would think himself injured by the fortifying too scrupulously the outward evidence of Christianity." In a similar manner, he redefined prophecy as only a "state of mind more sagacious than that of other men" and equated prophetic truth with insights like those of Bacon or Newton. By 1836, Emerson was ready to discard the external evidences.[37]

In 1836, the miracle controversy began. By that time it was becoming commonplace for Unitarian theologians who associated themselves with transcendentalist reform to dismiss the evidential value of the New Testament miracles. In his *Remarks on the Four Gospels* (1836), William Henry Furness (1802–96) in Philadelphia, a lifelong friend of Emerson, redefined miracle as a natural event not yet understood within a natural order in which everything manifested supernatural power. While he argued that the New Testament miracles might have occurred, Furness thought that their evidential use assumed "a mechanical philosophy—a philosophy of the senses." He thus connected the question of miracles to epistemological questions that intrigued the reformers.[38]

The main event in the Boston controversy came in an 1836 book review written for the *Christian Examiner* by George Ripley (1802–80), the pastor of the Purchase Street Church in Boston, who had far more than a superficial knowledge of both Coleridge and German thought. He had published a review in which he reported the dismissal of miracles as evidences by the German philosopher Johann Gottfried Herder and an essay on Schleiermacher in which he praised the effort to ground theology in "the religious consciousness." Now he used his review of an English Unitarian, James Martineau, to announce that "a firm faith in Christianity may be cherished independently of miracles." While he was not ready to deny the accuracy of the New Testament miracle stories, he was ready to declare it an "unsound method" to make belief in them the foundation of Christian faith. The review so enraged Andrews

Norton that he sent a letter to the local newspaper disputing Ripley's "ability to discuss the subject."[39]

Norton's letter inaugurated a series of exchanges with Ripley that intensified after Norton published his *Discourse on the Latest Form of Infidelity* in reply to Emerson's Divinity School Address. Ripley replied with three treatises in defense of a "spiritual faith." Rather than cast his lot explicitly with Emerson, however, Ripley chose to counter Norton's aspersions against German theology. The result was a more sophisticated defense of Schleiermacher than Americans had ever read, and though Ripley did not claim to agree on every point, he let it be known that he found in Schleiermacher a "vital, profound, and ennobling theology." Ripley's replies to Norton and his other theological reflections during the 1830s revealed a transcendentalist theology unlike Emerson's, more closely aligned with liberal Protestantism as it was being defined in Germany and more clearly rooted in earlier Unitarian thought.[40]

Ripley had no more use than Emerson for the external evidences, and he charged that Norton's reliance on miracle as proof merely demonstrated his allegiance to Lockean sensationalism. He shared with Emerson an intuitive epistemology founded on the distinction between the reason and the understanding, and he thought that the reason's power to perceive that truth differed from falsity, its ability to see that right differed from wrong, and its vision of "ideal perfectness" that enabled it to pursue a "diviner excellence" all entailed its participation in the divine nature, as did the capacity of the will for disinterested love. Like Emerson, he thought that religion had its grounding in a "sentiment" of human nature, a faculty for perceiving spiritual truth, though he was prone to use Schleiermacher's language about a feeling of dependence in order to express the sentiment's content.[41]

Ripley espoused, however, a Unitarian Christian form of transcendentalism. Even after 1838, he still affirmed a distinctive revelation of God in Jesus, still spoke of Jesus as a "savior" who was so filled with divine truth as to be identical with truth in "the Divine Mind," and still thought of the internal evidences — the "inherent marks of truth and divinity" in the New Testament — as warrant for a specifically Christian gospel. He never denied the historicity of the New Testament miracles, though he thought that the effort to make the truth of Christianity depend on "external support" had the unfortunate consequence of subjecting religion to "historical conditions."[42]

Ripley sympathized with Schleiermacher's hesitation to think of God as personal in any traditional sense; he recognized that it was "difficult to conceive of a personality as strictly infinite and impassible." But he insisted that Schleiermacher affirmed a "Living God," not a pantheist monism, and he apparently shared Schleiermacher's belief that "a religious faith in God may be cherished, independent of the human, personal form, in which he has been commonly represented," though he did not, like Emerson, shy away from personal metaphors for God, and in 1839, a year before his resignation from the Purchase Street Church, he still spoke of God as "the universal Father." What prompted the resignation was his awareness that his congregation disliked his position on miracles, on the wrongful exclusivity of belief in a historical biblical revelation, and on the implications of Christianity for social reform.[43]

Uppermost in Ripley's mind was the conviction that the older evidentialism no longer sufficed to provide the grounds for Christian belief. Most Unitarians could not accept that judgment. The conservative Orville Dewey spoke for them in an 1836 Dudleian Lecture at Harvard when he complained of a "presumption against miracles" and a "disposition of many to turn from miracles to what they call the internal evidence." Almost ten years later, N. L. Frothingham at First Church spoke for them again in his discourses on *Deism or Christianity?*, when he complained about theologians who denied that Jesus was "approved by God of miracles and signs which God did by him." But Frothingham also conceded that some external evidences, like the prophetic proofs, had been pressed with "undue minuteness," treating "accidental resemblances" between the Old and the New Testaments as prophetic fulfillments. Within a few years, even Unitarian moderates such as James Walker were admitting that not everyone, especially at places like Harvard, found "books on the evidences" to be any longer convincing. On that narrow point, the transcendentalists had won some allies.[44]

Theodore Parker

Among the auditors at Emerson's Divinity School Address, none was destined for greater celebrity and notoriety than Theodore Parker, the young minister at the Spring Street Church in West Roxbury near Boston. Parker returned home to record in his journal that Emerson's words had been "terribly sublime." A member of the transcendental club since its founding, Parker shared the excitement over the rediscovery of intuition. His career as a radical theologian began with his involvement in the miracle dispute. By the time it ended, he had formulated a style of transcendental theology quite different from Emerson's, one that reflected a self-conscious effort to combine the intuitive and the empirical, or as he was inclined to say, facts of consciousness and facts of observation.[45]

Parker entered the miracle controversy in 1840 with a pseudonymous essay in the form of a letter signed by "Levi Blodgett" in response to Andrews Norton's attacks on George Ripley. Parker agreed that the question of miracle as evidence for Christianity was a "subject of real moment," but he tried to frame it within a larger question about the evidence for any form of religious faith, which he found in the "religious sentiment," and especially the "sense of dependence," which was a part of human nature, rather than external proof. He found the evidence for Christianity, therefore, in the correspondence between the teachings of Jesus and the innate and universal sense or sentiment that supported belief in and dependence on God. While he still believed that Jesus wrought miracles, he thought that Christians valued Jesus not for the miracles but for his teaching and character.[46]

Even in the Levi Blodgett letter, Parker conceded that it was difficult to "establish a particular miracle" and that the gospel writers, products of their own age, might have been mistaken. In early 1840 he was immersed in the reading of David Friedrich Strauss's *Leben Jesu (Life of Jesus),* which he viewed as "an epoch in theological affairs." He found much to criticize in Strauss — the claim to have written without presuppositions, the conclusion that the gospels were not authentic, the notion that myths arise from ideas rather than from historical events — but Parker merely observed, without criticism, Strauss's assumptions about the impossibility of miracles in a universe governed by natural law, and in private correspondence he speculated that the miracles might belong to "the mythical part" of the New Testament. A clerical conference devoted to the question of whether differences of opinion on "the value and authority of miracles" should determine Christian fellowship left him depressed.[47]

By 1841, he was conceding that one could neither prove nor disprove the miracle stories of the New Testament, but it made no difference, he thought, because "this question of miracles, whether true or false, is of no religious significance." It was, in fact, clear that by that time Parker no longer believed in a universe in which specific miracles occurred, for he had decided that "we never in Nature see the smallest departure from Nature's law." But since he saw God as immanent in nature, he thought that this notion of uniformity in nature supported the religious faith that "God is always the same — his modes of action always the same." He eventually concluded that belief in miracles implied a finite God who had to alter his plans and contradict his own laws in order to achieve his ends.[48]

Parker's assumptions about the immutability of God stood behind his "Discourse of the Transient and Permanent in Christianity," delivered in 1841 at the ordination of Charles Shackleford at the Hawes Place Church in Boston. Looking back, he thought that the discourse helped make him the most hated man in America. Parker was prone to hyperbole, but the address did evoke a vehement and bitter reaction. Borrowing the title from an essay by Strauss,

Parker intended his discourse as an argument that the true religion of Christ would remain changeless. But he knew that he was defining the true religion of Christ in ways that cut against all the assumptions of traditional Christianity.

Parker argued that almost all the forms and doctrines of historical Christianity had proved themselves transitory. The Christianity of the nineteenth century had little relation to the Christianity of the fourth, the eleventh, or the sixteenth centuries, and the varied forms of Christianity espoused even by the American churches often differed so vastly from one another as to constitute virtually different religions. The lesson Parker wanted to draw from this observation was that Christianity should never be identified with its transient forms and doctrines.[49]

For Parker, the transient included what most American Protestants would have defined as the permanent: the unique authority of scripture and of Christ. While Parker was willing to read the Bible as a channel of religious insight, he thought it no longer possible to read it as the only certain rule of Christian faith and practice. While he was willing to think of Jesus as an "organ through which the Infinite spoke," a conveyer of a divine life, even a "Son of God" who embodied the divine image, he thought it no longer possible to rest the authority of his true teachings on his personal authority. "The authority of Jesus, as of all teachers, one would naturally think," he said, "must rest on the truth of his words, and not their truth on his authority."[50]

For Parker the permanent essence of Christianity consisted in the experience of love of God and the neighbor. The unchanging core was a certain quality of experience in which the soul recognized and loved God and fulfilled the divine law through love of the neighbor. What distinguished Parker's view from that of most other liberal theologians in America and Europe was his insistence that the experience that defined Christianity would remain possible even if Jesus had never lived.[51]

Parker was claiming that the prevailing Unitarian theology was mired in time-bound "conceptions." In his later writing, he distinguished four levels of religious apprehension. The two deepest were those of the reason and the religious sentiment, which produced an intuition and a sense of absolute dependence. Parker's "intuition" was much like Cousin's spontaneous rationality, an immediate awareness of the Infinite. His "sense of dependence" came directly from Schleiermacher. Both of these levels of religious experience together issued in the level of the "idea," specifically, the "idea of that on which we depend," which became the logical condition of other ideas. Parker's "ideas" were the eternal truths of reason, implicit in all discursive reasoning, which for him included the idea of God as "an Independent and Infinite Cause," the "being" of all existence, the "background" of all finite things. The final level — which was both more superficial and more transient than the others — was that of "conception," in which the senses, the understanding, and the imagination gave to the idea a concrete form, as if it occupied space and time. These conceptions, invariably inadequate, would change over time, and Parker thought that most, though not all, conceptions of God as personal implied limitations that diminished the idea of God. He felt that both Unitarian and popular theology had confused their conceptions of God with the divine reality.[52]

Like Emerson, Parker assumed that the purpose of religion was moral and religious growth. Its end was to lead men and women into harmony with God, which meant into a life devoted to truth, love, and right, a life that would continue in another form after death. The spiritual faculties therefore became means of supplying spiritual wants, and Parker thought it likely that the very existence of such spiritual desires indicated the reality of a God who made available the resources for satisfying them.[53]

His interest in the changing conceptions of religion led Parker to devote far more attention than other transcendental thinkers to the empirical and historical. This assumed one form in his introduction to his 1843 translation of W. M. L. DeWette's *Introduction* to the Old Testament, in which he used historical-critical methods to demonstrate the ways in which the Hebrew scripture carried the assumptions of its own era. He also issued a critical review of Isaac Dorner's *History of the Development of the Doctrine of Christ* (1839); the Tübingen theologian had argued that the idea of the God-Man was the central feature of Christianity and an implicit theme in all major religions. Parker argued that the book failed on both logical and historical grounds, but he admired the historical approach to the study of religion.[54]

He turned therefore with great interest to the writings of the positivist philosopher August Comte, and Parker's *Discourse of Matters Pertaining to Religion* (1842) was the first English-language book to use Comte's ideas. He followed Comte's example in distinguishing stages of religion, from fetishism to polytheism to monotheism. Unlike Comte, however, Parker did not believe that the scientific era had superseded the religious; he rather employed Comtean stages and notions of progress to argue that the growth of religious ideas had been progressive in ways that confirmed his distinction between the transient and permanent. He saw history as a movement guided by an "infinite love" that would not only create a just and loving society but also bring all humankind to bliss, "not a soul left behind, not a sparrow lost." He liked Comte because he believed in progress.[55]

Much of Parker's later influence came through his conception of religion and society as progressive, and some of his admirers also became admirers of

Comte. Parker's protégé Joseph Henry Allen, a Unitarian pastor in Washington, D.C., and Bangor, Maine, published in 1851 the first American appraisal of Comte's thought. Julia Ward Howe, a parishioner in Parker's congregation who was drawn by his willingness to employ maternal as well as paternal images of God, found in discussions of Comte with Parker, and in her own study of Comte, some of the ideas that shaped her later feminism. Parker's friend Elizabeth Peabody reviewed Comte in the *Christian Examiner* as an example of a writer whose ideas suggested that God was to be found in the study of society rather than in the older natural theology. For Parker, however, Comte was important as a thinker who showed how the historical and empirical study of religion might confirm confidence in the religious intuition.[56]

Outside New England, Philadelphia, and New York, transcendental ideas had little influence on theology. The Cincinnati group—James Freeman Clarke, William Henry Channing, and Christopher Pearse Cranch—remained in the West too short a time to exert much influence there. In Charleston, South Carolina, the Episcopal theologian James Warley Miles (1818–76) represented a conservative form of transcendental thought that followed the European mediating theologians—especially Hans Lassen Martenson of Copenhagen and Carl Nitzsch of Bonn and Berlin—who described the substance of Christianity as the reconciliation of finite and infinite. Miles believed that this reconciliation occurred because of God's self-revelation in Jesus, but his conviction that scripture contained myths and errors as well as religious truth was enough to drive him from his parish into the chair of philosophy at the College of Charleston. His *Philosophic Theology* (1849), which Augustus Neander in Germany praised as an important publication, employed the Coleridgian distinction between the reason and the understanding, and his denial that miracles had evidential value made him a lonely and isolated thinker in the South.[57]

In their critique of evidential Christianity, however, the transcendentalists were not alone. Theologians who were far more conservative than Emerson and Parker could see the point in an argument that an understanding of Christianity grounded on Lockean empiricism could not long endure the critical temper of the nineteenth century. The transcendentalists were among the first critics of the current forms of Baconian theology, but they were not the last.

22

Horace Bushnell: Christian Comprehensiveness

The transcendentalists were not alone in finding through intuition an alternative form of evidential Christianity. A few church theologians also felt stirrings of discontent with Baconian induction in theology and an eagerness for other ways of thinking about Christian reasonableness. In 1848, Horace Bushnell (1802–76) concluded that the "theologic method in New England has been essentially rationalistic" because of its bondage to the "logical under-standing." As an alternative, he urged theologians to attend to what he called the "Christian consciousness" and to think of theology as an exercise of the imagination.[1]

Bushnell's turn to religious experience as a source for theology has given him a place among the founders of American theological liberalism, and his disciples occupied prominent places within the circles of "progressive ortho-doxy" that marked the early stages of liberal theology. His critics accused him of tendencies toward naturalism. In fact, his notions of the Christian con-sciousness rested on an intense supernaturalism that distinguished him from the later liberal temperament. His belief in continuing miracles separated him even from both Old School and New School Calvinists of his own era. Yet Bushnell's swing toward experience as a source and norm of religious truth led to a view of theology that differed markedly from the accepted conventions.

Language, Nurture, and the Comprehensive Ideal

Bushnell never occupied an academic position. After completing the course of study at the Yale Law School in 1831, he underwent a religious conversion and entered Yale's Divinity School, where he studied none too happily under Nathaniel William Taylor, whom he found excessively fond of dry analysis. In 1833, he accepted an invitation from the North Congregational Church of Hartford, Connecticut, and he remained there as the pastor for the rest of his life. Yet he lived intellectually among the academic professionals. He lectured at Yale, Andover, and Harvard and published in Yale's *Christian Spectator* and *New Englander*. He was mentioned for Harvard's presidency, and the new College of California, which located in Berkeley after Bushnell chose and surveyed the site, tried to lure him as its first president.[2]

In any event, he never had much liking for the theological populists who rose out of the "rude-minded and ignorant masses." Only the prospect of social chaos on the western frontier led him to conclude, in his "Barbarism the First Danger" (1847), that it might be possible to work alongside the Methodists, at least the ones who were "now opposing the enemies of learning among themselves."[3]

The academic theologians, however, viewed him with some distrust and condescension. Taylor was alleged to have opined that Bushnell knew nothing, an opinion shared by Charles Hodge, who would call him "neither a philosopher nor [a] theologian." He was no systematic thinker, and one looks in vain in Bushnell for careful definitions or a deep knowledge of the Christian tradition. He was a preacher who fashioned a rhetorical style designed to stimulate the imagination. Yet he was also an insightful critic of orthodox rationalism.[4]

Much of Bushnell's theology came from his efforts to solve problems posed by the Unitarians. He felt so deeply the force of Unitarian objections to the New England orthodoxy that his critics always suspected him of being a secret Unitarian sympathizer. The Boston Unitarian Cyrus Bartol was an intimate friend, and he maintained congenial relations with others, including Theodore Parker. Bennet Tyler, who wanted Bushnell tried for heresy, accused him of being altogether too partial to Unitarian opinions. But Bushnell thought that the Unitarians and their opponents both shared the same rationalistic assumptions about theology, and he was evenhanded in his criticism of both groups. Just as his goal when he first went to Hartford was to overcome the division in his congregation between Taylorites and Tylerites, so also his aim as a writer was to overcome the larger religious divisions in the culture. He applied himself especially to the doctrines of the Trinity, Christology, and atonement because he thought that neither Unitarianism nor New England orthodoxy had seen them from the right perspective.[5]

Bushnell revealed his ambitions as a theologian when he published in 1848 his essay on "Christian Comprehensiveness." It drew on another aspect of Victor Cousin's philosophy, the eclectic way of thinking by which Cousin attempted to appropriate the best ideas from conflicting philosophical movements. In a similar manner, Bushnell argued that theologians should recognize the partial truth in opposed theological positions and move beyond the opposition toward a higher harmony. They should unite polar opposites, seeking the element of truth in both Calvinist election and Arminian synergism, both the Unitarian and the Trinitarian theology, both the Quaker trust in an Inner Light and the old Protestant confidence in the light of scripture, both the Catholic Real Presence and Zwinglian memorialism. All the Christian truths stood in "opposites, or extremes that need to be comprehended," and every sect held to a fragment of the truth. America, the land of many sects, had a special contribution to make to "the comprehensive church of the future."[6]

Bushnell had at least three reasons for seeming in 1848 to be so casual about doctrinal differences that others took to be irreconcilable. The first came from his own religious experience and his work as a pastor within a revivalist culture that he considered shallow; the second from a theory of religious knowledge that he learned partly from the Edwardean tradition and partly from Coleridge and Cousin; the third from an understanding of language that he had taken from his teacher of Greek and Hebrew at Yale, Josiah Willard Gibbs. All three contributed to his sense that the essential feature of the Christian life was an experience at a level deeper than the reflective understanding could fully grasp.

As a pastor he disliked the episodic nature of revivalist piety, and in 1836 he suggested in the *Christian Spectator* that the better option was to think of the aim of ministry as the steady growth of Christian character. Within a year he was preaching that growth of this kind was "the end of religion," and within a decade, the idea ripened into his *Discourses on Christian Nurture* (1847), an argument that children within the church ought to grow gradually into Christian maturity through the unconscious exertion of influence from the family, which Bushnell described as an "organic unity" bound together by a "law of connection" that shaped the character of all its members. The book assumed, on the one hand, the features of a Christian child-rearing manual and, on the other, a dissertation on the importance of infant baptism, which Bushnell defended by linking it to God's covenant with Abraham and his family. It was his answer both to Episcopal critics, whom he saw as advocates of an exaggerated doctrine of baptismal efficacy, and to Congregational revivalists, who failed to value the sacrament highly enough. It was also an effort to unite Congregational piety with the Unitarian insights into the importance of growth in character.[7]

The reaction was decidedly mixed. Bennet Tyler read the book through the lenses of the New Haven controversy, accusing Bushnell of error on native depravity and regeneration. From Princeton, Hodge praised the book for its covenantalism and its critique of religious individualism, but he worried about the implication that God operated in conversion through mere natural channels. The outcry persuaded the Sabbath School Society to suspend publication, but Bushnell republished the book in an expanded form as *Views of Christian Nurture* (1847), which elicited yet another open letter from Tyler. The *New Englander* — the voice of New Haven — worried openly that "the theological world of New England is again threatened with storm."[8]

Bushnell stood by the book and expanded it still further in 1860 under the title *Christian Nurture*. From the very beginning he tried to explain that he was talking about "a supernatural grace which inhabits the organic laws of nature and works its results in conformity with them." While he assumed that this supernatural grace operated with lawlike regularity, he saw himself as standing, on this point, within the tradition of Samuel Hopkins and the Edwardeans, who had also spoken of a "divine constitution" by which parents communicated holiness to children. New England Calvinists, however, were not accustomed to thinking of natural laws as vehicles of supernatural redemptive grace; to them it seemed that Bushnell was obliterating necessary distinctions. He thought that he was broadening a constricted vision of the supernatural. In any case, the book's ideal of religious growth and the formation of character guided almost everything he wrote about theology.[9]

It was probably a religious experience in 1848 that led Bushnell to give these convictions about religious growth a Christocentric interpretation. In the background stood the death of his son, the turmoil over his book, his reading of the French Quietists Madam Jeanne Marie Guyon and François Fénelon, and his immersion in the New Testament. The experience left Bushnell with the sense that he had suddenly seen "the gospel," and he referred to it throughout his life. Its meaning for him can probably be found in the sermon "Christ the Form of the Soul" (1848), written soon afterwards, in which he announced that "the grand object of the gospel plan" was that Christ be "formed within us" (Gal. 4:19), making us "like him in character."[10]

In 1848 this meant for Bushnell, fresh from his study of Quietism, that the disciple would allow Christ to crucify self-love. Later in life he would define the formation more positively as growth in "liberty, power, and greatness" or other such expansive qualities, but he held on to the idea that growth in

Christian character could provide the norm by which the adequacy of a theology could be judged. Assessing character by the degree of its conformity to the spirit of Christ in the gospels, he could then assess theological opinions by their effects on character.[11]

Even before he began his work in the parish, Bushnell had begun to explore romantic theories about religious knowledge. In college he read Coleridge's *Aids to Reflection* with little effect, but in a later reading he found the book filled with insights that would reappear throughout his own writings. Like Coleridge, Bushnell would think of Christianity as a matter more of "life" than of doctrine. Both saw language, especially etymology, as a clue to theological meaning; both asserted an analogy between nature and mind; both read the Bible as a stimulus to the religious imagination; both found the evidence for faith in the inner consciousness of the faithful; and both thought that the logical understanding could never comprehend spiritual truth. Of course, he read Coleridge through the filter of New England piety, which had long valorized the internal "sense" of the heart, and his free-floating style of thinking could not, in any case, remain long within the confines of another theologian's mind, but Bushnell acknowledged that he was more indebted to Coleridge than to any other author outside the Bible. In 1845–46, he toured Europe, and the tour also left its mark on his theology, especially after his long conversations with the Scottish philosopher of religion John Daniel Morell, whose writing helped introduce the work of Schleiermacher to the English-speaking world. Bushnell increasingly pondered the possibility that the core of religion was to be found at a level of experience deeper than linguistic conceptions.[12]

Some of those themes marked his 1848 lecture at Andover on "Dogma and Spirit," in which he argued that a vision of Christianity as "Life and Spirit" had far more promise than either revivalism or dogmatic purity as a stimulus for renewal in the churches. Speaking at a school that had enthroned the pious intellect as the guardian of Christian truth, Bushnell contrasted speculation and spirit, reason and sensibility, and the intellect and the heart, and announced that the sensibility was the better guide. To an audience well-trained in evidential reasoning, he argued that the apprehensions of faith created their own evidences. He was willing to concede that "opinion, science, systematic theology, or even dogma" had their place, but it was not the elevated place that they had occupied at Andover.[13]

The address produced grumbling, but Bushnell continued to claim that New England theology had become a dry rationalism. His reading of an excerpt from the German mediating theologian Richard Rothe helped him sharpen a distinction between "mere theology" and "divinity." Rothe had contended, in the manner of Schleiermacher, that theology was the logical exposition of the

Christian consciousness. For Bushnell this meant that theology should be grounded in "divinity," which he defined as an immediate knowledge of God, a "living consciousness" akin to the immediacy of self-consciousness, an experience of the life of God in the soul.[14]

The fullest exposition came in a sermon on "The Immediate Knowledge of God," not published until 1872 but preached at Yale earlier, in which Bushnell distinguished between an immediate, personal knowledge of God, attainable through a dimension of experience deeper than language and discursive thought, and a "medial" knowledge, available through reflection on nature and scripture. The distinction might have come from Cousin's notion of a prereflective or intuitive reason underlying the operations of reflective reason, though Bushnell did not employ Cousin's argument that the spontaneous level could be discerned by analysis of the presuppositions of reflection. It might have come from Schleiermacher by way of Morell or Rothe, for those theologians also believed that an unmediated consciousness, a prethematized layer of experience, operated beneath the forms of consciousness mediated through concepts. Whatever its source, Bushnell used it to point toward a precognitive awareness or feeling of an "otherness" within experience. While he did not disparage mediated knowledge — he even spoke of it as necessary to salvation — he valued it mainly because it helped make the immediate possible. The real value in "knowing about" God was that it pointed toward the possibility of "knowing God" in an unmediated experience.[15]

Bushnell acknowledged a "mystic element" in his distinction, but he hastened to add that the Bible remained for him the primary authority for Christian theology. Yet he no longer thought of the Bible as an infallible and verbally inspired repository of propositional truth. It was rather "the grand poem of salvation." It was the prime vehicle for the revelation of divine truth, but the God who authored it was an artist and not a logician, addressing the reader through stories and symbols drawn from the history of Israel. Although Bushnell asserted, against Strauss and Parker, the historical accuracy of the New Testament, and although he thought that the depiction of Jesus in the gospels proved him to be no "merely human character," he found the authority of the Bible to reside not in its origins or its accuracy but in its effect on the Christian consciousness. Proof that the Bible "bodied and expressed" the divine could be found only as the revelation became a source of saving experience.[16]

Bushnell's turn to experience meant that natural theology in the older sense, with its inferences from regularity to a divine designer, had no contribution to make. Even as a student he found Paley unconvincing, and his conviction grew that the God of the natural theologians was "not a being who meets the conditions of Christianity at all." For one thing, the "Paleyizing theologians" had no convincing explanation for the suffering and evil in nature and no answer for the objection that beaks and talons, claws and fangs, and stings and bags of venom seemed as much adapted to their destructive ends as anything else seemed to be. For another, a God derived from nature could never be more than a synonym for an abstract causation or one in an infinite series of creators.[17]

In a similar manner Bushnell recast the traditional evidences of revelation. He did not discard them. He often used the internal argument that the Bible was consistent with human need, and he adduced the miracles of Jesus as proofs that the gospel was a supernatural revelation. But he conceded that the miracles could not prove the doctrines, and he tried to push the whole machinery of rational proofs and evidences into the background. The true method of religion was "verification by the heart."[18]

Still another motive for Bushnell's departure from orthodox rationalism grew out of his reflections on language. In his "Preliminary Dissertation on the Nature of Language, as Related to Thought and Spirit," which he published in 1848 as the lead essay of his *God in Christ,* he announced that no one could enter fully into his position without knowing his views of language. He later described them as the "key to my real meaning." As a student at Yale he had probably learned from his teacher Josiah Willard Gibbs to think of all abstract terms in language as metaphors that had originated as terms for sensory experience. Gibbs's reading in German philology, especially the writing of Karl Ferdinand Becker, had convinced him that every word expressing "an intellectual or moral idea" originally had a physical referent: "right" had once meant "straight," "spirit" came from "breath," a "transgression" was once a "crossing over." Bushnell's unpublished manuscript on "Revelation" (1839) expressed his agreement that "the whole outward world" was "analogical to thought and truth."[19]

He derived from this insight a negative conclusion about the possibilities of theology as it had been conceived in rational orthodoxy and a positive conclusion about the metaphysical grounding of human communication. The negative conclusion attracted the most attention. Since words had their origins in the concrete forms of the world of sense, they could never refer precisely to the formless truths of the world of mind and spirit. As "faded metaphors," they always represented the invisible under the aspect of the visible, the formless under the aspect of form. They therefore revealed and misled at the same time. Bushnell found in all theological disputes a faulty assumption that theological language could be exact and that theology could be a science. He found theology far more akin to poetry. It consisted of metaphors and images that evoked experience rather than mirroring reality. Theology was devoid of literal truths, but it was filled with metaphorical insights that could expand human consciousness.[20]

The proper reaction, then, to ambiguity and contradiction in either theology or the Bible was to revel in the paradoxes. Since no single metaphor could convey theological truth, Bushnell thought that theologians came closest to the truth when they multiplied conflicting metaphors. He loved the gospel of John because its surface contradictions revealed the loftiest truths; he admired Paul precisely because his letters resisted system. He found the language of scripture suggestive of multiple possibilities of interpretation, with "meanings coming out of meanings, and second senses doubling upon first." In no way could they provide the material for a theological system. They were rather, as Bushnell noted in 1869, a "gift to the imagination."[21]

Defining the imagination as the power to glimpse and express truth through images, he redefined theology as an imaginative enterprise. He recognized the possibility that this left nothing "fixed or determinate" in theology. One system would always replace another; the many theologies would always struggle in vain to express the "one truth." When Edwards Amasa Park argued that the theologian should use a more abstract language that reconciled seemingly contradictory scriptural images, Bushnell replied that Park's abstractions were no more than metaphors themselves, as any survey of their etymology would demonstrate. "Instead of trying to get all the great truths in question, out of their symbols into others, and build them into sciences that are independent of the symbols," he said, "I am rather showing how to stay by the symbols or in them, as the best and holiest expressions of truth." Confident about the possibility of a prereflective and immediate experience of God and sure that the New Testament's depiction of Christ furnished the norms that could guide growth in character, Bushnell urged theologians not to worry overmuch about doctrinal precision.[22]

The positive metaphysical inference from this view of language came to Bushnell as he faced the problem of how minds limited to figures and images could nevertheless communicate with each other about spiritual truths. Even though the words bore multiple meanings, and each person's life story gave every word a different shade of subjective meaning, it still remained possible to converse about matters of spirit. The explanation could reside only in the sphere of the supernatural. God had created a physical world designed to give rise to signs that revealed the divine intention. The Logos in the outward world answered to the logos within. Like Emerson, Bushnell thought that the analogies between matter and mind revealed intelligence at work in the world. He speculated that physical science might refine the language of sense to such a degree that it would provide ever more precise and revealing metaphors. He thought that no series of textbooks in natural theology "piled even to the moon, could give a proof of God so immediate, complete, and conclusive" as could be found in the marvels of a nature that overflowed with analogies.[23]

Bushnell's theory seemed to dissolve any possibility of a criterion for theological truth, but he assumed that his ideal of Christian character ruled out "licentious vagaries." Sound theology, he said, was "health-giving theology." It strengthened "the practical doctrine of a godly life, as grounded in the living faith of Christ." Americans had always said that theology was practical; Bushnell was giving meanings to that conventional formula that it had rarely carried outside the confines of Unitarian and transcendentalist thought. He looked upon all the central Christian doctrines, from the Trinity to the person of Christ and the atonement, as practical aids to the living of a Christian life.[24]

Trinity, Atonement, and Character

In 1848, Bushnell published *God in Christ*. The book produced another outcry of criticism, and in the following year he defended his views before the Hartford Association. A year later a conference of ministers in western Connecticut tried to bring him to trial for heresy before the General Association of Connecticut, charging that the book was "destructive to the faith." In 1851 he published his Hartford defense in a second book, *Christ in Theology*, which in turn elicited more negative reviews in the learned journals and the popular religious press from theologians at Yale, Princeton, East Windsor, and Bangor. After the association refused to convict, some of his opponents formed a new Hartford association of ministers to escape his influence, and in 1852 his own congregation withdrew from the Hartford North Consociation of churches in order to prevent any heresy trial.[25]

The accusers believed, first, that Bushnell had denied the doctrine of the Trinity. In his 1848 "Discourse on the Divinity of Christ" at the Yale commencement, he had criticized the "confusion" of trying to assert "a real and metaphysical trinity of persons in the divine nature." Instead, he depicted the Trinity as the self-expression of the formless Absolute to finite minds whose apprehension required form. In the revelation of the Trinity, God made an accommodation to the limits of human thought in a way that both revealed something of the divine nature and preserved the mystery. The Father, Son, and Spirit were each manifestations of the Absolute in forms accommodated to the finite understanding.[26]

The theory sounded "modalist," conceiving of the Trinity simply as three modes in which the one God stood self-revealed. Bushnell preferred to speak of the threeness as instrumental to the divine self-expression, and while he defined it as "eternal," he would not speculate about the threeness internal to the Absolute itself. He said later that the New Haven address was a way of saying that in the battle between the Unitarians and the Trinitarians of New

England, no speculative solution was possible. He denied any attachment to Schleiermacher's modal Trinity, or to Moses Stuart's conclusion that a three-fold revelation could prove a God immanently three, or to the similar attempt of Neander and August Twesten in Germany to infer an immanent Trinity from the Christian consciousness of God as Creator, Redeemer, and Sanctifier. All presumed to know more about God's essential nature than Bushnell thought could be known.[27]

Acknowledging that the threeness in the revelation proved some vague "ground" of Trinity in the nature of God, he still said that no finite mind could know exactly what this meant, especially since the terms Father, Son, and Holy Spirit were analogies derived from human consciousness. Bushnell would not, in 1851, deny an immanent Trinity but neither would he affirm it. Trinitarian doctrine for him was still "for use and not for theory," practical rather than speculative. In his 1854 essay on "The Christian Trinity as Practical Truth," he repeated that the word "person" could be applied to God only by analogy.[28]

The doctrine's practical value lay for him in its superiority to both the pantheist's abstract infinity and the Unitarian's anthropomorphic Father. It kept open the possibility of a divine-human relationship that did not restrict the divine within the human. The pantheist's infinity was so inclusive of all reality as to lose any specific meaning, while the Unitarian's Divine Father too easily allowed a lapse into sentimentality. The doctrine of the Trinity asserted that God was the unfathomable Infinite and the winsome finite Christ as well as a source of power indwelling human life. As a "holy paradox," the doctrine safeguarded religious experience from either sentimentality or emptiness. In this way it served the ends of the growth of Christian character.[29]

Bushnell made a similar set of moves when he described the person of Christ. He hesitated to speculate about the internal composition of the divine and human in Christ. Like the Unitarians, he found the traditional notion of "two distinct subsistences" groundless. Rather than discarding faith in Christ's divinity, however, he proposed to redefine it: the uniqueness of Christ was to be found in what he expressed of God. Accused of denying both the distinct humanity and the eternity of Christ, Bushnell replied that he affirmed a "wholly mysterious" unity of the human and the divine in Christ but refused to speculate about "the ulterior psychology of Christ's person." He could affirm the traditional formula — two natures in one person — but define it to mean only that God was "mysteriously incarnate" in the human person of Christ.[30]

The duality was "instrumental." Bushnell was claiming that the value of both the incarnation and the words used to describe it rested in the "impressions" they made on the believer. Unlike most other Protestants, who valued the incarnation because it made possible the atoning death, unlike Catholics, who saw it chiefly as the foundation of the church, and unlike Nevin and Schaff at Mercersburg, who saw it as a saving transformation of human nature and the inner substance of the church, Bushnell valued the incarnation for what it revealed. It communicated God's desire to "draw himself into union with us, by an act of accommodation to our human sympathies and capacities." Like the Trinity, therefore, it humanized the Absolute while preserving enough of the sense of mysterious otherness to discourage a piety of sentimental familiarity. The importance of the doctrine came from its salutary effect on the Christian consciousness.[31]

Bushnell's inward turn, his emphasis on theology as an aid in the alteration of consciousness and the making of character, found clearest expression in his almost thirty years of intense meditation on the doctrine of atonement. In an address at Harvard in 1848 he characteristically sought a way of comprehending the truth — but omitting the error — in both the Calvinist and the Unitarian portrayals of the meaning of the death of Christ. Like the Unitarians, he defined the aim of the atonement as the renovation of character, a "moral effect, wrought in the mind of the race." It was designed to bring men and women "into union with God, to reconcile them unto God." Scripture itself, he argued, proposed this "subjective" end as the meaning of Christ's life and death. But he thought that Unitarian theology made Christ only an example rather than a source of saving power, and it also failed to compass the objective dimension of atonement in scripture.[32]

In designating the atonement as objective, Bushnell made no migration into Calvinist orthodoxy. He thought that the theory of atonement as the satisfaction of God's wrathful demand for punishment offended the moral sentiment by transferring penal evil to the innocent. The governmental theory, in turn, recognized the expressive character of atonement but made it only an expression of God's regard for public justice without taking its subjective end into account. It was too abstract, too much about transactions in "remote fields of being." Yet Bushnell thought that these older views had the virtue of fidelity to the language of scripture, the "terms of the altar" that described atonement as sacrifice, expiation, ransom, remission, and propitiation. This was a language of objectivity that pointed toward a divine transaction outside the boundaries of human subjectivity. Taken literally, the language misled. Taken as art, it made subjective atonement possible.[33]

He attributed at least three distinct meanings to the "altar form" of biblical language about the gospel. First he argued that only such an objective language had the aesthetic power to engage the affections and the will. It was for him a law of thought that the subjective must find representation in objective forms. Those forms then became the only media that could draw the self outside its subjectivity. A religion that limited itself to language expressive of subjectivity would dissolve into "inanity." It would lack the power to draw the adherent into any realm of experience outside the ordinary. It would serve only the energies of self-culture and therefore feed self-preoccupation. The biblical language, strange and alien, broke into each individual's experience from the outside in a way that could move the self off its own center.[34]

The second layer of meaning in the altar language moved even further beyond subjectivity. It pointed to a class of objective truths about the atonement. It meant that God really was in Christ reconciling the world, that the faithful really were delivered from the judicial consequences of their sin, and that Christ really was a "supernatural power" who raised the believer into a participation in the divine nature. It referred to the rightness of God, the wrongness of sin, the holiness of the law, and an absolution given from outside the self. Bushnell claimed that his theory, by signifying a power operating on the self from the outside, captured the intent of the older imputation theories without falling into subjection to their literal absurdity.[35]

The altar language then suggested a third level of meaning that further accentuated Bushnell's vision of atonement as an event beyond the reach of the natural. Just as his theory of language assumed that a supernatural Logos designed the physical world as a base for the language of spirit, so also his theory of atonement asserted that the "altar forms" of the Old Testament were the means by which God purposefully prepared the world to receive the truth about redemption. Bushnell modified the older typology, but he still saw the sacrificial rituals of ancient Israel as a source of forms and impressions that made it possible for the first-century world to understand the meaning of Christ's death. The Old Testament narratives came from a divine artistry in which God providentially instituted the forms that would reveal the divine intention in Christ.[36]

What Bushnell sought was a theory of atonement that would retain the language of scripture and then illustrate its potency by finding analogies to it. His quest for analogies, however, stood in a certain tension with his theory that the language of revelation was designed to maintain the mystery as well as reveal the truth. In 1866 he published *The Vicarious Sacrifice, Grounded in Principles of Universal Obligation* — a book resting on the premise that God and human beings were sufficiently similar in spiritual attributes that human experience could illumine divine intent. The book reinterpreted vicarious sacrifice — which had traditionally meant that Christ died as a substitute for sinful humanity — to mean that Christ, in obedience to the divine law of love, so identified himself with the sinful that his death could draw them from sinfulness and hence from its penalty. The atonement was an instance of the vicarious love that could be found any time a good human being acted self-sacrificially in love to restore a "bad or miserable" neighbor.[37]

Bushnell made no retreat from his earlier "subjective-objective" theory, and his critics again came out in force, ranging from the orthodox William Andrews, who said that Bushnell misrepresented the penal view, to Henry James, Sr., who said that he exaggerated the self-sacrificing quality of human love. The larger problem, though, was whether Bushnell had maintained his earlier recognition that theological language could not define its object. By suggesting that vicarious sacrifice in human experience could define the meaning of the sacrifice of Christ, he was coming close to suggesting that the divine was not quite as mysterious as it had once seemed.[38]

Both the attempt to preserve the objective side of atonement and the latent problem in his view of analogy became more pronounced when he published *Forgiveness and Law* (1874), in which Bushnell tried to assuage his critics by affirming that atonement meant not merely a change in human consciousness but also a "real propitiation of God." The leading argument was that just as real human forgiveness required a change in the offended party — an identification with the wrongdoer that was costly and risky — so also God's forgiveness implied a change in the disposition of God toward the sinner. The book moved Bushnell slightly closer to the older orthodoxy, but it also compromised his earlier willingness to live with ambiguity. He now affirmed that the principle of his theology was the analogy "or almost identity" between the moral nature of human beings and God. At the least, the principle stood in tension with his earlier accent on the mystery of divine activity.[39]

Yet this observation might not be entirely fair, for Bushnell had seemed earlier to overstate the likeness between the divine and the human when his intention was to reaffirm the distinctively supernatural. In his *Nature and the Supernatural as Together Constituting the One System of God* (1858), he drew, probably from Coleridge, a distinction between nature, a chain of causes and effects "determined from within the scheme itself," and the supernatural as that which transcended the cause-effect chain and acted on it from without. Since he thought that the human will could escape the natural chain of causes — and could act upon it from without — he found in human nature itself the evidence for a supernatural reality. The argument suggested to him that it made sense to talk of God's acting on nature, though it also seemed to reduce considerably the distance between the human and the divine.[40]

It is well to remember, however, that the book was an argument against naturalism. Its main contention was that the new naturalistic tone of American thought—he had in mind not only Emerson and Parker but also phrenology and mesmerism—wrongly assumed that religious capacities inherent in human nature defined the meaning of religion. He thought that their naturalism overlooked both the human conviction of sin and the need for a supernatural redemption. This was why he could never express any confidence in either social or individual progress that supposedly occurred through "mere laws of natural development." Yet he agreed, in good Calvinist fashion, that redemption should not be construed to violate nature. He wanted to show, just as he had argued earlier in *Christian Nurture,* that nature and the supernatural operated together as "the one system of God." This meant that he had to affirm the supernatural as distinct from the natural, and the affirmation took vivid form in his insistence that God continually intervened in the world miraculously. In the circles of academic theologians, he stood alone in his readiness to find the world still filled with divine miracles.[41]

It was certain, however, that Bushnell did not wish to claim the same degree of divine knowledge that theologians commonly claimed. His reticence found expression in his refusal to enter into the older debates over the order of salvation. Bushnell thought it futile to argue over the relative priority of faith and repentance or conversion and regeneration in religious experience, because all the arguments reduced the Bible to a series of propositions about philosophical matters. His confidence about experience, however, could sometimes produce its own forms of easy oversimplification. Dismissing the intricate debates in which theologians had tried to define the freedom and bondage of the will, he said that the question was reducible to a simple matter of consciousness. When agents felt free, they were.[42]

Whenever he did enter into the older debates over salvation, he redefined them in accord with his theory of character and growth. He insisted on justification by faith; he even claimed to retain the deeper meaning of the doctrine of imputation, though he redefined it to mean that the justified never had their righteousness as an inherent possession but only as a constant receptivity to God maintained by faith. But he did not accept the older forensic view of justification. He thought that justification was not merely a legal declaration of righteousness: "the true Christian justification is that which makes righteous." It was a "trusting of one's self" to Christ to be "new-charactered" by him. It was a quality of relationship that made possible the gradual healing that Bushnell still called sanctification, though he would not make the distinction between justification and sanctification too sharply, since both terms referred for him to different aspects of the one renewed life.[43]

Bushnell's refusal to make careful distinctions drew the scorn of other theologians, but he saw it as a strength. His significance lay partly in his willingness to question the overrefined distinctions that often marked theological debate, partly in his critique of current assumptions about language, and partly in his turn to experience as a source and norm of theological reflection. By reading him selectively, the later American liberals saw him as a forerunner, and his ideas about nurture helped redefine the meaning of Christian education within American Protestantism. In his own setting he represented a mounting dissatisfaction with the evidential view of Christian reasonableness, and he also joined a mounting chorus of objection to "the perfect sufficiency of formulas."[44]

23

The Mercersburg Theology: Communal Reason

In 1840 John Williamson Nevin (1803–86), an Old School Presbyterian graduate of Princeton Seminary, accepted an invitation to teach at the Theological Seminary of the German Reformed Church in Mercersburg, Pennsylvania. Four years later, he welcomed as his colleague Philip Schaff (1819–93), a native of Switzerland who had taught at the University of Berlin. The two men became the formative figures in what would be known as the Mercersburg theology, a school of thought that positioned itself against many of the assumptions that other American theologians took for granted. For Schaff and Nevin, the "problem of problems" in theology was "the Church Question," and they believed that the answer to it ought to recast every other question in Christian theology, including the question of reasonableness.[1]

Only a few American theologians took the Mercersburg theology seriously, and most of them fought against it. It seemed an alien implant, too absorbed with German modes of thought to fit the American context. It was Christocentric rather than bibliocentric; it elevated the incarnation over the atonement; it celebrated the corporate Christian "life" within the church rather than individual religious experience; it spoke of organic development in history rather than of the restitution of the primitive church; and it placed the sacraments rather than preaching at the forefront of Christian devotion. In all these ways, Nevin and Schaff stood apart from the majority, and they also had less in common with Catholics and high-church Episcopalians than it seemed to their opponents. In addition, they had a distinctive opinion about reason in theology. The Mercersburg theology added a conservative voice to the protest against the evidential apologetic.

Reason and Tradition

From a sociological perspective, the Mercersburg movement could be described as a reaction against populist forms of piety and theology. It began with Nevin's criticisms of revivalism as "coarse and vulgar." He charged the followers of Charles Finney with "popularizing" divine things, deplored the attraction of "the popular mind" to revivalist excess, and charged that the revivalist system seemed to discourage concern for an educated ministry. His distaste extended beyond revival techniques, for he included in his polemic not only Methodists, revivalist Lutherans, Mormons, and the revivalist party of John Winebrenner that had led a separatist movement out of the German Reformed Church but also Alexander Campbell's Disciples of Christ, who were themselves suspicious of revivalist methods. The dismay at the populist style was also evident in Schaff's description of America as a land of theological hucksters.[2]

Like the American Catholics, however, the Mercersburg theologians also disliked the notion that the isolated individual, educated or not, should presume to define religious truth. They disliked Protestant confidence in the principle of private judgment. Schaff argued that the "exaltation of private judgment" had never been the aim of the Protestant Reformation, which had tried rather to subject reason to the divine word. He thought that the principle of private judgment undermined biblical authority, since its defenders could accept only what their natural reason could approve. It also confirmed the wildest of American sectarians, since "by the Bible they always mean their own sense of it, and thus in fact follow merely their private judgment." Nevin agreed on both counts, and he also thought that the principle was hypocritical. Its defenders had "a scheme of notions already at hand, a certain system of opinion and practice, which is made to underlie all this boasted freedom in the use of the Bible, leading private judgment along by the nose, and forcing the divine text always to speak in its own way." To him the appeal to private judgment represented "a protest against the authority of all previous history."[3]

To most of their readers, this commendation of tradition would have sounded Catholic. Schaff spoke of the Bible as the product of church tradition; he conceded that Christ promised the church long before it had a Bible that his "uninterrupted presence" would preserve its "evangelical truth" (Matt. 16). But Schaff was not taking the Catholic view. He said that the church's decision about the canon was no more than recognition that certain books had attained authority, and he repeated Calvin's claim that the Bible's ultimate authority for the believer rested on the inner witness of the Spirit. For Schaff, tradition was normative insofar as it incorporated the "ever-deepening onward flow of the sense of Scripture itself, as it is carried forward in the consciousness of the Christian world." Rather than a source of doctrine parallel to the written word, tradition was synonymous with the history of interpretation.[4]

Nevin defended Schaff's appeal to "the bible as apprehended by the Church," but he moved beyond Schaff. Having read the German church historian August Neander, Nevin began even before joining the Mercersburg faculty to think about theology historically. After nine years at Mercersburg, he was able to publish a series of essays on "The Apostles' Creed" (1849), announcing that he no longer thought of the Bible as "the *principle* of Christianity." The principle, rather, was Christ; the creed was the crystallizing of the church's spontaneous witness to Christ's living presence, antedating and guiding decisions about the biblical canon; and the tradition that produced the creed became the "living stream into which continuously the sense of the Bible is poured." By the time the creed assumed written form in the fourth century, its affirmations had long constituted a living tradition expressing "the fundamental consciousness of the Church." One could not rightly interpret the Bible from outside that tradition, and fundamental doctrines and practices, from the Trinity to infant baptism, could be clearly discerned as in accord with biblical teaching only through the lenses it provided.[5]

The two men reached these conclusions about history and tradition partly as a result of their exposure to philosophical traditions different from the reigning Baconian empiricism. During the 1830s, Nevin immersed himself in the English Puritan mystics and Christian Platonists—like Henry Scougall, Robert Leighton, and John Howe. He felt drawn to Platonic thought because of its defense of "ideas" as objective forces rather than subjective fancies, and a Christian Platonism lingered throughout his career.[6]

Schaff had formed his philosophical perspectives under the tutelage of German Hegelians and romantics like F. W. Schelling, who had taught him to understand nature and history as progressive actualizations of the ideal. He had especially absorbed, during his study under Ferdinand Christian Baur in Tübingen, a Hegelian image of historical change as developmental, organic, and dialectical. It was developmental because it occurred in accord with inner laws that guided its progress, organic because it realized embryonic potentials by passing through stages that were integrally bound together, and dialectical because it proceeded through conflict and struggle between opposing forces and ideas.[7]

Nevin seriously encountered Hegelian thought when he went to Mercers-

burg and met Friedrich Augustus Rauch, a young German classicist and bud-
ding theologian who had earned a doctorate at Heidelberg. Rauch died a year
after Nevin's arrival, so he never contributed to the Mercersburg theology, but
his *Psychology* (1840) was the first English-language text to interpret Hegelian notions approvingly for an American audience, and Nevin studied the
book closely. It taught a conservative Hegelianism — a version friendly to a
traditional Christian view of God as personal — derived from Rauch's teacher
Karl Daub at Heidelberg. What impressed Nevin was its description of the
human body as the expression of an organic law, its insistence on the unity of
the self, and its definition of personality as a manifestation of both the general
life of the race and the individuality of each person. He would soon learn from
Schaff something of Hegel's developmental conception of history.[8]

The two men also bore a debt to the German "mediating theologians," who
sought to formulate an alternative to both the anti-supernaturalism of such
German Hegelian theologians as Baur and David Friedrich Strauss and the
supernaturalist orthodoxy of such German Lutheran confessionalists as Ernst
Hengstenberg. The mediating theologians built bridges between nineteenth-
century European secular culture and a Christian faith that retained its beliefs
in a personal God, the divine-human Christ, and redemption from sinfulness
through his life and death. Impressed by Schleiermacher's emphasis on corporate Christian experience as a foundation for theology, such mediating figures
as Isaac Dorner and Friedrich Schmid nonetheless held on to more traditional
ideas of biblical revelation. Schaff studied happily with both of them.[9]

For both Schaff and Nevin, the premier mediator was the Berlin church
historian August Neander, whom Schaff described as "an apostle of *mediation*, in the noblest sense of the word." Schaff studied with Neander in Berlin;
Nevin learned German in order to read Neander's history while teaching in
Pittsburgh. Neander taught them to think of church history as a discipline
concerned with "life and genetic development" rather than static facts. He also
helped them see it as a theological enterprise that united "science and Christian piety."[10]

With this background in idealist philosophy and mediating theology, neither Nevin nor Schaff had any intention of dismissing reason from theology.
Their objection was to the particular empiricist and rationalist temper underlying the evidential schemes. Nevin saw in evidentialism, whether Protestant
or Catholic, the assumption that "reason and revelation were only contiguous
spheres, the one ending where the other begins." To assume that reason concluded logically, from miracles or from forms of natural evidence, to the supernatural authority of the Bible, was to assume that the mind had to be moved by
motives extrinsic to the content of the revelation. Nevin had no doubts about

miracles and fulfilled prophecies, but he did not think that either could be abstracted from the "living revelation" as proofs for it.[11]

The Mercersburg alternative was to claim that Christ authenticated himself "by direct communication, in some way, with the rational nature of men, as being himself indeed the life of reason." The motives of assent lay in the revelation, in the Christ revealed, in the object presented to faith. The Bible contained a "living revelation" that authenticated itself without the "intermediate authority" of rational proofs. It was not that faith contradicted reason. Faith was a kind of intuition, operating in unity with a rationality that could grasp the "intrinsic reasonableness" of even mysteries like the Trinity. Like Nevin, Schaff accorded a limited secondary authority to the evidences while arguing that the Bible received its authorization finally from the "inward testimony of the Holy Spirit."[12]

Nevin may have derived some of these ideas from his reading during the 1830s of Samuel Taylor Coleridge, who disdained evidential reasoning in Christianity. Both he and Coleridge liked the Platonic notion that reason immediately beheld eternal ideas. He was also attracted to the common post-Kantian romantic distinction between an "understanding" that was limited to the phenomenal world and a "reason" able to grasp truths beyond the sensory and therefore akin to a faith that communed with higher realities. He wanted to overcome the dichotomy between faith and reason and to show that faith "includes in itself also, potentially at least, the force of reason and knowledge in regard to its own objects."[13]

It followed that Nevin also had little interest in traditional forms of natural theology. He thought that "mere logic" could make no leap from "the world of sense to the world of spirit," and that nature had to be read through the eyes of faith if it was to reveal its deeper secrets. Like Emerson and Bushnell, the Romantic poets, and earlier Christian Platonists, he thought of the outward creation as a repository of symbols and metaphors, and as a Christian he found in it signs of God's presence and glory, but he thought that the rational proofs of natural theology could never persuade the unbeliever to trust the God who was incarnate in Christ.[14]

Nevin thought of the subjective reason of the individual as a form of participation in an objective and universal reason. When it operated truly, it was not particular or private; it yielded to the authority of the universal. This was why private judgment had "no force of reason ever *as private*" but became rational "only by ceasing to be private and showing itself to be truly general." For the theologian this meant that reason functioned best as part of faith's search for understanding, and for both Schaff and Nevin this required a proper view of the church.[15]

The Church Question

The "church question" became during the 1840s an international preoccupation. In America it found expression among high-church Episcopalians, confessional Lutherans, and Presbyterians who claimed divine authority for their polity. It reappeared in Catholic debates over the possibility of salvation outside the church and in the claims of successionism among Landmark Baptists. It took another form in the restorationist movements and other efforts to overcome sectarian division. It stood behind the debates among Episcopalians, Presbyterians, and Methodists over episcopacy and polity. In England, its primary expression was the Oxford Movement; in Denmark, the Lutheran program led by N. S. F. Grundtvig. In Germany, it resulted in a Lutheran high-church movement that led the theologian Wilhelm Loehe to marvel that "everybody is talking about the church in our time." The German movement, led by Ernst Hengstenberg and the jurist Ludwig von Gerlach in Prussia, allied itself with resistance to revolution and the defense of hierarchy and authority in the society and the state as well as the church. It was within these conservative German circles that Schaff first developed his convictions about the importance of the church.[16]

In Mercersburg, Pennsylvania, the church question had humbler beginnings. Nevin first raised it there while criticizing the methods of revivalism. After a visiting preacher tried to employ Charles Finney's "new measures" in the German Reformed congregation in Mercersburg, Nevin published *The Anxious Bench* (1843), a "tract for the times" in which he argued that revivalist piety was part of an individualistic and unchurchly system that transmitted the worst features of American "puritanism." It created disorder, reduced faith to feeling, and shifted attention from the mysteries of conversion to the methods of the revivalist. A new edition the next year added a chapter in which he contrasted the revivalist "system of the bench" and the "system of the catechism," a piety of gradual nurture and instruction under the means of grace in the church. While he welcomed sober and intelligent appeals to the unconverted, he thought that the primary aim of ministry in the church should be "the growth of the Church itself in grace and living power." He later looked back to *The Anxious Bench* as proof that the Mercersburg theology owed its existence "not to any spirit of philosophical speculation as has been sometimes imagined, but to an active interest in practical Christianity."[17]

Within a year the issue for Nevin shifted to sectarian disunity. In 1844 he delivered to the joint Convention of the Reformed Dutch and the German Reformed Churches a sermon on "Catholic Unity" in which he defined the church as the body of Christ holding all of its members in an organic unity with him. Behind the sermon was Nevin's growing mastery of German theology but also a fresh awareness of the theme of union with Christ in the theology of Calvin. The thesis was that all Christians, mystically united with Christ's body, formed "one great spiritual whole," and they had an obligation to manifest their union by seeking the visible unity of the church catholic.[18]

Among Nevin's listeners was Philip Schaff, who had arrived in America twelve days earlier. As he wrote later in his journal, Schaff was delighted with Nevin: "I feared I might not find any sympathy in him for my views of the church; but I discover that he occupies essentially the same ground that I do and he confirms me in my position." But when Schaff delivered later that year his inaugural address before the Eastern Synod of the German Reformed Church, he discovered that Nevin was not typical.[19]

Published in 1845 as *The Principle of Protestantism*, Schaff's address proposed the entirely conventional thesis that the Protestant axioms were biblical authority and justification by faith. He linked this platitude, however, to an argument that the Protestant principle was also one of movement and growth, an "ever-deepening appropriation of Christianity as the power of a divine life which is destined to make all things new." What made this idea the occasion of a heresy trial in the German Reformed Church were two further contentions: first, that the Protestant churches had become rationalist and sectarian, and second, that this weakness could be overcome only through a course of historical development that would eventually reunite Protestant freedom and subjectivity with Catholic objectivity and authority. Nevin translated the address into English and published it alongside his sermon. The synod president, Joseph Berg, accused both men of "Romanizing tendencies," but the synod refused to convict them of heresy.[20]

Schaff's interests were always primarily historical, but he was interested in history as a clue to the future. His address outlined a vast cosmic progress in which the church would pass through different stages until its "Idea," already complete in Christ, would manifest itself fully in humanity and transform the spheres of science, art, government, and social life, bringing the world to its proper perfection. The Hegelian and romantic background of this would become clearer when Schaff published *What is Church History?* (1846), in which he introduced American students to the historiography of organic development.[21]

In contrast to both a traditional Christian view that exaggerated the changelessness of doctrines and a rationalism that dissolved all stability in change and flux, he presented the new Christian history as a recognition that the church, in both its doctrines and its practices, changed over time but in accord with a fixed divine purpose. He thought that John Henry Newman had failed to appreciate the extent of the changes; Ferdinand Christian Baur had failed to grasp the providential purpose. Even Neander had not seen the importance of the church as the arena of God's providential guidance. The new history would overcome these errors and transform theology. By showing the evolution of God's plan of redemption according to rational and necessary laws, the study of church history would show the inevitability of progress toward the millennium.[22]

Schaff adopted from Schelling, Schmid, and Neander a three-part typology that he used to interpret not only the apostolic church but also the whole course of Christian history. He saw the early church as a dialectical movement in which the Jewish Christianity of law and authority, typified by Peter and James, gave way to a Gentile Christianity of evangelical freedom, typified by Paul, with both finding their completion in a Christianity of harmony and union with Christ, typified by John. He contested Baur's view that the apostolic types represented contradictory forces; he saw them as complementing and completing each other. He found the same scheme in the larger history of the church: the Catholic principles of objectivity, authority, and obedience found a necessary corrective in the Protestant principles of freedom and subjectivity, but the church of the future would overcome the distortions on each side while preserving the essential ideas in a higher synthesis.[23]

In his descriptions of development, Schaff was not always consistent. Sometimes he emphasized romantic images of biological growth, cumulative through various stages of maturity, delayed by periodic disease. Sometimes he used a dialectical scheme in which logical contraries collided before giving way to a higher synthesis. Often he merely directed attention to a middle way between two extremes. These inconsistencies suggest that philosophical precision was not his driving aim. When in 1853 he published his *History of the Apostolic Church, with a General Introduction to Church History*, the aim came into clearer view in his praise of Neander for restoring "the religious and practical interest to its due prominence" in historical studies. For him, the practical interest required a belief that the church was "the depository and continuation of the earthly human life of the Redeemer."[24]

Schaff's historical training and research had convinced him that it was ludicrous for Protestants to dismiss the long history of the Catholic Church as nothing more than the maneuverings of the Antichrist. Whatever the distortions of the Catholic tradition, it had transmitted the life of Christ. Schaff therefore had to underscore the links that bound the Reformation to the earlier church, for otherwise, Protestantism became an aberration that lost touch with that life. Whatever the distortions of the Protestant movement, it still could count on Christ's promise of faithfulness to his church. Whether he described the church like Neander as the kingdom of God moving through history, or like the romantics as the organically developing Body of Christ, or like the idealists as the dialectical development of the "Idea" incarnate in Christ, he had come to see the church as the extended incarnation of the life of Christ in the world. All his historiography stood in service to that theological insight.[25]

Schaff was a resolutely historical thinker. Nevin combined his historical interests with an unusual penchant for thinking systemically. Although he never wrote a systematic theology, he was the most systematic American religious thinker of his era. He was captivated by what he called the "immanent logic of faith." When he looked back at his career, he conceded that the "Mercersburg System" grew into shape without calculation or plan, but he believed that it formed a system, self-consistent and interrelated in all its parts, and his main interest was in displaying its "inward structure . . . regarded as a whole." He believed that each doctrine had its "position, complexion, and quality in the system" and "it could not possibly have them in any other way." He spoke in much the same way at the outset of his career. In *The Spirit and Genius of the Heidelberg Catechism* (1847), composed of sermons delivered near the beginning of his tenure at Mercersburg, he observed that a theologian's stance on a single sacramental doctrine would have consequences on "the farthest limits of theology," and he added later that a change in the understanding of the Eucharist could alter the character of "the Christian system as a whole."[26]

For Nevin, the center of the system was the incarnation. This was the "cardinal principle." Nevin saw the incarnation of the second Person of the Trinity in Christ as "the true idea of the gospel." "No theology in the country," he said, had "made more of Christ as the centre of its thinking and acting" than the theology at Mercersburg. The only method for theology was to start "in Christ" and then follow the order in which the doctrines unfolded "with necessary connection from his Person." Nevin contended in 1849 that he was following the pattern of the Apostles' Creed, but he was also indebted to German models. While he thought that Schleiermacher had gone astray on other points, he recognized the importance of Schleiermacher's decision to place the Christian consciousness of redemption through Christ at the center of his system. This had sparked an interest in Christology that found expression in such historical accounts as Isaac Dorner's *History of the Development of the Doctrine of the Person of Christ* (1839). Nevin was the first American to reenvision theology from this perspective.[27]

He constructed his Christology on the Pauline contrast between the first and second Adam. Just as the human race had begun in Adam, so also it began anew in Christ. Just as Adam embodied the organic law of human nature that would manifest itself in the peopling of the world, so also the second Person of the Trinity, by assuming human nature, brought that principle into union with the Godhead. This was an event of universal force, transforming the law of human nature. It introduced into the generic idea of humanity a new source of life. Nevin could even speak of it as the completion of the human, a higher stage in a continuing process of divine creation. It was the unity of the human and the divine toward which all of creation had struggled. It introduced into the world a "divine supernatural order of existence" that elevated human nature to a new level, higher than it could ever have achieved through mere natural progress.[28]

Nevin could sound as if he were speaking of a Hegelian universe in which humanity gradually realized the primal Idea through its struggle toward consciousness of the truth, but he was no Hegelian. For Hegel, the Idea became incarnate in the human race. For Nevin, the Logos became incarnate in Christ alone, though its incarnation transformed the race. For Hegel, the biblical story of the miraculous birth, life, and death of Christ presented in pictorial form the philosophical truth that humanity embodied the progress of the Idea. For Nevin, the biblical story was literally true. For Hegel, humanity was a moment in the divine life. For Nevin, humanity remained ever distinct from God. Hegel recast Trinitarian thought as a rational description of the divine becoming. Nevin asserted the traditional Trinity of three Persons united in one nature, and called it a mystery. The Hegelian God was an impersonal principle except insofar as it reached self-consciousness through human consciousness. Nevin's God was personal.

Nevin never made a careful study of Hegel, but what the Hegelian thought-world provided him was a conceptuality that introduced dynamism and movement into a view of reality that still bore marks of Christian Platonism. He was, in scholastic terms, a moderate realist. He thought that the Ideal — whether it be the Idea of an oak tree or the church — existed only as possibility before it became actual in space and time, but as "the inmost substance of that which exists," the Ideal could not be reduced to the sum of the particulars in which it attained visibility. In Nevin's idealist philosophy, the general logically preceded the particular. The general ideal of treeness had a logical priority to any particular instance of it. The treeness, however, was no static abstraction but the dynamic law and power at work in the growth of each tree. It pressed forward toward embodiment and completion. It sought to externalize itself in the world, to unfold its presence and power. It was this philosophical vision that enabled Nevin to view the incarnation as an event that occurred in one divine-human person, recast the principle of human nature in which all people shared, and began to actualize the new ideal possibilities by drawing individuals into the working of its law.[29]

In making the incarnation the center of his system, Nevin altered the standard Protestant view of redemption. He thought that the incarnation redeemed humanity in principle. He spoke of it as "the mediatorial fact." To an American Protestant, this sounded odd at best, heretical at worst. Rather than setting the stage for a mediatorial atoning death of Christ, the incarnation itself was the redemptive medium of union between God and humanity. Nevin's opponents accused him of making the cross unnecessary, but he answered that the cross was a necessary crisis in which the principle of health decisively overcame the law of sin and death. His Calvinist colleagues accused him of deviating from orthodoxy about predestination and a limited atonement. He replied that it was a "vast mistake" to deny that Christian salvation was for "humanity as a whole" and a dangerous abstraction to think of redemption as having regard only to a "given number." But he was no universalist. He thought that believers had to receive the new life unto themselves, that not every person would, and that a mysterious "election of grace" made it possible, but he was unwilling to speculate about what "election" meant.[30]

The church was the extension of the incarnation through history. If the incarnation introduced a supernatural life into the world, then the church was the mystical body that actualized that life: "The Church is the historical continuation of the life of Jesus Christ in the world. By the Incarnation of the Son of God, a divine supernatural order of existence was introduced into the world, which was not in it as part of its own constitution before. . . . The new creation which revealed itself originally in his person is here made constant among men, with all its resources, as a real historical process, reaching forward to the end of time." Nevin described it by means of his distinction between the ideal and the actual. The ideal church was the power of the new supernatural creation; its principle was derived from the life of Christ. It contained all the possibility and potential that was latent in that life. Just as the life of Christ was a unitary divine-human life, of universal force, so also the church was holy, one, and catholic, free from sin and error. Apart from it there was no presence of Christ in the world: "No Church, no Christ." Outside it there was no salvation. But it could bear none of these features unless it was actual as well as ideal.[31]

The ideal for Nevin always pressed for embodiment, and the actual church embodied the force of the ideal. Without embodiment it would be only potential and not real. Like the theologians of the Catholic Church, Nevin rejected the Calvinist distinction between the visible and invisible church. An invisible church was to him an empty abstraction. The idea of the church included visibility just as much as the idea of the human being supposed a body. As actual, the church was holy, one, and catholic only in a fragmented and incomplete way; it required a process of historical evolution to actualize itself fully. But its ideal was not a distant goal; the ideal was immanent within the actual, a life struggling to come to its full manifestation. Just as the ideal could have no reality save under the form of the historical and actual, so the actual could have no truth and inner power except through the presence of the ideal within it.[32]

No theme marked Nevin's theology more than his persistent claim that Christianity was a life in which one participated, not a doctrine that one taught or learned. The church was the bearer of Christ's life; salvation was the partaking of this life. He derived the idea partly from Schleiermacher by way of reading Neander, Hermann Olshausen of Königsberg, and Carl Ullmann of Heidelberg. The purpose of the church was the mystical union in which the divine-human life of Christ flowed into its members. This was a gradual change in which the law of Christ's life slowly drew the believer into its power, lodging in the inmost core of the personality as a seed or principle that altered every faculty.[33]

Nevin's critics again espied Catholic tendencies. Both Charles Hodge and Joseph Berg charged that he had discarded the Calvinist doctrine of forensic justification through the imputation of Christ's righteousness to the believer. Nevin did, in fact, along with Schaff, reject imputation as Princeton understood it, though he never shared the Edwardean, New Haven, and New School inclination to abandon the doctrine. In his view of sin, he opted for mediate imputation: God imputed guilt and condemnation because every sinner shared in Adam's fallen life. So also he thought of the imputation of righteousness as a legal declaration grounded on the believer's union with the life of Christ. "In the very act of our justification," he argued, "it becomes ours in fact by our actual insertion into Christ himself." This was not a Catholic doctrine of inherent righteousness because it did not suppose a possibility of increasing righteousness through sacramental grace and good works, but it moved Nevin outside the circles of conservative Calvinism.[34]

His most important battle with his critics took place on the terrain of sacramental theology. In 1846 Nevin published *The Mystical Presence*. It was a vindication of what Nevin saw as the original Calvinist doctrine of the Eucharist, from which the "modern puritans" of American Calvinism had uniformly strayed. From his days at Western Seminary he had believed that Calvin and the best Reformed confessions taught the doctrine of the real spiritual presence of Christ in the Lord's Supper. In *The Mystical Presence,* he argued that this presence was the occasion for a special mystical union of the faithful with the whole person of Christ, the humanity and the divinity, the flesh and the spirit. He distinguished this view from Catholic doctrine and from the confessional Lutheran position, both of which he thought erred by designating the presence as local and corporeal. But both Catholics and the Lutheran confessionalists recognized, unlike most American Protestants, that the sacrament had an objective force and that its invisible grace was "the substantial life of the Saviour himself, particularly in his human nature."[35]

Nevin found in idealism a psychological theory that permitted a more adequate statement of Calvin's doctrine. Calvin had not clearly recognized that the principle of a body was not its matter but rather the organic law that maintained its identity even as its material volume changed. He had also not given proper emphasis to the unity of the person and thus to the "single indivisible life" of Christ, which ensured that his presence would always be "theanthropic," both divine and human at the same time. And he had not sufficiently noted the distinction between the individual and the generic life of Christ. Just as an oak tree included the force of a life capable of reaching far beyond its individual limits, able to repeat its life in a whole forest of trees, so also each human life was potentially the generic root or principle of a countless posterity. Christ was a singular man but also the generic source of a new creation. In these three ways, the new idealism made the sixteenth-century doctrine "more satisfactory to the understanding." But the doctrine still remained for Nevin a supernatural mystery beyond the comprehension of the natural reason.[36]

The book attracted little attention. Charles Hodge suggested that it took him two years to muster the energy to work his way through Nevin's murky obscurities. When Hodge finally replied, however, he spoke for the current evangelical consensus that the sacrament was a memorial and an occasion for communion with "the Spirit of Christ." He accused Nevin of leaving the Reformed tradition. By speaking of union with the divine-human Christ, by making the Lord's Supper a special and extraordinary means of Christ's presence, by overemphasizing the unity of Christ's two natures, and by superimposing philosophical idealism on doctrine, Nevin had fostered distortions and misunderstandings. When Nevin replied, however, he made it clear that Hodge had his own philosophical assumptions. In retrospect, Nevin was closer to Calvin on the Lord's Supper than Hodge was.[37]

The sacramental sensibility at Mercersburg extended to baptism. While he shied away from affirming baptismal regeneration in a Catholic sense, Nevin did find a gracious force in the sacrament that brought the infant into the church. He could therefore refer to it as "the washing of regeneration" for the "remission of sins." Schaff agreed that baptism was "in general necessary to salvation," though not without faith. Both argued for infant baptism as a fitting expression of a proper understanding of the church.[38]

The response to Mercersburg from most Protestant theologians was so uncomprehending and hostile that Nevin almost decided to convert to Catholicism. In 1851–52 he published a series of articles on "Early Christianity" and "Cyprian." The conclusion he drew from his studies was that the early church looked "very different from modern Protestantism." It knew nothing of "the Bible and private judgment" as the rule of faith; it accepted the primacy of the Roman pontiff; it conceived of a "purely Divine character belonging to the Church." It affirmed asceticism, celibacy, relics, miracles, purgatory, the veneration of saints, prayers for the dead, submission to the church, and faith in the sacraments as supernatural mysteries. He expressed sheer embarrassment at the ignorance of early Christianity that was revealed in the crude Protestant attacks on Rome. In 1851 Nevin resigned from his seminary position and seriously considered conversion. He entered into correspondence with both Orestes Brownson and John Hughes.[39]

Schaff never felt the same temptation, and he looked back at Nevin's essays on early Christianity as an unfortunate turning point in the Mercersburg movement. But Schaff also deplored the tone and content of Protestant attacks on Catholicism, and he exposed the students at Mercersburg to Catholic readings. One group of students left the seminary in disgust. Schaff was more interested, however, in the church of the future that would unite the best features of the Protestant and Catholic traditions, and he spoke later of delicate relations with Nevin during this period.

Finally for Nevin, as well as for Schaff, the decision to remain within Protestantism rested on the vision of historical development. Nevin conceded that "the idea of historical development" was the only possible escape from the difficulty of affirming the continuity of Protestantism with the early church. Convinced that it "must be one with the ancient church, to have any valid claim to its prerogatives and powers," he could accept it only because he was convinced that it stood in organic continuity with the previous history of the church. He took comfort from Schaff's notion that the Protestant churches were in a stage of transition toward "a higher and better state of the church."[40]

The practical influence of the Mercersburg theology was felt in the German Reformed Church mainly through the debates over the denomination's prayer book. The church in 1849 named Nevin the chair of a committee to study the introduction of liturgical forms that might replace or supplement the informal and free patterns of worship in the church. Under the leadership first of Nevin and then of Schaff, the committee produced a liturgy that embodied many of the features of Mercersburg thought. It never achieved wide favor, but after the Civil War Nevin's *Vindication of the Revised Liturgy* (1867) provided the best short summary of his thought and its practical implications.

By then Nevin had left Mercersburg Seminary behind. After his resignation, he continued as president of Marshall College, and in 1855 he moved to Lancaster, where he joined the faculty of Franklin and Marshall as a professor of philosophy, history, and aesthetics. After the Civil War, he became president. He maintained his theological interests, publishing widely on issues of the inspiration and interpretation of the scriptures, but the older themes of the Mercersburg theology now had less urgency for him. For a time he expressed interest in the interpretive theories of Emannuel Swedenborg, who found the Bible and the world filled with symbols of Spirit, but his attachment to historic Christianity maintained its hold on him.

By 1861, Schaff's changing intellectual interests could be seen in his book on *The Person of Christ,* in which he argued that the best argument for Christ's divinity could be found in his superlative moral character. Instead of writing Christology "from above," moving from the Trinity and the incarnation outwards, he turned his attention to the "human character" of Christ — "the man, Jesus of Nazareth" — with the intention of showing that it was "singularly perfect."[41]

In 1862 Schaff taught as a visiting professor at Andover, and the following year he left Mercersburg permanently to live in New York City. After serving as an executive for the New York Sabbath Committee, he joined the faculty of Union Theological Seminary in 1870. His three-volume *Creeds of Christendom* (1877), his twelve-volume *History of the Christian Church* (1883–93), and his voluminous contributions to the cause of ecumenical union made him one of the most influential American church leaders of the late nineteenth century.

The original Mercersburg impulse continued for a time in the work of Nevin's students E. V. Gerhart and Theodore Appel, but after the liturgical dispute it faded away, to be rediscovered only in the twentieth century when renewed interest in church union made it seem like a forerunner to the ecumenical movement. In its own setting, however, the Mercersburg theology advanced a conception of the incarnation, the church, and the sacraments that countered the prevailing trends of its era. Its criticisms of evidentialism and its argument for the "self-authenticating" Christ foreshadowed some of the central directions of later Protestant thought.

24

Orestes Brownson and Isaac Hecker: Transcendental Catholicism

In 1844 Orestes Brownson joined the Catholic Church. Disillusioned with the romantic individualism of the American transcendentalists, he became convinced that apart from Catholic authority the mind sank in a sea of subjectivity. A similar background in transcendentalism marked the career of Isaac Thomas Hecker, who converted to Catholicism in the same year. They became the two best-known American converts of the decade, Brownson because of his essays in *Brownson's Quarterly Review,* Hecker because of his founding of the Paulist fathers. Both exemplified the influence of romantic ideals on Catholic theology in the early nineteenth century. Both also represented the turn toward new arguments for the reasonableness of Catholicity. To both of them, the Catholic tradition was the voice of reason against a Protestantism that claimed to be rational but subverted rationality. And both agreed that the older evidentialism, in both its Protestant and its Catholic forms, no longer sufficed as the primary mode of apologetic for Christian faith.

The Catholic Brownson

Brownson was the most imaginative and provocative American Catholic thinker of the nineteenth century. Overflowing with ideas and energy, he wrote seven books, twenty-five pamphlets, and more than fifteen hundred essays and edited four journals. He had a broad and deep knowledge of European theology and philosophy, and no American contemporary matched him as a philosophical theologian. He was a relentlessly independent thinker, even after submitting to the authority of the church, and although the Catholic bishops sent him in 1849 a letter praising and encouraging his literary work in defense of the faith, they soon regretted their endorsement and asked him to remove their names from his journal. He was rigorously logical, fiercely polemical, and seemingly fearless, and just as his conversion to Catholicism drew ridicule and contempt from his erstwhile friends in New England, so also his blunt commentary on social and ecclesiastical trends alienated allies in the church.[1]

In some ways he epitomized the ideals of the theological populists. Born in Vermont, he spent his childhood in rural poverty, and neither his widowed mother nor the elderly couple who boarded him until he was fourteen could afford schooling. A move to New York with his mother enabled him to spend a year in an academy, but he read incessantly throughout his life, eventually teaching himself German, French, Italian, Latin, and Greek in order to expand his horizons. Yet he remained suspicious of the "literary class" and early adopted as his life work the promotion of social and political equality.

As a literary critic he espoused a democratic aesthetic that judged art in accord with its sympathy for common people, and his admiration for the scholar who shared and expressed the life of the people set him against Emerson's ideal of the solitary scholar battling mediocrity. As a reformer he defended wage earners, and his essay on "The Laboring Classes" (1840), predicting class struggle and censuring both the capitalist and the clerical elite, reflected his belief that equality and democracy were the true ideals of Jesus. As a popular theologian, he spent his early career defending a democratic Christianity that identified the kingdom of God with the reign of equality on earth. He also argued that professional theologians — even a separate clerical profession — were no longer needed and that college professors were a corrupt aristocracy. "True and holy for us," he wrote, "are the instincts of the masses."[2]

The Whig victory over the Democrats in the presidential election of 1840, which tapped the instincts of the masses for what Brownson saw as unholy ends, shook his "belief in the divinity of the people." He began to elevate justice and order over equality, though he still remained an ally of working people. His views of theological authority also shifted. In early 1844 he was ready to appeal to the cultivated few rather than the mass mind; only an elite could lead the way toward progress. After he became a Catholic later that year he affirmed the church's position that the laity should recognize "the rights of authority" by following the guidance of the bishops and clergy. He continued to write as a lay theologian, even though he occasionally apologized and always pledged to follow his bishop's mandates, but his increasingly abstruse explorations of philosophical themes moved him away from what he was calling by 1857 "the popular mind."[3]

In his intellectual biography, *The Convert* (1857), Brownson described his life pilgrimage as a quest for a reasonable faith and his conversion to the church as a proof that no Catholic had any need to abandon the exercise of reason. "In becoming a Catholic," he said, "I used my reason." He had concluded that the "fundamental vice" of Protestants was their "rejection of reason," a rejection grounded in their belief in total depravity. As a young man, he had understood reason as the exercise of "private understanding" by an isolated individual; as a transcendentalist he viewed it as a form of participation in an impersonal divine reason; as a Catholic he saw it as a "communion" with the infinite reason of a personal God. Both as a transcendentalist and as a Catholic, he viewed it as the manifestation of a principle of intelligibility that preceded individual reasoning and made it possible.[4]

Always implicit in Brownson's quest was the problem of authority: "on what authority I was to take my belief." In addition to his search for authority and a reasonable faith, however, Brownson sought a way to understand and promote human progress. He viewed all his exertions as a religious and social reformer as part of the quest for progress. His labor for the Church of the Future taught him, though, that ideas, by themselves, were impotent for nurturing progress; it also taught him that progress could occur only when something drew men and women beyond themselves. But this raised a problem with his transcendental religion. In 1841 he attended the lectures of Theodore Parker, who also grounded religion in a natural religious sentiment. In pondering them, Brownson began to see transcendentalist subjectivity as a trap. In making religion depend on a natural sentiment, Parker and Emerson made it purely subjective. It was merely an outflowing of human nature. But then it could never be an encounter with a reality that drew human nature beyond itself. And so it could never nurture human progress.[5]

His close reading of Kant's *Critique of Pure Reason* raised a similar problem, for in arguing that the forms and categories of the mind structured all knowing, Kant also found no way, as Brownson read him, that the mind could be assured of grasping an object that was more than a projection of its own internal structure. In saying that the mind could never grasp reality in itself, Kant suggested that human subjectivity would always limit the scope of human claims to knowledge. Brownson wanted to get outside the prison of subjectivity.[6]

He began to move toward a solution as early as 1833, when he started reading Cousin. He liked Cousin's suggestion that philosophy synthesized seemingly competing truths. He also liked the argument that the philosopher could discover in consciousness a synthesis that included the subject or thinker, the object thought, and the relation between them. Since no element was prior to the other, Cousin argued, it was a false abstraction to assume a subject isolated from the object. The mind grasped the object with the same directness that marked its grasp of its own subjectivity. Moreover, Brownson relished Cousin's "psychological method," which seemed to show that ideas of the good, the true, and the beautiful were contained within an impersonal reason that transcended, though it also included, individual minds. By 1842, however, Brownson concluded that Cousin had only asserted, not demonstrated, his argument.[7]

He read in that year the works of Pierre Leroux (1797–1871), a French St.-Simonian who expanded the analysis of thought as a synthesis of subject, object, and relation. If one was as certain as the other, Leroux claimed, then the subject depended on the object as much as the object on the subject. And just as knowing entailed both, so also every other dimension of human life required the concurrence of an object outside the self. Life was communion, and human beings could live only by communion with what was not themselves, communion between the "me" and the "not-me." Brownson argued in his essays on "Synthetic Philosophy" (1842–43) that both the subject and the object preceded thought as its conditions, that the transcendental and eternal "ideas of reason" were therefore, as objects of thought, more than modes of the subject, and that our knowledge of them was a dim knowledge of the divine reason itself.[8]

Leroux's scheme of life by communion offered a way out of subjectivism. It also explained how progress could occur: by bringing humanity into relation with a higher object. But Leroux's pantheistic divinity immanent in the race would not suffice; progress required a relation to a transcendent other with whom the race stood in communion and which could draw it beyond itself. To link humanity with this transcendent other, Brownson returned to the idea of divine providential intervention. He adopted Leroux's notion that certain "providential" people had such an extraordinary communion with God that they elevated all who came into relation with them. This elevation continued in the traditions that bore their life into future generations. In 1842, Brownson thought that Jesus was one among several such providential personalities, but his thinking was now drawing him to the doorway of Catholicity.[9]

In 1842 he wrote "The Mediatorial Life of Jesus: A Letter to the Rev. William Ellery Channing." He had concluded that men and women needed a mediator in order to commune with God; that the mediator must be both divine and human, as Jesus was; and that the life of Jesus had passed from generation to generation through the witness of the apostles and their successors. Only by living within this life could the faithful attain an "eternal" — or full and normal — life. By 1844 he concluded that the church, which bore that life, was necessary for salvation, though he still sought to discern an ideal church that was not identifiable with any existing historical institution, an organic but hidden reality bearing the life of Christ, an extension, in fact, of the incarnation. Only toward the end of that year did he decide that the church about which he was talking had to be visible and that the Catholic Church made the best argument.[10]

Bishop John Bernard Fitzpatrick, who became his mentor, discouraged his philosophical speculation and turned his reading in traditional scholastic directions. By 1845 he was advancing the familiar claims of evidential Catholicity by outlining the standard "motives of credibility." His essay on "The Church Against No-Church" contended that faith required extrinsic evidence, or testimony; that the witness must be infallible; that neither reason nor the Bible nor inner illumination could alone provide that infallible witness; and that rationally convincing evidence could show that Jesus had commissioned a body of teachers, the *ecclesia docens*, and promised the Spirit of Truth that ensured infallibility (John 14:16–17). The argument from antiquity — and from miracles — proved that the Roman Catholic Church was the recipient of this divine promise.[11]

He did not, however, abandon fully his conviction that philosophical argument was the better apologetic. He decided that Protestantism was merely latent transcendentalism, since its doctrine of private judgment made each isolated individual "the exact measure of truth and goodness." Protestants could never reach the truth without "a sound and adequate philosophy." Their beloved Scottish philosophers, Reid and Stewart, had failed to establish the principles of reason. They had only asserted them as necessary for assured knowledge. But even Hume had acknowledged this. Protestants were rationalists without a philosophy. Even their rationalism made no sense, because their doctrine of total depravity contradicted their Realist philosophy. And when they moved away from Calvinism, as Bushnell had done, they fell still into subjectivism because of their philosophical errors.[12]

His musings on reason and faith became increasingly subtle and even risky. In 1845 he argued that reason could not attain supernatural truths without the aid of revelation; it could only judge the credibility of the church's testimony. He later explained that his long association with rationalists had caused him at first to emphasize the necessity of revelation, and he was inclined toward the traditionalist Louis de Bonald, who thought that even philosophy depended on a primal revelation transmitted through the human languages. In 1855, however, the Papacy condemned this form of traditionalism, and Brownson reexamined the question. He determined that his task now was to follow the example of H. L. C. Maret, the dean of the theological faculty at the University of Paris, and defend "the Dignity of human Reason against the Sceptics and Traditionalists and the necessity of Divine Revelation against the Rationalists."[13]

His thinking now increasingly employed a distinction between the natural and the supernatural orders. He found reason entirely sufficient for the natural order, revelation necessary for knowledge of the supernatural. He thought that the traditionalists were right when they said that reason could not even recognize the supernatural without revelation. But he also contended that God was present in the natural order and that reason could grasp that presence, so he followed the Vatican in affirming natural theology. Reason could prove the existence of God, freedom, and immortality. But this was not the autonomous or the impersonal reason of his transcendentalist period.

He understood reason in the light of the distinction between reflection and intuition. Brownson had found it in Cousin, but he thought that Cousin had not understood it properly. As Brownson saw it, reflection was explicit discursive reasoning, making distinctions, comparisons, and contrasts with the aid of language. Intuition was a prereflective apprehension. Brownson was not entirely consistent in his use of the concept, but he usually meant that intuition was the mind's prereflective apprehension of the universal ideas implicit in reflection. These included such ideas as causation, existence, necessity, substance, infinity, goodness, beauty, and perfection, and for Brownson they were not merely subjective ideas. He was a Platonic Realist who believed that the ideas had an objective foundation in the order of things.[14]

They constituted what he called "the intelligible" because without them neither sensory experience nor reflective cognition would be possible. They were transcendental ideas, presuppositions of any possible experience. One became consciously aware of them through reflection, but strictly speaking, reflection neither created nor discovered them. They could not be sought and discovered because the mind without them was incapable of even seeking. It was rather that they revealed and affirmed themselves to our intuition. The objective intelligible order constituted our subjective intelligence by its affirming of itself to us.[15]

For Brownson, the point was theological. The intuitive principles were necessary and eternal ideas; ideas presupposed mind; so they were the ideas of a necessary and eternal mind. Our intuitions therefore brought us into immediate relation to the ideas of God, and since God and God's ideas were not separated, it brought us into an immediate relation to "that which is God." At a prereflective level, reason had an immediate intuition of aspects of the divine being. For intuitive reason, God was "the intelligible" that made reasoning possible.[16]

These notions linked Brownson to Platonic and Augustinian modes of argument. They also had a family resemblance, which he recognized, to the Scottish philosophy's first principles and Kant's categories of the understanding, but he criticized Kant and the Scots for viewing the ideas merely as principles of subjective reason rather than as objective principles that made subjective reasoning possible. In 1850 he was reading the Italian philosopher Vincenzo Gioberti, who furnished him with a vocabulary for refining his epistemology. This was a problem, because Gioberti's belief that the mind had an immediate apprehension of God — a position that became known as ontologism — seemed to make revelation superfluous, and it also appeared to suggest an implicit pantheism, since the principles that he (and Brownson) located within the divine mind were the principles underlying and immanent within the phenomenal world. From the beginning, Brownson had reservations about Gioberti, but he continued to defend him against blanket condemnations. He found within Gioberti's own thought the solutions to the Vatican's problems.[17]

He countered charges of pantheism by adapting the Giobertian formula *Ens creat existentias* (Being, or God, creates existences). He argued that the intuition itself, constituted in part by such ideas as necessity and infinity, entailed contingency and finitude, an order of existence distinct from God. The idea of necessary being made sense only when contrasted to the idea of contingent existence; the idea of infinity could be understood only in contrast to the idea of finitude. Moreover, the intuition apprehended real and necessary being only in relation to finite and contingent realities in the world, including the finite thinker. And finally, in identifying the principles that made thought possible, reflective reason could show that the intuition brought the mind into relation to an objective creativity that had created the very possibility of thought itself. Implicit within the intuition of God, in short, was the distinction between God and finite existence. To intuit God was also to intuit a world separate from God.[18]

He also countered the charge that the ontologist view accorded to the finite and fallen mind a capacity reserved only for the heavenly saints. An intuition of God, he argued, was different from a vision of the divine essence. It apprehended God only as the intelligible; this apprehension, moreover, never occurred apart from the mind's ordinary awareness of sensory objects and mental signs. It was always indirect, obscure, and indistinct. Brownson preferred to say that the intuition merely asserted "that which is God" rather than the full divine reality. In fact, it did not recognize the eternal ideas as "that which is God." Only a subsequent act of the reflective reason could prove the object of the intuition to be an aspect of the divine being, and Brownson agreed with the traditionalists that reflection directed toward the divine contained the dim memory of the original revelation. Despite Vatican condemnations of ontologism and traditionalism, Brownson employed elements of both views throughout his career.[19]

His argument led him away from the prevailing sympathy with natural theology. He had to accept the argument from design, for the Vatican affirmed it, but he pointed out that it presupposed the intuition of the intelligible and therefore assumed God's reality from the outset. The mind could not recognize design in nature unless it already possessed the idea of causality, an idea furnished through intuition. Inductive reason could not prove universal truths unless they were already implicit within the reasoning. One could not reach God through logic unless God was implicitly present in the premises. By 1857, Brownson was again ready to say that a philosophy like the one that had brought him to the church—the philosophy of life by communion—was the best way to "remove obstacles" to Catholic faith.[20]

Notions of revelation still permeated Brownson's theories of knowledge. The intuition apprehended "that which is God" because God revealed that much of himself in the natural order. But natural reason—intuitive or reflective—could grasp God only as the author of nature, not as the author of grace. Though reason could know its own incompleteness, it could by itself not even know that a supernatural order of grace existed. To know the supernatural mysteries, it had to depend on a special revelation. It could trust that revelation because it could show that the witness, the church, was authorized to transmit it truthfully, but then it had to submit to the revealed truth.[21]

As he matured as a Catholic thinker, Brownson became ever more confident that Catholicity was an organic whole in which all the elements logically cohered. From the mystery of the Trinity to the humblest act of worship, every Catholic truth and practice formed an unbroken chain. And the truths in that chain, though often above reason, never contradicted reason.[22]

Trinity, for example, was a truth of revelation, though reason, instructed by revelation, could show that a creative God must embody a principle of multiplicity if he creates according to ideas eternal in his mind. In trying to explain the superintelligible Trinity by reducing it to intelligible categories, he thought, Protestants like Bushnell and Stuart had lost sight of it, but reason properly submissive to the church could retain the mystery even as it showed that eternal distinctions in God did not need to compromise God's absolute unity.[23]

Trinity was linked to incarnation, "the hypostatic union of the divine substance and human nature," another supernatural mystery that nonetheless reflected the intuitive rational truth that the divine and human remained distinct but not separable. The incarnation, in turn, implied the church as the body of Christ, a truth consistent with the rational demonstration of the church's authority. The authority of the church then validated the church's worship, from its sacramental practice to its specific forms of devotion. In Catholic theology and worship, in other words, there was "a reason for everything," and Catholicity proved itself to be the supremely logical religion.[24]

Brownson's enthusiasm, however, created problems. First, he took with great seriousness as a new convert the belief that there was no salvation outside the church. If the church was an organic body giving life to its members, they had to be in communion with it. He conceded that Catholics need not consign to perdition all who were not visibly in communion, but he disliked the common distinction, popular among American Catholics since the eighteenth century, between the "soul" and the "body" of the church, which had provided a way of explaining that non-Catholics might be saved. Deploring "latitudinarianism," he emphasized that salvation outside the visible body would require a perfect charity and supernatural faith that were hardly to be found among American Protestants. A few of the theologian-bishops, including Kenrick and Fitzpatrick, tended to agree, but most felt that Brownson was needlessly stirring up trouble.[25]

He upset other Catholics with his criticisms of John Henry Newman. The most celebrated convert of the era, Newman had made his decision to become Catholic after concluding that Catholic beliefs not contained in the New Testament could be explained as the results of a legitimate historical development of doctrine. Brownson thought that Newman's view implied a "deficiency in the apostolic doctrine." This was incompatible with infallibility and too closely allied with the Protestant assumption that doctrine could be found only in the written word. Newman had neglected the oral tradition as the source of what seemed to be later developments.[26]

Brownson found even worse errors in the work of Nevin and Schaff, who saw Protestantism as a development from Catholicism and both as stages pointing to an even higher form of Christianity. For Brownson, Catholic doctrine was "fixed and permanent." By 1862 he conceded that perhaps some things were only implicitly revealed to the primitive church and that faith could acquire more "light, evidence, and distinction" — that the "human element" in dogma was variable and that maybe this was what Newman meant. He always agreed that theology developed, but he found it hard to say that doctrine developed as well. So also did the other Catholic theologians in America, but it still made them uneasy when Brownson came down hard on Newman.[27]

They became even more uncomfortable when he persisted in arguing for the temporal power of the Papacy. In 1853 he wrote that the Pope could depose civil leaders for crimes against the spiritual order. The typical position of American Catholic theologians had been that the Pope's temporal power was merely an acquired, not a divine, right, exercised in medieval society because conditions then required it. Brownson thought that the Americans — and he named Carroll, England, and Spalding — were too inclined to deny the spiritual independence of the Pope, as well as to accept the separation of church and state.[28]

Michael O'Connor, the bishop in Pittsburgh, condemned his views, and Brownson backed down, but his zeal cost him with the other bishops, who used the occasion to ensure that their names disappear from his journal. By this time, he was also locked in conflict with Bishop Hughes in New York, who disliked his criticisms of the Irish masses and his push for the Americanization of the church. For a while, he considered withdrawing from theological commentary altogether.[29]

Brownson and Hecker

Brownson became increasingly at odds even with his fellow convert Isaac Thomas Hecker, to whom he had been both mentor and friend since 1841. Hecker had followed a path similar to Brownson's. Attracted to radical Jacksonian politics, intrigued for a time by Mormonism, drawn to Unitarianism, and then allied with the transcendentalists, Hecker converted to Catholicism in 1844. He was influenced by some of the same authors who influenced Brownson, from Victor Cousin to Johann Moehler. After an unhappy period in the Redemptorist order, Hecker founded in 1815 the Paulist fathers, an order designed to present Catholicism as the faith for Americans.

In 1855, he tried a new style of theological apologetic. His *Questions of the Soul* tried to show that American spiritual seekers, the sort of people with whom he had briefly associated at the Brook Farm and Fruitlands communal experiments, could fulfill the wants of their hearts only in Catholicism. This made conversion "a supreme act of reason" because it offered the promise of a way of life in which all the human faculties could be harmoniously united. Hecker wanted to reach the people who read Emerson and the transcendentalists and to show them that the church had no antagonism to nature but rather fulfilled its aspirations: "For the end of man is not in himself, nor in his instincts, nor in his soul, but in God."[30]

Brownson wrote an admiring review in which he praised Hecker for presenting Catholicism "in its purely affirmative or positive character, as the adequate object of the heart." He contrasted his own logical style with Hecker's appeal to the heart and confessed that Hecker had felt the spirit of the times more clearly than he had: "This is the book I would have written if God had given me the genius and ability."[31]

Two years later, however, Hecker published his *Aspirations of Nature* (1857), which followed the same approach as the first book. Now the focus of concern was reason, and Brownson felt alarmed. Hecker's argument was that the aspiration of the soul was to find a religion that did not "contradict the universal dictates of reason." Unlike Protestants, whose doctrines of depravity and disparagement of free will and good works signified a repudiation of reason, Catholics offered a religion that respected reason and its powers. Confident that reason could demonstrate the reality of God, the spirituality of the soul, and human freedom, they affirmed that the right exercise of reason would lead the pure heart to Catholic faith. Hecker cited Brownson's own earlier argumentation that Catholicity satisfied "the demands of the most rigid Reason."[32]

Brownson's review was this time far more reserved. Drawing on the traditionalist side of his heritage, he said that reason attained to religious truth only because it had the aid of revelation. If reason seemed to grasp Catholic truths, this was only because it had been predisposed by the culture and habits of Christendom. Hecker had understated "the aberrations of reason" and underestimated "the real loss by the fall." He therefore overrated both the powers of reason and the natural desire of the American mind for Catholic truth. Reason, he said, can assent to the revelation, can even see its reasonableness, but it cannot "apprehend and conduct us toward our appointed end."[33]

Brownson may have been trying to assure Bishop Hughes that he recognized the limits of Americanization. He had in the past, and would in the future, praise the dignity of reason as highly as Hecker. The review bothered Hecker, however, and though the two men would unite again after the Civil War, it foreshadowed future tensions. They would disagree over original sin, exclusive salvation, and ontologism, as well as reason and revelation, and Brownson would eventually resign as a contributor to Hecker's journal.[34]

Brownson stood apart from all his fellow theologians, partly because of his prickly personality and partly because of a fearless willingness to follow logic wherever it might lead. But his essays reflected the broader desire of Catholic theologians to show that reason stood on the side of the Catholic tradition and that the evidences, to which Protestants unceasingly appealed, pointed toward Rome. Despite his willingness to employ evidential thinking when his superiors in the church urged him to follow in conventional paths, Brownson never fully abandoned a particular form of transcendental philosophy. He felt confident that the unearthing of presuppositions brought one nearer the truth of divine revelation than the appeal to miracles, prophecies, and the internal evidences that held the confidence of most American theologians, Protestant or Catholic. But it was telling that Brownson's mentors in the church insisted that he not discard the older evidences entirely. The evidential tradition could not be treated with disrespect, especially in an American theological world that had taken it so seriously for so long. Brownson wanted to move beyond it. He managed to make it only part of the way.

25

The Dilemma of Slavery

American Christians believed that the Bible taught them how to attain a saving knowledge of God and live ethically. Theologians had both ideas in mind when they said that theology was practical. Most American Christians assumed, as well, that the same precepts that guided the individual could lead the nation toward righteousness. When the great struggle over slavery in America intensified in the early nineteenth century, it was natural for Americans on both sides of the issue to appeal to the Bible. The proslavery Virginia Baptist Thornton Stringfellow, confident that the Bible would support his position, claimed that everyone "ought to look into the Bible, and see what is in it about slavery." The antislavery New School Presbyterian Albert Barnes, on the other hand, felt that future generations would "look back upon the defenses of slavery drawn from the Bible, as among the most remarkable instances of mistaken interpretation and unfounded reasoning furnished by the perversities of the human mind." Barnes believed that the Bible offered unimpeachable evidence against the morality of slavery.[1]

Before the debate over slavery ended, it would raise questions about the practicality of theology, the interpretation and authority of the Bible, and the Baconian ideal of theological rationality. Long before biblical criticism made significant inroads into the consciousness of most Christian thinkers, the debate over slavery would introduce American readers to critical questions about history, doctrinal development, and hermeneutics. It compelled some theologians to recognize that they had to choose between biblical literalism and a form of interpretation that took into account historical criticism, the social and cultural context of the biblical writings, diversity and development within the canon, and the force of presuppositions in biblical scholarship.

The Biblical Argument

The debate over slavery in America extended back into the seventeenth century, and the earliest treatises against the enslavement of Africans employed biblical arguments. The lawyer Samuel Sewall in Boston, writing in the midst of a struggle over restrictions on slavery in the city, laid out in 1700 the biblical case for emancipation. Observing that Old Testament laws forbade Israelites to enslave one another and mandated the death penalty for stealing and selling human beings, Sewall argued that such laws were of "everlasting equity." He challenged the argument that Africans, as the posterity of Ham, stood under the curse of slavery, pointing out that Noah in Genesis 9 imposed the curse not on Ham but on Canaan, who Sewall saw as the ancestor of the Canaanites of Palestine. Sewall also drew on New Testament passages that would anchor the antislavery argument all the way up to the Civil War: God created "of One Blood, all Nations of Men," and Christians were required to do unto others as they would have others do unto them.[2]

The reply by John Saffin, who was, like Sewall, a Boston lawyer, laid out counterarguments that would also echo for the next 150 years. The patriarchs of the Old Testament, including Abraham, "the Father of all them that believe," owned slaves, and the Mosaic law regulated — and therefore accepted — enslavement. Old Testament law taught that "any lawful Captives of other Heathen Nations may be made Bond men." In the New Testament, moreover, Paul accepted the distinction between bondage and freedom and urged slaves to remain in their station. As for any demand that equal "love and respect" be accorded every person, Saffin said that the sentiment, taken literally, was absurd. It would require that the rich give to the poor "so much of our Estates, as to make them equal with our selves." Saffin argued that American slavery was a positive good, for it enabled Africans to accept Christian truth.[3]

For much of the eighteenth century, the antislavery reading of the Bible found a sympathetic hearing in groups drawn by the populist theological impulse. Mennonites and Quakers gradually purged slaveholders from their communities. A number of Baptist associations in the South protested against enslavement, and Methodists declared, for a brief moment, that their members must free their slaves or accept exclusion from the sacraments. In New

England, Samuel Hopkins decried slavery as "contrary to the whole tenor of divine revelation." Hopkins considered it a "horrid reproach of divine revelation" to suppose that the Bible should be used to support enslavement.[4]

The proslavery biblical argument in the early eighteenth century found its strongest theological proponents among the clergy of the Church of England. In their sermons to slaves and slaveholders, Anglican clergymen like Thomas Bacon in Maryland employed, by way of exhortation, many of the arguments that would recur in later debates, including ample quotation from New Testament passages instructing slaves to be obedient to their masters. But even some of the populist traditions, led by the Methodists, also backed away soon enough from their opposition to slavery. The Methodists recanted within months of taking their stand, overwhelmed by resistance from members in the South.[5]

By the 1830s, theologians on both sides developed a repertoire of arguments that followed, for the most part, the canons of biblical literalism and the Baconian habit of assembling proof-texts. The problem was that the battle, when fought on literalist and Baconian terrain, always seemed to end in stalemate. Proslavery theologians returned to the curse of Canaan (Gen. 9:25–27), arguing that Africans were Canaan's offspring. Abolitionists replied that Canaan's offspring were the Canaanites, who suffered the consequences of the curse when they lost their land to the armies of Joshua. Proslavery writers pointed out Old Testament narratives showing that Abraham — a "Friend of God" — and the other patriarchs of Israel owned slaves (Gen. 12:5, 17:13). The abolitionist answer was that the patriarchs also practiced polygamy and divorce, actions that carried no exemplary force for Christians. Proslavery writers noted that God commanded the Israelites to take servants from surrounding nations as "bondmen forever" and prescribed laws for the punishment of slaves (Lev. 25:44–46, Exod. 21:20). Antislavery theologians replied that the command referred only to the seven surrounding nations whose sins had destined them for destruction (Deut. 7:1–2) and that the Old Testament regulated slavery only because the institution lingered as a social remnant from the pre-Mosaic era, not because God approved of it.[6]

Abolitionist theologians pointed out that Leviticus mandated a year of rest for servants every seven years and a jubilee every fifty years in which the enslaved would be freed (Lev. 25). Proslavery writers countered that such regulations applied only to Hebrew slaves held by other Hebrews. When abolitionists brought up the law that whoever stole a human being should be put to death (Exod. 21:16), Moses Stuart furnished the proslavery rebuttal: the passage referred only to the stealing of other Hebrews, not captives from foreign nations. After the fugitive slave act of 1850 required Americans to return runaway slaves, abolitionists made much of Deuteronomy 23:15–16, which decreed that Israelites should not return slaves who had escaped. Proslavery writers contended that the law referred only to slaves escaping from a master who failed to worship God, a restriction exempting the Christian masters of the American South.[7]

The standoff continued when the theologians moved to the New Testament. Proslavery writers appealed to the pastoral epistles, which exhorted slaves to obey their masters (Eph. 6:5; Col. 3:22, 4:1; Titus 2:9–10; 1 Pet. 2:18). Abolitionists replied that the passages required masters to render unto their servants what was "just and equal" — a requirement nowhere observed among southern slaveholders. They insisted that the golden rule requiring Christians to do unto others as they would have others do unto them subverted the principle of slavery. Proslavery writers replied that the golden rule mandated only that masters should treat slaves as masters would wish to be treated if they were slaves, adding that it would be inhumane to free slaves if they were unable to care for themselves in a competitive society.[8]

Paul's letter to Philemon, with which he sent the slave Onesimus back to his master "forever," became a mainstay for proslavery arguments, but abolitionists also claimed the letter on the grounds that Paul instructed Philemon to receive Onesimus "as a brother" rather than merely as a slave. Abolitionists also found support in Paul's affirmation that in Christ there was neither male nor female, Jew nor Greek, bond nor free (Gal. 3:28), a passage that proslavery writers would interpret only as evidence for commonality in faith. For the proslavery writers, however, the argument that clinched the case was that Jesus never condemned slavery and that his parables took servitude for granted. The Baptist Richard Fuller noted that slavery was everywhere in the first century. If Jesus had considered it sinful, he would have challenged it. For the abolitionists, however, the silence of Jesus meant only that he taught principles that undermined all oppression, slavery included.[9]

In short, the issue was not amenable to solution through the inductive gathering of biblical passages that had long characterized Baconian interpretation. The problem was how to interpret the passages. When clashing literal interpretations no longer convinced, the theologians had to turn to hermeneutics, the theory of interpretation.[10]

The Hermeneutical Turn

When William Ellery Channing published *Slavery* in 1835, he argued that the prerequisite for adequate interpretation was to recognize that certain biblical principles lay deeper than the surface ambiguities. The requirement that Christians do unto others as they would have others do unto them took precedence over both Old Testament laws and the New Testament epistles calling on servants to be obedient. "But is not slavery condemned by . . . the many passages which make the new religion to consist in serving one another, and in doing to others what we would that they should do to themselves?" he asked. Channing thought that while Paul could not openly oppose the slavery of his day without hindering the progress of Christian teaching, he spread principles destined to subvert the institutions of enslavement. The "general tenor and spirit" of the New Testament opposed slavery even though not every New Testament writer recognized the implications of that spirit.[11]

It became, therefore, a commonplace of abolitionist argument that not everything in the Bible had equal authority. Even Francis Wayland, otherwise drawn to the theory of an infallible text, contended that the "law of universal love," elaborated in the New Testament and embodied in the narrative of the Christ who "died for all," counted for more than all the passages that appeared on the surface to suggest that slavery was consistent with God's will.[12]

This appeal to deeper principle drew the scorn of the proslavery theologians. Fuller ridiculed it as an exercise in subjectivism: "The 'principle' is to be known only by deduction and argument, in which men will differ." In his view, Channing and Wayland made the Bible "contradict itself," employing the Bible's alleged "principles" in a way that cast doubt on the Bible's express commands and permissions. The meaning of the principles, argued Albert Taylor Bledsoe, could be known only through the express precepts in which they found expression, including the precepts to slaves that they should obey their masters. Stringfellow observed that the principle on which Channing relied — the golden rule — also appeared in Leviticus (Lev. 19:18), the Old Testament book that contained the clearest legitimization of slavery. It made no sense, Richard Fuller argued, to say that the apostles delivered principles against slavery and still admitted slaveholders to the primitive churches and pronounced them "faithful and beloved."[13]

The attack on the hermeneutic of principle drove some proslavery writers further toward literalism than they would have preferred to go. When Channing claimed that defenders of slavery should, if consistent, approve of divorce and polygamy because the Deuteronomic legislation permitted both, Bledsoe conceded that polygamy and divorce were not in themselves sinful, always and everywhere. Such concessions came hard for antebellum conservatives. Most proslavery writers took another route, pointing out that Jesus equated divorce and remarriage with adultery (Mark 10:10–12), that Paul forbade wives to separate from their husbands and husbands to divorce their wives (1 Cor. 7:10–11), and that the same passages that forbade divorce also, by inference, condemned polygamy. On these points, the New Testament superseded the Old. But the rebuttal did not entirely dispense with Channing's demand that literalists be consistent.[14]

Channing emphasized the point by noting Paul's insistence that Christians be subject to the higher powers of the magistrate (Rom. 13). Written during the reign of a despotic emperor, the Pauline admonition created a problem for theologians who insisted on literal readings of scripture and yet approved of the American Revolution. The problem compelled Charles Hodge, who recognized its cogency, to revert to a distinction between despotism, which Christians were obliged to accept and honor, and the misuse of despotic power, which they could resist. But neither Hodge nor other proponents of literal interpretation cherished the position of having to defend despotism, and Hodge insisted that a magistrate acting "beyond his limits as magistrate" — requiring, for example, the worship of idols — was not to be obeyed. More tellingly, Hodge claimed that everyone had to "determine for himself" when to resist despotism. Yet Channing's point had been that respect for biblical principles sometimes made it necessary to disregard specific biblical admonitions, such as exhortations to Christians always to obey their rulers or to slaves always to obey their masters, as reflections of ancient culture rather than expressions of the divine will. Hodge's reply placed him closer to Channing's position than he wished to be.[15]

While the proslavery theologians could give a plausible answer to Channing's point about polygamy and divorce, they had no way to answer consistently the criticism that they chose to be literal when it served their purposes but more flexible when biblical commands seemed unreasonable by nineteenth-century standards. In the slavery debates it always remained ambiguous why Old Testament laws regulating slavery should be deemed expressions of the divine will for the nineteenth century but Old Testament laws regulating food and clothing should be considered as restricted to the old covenant. Channing's issue was even more acute for Christians who argued for slavery from the New Testament. The proslavery theologians never felt compelled to take literally, as a rule for their behavior, Jesus' command to the rich young ruler to sell all he had and give the money to the poor or his injunctions to the people of Israel to lend money to anyone who asked and to expect no return, to give to everyone who begged of them, to surrender their coats upon demand, or to practice nonresistance to physical attacks (Luke 6:35–36, 18:22; Matt. 6:38–42). Since this sword cut against the abolitionists, as well, neither side gave it serious attention, but it exemplified the force of Channing's questions about proslavery consistency.

While Channing appealed to scriptural principles, other antislavery theologians complemented his argument with a hermeneutic of development. Francis Wayland, for instance, conceded that the ancient patriarchs held slaves, but he claimed that God had "seen fit to enlighten our race progressively" and that the earliest periods of biblical history did not always provide good examples for Christians to follow. The slaveholding patriarchs were not sinful, for they had no way of knowing that slavery was a sin, but they were nonetheless wrong, as later stages of biblical revelation would make clear. God revealed more of his will to Moses, who regulated and softened enslavement, and even more to the prophets, who condemned oppression, and finally even more to the authors of the New Testament, who promulgated the principles that subverted slavery as an institution.[16]

Proslavery theologians were of a divided mind about progressive revelation. Bledsoe found it unacceptable because it implied that God allowed early Israelites to sin by withholding knowledge of the divine will from them. Stringfellow observed that the later prophets, in any case, never condemned slavery. For Fuller, right and wrong were immutable. If slavery was no sin in the patriarchal era it could not be sinful now. All agreed that revelation was progressive insofar as the New Testament fulfilled the Old, but the defenders of slavery found sufficient evidence for the justice of slavery in the New Testament to conclude that God even at the highest stage of revelation displayed approval for slavery as an institution. The danger in the idea of progressive revelation, from Fuller's perspective, was that it opened the possibility for the New Testament to be superseded or for its adherents to reinterpret its teachings in accord with current fashion. The gospel, in his view, did not "adjust itself to the times." Slavery remained as right in the first century — or the nineteenth — as it had been in the era of the patriarchs.[17]

Unitarians had long accepted the idea of progressive revelation, often using it to question the authority of the Old Testament for the Christian church. The antislavery controversy, however, helped popularize the idea among more conventional Protestant theologians, at least those who found it a useful weapon against the proslavery argument. The proslavery authors saw that the idea could imply error or inadequacy in the earliest strata of biblical revelation, and they knew that the suggestion of error contradicted a belief in biblical infallibility. After the Civil War, critics of the older orthodoxy would regularly employ the idea of progressive revelation in order to free Christians from having to believe literal readings of the Old Testament. For some of them, the struggle over slavery helped prepare the way for new ways of reading the Bible.

Such notions of progressive revelation intensified an awareness of history and historical change, and no hermeneutical strategy had more potential influence on the understanding of theology than the historical turn taken by both sides. For abolitionists, historical consciousness undermined the proslavery reading. Wayland contended that God intended many of his commands for a particular people at a particular time. Nineteenth-century Christians, for instance, had no right to destroy Canaanites even though God had commanded ancient Israel to slay its enemies. So also, the laws regulating slavery were meant for the ancient world, not the modern one. The proslavery response was that every divine command in the Bible, including the ten commandments and the words of Christ, had been directed to a specific audience at a specific time but that the specificity did not lessen the obligation of the rule for later generations. As the proslavery theologians saw it, Wayland's argument about historical specificity would mean that the Bible could no longer reveal to later generations "the character and will of God."[18]

A portentous historical turn in the debate occurred, however, when both sides moved beyond the text toward a historical examination of slavery in the ancient world. For both, the meaning of the biblical accounts of slavery depended on an answer to historical questions. Did the ancient Israelites permit perpetual servitude? How did the Israelite treatment of slaves compare with the way Romans or Syrians treated their slaves? And especially, how did Israelite slavery compare with American slavery? In 1846, Albert Barnes argued in his *Inquiry into the Scriptural Views of Slavery* that the relatively mild forms of ancient Israelite slavery should not be compared with the harsher forms of slavery in the Americas. Such arguments produced a flood of polemics in which debaters on both sides produced biblical and extrabiblical evidence to illustrate the nature of slavery in the ancient world.[19]

The historical dispute produced some modest abolitionist victories, compelling some defenders of slavery to acknowledge that southern slavery stood in need of reform. Northern moderates like Charles Hodge used the controversy as an occasion to let it be known that they did not regard slavery as a "desirable institution" or "approve of the slave laws of the Southern states," even though they opposed the view that slavery was evil in itself. Other proslavery writers, however, took the position that Israelite slavery had been far harsher than the slavery of the South.[20]

Although the disputants never raised the questions of historical criticism with which theologians in Germany had located the biblical texts squarely in the context of ancient near-eastern culture, the debate over slavery forced them to abandon, for the moment, a Baconian hermeneutic that had largely disregarded the historical setting of the biblical writings. Baconians often collected texts without regard for the differences in time and place among the biblical writings. The debate over slavery compelled a greater awareness of the

historical background of the biblical books. It introduced a historical consciousness among conservative Protestants that would lead some of them,
after the war, to repudiate the rational orthodoxy in which they had been
schooled.

More than most other theological debates of the period, moreover, the
slavery controversy displayed the extent to which cultural assumptions governed biblical interpretation. Especially visible was the intrusion into theology
of assumptions about race. Even Channing, speaking for the abolitionists,
argued that Paul could not have approved of slavery because it was inconceivable that he could have accepted the enslavement of Greeks. The enslavement
of whites was unthinkable. Proslavery theologians were more blatant in their
assumption that the color and culture of the enslaved provided grounds for
preserving the institution. The southern Methodist William Smith, who combined his exegesis with a defense of inequality, added that the inferiority of
Africans — an inferiority not innate but cultural — suited them for a slave system. Bledsoe contended that blacks were "unfit for a higher and nobler state
than one of slavery." James Henley Thornwell went out of his way to assert the
common humanity of blacks and whites, and he deplored the irresponsibility
of masters, but he combined his reading of the Bible with a conviction that
black people were destined for slavery. Claiming to ground their position
solely on the word of God, the proslavery theologians remained blind to the
force of racial assumptions on their reading of the word.[21]

Even more, the proslavery reading of scripture reflected the southern commitment to a hierarchical, organic social ideology that considered relations of
dependence a necessary part of the natural ordering of things. This was one
reason that the defenders of slavery so often linked their defense of slavery
with their belief that children should be subordinate to adults and women
should be subordinate to men. Charles Hodge argued that slaves could be
property without being considered objects because property varied in quality:
"A man has property in his wife, in his children, in his domestic animals, and
in his forests. That is, he has the right to the possession and use of these several
objects, according to their nature." The slaveholders' interpretation of the
golden rule — that it required that Christian masters do unto their slaves as
they would have their slaves do unto them if the masters had been destined to
occupy the lowest rung of the social ladder — revealed the extent to which
nonegalitarian cultural biases shaped their reading of scripture.[22]

The cultural biases of the slaveholders, however, enabled them to see that
the abolitionists also read scripture through lenses formed by the commonplaces of a capitalist society. Arguing that property in a slave was nothing
more than a right to the slave's service without consent or contract, they

pointed out that the northern economy rested on a de facto enslavement of the urban laboring classes without any custom of patriarchal care to mitigate the harshness. Thornwell charged that many a laborer in the northern market was also doomed to "involuntary servitude." The abolitionist reading of scripture glossed over the multiple layers of servitude throughout American culture. Unable to see the validity of the charge, the abolitionists also could not recognize the degrees of servitude in ancient Israelite culture. In the debates with slaveholders over the meaning of the Greek word *doulos* and the Hebrew *ebed* — words that proslavery writers read as meaning "slave" and antislavery writers often translated as voluntary "servant" — the abolitionists usually could recognize only two classes of people in ancient Israel, slave or free. Their cultural assumptions blinded them to economic relations within an ancient society that was accustomed to gradations of servitude.[23]

Just as the proslavery argument rested on prior beliefs about natural inequality, moreover, the antislavery argument depended on assumptions about equality drawn from philosophies of the enlightenment. On all sides, the theologians appealed, in Scottish fashion, to the "moral consciousness." For Francis Wayland, moral consciousness gave immediate evidence of a common human nature and a doctrine of natural rights, though a theory of natural rights could be found in the biblical text only through creative interpretation. Channing imported into his exegesis the "intuition" that all people naturally have equal rights. On the basis of "consciousness," the Declaration of Independence became, in effect, a glass through which scripture could be read. When proslavery writers looked to their intuitions, however, they discovered that "inequality is the law of heaven," and therefore they read the Bible with inegalitarian presuppositions. The Scottish appeal to consciousness had failed to determine the battle between the Calvinists and the Arminians; it also failed to overcome the gap between slaveholders and their critics. It rather revealed the extent to which cultural assumptions filled the content of "consciousness."[24]

To a segment of American intellectuals, the theological impasse meant that theology could no longer articulate the moral vision that held the culture together. Abolitionists warned that "we must give up the point that the New Testament defends slavery, or we must give up a very large — and an increasingly large — portion of this land to infidelity; for they neither can, nor will, nor ought, to be convinced that a book that sanctions slavery is from God." Barnes thought that a victory by the proslavery exegetes would "make thousands of infidels, for multitudes see that slavery is against all the laws which God has written on the human soul." In fact, some of the abolitionists publicly repudiated Christian scripture. Like earlier deists, they found the Bible objectionable for moral reasons.[25]

Nonetheless, the debates over slavery revealed the importance of theology in American cultural disputes. Political economists and politicians debated about slavery in their own language of constitutionalism and power, but the theologians spoke in the language that made sense to the largest number of Americans. The irony is that the slavery controversy among the theologians revealed, as well, the inability of theology to unite Americans or to help them transcend the pull of economic and political interests. The cultural language that supposedly united Americans proved itself able to contribute even more forcefully to their division.

The debate helped to subvert the particular form of theological discourse in which it was conducted. By forcing the theologians to adopt alternative ways of reading the biblical text, it introduced a larger educated public to ideas of historical development, the cultural setting of the biblical writings, and conceptual tensions within the Bible. Long before German biblical criticism attained wide currency in the theological seminaries, the debate over slavery called into question some of the assumptions of the Baconian style.

26

Afterword

In 1882, the liberal Congregationalist Newman Smyth looked back on the "orthodox rationalism" of previous generations of American theologians and decided that it had to be discarded: "Every doctrine is to be thought out afresh and taught in methods better suited to the temper of the times." The older theologians had divided the mind into faculties of intellect, will, and sensibilities and failed to see that mind was an organic unity. Adhering to conventional proofs for the existence of God, they had also failed to see that God's self-revelation was the presupposition of any thought about God. Relying on the "evidences" of revelation, especially the external evidences of prophecy and miracle, they had promulgated a "rationalistic view of revelation as the enforcement of truth upon the human reason from without." A new start was necessary.[1]

By 1901, the president of Oberlin College, Henry Churchill King, felt confident that the new start had led to an innovative and "constructive period in theology," and he was impressed by the thoroughness of the transition: "The way in which elaborate systems of theology, of comparatively recent date, have simply disappeared from the practical use and thought of men is one of the remarkable phenomena of our time." Particularly among Protestant liberals, the conviction was strong that the older forms of theology had now succumbed to better ones. The learned Boston pastor George A. Gordon observed that the New England theology, for example, had suffered sheer "collapse," giving way to theologies that fit the new "religious consciousness."[2]

The transitions were indeed important, but King and Gordon overstated the extent of the changes. Earlier battles between Unitarians and Calvinists, deists and defenders of biblical revelation, and the antagonists in the debates over slavery had raised many of the questions that prompted the rise of the new theology. While some theologians after the mid-nineteenth century took new paths, moreover, others implicitly retained ideas and strategies that had guided theology for the previous three centuries and still others remained fully attuned to the older systems. Theology changed in accord with the intellectual transitions of the later nineteenth century, but it also bore the heritage of its past.

Transitions

Writing in 1916, Arthur Cushman McGiffert, the president of Union Seminary in New York, identified the trends that had most deeply influenced theology in the previous fifty years. He emphasized evolutionary theory, especially in its Darwinian forms; the growing influence of historical consciousness, especially in biblical criticism; an expanding interest in the social character of human life and knowledge, expressed both in social reform and in philosophies that recognized the social context of thinking; and the changing fashions of philosophical teaching in the American universities, especially the rise of philosophical idealism and pragmatism.[3]

With a few prominent exceptions, the antebellum theologies declined most rapidly among the academic theologians in the older seminaries and the private universities. It was a matter of consequence that academic theologians — the full-time professionals — became after the war the recognized authorities in most of the large denominations. George Gordon, serving in 1903 as the pastor of the Old South Congregational Church in Boston, conceded in his Beecher Lectures at Yale Divinity School that "the professional theologian has played an immense part during the last fifty years," as the training of clergy "passed entirely into the hands of the professional scholar." The most severe criticisms of the Baconian style of theology came from these academic professionals, who followed closely the scholarly trends in European universities.[4]

In 1906 the *American Journal of Theology,* edited by the theology faculty at the University of Chicago, began to publish a series of articles describing the changes in theology within five large Protestant denominations: the Methodists, Baptists, Congregationalists, Presbyterians, and Episcopalians. The essays focused on the alterations wrought by adherents of the "New Theology."

The changes cut across denominational boundaries, and the authors recognized that denominational distinctions had grown less prominent as markers of theological identity. William Adams Brown of Union Seminary in New York pointed out that "the present generation has witnessed a growing disposition to break down denominational lines." While the Protestant and Catholic divide remained high, the denominational setting for theology otherwise became less important.[5]

To these authors, moreover, it appeared that preoccupations with Calvinism had also faded. Williston Walker at Yale said that most Congregationalist theologians now "recoiled" at the notion of an "arbitrary selection for salvation of a portion of an equally guilty race." He acknowledged that some congregations retained a Calvinist identity, but he pointed out that in the debates over the new Congregationalist statement of faith in 1883, "none of the theological controversies that had agitated these churches half a century before" evoked any interest. In particular, the Edwardean theology, "generally accepted during the first half of the nineteenth century," had undergone such "extensive modification" that it could no longer be found intact. Speaking for the Presbyterians, William Adams Brown said that the doctrine of reprobation, at least, had "disappeared altogether" and that most theologians in his circles within this once-Calvinist denomination affirmed an "all-sufficient salvation freely offered" to all men and women.[6]

The essays suggested that the theologians who championed the new theology disliked older conceptions of original sin, emphasized human freedom, and replaced the older millennial theories with a doctrine of the kingdom of God that accented the ethical strands within the prophetic tradition. While adhering to the confession of a divine Christ, they honored the historical Jesus more than the Christ of the creeds and thought of atonement more as a moral change in the Christian, generated by Jesus' example of self-sacrifice, than as either an act of satisfaction to a wrathful God or a governmental transaction preserving cosmic integrity.

The new theologians were far more reluctant than their predecessors to make pronouncements about either the meaning of "eternal life" or the conditions requisite for attaining it. They embraced biblical criticism and had no reluctance in acknowledging that the Bible contained diverse layers of material, including ideas that contradicted each other, which they tended to interpret with developmental categories. They discarded any notion of biblical infallibility. They thought of God much more as loving Father than as Sovereign Judge, and they often justified their departures from older views as proper responses to the changing "spirit of the age." Many of them adopted a "modernist principle" — an insistence that theology had to change its formulations in accord with intellectual and social change — that most antebellum theologians would have resisted.[7]

The essays traced Protestant trends alone, but they might have added that Catholic liberals, as well, felt the appeal of a position like that of William Kerby of Catholic University, who urged in 1900 that the social sciences could be employed to help Catholics understand the personality of the historical Jesus, the laws of social growth that shaped the Christian movement, and a proper historical interpretation of the gospel. Catholic modernism never created the stir in America that it created in Europe, but Catholics of the "Americanist" party, such as Bishop John Ireland of Minneapolis, shared at least the conviction that in a changing world "the Church must herself be new, adapting herself in manner of life and in method of action to the conditions of the new order."[8]

Continuities

The story, however, was far more complex than any simple narrative of a transition to liberalism might seem to suggest. The most accurate way of talking about the history of theology after the Civil War in America is to recognize the emergence of distinct theological subcultures, often cutting across denominational boundaries and older confessional lines. In some of those subcultures, like those of the liberal seminaries and private universities, the theological transitions could be quite pronounced. In others, many of the older themes persisted. In 1879, the educational reformer G. Stanley Hall reported, after a survey of American colleges and universities, that even in philosophy departments the students often learned more about the theology of Edwards Amasa Park and Charles Hodge than about Plato and Kant.[9]

The older theologies proved even more tenacious in churches and seminaries, and the essayists in the *American Journal of Theology* conceded that strong currents flowed against theological change. Henry Sheldon of Boston University pointed to the continuation of older theories of atonement and biblical inerrancy among the Methodists. Brown noted the ability of Presbyterian conservatives to convict prominent liberal Presbyterian scholars of heresy and to persuade the General Assembly to support doctrines of verbal inerrancy in the 1890s. Had Brown written his essay twenty years later, he might have added that Old School Presbyterian theology, only slightly revised, retained a hold at Princeton Seminary until the early 1920s and that a traditional Calvinist theology continued to prevail even after that in many other Reformed seminaries, colleges, and churches, especially in the South and Midwest. The Baptist historian Albert Newman added that most Baptist authors outside the Northeast rejected the new theology, and he thought that the activity of "aggressive premillennialists," allied with theologians outside Baptist circles, more than counterbalanced the influence of liberal Baptists. The older manuals of theology continued to inform pedagogy in Catholic seminaries throughout the nineteenth century, and among the Lutherans of the Midwest the struggles over confessions, biblical authority, and predestination still raged in the twentieth.[10]

Above all, the evidential style persisted. When the Boston Methodist Henry Sheldon, for example, published a *System of Christian Doctrine* in 1903, he laid out the familiar rational arguments for the existence of God, presented the traditional evidences of Christianity, including the evidence from miracle and prophecy, and defined the functions of reason in relation to revelation. He still pondered the relation of the speculative and the practical in theology, still continued to fight the battle over "Calvinistic predestinarianism," and still argued about the Edwardean distinction between moral and natural ability. He still was interested in the relation between Genesis and natural science, still reasoned about the order of salvation, and gave ethics a prominent place in his theological system. Although looking mainly to European theologians as his authorities, he still engaged the ideas of Jonathan Edwards, Charles Hodge, and Horace Bushnell. When even more conservative theologians published in 1910 the multiple volumes of *The Fundamentals* that later helped popularize the concept of "fundamentalism," no fewer than ten of the articles were standard expositions of the evidences of revelation.[11]

Most striking, however, was the way in which even the advocates of the new theology continued patterns of thought from earlier periods. Theodore Thornton Munger, a Congregationalist whose 1883 essay on the "New Theology" was a manifesto for theological change, emphasized continuities as well as discontinuities between the old and the new. Munger saw the new theology as the revision of an older system, not its abandonment, a "transfer of emphasis, a change of temper, a widened habit of thought," grounded on "a broader research." He saw that even the liberals retained crucial features of the evidential style.[12]

Although the proponents of the new Protestant theology criticized the "rationalism" of their predecessors, they still pursued the quest for reasonableness, seeking only, in Munger's words, "a somewhat larger and broader use of reason." Munger explained that they wanted a conception of reason that moved beyond the static logic of evidentialism, in which reason offered proofs and demonstrations of a revelation to which it then submitted. But when they promoted a conception of reason that included "the intuitions — the universal and spontaneous verdicts of the soul," the whole "inner being," they were not abandoning the evidential style of theology but attempting to bring it up-to-date.[13]

When Newman Smyth, for example, published *The Religious Feeling* (1877), one of the landmark books of early American liberal theology, he wrote that the older evidentialism, built on "Paley's formidable array of evidences," no longer sufficed, but he also described his book, quite properly, as proposing only "a slight departure from the usual forms in which the evidences of faith are presented." Like the Baconians, Smyth saw the issue as one of "facts," determined by "observation and testimony." He merely wanted to turn attention to the facts of the immediate consciousness — the unmediated, prethematized awareness that, according to Schleiermacher, underlay the formulation of concepts — rather than to miracles, prophecies, and the internal unity of the Bible. He was advocating, like some earlier antebellum thinkers, a revised form of the internal argument. The earlier theologians had found internal evidence not only in the unity of the Bible but also in its consistency with religious and moral experience. Smyth was advancing a similar argument.[14]

Like earlier theologians, moreover, the liberals continued to emphasize the ethical import of theology. George Harris, who brought the new theology to Andover, thought that the New Testament's depiction of Jesus as the purest type of virtue, its ethic of self-sacrificing love, and the doctrine of the ethical kingdom of God could withstand any challenge to biblical authority. When Henry Churchill King tried to restate theology "in terms of personal relation," he moved the ethical closer to the center of theology. A similar turn marked the Catholic Americanist movement and the Protestant Social Gospel. The degree of emphasis on ethics was new, but the turn to the ethical in late-nineteenth-century theology was more a continuation than an alteration of the older theologies, which had always maintained a special place for "moral science."[15]

When the liberals called for theologians to adopt "a new relation to natural science," they saw themselves as overcoming "the long apparent antagonism between the kingdoms of faith and of natural law." But the openness to science was no innovation. Antebellum theologians had long ago reinterpreted Genesis to conform to the findings of geology. John Augustine Zahm at Notre Dame was one of the first Catholic theologians to call, in 1896, for Catholics to appropriate evolutionary theory, but Francis Patrick Kenrick had already signified, as early as 1860, the Catholic willingness to reinterpret the Bible in accord with scientific learning. In principle, the liberal determination to be more open to natural science did not veer far from the position of the antebellum theologians.[16]

When George Gordon delivered his Beecher Lectures at Yale in 1903, he acknowledged that for him, and for many in his audience, the theology that once echoed in the divinity school's lecture rooms had "lost its authority." The "ponderous volumes of divinity" produced by the earlier New England theologians no longer commanded interest at Yale. Gordon was not nostalgic, for he knew that "all things human pass" and that the theologies of his own era would also pass away. But he could look back at the older theologians and recognize the force that they had once exerted on the religious culture of the nation. He thought it was a history worth remembering.[17]

Notes

Preface

1. Sydney E. Ahlstrom, "Theology in America: A Historical Survey," *The Shaping of American Religion, Religion in American Life*, 3 vols., ed. James Ward Smith and A. Leland Jamison (Princeton, N.J.: Princeton University Press, 1971), 1:232–321, 319; Sydney Ahlstrom, ed., *Theology in America: The Major Protestant Voices from Puritanism to Neo-Orthodoxy* (Cincinnati, Ohio: Bobbs-Merrill, 1967), 23–107. See also Mark G. Toulouse and James O. Duke, eds., "General Introduction," *Makers of Christian Theology in America* (Nashville, Tenn.: Abingdon Press, 1997), 13–19; Thomas B. Harbottle, ed., *Dictionary of Quotations (Classical)* (New York: Frederick Ungar, 1958), 308.

Chapter 1. Introduction: Theology in America

1. Hugh Amory and David D. Hall, eds., *A History of the Book Volume One: The Colonial Book in the Atlantic World* (Cambridge: Cambridge University Press, 2000), 520; Robert Baird, *Religion in America*, ed. Henry Warner Bowden (New York: Harper), 159.

2. Jarena Lee, *Religious Experience and Journal of Mrs. Jarena Lee*, in *Black Women in Nineteenth-Century American Life*, ed. Bert. J. Lowenberg and Ruth Bogin (University Park: Pennsylvania State University Press, 1976), 136–41.

3. Alexis de Tocqueville, *Democracy in America*, 2 vols. (New York: Schocken, 1961), I:11, 48; "Review of Lectures on Christian Theology," *Spirit of the Pilgrims* 5

(1832):524; [E. A. Park], "Thoughts on the State of Theological Education in our Country," *Bibliotheca Sacra* 1 (1844):735–36, 741, 745, 750, 766.

4. Tocqueville, *Democracy in America,* I:65; Horace Bushnell, "The Age of Homespun," *Work and Play* (New York: Charles Scribner's Sons, 1883), 395; George W. Burnap, "The Importance of Systematic Theology and the Duty of the Unitarian Clergy in Relation to it," *Christian Examiner,* 4th ser., 50 (1850):170; E. Brooks Holifield, "Theology as Entertainment: Oral Debate in American Religion," *Church History* 67 (1998): 499–520.

5. John T. Wayland, *The Theological Department in Yale College 1822–1858* (New York: Garland, 1987), 180.

6. William Ames, *The Marrow of Theology,* trans. John D. Eusden (Boston: Pilgrim Press, 1968), 1, 188; Samuel Willard, *Brief Directions for a Young Scholar Designing the Ministry, for the Study of Divinity* (Boston: Draper, 1735), 1, 6; Charles Hodge, *Systematic Theology,* 2 vols. (New York: Scribner, Armstrong, 1874), I:2; Thomas Ralston, *Elements of Divinity* (Nashville, Tenn.: Redford, 1871), 14; Henry P. Tappan, "Progress of Educational Development in Europe," *American Journal of Education* 1 (1856):252.

7. Avery Dulles, *A History of Apologetics* (New York: Corpus, 1971), 99–101, 113–30.

8. Edward, Lord Herbert of Cherbury, *De Veritate, Deism: An Anthology,* ed. Peter Gay (Princeton, N.J.: D. Van Nostrand, 1968), 29; John Locke, *On the Reasonableness of Christianity,* ed. George Ewing (Chicago: Henry Regnery, n.d.), 18, 35, 39–49.

9. Holifield, "Theology as Entertainment," 512.

10. Thomas Whittemore, *The Early Days of Thomas Whittemore* (Boston: James Usher, 1859), 175–76, 180.

11. Henry Boynton Smith, *Faith and Philosophy* (New York: Scribner and Armstrong, 1977), 145.

12. David H. Kelsey, *To Understand God Truly* (Louisville, Ky.: Westminster/John Knox, 1992), 34–59.

13. Richard A. Muller, *Post-Reformation Reformed Dogmatics,* 2 vols. (Grand Rapids, Mich.: Baker Book House, 1987), 1:218; Richard A. Muller, *God, Creation, and Providence in the Thought of Jacob Arminius* (Grand Rapids, Mich.: Baker Book House, 1991), 64.

14. Muller, *God, Creation, and Providence,* 271; Muller, *Post-Reformation Reformed Dogmatics,* 1:219, 223.

15. Muller, *God, Creation, and Providence,* 16, 68; E. P. Meijering, *Melanchthon and Patristic Thought* (Leiden: E. J. Brill, 1983), 5– 12; Denis R. Janz, *Luther on Thomas Aquinas* (Stuttgart: Franz Steiner, 1989), 15.

16. [Park], "Thoughts on the State of Theological Education in our Country," 736.

17. Baird, *Religion in America,* 160.

18. Ibid., 161.

19. Ibid., 161.

20. Glenn T. Miller, *Piety and Intellect* (Atlanta, Ga.: Scholars Press, 1990), 201, 213; Joseph M. White, *The Diocesan Seminary in the United States* (Notre Dame, Ind.: University of Notre Dame Press, 1989), 50, 58; Philip Schaff, *America: A Sketch of its Political, Social, and Religious Character* (Cambridge, Mass.: Harvard University Press, 1961), 62.

21. Schaff, *America*, 62–63.

22. [Park], "Thoughts on the State of Theological Education in our Country," 752.

23. Ebenezer Porter, *A Sermon, Delivered Sept. 22, 1818* (Andover, Mass.: Flagg and Gould, 1818), 9; Elwyn Allen Smith, *The Presbyterian Minister in American Culture* (Philadelphia: Westminster Press, 1962), 183; Philip Lindsley, *A Plea for the Theological Seminary at Princeton, N.J.* (Trenton, N.J.: George Sherman, 1821), 9, 14.

24. Philip Schaff, *The Principle of Protestantism* (Philadelphia: United Church Press, 1964), 150; Burnap, "Importance of Systematic Theology," 171.

25. Tertullian, *The Prescriptions Against the Heretics, Early Latin Theology,* ed. S. L. Greenslade (Philadelphia: Westminster Press, 1961), 36.

26. Barbara A. Johnson, *Reading Piers Plowman and The Pilgrim's Progress* (Carbondale: Southern Illinois University Press, 1992), 76, 85, 96; Carol Edington, " 'To Speik of Preistis be sure it is na bourds': Discussing the Priesthood in pre-Reformation Scotland," *The Reformation of the Parishes,* ed. Andrew Pettegree (Manchester: Manchester University Press, 1993), 29–30.

27. Johnson, *Reading Piers Plowman,* 97; George Fox and James Nayler, *Soul's Errand to Damascus* (1653), in *Early Quaker Writings 1650– 1700,* ed. Hugh Barbour and Arthur O. Roberts (Grand Rapids, Mich.: William B. Eerdmans, 1973), 259.

28. Benjamin S. Youngs and Calvin Green, *Testimony of Christ's Second Appearing,* 4th ed. (Albany, N.Y.: Van Benthuysen, 1856), viii, xiii, 134; Nathan Hatch, *The Democratization of American Christianity* (New Haven, Conn.: Yale University Press, 1989), 49–122.

Chapter 2. The New England Calvinists

1. Thomas Shepard, *Theses Sabbaticae: Or the Doctrine of the Sabbath* (London: John Rothwell, 1649), Part I:6.

2. Thomas Hooker, *The Paterne of Perfection* (London: F. Clifton, 1640), 43–46; Thomas Shepard, *God's Plot: The Paradoxes of Puritan Piety,* ed. Michael McGiffert (Amherst: University of Massachusetts Press, 1972), 84; Thomas Shepard, *The Sound Believer: A Treatise of Evangelical Conversion* (London: R. Dawlman, 1645), 26; Thomas Shepard, *Certain Select Cases Resolved* (London: W. Hunt, 1650), 61.

3. George Selement, "Publication and the Puritan Minister," *William and Mary Quarterly,* 3d ser., 37 (1980):219–41. Baird Tipson graciously brought the Stone manuscript to my attention.

4. Everett H. Emerson, *John Cotton* (New York: Twayne, 1965), 19, 68; John Cotton, *Gods Mercie Mixed With His Justice* (London: Brewster and Hood, 1641), A2; John Norton, *Abel being Dead Yet Speaketh* (London: Lodowick Lloyd, 1658), 13.

5. George Leon Walker, *Thomas Hooker: Preacher, Founder, Democrat* (New York: Dodd, Mead, 1891), 58.

6. John Adams Albro, ed., *The Works of Thomas Shepard,* 3 vols. (Boston: Doctrinal Tract and Book Society, 1853), 1:clxxv; Edward Johnson, *Wonder-Working Providence of Sions Saviour in New England* (1st ed. 1654, Andover, Mass.: Warren Draper, 1867), 77.

7. Norton, *Abel being Dead Yet Speaketh,* 41.

8. Cotton Mather, *Magnalia Christi Americana, Or the Ecclesiastical History of New England,* 2 vols. (New York: Russell and Russell, 1967), 2:399–404.

9. Ibid., 452.

10. David D. Hall, *Worlds of Wonder, Days of Judgment: Popular Religious Belief in Early New England* (New York: Alfred A. Knopf, 1989), 8.

11. Norton, *Abel being Dead Yet Speaketh,* 24.

12. John Cotton, *A Treatise of the Covenant of Grace* (London: James Cottrell, 1659), 186; Shepard, *Certain Select Cases Resolved,* 46.

13. Thomas Shepard, *A defence of the Answer made unto the nine questions sent from England* (London: n.p., 1645), 4; John Cotton, *A Commentary Upon the First Epistle General of John* (London: Thomas Parkhurst, 1658), 77–78; Theodore Dwight Bozeman, *To Live Ancient Lives: The Primitivist Dimension in Puritanism* (Chapel Hill: University of North Carolina Press, 1988), 120–50.

14. Thomas Hooker, *The Covenant of Grace Opened* (London: G. Dawson, 1649), 63.

15. John Cotton, *The Churches Resurrection, Or the Opening of the Fift and sixt verses of the 20th chap of the Revelation* (London: R.O., 1642), 7; John Cotton, *A Brief Exposition with Practical Observations Upon the Whole Book of Canticles* (London: Ralph Smith, 1655), 27; John Whitgift, *The Works of John Whitgift,* 3 vols. (Cambridge: Cambridge University Press, 1853), 1:208, 315–16, 322, 469–70; Thomas Shepard, *The Sincere Convert and the Sound Believer* (Paisley: Stephen and Andrew Young, 1812), 94.

16. Samuel Mather, *The Figures or Types of the Old Testament* (1st ed. 1683; New York: Johnson Reprint Corporation, 1969), 52, 75, 155; Cotton, *Brief Exposition,* 27.

17. John Cotton, *The Result of a Synod at Cambridge in New England, Anno 1646* (London: n.p., 1654), 21, 25; John Cotton, *Singing of Psalmes a Gospel-Ordinance* (London: M.S., 1647), 23–24.

18. John Cotton, *The Grounds and Ends of the Baptisme of the Children of the Faithful* (London: Andrew Crooke, 1647), 4, 167; John Cotton, *The Way of the Churches of Christ in New England* (London: Matthew Simmons, 1645), 72–73; Thomas Hooker, *A Survey of the Summe of Church-Discipline* (London: John Bellamy, 1648), Part 1:9.

19. Thomas Shepard, *The Sincere Convert, Works of Thomas Shepard,* 1:10; Cotton, *Commentary Upon the First Epistle General of John,* 16– 17.

20. Petrus Ramus, *Petrus Ramus, His Logick in two books,* trans. Roger Fage (London: Nicholas Vavafour, 1636), 29.

21. Ibid., 2, 9; Alexander Richardson, *The Logicians School-Master; Or, A Comment upon Ramus Logicke* (London: John Bellamine, 1629), 49.

22. Richardson, *Logicians School-Master,* 34–66.

23. Ibid., 12–16; Perry Miller, *The New England Mind: The Seventeenth Century* (Boston: Beacon Press, 1961), 111–53.

24. Thomas Hooker, *The Saints Guide* (London: John Stafford, 1645), 97; Thomas Hooker, *The Unbelievers Preparing for Christ* (London: Andrew Crooke, 1638), 87; Thomas Shepard, *The Parable of the Ten Virgins Opened and Applied* (London: John Rothwell, 1660), Part 1:141; Shepard, *Sincere Convert, Works,* 1:10; John Norton, *The Orthodox Evangelist* (London: John Mocock, 1654), 152–53.

25. Hooker, *Unbelievers Preparing for Christ,* 87; Norton, *Orthodox Evangelist,* 152; Shepard, *Sincere Convert, Works,* 1:12; Hooker, *Saints Guide,* 102.

26. Cotton, *Treatise of the Covenant of Grace,* 209; Shepard, *Certain Select Cases Resolved,* 44; Hooker, *Unbelievers Preparing for Christ,* 42.

27. Thomas Hooker, *The Soules Vocation or Effectual Calling to Christ* (London: Andrew Crooke, 1638), 65; Shepard, *Parable of the Ten Virgins,* 1:76.

28. Cotton, *Commentary Upon the First Epistle General of John,* 58, 373.

29. Norton, *Orthodox Evangelist,* 2.

30. Shepard, *Parable of the Ten Virgins,* Part 1:28.

31. Shepard, *Sincere Convert, Works,* 1:9; John Murray, *The Imputation of Adam's Sin* (Grand Rapids, Mich.: William B. Eerdmans, 1959), 12–18.

32. Norton, *Orthodox Evangelist,* 138.

33. Ibid., 5, 23; Shepard, *Sincere Convert, Works,* 1:2.

34. Thomas Hooker, *An Exposition of the Principles of Religion* (London: R. Dawlman, 1645), 5; Norton, *Orthodox Evangelist,* 24; Shepard, *Sincere Convert, Works,* 1:17.

35. Shepard, *Sincere Convert, Works,* 1:17; Hooker, *Paterne of Perfection,* 20; Shepard, *Certain Select Cases Resolved,* 67; Thomas Hooker, *The Saints Dignitie and Dutie* (London: Francis Eglesfield, 1651), 29.

36. Hooker, *Saints Dignitie,* 3; John Cotton, *Christ the Fountaine of Life* (London: Robert Ibbitson, 1651), 63.

37. Norton, *Orthodox Evangelist,* 1.

38. Cotton, *Gods Mercie Mixed with His Justice,* 90, 99; Shepard, *Sound Believer,* 217; Hooker, *Unbelievers Preparing for Christ,* 160; Shepard, *God's Plot,* 58, 64.

39. Jacobus Arminius, "A Declaration of the Sentiments of Arminius," *The Works of James [Jacobus] Arminius,* ed. William Nichols, 3 vols. (London: Longman, 1825–75), 1:555, 589, 600; Jacobus Arminius, "Nine Questions," ibid., 2:66; "The Canons of the Synod of Dort," *The Creeds of Christendom,* ed. Philip Schaff, 3 vols. (1st ed. 1877; Grand Rapids, Mich.: Baker Book House, 1966), 3:581–97.

40. Norton, *Orthodox Evangelist,* 57; John Cotton, *The Way of Congregational Churches Cleared* (London: Matthew Simmons, 1648), 33; Shepard, *Sincere Convert, Works,* 1:45.

41. Norton, *Orthodox Evangelist,* 35–40, 48–50; Hooker, *Saints Dignitie,* 3–75; Hooker, *Exposition of the Principles of Religion,* 40, 49.

42. Norton, *Orthodox Evangelist,* 270–71; Hooker, *Paterne of Perfection,* 120, 150, 232; Hooker, *Unbelievers Preparing for Christ,* 202; Thomas Hooker, *The Christians Two Chiefe Lessons* (London: Stephens and Meredith, 1640), 248; Norman Fiering, *Moral Philosophy at Seventeenth-Century Harvard* (Chapel Hill: University of North Carolina Press, 1981), 104–46; William K. B. Stoever, *A Faire and Easie Way to Heaven: Covenant Theology and Antinomianism in Early Massachusetts* (Middletown, Conn.: Wesleyan University Press, 1978), 100–17.

43. Thomas Hooker, *The Application of Redemption* (London: Peter Cole, 1656), 353, 387; Norton, *Orthodox Evangelist,* 65, 74, 114, 214; Hooker, *Unbelievers Preparing for Christ,* 27, 126.

44. William Ames, *The Marrow of Sacred Divinity* (London: Edward Griffin, 1642), 51; David A. Weis, *Foedus Naturale: The Origins of Federal Theology in Sixteenth Century Reformation Thought* (New York: Oxford University Press, 1989), 35–80; Mi-

chael McGiffert, "Grace and Works: The Rise and Division of Covenant Divinity in Elizabethan Puritanism," *Harvard Theological Review* 75 (1982):463–502.

45. Peter Bulkeley, *The Gospel Covenant; Or the Covenant of Grace Opened* (London: Matthew Simmons, 1651), 31–34, 114.

46. Ibid., 56–61.

47. Thomas Hooker, *The Faithful Covenanter* (London: C. Meredith, 1644), 13; Bulkeley, *Gospel Covenant,* 56; Shepard, *Parable of the Ten Virgins,* Part 1:5, 28; John Cotton, *The Covenant of Grace: Discovering the Great Work of a Sinners Reconciliation to God* (London: John Allen, 1655), 21.

48. Hooker, *Soules Vocation,* 514, 608; Norton, *Orthodox Evangelist,* 313, 323–24; Shepard, *Parable of the Ten Virgins,* Part 1:130.

49. Cotton, *Covenant of Grace,* 18, 29; Shepard, *Certain Select Cases Resolved,* 13; Hooker, *Unbelievers Preparing for Christ,* 40; Hooker, *Soules Vocation,* 40; Bulkeley, *Gospel Covenant,* 80, 382.

50. Bulkeley, *Gospel Covenant,* 383.

51. Shepard, *Defence of the Answer,* 2, 106; Hooker, *Survey,* 23, 46; Thomas Shepard, *Subjection to Christ in All His Ordinances, and Appointments* (London: John Rothwell, 1652), 55.

52. Norton, *Orthodox Evangelist,* 19.

53. John Cotton, *The Way of Life* (London: Fawne, 1641), 12; Cotton, *Covenant of Grace,* 53; Bulkeley, *Gospel Covenant,* 334–35, 370; Norton, *Orthodox Evangelist,* 132.

54. Cotton, *Way of Life,* 39.

55. Giles Firmin, *The Real Christian* (London: Dorman Newman, 1670), 2, 8, 108; Shepard, *Certain Select Cases Resolved,* 77; Thomas Hooker, *The Soules Humiliation,* 2d ed. (London, Andrew Crooke, 1638), 112; Hooker, *Saints Guide,* 160; Thomas Hooker, *The Soules Ingrafting into Christ* (London: Andrew Crooke, 1637), 6; Shepard, *Sound Believer,* 125.

56. Hooker, *Christians Two Chiefe Lessons,* 251; Hooker, *Soules Vocation,* 344; Charles L. Cohen, *God's Caress* (New York: Oxford University Press, 1986), 87, n.35; David D. Hall, ed., *The Antinomian Controversy, 1636–38* (Middletown, Conn.: Wesleyan University Press, 1968), 177; Cotton, *Way of Congregational Churches,* 76; Norton, *Orthodox Evangelist,* 169.

57. Hooker, *Unbelievers Preparing for Christ,* 2, 8, 10; Hooker, *Application of Redemption,* 151; Hooker, *Soules Vocation,* 289, 338; Shepard, *Certain Select Cases Resolved,* 42.

58. Cotton, *Way of Congregational Churches,* 32.

59. Cotton, *Covenant of Grace,* 75–77, 141, 147; Cotton, *Treatise of the Covenant of Grace,* 210, 213.

60. Hall, ed., *Antinomian Controversy,* 26–27, 30.

61. Ibid., 38, 40; Stoever, *Faire and Easie Way to Heaven,* 41–44, 65.

62. Hall, ed., *Antinomian Controversy,* 99; Stoever, *Faire and Easie Way to Heaven,* 48, 66.

63. Hall, ed., *Antinomian Controversy,* 102–03.

64. Ibid., 183, 186.

65. Ibid., 205–06, 209; Johnson, *Wonder-Working Providence*, 92–99.

66. Hall, ed., *Antinomian Controversy,* 308.

67. Ibid., 164, 302, 306.

68. Ibid., 235, 264, 326, 333.

69. Ibid., 361.

70. Ibid., 216, 333, 339.

71. Ibid., 405, 417; Shepard, *God's Plot,* 74; Johnson, *Wonder-Working Providence,* 125; Jonathan Mitchell and Thomas Shepard, Jr., "To the Reader," Shepard, *Parable of the Ten Virgins,* n.p.

72. John Cotton, *A Brief Exposition of the Whole Book of Canticles* (London: Philip Nevil, 1642), 10; Cotton, *Commentary upon the First Epistle General of John,* 143.

73. John Cotton, *The Pouring Out of the Seven Vials: Or an Exposition of the 16. Chapter of the Revelation* (London: R.S., 1642); Cotton, *Churches Resurrection* (1642); John Cotton, *An Exposition Upon the Thirteenth Chapter of the Revelation* (London: Livewell Chapman, 1655); Cotton, *Brief Exposition . . . of Canticles* (1655).

74. Cotton, *Churches Resurrection,* 5, 16, 20, 30; Cotton, *Brief Exposition . . . of Canticles* (1655), 223.

75. Bozeman, *To Live Ancient Lives,* 199–204.

76. Ibid., 205–12.

77. James F. Maclear, "New England and the Fifth Monarchy," *William and Mary Quarterly,* 3d ser., 32 (1975):234–36; Shepard, *Parable of the Ten Virgins,* 1:9–10, 2:105; Thomas Shepard, *The Clear Sun-shine of the Gospel Breaking Forth Upon the Indians of New England* (London, 1648), *Massachusetts Historical Society Collections,* 3d ser., 4 (1834):30.

78. Maclear, "New England and the Fifth Monarchy," 237; Johnson, *Wonder-Working Providence,* 34.

79. John Winthrop, *Winthrop's Journal: "History of New England," 1630–1649,* ed. James Kendall Hosmer, 2 vols. (New York: Charles Scribner's Sons, 1908), 1:62; Roger Williams, *Mr. Cotton's Letter Lately Printed, Examined, and Answered* (London, 1644), *Publications of the Narragansett Club,* 1st ser., 6 vols. (Providence, R.I., 1866), 1:97.

80. Nathaniel Morton, *New Englands Memorial,* ed. Howard J. Hall (New York: Scholars' Reprints, 1937), 79, 82; Winthrop, *Winthrop's Journal,* 1:149; Williams, *Mr. Cotton's Letter,* 105; Edmund S. Morgan, *Roger Williams* (New York: Harcourt, Brace, and World, 1967), 29–33.

81. Roger Williams, *The Bloudy Tenet of Persecution, for Cause of Conscience* (London, 1644), *Publications of the Narragansett Club,* 3:334; John Cotton, *A Letter of Mr. John Cotton* (London, 1643), *Publications of the Narragansett Club,* 1:14–21; Williams, *Mr. Cotton's Letter,* 74–90; Leonard Allen, " 'The Restauration of Zion': Roger Williams and the Quest for the Primitive Church" (Ph.D. diss., University of Iowa, 1984).

82. Williams, *Bloudy Tenet of Persecution,* 77, 97, 119, 129, 146.

83. Ibid., 354; John Cotton, *The Bloudy Tenent, Washed, and Made White in the Bloud of the Lambe* (London: Matthew Simmons, 1647), 68; Roger Williams, *The Bloody Tenent Yet More Bloody* (London, 1642), *Publications of the Narragansett Club,* 4:450; W. Clark Gilpin, *The Millenarian Piety of Roger Williams* (Chicago: University of Chicago Press, 1979): 40–42.

84. Roger Williams, *The Hireling Ministry None of Christs* (London, 1652), *The Complete Writings of Roger Williams*, ed. Perry Miller, 7 vols. (New York: Russell and Russell, 1963), 7:158, 160; Roger Williams, *Queries of Highest Consideration* (London, 1644), *Publications of the Narragansett Club*, 2:21, 29.

85. Williams, *Bloody Tenent Yet More Bloody*, *Complete Writings*, 4:45; Roger Williams, *Christenings Make Not Christians* (London, 1645), *Complete Writings*, 7:40; Gilpin, *Millenarian Piety of Roger Williams*, 81–137.

86. Roger Williams, *The Hireling Ministry None of Christs* (London, 1652), *Complete Writings*, 7:169; Roger Williams, *The Examiner Defended* (London, 1652), *Complete Writings*, 7:224.

87. Bulkeley, *Gospel Covenant*, 23; Hooker, *Covenant of Grace Opened*, 10.

88. Hooker, *Covenant of Grace Opened*, 2, 20; Thomas Shepard, *The Church Membership of Children and their Right to Baptism* (Cambridge: Samuel Green, 1662), 2, 6; John Cotton, *The Grounds and Ends of the Baptisme of the Children of the Faithful* (London: Andrew Crooke, 1647), 45, 53.

89. Williston Walker, ed., *Creeds and Platforms of Congregationalism* (Boston: Pilgrim Press, 1960), 224; Cotton, *Grounds and Ends*, 125, 145–46; Thomas Shepard, *Theses Sabbaticae*, *Works*, 3:75; Shepard, *Church Membership of Children*, 5, 22.

90. Increase Mather, *The First Principles of New England, Concerning the Subject of Baptisme and Communion of Churches* (Cambridge: Samuel Green, 1675), 2; John Cotton, *The Way of the Churches of Christ in New England* (London: n.p., 1645), 81; Nathaniel Shurtleff, ed., *Records of the Governor and Company of the Massachusetts Bay in New England*, 5 vols. (Boston: W. White, 1853–54), 3:71; [Nathanael Mather?], "A Disputation Concerning Church-Members and their Children," *Answer to XXI Questions* (London: n.p., 1659), 31.

91. Walker, ed., *Creeds and Platforms*, 325.

92. [Richard Mather], *A Defence of the Answer and Arguments of the Synod Met at Boston* (Cambridge: Samuel Green and Marmaduke Johnson, 1664), 62; John Davenport, *Another Essay for the Investigation of the Truth* (Cambridge: Samuel Green and Marmaduke Johnson, 1663), 35; John Davenport, "The Third Essay containing a Reply to the Answer unto the other Essay" (1665), pp. 111, 127, 139, manuscript in the American Antiquarian Society.

93. Jonathan Mitchell, "An Answer to the Apologetical Preface," in [Mather], *A Defence of the Answer and Arguments*, 44–45; John Allin, *Animadversions Upon the Antisynodalia Americana* (Cambridge: Samuel Green and Marmaduke Johnson, 1664), 58; Davenport, *Another Essay*, 6, 29–30, 39.

94. [Charles Chauncy], *Anti-Synodalia Scripta Americana*, in *Propositions Concerning the Subject of Baptism and Consociation of Churches* (London: n.p., 1662), 14, 17, 32, 34; Davenport, *Another Essay*, 4; Increase Mather, "Apologeticall Preface," Davenport, *Another Essay*, n.p.

Chapter 3. Rationalism Resisted

1. C. Fitzsimmons Allison, *The Rise of Moralism* (New York: Seabury, 1966), 116–18; Herbert Thorndike, "Of the Covenant of Grace" (1659), *Thorndike's Works*, 6 vols.

(Oxford: John Parker, 1849), 3:565– 85; George Bull, *Harmonia Apostolica, The Works of George Bull,* ed. Edward Burton, 8 vols. (Oxford: Oxford University Press, 1846), 3:13, 16.

2. Allison, *Rise of Moralism,* 54–56; Richard Baxter, *Aphorisms of Justification* (The Hague: Abraham Brown, 1655), 153, 185; Richard Baxter, *A Treatise of Justifying Righteousness* (London: For Nevil Simons, 1676), 91–103, 163, 176–77.

3. Michael R. Watts, *The Dissenters: From the Reformation to the French Revolution* (Oxford: Clarendon Press, 1978), 291–97.

4. Bryan G. Armstrong, *Calvinism and the Amyraut Heresy: Protestant Scholasticism and Humanism in Seventeenth-Century France* (Madison: The University of Wisconsin Press, 1969), 91, 94, 215–16.

5. Ibid., 104–05.

6. Nathanael Culverwell, "An Elegant and Learned Discourse of the Light of Nature," *The Cambridge Platonists,* ed. Gerald Cragg (New York: Oxford University Press, 1968), 54; Henry More, "An Antidote Against Atheism," ibid., 169; Ralph Cudworth, "The Demonstration of the Existence of a God," ibid., 199.

7. Cudworth, "The Demonstration of the Existence of a God," 198.

8. Gerald Cragg, *From Puritanism to the Age of Reason* (Cambridge: Cambridge University Press, 1966), 61–86; Gerard Reedy, S.J., *The Bible and Reason: Anglicans and Scripture in Late-Seventeenth Century England* (Philadelphia: University of Pennsylvania Press, 1985), 35– 36; John Spurr, " 'Latitudinarianism' and the Restoration Church," *Historical Journal* 31 (1988):61–82.

9. John Ray, *The Wisdom of God Manifested in the Works of the Creation* (1st ed. 1691; London: William Innys, 1714), 107–13, 117–47, 248–344; William Derham, *Physico-Theology,* 2 vols. (1st ed. 1713; London: For A. Strahan, 1798), 1:135–238.

10. Charles Blount, "A Summary Account of the Deists Religion," *The Miscellaneous Works of Charles Blount, Esq.* (1st ed. 1695; New York: Garland, 1979), 91; Robert E. Sullivan, *John Toland and the Deist Controversy* (Cambridge, Mass.: Harvard University Press, 1982), 209– 15.

11. Walker, ed., *Creeds and Platforms,* 439.

12. David D. Hall, *The Faithful Shepherd: A History of the New England Ministry in the Seventeenth Century* (Chapel Hill: The University of North Carolina Press, 1972), 168–69.

13. Seaborn Cotton, *A Brief Summe of the Chief Articles of our Christian Faith* (Cambridge: Samuel Green, 1663), 1; James Noyes, *A Short Catechism Composed by Mr. James Noyes* (Cambridge: Samuel Green and Marmaduke Johnson, 1661), 3; John Norton, *A Brief Catechism Containing the Doctrine of Godliness or Living Unto God* (Cambridge: Samuel Green and Marmaduke Johnson, 1660), 3; "New Haven Catechism," in John Davenport and William Hooke, *Ancient Waymarks,* ed. Leonard Bacon (New Haven, Conn.: B. L. Hamden, 1853), 3.

14. Samuel Willard, *A Compleat Body of Divinity in Two Hundred and Fifty Expository Lectures on the Assembly's Shorter Catechism* (Boston: B. Green and S. Kneeland, 1726), 600–01.

15. Cotton Mather, *Bonifacius* (Boston: B. Green, 1710), 23, 34, 50; Cotton Mather, *The Diary of Cotton Mather, II, 1709-1724, Massachusetts Historical Society Collec-*

tions, 7th ser., 8 (Boston, 1912), 357; Cotton Mather, *Manuductio ad Ministerium,* ed. Thomas J. Holmes and Kenneth B. Murdock (New York: Columbia University Press, 1938), 37– 38; Ames, *Marrow of Sacred Divinity,* 226–27; Fiering, *Moral Philosophy at Seventeenth-Century Harvard,* 40.

16. Seymour Van Dyken, *Samuel Willard: Preacher of Orthodoxy in an Era of Change* (Grand Rapids, Mich.: William B. Eerdmans, 1972), 43; Ernest Benson Lowrie, *The Shape of the Puritan Mind: The Thought of Samuel Willard* (New Haven, Conn.: Yale University Press, 1974), 3–19.

17. Samuel Willard, *Covenant-Keeping the Way to Blessedness* (Boston: James Glen, 1682), 31; Samuel Willard, *The Law Established by the Gospel* (Boston: Bartholomew Green, 1694), preface, 29–32, 39.

18. Willard, *Compleat Body,* 253–71.

19. Ibid., 7–10.

20. Solomon Stoddard, *The Inexcusableness of Neglecting the Worship of God* (Boston: B. Green, 1708), 14; Solomon Stoddard, *An Appeal to the Learned* (Boston: B. Green, 1709), 9.

21. Stoddard, *Appeal to the Learned,* 25–26, 43, 49, 72; Stoddard, *Inexcusableness of Neglecting,* 27–28.

22. Solomon Stoddard, *A Guide to Christ* (Boston: J. Allen, 1714), 2, 4, 6, 86; Solomon Stoddard, *The Efficacy of the Fear of Hell to Restrain Men from Sin* (Boston: Thomas Fleet, 1713), 67; Solomon Stoddard, *The Defects of Preachers Removed* (New London, Conn.: Kneeland and Green), 13.

23. Solomon Stoddard, *The Safety of Appearing at the Day of Judgment in the Righteousness of Christ* (Boston: Samuel Green, 1687), 205, 282; Solomon Stoddard, *A Treatise Concerning Conversion* (Boston: Franklin, 1719), 7.

24. Increase Mather, "An Apologeticall Preface," in John Davenport, *Another Essay for Investigation of the Truth* (Cambridge, Mass.: Samuel Green and Marmaduke Johnson, 1663), n.p.

25. Increase and Cotton Mather, "A Defence of the Evangelical Churches," in John Quick, *The Young Mans claim upon the Sacrament of the Lords Supper* (Boston: B. Green and J. Allen, 1700), 48–50; Increase Mather, *A Dissertation Wherein the Strange Doctrine Lately Published in a Sermon, the Tendency of Which is to Encourage Unsanctified Persons (while such) to Approach the Holy Table of the Lord, is Examined and Confuted* (Boston: B. Green, 1707), 28–30.

26. Increase Mather, *Five Sermons on Several Subjects* (Boston: B. Green, 1719), preface; Increase Mather, "To the Reader," *Practical Truths Tending to Promote Holiness in the Hearts and Lives of Christians* (Boston: B. Green, 1704), n.p.; Increase Mather, "Preface," Stoddard, *Guide to Christ,* vi; Increase Mather, *Pray for the Rising Generation* (Boston: John Foster, 1679), 12.

27. Compare Perry Miller, *The New England Mind: From Colony to Province* (Boston: Beacon Press, 1961), 66–67, 214–15, with Richard F. Lovelace, *The American Pietism of Cotton Mather* (Grand Rapids, Mich.: W. B. Eerdmans, 1979), 83–84. See also Robert Middlekauff, *The Mathers: Three Generations of Puritan Intellectuals 1565–1728* (New York: Oxford University Press, 1971), 294–304.

28. Cotton Mather, *A Seasonable Testimony to the Glorious Doctrines* (Boston: n.p.,

1702), 6–12; Cotton Mather, *Free Grace* (Boston: B. Green, 1706), 2; Cotton Mather, *The Spirit of Life Entering into the Spiritually Dead* (Boston: Timothy Green, 1707), 35; Cotton Mather, *The Greatest Concern in the World* (Boston: Timothy Green, 1707), 13.

29. Lovelace, *American Pietism of Cotton Mather,* 33–34; Kenneth Silverman, *The Life and Times of Cotton Mather* (New York: Harper and Row, 1984), 301–02.

30. Willard, *Compleat Body,* 16–20; Increase Mather, *A Discourse Proving that the Christian Religion is the only True Religion* (Boston: The Booksellers, 1702), 3, 4, 85; Cotton Mather, *Reasonable Religion: The Truth of the Christian Religion, Demonstrated* (Boston: T. Green, 1700), 14–56; Cotton Mather, *Reason Satisfied and Faith Established: The Resurrection of a Glorious Jesus Demonstrated* (Boston: John Allen, 1712), 9–22.

31. Increase Mather, *A Discourse Proving,* 6, 8, 87; Cotton Mather, *Reason Satisfied,* 9, 20–62.

32. Increase Mather, *The Mystery of Christ Opened and Applied* (Boston: n.p., 1686), 1; Increase Mather, *Several Sermons* (Boston: B. Green, 1715), v.

33. Cotton Mather et al., *The Principles of the Protestant Religion Maintained* (Boston: Richard Pierce, 1690), 55–57; Van Dyken, *Samuel Willard,* 156–69; Increase Mather, *A Discourse Proving,* 3.

34. John Eliot, *The Harmony of the Gospels* (Boston: John Foster, 1678), 5–34.

35. Increase Mather, *The Mystery of Christ,* 1–2; Silverman, *Life and Times of Cotton Mather,* 330.

36. Willard, *Compleat Body,* 33–40, 109.

37. Cotton Mather, *A Man of Reason* (Boston: John Edwards, 1718), 7.

38. John Cotton, *A Brief Exposition with Practicall Observations upon the Whole Book of Ecclesiastes* (London: Ralph Smith, 1654), 13, 16, 23; Theodore Hornberger, "Puritanism and Science: The Relationships Revealed in the Writings of John Cotton," *New England Quarterly* 10 (1937):503–15; Samuel Eliot Morison, "The Harvard School of Astronomy in the Seventeenth Century," *New England Quarterly* 7 (1934):12; Rose Lockwood, "The Scientific Revolution in Seventeenth-Century New England," *New England Quarterly* 52 (1980):78.

39. Morison, "Harvard School," 13; Silverman, *Life and Times of Cotton Mather,* 253.

40. Silverman, *Life and Times of Cotton Mather,* 41, 167; Middlekauff, *The Mathers,* 290.

41. Cotton Mather, *The Christian Philosopher* (London: E. Matthews, 1721), 7, 85.

42. Increase Mather, "To the Reader," *Kometographia: Or, A Discourse Concerning Comets* (Boston: Samuel Green, 1683), ii; Increase Mather, *An Essay for the Recording of Illustrious Providences* (Boston: George Calvert, 1684), 220; Increase Mather, *Heaven's Alarm to the World* (1st ed. 1681; Boston: John Foster, 1682), 7.

43. Increase Mather, *The Doctrine of Divine Providence Opened and Applied* (Boston: Richard Pierce, 1684), 11, 46; Increase Mather, *Essay for the Recording of Illustrious Providences,* "Preface," 135, 168.

44. Willard, *Compleat Body,* 110–13; Increase Mather, *Angelographia* (Boston: Green and Allen, 1696), 63; Cotton Mather, *Coelestinus* (Boston: S. Kneeland, 1723), 13; Silverman, *Life and Times of Cotton Mather,* 24.

45. Increase Mather, *Essay for the Recording of Illustrious Providences,* 186, 199.

46. Henry J. Cadbury, ed., *George Fox's Book of Miracles* (Cambridge: Cambridge University Press, 1948), 75, 81; Willard, *Compleat Body,* 138.

47. John Richardson, *The Necessity of a Well-Experienced Souldiery* (Cambridge: Samuel Green, 1679), 6; John Davenport, *The Knowledge of Christ Indispensably Required of All Men that Would be Saved* (London: L. Chapman, 1653), 70.

48. Increase Mather, *The Doctrine of Divine Providence* (Boston: Richard Pierce, 1684), 46; Increase Mather, "An Historical Discourse Concerning the Prevalency of Prayer," in the appendix to Richard Alleine, *A Companion for Prayer* (Boston: S. Kneeland, 1750), n.p.; Increase Mather, *The Mystery of Israel's Salvation* (London: John Allen, 1669), 90; Cadbury, ed., *George Fox's Book of Miracles*, 82.

49. Cotton Mather, *Things for a Distress'd People to Think Upon* (Boston: B. Green and J. Allen, 1696), 36, 69, 73, 80, 84.

50. Samuel Willard, *The Fountain Opened* (Boston: B. Green and J. Allen, 1700), 114.

51. Increase Mather, *Mystery of Israel's Salvation*, "Preface," 1, 76; Increase Mather, *A Discourse Concerning Earthquakes* (Boston: Timothy Green, 1706), 3, 24; Increase Mather, *A Dissertation Concerning the Future Conversion of the Jewish Nation* (London: R. Toobey, 1709), 17.

52. Increase Mather, *A Dissertation Concerning the Future Conversion*, 15, 34; Mason I. Lowance and David Watters, eds., "Increase Mather's 'New Jerusalem': Millennialism in Late Seventeenth-Century New England," *Proceedings of the American Antiquarian Society,* 87 (1977):386, 405; Increase Mather, *Mystery of Israel's Salvation*, "Preface," 139.

53. Increase Mather, *Dissertation Concerning the Future Conversion*, 33; Increase Mather, "New Jerusalem," ed. Lowance and Watters, 370, 379; Increase Mather, *The Day of Trouble is Near* (Cambridge: Marmaduke Johnson, 1674), 26; Increase Mather, *A Call from Heaven to the Present and Succeeding Generations* (Boston: John Foster, 1679), 56.

54. Reiner Smolinski, "*Israel Redivivus:* The Eschatological Limits of Puritan Typology in New England," *New England Quarterly* 63 (1990):370; Michael G. Hall, *The Last American Puritan: The Life of Increase Mather, 1639–1723* (Middletown, Conn.: Wesleyan University Press, 1988), 283; Increase Mather, *Dissertation Concerning the Future Conversion*, 32.

55. Samuel Sewall, *Phaenomena quaedam Apocalyptica* (Boston: B. Green and J. Allen, 1697), 2.

56. Increase Mather, "New Jerusalem," ed. Lowance and Watters, 364; Reiner Smolinski, "An Authoritative Edition of Cotton Mather's Unpublished Manuscript 'Triparadisus,'" 2 vols. (Ph.D. diss., Pennsylvania State University, 1987), 2:506.

57. Cotton Mather, *Theopolis Americana* (Boston: B. Green, 1710), 50; Smolinski, "An Authoritative Edition," 1:lxxxix.

58. Smolinski, "An Authoritative Edition," 1:cxxxxi, 202, 263, 307, 314, 328, 2:364, 422, 432; Smolinski, "Israel Redivivus," 375.

Chapter 4. Nature, the Supernatural, and Virtue

1. Thomas Foxcroft, *Observations Historical and Practical on the Rise and Primitive State of New England* (Boston: S. Kneeland and T. Green, 1730), 41; Ebenezer Turell, *The Life and Character of the Reverend Benjamin Colman* (Boston: Rogers and Fowle,

1749), 123; Hall, *Last American Puritan,* 284; John Corrigan, *The Prism of Piety: Catholic Congregational Clergy at the Beginning of the Enlightenment* (New York: Oxford University Press, 1991), 9–31.

2. Fiering, *Moral Philosophy at Seventeenth-Century Harvard,* 210.

3. John Higginson and Nicholas Noyes, "Letter to the Brattle Street Church, Dec. 30, 1699," in Corrigan, *Prism of Piety,* 28–30; Turell, *Life of Colman,* "Preface," 169.

4. Benjamin Colman, *The Glory of God in the Firmament of His Power* (Boston: S. Kneeland and T. Green, 1743), 2–3, 10, 17; Benjamin Colman, *The Credibility of the Christian Doctrine of the Resurrection* (Boston: Thomas Hancock, 1729), 14; James West Davidson, *The Logic of Millennial Thought* (New Haven, Conn.: Yale University Press, 1977), 27; Turell, *Life of Colman,* 168.

5. John Wise, *Vindication of the Government of New England Churches* (1717), *The Puritans: A Sourcebook of their Writings,* ed. Perry Miller and Thomas H. Johnson, 2 vols. (New York: Harper, 1963), 1:257–60.

6. John Bulkley, *The Usefulness of Reveal'd Religion, to Preserve and Improve that which is Natural* (New London: T. Green, 1730), 5, 15, 28.

7. Benjamin Colman, *The Hainous Nature of the Sin of Murder* (Boston: John Allen, 1713), 10; Benjamin Wadsworth, *The Benefits of a Good, and the Mischiefs of an Evil Conscience* (Boston: B. Green, 1719), 24; Benjamin Wadsworth, *The Imitation of Christ a Christian Duty* (Boston: B. Green, 1722), 10–16; John Barnard, *The Lord Jesus Christ the only, and Supreame Head of the Church* (Boston: S. Kneeland and T. Green, 1738), 29.

8. Harry S. Stout, *The New England Soul: Preaching and Religious Culture in Colonial New England* (New York: Oxford University Press, 1986), 148–65.

9. Cotton Mather, *Ratio Disciplinae Fratrum Nov-Anglorum* (Boston: S. Gerrish, 1726), 5; John White, *New England's Lamentations* (Boston: T. Fleet, 1734), 16; Jonathan Edwards, *A Faithful Narrative of the Surprising Work of God,* in *Jonathan Edwards: The Great Awakening,* ed. C. C. Goen (New Haven, Conn.: Yale University Press, 1972), 16.

10. H. Shelton Smith, *Changing Conceptions of Original Sin* (New York: Scribner, 1955), 10–19.

11. Charles Chauncy, *Seasonable Thoughts on the State of Religion in New England* (Boston: Rogers and Fowle, 1743), 274, 398; Robert J. Wilson III, *The Benevolent Deity: Ebenezer Gay and the Rise of Rational Religion in New England, 1696–1787* (Philadelphia: University of Pennsylvania Press, 1984), 63–64; Conrad Wright, *The Beginnings of Unitarianism in America* (Boston: Beacon Press, 1955), 23; Samuel Osborn, *The Case and Complaint of Mr. Samuel Osborn* (Boston: n.p., 1743), 4–20, 25.

12. *The Testimony and Advice of a Number of Laymen* (Boston: n.p., 1743), 3; William Balch, *The Apostles St. Paul and St. James Reconciled With Respect to Faith and Works* (Boston: D. Fowle, 1743), 8, 13, 26; William Balch, *Vindication of Some Points of Doctrine* (Boston: Rogers and Fowle, 1746), 82; Experience Mayhew, *Grace Defended* (Boston: B. Green, 1744), 137, 139, 155, 198.

13. Lemuel Briant, *The Absurdity and Blasphemy of Depretiating Moral Virtue* (Boston: J. Green, 1749), 7, 20; *The Result of a Late Ecclesiastical Council* (Boston: n.p., 1753), 7; Samuel Niles, *A Vindication of Several Important Gospel-Doctrines* (Boston: S.

Kneeland, 1752), 26, 69; *The Report of a Committee of the First Church in Braintree* (Boston: n.p., 1753), 5; John Bass, *A True Narrative of an Unhappy Contention in the Church of Ashford,* in Alan Heimert and Perry Miller, eds., *The Great Awakening* (Indianapolis, Ind.: Bobbs-Merrill, 1967), 470, 478.

14. Robert Prichard, *A History of the Episcopal Church* (Harrisburg, Pa.: Morehouse, 1991), 34.

15. Thomas Bray, *Several Circular Letters to the Clergy of Maryland* (1701), in Bernard C. Steiner, ed., *Rev. Thomas Bray: His Life and Selected Works Related to Maryland* (Baltimore: Maryland Historical Society, 1901), 133; Thomas Bray, *A Short Discourse Upon the Doctrine of our Baptismal Covenant,* 4th ed. (London: S. Hole, 1704), 2, 3, 39, 50, 141.

16. Alexander Garden, *The Doctrine of Justification* (Charlestown, S.C.: Peter Timothy, 1752), 15, 35, 43; Alexander Garden, *Six Letters,* 2d ed. (Boston: T. Fleet, 1740), 6, 9.

17. Garden, *Six Letters,* 26, 16–28; Alexander Garden, *Regeneration and the Testimony of the Spirit* (Charlestown, S.C.: Peter Timothy, 1740), 1, 16.

18. Samuel Quincy, *Twenty Sermons* (Boston: John Draper, 1750), 35, 134, 252, 325.

19. Devereux Jarratt, *The Life of the Reverend Devereux Jarratt,* ed. David L. Holmes (Cleveland, Ohio: The Pilgrim Press, 1995), 49–50.

20. Joseph J. Ellis, *The New England Mind in Transition: Samuel Johnson of Connecticut, 1696–1772* (New Haven, Conn.: Yale University Press, 1973), 125; Samuel Johnson, *A Letter from a Minister of the Church of England to his Dissenting Parishioners* (1733), in Herbert and Carol Schneider, eds., *Samuel Johnson, President of King's College: His Career and Writings,* 4 vols. (New York: Columbia University Press, 1929), 3:26.

21. Samuel Johnson, "Memoirs of the Life of the Rev. Dr. Johnson," *Career and Writings,* 2:6–7; Samuel Johnson, "Technology or Technometry," ibid., 2:186.

22. George E. DeMille, *The Catholic Movement in the American Episcopal Church* (Philadelphia: Church Historical Society, 1941), 10; E. Clowes Chorley, *Men and Movements in the Episcopal Church* (New York: Scribner's Sons, 1946), 136.

23. Samuel Johnson, *A Second Letter from a Minister of the Church of England to His Dissenting Parishioners* (1743), *Career and Writings,* 3:51–52, 89; Johnson, *Letter from a Minister,* ibid., 3:26.

24. Samuel Johnson, *A Letter to Mr. Samuel Browne of Waterbury,* ibid., 3:163.

25. Johnson, *Letter to Mr. Samuel Browne,* ibid., 3:150, 180; Samuel Johnson, *A Letter to Mr. Jonathan Dickinson* (1747), ibid., 3:199.

26. Johnson, *Letter to Dickinson,* ibid., 3:202, 204.

27. Johnson, *Letter to Browne,* ibid., 3:149, 171.

28. Samuel Johnson, *Ethices Elementa: Or, the First Principles of Moral Philosophy* (2nd ed. 1752), ibid., 2:444; Johnson, *Letter to Browne,* ibid., 3:150, 166; Ralph Cudworth, *Treatise Concerning Eternal and Immutable Morality, British Moralists,* ed. L. A. Selby-Bigge, 2 vols. (Indianapolis, Ind.: Bobbs-Merrill, 1964), 1:258.

29. Samuel Clarke, *A Discourse Concerning the Unchangeable Obligations of Natural Religion, The Works of Samuel Clarke,* 4 vols. (London: Knapton, 1738), 2:596, 608, 622–23, 640; William Wollaston, *The Religion of Nature Delineated* (1724), *British Moralists,* 2:364–65.

30. Johnson, *Ethices Elementa,* 2:448–49, 454–89, 497.

31. Ibid., 443, 486; Samuel Johnson, "Samuel Johnson to Benjamin Colman, 1746," *Career and Writings,* 3:325; Mark Valeri, *Law and Providence in Joseph Bellamy's New England* (New York: Oxford University Press, 1994), 47.

32. Norman S. Fiering, "President Samuel Johnson and the Circle of Knowledge," *William and Mary Quarterly,* 3d ser., 28 (1971):200–23; Johnson, *Technologia sive Technometria, Career and Writings,* 2:364– 65; Edwin S. Gaustad, *George Berkeley in America* (New Haven, Conn.: Yale University Press, 1979), 59–65.

33. Samuel Johnson, *Memoirs, Career and Writings,* 1:24.

34. Ibid., 1:25; John Locke, *An Essay Concerning Human Understanding,* 2 vols. (New York: Dover, 1959), 1:168–77.

35. Locke, *Essay Concerning Human Understanding,* 1:178–82.

36. George Berkeley, *Treatise Concerning the Principles of Human Knowledge* (1710), *The Works of George Berkeley,* ed. Alexander C. Fraser, 2 vols. (Oxford: Clarendon Press, 1871), 1:160–65, 232–34.

37. George Berkeley, "Letter to Samuel Johnson, Nov. 25, 1729," *Career and Writings,* 2:272.

38. Samuel Johnson, *Elementa Philosophica* (1752), ibid., 2:378.

39. Ibid., 2:379, 381, 383, 432.

40. Ibid., 2:464, 466.

41. Ellis, *New England Mind in Transition,* 228.

42. Gilbert Tennent, *The Unsearchable Riches of Christ* (Boston: J. Draper, 1739), "Preface," 137.

43. Jonathan Dickinson, *A Display of God's Special Grace* (Boston: Rogers and Fowle, 1742), 2.

44. David Harlan, *The Clergy and the Great Awakening in New England* (Ann Arbor, Mich.: UMI Research Press, 1979), 4.

45. Charles Chauncy, *Enthusiasm Described and Cautioned Against* (1742), *Great Awakening,* 241; Chauncy, *Seasonable Thoughts,* 103, 168, 299, 302.

46. Samuel Finley, *Christ Triumphing and Satan Raging* (1741), *Great Awakening,* 157; Chauncy, *Seasonable Thoughts,* 251; Christopher Grasso, *A Speaking Aristocracy: Transforming Public Discourse in Eighteenth-Century Connecticut* (Chapel Hill: University of North Carolina Press, 1999), 102.

47. Gilbert Tennent, *The Association for Defence Farther Encouraged, or Defensive War Defended* (Philadelphia: B. Franklin and D. Hall, 1748), 22, 27.

48. Jonathan Dickinson, *The Reasonableness of Christianity* (Boston: S. Kneeland and T. Green, 1732), 64; Leigh Eric Schmidt, "Jonathan Dickinson and the Making of the Moderate Enlightenment," *American Presbyterians* 63 (1985):342.

49. Dickinson, *Reasonableness of Christianity,* 2, 17, 25, 38, 40, 64, 68, 76, 116, 141.

50. Gilbert Tennent, *The Danger of an Unconverted Ministry* (1741), *Great Awakening,* 82; Chauncy, *Seasonable Thoughts,* "Preface," iii.

51. Jonathan Edwards, "Justification by Faith Alone" (1738), *Great Awakening,* 8; George Whitefield, *Journal,* ibid., 43; Tennent, "Danger of an Unconverted Ministry," ibid., 82; David McGregore, *The Spirits of the Present Day Trial* (1742), ibid., 219.

52. William Cooper, *The Doctrine of Predestination Unto Life* (Boston: J. Draper,

1740), "Preface"; Samuel Blair, *The Doctrine of Predestination* (Philadelphia: Franklin, 1742), 2; Jonathan Dickinson, *The True Scripture-Doctrine Concerning Some Important Points of Christian Faith* (Boston: G. Rogers, 1741), xi.

53. Dickinson, *True Scripture-Doctrine*, 31–38.

54. Samuel Blair, *The Gospel Method of Salvation* (New York: Bradford, 1737), 10; Dickinson, *True Scripture-Doctrine*, 71; Thomas Foxcroft, *Some Seasonable Thoughts on Evangelic Preaching* (Boston: G. Rogers and D. Fowle, 1740), 29, 34; Tennent, "Danger of an Unconverted Ministry," *Great Awakening*, 79.

55. Andrew Croswell, *An Answer to the Rev. Mr. Garden's Three First Letters to the Rev. Mr. Whitefield* (Boston: S. Kneeland and T. Green, 1741), 16, 32, 58–59; Leigh Eric Schmidt, "'A Second and Glorious Reformation': The New Light Extremism of Andrew Croswell," *William and Mary Quarterly*, 3d ser., 43 (1986):222.

56. Chauncy, *Seasonable Thoughts*, 31, 279, 282.

57. Jonathan Dickinson, *The Nature and Necessity of Regeneration* (New York: James Parker, 1743), 5–6, 18.

58. Milton J. Coalter, Jr., *Gilbert Tennent: Son of Thunder* (Westport, Conn.: Greenwood Press, 1986), 23; John Thomson, *The Doctrine of Convictions* (Philadelphia: Bradford, 1741), 15.

59. Jonathan Dickinson, *The Witness of the Spirit* (Boston: Kneeland and Green, 1740), 7; Tennent, *Unsearchable Riches*, 27, 175.

60. Chauncy, *Seasonable Thoughts*, 5, 109; Thomson, *Doctrine of Convictions*, 12, 39, 41; McGregore, *Spirits of the Present Day Trial, Great Awakening*, 219.

61. John Thomson, *The Government of the Church of Christ* (1741), *Great Awakening*, 115–16; Tennent, *Unsearchable Riches*, 22, 27.

62. Chauncy, *Seasonable Thoughts*, 3, 109; Gilbert Tennent, *Remarks Upon a Protestation Presented to the Synod of Pennsylvania* (1741), *Great Awakening*, 171; Tennent, *Unsearchable Riches*, 96; Dickinson, *Nature and Necessity of Regeneration*, 14–15.

63. Dickinson, *Witness of the Spirit*, 8–19, 20–21.

64. Thomson, *Doctrine of Convictions*, 49, 55, 60.

65. Tennent, *Remarks Upon a Protestation*, 173.

66. Dickinson, *Display of God's Special Grace*, 90, 92, 99, 104; Andrew Croswell, *Mr. Croswell's Reply to a Book Lately Published* (Boston: Rogers and Fowle, 1742), 11–12, 23.

67. Chauncy, *Seasonable Thoughts*, 124.

68. Jonathan Dickinson, *A Defence of the Dialogue* (Boston: J. Draper, 1743), 18, 23, 29.

69. Croswell, *Mr. Croswell's Reply*, 23; Dickinson, *Defence of the Dialogue*, 37; Andrew Croswell, *What Is Christ to Me, If He Is Not Mine?* (1745), *Great Awakening*, 508, 511, 513.

70. Schmidt, "'A Second and Glorious Reformation,'" 230, 234; Solomon Williams, *A Vindication of the Gospel-Doctrine of Justifying Faith* (Boston: Rogers and Fowle, 1746), 36, 45.

Chapter 5. Jonathan Edwards

1. Jonathan Edwards, "Christian Knowledge: Or, the Importance and Advantage of a Thorough Knowledge of Divine Truth," *The Works of President Edwards in Eight Volumes*, ed. John Erskine (Leeds: Edward Baines, 1811), 5:408.

2. Ibid., 409; Jonathan Edwards, *Fifteen Sermons on Various Subjects, Works* (Leeds edition), 7:416; William Sparkes Morris, *The Young Jonathan Edwards: A Reconstruction* (Brooklyn, N.Y.: Carlson, 1991), 247.

3. Edwards, "Christian Knowledge," 419; Gerald R. McDermott, *One Holy and Happy Society: The Public Theology of Jonathan Edwards* (University Park: The Pennsylvania State University Press, 1992), 155–60; Jonathan Edwards, "Narrative of Communion Controversy," *Jonathan Edwards: Ecclesiastical Writings,* ed. David D. Hall, *Works of Jonathan Edwards* (New Haven, Conn.: Yale University Press, 1994), 12:565; David D. Hall, "Editor's Introduction," ibid., 12:48, 79; George S. Claghorn, ed., *Jonathan Edwards, Letters and Personal Writings, Works of Jonathan Edwards* (New Haven, Conn.: Yale University Press, 1998), 16:102.

4. Wallace E. Anderson, ed., *Jonathan Edwards, Scientific and Philosophical Writings, Works of Jonathan Edwards* (New Haven, Conn.: Yale University Press, 1980), 6:36; Jonathan Edwards, "A Rational Account of the Main Doctrines of the Christian Religion Attempted," ibid., 6:397.

5. Samuel Hopkins, *The Life of the Late Reverend, Learned and Pious Mr. Jonathan Edwards* (Boston: S. Kneeland, 1765), 40; Stephen J. Stein, "The Spirit and the Word: Jonathan Edwards and Scriptural Exegesis," *Jonathan Edwards and the American Experience,* ed. Nathan O. Hatch and Harry S. Stout (New York: Oxford University Press, 1988), 120–23; Roland Andre Delattre, *Beauty and Sensibility in the Thought of Jonathan Edwards* (New Haven, Conn.: Yale University Press, 1968), 15–57; Robert E. Brown, *Jonathan Edwards and the Bible* (Bloomington: Indiana University Press, 2002), 88–128.

6. Jonathan Edwards, "Personal Narrative," *Jonathan Edwards: Representative Selections,* ed. Clarence H. Faust and Thomas H. Johnson (New York: Hill and Wang, 1962), 58–67; Jonathan Edwards, "The Mind," *The Philosophy of Jonathan Edwards From His Private Notebooks,* ed. Harvey Townsend (Eugene: University of Oregon Press, 1955), 21; Thomas A. Schafer, ed., *The "Miscellanies," Works of Jonathan Edwards* (New Haven, Conn.: Yale University Press, 1994), 13:14–15.

7. Jonathan Edwards, "The Final Judgment: Or, The World Judged Righteously by Jesus Christ," *Works* (Leeds edition), 4:85–102, 394; Samuel Clarke, *On Natural Religion, British Moralists,* 2:2, 3–12; Fiering, *Moral Philosophy at Seventeenth-Century Harvard,* 90, 96; Norman Fiering, *Jonathan Edwards's Moral Thought and Its British Context* (Chapel Hill: University of North Carolina Press, 1981), 70, 86.

8. Edwards, "The Mind," 25, 47; Elizabeth Flower and Murray G. Murphey, *A History of Philosophy in America,* 2 vols. (New York: G. P. Putnam's Sons, 1977), 1:154; Jonathan Edwards, *Images or Shadows of Divine Things,* ed. Perry Miller (New Haven, Conn.: Yale University Press, 1948), 135.

9. Jonathan Edwards, *Letters and Personal Writings,* 38, 52, 59, 68, 121–25, 127, 380–81, 480, 558, 564; Patricia J. Tracy, *Jonathan Edwards: Religion and Society in Eighteenth-Century Northampton* (New York: Hill and Wang, 1979), 147–70.

10. Jonathan Edwards, "Miscellaneous Observations on Important Theological Subjects," *Works* (Leeds edition), 8:155, 157, 209; Gerald R. McDermott, "A Possibility of Reconciliation: Jonathan Edwards and the Salvation of Non-Christians," *Edwards in Our Time: Jonathan Edwards and the Shaping of American Religion,* ed. Sang Hyun Lee and Allen C. Guelzo (Grand Rapids, Mich.: William B. Eerdmans, 1999), 179–82;

Gerald R. McDermott, *Jonathan Edwards Consults the Gods* (New York: Oxford University Press, 1999), 6–10.

11. Jonathan Edwards, *Dissertation Concerning the End for Which God Created the World, Works of President Edwards in Four Volumes* (reprint of 1808 Worcester edition; New York: Leavitt and Allen, 1855), 2:199– 202.

12. Jonathan Edwards, "Miscellanies," *Philosophy of Jonathan Edwards,* 74 (Misc. #91), 76 (Misc. #149), 76 (Misc. #199), 78 (Misc. #200, Misc. #268).

13. Morris, *Young Jonathan Edwards,* 313–14; Jonathan Edwards, "Of Being," *Philosophy of Jonathan Edwards,* 1; Schafer, ed., *The "Miscellanies,"* 40–41.

14. Edwards, "Miscellanies," *Philosophy of Jonathan Edwards,* 253 (Misc. #94); Morris, *Young Jonathan Edwards,* 476, 478; Fiering, *Jonathan Edwards's Moral Thought,* 83.

15. Edwards, "Miscellanies," *Philosophy of Jonathan Edwards,* 224 (Misc. #1340).

16. Edwards, "Miscellaneous Observations," 284; Edwards, "Christian Knowledge," 408; Jonathan Edwards, *Sermons on Various Important Subjects* (Boston: S. Kneeland, 1765), 61; Jonathan Edwards, "Justification by Faith Alone," *Five Important Discourses on Important Subjects, Works* (Leeds edition), 6:231.

17. Edwards, *Fifteen Sermons, Works* (Leeds edition), 7:458; Jonathan Edwards, *A History of the Work of Redemption,* ibid., 5:297; Edwards, "Miscellaneous Observations," 8:24, 178.

18. Jonathan Edwards, "To the Trustees of the College of New Jersey," *A Jonathan Edwards Reader,* ed. John E. Smith, Harry S. Stout, and Kenneth P. Minkema (New Haven, Conn.: Yale University Press, 1995), 323– 24; Kenneth P. Minkema, "The Other Unfinished 'Great Work': Jonathan Edwards, Messianic Prophecy, and 'The Harmony of the Old and New Testament,'" *Jonathan Edwards's Writings: Text, Context, Interpretation,* ed. Stephen J. Stein (Bloomington: Indiana University Press, 1996), 52– 61.

19. Edwards, *Sermons on Various Important Subjects,* 234; Edwards, "Miscellaneous Observations," 154; Edwards, *History of the Work of Redemption,* 133; Edwards, "Miscellanies," *Philosophy of Jonathan Edwards,* 233 (Misc. #1340).

20. Stephen J. Stein, ed., "Editor's Introduction," *Notes on Scripture, The Works of Jonathan Edwards* (New Haven, Conn.: Yale University Press, 1998), 15:1–36.

21. Edwards, *Images or Shadows of Divine Things,* 50, 57, 69– 70, 109.

22. Jonathan Edwards, "A Divine and Supernatural Light," *Five Sermons on Different Occasions, Works* (Leeds edition), 8:8, 19.

23. Edwards, "Miscellanies," *Philosophy of Jonathan Edwards,* 113–24 (Misc. #782).

24. Ibid., 118; Anderson, "Introduction," *Scientific and Philosophical Writings,* 53.

25. Edwards, "Of Being," 7, 9–20; Edwards, "The Mind," 37 (#27), 32 (#13).

26. George Rupp, "The 'Idealism' of Jonathan Edwards," *Harvard Theological Review* 62 (1969):214; Morris, *Young Jonathan Edwards,* 314, 356; Wallace E. Anderson, "Immaterialism in Jonathan Edwards' Early Philosophical Notes," *Journal of the History of Ideas* 25 (1964):191; Flower and Murphey, *History of Philosophy,* 1:151; Sang Hyun Lee, *The Philosophical Theology of Jonathan Edwards* (Princeton, N.J., Princeton University Press, 1988), 62.

27. Jonathan Edwards, *Original Sin,* ed. Clyde A. Holbrook, *Works of Jonathan Edwards* (New Haven, Conn.: Yale University Press, 1970), 3:400, 401; Edwards, *The "Miscellanies,"* 210 (Misc. #18).

28. Edwards, "Miscellanies," *Philosophy of Jonathan Edwards,* 186–87, 190 (Misc. #1263); Edwards, *The "Miscellanies,"* 235 (Misc. #64).

29. Edwards, "Miscellanies," *Philosophy of Jonathan Edwards,* 87 (Misc. #880), 262 (Misc. #697), 74 (Misc. #27a); Jonathan Edwards, *The Nature of True Virtue, Works of President Edwards* (Worcester edition), 2:278; Edwards, *Dissertation Concerning the End for Which God Created the World,* ibid., 2:217, 220.

30. Edwards, *Dissertation Concerning the End for Which God Created the World,* 207–08, 220, 257; Edwards, "Miscellanies," *Philosophy of Jonathan Edwards,* 253 (Misc. #94); Egbert Smyth, "Jonathan Edwards' Idealism," *American Journal of Theology,* 1 (1897):959; Michael J. McClymond, *Encounters with God* (New York: Oxford University Press, 1998), 30–32.

31. Jonathan Edwards, "An Essay on the Trinity," *Jonathan Edwards,* ed. Faust and Johnson, 375–81; Edwards, "Miscellanies," *Philosophy of Jonathan Edwards,* 252–61 (Misc. #94); Schafer, ed., *The "Miscellanies,"* 14, 20.

32. Edwards, "Miscellanies," *Philosophy of Jonathan Edwards,* 254–58 (Misc. #117); Schafer, ed., *The "Miscellanies,"* 28; Edwards, *The "Miscellanies,"* 476 (Misc. #402).

33. Edwards, *Dissertation Concerning the End for Which God Created the World,* 200–01, 203, 206, 255.

34. Edwards, *Sermons on Various Important Subjects,* 171; Edwards, "Miscellaneous Observations," 413, 500, 502, 533.

35. Edwards, "Miscellaneous Observations," 507, 533; Jonathan Edwards, *Seven Sermons on Important Subjects, Works* (Leeds edition), 6:529; Edwards, *History of the Work of Redemption,* 150.

36. Edwards, "Miscellaneous Observations," 517, 524; Edwards, "Justification by Faith Alone," 240, 247, 252; Alister E. McGrath, *Justitia Dei* (Cambridge: Cambridge University Press, 1986), 37.

37. Jonathan Edwards, "The Excellency of Christ," *Five Important Discourses on Important Subjects,* 6:433, 440–48; Edwards, *Sermons on Various Important Subjects,* 178.

38. Jonathan Edwards, *Some Thoughts Concerning the Present Revival of Religion in New England, The Great Awakening,* ed. Goen, 464.

39. Edwards, "Miscellaneous Observations," 416–18, 427.

40. Edwards, *Original Sin,* 103, 167.

41. Ibid., 128, 130, 143–44.

42. Ibid., 381, 397, 399.

43. Ibid., 23, 392, 408.

44. Edwards, "Miscellaneous Observations," 427, 445; Edwards, "Divine and Supernatural Light," 7; Anri Morimoto, *Jonathan Edwards and the Catholic Vision of Salvation* (University Park: Pennsylvania State University Press, 1995), 18–19; Conrad Cherry, *The Theology of Jonathan Edwards* (Bloomington: Indiana University Press, 1990), 36; Morris, *Young Jonathan Edwards,* 632.

45. Lee, *Philosophical Theology of Jonathan Edwards,* 3–46; Morimoto, *Jonathan Edwards and the Catholic Vision,* 31, 32–59; John Smith, "Editor's Introduction," *A Treatise Concerning Religious Affections,* by Jonathan Edwards, *Works of Jonathan Edwards* (New Haven, Conn.: Yale University Press, 1959), 2:56.

46. Edwards, *Religious Affections,* 111; Jonathan Edwards, *Charity and Its Fruits,*

Jonathan Edwards, Ethical Writings, ed. Paul Ramsey, *Works of Jonathan Edwards* (New Haven, Conn.: Yale University Press, 1989), 8:129, 131; Edwards, *Original Sin,* 169; Jaroslav Pelikan, *Christian Doctrine and Modern Culture, The Christian Tradition: A History of the Development of Doctrine,* 5 vols. (Chicago: University of Chicago Press, 1989), 5:129, 151.

47. Edwards, *Ethical Writings,* 294; Edwards, *Religious Affections,* "Preface," 240, 421; Hall, "Editor's Introduction," *Ecclesiastical Writings,* 49.

48. Nathanael Emmons, *A System of Divinity,* ed. Jacob Ide, 2 vols. (Boston: Crocker and Brewster, 1842), 2:159, 165; Samuel Hopkins, *Two Discourses* (Boston: William McAlpine, 1768), 16; Edwards, *Charity and Its Fruits,* 329.

49. Edwards, *Religious Affections,* 154, 161–62; Jonathan Edwards, *A Faithful Narrative of the Surprising Work of God, The Great Awakening,* ed. Goen, 163; Edwards, "Divine and Supernatural Light," 6; Edwards, *Charity and Its Fruits,* 332.

50. Edwards, "Justification by Faith Alone," 235–36.

51. Ibid., 241–48, 252, 303.

52. Jonathan Edwards, *The Nature of True Virtue,* ed. William Frankena (Ann Arbor: University of Michigan Press, 1960), 3, 23; Edwards, *Dissertation Concerning the End for Which God Created the World,* 203, 206.

53. Edwards, *Nature of True Virtue,* 3, 18–21.

54. Jonathan Edwards, *Freedom of the Will,* ed. Paul Ramsey, *Works of Jonathan Edwards* (New Haven, Conn.: Yale University Press, 1957), 1:164, 191, 197, 270–73.

55. Ibid., 144–45, 164, 226, 427.

56. Ibid., 159.

57. Edwards, *History of the Work of Redemption,* 18, 294, 297; Edwards, "Miscellaneous Observations," 334.

58. Jonathan Edwards, "Notes on the Apocalypse," *Jonathan Edwards, Apocalyptic Writings,* ed. Stephen J. Stein, *Works of Jonathan Edwards* (New Haven, Conn.: Yale University Press, 1977), 5:107, 129.

59. Davidson, *Logic of Millennial Thought,* 129–32; Jonathan Edwards, *A History of the Work of Redemption,* ed. John Wilson, *Works of Jonathan Edwards* (New Haven, Conn.: Yale University Press, 1989), 9:354, 372, 456, 479, 486; Wilson, "Editor's Introduction," ibid., 13.

60. Edwards, *Some Thoughts Concerning the Present Revival of Religion,* 353–54; Chauncy, *Seasonable Thoughts,* 272; Jonathan Edwards, *An Humble Attempt to Promote Explicit Agreement and Visible Union of God's People in Extraordinary Prayer, Apocalyptic Writings,* 411, 533; Stein, "Editor's Introduction," ibid., 28; McDermott, *One Holy and Happy Society,* 77–90.

61. Edwards, *Humble Attempt,* 339, 346; Edwards, *History of the Work of Redemption,* 467, 483–84.

62. Edwards, "Notes on the Apocalypse," 129, 141, 177, 183– 84; Edwards, *History of the Work of Redemption,* 490; Jonathan Edwards, "The End of the Wicked Contemplated," *Works* (Leeds edition), 4:510; Edwards, "Final Judgment," 466, 467–72.

63. Hall, "Editor's Introduction," *Ecclesiastical Writings,* 51– 62.

64. Edwards, "Miscellaneous Observations," 477; Edwards, *Sermons on Various Important Subjects,* 207, 524; Jonathan Edwards, *An Humble Inquiry, Ecclesiastical Writings,* 205.

65. Edwards, *An Humble Inquiry,* 196; Edwards, "Divine and Supernatural Light," 13; Edwards, *Sermons on Various Important Subjects,* 246.

66. Jonathan Edwards, *Misrepresentations Corrected, and Truth Vindicated, Ecclesiastical Writings,* 351, 358.

Chapter 6. Fragmentation in New England

1. Robert L. Ferm, "Jonathan Edwards the Younger and the American Reformed Tradition" (Ph.D. diss., Yale University, 1958), 230.

2. William A. Hart, *A Discourse Concerning the Nature of Regeneration* (New London, Conn.: T. Green, 1742), 38, 40; Thomas Andros, *An Essay in which the Doctrine of a Positive Divine Efficiency . . . is Candidly Discussed* (Boston: Crocker and Brewster, 1820), v–vi; Allen C. Guelzo, *Edwards on the Will: A Century of American Theological Debate* (Middletown, Conn.: Wesleyan University Press, 1989), 88; Joseph A. Conforti, *Samuel Hopkins and the New Divinity Movement* (Grand Rapids, Mich.: Christian University Press, 1981), 73–74; Ferm, "Jonathan Edwards the Younger," 166.

3. Jedediah Mills, *An Inquiry Concerning the State of the Unregenerate Under the Gospel* (New Haven, Conn.: B. Mecom, 1767), 121.

4. Ebenezer Gay, *The True Spirit of a Gospel-Minister Represented and Urged* (Boston: D. Gookin, 1746), 10, 32; Wilson, *Benevolent Deity,,* 76, 156–60.

5. Ebenezer Gay, *Natural Religion, as Distinguish'd from Revealed* (Boston: John Draper, 1759), 5, 11, 16.

6. Ebenezer Gay, *A Beloved Disciple of Jesus Christ Characterized* (Boston: R. & S. Draper, 1766), 7, 12, 19, 22, 30, 31.

7. Samuel Webster, *A Winter Evening's Conversation Upon the Doctrine of Original Sin* (Boston: Green and Russell, 1757), 6–8, 27.

8. Samuel Niles, *The True Scripture-Doctrine of Original Sin* (Boston: S. Kneeland, 1757), 41, 150; Peter Clark, *The Scripture-Doctrine of Original Sin Stated and Defended, in a Summer Morning's Conversation* (Boston: S. Kneeland, 1758), 4, 16–25.

9. Clark, *Scripture-Doctrine of Original Sin,* 8; [Charles Chauncy], *The Opinion of One That Has Perused the Summer Morning's Conversation* (Boston: Green and Russell, 1758), 8, 17.

10. Charles W. Akers, *Called Unto Liberty: A Life of Jonathan Mayhew, 1720–1766* (Cambridge, Mass.: Harvard University Press, 1964), 51.

11. Jonathan Mayhew, *Seven Sermons* (Boston: Rogers and Fowle, 1749), 5, 97, 146, 154–55.

12. Ibid., 36, 47, 72.

13. Ibid., 100, 102, 120, 127.

14. Jonathan Mayhew, *Striving to Enter in at the Strait Gate* (Boston: Richard Draper, 1761), 46, 51; Akers, *Called Unto Liberty,* 72.

15. Jonathan Mayhew, *Two Sermons on the Nature, Extent, and Perfection of the Divine Goodness* (Boston: D. & J. Kneeland, 1763), 42, 60; Mayhew, *Striving to Enter,* 12, 22; Conforti, *Samuel Hopkins,* 118.

16. Mayhew, *Two Sermons on . . . Divine Goodness,* 65.

17. Jonathan Mayhew, *On Hearing the Word* (Boston: R. Draper), 267–68, 269, 276–

77, 403–04, 417–18; Jonathan Mayhew, *Christian Sobriety* (Boston: Richard and Samuel Draper, 1763), 59–61.

18. Samuel Clarke, *The Scripture Doctrine of the Trinity* (London: For J. Knapton, 1712), 243; Akers, *Called Unto Liberty,* 118–21.

19. Mayhew, *Two Sermons on . . . Divine Goodness,* 84; Davidson, *Logic of Millennial Thought,* 111–13; Valeri, *Law and Providence,* 61.

20. Charles Chauncy, *The Mystery hid from Ages and Generations, made Manifest by the Gospel Revelation: Or, the Salvation of All Men* (London: For C. Dilly, 1784), 12–13; Edward M. Griffin, *Old Brick: Charles Chauncy of Boston, 1705–1787* (Minneapolis: University of Minnesota Press, 1980), 111.

21. John Clarke [and Charles Chauncy], *Salvation for All Men* (Boston: T. & J. Fleet, 1782), 4, 7, 9; Charles Chauncy, *The Benevolence of the Deity* (Boston: Powars and Willis, 1784), 1, 16, 58, 60, 68, 70–71.

22. Chauncy, *The Mystery hid from Ages and Generations,* 2; Charles Chauncy, *Five Dissertations on the Scripture Account of the Fall* (London: C. Dilly, 1785), 50–61; Griffin, *Old Brick,* 123; Davidson, *Logic of Millennial Thought,* 108–11.

23. Griffin, *Old Brick,* 172; Akers, *Called Unto Liberty,* 104, 132.

24. Nathanael Emmons, *The Works of Nathanael Emmons,* ed. Jacob Ide, 2 vols. (Boston: Crocker and Brewster, 1842), 1:286. See Bruce Kuklick, *Churchmen and Philosophers: From Jonathan Edwards to John Dewey* (New Haven, Conn.: Yale University Press, 1985), 43–65.

25. Samuel Hopkins, "Life of Samuel Hopkins, D.D.," in Stephen West, ed., *Samuel Hopkins: Sketches of the Life of the Late Rev. Samuel Hopkins* (Hartford, Conn.: Hudson and Goodwin, 1805), 103; Guelzo, *Edwards on the Will,* 181, 189, 197.

26. Samuel Hopkins, *An Inquiry Into the Nature of True Holiness* (1st ed. 1773; Newport, R.I.: William Durrell, 1791), 9, 100; Samuel Hopkins, *Twenty-One Sermons on a Variety of Interesting Subjects* (Salem, Mass.: Joshua Cushing, 1803), 7; Emmons, *Works of Nathanael Emmons,* 1:277, 283.

27. Emmons, *Works of Nathanael Emmons,* 1:cliii; James Hoopes, "Calvinism and Consciousness from Edwards to Beecher," *Jonathan Edwards and the American Experience,* 216.

28. Samuel Hopkins, *The System of Doctrines,* 2 vols. (Boston: I. Thomas and E. Andrews, 1793), 1:88.

29. Hopkins, "Life of Samuel Hopkins," 88, 103; Hopkins, *System of Doctrines,* 1:A3; Nathanael Emmons, *Hopkinsian Calvinism* (Providence, R.I.: n.p., 1858), 4; George Nye Boardman, *A History of New England Theology* (New York: Randolph, 1899), 33; Conforti, *Samuel Hopkins,* 108.

30. Glenn Paul Anderson, "Joseph Bellamy (1719–1790): The Man and His Works," 2 vols. (Ph.D. diss, Boston University, 1971), 1:198; Conforti, *Samuel Hopkins,* 10; Valeri, *Law and Providence,* 9–40.

31. Valeri, *Law and Providence,* 76–90; Conforti, *Samuel Hopkins,* 98–99.

32. Joseph Bellamy, *True Religion Delineated* (Boston: S. Kneeland, 1750), 90–91.

33. Ibid., 1, 7, 15, 61; Hopkins, *Two Discourses,* 7, 9; Emmons, *System of Divinity,* 1:143.

34. Bellamy, *True Religion Delineated,* 421.

35. Sarah Osborn, *The Nature, Certainty, and Evidence of True Christianity* (Danbury, Conn.: Douglas, 1793), 13; Catherine A. Brekus, *Strangers and Pilgrims: Female Preaching in America 1740–1845* (Chapel Hill: University of North Carolina Press, 1998), 74.

36. Valeri, *Law and Providence,* 65.

37. Joseph Bellamy, *Theron, Paulinas, and Aspasio* (Boston: S. Kneeland, 1759), 16, 48, 135; Joseph Bellamy, *A Blow at the Root of the Refined Antinomianism of the Present Age* (Boston: S. Kneeland, 1763), 45; Joseph Bellamy, *Remarks on the Rev. Mr. Croswell's Letter to the Reverend Mr. Cumming* (Boston: S. Kneeland, 1763), 17; Emmons, *System of Divinity,* 2:159, 165.

38. Hopkins, *Two Discourses,* 16, 21; Emmons, *System of Divinity,* 2:46, 52.

39. Hopkins, *Inquiry Into the Nature of True Holiness,* vi, 60, 82.

40. Ibid., 197; Hopkins, "Life of Samuel Hopkins," 149, 162.

41. Samuel Hopkins, *An Enquiry Concerning the Promises of the Gospel* (Boston: McAlpine and Fleming, 1765), 27, 91.

42. Ibid., 77; Morimoto, *Jonathan Edwards and the Catholic Vision,* 34.

43. Hopkins, *Two Discourses,* 39, 56; Hopkins, *Enquiry Concerning the Promises,* 56.

44. Hopkins, *Enquiry Concerning the Promises,* 125, 139; Bellamy, *True Religion Delineated,* 175; Guelzo, *Edwards on the Will,* 120.

45. Joseph Bellamy, *That There is But One Covenant, Whereof Baptism and the Lord's Supper are Seals* (New Haven, Conn.: Green, 1769), 5, 7; Conforti, *Samuel Hopkins,* 82; Guelzo, *Edwards on the Will,* 125.

46. Hopkins, *System of Doctrines,* 1:84, 88.

47. John Smalley, *The Inability of the Sinner to Comply with the Gospel, Theological Tracts,* ed. John Brown, 3 vols. (London: A. Fullerton, 1853), 1:273; Daniel C. Garver, "John Smalley (1734–1820)," *American Writers Before 1800,* ed. James Levernier and Douglas R. Wilmes (Westport, Conn.: Greenwood, 1983), 1326–27; Emmons, *Works of Nathanael Emmons,* 1:xiii.

48. Smalley, *Inability of the Sinner,* 274, 279.

49. Emmons, *System of Divinity,* 1:307.

50. Smalley, *Inability of the Sinner,* 279, 282, 284, 331.

51. Emmons, *System of Divinity,* 1:305; Frank Hugh Foster, *A Genetic History of the New England Theology* (Chicago: University of Chicago Press, 1907), 167; Hopkins, *Twenty-One Sermons,* 208; Smalley, *Inability of the Sinner,* 95–96.

52. Joseph Bellamy, *A Letter to the Reverend Author of the Winter-Evening Conversation* (Boston: S. Kneeland, 1758), 12; Ferm, "Jonathan Edwards the Younger," 214; Samuel Hopkins, *System of Doctrines, The Works of Samuel Hopkins,* 3 vols. (Boston: Doctrinal Tract and Book Society, 1852), 1:218.

53. Bellamy, *True Religion Delineated,* 256; Foster, *Genetic History,* 174; Emmons, *System of Divinity,* 1:488–89.

54. Hopkins, *Two Discourses,* 37, 48; Smalley, *Inability of the Sinner,* 292, 305, 311; Emmons, *System of Divinity,* 1:519.

55. Samuel Hopkins, "A Particular and Critical Inquiry into the Cause, Nature, and Means of Regeneration," *Two Sermons, Works,* 3:553; Edwards Amasa Park, "Memoir [of Hopkins]," *Works,* 1:200; Stephen West, *An Essay on Moral Agency* (New Haven, Conn.: T. & S. Green, 1772), 23, 56.

56. John T. Shawcross, "Nathanael Emmons (1745–1840)," *American Writers Before 1800*, 533–36; Guelzo, *Edwards on the Will*, 111.

57. Emmons, *System of Divinity*, 1:351, 355, 384, 522; 2:114– 19, 124–28; Joseph Conforti, *Jonathan Edwards, Religious Tradition, & American Culture* (Chapel Hill: University of North Carolina Press), 128.

58. Emmons, *System of Divinity*, 1:364–73.

59. Guelzo, *Edwards on the Will*, 111.

60. Bellamy, *True Religion Delineated*, 38; Boardman, *History of New England Theology*, 80; Valeri, *Law and Providence*, 119–20.

61. Joseph Bellamy, *Sermons Upon the Following Subjects, viz., The Divinity of Jesus Christ, The Millennium, The Wisdom of God in the Permission of Sin* (Boston: Edes and Gill, 1758), 95, 104, 108, 126, 145, 159, 199.

62. Samuel Hopkins, *Sin, through Divine Interposition, an Advantage to the Universe, Works*, 2:506, 521, 534–35; Hopkins, "Life of Samuel Hopkins," 93; Hopkins, *Twenty-One Sermons*, 343, 347.

63. West, *Essay on Moral Agency*, 173–202; Emmons, *System of Divinity*, 1:213; Boardman, *History of New England Theology*, 88.

64. Bellamy, *True Religion Delineated*, 72, 308; Foster, *Genetic History*, 116, 181; Conforti, *Samuel Hopkins*, 164.

65. Ferm, "Jonathan Edwards the Younger," 92, 152, 172.

66. Jonathan Edwards, Jr., "The Necessity of the Atonement and the Consistency Between that and Free Grace, in Forgiveness," *Theological Tracts,* 3 vols., ed. John Brown (London: Fullarton, 1853), 1:337, 358, 368.

67. Joseph Bellamy, "The Divinity of Jesus Christ," *Sermons Upon the Following Subjects*, 38–41; Samuel Hopkins, *The Importance and Necessity of a Christians considering Jesus Christ in the Extent of his high and glorious Character* (Boston: Kneeland and Adams, 1768), 15, 23.

68. Samuel Hopkins, *An Inquiry Concerning the Future State of Those Who Die in their Sins* (Newport, R.I.: Solomon Southwick, 1783), 137, 142.

69. Samuel Hopkins, *A Treatise on the Millennium* (Edinburgh: G. Caw, 1806), 52, 116, 145; Bellamy, "The Millennium," *Sermons Upon the Following Subjects*, 65, 68.

70. David W. Kling, *A Field of Divine Wonders* (University Park: Pennsylvania State University Press, 1993), 59–60; Nathan O. Hatch, *The Sacred Cause of Liberty* (New Haven, Conn.: Yale University Press, 1977), 36, 41; Stout, *New England Soul*, 233–55.

71. Conforti, *Jonathan Edwards, Religious Tradition, & American Culture*, 36–107.

72. Mills, *Inquiry Concerning the State of the Unregenerate*, 7, 42, 117, 118.

73. Moses Hemmenway, *A Discourse Concerning the Church* (Boston: Thomas & Andrews, 1792), 8, 51; Moses Mather, *A Systematic View of Divinity; Or, the Ruin and Recovery of Man* (Stanford, Conn.: Nathan Weed, 1813), 196–98.

74. Edmund S. Morgan, *The Gentle Puritan: A Life of Ezra Stiles, 1727–1795* (New Haven, Conn.: Yale University Press, 1962), 175.

75. William Hart, *A Letter to the Rev. Samuel Hopkins* (New London, Conn.: T. Green, 1770), 11; William Hart, *Remarks on President Edwards's Dissertations Concerning the Nature of True Virtue* (New Haven, Conn.: T. & S. Green, 1771), 23, 52;

Moses Hemmenway, *Seven Sermons* (Boston: Kneeland and Adams, 1767), 11, 56; Moses Hemmenway, *Remarks on Mr. Hopkins's Answer* (Boston: J. Kneeland, 1774), 13, 44, 49.

76. Hart, *Remarks,* 40, 51; Hemmenway, *Remarks,* 17, 103; Moses Hemmenway, *A Vindication of the Power, Obligation, and Encouragement of the Unregenerate to Attend the Means of Grace* (Boston: J. Kneeland, 1772), 46, 50.

77. Hart, *Remarks,* 7, 9, 19, 29, 33–34.

78. Hemmenway, *Remarks,* 145; Ezra Stiles Ely, *A Contrast Between Calvinism and Hopkinsianism* (New York: S. Whiting, 1811), 74.

79. Hemmenway, *Vindication,* 12, 21, 77; Hemmenway, *Remarks,* 127– 28; Mather, *Systematic View of Divinity,* 60.

80. James Dana, *The "Examination of the Late Revd. President Edwards's Enquiry on the Freedom of the Will" Continued* (New Haven, Conn.: Thomas and Samuel Green, 1773), v–vi, 34–35, 37, 54.

81. James Dana, *Examination of the Late Revd. President Edwards's Enquiry on the Freedom of the Will* (Boston: Daniel Kneeland, 1770), 48– 49.

82. Dana, *Examination Continued,* 93; Foster, *Genetic History,* 234; Mather, *Systematic View of Divinity,* 234.

83. Hemmenway, *Remarks,* 42 110, 125; Samuel Moody, *An Attempt to Point Out the Fatal and Pernicious Consequences of the Rev. Mr. Joseph Bellamy's Doctrines Respecting Moral Evil* (Boston: Edes and Gill, 1759), 25.

84. Hemmenway, *Remarks,* 128, 131; Hemmenway, *Seven Sermons,* 30.

85. Mills, *Inquiry,* 55; William Hart, *Brief Remarks On a Number of False Propositions and Dangerous Errors* (New London, Conn.: Timothy Green, 1769), 41; Hemmenway, *Seven Sermons,* 84.

86. Hart, *Brief Remarks,* 45; Hemmenway, *Seven Sermons,* 78; Hart, *Letter,* 5–9; Ely, *Contrast,* 131, 146.

87. Samuel Hopkins, "An Answer to the Rev. Mr. Hemmenway's 'Vindication,'" *Inquiry Into the Nature of True Holiness,* 208; Hemmenway, *Remarks,* 141.

88. Hart, *Brief Remarks,* 58; Ely, *Contrast,* 224.

89. Ely, *Contrast,* 94–107; Morgan, *Gentle Puritan,* 169.

90. Foster, *Genetic History,* 174; Thomas Clap, *An Essay on the Nature and Foundation of Moral Virtue and Obligation* (New Haven, Conn.: B. Mecom, 1765), ii; Mark A. Noll, "Moses Mather (Old Calvinist) and the Evolution of Edwardseanism," *Church History* 49 (1980):281.

91. Ezra Stiles, *The Literary Diary of Ezra Stiles,* ed. Franklin Bowditch, 3 vols. (New York: Charles Scribner's Sons, 1901), 3:274.

Chapter 7. The Deists

1. Edward, Lord Herbert of Cherbury, *De Veritate,* trans. Merick H. Carré (Bristol: Arrowsmith, 1937), 308.

2. John Toland, *Christianity Not Mysterious* (1696), *Deism and Natural Religion,* ed. E. Graham Waring (New York: Frederick Ungar, 1967), 4.

3. Anthony Collins, *A Discourse of the Grounds and Reasons of the Christian Religion* (London: n.p., 1724), 31, 37, 48; Sullivan, *John Toland and the Deist Controversy,* 208, 217–18, 221.

4. Thomas Woolston, *Discourses on the Miracles of our Saviour* (1728), *Deism and Natural Religion,* 66, 70, 75; Thomas Woolston, *Defense* (1729), ibid., 79.

5. Matthew Tindal, *Christianity as Old as the Creation, Deism and Natural Religion,* 109, 149, 161.

6. G. Adolph Koch, *Republican Religion: The American Revolution and the Cult of Reason* (1st ed. 1933; Gloucester, Mass.: Peter Smith, 1964), 55; Herbert M. Morais, *Deism in Eighteenth-Century America* (1st ed. 1934; New York: Russell and Russell, 1960), 120. Henry May, *The Enlightenment in America* (New York: Oxford University Press, 1976), 116–32, does not emphasize the distinction, and Kerry S. Walters, "Elihu Palmer and the Religion of Nature," *Elihu Palmer's 'Principles of Nature': Text and Commentary* (Wolfeboro, N.H.: Longwood Academic, 1990), 24, warns that it can be misleading if it suggests a theological difference as opposed to a difference in public self-presentation. See also Kerry S. Walters, ed., *The American Deists* (Lawrence: University Press of Kansas, 1992), 26– 27. I employ the distinction to suggest a difference in style and attitude.

7. Ethan Allen, *Reason the Only Oracle of Man, Or a Compendious System of Natural Religion* (Bennington, Vt.: Haswell and Russell, 1784), "Preface," 200; Blount, *Miscellaneous Works,* 91; Elihu Palmer, *Principles of Nature; Or, a Development of the Moral Causes of Happiness and Misery Among the Human Species* (1st ed. 1801/1802; London: R. Carlile, 1819), 198; Thomas Paine, *The Age of Reason,* ed. Philip S. Foner (Secaucus, N.J.: Citadel Press, 1974), 84.

8. Anthony Collins, *A Discourse of Freethinking* (1713), *Deism and Natural Religion, 63;* Toland, *Christianity Not Mysterious,* ibid., 2.

9. Allen, *Reason the Only Oracle,* "Preface," n.p.

10. Palmer, *Principles of Nature,* 97–99; Kerry S. Walters, "Elihu Palmer's Crusade for Rational Religion," *Religious Humanism* 24 (1990):121.

11. Paine, *Age of Reason,* 69; Kerry S. Walters, *Rational Infidels: The American Deists* (Durango, Colo.: Longwood Academic, 1992), 124– 25; Palmer, *Principles of Nature,* 17; Benjamin Franklin, *Papers of Benjamin Franklin,* 35 vols., ed. L. W. Labaree et al. (New Haven, Conn.: Yale University Press, 1961), 3:88–89; Benjamin Franklin, *Writings of Benjamin Franklin,* ed. Albert Henry Smith, 10 vols. (New York: Macmillan, 1905–07), 10:84; Thomas Jefferson, *The Writings of Thomas Jefferson,* ed. A. A. Lipscomb and A. E Bergh, 20 vols. (Washington, D.C.: Jefferson Memorial Association, 1904), 14:149, 15:323.

12. Allen, *Reason the Only Oracle,* 159; Palmer, *Principles of Nature,* 111.

13. Jefferson, *Writings,* 15:272–76, 426; Daniel Boorstin, *The Lost World of Thomas Jefferson* (New York: Beacon Press, 1960), 27– 56.

14. Paine, *Age of Reason,* 55–57; Palmer, *Principles of Nature,* 18.

15. Jefferson, *Writings,* 14:149, 15:323–24.

16. Ibid., 15:75; Paine, *Age of Reason,* 92–94.

17. Allen, *Reason the Only Oracle,* 468; Palmer, *Principles of Nature,* iv, 12, 168, 178.

18. Benjamin Franklin, *The Autobiography of Benjamin Franklin,* ed. Benjamin W.

Labaree et al. (New Haven, Conn.: Yale University Press, 1964), 113; Franklin, *Papers*, 1:104; Walters, *Rational Infidels*, 72.

19. Franklin, *Papers*, 2:28–33; Norman S. Fiering, "Benjamin Franklin and the Way to Virtue," *American Quarterly* 30 (1978):217–18.

20. Franklin, *Papers*, 4:504–06; Franklin, Writings, 10:84; Alfred Owen Aldridge, *Benjamin Franklin and Nature's God* (Durham, N.C.: Duke University Press, 1967), 174.

21. Jefferson, *Writings*, 10:380, 13:350, 12:236, 14:233.

22. Franklin, *Writings*, 10:84; Jefferson, *Writings*, 10:380; Paine, *Age of Reason*, 53–55; Palmer, *Principles of Nature*, 25, 87, 90–91.

23. Allen, *Reason the Only Oracle*, 188, 200; Palmer, *Principles of Nature*, 22; Paine, *Age of Reason*, 66, 69.

24. Allen, *Reason the Only Oracle*, 426; Paine, *Age of Reason*, 63, 68.

25. Paine, *Age of Reason*, 105–06, 110–12, 141, 164–67.

26. Allen, *Reason the Only Oracle*, 285; Palmer, *Principles of Nature*, 76, 79; Paine, *Age of Reason*, 96–97.

27. Palmer, *Principles of Nature*, 65, 69; Allen, *Reason the Only Oracle*, 235.

28. Jefferson, *Writings*, 10:174; 15:240, 269–76; Franklin, *Papers*, 1:102–04; Allen, *Reason the Only Oracle*, 51, 83, 247; Palmer, *Principles of Nature*, 53, 198. Elizabeth E. Dunn, "From a Bold Youth to a Reflective Sage: A Reevaluation of Benjamin Franklin's Religion," *Pennsylvania Magazine of History and Biography* 111 (1987):512, suggests that Franklin's polytheistic comments had an ironic edge; Kerry S. Walters, *Benjamin Franklin and His Gods* (Urbana: University of Illinois Press, 1999), 75–92, argues that he was referring to diverse cultural perspectives on God; Aldridge, *Benjamin Franklin and Nature's God*, 28–29, contends for a literal polytheism.

29. Allen, *Reason the Only Oracle*, 113, 117, 176, 388; Palmer, *Principles of Nature*, 32, 35, 104; Ronald L. Bosco, " 'He that best understands the World, least likes it': The Dark Side of Benjamin Franklin," *Pennsylvania Magazine of History and Biography* 111 (1987):526–48.

30. Philip Freneau, *Letters on Various Interesting and Important Subjects* (Philadelphia: D. Hogan, 1799), 37–38; Walters, "Elihu Palmer and the Religion of Nature," 11; Richard H. Popkin, "The Age of Reason versus the Age of Revelation," *Deism, Masonry, and the Enlightenment*, ed. J. A. Leo Lemay (Newark: University of Delaware Press, 1987); 158–70; Mark C. Carnes, "Manmade Religion: Victorian Fraternal Rituals," *Religion and American Culture*, ed. David G. Hackett (New York: Routledge, 1995), 317–26.

31. Frances Wright, *Life, Letters, and Lectures, Women Without Superstition: The Collected Writings of Women Freethinkers of the Nineteenth and Twentieth Centuries*, ed. Annie Laurie Gaylor (Madison, Wisc.: Freedom from Religion Foundation, 1997), 38–39.

32. Stiles MSS, Yale University, p. 460, as cited in I. Woodbridge Riley, *American Philosophy: The Early Schools* (New York: Dodd, Mead, 1907), 217; Joseph Butler, *Analogy of Religion, Natural and Revealed, to the Constitution and Course of Nature* (1st ed. 1736; New York: Ivison, Blakeman, Taylor, 1872), 273–319.

33. Uzal Ogden, *Antidote to Deism: The Deist Unmasked*, 2 vols. (Newark, N.J.: John Woods, 1795), 1:67; Elias Boudinot, *The Age of Revelation, or the Age of Reason Shown to be an Age of Infidelity* (Philadelphia: Asbury Dickens, 1801), xix–xxi.

34. Andrew Broaddus, *The Age of Reason and Revelation* (Richmond, Va.: Dixon, 1795), 9, 43; James H. Smylie, "Clerical Perspectives on Deism: Paine's *The Age of Reason* in Virginia," *Eighteenth-Century Studies* 6 (1972–73):203–20; Alfred Owen Aldridge, *Man of Reason: The Life of Thomas Paine* (Philadelphia: J. B. Lippincott, 1959), 234.

35. Broaddus, *Age of Reason and Revelation*, 9, 12, 44, 49, 63; James Muir, *An Examination of the Principles Contained in the Age of Reason* (Baltimore, Md.: S. & J. Adams, 1795), 119; Ogden, *Antidote to Deism*, 1:127.

36. Ogden, *Antidote to Deism*, 33; Broaddus, *Age of Reason and Revelation*, 51.

37. Muir, *Examination of the Principles*, 114; Broaddus, *Age of Reason and Revelation*, 24.

38. Broaddus, *Age of Reason and Revelation*, 26; Ogden, *Antidote to Deism*, 1:165–70.

Chapter 8. Evidential Christianity

1. Samuel Miller, *A Brief Retrospect of the Eighteenth Century,* 2 vols. (New York: T. & J. Swords, 1803), 2:431, 433–34.

2. Leonard Woods, *The Works of Leonard Woods,* 5 vols. (Andover, Mass.: Flagg and Wardwell, 1849), 1:33, 53, 86; Leonard Woods, *A Course of Study in Christian Theology, Mental Discipline,* ed. Henry F. Burden (New York: Jonathan Leavitt, 1830), 211–12.

3. Miller, *Brief Retrospect,* 1:202; Theodore Dwight Bozeman, *Protestants in an Age of Science: The Baconian Ideal and Antebellum American Religious Thought* (Chapel Hill: University of North Carolina Press, 1977), 3; Samuel Tyler, *A Discourse of the Baconian Philosophy* (Frederick City, Md.: Ezekiel Hughes, 1844), ix, 3.

4. George H. Daniels, *American Science in the Age of Jackson* (New York: Columbia University Press, 1968), 65; B. B. Smith, "Theology, A Strictly Inductive Science," *Literary and Theological Review* 2 (1835):89–95.

5. Miller, *Brief Retrospect,* 2:1803.

6. Herbert Hovenkamp, *Science and Religion in America 1800–1860* (Philadelphia: University of Pennsylvania Press, 1978), 19; Nathan Bangs, "Introduction," *The Works of Thomas Reid,* ed. Nathan Bangs, 3 vols. (New York: N. Bangs and T. Mason, 1822), 1:iii; "The Collected Works of Dugald Stewart," *Quarterly Review of the Methodist Episcopal Church, South* 11 (1857):619.

7. Thomas Reid, *Works of Thomas Reid,* 2:25.

8. Ibid., 1:131–32.

9. Ibid., 2:44, 83.

10. Ibid., 1:152, 2:260.

11. Ibid., 1:362–63, 2:311–71; Andrew Seth Pringle-Pattison, *Scottish Philosophy* (Edinburgh: William Blackwood, 1885), 73–141; Selwyn A. Grave, *The Scottish Philosophy of Common Sense* (Oxford: Oxford University Press, 1960).

12. Reid, *Works,* 1:131, 191, 362–63; 2:311.

13. Ibid., 3:264, 204–05, 307, 309; Thomas Reid, *Essays on the Active Powers of the Mind* (Cambridge, Mass.: MIT Press, 1969), 463.

14. Dugald Stewart, *Elements of the Philosophy of the Human Mind* (Brattleborough, Vt.: William Fessenden, 1813), 17, 86.

15. William Hamilton, *Lectures on Metaphysics,* 2 vols. (Boston: Gould and Lincoln, 1860), 1:34, 2:530.

16. Stewart, *Elements,* 92.

17. Tyler, *Discourse,* 116; Miller, *Brief Retrospect,* 2:4; Alexander H. Everett, *History of Intellectual Philosophy, The Transcendentalists,* ed. Perry Miller (Cambridge, Mass.: Harvard University Press, 1950), 29.

18. Edwards A. Park, *Duties of a Theologian* (New York: American Biblical Repertory, 1839), 12; "Elements of Mental Philosophy," *Biblical Repertory* 2, n.s. (1830):183–210.

19. Joseph Haven, *Mental Philosophy: Including the Intellect, Sensibilities, and Will* (Boston, Mass.: Gould and Lincoln, 1857), 23.

20. Edward Robinson, *The Bible and Its Literature: An Inaugural Address* (New York: American Biblical Repository, 1841), 16, 32; Wayland, *Theological Department in Yale College,* 189; Stanley G. French, Jr., "Some Theological and Ethical Uses of Mental Philosophy in Early Nineteenth Century America" (Ph.D. diss., University of Wisconsin, 1967), 130.

21. Samuel Stanhope Smith, *A Comprehensive View of the Leading and Most Important Principles of Natural and Revealed Religion* (New Brunswick, N.J.: Deare and Myer, 1815), 217.

22. Ibid., 3–5.

23. Francis Bowen, *Critical Essays on a Few Subjects Connected with the History and Present Condition of Speculative Philosophy* (Boston: H. B. Williams, 1842), 182; Woods, *Theological Lectures, Works,* 1:207; [E. A. Park and B. B. Edwards], "Natural Theology," *Bibliotheca Sacra* 3 (1846):256; Charles Hodge, *Systematic Theology,* 2 vols. (New York: Scribner, Armstrong, 1874), 1:205; Smith, *Comprehensive View,* 4.

24. Smith, *Comprehensive View,* 5, 8.

25. William Paley, *Natural Theology: Selections,* ed. Frederick Ferré (New York: Bobbs-Merrill, 1963), xiii. The publishing data came from Orville Roorbach, *Bibliotheca Americana,* 4 vols. (New York: O. A. Roorbach, 1852).

26. Paley, *Natural Theology,* 3–6, 13–19; James B. Walker, *God Revealed in the Process of Creation and By the Manifestation of Jesus Christ* (Boston: Gould and Lincoln, 1857), viii.

27. W. C. Dana, "A Reasonable Answer to the Sceptics," *Southern Presbyterian Review* 11 (1858):391; A. B. Van Zandt, "The Necessity of a Revelation and the Condition of Men Without It," *Lectures on the Evidences of Christianity Delivered at the University of Virginia,* ed. W. H. Ruffner (New York: Robert Carter, 1852), 52.

28. [Park and Edwards], "Natural Theology," 267; "The Progress of Science and Its Connection with Scripture," *Quarterly Review of the Methodist Episcopal Church, South* 11 (1857):44–73; E. A. Rockwell, "The Alphabet of Natural Theology," *Southern Presbyterian Review* 10 (1857):411–36; E. Brooks Holifield, "Science and Religion in the Old South," *Science and Medicine in the Old South,* ed. Ronald L. Numbers and Todd L. Savitt (Baton Rouge: Louisiana State University Press, 1989), 127–43.

29. Edward Hitchcock, *The Religion of Geology and Its Connected Sciences* (Boston: Phillips, Sampson, 1854), ix–x, 177, 252.

30. Ibid., 13–93, 146–218, 248, 252–84.

31. Ibid., 176, 327–70; Edward Hitchcock, "Remarks on Professor Stuart's Examination of Genesis 1 in Reference to Geology," *The Biblical Repository and Quarterly Observer* 7 (1836):482–85; D. W. Martindale, "Footprints of the Creator," *Quarterly Review of the Methodist Episcopal Church, South* 5 (1851):507.

32. Miller, *Brief Retrospect*, 1:174.

33. "Hugh Miller on the Testimony of the Rocks," *Quarterly Review of the Methodist Episcopal Church, South* 11 (1857):626.

34. Edward Hitchcock, "The Connection Between Geology and the Mosaic History of the Creation," *American Biblical Repository* 6 (1835):318; Hitchcock, *Religion of Geology*, 39.

35. Moses Stuart, "Critical Examination of Genesis 1 With Reference to Geology," *American Biblical Repertory* 7 (1836):49; Hovenkamp, *Science and Religion*, 129.

36. Hitchcock, "Remarks on Professor Stuart's Examination," *Biblical Repository*, 452; Edward Hitchcock, "The Historical and Geological Deluge Compared," *American Biblical Repository* 9 (1837):92, 100.

37. Hitchcock, "Remarks on Professor Stuart's Examination," *American Biblical Repository*, 73; Rufus P. Stebbins, "The Religion of Geology," *Christian Examiner* 53 (1852):60; Hovenkamp, *Science and Religion*, 143.

38. Hitchcock, "Remarks on Professor Stuart's Examination," *Biblical Repository*, 484.

39. John Bachman, *The Unity of the Human Race Examined on the Principles of Science* (Charleston, S.C.: C. Canning, 1850), 9, 292; Thomas Smyth, *The Unity of the Human Races, The Complete Works of the Rev. Thomas Smyth*, ed. J. W. Flinn, 10 vols. (Columbia, S.C.: R. L. Bryan, 1909– 12), 8:116–40, 319–24.

40. N. W. Taylor, "On the Authority of Reason in Theology," *Quarterly Christian Spectator* 9 (1837):125; L. W. Green, "The Harmony of Revelation and Natural Science," *Lectures on the Evidences*, 463; Albert Barnes, "Introductory Essay," *The Analogy of Religion*, by Joseph Butler (New York: Mark H. Newman, 1848), xv.

41. Taylor, "On the Authority of Reason," 152; Van Zandt, "Necessity of a Revelation," 55.

42. See, for example, Henry B. Bascom, "Lectures on the Relative Claims of Christianity and Infidelity," *Posthumous Works of the Reverend Henry B. Bascom*, 3 vols. (Nashville, Tenn.: M. E. Church South, 1917), 2:62–64.

43. Joseph Butler, *The Analogy of Religion, Natural and Revealed, to the Constitution and Course of Nature* (London: George Bell, 1889), 254; Barnes, "Introductory Essay," viii.

44. Mark Hopkins, *Lectures on the Evidences of Christianity* (Boston: T. R. Marvin, 1846), 41; "Evidences of Revealed Religion," *Christian Spectator* 7 (1825):458.

45. Lyman Beecher, "Letter from Dr. Beecher to Dr. Woods," *Spirit of the Pilgrims* 5 (1832):396; Charles Pettit McIlvaine, *Evidences of Christianity, in their External, or Historical Division* (1st ed. 1832; Philadelphia: Smith and English, 1855), 23, 25; Hopkins, *Lectures on the Evidences*, 15.

46. Van Zandt, "Necessity of a Revelation," 31; William S. Plumer, "Man Responsible for his Belief," *Lectures on the Evidences*, 16.

47. John Gorham Palfrey, *Lectures on the Evidences of Christianity,* 2 vols. (Boston: James Munroe, 1843), 1:8, 26; Archibald Alexander, *Evidences of the Authenticity, Inspiration, and Canonical Authority of the Holy Scriptures* (Philadelphia: Presbyterian Board of Publications, 1832), 186–90.

48. Harvey Newcomb, *Christianity Demonstrated* (Boston, Mass.: Kendall and Lincoln, 1848), 82; R. J. Breckinridge, "The General Internal Evidence of Christianity," *Lectures on the Evidences,* 346; James W. Alexander, "The Character of Jesus Christ an Argument for the Divine Origin of Christianity," ibid., 195; Smith, *Comprehensive View,* 197.

49. McIlvaine, *Evidences of Christianity,* 184.

50. Ibid., 193, 208; Alexander T. McGill, "Prophecy," *Lectures on the Evidences,* 112, 120.

51. Palfrey, *Evidences of Christianity,* 1:38, 46; Henry Ruffner, "Miracles, Considered as an Evidence of Christianity," *Lectures on the Evidences,* 61.

52. David Hume, "Of Miracles," *Hume on Religion,* ed. Richard Wollheim (London: Meridian, 1963), 211–12.

53. Thomas Ralston, *Elements of Divinity* (1st ed. 1847; Nashville, Tenn.: A. H. Redford, 1878), 611; Hovenkamp, *Science and Religion,* 84.

54. Hopkins, *Lectures on the Evidences,* 39; Palfrey, *Evidences of Christianity,* 1:55.

55. Ruffner, "Miracles," 86–102.

56. John Stone, "The Mysteries Opened, or Scriptural Views of Preaching," *Biblical Repertory and Princeton Review* 17 (1845):405.

57. Jerry Wayne Brown, *The Rise of Biblical Criticism in America, 1800–1870* (Middletown, Conn.: Wesleyan University Press, 1969), 21, 48.

58. Joseph Stevens Buckminster, *Sermons by the Late Rev. J. S. Buckminster* (Boston: John Eliot, 1814), 1–37, 105–07.

59. John H. Giltner, *Moses Stuart: The Father of Biblical Science in America* (Atlanta, Ga.: Scholars Press, 1988), 52–53.

60. Ibid., 29–47, 54, 66, 74.

61. Andrews Norton, *The Evidences of the Genuineness of the Gospels,* 2 vols. (London: John Chapman, 1847), 2:27; Brown, *Rise of Biblical Criticism,* 76, 90.

62. Norton, *Evidences of the Genuineness,* 1:36–58, 156–63; Brown, *Rise of Biblical Criticism,* 80.

63. Brown, *Rise of Biblical Criticism,* 92–93.

64. William Henry Furness, *Jesus and His Biographers; Or Remarks on the Four Gospels Revised* (Philadelphia: Carey, Lea, & Blanchard, 1838), 9, 107, 125, 238, 434.

65. Brown, *Rise of Biblical Criticism,* 125–36.

66. Stephen Bullfinch, "Strauss's Life of Jesus — The Mythic Theory," *Christian Examiner* 39 (1845):145–69; George Edward Ellis, "The Mythical Theory Applied to the Life of Jesus," *Christian Examiner* 41 (1846):313–54.

67. Theodore Parker, "Strauss's Life of Jesus" (1837), *The Critical and Miscellaneous Writings of Theodore Parker* (Boston: Little, Brown, 1856), 329–37, 339–40.

68. Gerald P. Fogarty, S.J., *American Catholic Biblical Scholarship: A History from the Early Republic to Vatican II* (San Francisco: Harper and Row, 1989), 14–34.

69. Alexander, *Evidences,* 10.

70. Smith, *Faith and Philosophy,* 27; Charles G. Finney, *Finney's Lectures on Systematic Theology* (Grand Rapids, Mich.: Eerdmans, 1951), 10; "On Christianity Considered as a Practical System," *Virginia Evangelical and Literary Magazine* 5 (1822):115.

Chapter 9. Unitarian Virtue

1. W. E. Channing, "Evidences of Christianity," *A Selection from the Works of William E. Channing* (Boston: American Unitarian Association, 1855), 151.

2. William Ware, "Antiquity and Revival of Unitarian Christianity," *An American Reformation: A Documentary History of Unitarian Christianity,* ed. Sydney E. Ahlstrom and Jonathan S. Carey (Middletown, Conn.: Wesleyan University Press, 1985), 138, 146; George E. Ellis, *A Half Century of the Unitarian Controversy* (Boston: Crosby, Nichols, 1857), 15–16, 19, 24; Conrad Wright, *The Beginnings of Unitarianism in America* (Boston: Beacon Press, 1955), 5–8.

3. Ellis, *Half Century,* xxix, xx, 25; Edward B. Hall, *What Is It To Be a Unitarian?* (Boston: Gray and Bowen, 1832), 6; Alvan Lamson, "A Plea for Theology," *Christian Examiner* 39 (1845):291; Lawrence Buell, "The Literary Significance of the Unitarian Movement," *American Unitarianism 1805–1865,* ed. Conrad Wright (Boston: Northeastern University Press, 1989), 165–68.

4. Hall, *What Is It To Be a Unitarian?,* 6; Ellis, *Half Century,* 15–16; George W. Burnap, "The Importance of Systematic Theology and the Duty of the Unitarian Clergy in Relation to It," *Christian Examiner* 50 (1850):168.

5. Ellis, *Half Century,* xx, 27, 43, 71, 321.

6. George Wills Cooke, *Unitarianism in America* (Boston: American Unitarian Association, 1902), 118.

7. W. E. Channing, "A Letter to the Rev. Samuel C. Thacher" (1815), *American Reformation,* 81.

8. Paul K. Conkin, "Priestley and Jefferson," *Religion in a Revolutionary Age,* ed. Ronald Hoffman and Peter J. Albert (Charlottesville: University Press of Virginia, 1994), 290–307; Elizabeth M. Geffen, *Philadelphia Unitarianism 1796–1861* (Philadelphia: University of Pennsylvania Press, 1961), 17–85; David P. Edgell, *William Ellery Channing: An Intellectual Portrait* (Boston: Beacon Press, 1955), 106; Channing, "Letter to Thacher," 78.

9. W. E. Channing, *Unitarian Christianity* (1817), *Works* (1855), 182, 187, 217.

10. Moses Stuart, *Letters to the Rev. Wm. E. Channing* (1st ed. 1819; Andover, Mass.: Flagg and Gould, 1846), 20, 24, 49, 52; Moses Stuart, *Letters on the Eternal Generation of the Son* (Andover, Mass.: Flagg and Gould, 1822), 92–94; Foster, *Genetic History,* 229.

11. Andrews Norton, *A Statement of Reasons for Not Believing the Doctrines of the Trinitarians,* 3d ed. (Boston: American Unitarian Association, 1867), xlviii, 48, 57; Lilian Handlin, "Babylon est delenda — the Young Andrews Norton," *American Unitarianism,* 64.

12. Norton, *Statement of Reasons,* 40, 50, 72, 95, 156, 164.

13. Ibid., 377; Leonard Woods, *Letters to Unitarians Occasioned by the Sermons of the Reverend William C. Channing* (Andover, Mass.: Flagg and Gould, 1820), 31.

14. Woods, *Letters to Unitarians,* 27, 41.

15. Henry Ware, *Letters Addressed to Trinitarians and Calvinists* (Cambridge, Mass.: Hilliard and Metcalf, 1820), 20, 32, 37.

16. Woods, *Letters to Unitarians,* 23; Ware, *Letters,* 125; Henry Ware, *An Answer to Dr. Woods' Reply, In a Second Series of Letters Addressed to Trinitarians and Calvinists* (Cambridge, Mass.: Hilliard and Metcalf, 1822), 99; Jared Sparks, "The Comparative Moral Tendency of the Leading Doctrines of Calvinism and the Sentiments of Unitarians" (1823), *American Reformation,* 338.

17. W. E. Channing, *The Perfect Life, The Works of William E. Channing,* ed. William Henry Channing (Boston: American Unitarian Association, 1896), 1010.

18. W. E. Channing, "Christian Worship," *The Works of William E. Channing,* 6 vols. (Boston: George G. Channing, 1849), 4:342–43, 347–54; Conrad Wright, *The Liberal Christians* (Boston: Beacon Press, 1970), 25.

19. Richard Price, *A Review of the Chief Questions and Difficulties of Morals, British Moralists,* 2:106, 114; Edgell, *William Ellery Channing,* 12.

20. Price, *Review,* 106, 114, 124, 142–43, 144–49; Elizabeth Peabody, *Reminiscences of Rev. Wm. Ellery Channing* (Boston: Roberts Brothers, 1880), 368.

21. W. E. Channing, *Unitarian Christianity, Works* (1849), 3:64–65; W. E. Channing, "Christianity a Rational Religion," *Works* (1855), 32–38; W. E. Channing, "The Evidences of Revealed Religion," ibid., 65–93.

22. Channing, "Evidences of Christianity," *Works* (1855), 115; Channing, *Unitarian Christianity* (1849), 75, 82, 88, 94; Channing, "Letter to Thacher," 82; Channing, *The Perfect Life,* 1001 (quotation), 1004.

23. Channing, *The Perfect Life,* 988, 1010; Channing, *Unitarian Christianity* (1855), 215–17; Wright, *The Liberal Christians,* 28; Daniel Walker Howe, "The Cambridge Platonists of Old England and the Cambridge Platonists of New England," *American Unitarianism,* 87–110; Daniel Walker Howe, *The Unitarian Conscience: Harvard Moral Philosophy, 1805–1861* (Cambridge, Mass.: Harvard University Press, 1970), 22–43.

24. W. E. Channing, "The Evil of Sin," *Works* (1849), 3:221; W. E. Channing, "Likeness to God," *Works* (1849), 3:231, 247; Channing, *The Perfect Life,* 931.

25. W. E. Channing, "Unitarian Christianity Most Favorable to Piety," *Works* (1855), 229; Channing, *Unitarian Christianity* (1855), 190–95; Robert Leet Patterson, *The Philosophy of William Ellery Channing* (New York: Bookman, 1952), 70; Channing, *The Perfect Life,* 936.

26. Channing, "Likeness to God," 228, 240, 241.

27. Ibid., 233, 238, 239; Channing, *The Perfect Life,* 931, 970.

28. Channing, *The Perfect Life,* 996; Channing, "Likeness to God," 479.

29. Channing, "Likeness to God," 470; Channing, "Letter to Thacher," 78, 79, 81; W. E. Channing, "Extract from a Letter on Creeds," *Works* (1855), 343; Channing, *The Perfect Life,* 1008; W. E. Channing, "Love to Christ," *Works* (1849), 4:193.

30. Channing, "Unitarian Christianity Most Favorable to Piety," 259; Channing, *Unitarian Christianity* (1849), 89, 92.

31. W. E. Channing, "The Moral Argument Against Calvinism," *Works* (1855), 290; Channing, *The Perfect Life,* 972, 1009; W. E. Channing, "Objections to Unitarian Christianity Considered," *Works* (1855), 276; Channing, *Unitarian Christianity* (1855), 214–15.

32. Patterson, *Philosophy of Channing*, 65.

33. John Brazer, *The Power of Unitarianism Over the Affections* (Boston: Bowles, 1829), 3, 8; Samuel Barrett, *The Doctrine of Religious Experience* (Boston: Bowles, 1829), 5, 11; *An Experimental Religion* (Boston: Bowles and Dearborn, 1827), 3; Ezra Stiles Gannett, *Unitarian Christianity—What It Is and What It Is Not* (Boston: William Crosby, 1840), 32; Howe, *Unitarian Conscience*, 151–73.

34. Henry Ware, Jr., *On the Formation of the Christian Character* (Boston: J. Munro, 1845), 7, 9, 105, 106; Howe, *Unitarian Conscience*, 106–12.

35. Lydia Maria Child, *The Progress of Religious Ideas Through Successive Ages*, 3 vols. (New York: C. S. Francis, 1855), 3:433, 450–51.

36. Ezra Stiles Gannett, *Christian Unitarianism Not a Negative System* (Boston: Charles Bowen, 1835), 4.

37. Gannett, *Unitarian Christianity*, 4, 8, 15, 33; N. L. Frothingham, *Deism or Christianity? Four Discourses* (Boston: Crosby and Nichols, 1845), 26.

38. James Walker, *Reason, Faith, and Duty* (Boston: Roberts Brothers, 1877), 37–61; Francis Bowen, "Emerson's Nature," *The Transcendentalists*, 174; Francis Bowen, "Locke and Transcendentalists," ibid., 176.

39. Howe, *Unitarian Conscience*, 69–81.

40. Orville Dewey, "On Miracles," *Discourses and Reviews Upon Questions in Controversial Theology and Practical Religion* (New York: C. S. Francis, 1846), 232, 244; Andrews Norton, *A Discourse on the Latest Form of Infidelity* (Cambridge, Mass.: John Owen, 1839), 11, 13, 23, 55.

41. Andrew Preston Peabody, *An Essay on the Prophecies Relating to the Messiah* (Boston: James Munroe, 1835), 22; Frothingham, *Deism or Christianity?*, 14, 43; Brown, *Rise of Biblical Criticism*, 125–36.

42. William Ware, "Antiquity and Revival of Unitarian Christianity," *American Reformation*, 137; Orville Dewey, *Remarks on the Sacred Scriptures, and on Belief and Unbelief* (Boston: James Munroe, 1839), 18; Andrew P. Peabody, *Lectures on Christian Doctrine* (Boston: James Munroe, 1844), 20, 55; Abiel Abbot Livermore, "The Epistle of Paul to the Romans," *American Reformation*, 276.

43. Henry Ware, Jr., "The Personality of the Deity," *The Works of Henry Ware, Jr.* (Boston: James Munroe, 1847), 3:27, 32; Ezra Stiles Gannett, *The Faith of the Unitarian Christian Explained, Justified, and Distinguished* (Boston: Crosby and Nichols, 1845), 8.

44. Henry Ware, Jr., *The Life of the Saviour* (1st ed. 1833; Boston: James Munroe, 1836), 269.

45. Samuel Gilman, *Unitarian Christianity Free from Objectionable Extremes* (Boston: Gray and Bowen, 1829), 7, 8, 10; Ellis, *Half Century*, 144; Earl Morse Wilbur, *A History of Unitarianism in Transylvania, England, and America* (Boston: Beacon Press, 1945), 463; Gannett, *Unitarian Christianity*, 25; William G. Eliot, *Discourses on the Doctrines of Christianity* (Boston: American Unitarian Association, 1857), 101–26.

46. Ellis, *Half Century*, xv; Gannett, *Faith of the Unitarian Christian*, 26; Gannett, *Unitarian Christianity*, 27; Eliot, *Discourses*, 127–28.

47. Dewey, *Discourses and Reviews*, 319; F. W. P. Greenwood, *Sermons* (Boston: Charles Little, 1844), 278.

48. Henry Ware, Jr., "The Doctrine of Probation," *Works*, 3:412, 424; William Ware, *The Danger of Delay* (Boston: Gray and Bowen, 1829), 5, 14.

49. Ware, "Doctrine of Probation," 426, 428; Gannett, *Unitarian Christianity,* 29; James Walker, "The Day of Judgment," *American Reformation,* 308.

50. W. E. Channing, *The Future Life* (London: John Mardon, 1836), 8–22; Colleen McDannell and Bernhard Lang, *Heaven: A History* (New York: Random House, 1988), 69–110, 228–75.

51. Andrew Preston Peabody, *Christian Consolations* (Boston: William Crosby and H. P. Nichols, 1847), 189; F. W. P. Greenwood, *Sermons of Consolation* (Boston: Little and Brown, 1844), 202; Walker, "The Day of Judgment," *American Reformation,* 303–07.

52. Frederic Henry Hedge, "The Broad Church," *Christian Examiner* 69 (1860):54–66; F. H. Hedge, ed., *Recent Inquiries in Theology, by English Churchmen* (Boston: Walker, Wise, 1860).

53. James Freeman Clarke, *Orthodoxy: Its Truths and Errors* (Boston: American Unitarian Association, 1866), 439; James Freeman Clarke, *Ten Great Religions: An Essay in Comparative Theology,* 2 vols. (Boston: Houghton, Mifflin, 1871), 2:361; Frederic Henry Hedge, *Reason in Religion* (Boston: Walker, Fuller, 1865), 4–17, 197–223.

54. F. H. Hedge, *An Address Delivered Before the Graduating Class of the Divinity School in Cambridge* (Cambridge, Mass.: John Bartlett, 1849), 17.

55. James Freeman Clarke, *The Church — As It Is, As It Was, and As It Ought to Be* (Boston: Greene, 1848), 23–25; James Freeman Clarke, *The Church of the Disciples in Boston* (Boston: Greene, 1846), 12– 15; James Freeman Clarke, "Orestes Brownson's Argument for the Roman Church," *Christian Examiner* 48 (1850):227–47.

56. Frederic Henry Hedge, "Coleridge," *The Transcendentalists,* 66–72; Henry A. Pochman, *German Culture in America* (Madison: University of Wisconsin Press, 1957), 47; Hedge, *Address,* 9, 10, 15; Frederic Henry Hedge, "Ecclesiastical Christendom," *Christian Examiner* 51 (1851):113.

57. Hedge, "Ecclesiastical Christendom," 129; Hedge, "Broad Church," 59, 62–63; Hedge, *Address,* 7; George H. Williams, *Rethinking the Unitarian Relationship with Protestantism: An Examination of the Thought of Frederic Henry Hedge* (Boston: Beacon Press, 1949).

58. Henry W. Bellows, "The Suspense of Faith: A Discourse on the Nature of the Church," *American Reformation,* 389–90, 395– 96.

59. Hedge, *Address,* 9, 14; Williams, *Rethinking,* 26.

60. Norton, *Statement of Reasons,* 6; "The First Annual Report of the Executive Committee," *American Reformation,* 170; Ware, *Letters,* 148.

61. W. E. Channing, "The System of Exclusion and Denunciation in Religion Considered," *Works* (1849), 5:375; Norton, *Statement of Reasons,* 18; Handlin, "Babylon est delenda," 56, 60; Howe, *Unitarian Conscience,* 178, 181; Hall, *What Is It to Be a Unitarian?,* 3.

Chapter 10. Universal Salvation

1. Hosea Ballou, *Commendation and Reproof of Unitarians* (Boston: Henry Bowen, 1829), 10, 15.

2. Ibid., 6; Hosea Ballou, *A Series of Letters in Defence of Divine Revelation* (Boston: Henry Bowen, 1820), 23, 65; Elhanan Winchester, *Ten Letters Addressed to Mr. Paine* (New York: Samuel Campbell, 1794), 48– 64.

3. Joseph R. Sweeney, "Elhanan Winchester and the Universal Baptists" (Ph.D. diss., University of Pennsylvania, 1969), 108, 150; David Robinson, *The Unitarians and the Universalists* (Westport, Conn.: Greenwood, 1985), 47–48.

4. Ballou, *Commendation,* 8; Hosea Ballou, *Feast of Knowledge* (Boston: Henry Bowen, 1822), 4; Russell Streeter, *A Sermon Delivered at the Installation of the Rev. Sebastian Streeter* (Boston: Henry Bowen, 1824), 6; Ann Lee Bressler, *The Universalist Movement in America, 1770–1880* (New York: Oxford University Press, 2000), 60–65.

5. Stephen A. Marini, *Radical Sects of Revolutionary New England* (Cambridge, Mass.: Harvard University Press, 1982), 68; Ernest Cassara, ed., *Universalism in America: A Documentary History* (Boston: Beacon Press, 1971), 33; Matthew Hale, *Universalism Examined, Renounced, and Exposed* (Boston: Tappen and Dennet, 1844), quoted in Foster, *Genetic History,* 326; John Murray, *The Life of the Rev. John Murray, Preacher of Universal Salvation, Written by Himself* (Boston, Mass.: A. Tompkins, 1844), 198; John Murray, *Some Hints Relative to the Forming of a Christian Church* (Boston: Joseph Bumstead, 1791), 47; Richard Eddy, *Universalism in America: A History,* 2 vols. (Boston: Universalist Publishing House, 1891–94), 2:446–69.

6. Eddy, *Universalism in America,* 1:381; Bressler, *Universalist Movement,* 97–115.

7. John L. Brooke, *The Refiner's Fire: The Making of Mormon Cosmology, 1644–1844* (Cambridge: Cambridge University Press, 1994), 48–49.

8. George de Benneville, *The Life and Trance of Dr. George de Benneville,* ed. Ernest Cassara, *Journal of the Universalist Historical Society* 2 (1960–61):82–83.

9. Georg Paul Siegvolck, *The Everlasting Gospel* (Philadelphia: n.p., 1807), 14, 23, 56, 61, 70; Robinson, *Unitarians and Universalists,* 53.

10. John Murray, *Records of the Life of the Rev. John Murray* (Boston: Bowen and Cushing, 1827), 81–128.

11. Murray, *Life of Rev. John Murray,* 109, 137, 242.

12. Ibid., 66, 202; Murray, *Some Hints,* 44.

13. John Murray, *Universalism Vindicated* (Charlestown, Mass.: J. Lamson, 1798), 14; Murray, *Life of Rev. John Murray,* 280; James Relly, *Union: Or a Treatise on the Consanguinity and Affinity Between Christ and his Church, Universalism in America,* 22–23; Sweeney, "Elhanan Winchester," 180.

14. Judith Sargent Stevens [Murray], *Some Deductions from the System Promulgated in the Page of Divine Regulation Ranged in the Form of a Catechism* (Portsmouth, N.H.: n.p., 1782), 13, 23; Sharon M. Harris, ed., *Selected Writings of Judith Sargent Murray* (New York: Oxford University Press, 1995), 3–13, 81–84.

15. John Murray, *Life of Rev. John Murray,* 266; Judith Murray, *Some Deductions,* 20.

16. Eddy, *Universalism in America,* 1:156–58; Judith Murray, *Some Deductions,* 18.

17. John Cleaveland, *An Attempt to Nip in the Bud, the Unscriptural Doctrine of Universal Salvation* (Salem, Mass.: Russell, 1776), 19, 41; Isaac Backus, *The Doctrine of Universal Salvation Examined and Refuted* (Providence, R.I.: John Carter, 1782), 3; Judith Murray, *Some Deductions,* 29–30.

18. Andrew Croswell, *Mr. Murray Unmasked* (Boston: J. Kneeland, 1775), 5; Cleaveland, *Attempt to Nip,* 30; Backus, *Doctrine of Universal Salvation,* 20.

19. Eddy, *Universalism in America,* 1:212–57.

20. Edwin Martin Stone, *Biography of Rev. Elhanan Winchester* (Boston: H. R. Brews-

ter, 1836), 27, 62; Elhanan Winchester, *A Course of Lectures on the Prophecies that Remain to be Fulfilled* (Norwich, Conn.: John Trumbull, 1789), 24; Elhanan Winchester, *The Seed of the Woman Bruising the Serpent's Head* (Philadelphia: n.p., 1781), 9, 19–34; Eddy, *Universalism in America*, 1:248, 341.

21. Winchester, *Seed of the Woman*, 19–34; Elhanan Winchester, *An Attempt to Collect the Scripture Passages in Favor of the Universal Restoration* (Providence, R.I.: Bennett Wheeler, 1786).

22. Winchester, *Seed of the Woman*, 18–19; Elhanan Winchester, *The Universal Restoration Exhibited in Four Dialogues Between a Minister and His Friend* (1st ed. 1788; Philadelphia.: T. Dobson, 1792), 1–45, 93, 174; Stone, *Biography*, 142; Sweeney, "Elhanan Winchester," 83.

23. Murray, *Life of Rev. John Murray*, 291, 293, 295; Murray, *Some Hints*, 40; Murray, *Records*, 346.

24. Elhanan Winchester, *An Elegy on the Death of John Wesley* (Philadelphia: Johnson and Justice, 1792), 5; Winchester, *Seed of the Woman*, 18; Elhanan Winchester, *The Mystic's Plea* (Philadelphia: n.p., 1781), 12.

25. Winchester, *Seed of the Woman*, 10, 12, 16; Winchester, *Mystic's Plea*, 12.

26. Winchester, *Mystic's Plea*, 8; Winchester, *Universal Restoration*, 207; Brooke, *Refiner's Fire*, 140, 206.

27. Stone, *Biography*, 67; Winchester, *Lectures on the Prophecies*, 18, 133, 135; Elhanan Winchester, *Two Lectures on the Prophecies* (Norwich, Conn.: Trumbull, 1792), 3.

28. Stone, *Biography*, 73; Winchester, *Universal Restoration*, 93; Bressler, *Universalist Movement*, 21.

29. Robinson, *Unitarians and Universalists*, 56.

30. Hosea Ballou, *Sermons on Important Doctrinal Subjects* (Boston: G. W. Bazin, 1832), xi–xv.

31. Ibid., xv; Ballou, *Defence of Divine Revelation*, 11; Hosea Ballou, *A Treatise on Atonement* (Portsmouth, N.H.: Charles Pierce, 1812), 34, 47, 116, 118.

32. Thomas Whittemore, *The Early Days of Thomas Whittemore: An Autobiography* (Boston: James Usher, 1859), 174; Ballou, *Defence of Divine Revelation*, 11, 23–67, 114, 117, 188; Ballou, *Treatise on Atonement*, v.

33. Ballou, *Treatise on Atonement*, xi.

34. Ibid., 19, 90, 99, 116, 123.

35. Ibid., 95–106.

36. Ballou, *Sermons*, 38; Ballou, *Treatise on Atonement*, 36–37, 45; Robinson, *Unitarians and Universalists*, 64; Hosea Ballou, *A Candid Review of a Pamphlet Entitled a Candid Review* (Portsmouth, N.H.: Weeks and Floyd, n.d.), 65.

37. Ballou, *Treatise on Atonement*, 66.

38. Cassara, "Introduction," *Universalism in America*, 24; Hosea Ballou, *Examination of the Doctrine of Future Retribution* (1834), ibid., 150.

39. Ballou, *Doctrine of Future Retribution*, 151–52; Bressler, *Universalist Movement in America*, 35–36.

40. Charles Hudson, *A Series of Letters Addressed to the Rev. Hosea Ballou* (1827), *Universalism in America*, 155, 160.

41. Walter Balfour, *An Inquiry into the Scriptural Import of the Words Sheol, Hades,*

Tartarus, and Gehenna (Charlestown, Mass.: G. Davidson), 24, 88; Walter Balfour, *Three Essays on the Intermediate State of the Dead* (1828), *Universalism in America,* 162; Bressler, *Universalist Movement in America,* 42.

42. Abner Kneeland, *An Introduction to the Defence of Abner Kneeland* (1834), *Universalism in America,* 166–67; Bressler, *Universalist Movement in America,* 46.

43. Hosea Ballou 2ᵈ, *The Ancient History of Universalism* (Boston: Marsh and Capen, 1829), 83, 256.

44. Thomas Whittemore, *The Modern History of Universalism from the Era of the Reformation to the Present Time* (Boston: The Author, 1830); Thomas Baldwin Thayer, *The Origin and History of the Doctrine of Endless Punishment* (Boston: J. M. Usher, 1855).

45. Bressler, *Universalist Movement in America,* 97–126.

46. Russell E. Miller, *The Larger Hope: The First Century of the Universalist Church in America 1770–1870,* 2 vols. (Boston, Mass.: Unitarian Universalist Association, 1979), 1:127–30; Holifield, "Theology as Entertainment," 506–08.

47. Bressler, *Universalist Movement in America,* 148–54.

48. Thomas Baldwin Thayer, *Theology of Universalism* (Boston: Universalist Publishing House, 1862), 20, 82.

49. Murray, *Some Hints,* 12; Whittemore, *Early Days of Thomas Whittemore,* 188.

Chapter 11. Episcopal Theology and Tradition

1. William White, "The Source of Knowledge" (1823), *The Common Sense Theology of Bishop White,* ed. Sydney A. Temple (Morningside Heights, N.Y.: King's Crown, 1946), 60, 61, 63; E. Clowes Chorley, *Men and Movements in the Episcopal Church* (Hamden, Conn.: Archon, 1961), 150, 159.

2. Robert W. Prichard, *The Nature of Salvation: Theological Consensus in the Episcopal Church, 1801–73* (Urbana: University of Illinois Press, 1997), 25; George L. Blackman, *Faith and Freedom: A Study of Theological Education and the Episcopal Theological School* (New York: Seabury, 1967), 7–15.

3. Robert Bruce Mullin, *Episcopal Vision/American Reality: High Church Theology and Social Thought in Evangelical America* (New Haven, Conn.: Yale University Press, 1986), 16–25.

4. Mullin, *Episcopal Vision/American Reality,* 61–96.

5. Devereux Jarratt, *The Life of the Reverend Devereux Jarratt* (1806), ed. David L. Holmes (Cleveland, Ohio: Pilgrim Press, 1995), 51–56; Diana Hochstedt Butler, *Standing Against the Whirlwind: Evangelical Episcopalians in Nineteenth-Century America* (New York: Oxford University Press, 1995), 24, 28–30; Chorley, *Men and Movements,* 6–8.

6. Butler, *Standing Against the Whirlwind,* 24–35.

7. Ibid., 39, 45, 69, 95–99.

8. Ibid., 135–38; George E. DeMille, *The Catholic Movement in the American Episcopal Church* (Philadelphia: Church Historical Society, 1941), 35, 69, 90, 106.

9. Prichard, *Nature of Salvation,* 12–16.

10. Ibid., 36–38.

11. William White, *Comparative Views of the Controversy Between the Calvinists and Arminians,* 2 vols. (Philadelphia: M. Thomas, 1817), 1:1, 2:29; Robert W. Prichard, "Nineteenth Century Episcopal Attitudes on Predestination and Election," *Historical Magazine of the Protestant Episcopal Church* 51 (1982):32, 46.

12. White, *Comparative Views,* 1:97, 183, 454.

13. John Henry Hobart, *The Excellence of the Church* (New York: T. & J. Swords, 1810), 2; Thomas Y. How, *Letters Addressed to the Rev. Samuel Miller* (Utica, N.Y.: Seward and Williams, 1808), 30; Prichard, *Nature of Salvation,* 21, 42.

14. William H. Wilmer, *The Episcopal Manual* (Baltimore: E. J. Coale, 1829), 45, 46, 47, 49.

15. Butler, *Standing Against the Whirlwind,* 29; Chorley, *Men and Movements,* 77.

16. Reuel Keith, *Lectures on those Doctrines in Theology Usually Called Calvinistic* (New York: J. Inglis, 1868), 20, 26–28, 35; Prichard, "Nineteenth-Century Episcopal Attitudes," 43.

17. White, *Comparative Views,* 1:274, 185.

18. Richard Hooker, *Of the Laws of Ecclesiastical Polity, The Works of that Learned and Judicious Divine, Mr. Richard Hooker,* 3 vols., ed. Isaac Walton (New York: Burt Franklin, 1970), 1:376.

19. May, *Enlightenment in America,* 73, 138; Flower and Murphey, *History of Philosophy in America,* 1:268, 281.

20. Robert Prichard, *A History of the Episcopal Church* (Harrisburg, Pa.: Morehouse-Barlow, 1991), 96; Temple, "Introduction," *Common Sense Theology,* 15–19, 39.

21. William White, "An Argument in Favor of Divine Revelation," *Common Sense Theology,* 69; Wilmer, *Episcopal Manual,* 62.

22. John Henry Hopkins, *Christianity Vindicated, in Seven Discourses on the External Evidences of the New Testament* (Burlington, Vt.: E. Smith, 1833); Alonzo Potter, ed. *Lectures on the Evidences of Christianity Delivered in Philadelphia by Clergymen of the Protestant Episcopal Church* (Philadelphia: E. H. Butler, 1855); Butler, *Standing Against the Whirlwind,* 39; Chorley, *Men and Movements,* 39, 58, 214.

23. White, "Source of Knowledge," 56; John Jewel, *An Apologie of the Church of England, English Reformers,* ed. T. H. L. Parker (Philadelphia: Westminster, 1966), 39; John Whitgift, *Works of John Whitgift,* ed. John Ayre, 3 vols. (Cambridge: Cambridge University Press, 1851), 2:182, 238.

24. John Henry Hobart, *An Apology for Apostolic Order and Its Advocates* (New York: Stanford and Swords, 1844), 158, 163, 173; John Henry Hopkins, *The Primitive Church, Compared with the Protestant Episcopal Church of the Present Day* (Burlington, Vt.: Smith and Harrington, 1835), viii.

25. William Ingraham Kip, *The Double Witness of the Church* (New York: Stanford and Delisser, 1858), 253, 256, 259–60.

26. George Washington Doane, "The Faith Once Delivered to the Saints" (1840), *The Episcopal Writings of the Rt. Rev. George Washington Doane,* ed. W. C. Doane (New York: D. Appleton, 1860), 330, 333, 337; Chorley, *Men and Movements,* 189.

27. John S. Stone, *The Contrast, or the Evangelical and Tractarian Systems Compared* (New York: Protestant Episcopal Society for the Promotion of Evangelical Knowledge, 1853), 24; Mullin, *Episcopal Vision/American Reality,* 158; Prichard, *Nature of Salvation,* 39.

28. Charles Pettit McIlvaine, *Oxford Divinity Compared with that of the Romish and Anglican Churches with a Special View to the Doctrine of Justification by Faith* (London: Seeley and Burnside, 1841), 9–12; Stone, *Contrast,* 83.

29. John Henry Hobart, *A Companion for the Festivals and Fasts of the Protestant Episcopal Church* (1st ed. 1804; New York; Stanford and Swords, 1831), 20.

30. Hobart, *Apology for Apostolic Order,* 144–46.

31. Ibid., 115; Hobart, *Excellence of the Church,* 23; Hopkins, *Christianity Vindicated,* 189; James Hervey Otey, *Unity of the Church* (Nashville, Tenn.: W. F. Bangs, 1843), 9–85.

32. William White, *The Case of the Episcopal Church in the United States Considered* (1782), *Common Sense Theology,* 74; Wilmer, *Episcopal Manual,* 31; Chorley, *Men and Movements,* 68, 70.

33. How, *Letters Addressed to the Rev. Samuel Miller,* 79; Samuel Miller, *Letters Concerning the Constitution and Order of the Christian Ministry* (1st ed. 1807; Philadelphia: Towar and Hogan, 1830), 470–84.

34. How, *Letters Addressed to the Rev. Samuel Miller,* 79.

35. Hobart, *Apology for Apostolic Order,* 54, 57–58; How, *Letters Addressed to the Rev. Samuel Miller,* 17, 27; John Stark Ravenscroft, *The Works of the Right Rev. John Stark Ravenscroft,* 2 vols. (New York: Protestant Episcopal Press, 1830), 1:253, 284–85.

36. Williams Adams, *Mercy to Babes* (New York: Stanford and Swords, 1847), 17; Hobart, *Apology for Apostolic Order,* 256; Mullin, *Episcopal Vision/American Reality,* 256.

37. Wilmer, *Episcopal Manual,* 84; McIlvaine, *Oxford Divinity,* 201.

38. William White, *Lectures on the Catechism of the Protestant Episcopal Church* (Philadelphia: Bradford and Inskeep, 1813), 221; Wilmer, *Episcopal Manual,* 110; Hobart, *Excellence of the Church,* 15; Prichard, *Nature of Salvation,* 71–96.

39. White, *Comparative Views, Common Sense Theology,* 107, 112–13; Temple, "Introduction," *Common Sense Theology,* 39; White, *Lectures on the Catechism,* 213.

40. White, *Lectures on the Catechism,* 219; Charles Pettit McIlvaine, *Spiritual Regeneration with Reference to Present Times* (New York: Harper and Brothers, 1851), 34; Wilmer, *Episcopal Manual,* 113, 142–45; William Meade, *Companion to the Font and Pulpit* (Washington, D.C.: Gideon, 1846), 13, 29, 45, 52–55, 78; William Meade, *Lectures on the Pastoral Office* (New York: Stanford and Swords, 1849), 171; Prichard, *Nature of Salvation,* 71–136.

41. Hobart, *Excellence of the Church,* 9, 25; Richard Channing Moore, *The Doctrines of the Church* (Philadelphia: William Fry, 1820), 13.

42. Wilmer, *Episcopal Manual,* 113; McIlvaine, *Oxford Divinity,* 392; John Stark Ravenscroft, Letters, 11 July 1820, 16 July 1821, John Stark Ravenscroft Papers, University of North Carolina; Ravenscroft, *Works,* 1:30; Prichard, *Nature of Salvation,* 88.

43. L. Sullivan Ives, *The Obedience of Faith* (New York: Stanford and Swords, 1849), 12, 125; Mullin, *Episcopal Vision/American Reality,* 131–32; Prichard, *Nature of Salvation,* 180–87.

44. Hobart, *Excellence of the Church,* 26; Wilmer, *Episcopal Manual,* 130; McIlvaine, *Oxford Divinity,* 74; Mullin, *Episcopal Vision/American Reality,* 74.

45. DeMille, *Catholic Movement,* 54, 56, 84.

46. McIlvaine, *Oxford Divinity*, 36; Wilmer, *Episcopal Manual*, 58, 61, 72; Hobart, *Excellence of the Church*, 6, 7, 18; How, *Letters Addressed to the Rev. Samuel Miller*, 26; Hobart, *Apology for Apostolic Order*, 63.

47. John Henry Newman, *Lectures on Justification* (London: Rivington, 1838), 67, 256, 286, 315; Charles P. McIlvaine, *Justification by Faith* (Columbus, Ohio: Isaac N. Whiting, 1840), 153.

48. McIlvaine, *Justification by Faith*, 81–82, 102, 131; McIlvaine, *Oxford Divinity*, 2, 346.

49. Ives, *Obedience of Faith*, 20, 77.

50. McIlvaine, *Justification by Faith*, 82; William White, "The Analogy of the Understanding and the Will," *Common Sense Theology*, 89; Hobart, *Apology for Apostolic Order*, 252; Wilmer, *Episcopal Manual*, 56.

51. William White, "The Analogy of the Understanding and the Will," *Common Sense Theology*, 88; Hobart, *Excellence of the Church*, 11–19; Ives, *Obedience of Faith*, 14; McIlvaine, *Spiritual Regeneration*, 11–17.

52. Prichard, *Nature of Salvation*, 137–54.

53. Ibid., 144–46.

54. William White, "Cautionary Letters to a Young Lady," Appendix, *Memoir of the Life of the Right Reverend William White*, by Bird Wilson (Philadelphia: James Kay, Jr., 1839), 423.

55. John Henry Hobart, *The State of the Departed, Set Forth in a Funeral Address* (1st ed. 1816; New York: T. & J. Swords, 1825), 6, 36, 54, 96.

56. "The Intermediate State," *Princeton Review* 11 (1839):455, 478.

57. Prichard, *Nature of Salvation*, 151–64.

58. Hobart, *Excellence of the Church*, 5, 12; Wilmer, *Episcopal Manual*, v, 46, 49; White, *Comparative Views*, *Common Sense Theology*, 108; Jasper Adams, *Elements of Moral Philosophy* (Cambridge, Mass.: Folsom, Wells, Thurston, 1837), 11.

Chapter 12. Methodist Perfection

1. Peter Cartwright, *Autobiography of Peter Cartwright*, ed. W. P. Strickland (New York: Methodist Book Concern, 1856), 79–80.

2. James E. Cobb, *Philosophy of Faith* (St. Louis, Mo.: Methodist Book Depository, 1859), 89; Asa Shinn, *An Essay on the Plan of Salvation* (Baltimore: Neal, Wills, Cole, 1812), "Preface," n.p.; James Jenkins, *Experience, Labours, and Sufferings of Rev. James Jenkins* (Columbia, S.C.: James Jenkins, 1842), 10; John Ffirth, *Truth Vindicated* (New York: J. C. Totten, 1814), 69, 130; Nathan Bangs, *A History of the Methodist Episcopal Church*, 4 vols. (New York: Carlton and Porter, 1857), 1:269, 301, 321.

3. Bangs, *History*, 2:349–51, 3:12.

4. Joshua Soule and Timothy Mason, "Address of the Editors," *Methodist Magazine* 1 (1818):4.

5. Bangs, *History*, 1:364.

6. Nathan Bangs, "The Importance of Study to a Minister of the Gospel," *Methodist Magazine* 6 (1832):32; Thomas N. Ralston, *Elements of Divinity* (1st ed. 1847; Nashville, Tenn.: A. H. Redford, 1871), 3.

7. Shinn, *Essay on the Plan of Salvation,* "Preface," n.p.; Ralston, *Elements of Divinity,* 4; "Review of *Elements of Divinity," Quarterly Review of the Methodist Episcopal Church, South* 1 (1847):422–51; Asbury Lowrey, *Positive Theology* (Cincinnati, Ohio: Applegate, 1853), "Preface," n.p.; Luther Lee, *Elements of Theology* (1st ed. 1859; Syracuse, N.Y.: Wesleyan Book Room, 1865), iv–viii; A. A. Jimeson, *Notes on the Twenty-Five Articles of Religion* (Cincinnati, Ohio: Applegate, 1853), "Preface," n.p. Other Methodist texts are noted in Leland Scott, "The Concern for Systematic Theology, 1840–1870," *Perspectives on American Methodism,* ed. Russell E. Richey, Kenneth E. Rowe, and Jean Miller Schmidt (Nashville, Tenn.: Abingdon Press, 1993), 277–85.

8. Samuel Wakefield, *A Complete System of Christian Theology* (1st ed. 1862; Cincinnati, Ohio: Cranston and Curts, 1869), 4; [Daniel Whedon], "Complete System of Christian Theology," *Methodist Quarterly Review* 45 (1863):165–66.

9. William F. Warren, *Systematische Theologie einheitlich behandelt: Einleitung* (Cincinnati, Ohio: Poe and Hitchcock, 1865), "Preface," n.p.

10. Shinn, *Essay on the Plan of Salvation,* 17; Ralston, *Elements of Divinity,* 10, 176; Wakefield, *Complete System,* 44; Wilbur Fisk, *Calvinistic Controversy* (1st ed. 1835; New York: Lane and Scott, 1851), 139; Nathan Bangs, ed., "Introduction," *The Works of Thomas Reid,* 3 vols. (New York: N. Bangs and T. Mason, 1822), 1:iii; Scott, "Concern for Systematic Theology," 281–82.

11. Freeborn Garrettson, "Union of Fear, Hope, Love, and Joy in the Believer," *Methodist Magazine* 8 (1825):251; Shinn, *Essay on the Plan of Salvation,* 88; Ffirth, *Truth Vindicated,* 25; Wakefield, *Complete System,* 20; Ralston, *Elements of Divinity,* 10–12.

12. B. F. Cocker, "Metaphysics of Watson's Institutes," *Methodist Quarterly Review* 44 (1862):184–88; Leland Howard Scott, "Methodist Theology in America in the Nineteenth Century" (Ph.D. diss., Yale University, 1954), 146; M. M. Henkle, *The Life of Henry Bidleman Bascom* (Louisville, Ky.: Morton and Griswold, 1854), 137–39, 230, 254, 270, 326; Henry Bidleman Bascom, "Lectures on the Relative Claims of Christianity and Infidelity," *Posthumous Works of the Rev. Henry B. Bascom,* 3 vols. (Nashville, Tenn.: Publishing House of the Methodist Episcopal Church, South, 1917), 2:62, 64.

13. Wakefield, *Complete System,* 71–82; Ralston, *Elements of Divinity,* 598–99; Samuel Luckey, "The More Sure Word of Prophecy," *Methodist Magazine* 9 (1828):41–52.

14. Wakefield, *Complete System,* 40–123; Ralston, *Elements of Divinity,* 604–731; William McKendrie Bangs, "Observations on Watson's Theological Institutes," *Methodist Quarterly Review* 19 (1837):332, 339.

15. Nathan Bangs, *Vindication of Methodist Episcopacy* (New York: Methodist Episcopal Church, 1820); Nathan Bangs, *An Original Church of Christ* (New York: Mason and Lane, 1837); Alexander M'Caine, *The History and Mystery of Methodist Episcopacy* (Baltimore: Matchett, 1827); John Emory, *A Defence of "Our Fathers"* (New York: Carlton and Porter, 1827); Alexander M'Caine, *A Defence of the Truth* (Baltimore: Matchett, 1829).

16. Stephen Remington, *Anti-Universalism: Or Universalism Shown to be Unscriptural* (New York: Harper and Brothers, 1837), xi; Timothy Merritt, *A Discussion of Universal Salvation* (New York: Lane and Tippett, 1846), 5–10; Luther Lee, *Universalism Examined and Refuted* (Watertown, N.Y.: Knowlton and Rice, 1836), 125–26.

17. Orestes Brownson, *The Convert; or Leaves from My Experience, Works of Orestes*

Brownson, 20 vols., ed. Henry F. Brownson (New York: AMS Press, 1966), 5:7; Anne C. Loveland, *Southern Evangelicals and the Social Order 1800–1860* (Baton Rouge: Louisiana State University Press, 1980), 33.

18. Lee, *Universalism,* 123; Merritt, *Discussion,* 16, 204; Wilbur Fisk, "Two Discourses," in Merritt, *Discussion,* 291; Wilbur Fisk, "Future Rewards and Punishments," *Methodist Magazine* 6 (1823):369; Timothy Merritt, "Discourse on Future Punishment," *Methodist Magazine* 6 (1823):203; Remington, *Anti-Universalism,* 82.

19. Fisk, "Two Discourses," 297; Lee, *Universalism,* 200; Remington, *Anti-Universalism,* 159; Ralston, *Elements of Divinity,* 519.

20. Clarence L. Bence, "Processive Eschatology: A Wesleyan Alternative," *Wesleyan Theological Journal* 14 (1979):46; Wakefield, *Complete System,* 630; Ralston, *Elements of Divinity,* 496–543.

21. Ralston, *Elements of Divinity,* 4.

22. Abel Stevens, *Life and Times of Nathan Bangs* (New York: Carlton and Porter, 1863), 209; Nathan Bangs, *The Errors of Hopkinsianism* (New York: John Totten, 1815).

23. Ralston, *Elements of Divinity,* 323.

24. Fisk, *Calvinistic Controversy,* 19, 33; Bangs, *Errors of Hopkinsianism,* 25, 98, 123.

25. Ralston, *Elements of Divinity,* 123, 125; Bangs, *Errors of Hopkinsianism,* 93; Shinn, *Essay on the Plan of Salvation,* 294–310; Fisk, *Calvinistic Controversy,* 160; Ffirth, *Truth Vindicated,* 135; Lee, *Universalism,* 32–33.

26. Fisk, *Calvinistic Controversy,* 176, 185; Ralston, *Elements of Divinity,* 130–36.

27. Fisk, *Calvinistic Controversy,* 181, 257; Ralston, *Elements of Divinity,* 257; Wakefield, *Complete System,* 295; Daniel D. Whedon, "Doctrines of Methodism," *Bibliotheca Sacra* 74 (1862):257.

28. Fisk, *Calvinistic Controversy,* 162; Arminius, "Declaration of the Sentiments of the Arminians," *Works,* 1:589; "Articuli Arminiani sive Remonstrantia" (1610), *The Creeds of Christendom,* 3 vols., ed. Philip Schaff (Grand Rapids, Mich.: Baker Book House, 1966), 3:547.

29. Nathan Bangs, *An Examination of the Doctrine of Predestination* (New York: J. C. Totten, 1817), 87–107; Fisk, *Calvinistic Controversy,* 243; Robert E. Chiles, *Theological Transition in American Methodism* (Nashville, Tenn.: Abingdon Press, 1965), 4–27.

30. John M'Clintock, "German Literature: Professor Tholuck," *Methodist Magazine* 22 (1840):212–26; John M'Clintock, "A Review of Edwards' 'Inquiry into the Freedom of the Will,'" *Methodist Quarterly Review* 26 (1844):61–85; "Review of an Examination of President Edwards' Inquiry into the Freedom of the Will," *Methodist Quarterly Review* 28 (1846):605.

31. Albert Taylor Bledsoe, *An Examination of President Edwards' Inquiry Into the Freedom of the Will* (Philadelphia: H. Hooker, 1845), 36, 43, 50, 57–58.

32. Ibid., 87, 101, 103.

33. Albert Taylor Bledsoe, *A Theodicy; or Vindication of the Divine Glory, as Manifested in the Constitution and Government of the Moral World* (New York: Carlton and Phillips, 1856), 97, 150–75; Albert Taylor Bledsoe, "The Divine Government," *Methodist Quarterly Review* 6 (1852):281–90; "Bledsoe's Theodicy," *Methodist Quarterly Review* 8 (1854):132; "Bledsoe's Theodicy," *Southern Presbyterian Review* 8 (1854– 55): 230.

34. Daniel D. Whedon, *The Freedom of the Will as a Basis of Human Responsibility and a Divine Government* (New York: Carlton and Lanahan, 1864), 4, 113, 161, 207, 366.

35. Whedon, "Doctrines of Methodism," 257; Ralston, *Elements of Divinity,* 263–64; Lee, *Universalism,* 45; Fisk, *Calvinistic Controversy,* 47.

36. Borden Parker Bowne, *Studies in Christianity* (Boston: Houghton Mifflin, 1909). For satisfaction theories, see Joshua Soule, "The Perfect Law of Liberty," *The Methodist Pulpit South,* ed. W. T. Smithson (Washington, D.C.: Henry Polkinhorn, 1858), 149–66; Lee, *Universalism,* 44– 83; for governmental theories, see Shinn, *Essay on the Plan of Salvation,* 203; Timothy Merritt, "An Essay on Atonement," *Methodist Magazine* 7 (1824):200–44; for views combining both, see Wakefield, *Complete System,* 260–68; Ralston, *Elements of Divinity,* 193, 277.

37. John Wesley, "Salvation by Faith" (1738), *The Works of John Wesley,* ed. Albert Outler and Frank Baker, 26 vols. (Nashville, Tenn.: Abingdon Press, 1984), 1:109–30; John Wesley, "Minutes of Some Late Conversations" (1745), *The Works of John Wesley,* ed. Thomas Jackson, 14 vols. (reprint of 1872 London edition; Peabody, Mass.: Hendrickson, 1984), 8:282; John Wesley, "Minutes of Several Conversations" (1744–89), ibid., 8:336; John Wesley to Elizabeth Bennis, 1 March 1774, ibid., 12:399; John Wesley, "Thoughts on Salvation by Faith" (1779), ibid., 11:494– 95; Henry Rack, *Reasonable Enthusiast: John Wesley and the Rise of Methodism* (Philadelphia: Trinity Press, 1989), 390–93.

38. Compare Ralston, *Elements of Divinity,* 358, 393, and Wakefield, *Complete System,* 415, with Bangs, *History,* 1:193.

39. Merritt, *Discussion,* 46; Ffirth, *Truth Vindicated,* 34.

40. Ralston, *Elements of Divinity,* 375, 387; "Thoughts on St. Paul's Doctrine of Justification," *Methodist Magazine,* 1 (1818):418; Wakefield, *Complete System,* 418–19.

41. Ralston, *Elements of Divinity,* 359, 417, 423; Wakefield, *Complete System,* 427, 428–30.

42. John Wesley, "On Baptism," *John Wesley,* ed. Albert Outler (New York: Oxford University Press, 1964), 321–22; Wakefield, *Complete System,* 431–32; Leonidas Rosser, *Baptism* (Richmond, Va.: The Author, 1854), 17, 19; Thomas O. Summers, *Baptism* (Richmond, Va.: John Early, 1853), 141, 148; James Chapman, *Baptism* (Nashville, Tenn.: Stevenson and Owen, 1856), 322.

43. Ralston, *Elements of Divinity,* 436, 442; Wakefield, *Complete System,* 440.

44. John Wesley, "The New Birth," *Forty-Four Sermons* (London: Epworth Press, 1944), 523; John Wesley, "The Scripture Way of Salvation," *John Wesley,* 247; Ralston, *Elements of Divinity,* 458, 461.

45. See, for example, the reports in *Methodist Magazine* 3 (1820):471.

46. Bangs, *Errors of Hopkinsianism,* 157–200; Allan Coppedge, "Entire Sanctification in Early American Methodism, 1812–1835," *Wesleyan Theological Journal* 13 (1978): 34–50; John Leland Peters, *Christian Perfection and American Methodism* (Nashville, Tenn.: Abingdon Press, 1961), 12–45.

47. Timothy Merritt, *The Christian's Manual: A Treatise on Christian Perfection* (1st ed. 1825; New York: Emory and Waugh, 1828), 18, 75, 93– 103.

48. Phoebe Palmer, *The Way of Holiness* (1st ed. 1843; New York: For the Author,

1854), 32, 62–64; Thomas C. Oden, ed., *Phoebe Palmer: Selected Writings* (New York: Paulist Press, 1988), 120, 121; Harold E. Raser, *Phoebe Palmer: Her Life and Thought* (Lewiston, N.Y.: Edwin Mellen, 1987), 44, 187; Charles Edward White, *The Beauty of Holiness* (Grand Rapids, Mich.: Zondervan, 1986), 20, 25, 136; Donald W. Dayton, *Theological Roots of Pentecostalism* (Grand Rapids, Mich.: Zondervan, 1987), 35–86.

49. Charles Edward White, "What the Holy Spirit Can and Cannot Do: The Ambiguities of Phoebe Palmer's Theology of Experience," *Wesleyan Theological Journal* 20 (1985):108–21; Raser, *Phoebe Palmer,* 229–54; John A. Knight, "John Fletcher's Influence on the Development of Wesleyan Theology in America," *Wesleyan Theological Journal* 13 (1978):13–29; Timothy L. Smith, "How John Fletcher Became the Theologian of Wesleyan Perfectionism, 1770–1776," *Wesleyan Theological Journal* 15 (1980): 68–87.

50. George Peck, *The Scripture Doctrine of Christian Perfection* (New York: Lane and Sandford, 1843), 446, 449, 451.

51. Randolph Sinks Foster, *The Nature and Blessedness of Christian Purity* (New York: Harper and Brothers, 1851), 8–35; Hiram Mattison, *Thoughts on Entire Sanctification* (New York: Land and Scott, 1852), 6– 28; Raser, *Phoebe Palmer,* 267–72.

52. White, *Beauty of Holiness,* 180; Frances Bumpass, "Editorial," *The Weekly Message* (15 March 1855), 4:2, cited in Cheryl Junk, "Strangers in a Strange Land," unpub. essay, 12.

53. Shinn, *Essay on the Plan of Salvation,* "Preface," n.p.

Chapter 13. The Baptists and Calvinist Diversity

1. David Benedict, *Fifty Years Among the Baptists* (New York: Sheldon, 1860), 33, 68; Isaac Backus, *A Discourse Showing the Nature and the Necessity of an Internal Call to Preach the Everlasting Gospel* (1754), *Isaac Backus on Church, State, and Calvinism,* ed. William G. McLoughlin (Cambridge, Mass.: Harvard University Press, 1968), 75; John Leland, "The Rights of Conscience Inalienable," *The Writings of the Late Elder John Leland* (New York: G. W. Wood, 1845), 185.

2. Richard Furman, "Circular Letter," *A Baptist Source Book,* ed. Robert A. Baker (Nashville, Tenn.: Broadman Press, 1966), 29–30; Robert B. C. Howell, *The Evils of Infant Baptism* (Charleston, S.C.: Southern Baptist Publication Society, 1852), 279–80.

3. Francis Wayland, *Notes and the Principles and Practices of Baptist Churches* (New York: Sheldon, Blakeman, 1857), 123, 132.

4. Broaddus, *Age of Reason and Revelation,* 9, 26; John L. Dagg, *A Manual of Theology* (Charleston: Southern Baptist Publication Society, 1857), 20, 30–36, 61, 68, 112, 123, 125; Wayland, *Principles and Practices,* 286.

5. Wayland, *Principles and Practices,* 47; John Leland, "Budget of Scraps," *Writings of Leland,* 345; W. Wiley Richards, *Winds of Doctrine: The Origin and Development of Southern Baptist Theology* (Lanham, Md.: University Press of America, 1941), 47, 91; William L. Lumpkin, *Baptist Confessions of Faith* (Philadelphia: Judson Press, 1959), 248, 362; Thomas J. Nettles, "Richard Furman," *Baptist Theologians,* ed. Timothy George and David S. Dockery (Nashville, Tenn.: Boardman Press, 1990), 149; Timothy George, "James Petigru Boyce," ibid., 258.

6. Wayland, *Principles and Practices,* 14, 87, 132.

7. Robert Fleming, ed., *The Georgia Pulpit* (Richmond, Va.: H. K. Ellyson, 1847), 139.

8. Isaac Backus, *A Short Description of the Difference Between the Bondwoman and the Free* (1756), *Backus on Church, State, and Calvinism,* 148–67; Dagg, *Manual of Theology,* 194; Howell, *Evils of Infant Baptism,* 85; Patrick Hues Mell, *Baptism in its Mode and Subject* (Charleston, S.C.: Southern Baptist Publication Society, 1853), 290.

9. Norman H. Maring, "The Individualism of Francis Wayland," *Baptist Concepts of the Church,* ed. Winthrop S. Hudson (Philadelphia: The Judson Press, 1959), 148; Edwin S. Gaustad, "The Leland-Backus Tradition," ibid., 108–10.

10. Robert T. Handy, "The Philadelphia Tradition," ibid., 36.

11. Robert G. Torbet, "Landmarkism," ibid., 192; James Robinson Graves, "Introductory Essay," *A Concise History of Foreign Baptists,* by G. H. Orchard, 11th ed. (Nashville, Tenn.: Graves, Marks, and Rutland, 1855), v, xii; Thomas Crosby, *The History of the English Baptists,* 4 vols. in 2 (reprint of 1738–40 edition; Lafayette, Tenn.: Church History Research and Archives, 1978), 1:3–27.

12. Orchard, *Concise History,* 2–5, 372–76; W. Morgan Patterson, *Baptist Successionism: A Critical View* (Valley Forge, Pa.: The Judson Press, 1969), 24–25; Hosea Holcombe, *A History of the Rise and Progress of the Baptists in Alabama* (Philadelphia: King and Baird, 1840), 14–15; Richards, *Winds of Doctrine,* 67; Keith E. Eitel, "James Madison Pendleton," *Baptist Theologians,* 195.

13. Graves, "Introductory Essay," ii–xxiv; James Robinson Graves, *The Great Iron Wheel; or Republicanism Backwards and Christianity Reversed* (Nashville, Tenn.: Graves and Marks, 1855), 436–70, 498; James Robinson Graves, "Introduction," *Pedobaptist and Campbellite Immersions,* by A. C. Dayton (1st ed. 1858; Louisville, Ky.: Baptist Book Concern, 1903), iii–xi.

14. Graves, *Great Iron Wheel,* 415–27, 451–70; Graves, *The Trilemma; or, Death by Three Horns* (1st ed. 1860; Texarkana, Ark.: Baptist Sunday School Committee, 1928), 9, 25, 79; John L. Dagg, *A Treatise on Church Order* (Charleston, S.C.: Southern Baptist Publication Society, 1858), 120, 286–88, 291; Keith Eitel, "James Madison Pendleton," *Baptist Theologians,* 195, 198; Harold S. Smith, "J. R. Graves," ibid., 239; James E. Tull, *Shapers of Baptist Thought* (Valley Forge, Pa.: Judson Press, 1972), 30; Richards, *Winds of Doctrine,* 71.

15. John Smyth, "Short Confession of Faith in XX Articles by John Smyth," *Baptist Confessions of Faith,* ed. William L. Lumpkin (Philadelphia: Judson Press, 1959), 100–01; "A Short Confession of Faith" (1610), ibid., 103; John Smyth, *The Character of the Beast, The Works of John Smyth,* ed. W. T. Whitley (Cambridge: Cambridge University Press, 1915), 21, 28.

16. I. D. Stewart, *The History of the Freewill Baptists,* 2 vols. (Dover, N.H.: Freewill Baptist Printing, 1862), 1:28, 32–53.

17. Marini, *Radical Sects,* 3–10; Henry Alline, *Two Mites Cast Into the Offering of God, for the Benefit of Mankind* (with amendments by Benjamin Randall) (Dover, N.H.: Samuel Bragg, 1804), 80, 96; George A. Rawlyk, ed., *Henry Alline: Selected Writings* (New York: Paulist Press, 1987), 28.

18. "The Confession of Faith of those Churches which are Commonly (though falsly) Called Anabaptists" (1644), *Baptist Confessions of Faith,* 153–69.

19. Geoffrey F. Nuttall, "Northamptonshire and *The Modern Question:* A Turning Point in Eighteenth-Century Dissent," *Journal of Theological Studies,* n.s., 16 (1965): 101–23; Thomas J. Nettles, *By His Grace and For His Glory* (Grand Rapids, Mich.: Baker Book House, 1986), 91–104.

20. John Gill, *A Body of Doctrinal Divinity,* 2 vols. (London: For the Author, 1769–70), 1:332, 337, 348, 526; 2:741, 754, 850; Nettles, *By His Grace and for His Glory,* 93–99; Timothy George, "John Gill," *Baptist Theologians,* 91–92.

21. Andrew Fuller, *The Gospel Worthy of All Acceptation* (1st ed. ca. 1785; New York: Isaac Collins, 1801), "Preface," vi–xiii, 109, 110–11, 148, 196; Nettles, *By His Grace and for His Glory,* 113–29; Tull, *Shapers of Baptist Thought,* 79–80.

22. Fuller, *Gospel Worthy,* 44, 109, 110–11; Phil Roberts, "Andrew Fuller," *Baptist Theologians,* 121–26.

23. Benedict, *Fifty Years Among the Baptists,* 135–36, 141; Wayland, *Principles and Practices,* 18; Fuller, *Gospel Worthy,* 53–59, 196.

24. McLoughlin, ed., *Backus on Church, State, and Calvinism,* 22, 53; Isaac Backus, *A Fish Caught in His Own Net* (1768), ibid., 175–78.

25. Backus, *Difference Between the Bondwoman and the Free,* 148–57.

26. Isaac Backus, *The Doctrine of Particular Election and Final Perseverance* (1789), *Backus on Church, State, and Calvinism,* 483; Isaac Backus, *The Sovereign Decrees of God* (1773), ibid., 295–99; Isaac Backus, *Truth is Great and Will Prevail* (1781), ibid., 411.

27. Jonathan Maxcy, "A Discourse Designed to Explain the Doctrine of Atonement" (1796), *The Atonement: Discourses and Treatises,* ed. Edwards A. Park (Boston: Congregational Publishing Society, 1859), 89, 95, 105, 106; William B. Johnson, Letter to J. S. Mims, 25 March 1848, 6 October 1851, William B. Johnson Papers, Furman University, in Gregory A. Wills, "Neglected Influences: New England Theology, Moderate Calvinism, and Baptist Identity," 1, 3. I am grateful to Dr. Wills for allowing me to read this unpublished essay.

28. Wayland, *Principles and Practices,* 19–20, 21.

29. Benedict, *Fifty Years Among the Baptists,* 135.

30. Jesse Mercer, *Ten Letters Addressed to the Rev. Cyrus White* (Washington, Ga.: Wilkes County News Office, 1830), 11–12, 27, 37, 39.

31. Patrick Hues Mell, *Predestination and the Saints' Perseverance Stated and Defended* (Charleston, S.C.: Southern Baptist Publication Society, 1858), 20, 23, 25, 26, 56, 71, 73, 80; Paul A. Basden, "Patrick Hues Mell," *Baptist Theologians,* 205.

32. Robert B. C. Howell, *The Covenants* (Charleston, S.C.: Southern Baptist Publication Society, 1855), 22, 39; N. M. Crawford, *Christian Paradoxes* (Nashville, Tenn.: Graves, Marks, 1859), 31, 180; Robert B. C. Howell, *The Way of Salvation* (Charleston, S.C.: Southern Baptist Publication Society, 1856), 87–101; George, "James Petigru Boyce," 252–54.

33. Dagg, *Manual of Theology,* 34, 121, 124, 128, 324; Mark E. Dever, "John L. Dagg," *Baptist Theologians,* 170–79.

34. Bertram Wyatt-Brown, "The Antimission Movement in the Jacksonian South," *Journal of Southern History* 36 (1970):501–29; Byron Cecil Lambert, *The Rise of the Anti-Mission Baptists: Sources and Leaders, 1800–1840* (New York: Arno Press, 1980), 21–57.

35. Lambert, *Anti-Mission Baptists,* 63–108, 153–220, 227.

36. John Leland, "The Government of Christ a Christocracy" (1804), *Writings of Leland,* 275, 278; "An Oration Delivered at Cheshire" (1802), ibid., 251.

37. John Leland, "Letter of Vindication, on Leaving Virginia" (1791), ibid., 172; John Leland, "The First Rise of Sin Neither from a Holy nor Sinful Cause" ibid., 141–42, 167, 169; Leland, "Government of Christ," 276.

38. John Leland, *Writings of Leland,* 571; John Leland, "The Virginia Chronicle" (1790), ibid., 111; John Leland, "Sermon Preached at Ankram" (1806), ibid., 310; John Leland, "Budget of Scraps," ibid., 341; John Leland, "A Short Narrative" (1811), ibid., 369.

39. John Taylor, *Thoughts on Missions* (Franklin County, Ky.: n.p., 1820), 23, 26–29; John Taylor, *A History of Ten Baptist Churches* (Frankfurt, Ky.: J. H. Holman, 1823), 138–40.

40. Daniel Parker, *A Public Address to the Baptist Society* (Vincennes, Ill.: Stuart and Osborn, 1820), 5; Lambert, *Anti-Mission Baptists,* 275.

41. Daniel Parker, *Views on the Two Seeds, Baptist Source Book,* 79–84; Wyatt-Brown, "Antimission Movement," 502–27; Lambert, *Anti-Mission Baptists,* 275–81.

42. Brooke, *Refiner's Fire,* 23–24.

43. Lambert, *Anti-Mission Baptists,* 376–98.

44. Jeremiah Jeter, *Campbellism Examined* (Boston: Gould and Lincoln, 1855), 23–30, 78–94, 212–40.

Chapter 14. Restoration

1. Michael G. Kenny, *The Perfect Law of Liberty: Elias Smith and the Providential History of America* (Washington, D.C.: Smithsonian Institution Press, 1994), 118; Nathan O. Hatch, "The Christian Movement and the Demand for a Theology of the People," *Journal of American History* 67 (1980):545–67; Hatch, *Democratization of American Christianity,* 68–81.

2. Richard McNemar, *The Kentucky Revival* (New York: E. O. Jenkins, 1846), 59; William Garrett West, *Barton Warren Stone: Early American Advocate of Christian Unity* (Nashville, Tenn.: The Disciples of Christ Historical Society, 1954), 101.

3. Robert Richardson, *Memoirs of Alexander Campbell,* 2 vols. (Philadelphia: J. B. Lippincott, 1868–70), 2:56.

4. Alexander Campbell, *The Christian System* (1st ed. 1835; St. Louis, Mo.: Christian Publishing Company, 1890), 131, 200; Elias Smith, *A New Testament Dictionary* (Philadelphia: For the Author, 1812), 4; Alexander Campbell and Robert Owen, *Debate on the Evidences of Christianity,* 2 vols. (Bethany, Va.: Alexander Campbell, 1829), 1:4; Timothy Earl Fulop, "Elias Smith and the Quest for Gospel Liberty" (Ph.D. diss., Princeton University, 1992), 141; Kenny, *Perfect Law of Liberty,* 164.

5. Alexander Campbell, "Tracts for the People: Flesh and Spirit," *Millennial Harbinger,* 3d ser., 3 (1846):307–08 (hereafter *MH*); Alexander Campbell, *Addresses, A Compend of Alexander Campbell's Theology,* ed. Royal Humbert (St. Louis, Mo.: Bethany Press, 1961), 152; Kenny, *Perfect Law of Liberty,* 81.

6. Campbell, "Tracts for the People," 307.

7. David Edwin Harrell, Jr., *Quest for a Christian America* (Nashville, Tenn.: The Disciples of Christ Historical Society, 1966), 64; Richard M. Tristano, *The Origins of the Restoration Movement* (Atlanta, Ga.: Glenmary Research Center, 1988), 59.

8. Tristano, *Origins,* 95; Kenny, *Perfect Law of Liberty,* 63; Jean-Frédéric Ostervald, *A Compendium of Christian Theology* (Hartford, Conn.: Patten, 1789), 45, 48.

9. Smith, *New Testament Dictionary,* 5.

10. Alexander Campbell, *Memoirs of Elder Thomas Campbell* (Cincinnati, Ohio: H. S. Bosworth, 1861), 18, n.4; Richard T. Hughes and C. Leonard Allen, *Illusions of Innocence: Protestant Primitivism in America, 1630– 1875* (Chicago: University of Chicago Press, 1988), 178; Alexander Campbell, "Instrumental Music," *MH,* 4th ser., 1 (1851): 581–82; Benjamin Lyon Smith, *Alexander Campbell* (St. Louis, Mo.: Bethany Press, 1930), 123.

11. Alexander Campbell, "Essays on Man," *The Christian Baptist,* 2d ed., ed. D. S. Burnet (Cincinnati, Ohio: H. S. Bosworth, 1861), 658; Campbell, *Christian System,* 168– 69, 330; Dale A. Jorgenson, *Theological and Aesthetic Roots in the Stone-Campbell Movement* (Kirksville, Mo.: Thomas Jefferson University Press, 1989), 30–31.

12. Alexander Campbell, "Sermon on the Law," *MH,* 3d ser., 3 (1846):493–521.

13. Alexander Campbell and Robert Owen, *Debate on the Evidences of Christianity* (Nashville, Tenn.: McQuiddy, 1959), 388.

14. M. Eugene Boring, *Disciples and the Bible* (St. Louis, Mo.: Chalice Press, 1997), 77.

15. Alexander Campbell and N. L. Rice, *A Debate Between Rev. A. Campbell and Rev. N. L. Rice, On the Action, Subject, Design, and Administration of Christian Baptism* (Lexington, Ky.: Skillman, 1844), 49; Campbell, *Christian System,* 134.

16. Alexander Campbell, "To Mr. Skinner," *MH,* n.s., 1 (1837):397; Campbell and Owen, *Debate on the Evidences,* 1:142; Boring, *Disciples and the Bible,* 81–82.

17. Alexander Campbell, "Directions to the Reader," *The Living Oracles* (Buffaloe, Va.: Alexander Campbell, 1826), n.p.; Alexander Campbell, "The Bible: Principles of Interpretation," *MH,* 3d ser., 3 (1846):13– 24; Alexander Campbell, *Lectures on the Pentateuch* (St. Louis, Mo.: Christian Publication Society, 1867), 69; W. E. Garrison, *Alexander Campbell's Theology* (St. Louis, Mo.: Christian Publishing Company, 1900), 189.

18. Hughes and Allen, *Illusions of Innocence,* 124, 156.

19. Campbell, *Christian System,* 18; Alexander Campbell, "The Confirmation of the Testimony," *MH* 1 (1830):9; Hughes and Allen, *Illusions of Innocence,* 117; Campbell and Owen, *Debate on the Evidences,* 1:185.

20. Campbell and Owen, *Debate on the Evidences,* 1:50, 149, 166.

21. Ibid., 1:62; Alexander Campbell, "To 'An Occasional Reader,'" *Christian Baptist,* 197; S. Morris Eames, *The Philosophy of Alexander Campbell* (Bethany, Va.: Bethany College, 1966), 36.

22. Campbell, *Christian System,* 9, 115; West, *Barton Warren Stone,* 107; Smith, *New Testament Dictionary,* 168; Campbell and Owen, *Debate on the Evidences,* 1:109–10.

23. Campbell and Owen, *Debate on the Evidences,* 1:162, 168, 262; 2:5; Alexander Campbell, "Introductory Lecture," *Introductory Addresses Delivered at the Organization of Bethany College* (Bethany, Va.: A. Campbell, 1841), 61–86.

24. Campbell, *Christian System*, 20; Campbell and Owen, *Debate on the Evidences*, 1:214; 2:3, 10, 26, 43–45, 63; Alexander Campbell, "Evidences of the Gospel," *MH* 6 (1835):201; Eames, *Philosophy of Alexander Campbell*, 38.

25. Smith, *New Testament Dictionary*, 68; Alexander Campbell, "Reply," *Christian Baptist*, 142; Campbell, *Christian System*, 56, 130; Alexander Campbell, "To Amicus," *Christian Baptist*, 253; West, *Barton Warren Stone*, 96–97; Alexander Campbell, "A Review of a Review," *MH*, n.s., 3 (1839):505.

26. Alexander Campbell, "Experimental Religion," *MH*, 5th ser., 4 (1861):327; Alexander Campbell, "Christian Experience," *MH* 1 (1830):498–99.

27. Boring, *Disciples and the Bible*, 395; Walter Scott, *The Gospel Restored* (1st ed. 1836; Joplin, Mo.: College Press Publishing, 1986), v–vi.

28. West, *Barton Warren Stone*, 96, 97, 180–81, 198.

29. Campbell, *Christian System*, 68; Alexander Campbell, "Dialogue Between a Disciple of Christ and a Presbyterian," *MH*, 4th ser., 4 (1854):512–15; Hughes and Allen, *Illusions of Innocence*, 119, 120–21; Smith, *Alexander Campbell*, 327.

30. Alexander Campbell, "The Apocalypse Explained," *Christian Baptist* 2 (1825): 136–37; Alexander Campbell, "The Coming of the Lord," *MH*, n.s., 5 (1841):9, 97–98, *MH*, n.s., 6 (1842):220–21, 295–96, 305, *MH*, n.s., 7 (1843):74; Campbell and Owen, *Debate on the Evidences*, 1:105; Campbell, *Christian System*, 310; Alexander Campbell, "Preface," *MH* 4 (1833):1–2; Hughes and Allen, *Illusions of Innocence*, 173; Harrell, *Quest*, 44.

31. Smith, *New Testament Dictionary*, 237; Fulop, "Elias Smith," 151, 153–54; Kenny, *Perfect Law of Liberty*, 65; Barton W. Stone, "The Millennium," *Christian Messenger* 7 (1833):312–14; 8 (1834):145–48; Harrell, *Quest*, 41–43; Campbell, "Coming of the Lord," *MH* (1843):220–21, 295–96.

32. Alexander Campbell, "Everlasting Gospel," *MH* 4 (1833):121–22; Eames, *Philosophy of Alexander Campbell*, 73; Hughes and Allen, *Illusions of Innocence*, 186; Richard T. Hughes, "From Primitive Church to Civil Religion: The Millennial Odyssey of Alexander Campbell," *Journal of the American Academy of Religion* 44 (1976):87–103.

33. Campbell, *Christian System*, 149, 157, 173, 184; Alexander Campbell, "Periodical Conventions," *MH*, 4th ser., 3 (1853):106; Barton W. Stone, "The Kingdom of Heaven, or Church of God," *Christian Messenger* 11 (1840):28–30; Clark Gilpin, "The Integrity of the Church: The Communal Theology of Disciples of Christ," *Classic Themes of Disciples Theology*, ed. Kenneth Lawrence (Ft. Worth: Texas Christian University, 1986), 33.

34. Campbell, *Debate on Baptism*, 611; Fulop, "Elias Smith," 79.

35. Barton W. Stone, *The Biography of Eld. Barton Warren Stone, Written by Himself*, ed. John Rogers (Cincinnati, Ohio: James, 1847), 29–30; Richardson, *Memoirs*, 2:190; Campbell, *Christian System*, viii, 4; Alexander Campbell, "John M. Duncan on Foreknowledge," *MH*, n.s., 4 (1840):490–91; Smith, *New Testament Dictionary*, 142–43.

36. Campbell, *Christian System*, 35; Alexander Campbell, "Remarks," *MH*, 3d ser., 3 (1846):325–29; Smith, *New Testament Dictionary*, 305.

37. Campbell, *Christian System*, 30; Smith, *New Testament Dictionary*, 168, 171, 202, 258; Alexander Campbell, "Reply to Mr. J. A. Waterman," *MH* 4 (1833):246–47; Campbell, "To Amicus," *Christian Baptist*, 254; Barton W. Stone, *Atonement: The Substance of Two Letters Written to a Friend* (Lexington, Ky.: J. Charless, 1805), 8–9.

38. Alexander Campbell, "Christian Union," *MH,* 3d ser., 4 (1847):169; Campbell, *Christian System,* 204–07.

39. Hughes and Allen, *Illusions of Innocence,* 115.

40. Campbell, *Christian System,* 204; Tristano, *Origins,* 90– 91; West, *Barton Warren Stone,* 179.

41. Alexander Campbell and John B. Purcell, *A Debate on the Roman Catholic Religion* (Nashville, Tenn.: McQuiddy, 1914), 61; Alexander Campbell, "Any Christians Among Protestant Parties," *MH,* n.s., 1 (1837):411–14; Campbell, *Debate on Baptism,* 522.

42. Campbell, *Christian System,* 268–74; Barton W. Stone, "The Lord's Supper," *Christian Messenger* 8 (1834):176–77.

43. Kenny, *Perfect Law of Liberty,* 227–29.

44. Smith, *New Testament Dictionary,* 53; Barton W. Stone, *An Address to the Christian Churches in Kentucky, Tennessee, and Ohio on Several Important Doctrines of Religion* (Lexington, Ky.: Cavins, 1821), 57– 60, 65, 76; Stone, *Atonement,* 20, 25; Barton W. Stone, "Atonement," *MH,* n.s., 4 (1840):243–46, 289–93, 387–90; Alexander Campbell, "Letter to B. W. Stone," *MH,* n.s., 4 (1840):246–50, 294–98, 391–96; Campbell, *Christian System,* 39, 41, 44–45; William R. Barr, "Christology in Disciples Tradition," *Classic Themes,* 10.

45. Smith, *New Testament Dictionary,* 95; West, *Barton Warren Stone,* 185, 187.

46. Stone, *Address,* 12, 14; Thomas Cleland, *Letters to Barton W. Stone* (Lexington, Ky.: Skillman, 1822), 40, 80.

47. Alexander Campbell, "Christian Psalmody," *MH,* 3d ser., 1 (1844):292; Alexander Campbell, "Unitarianism as Connected with Christian Union," *MH,* 3d ser., 3 (1846): 451–52; Campbell, "A Restoration of the Ancient Things," *Christian Baptist,* 362; Barton W. Stone, "To the Christian Baptist," *Christian Messenger* 1 (1827):204–09.

48. Stone, *Biography,* 29; Smith, *New Testament Dictionary,* 141– 42; Campbell and Owen, *Debate on the Evidences,* 2:108, 114; West, *Barton Warren Stone,* 190.

Chapter 15. Roots of Black Theology

1. James H. Cone, "Black Theology in American Religion," *Journal of the American Academy of Religion* 53 (1985):755–71; Gayraud Wilmore, *Black Religion and Black Radicalism* (Garden City, N.Y.: Doubleday, 1973), 103–86.

2. William E. Hatcher, *John Jasper* (New York: Fleming Revell, 1908), 122; David W. Wills, "Womanhood and Domesticity in the A.M.E. Tradition," *Black Apostles at Home and Abroad,* ed. David W. Wills and Richard Newman (Boston: G. K. Hall, 1982), 138; Daniel A. Payne, *History of the African Methodist Episcopal Church* (Nashville, Tenn.: AME Sunday School Union, 1891), 117, 155, 396; "Outdoor Preaching," *Christian Recorder* 1 (18 October 1854):85.

3. Payne, *History,* 141.

4. Sondra A. O'Neale, ed., *Jupiter Hammon and the Biblical Beginnings of African American Literature* (Metuchen, N.J.: Scarecrow Press, 1993), 89.

5. Jupiter Hammon, *A Winter Piece,* ibid., 105, 106, 108; Jupiter Hammon, *An Evening's Improvement,* ibid., 173, 174; Jupiter Hammon, *An Address to the Negroes of the State of New York,* ibid., 238.

6. Hammon, *Winter Piece,* 100, 101, 107, 113; Hammon, *Evening's Improvement,* 164.

7. Hammon, *Evening's Improvement,* 164; Hammon, *Address,* 239; Hammon, *Winter Piece,* 99.

8. Helen McLam, "Black Puritan on the Northern Frontier," *Black Preacher to White America: The Collected Writings of Lemuel Haynes, 1773–1833* (Brooklyn, N.Y.: Carlson, 1990), xxii.

9. Lemuel Haynes, *Collected Writings,* 33, 35, 40.

10. Ibid., 86, 91, 96.

11. Ibid., 135, 136, 137

12. "Letters Showing the Rise and Progress of the Early Negro Churches of Georgia and the West Indies," *Journal of Negro History* 1 (1916):73; Mechal Sobel, *Trabelin' On: The Slave Journey to an Afro-Baptist Faith* (Princeton, N.J.: Princeton University Press, 1979), 140–81.

13. James M. Simms, *The First Colored Baptist Church in North America* (Philadelphia: J. B. Lippincott, 1888), 80, 124; Gregory L. Wills, *Democratic Religion: Freedom, Authority, and Church Discipline in the Baptist South, 1785–1900* (New York: Oxford University Press, 1997), 77–78. See Carter G. Woodson, *The History of the Negro Church* (Washington, D.C.: The Associated Publishers, 1921), 54, 69, for evidence of Calvinist theology among black Presbyterian clergy.

14. Richard Allen and Jacob Tapsico, *The Doctrines and Disciplines of the African Methodist Episcopal Church* (Philadelphia: John Cunningham, 1817), 11–25, 26–30; Richard Allen, *The Life Experience and Gospel Labors of the Rt. Rev. Richard Allen* (1st ed. 1833; Nashville, Tenn.: Abingdon Press, 1960), 83, 89.

15. George White, *A Brief Account of the Life, Experience, Travels, and Gospel Labors of George White* (New York: John C. Totter, 1810), 9, 15, 46–48; Noah C. Cannon, *A History of the African Methodist Episcopal Church* (Rochester, N.Y.: Strong & Dawson, 1842), 33; William Aikman, "Religious Value of Obedience," *Christian Recorder,* n.s., 1 (9 Feb. 1861):17; "A Divine Saviour," ibid., n.s., 1, (14 Dec. 1861):193; Daniel A. Payne, "Who is Sufficient for these things?" (1852), *Daniel A. Payne: Sermons and Addresses, 1853–1891,* ed. Charles Killiam (New York: Arno Press, 1972), 270; Daniel A. Payne, "God," *Repository of Religion and Literature* 2 (1859):4; Daniel A. Payne, *Welcome to the Ransomed* (Baltimore: Bull and Tuttle, 1862), 7.

16. Noah Calwell W. Cannon, *Rock of Wisdom* (New York?: n.p., 1833), 39, 40, 48, 80–95; Cannon, *History of the African Methodist Episcopal Church,* 31–34.

17. William Douglass, *Annals of the First African Church in the United States of America* (Philadelphia: King and Baird, 1862), 96.

18. William Douglass, *Sermons Preached in the African Protestant Episcopal Church* (Philadelphia: King & Baird, 1854), 19, 25, 68, 80, 231; Douglass, *Annals,* 131, 147.

19. [Samuel Cornish], "A Virtuous Life," *The Colored American* (29 July 1839), n.p.; "Moral Character," ibid. (25 April 1840), n.p.; "Inducement to Virtue," ibid. (1 October 1837), n.p.; Peter Williams, Jr., *A Discourse Delivered on the Death of Capt. Paul Cuffe* (New York: B. Young, 1817), 16.

20. Hammon, *Evening's Improvement,* 106; Allen, *Life Experience,* 42; Payne, *History,* 169, 394; Payne, "God," 2; Douglass, *Sermons,* 215.

21. Hatcher, *John Jasper,* 133; H. Dean Trulear and Russell E. Richey, eds., "Two Sermons by Brother Carper: 'The Eloquent Negro Preacher,'" *American Baptist Quarterly* 6 (1987):7, 12; William S. White, *The African Preacher* (Philadelphia: Presbyterian Board of Publication, 1849), 11, 25.

22. Haynes, *Collected Writings,* 79–102; Allen, *Life Experience,* 70; Daniel Coker, *A Dialogue Between a Virginian and an African Minister* (1810), *Pamphlets of Protest,* ed. Richard Newman, Patrick Rael, and Philip Lapsansky (New York: Routledge, 2001), 54–61.

23. Absalom Jones, "A Thanksgiving Sermon" (1808), *Early Negro Writing, 1760–1837,* ed. Dorothy Porter (Boston: Beacon Press, 1971), 337; Maria W. Stewart, "An Address Delivered at the African Masonic Hall" (1833), ibid., 133; James Forten, "An Address Delivered Before the American Reform Society" (1837), ibid., 231; "The Sons of Africans" (1808), ibid., 17; Noah Davis, *A Narrative of the Life of the Rev. Noah Davis* (Baltimore: Weishampel, 1859), 76; Eddie S. Glaude, Jr., *Exodus! Religion, Race, and Nation in Early Nineteenth-Century Black America* (Chicago: University of Chicago Press, 2000), 3–18.

24. William Whipper, "Minutes of the First Annual Meeting of the American Reform Society" (1837), *Early Negro Writing,* 202; Richard P. McCormack, "William Whipper: Moral Reformer," *Pennsylvania History* 43 (1976):23–48; John W. Lewis, "Essay on the Character and Condition of the African Race" (1852), *Pamphlets of Protest,* 190, 192; Joseph M. Carr, "Address Delivered Before the Humane Mechanics Association" (1834), *Early Negro Writing,* 14; William Hamilton, "An Oration Delivered in the African Zion Church" (1827), ibid., 101.

25. Cornish, ed., *The Colored American* (8 July 1837), n.p.; ibid. (6 May 1837), n.p.; Glaude, *Exodus!,* 136–42.

26. Daniel Payne, "Bishop Daniel Alexander Payne's Protestation of American Slavery," *Journal of Negro History* 52 (1967):60; Nathaniel Paul, *An Address Delivered on the Celebration of the Abolition of Slavery, In the State of New York* (Albany, N.Y.: Van Steenberon, 1827), 12–13.

27. Payne, "Protestation," 63; Paul, *Address,* 10–11.

28. J. W. C. Pennington, "To My Father, Mother, Brother, and Sisters," *The Mind of the Negro as Reflected in Letters Written During the Crisis 1800–1860,* ed. Carter G. Woodson (Washington, D.C.: Association for the Study of Negro Life and History, 1926), 642–45, 647. See also Lewis, "Essay," 192.

29. David Walker, *David Walker's Appeal, in Four Articles,* ed. Charles M. Wiltse (New York: Hill and Wang, 1965), 5, 9, 35, 37, 72.

30. H. H. Garnet, "An Address to the Slaves of the United States of America," *Negro Orators and their Orations,* ed. Carter G. Woodson (New York: Russell and Russell, 1969), 153; H. H. Garnet, "A Memorial Discourse," *Masterpieces of Negro Eloquence,* ed. Alice Moore Dunbar (New York: Bookery, 1914), 111.

31. Martin R. Delany, *The Condition, Elevation, Emigration, and Destiny of the Colored People of the United States* (Philadelphia: For the Author, 1852), 61–62.

32. Alexander Crummell, *Destiny and Race: Selected Writings 1840– 1898,* ed. Wilson J. Moses (Amherst: University of Massachusetts Press, 1992), 98, 100, 112–13, 161.

33. Albert J. Raboteau, *Slave Religion: The "Invisible Institution" in the Antebellum*

South (New York: Oxford University Press, 1978), 44– 92; Walter F. Pitts, *Old Ship of Zion: The Afro-Baptist Ritual in the African Diaspora* (New York: Oxford University Press, 1993), 91–131.

Chapter 16. The Immediacy of Revelation

1. H. Larry Ingle, *Quakers in Conflict: The Hicksite Reformation* (Knoxville: University of Tennessee Press, 1986), 46.

2. Melvin B. Endy, *William Penn and Early Quakerism* (Princeton, N.J.: Princeton University Press, 1973), 63, 71.

3. Hugh Barbour and Arthur O. Roberts, eds., *Early Quaker Writings 1650–1700* (Grand Rapids, Mich.: William B. Eerdmans, 1973), 14.

4. Ibid., 6.

5. Robert Barclay, *An Apology for the True Christian Divinity* (London: Robert Barclay, 1678), 4; Endy, *William Penn*, 240.

6. Margaret Fell, *Womens Speaking Justified, Proved and Allowed of by the Scriptures* (1st ed. 1666; London: n.p., 1667), 1–18; William Penn, *Primitive Christianity Revived In the Faith and Practice of the People Called Quakers* (Salem, Mass.: George Read, 1844), 14; Barclay, *Apology*, 4.

7. Endy, *William Penn*, 239; Hugh Barbour and J. William Frost, *The Quakers* (Westport, Conn.: Greenwood Press, 1988), 29; Henry J. Cadbury, ed., *George Fox's Book of Miracles* (Cambridge: Cambridge University Press, 1948), 44.

8. Isaac Pennington, "Letters of Council," *Early Quaker Writings,* 241; George Whitehead, "Christian Doctrine," ibid., 561; Howard H. Brinton, *The Religion of George Fox as Revealed by His Epistles* (Lebanon, Pa.: Pendle Hill, 1968), 121; J. William Frost, ed., *The Keithian Controversy in Early Pennsylvania* (Norwood, Pa.: Norwood Editions, 1980), ix; Penn, *Primitive Christianity Revived,* 40; Endy, *William Penn,* 82.

9. Endy, *William Penn,* 65; Brinton, *Religion of George Fox,* 11.

10. Francis Daniel Pastorius, *Four Boasting Disputers of this World Briefly Rebuked* (New York: William Bradford, 1697), 9.

11. Ibid., 3–15; Marion Dexter Learned, *The Life of Francis Daniel Pastorius* (Philadelphia: W. Campbell, 1908), 219.

12. Ingle, *Quakers in Conflict,* 17–33, 69.

13. Ibid., 79, 120, 146.

14. Thomas D. Hamm, *The Transformation of American Quakerism, 1800–1907* (Bloomington: Indiana University Press, 1988), 175.

15. Elias Hicks, *Letters of Elias Hicks Including Also a Few Short Essays* (New York: Isaac T. Hopper, 1834), 26, 69; Elias Hicks, *A Series of Extemporaneous Discourses* (Philadelphia: J. and E. Parker, 1825), 54, 305.

16. Hicks, *Letters,* 26, 44, 45, 64; Hicks, *Extemporaneous Discourses,* 119, 316.

17. Hicks, *Letters,* 57, 58, 94; Hicks, *Extemporaneous Discourses,* 37, 256, 318.

18. Hicks, *Letters,* 41, 51; Hicks, *Extemporaneous Discourses,* 207.

19. Ralph Waldo Emerson, "Natural Religion," *Uncollected Lectures by Ralph Waldo Emerson,* ed. Clarence Gohdes (New York: W. E. Rudge, 1932), 57.

20. Hicks, *Letters*, 123; Hicks, *Extemporaneous Discourses*, 147, 260.

21. Hicks, *Letters*, 55, 117; Hicks, *Extemporaneous Discourses*, 317.

22. Hicks, *Letters*, 205; Hicks, *Extemporaneous Discourses*, 103, 131, 161, 203, 267.

23. Hicks, *Letters*, 127; Hicks, *Extemporaneous Discourses*, 103, 117.

24. Allen, *Reason the Only Oracle*, 326.

25. Elder John Lyon, "Certain Important Points of Religious Doctrine" (1844), *The Shakers: Two Centuries of Spiritual Reflection,* ed. Robley E. Whitson (New York: Paulist Press, 1983), 103, 107; Stephen J. Stein, ed., *Letters From a Young Shaker* (Lexington: University Press of Kentucky, 1985), 111; Benjamin S. Youngs, Calvin Green et al., *Testimony of Christ's Second Appearing* (1st ed. 1808; Albany, N.Y.: Van Benthuysen, 1856), 460–65, 521.

26. Stephen J. Stein, *The Shaker Experience in America* (New Haven, Conn.: Yale University Press, 1992), 2–38.

27. Stein, *Shaker Experience*, 66–78.

28. Youngs et al., *Testimony*, viii, xiii, 134, 236, 346.

29. Roxalana Grosvenor, *Sayings of Mother Ann and the First Elders* (1845), *The Shakers*, 47; Seth Y. Wills, *Testimonies of the Life, Revelations and Doctrines of our Ever Blessed Mother Ann Lee* (1816), ibid., 162.

30. Joseph Meacham, *A Concise Statement of the Principles of the Only True Church* (1790), ibid., 61–66.

31. Youngs et al., *Testimony*, 375, 388; Calvin Green, *A Summary View of the Millennial Church* (1823), *The Shakers*, 216.

32. Grosvenor, *Sayings, The Shakers*, 213; George A. Sterling, *The Day Star* (1847), ibid., 240; John Dunlavy, *The Manifesto* (1818), ibid., 74; Calvin Green, "Atheism, Deism, Universalism, and Fatalism Refuted" (1830), ibid., 80.

33. Youngs et al., *Testimony*, 109, 110, 112, 415.

34. Dunlavy, *Manifesto*, 67–70, 74; Youngs, et al., *Testimony*, 477, 562–76.

35. Youngs et al., *Testimony*, 179, 572, 585; Green, *Summary View*, 117; Meacham, *Concise Statement*, 61–66.

36. Youngs et al., *Testimony*, 492.

37. Calvin Green, *Biography of Father Joseph* (1827), *The Shakers*, 214; Youngs et al., *Testimony*, 478, 479–503; Whitson, ed., *The Shakers*, 211.

38. Youngs et al., *Testimony*, 588–91.

39. Ibid., iii, iv, xxi; Dunlavy, *Manifesto*, 128–29.

40. F. Mark McKiernan, *The Voice of One Crying in the Wilderness: Sidney Rigdon, Religious Reformer* (Lawrence, Kan.: Coronado Press, 1971), 47; Joseph Smith, "Revelation of May 1831," *Joseph Smith: Selected Sermons and Writings,* ed. Robert L. Millet (New York: Paulist Press, 1989), 159.

41. McKiernan, *Voice of One Crying*, 191.

42. Joseph Smith et al., *Doctrines and Covenants of the Church of the Latter Day Saints* (Kirtland, Ohio: F. G. Williams, 1835), Sect. 4, 95; Joseph Smith, "The King Follett Discourse," *Selected Sermons and Writings,* 133; Charles Thompson, *Evidences in Proof of the Book of Mormon* (Batavia, N.Y.: D. D. Waite, 1841), 184; Richard L. Bushman, *Joseph Smith and the Beginnings of Mormonism* (Urbana: University of Illinois Press, 1984), 148.

43. Joseph Smith, "Letter to John Wentworth," *Selected Sermons and Writings,* 103.

44. *The Book of Mormon,* trans. Joseph Smith, Jr. (Salt Lake City, Utah: Church of Jesus Christ of Latter-day Saints, 1964), 2 Nephi 30:3– 6; Alexander Campbell, *Delusions: An Analysis of the Book of Mormon* (Boston: Benjamin Greene, 1832), 13.

45. *Book of Mormon,* Helaman 9:24; Parley Pratt, *A Voice of Warning and Instruction to All People* (1st ed. 1836; New York: Eastern States Mission, 1846), 126; Thompson, *Evidences,* 1, 112, 143.

46. *Doctrines and Covenants,* Sect. 24, 38, Sect. 63, 101, Sect. 84, 139; *Book of Mormon,* Mormon 8:26, 9:11; McKiernan, *Voice of One Crying,* 71; Brooke, *Refiner's Fire,* 228; Joseph Smith, "Revelation," *Selected Sermons and Writings,* 156; Pratt, *Voice of Warning,* 112, 128.

47. Brooke, *Refiner's Fire,* 149–262; D. Michael Quinn, *Early Mormonism and the Magic World View* (Salt Lake City, Utah: Signature Books, 1987), 192–224.

48. Pratt, *Voice of Warning,* 26; Thompson, *Evidences,* 143; Millett, ed., *Selected Sermons and Writings,* 238; *Book of Mormon,* 2 Nephi 3:11– 15; Steven C. Harmper, "Infallible Proofs, Both Human and Divine: The Persuasiveness of Mormonism for Early Converts," *Religion and American Culture* 10 (2000):99–118.

49. Klaus Hansen, *Mormonism and the American Experience* (Chicago: University of Chicago Press, 1981), 32.

50. *Doctrines and Covenants,* Sect. 64, 106; Bushman, *Joseph Smith,* 170; Grant Underwood, *The Millenarian World of Early Mormonism* (Urbana: University of Illinois Press, 1993), 8–19.

51. *Doctrines and Covenants,* Sect. 29, 43, Sect. 45, 73, Sect. 57, 89, Sect. 78, 130; *Book of Mormon,* Ether 13; Underwood, *Millenarian World,* 29.

52. Pratt, *Voice of Warning,* 62; Underwood, *Millenarian World,* 27.

53. Underwood, *Millenarian World,* 120.

54. *The Pearl of Great Price, Being a Choice Selection from the Revelations, Translations, and Narratives of Joseph Smith* (Salt Lake City, Utah: Deseret News, 1888), 121; *Doctrines and Covenants,* Sect. 35, 52; Jan Shipps, *Mormonism: The Story of a New Religious Tradition* (Urbana: University of Illinois Press, 1985), 76; Dean C. Jessee, ed., *The Personal Writings of Joseph Smith* (Salt Lake City, Utah: Deseret Books, 1984), 182.

55. *Pearl of Great Price,* 122; Brooke, *Refiner's Fire,* 195, 213; Bushman, *Joseph Smith,* 71; Shipps, *Mormonism,* 67–85.

56. *Doctrines and Covenants,* Sect. 76, 124; Quinn, *Early Mormonism,* 173.

57. Brooke, *Refiner's Fire,* 242; Hansen, *Mormonism,* 103.

58. *Doctrines and Covenants,* Sect. 93, 160; Smith, "King Follett Discourse," 139, 162, n.10; Smith, "Letter to Wentworth," 107.

59. Joseph Smith, "Revelation of May 1833," *Selected Sermons and Writings,* 178; *Doctrines and Covenants,* Sect. 76, 126.

60. Smith, "King Follett Discourse," 132, 139.

61. *Doctrines and Covenants,* Sect. 132, 239–45; Brooke, *Refiner's Fire,* 254.

62. Parley Pratt, *Key to the Science of Theology* (1st ed. 1855; Salt Lake City, Utah: Deseret, 1948), 8, 41, 76, 106, 131–48, 159– 68; Brooke, *Refiner's Fire,* 275; Shipps, *Mormonism,* 131–49.

Chapter 17. Calvinism Revised

1. Williston Walker, *Ten New England Leaders* (New York: Silver, Burdett, 1901), 362; Douglas Sweeney, *Nathaniel Taylor, New Haven Theology, and the Legacy of Jonathan Edwards* (New York: Oxford University Press, 2003), 5–12; Conforti, *Jonathan Edwards,* 9–10; E. A. Park, "New England Theology," *Bibliotheca Sacra* 9 (1852): 192.

2. Timothy Dwight, *Theology Explained and Defended in a Series of Sermons,* 4 vols. (New York: Harper and Brothers, 1858), 4:524–26; Park, *Duties of a Theologian,* 5; Catholic Layman, *A Letter to Edwards A. Park* (Boston: Charles Stimson, 1844), 4.

3. Leonard Woods, *Theology of the Puritans* (Boston: Woodbridge, Moore, 1851), 14; Enoch Pond, *Sketches of the Theological History of New England* (Boston: Congregational Publishing, 1880), 58; Lyman Beecher, "Letter from Dr. Beecher to Dr. Woods," *Spirit of the Pilgrims* 5 (1832):394.

4. Park, "New England Theology," 212.

5. Woods, *Theology of the Puritans,* 12, 15.

6. Park, "New England Theology," 174–75.

7. Pond, *Sketches,* 57, 66, 74; Conforti, *Jonathan Edwards,* 116.

8. Woods, *Theology of the Puritans,* 13, 34, 35; Pond, *Sketches,* 64; Conforti, *Jonathan Edwards,* 126–27; Anthony Cecil, Jr., *The Theological Development of Edwards Amasa Park* (Atlanta, Ga.: Scholars Press, 1974), 221–25.

9. Park, "New England Theology," 208.

10. Woods, *Works,* 1:95, 187; 5:11, 14.

11. Stuart, *Letters to Channing,* 13; Moses Stuart, *Critical History and Defense of the Old Testament Canon* (Andover, Mass.: Allen, 1845), 191–94; Giltner, *Moses Stuart,* 50.

12. Stuart, *Letters to Channing,* 13, 57; Woods, *Works,* 1:95; 5:8, 13; Woods, *Letters to Unitarians,* 26, 90.

13. Park, *Duties of a Theologian,* 5; Cecil, *Theological Development,* 8–17.

14. Park, "Natural Theology," 241, 244, 248; Cecil, *Theological Development,* 22; Giltner, *Moses Stuart,* 54.

15. Smith, *Faith and Philosophy,* 29; Edwards Amasa Park, "The Theology of the Intellect and that of the Feelings," *Bibliotheca Sacra* 7 (1850):533–69.

16. Park, "Theology of the Intellect," 534, 545, 548–49.

17. Horace Bushnell, "Our Gospel a Gift to the Imagination," *Building Eras in Religion* (New York: Charles Scribner's Sons, 1881), 265, 269–72; Charles Hodge, "The Theology of the Intellect and that of the Feelings," *Essays and Reviews* (New York: Robert Carter, 1857), 539–69; Woods, *Letters to Unitarians,* 90, 95, 99.

18. Stuart, *Letters to Channing,* 19, 32, 36, 52.

19. Woods, *Works,* 1:438, 440, 445, 457; Stuart, *Letters to Channing,* 36; Leonard Woods, "Dr. Woods's Letter to Dr. Beecher," *Spirit of the Pilgrims* 5 (1832):455–72.

20. Woods, *Letters to Unitarians,* 19; Woods, *Works,* 4:367, 442; Boardman, *History of New England Theology,* 88.

21. Edward Dorr Griffin, *The Doctrine of Divine Efficiency Defended* (New York: Jonathan Leavitt, 1833), 180.

22. Edward Dorr Griffin, "An Humble Attempt to Reconcile the Differences of Chris-

tians Respecting the Extent of the Atonement," *The Atonement: Discourses and Treatises,* ed. Edwards A. Park (Boston: Congregational Publishing, 1859), 295–97, 298; Griffin, *Doctrine of Divine Efficiency,* 189; Bennet Tyler, *A Discourse on Human Ability and Inability* (Hartford, Conn.: Case, Tiffany, 1854), 20–21.

23. Park, ed., *The Atonement,* ix–lxxix.

24. Joseph Harvey, *A Letter to the Rev. Dr. Tyler on Human Ability and Inability* (Springfield, Mass.: Bowles, 1855), 21; Tyler, *Discourse on Human Ability,* 16–17.

25. Park, "New England Theology," 180; Conforti, *Jonathan Edwards,* 121.

26. Asa Burton, *Essays on Some of the First Principles of Metaphysicks, Ethicks, and Theology* (Portland, Maine: Shirley, 1824), 84–94, 131–38.

27. Park, *Duties of a Theologian,* 13; Enoch Pond, "The Character of Infants," *Bibliotheca Sacra* 9 (1852):755; Enoch Pond, *Lectures in Christian Theology* (1st ed. 1866; Boston: Congregational Publishing, 1874), 388.

28. Leonard Woods, *An Essay on Native Depravity* (Boston: William Peirce, 1835), 218; Joseph Harvey, *Review of a Sermon, Delivered in the Chapel of Yale College* (Hartford, Conn.: Goodwin, 1829), 16, 29; Bennet Tyler, *Letters on the Origin and Progress of the New Haven Theology* (New York: Carter and Collier, 1837), 19.

29. Pond, *Sketches,* 64.

30. Woods, "Dr. Woods's Letter to Dr. Beecher," 460; Woods, *Essay on Native Depravity,* 197; Conforti, *Jonathan Edwards,* 129.

31. Bennet Tyler, "Dr. Taylor's Theological Views," *Spirit of the Pilgrims* 5 (1832):329; Woods, *Essay on Native Depravity,* 81.

32. Moses Stuart, *A Commentary on the Epistle to the Romans* (Andover, Mass.: Flagg and Gould, 1832), 215–16, 541.

33. Park, "New England Theology," 177; N. W. Taylor, "Spring on the Means of Regeneration," *Quarterly Christian Spectator* 1 (1829):19; Bennet Tyler, *Strictures on the Review of Dr. Spring's Dissertation on the Means of Regeneration* (Portland, Maine: Shirley and Hyde, 1829), 11; Griffin, *Doctrine of Divine Efficiency,* 189.

34. Tyler, *Strictures,* 8; Pond, *Sketches,* 62.

35. Walker, *Ten New England Leaders,* 374; David W. Kling, *A Field of Divine Wonders* (University Park: The Pennsylvania State University Press, 1993), 110–68.

36. Tyler, *Letters on the Origin,* 103; Sweeney, *Nathaniel Taylor,* 21–45.

37. Wayland, *Theological Department in Yale College,* 47; "Jonathan Edwards and the Successive Forms of New Divinity," *Biblical Repertory and Princeton Review* 30 (1858): 606.

38. Dwight, *Theology Explained and Defended,* 1:256, 260; 2:219– 29, 400, 405; 4:26, 215, 312; John R. Fitzmier, *New England's Moral Legislator: Timothy Dwight, 1752–1817* (Bloomington: Indiana University Press, 1998), 17–18, 105–29.

39. Dwight, *Theology Explained and Defended,* 1:254–56, 366, 434, 478, 486; 2:419.

40. Ibid., 2:418–19, 465, 467; 3:100.

41. Ibid., 4:38–60, 71.

42. Ibid., 1:369, 371; 2:230, 315.

43. Timothy Dwight, *The Nature and Danger of Infidel Philosophy* (New Haven, Conn.: George Bunce, 1798), 35, 50.

44. Sidney Earl Mead, *Nathaniel William Taylor 1786–1858* (Chicago: University of

Chicago Press, 1942), 6–84; Sweeney, *Nathaniel Taylor,* 46–65; Wayland, *Theological Department in Yale College,* 5–90; N. W. Taylor, "Letter from Rev. Dr. Taylor," *Spirit of the Pilgrims* 5 (1832):177; Kuklick, *Churchmen and Philosophers,* 94–111.

45. Taylor, "Spring on the Means of Regeneration," 13, 703; Taylor, "Letter from the Rev. Dr. Taylor," 177.

46. Taylor, "Letter from the Rev. Dr. Taylor," 177–78.

47. Taylor, "On the Authority of Reason in Theology," 151.

48. Woods, *Works,* 4:352; Harvey, *Review of a Sermon,* 12; Taylor, "On the Authority of Reason," 157–58; N. W. Taylor, "The Trinity," *Essays, Lectures, Etc. Upon Select Topics in Revealed Theology* (New York: Clark, Austin, Smith, 1859), 2; N. W. Taylor, "Application of the Principles of Common Sense to Certain Disputed Doctrines," *Christian Spectator* 3 (1831):475.

49. Taylor, "On the Authority of Reason," 156.

50. Tyler, *Letters on the Origin,* 6; Taylor, "The Trinity," 40; N. W. Taylor, "Review of Norton's Views of Calvinism," *Quarterly Christian Spectator* 5 (1823):196–224.

51. E. Porter, "Review of the Doctrine and Discipline of the Methodist Episcopal Church," *Quarterly Christian Spectator* 2 (1830):488, 483–504; "Review of the Economy of Methodism," ibid., 1 (1829):509–26; see also *Quarterly Christian Spectator* 3 (1831):597–640, 1 (1829):566–72; N. W. Taylor, *Man a Free Agent Without the Aids of Divine Grace* (New Haven, Conn.: American Tract Society, 1818), 4–14.

52. Wayland, *Theological Department in Yale College,* 206; N. W. Taylor, *Lectures on the Moral Government of God,* 2 vols. (New York: Clark, Austin, Smith, 1859), 1:2, 47, 257.

53. Taylor, *Lectures on the Moral Government,* 2:29, 137–38; Taylor, "Letter from Rev. Dr. Taylor," 174.

54. Eleazar Fitch, *Two Discourses on the Nature of Sin* (New Haven, Conn.: Treadway, Adams, 1826), 4; Tyler, *Letters on the Origin,* 7; Sweeney, *Nathaniel Taylor,* 70–71.

55. N. W. Taylor, *Concio ad Clerum: A Sermon Delivered in the Chapel of Yale College* (New Haven, Conn.: Maltby, Hallock, 1842), 5, 8, 13, 37.

56. Ibid., 36–37; Harvey, *Review of a Sermon,* 37; Taylor, "Letter from Rev. Dr. Taylor," 176.

57. Taylor, "Letter from Rev. Dr. Taylor," 175–76; N. W. Taylor, "Dr. Taylor's Reply to Dr. Tyler's Examination," *Spirit of the Pilgrims* 5 (1832):428; Joseph Harvey, *Examination of a Review of Dr. Taylor's Sermon* (Hartford, Conn.: Goodwin, 1829), 6.

58. Taylor, *Concio ad Clerum,* 25; Harvey, *Examination,* 20; N. W. Taylor, *Review of Spring's Dissertation on Native Depravity* (New Haven, Conn.: Cooke, 1833), 7.

59. Taylor, *Lectures on the Moral Government,* 1:134, 195; N. W. Taylor, *Regeneration the Beginning of Holiness in the Human Heart* (New Haven, Conn.: Whiting, 1816), 11; Taylor, "Spring on the Means of Regeneration," 223, Sweeney, *Nathaniel Taylor,* 74–76.

60. Letter from Taylor, in Lyman Beecher, *The Autobiography of Lyman Beecher,* ed. Barbara M. Cross, 2 vols. (Cambridge, Mass.: Harvard University Press, 1961), 1:284–87.

61. Ibid., 1:285; Taylor, "Spring on the Means of Regeneration," 225; Taylor, *Lectures on the Moral Government,* 1:194; Sweeney, *Nathaniel Taylor,* 76–83.

62. Taylor, "Spring on the Means of Regeneration," 20, 209; Taylor, "Letter from Rev. Dr. Taylor," 6.

63. Dwight, *Theology Explained and Defended,* 1:462; Taylor, "Spring on the Means of Regeneration," 210; Sweeney, *Nathaniel Taylor,* 116– 17.

64. Bennet Tyler, *A Vindication of the Strictures on the Review of Dr. Spring's Dissertation* (Portland, Maine: Shirley, Hyde, 1830), 19; Tyler, "Dr. Taylor's Theological Reviews," 333.

65. Taylor, *Regeneration the Beginning,* 12; Jonathan Edwards, "Remarks on the Principles of Morality and Natural Religion," *Freedom of the Will,* ed. Ramsey, 456; Taylor, "Spring on the Means of Regeneration," 19, 700; Taylor, "Letter from Rev. Dr. Taylor," 174; Conforti, *Jonathan Edwards,* 50.

66. Taylor, "Spring on the Means of Regeneration," 491; Taylor, "Letter from Rev. Dr. Taylor," 175–76; N. W. Taylor, "Dr. Taylor's Reply to Dr. Tyler's Examination," *Spirit of the Pilgrims* 5 (1832):429.

67. Tyler, *Letters on the Origin,* 34.

68. Catharine Beecher, *Letters on the Difficulties of Religion* (Hartford, Conn.: Belknap, Hammersly, 1836), 50; "Letters on the Difficulties of Religion," *Quarterly Christian Spectator* 8 (1836):671– 72.

69. Catharine Beecher, *Truth Stronger than Fiction* (New York: For the Author, 1850), 158, 291; Catharine Beecher, *Common Sense Applied to Religion, or, The Bible and the People* (New York: Harper, 1857), 306– 07; Mark David Hall, "Catharine Beecher: America's First Female Philosopher and Theologian," *Fides et Historia* 32 (2000):65–80; Sweeney, *Nathaniel Taylor,* 137–39.

70. Charles G. Finney, *Lectures on Revivals of Religion,* ed. William G. McLoughlin (1st ed. 1835; Cambridge, Mass.: Harvard University Press, 1960), 185–88; Charles G. Finney, *The Memoirs of Charles G. Finney,* ed. Garth M. Rosell and Richard A. G. Dupuis (Grand Rapids, Mich.: Zondervan, 1989), 89–90; Keith J. Hardman, *Charles Grandison Finney 1792–1875: Revivalist and Reformer* (Syracuse, N.Y.: Syracuse University Press, 1987), 282–83, 186–87; Allen C. Guelzo, "An Heir or a Rebel? Charles Grandison Finney and the New England Theology," *Journal of the Early Republic* 17 (1997):90.

71. Finney, *Memoirs,* 57; George Frederick Wright, *Charles Grandison Finney* (Boston: Houghton, Mifflin, 1891), 179; Sweeney, *Nathaniel Taylor,* 150–51.

72. A. T. Swing, "President Finney and the Oberlin Theology," *Bibliotheca Sacra* 57 (1900):465–82; M. L. Vulgamore, "Charles G. Finney: Catalyst in the Dissolution of American Calvinism," *Reformed Review* 17 (1964):39; Hardman, *Finney,* 234, 287; Douglas Sweeney, "Finney and Edwardsean Culture," *Wesleyan/Holiness Studies Center Bulletin* 6 (1998):2; Allen Guelzo, "Are There Two Roads to Holiness?" ibid., 3; Guelzo, "An Heir or a Rebel?" 68; Boardman, *History of New England Theology,* 145; Foster, *Genetic History,* 467.

73. Wright, *Finney,* 161, 181; Finney, *Memoirs,* 143, 176, 251; Charles G. Finney, *Finney's Lectures on Systematic Theology,* ed. J. H. Fairchild (1st ed. 1851; Grand Rapids, Mich.: Eerdmans, 1951), 334. An earlier 1846 version of the lectures differed in scope from the expanded 1851 edition.

74. Finney, *Finney's Lectures,* ix, x, 8, 12, 113, 185, 219, 262, 339; Wright, *Finney,* 182–86; Charles G. Finney, "Sinners Bound to Change Their Own Hearts," *Sermons on Important Subjects* (New York: Taylor, 1836), 40.

75. Finney, *Finney's Lectures,* ix, xi, 2, 3–35, 61.

76. Swing, "President Finney," 470; Charles G. Finney, "Traditions of the Elders," *Sermons on Important Subjects,* 65, 69; Finney, *Finney's Lectures,* 259, 270, 275; Finney, *Memoirs,* 50.

77. Finney, *Finney's Lectures,* 215, 231, 252; Finney, *Memoirs,* 152.

78. Finney, *Finney's Lectures,* 256; Charles G. Finney, "Why Sinners Hate God," *Sermons on Important Subjects,* 156; Wright, *Finney,* 230.

79. Asa Rand, *The New Divinity Tried* (Boston: Lyceum Press, 1832), 11; Finney, "Sinners Bound," 23–24; Finney, *Finney's Lectures,* 282; Finney, *Memoirs,* 350.

80. Finney, *Finney's Lectures,* 117, 120, 391, 392.

81. Finney, *Lectures on Revivals of Religion,* 13; Finney, *Finney's Lectures,* 14; Charles G. Finney, *Lectures to Professing Christians* (1st ed. 1837; New York: Fleming H. Revell, 1878), 108; Finney, "Sinners Bound," 49; Finney, "Traditions of the Elders," 75; Finney, *Memoirs,* 80, 190, 265.

82. Finney, *Finney's Lectures,* x, 15, 328, 329, 333.

83. Finney, "Sinners Bound," 25, 29; Finney, *Lectures to Professing Christians,* 287, 342–44; Finney, *Finney's Lectures,* 321, 322–24.

84. Finney, *Finney's Lectures,* 342.

85. Finney, *Finney's Lectures,* 483, 490, 492, 552; Charles G. Finney, "Doctrine of Election," *Sermons on Important Subjects,* 214; Finney, "Reprobation," ibid., 552.

86. Finney, *Lectures to Professing Christians,* 339.

87. Finney, *Memoirs,* 391–92; Dayton, *Theological Roots of Pentecostalism,* 50, 71; Asa Mahan, *Scripture Doctrine of Christian Perfection* (Boston: King, 1839), 10, 16; Guelzo, "An Heir or a Rebel?" 83; Hardman, *Finney,* 328; Finney, *Finney's Lectures,* 455.

88. Finney, *Lectures to Professing Christians,* 341, 345, 346, 407; Finney, *Finney's Lectures,* 433.

89. Finney, *Finney's Lectures,* 96; Wright, *Finney,* 210, 221.

90. Finney, *Lectures to Professing Christians,* 57, 356; Finney, *Memoirs,* 453; Hardman, *Finney,* 273; Charles G. Finney, "Stewardship," *Sermons on Important Subjects,* 203.

91. Smith, *Faith and Philosophy,* 33, 32, 117.

92. William K. B. Stoever, "Henry Boynton Smith and the German Theology of History," *Union Seminary Quarterly Review* 24 (1968):68–89; Smith, *Faith and Philosophy,* 19.

93. Smith, *Faith and Philosophy,* 57; Stoever, "Henry Boynton Smith," 84.

94. Smith, *Faith and Philosophy,* 60, 90, 215–62, 385; Foster, *Genetic History,* 440–42.

95. George Park Fisher, *Discussions in History and Theology* (New York: Charles Scribner's Sons, 1880), 311; Foster, *Genetic History,* 247.

96. Smith, *Faith and Philosophy,* 12, 27.

Chapter 18. "True Calvinism" Defended

1. John C. Vander Stelt, *Philosophy and Scripture: A Study in Old Princeton and Westminster Theology* (Marlton, N.J.: Mack, 1978), 93.

2. A. A. Hodge, *The Life of Charles Hodge* (1st ed. 1881; New York: Arno Press, 1969), 308.

3. Ibid., 81, 269, 308–310.

4. Charles Hodge, "Public Education," *Biblical Repertory* 1 (1829):371 (hereafter *BR*); Archibald Alexander, "A Sermon Delivered at the Opening of the General Assembly" (1808), in Mark Noll, ed. *The Princeton Theology 1812–1891* (Grand Rapids, Mich.: Baker Book House, 1983), 54; Charles Hodge, "Suggestions to Theological Students," *Biblical Repertory and Theological Review* 5 (1833):112 (hereafter *BRTR*); Samuel Miller, *Letters on Clerical Manners and Habits* (New York: Carvill, 1827), 42; E. Brooks Holifield, *The Gentlemen Theologians* (Durham, N.C.: Duke University Press, 1978), 15; Hodge, "Suggestions to Theological Students," 106; Charles Hodge, "The Latest Form of Infidelity," *Biblical Repertory and Princeton Review* 12 (1840):36 (hereafter *BRPR*); Charles Hodge, "Finney's Lectures on Theology," *Essays and Reviews* (New York: Robert Carter, 1857), 248.

5. B. M. Palmer, *The Life and Letters of James Henley Thornwell* (Richmond, Va.: Whittet, Shepperson, 1875), 90; David F. Wells, ed., *The Princeton Theology* (Grand Rapids, Mich.: Baker Book House, 1989), 59, n.1; Holifield, *Gentlemen Theologians,* 204; Charles Hodge, "Presbyterian Reunion," *BRPR* 40 (1868):61; Leonard J. Trinterud, "Charles Hodge (1797–1878)," *Sons of the Prophets,* ed. Hugh T. Kerr (Princeton, N.J.: Princeton University Press, 1963), 34.

6. Lefferts A. Loetscher, *Facing the Enlightenment and Pietism* (Westport, Conn.: Greenwood, 1983), 74, 76; Elwyn Allen Smith, *The Presbyterian Minister in American Culture* (Philadelphia: Westminster Press, 1962), 130; James Oscar Farmer, Jr., *The Metaphysical Confederacy* (Macon, Ga.: Mercer University Press, 1986), 51; A. A. Hodge, *Life,* 81, 269.

7. Loetscher, *Facing the Enlightenment,* 44; Earl A. Pope, *New England Calvinism and the Disruption of the Presbyterian Church* (New York: Garland, 1987), 127; Charles Hodge, "Professor Park and the Princeton Review," *Princeton Review* 23 (1851):685, 694 (hereafter *PR*).

8. Charles Hodge, *Systematic Theology,* 3 vols. (New York: Scribner, Armstrong, 1871–73), 2:192, 207, 220, 225–26, 285, 289, 303, 319; Charles Hodge, "Free Agency," *BRPR* 29 (1857):118; Charles Hodge, "Clap's Defence of the Doctrines of the New England Churches," *BRPR* 11 (1939):394–95; Charles Hodge, "Inquiries Respecting the Doctrine of Imputation," *BRTR* 2 (1830):436, 454.

9. Ely, *Contrast,* viii; Smith, *Presbyterian Minister,* 109, 166; Holifield, *Gentlemen Theologians,* 195.

10. J. H. Thornwell, "Election and Reprobation," *The Collected Writings of James Henley Thornwell,* ed. John B. Adger, 3 vols. (Richmond: Presbyterian Committee of Publication, 1871), 2:108; J. H. Thornwell, "Necessity of the Atonement," ibid., 2:223, 251; J. H. Thornwell, "Lectures in Theology," ibid., 1:332; Smith, *Presbyterian Minister,* 130; Pope, *New England Calvinism,* 226, 379.

11. Charles Hodge, "Barnes on the Epistle to the Romans," *BRTR* 7 (1835):289; Hodge, "Park and the Princeton Review," 694; Hodge, "Clap's Defence," 399.

12. Pope, *New England Calvinism,* 109; George Marsden, *The Evangelical Mind and the New School Presbyterian Experience* (New Haven, Conn.: Yale University Press, 1970), 59–89.

13. Lyman Beecher, *Views in Theology* (Cincinnati, Ohio: Truman, Smith, 1836), 125.

14. Nathan S. S. Beman, *Four Sermons on the Doctrine of the Atonement* (Troy, N.Y.: Parker, 1825), vi, 30, 77, 107, 121, 122.

15. Albert Barnes, *The Way of Salvation* (New York: Leavitt, Lord, 1836), 19–21, 25, 52, 60, 63, 74, 134, 154, 169; Pope, *New England Calvinism,* 171, 186, 265.

16. Beecher, *Autobiography,* 412–17.

17. Beecher, *Views in Theology,* 14, 21, 31, 117, 155, 193–94, 237–38.

18. George Duffield, *Spiritual Life, or, Regeneration* (Carlisle, Pa.: George Fleming, 1832), 202, 247, 274, 317, 363, 545.

19. Pope, *New England Calvinism,* 284; Samuel J. Baird, *History of the New School and of the Questions Involved in the Disruption of the Presbyterian Church in 1838* (Philadelphia: Claxton, Remsen, Haffelfinger, 1868), 175; Samuel J. Baird, *The First Adam and the Second* (Philadelphia: Lindsay, Blakeston, 1860), 49, 50, 474.

20. Vander Stelt, *Philosophy and Scripture,* 90; A. A. Hodge, *Life,* 521.

21. Loetscher, *Facing the Enlightenment,* 108, 174, 199.

22. Charles Hodge, *The Constitutional History of the Presbyterian Church in the United States of America, Part I and II* (Philadelphia: William Martien, 1839), 160, 209, 219.

23. Hodge, "Inquiries Respecting Imputation," 428.

24. Trinterud, "Charles Hodge," *Sons of the Prophets,* 37.

25. Charles Hodge, "Inspiration," *BRPR* 29 (1857):669–70; Archibald Alexander, "The Sermon Delivered at the Inauguration" (1812), *Princeton Theology,* 80; Hodge, *Systematic Theology,* 1:151–88; Charles Hodge, "On the Sonship of Christ," *BR* (1829): 429.

26. Richard A. Muller, *Post-Reformation Reformed Dogmatics, 2: Holy Scripture* (Grand Rapids, Mich.: Baker Book House, 1993), 433; Randall Balmer, "The Princetonians and Scripture: A Reconsideration," *Westminster Theological Journal* 44 (1982): 354–62.

27. Alexander, "Sermon," *Princeton Theology,* 53; Archibald Alexander, "The Bible, A Key to the Phenomena of the Natural World," ibid., 95; Hodge, *Systematic Theology,* 1:125, 38–39; Loetscher, *Facing the Enlightenment,* 21; Charles Hodge, *The Way of Life,* ed. Mark Noll (New York: Paulist Press, 1987), 56, 59, 64–76.

28. A. A. Hodge, *Life,* 99; Hodge, *Systematic Theology,* 1:10–15, 25, 60; Charles Hodge [and Francis A. March?], "Sir William Hamilton's Philosophy of the Conditioned," *BRPR* 32 (1860):472–510.

29. Hodge, *Systematic Theology,* 1:171; Jonathan Wells, "Charles Hodge on the Bible and Science," *American Presbyterians: The Journal of Presbyterian History* 66 (1998): 157–65.

30. Charles Hodge, "The Unity of Mankind," *BRPR* 31 (1859):130; Charles Hodge, *What is Darwinism?* (London: T. Nelson, 1874), 141, 176–77; John W. Stewart, *Mediat-*

ing the Center: Studies in Reformed Theology and History (Princeton, N.J.: Princeton Seminary, 1995), 36–44.

31. A. A. Hodge, *Life,* 47, 391; Noll, ed., *Princeton Theology,* 13; Charles Hodge, "Remarks on Dr. Cox's Communication," *BRPR* 3 (1831):524.

32. Pope, *New England Calvinism,* 117, 216; Charles Hodge, "Adoption of the Confession of Faith," *BRPR* 30 (1858):671, 680.

33. Hodge, *Systematic Theology,* 2:198, 354; Hodge, "Inquiries Respecting Imputation," 437.

34. Archibald Alexander, "The Early History of Pelagianism," *BRPR* 2 (1830):93; Hodge, "Inquiries Respecting Imputation," 431, 468.

35. Charles Hodge, "The Christian Spectator on the Doctrine of Imputation," *BRTR* 3 (1831):421, 424; Hodge, "Inquiries Respecting Imputation," 442, 449; Charles Hodge, "The First and Second Adam," *BRPR* (1860):347; Charles Hodge, "Stuart on the Romans," *BRPR* (1833):386.

36. Hodge, "Regeneration," *Essays and Reviews,* 35; Hodge, "Finney's Lectures," ibid., 247, 258, 283; Hodge, "Remarks on Dr. Cox's Communication," 518; Hodge, "Free Agency," 118; Charles Hodge, "Narrative of the Visit to the American Churches by Andrew Reed," *BRTR* 7 (1835):614, 617.

37. Charles Hodge, "Beman on the Atonement," *BRPR* 17 (1845):87– 96, 109, 112, 116; Hodge, "Clap's Defence," 386.

38. Hodge, "Finney's Lectures," *Essays and Reviews,* 253, 255, 258, 259; Charles Hodge, "The New Divinity Tried," *BRTR* 4 (1832):291–98.

39. Hodge, "Finney's Lectures," *Essays and Reviews,* 261; Hodge, "New Divinity Tried," 288; Hodge, "Free Agency," 112.

40. Charles Hodge, "Professor Park's Remarks on the Princeton Review," *PR* 23 (1851):313.

41. Hodge, *Systematic Theology,* 2:61.

42. Charles Hodge et al., "Transcendentalism of the Germans and Cousin," *The Transcendentalists,* ed. Miller, 238–39; Charles Hodge, "The Latest Form of Infidelity," *BRPR* 12 (1840):31, 37.

43. Charles Hodge, "Schaf's Protestantism," *PR* 17 (1845):626– 27; Charles Hodge, "What is Christianity?" *BRPR* 32 (1860):121.

44. J. W. Nevin, *The Mystical Presence: A Vindication of the Reformed or Calvinistic Doctrine of the Holy Eucharist* (Philadelphia: Lippincott, 1846), 146–77; Charles Hodge, "Doctrine of the Reformed Church on the Lord's Supper," *Essays and Reviews,* 374.

45. Philip Schaff, *Theological Propadeutic* (New York: Charles Scribner's Sons, 1894), 394; George H. Shriver, "Passages in Friendship: John W. Nevin to Charles Hodge," *Journal of Presbyterian History* 58 (1980):121; Charles Hodge, "History of the Apostolic Church," *BRPR* 26 (1854):151; Hodge, *Systematic Theology,* 2:201, 202, 210, 446–47; 3:655.

46. Hodge, "History of the Apostolic Church," 159, 166; Walter H. Conser, Jr., *God and the Natural World: Religion and Science in Antebellum America* (Columbia: University of South Carolina Press, 1993), 37–64.

47. Hodge, "History of the Apostolic Church," 171; Charles Hodge, "God in Christ," *Essays and Reviews,* 440, 448.

48. Charles Hodge, "Bushnell on Christian Nurture," *Essays and Reviews,* 302–09;

Hodge, "God in Christ," ibid., 436, 453; Charles Hodge, "Bushnell on Vicarious Sacrifice," *BRPR* 38 (1866):172–84.

49. Charles Hodge, "The Theology of the Intellect and that of the Feelings," *Essays and Reviews,* 538–40, 549.

50. Philip Schaff, *What is Church History?* (Philadelphia: J. B. Lippincott, 1846), 9; Hodge, "The Responsibilities of Boards of Missions," *Essays and Reviews,* 397; Charles Hodge, "Bishop Doane and the Oxford Tracts," *BRPR* 13 (1841):456.

51. Charles Hodge, "Is the Church of Rome a Part of the Visible Church?" *Essays and Reviews,* 229; Hodge, *Systematic Theology,* 3:545; Charles Hodge, "The Visibility of the Church," *BRPR* 25 (1853):682; Charles Hodge, "The Tecnobaptist: The Church Membership of Infants," *BRPR* 30 (1858):349–50.

52. Hodge, *Systematic Theology,* 3:545.

53. Charles Hodge, "Tracts for the Times," *BRPR* 10 (1838):87, 105; Hodge, "Bushnell on Christian Nurture," *Essays and Reviews,* 397; Charles Hodge, "Idea of the Church," *BRPR* 25 (1853):340; Charles Hodge, "The Church of England and Presbyterian Orders," *BRPR* 26 (1854):380; Charles Hodge, "On the Permanency of the Apostolic Office," *BRPR* 28 (1856):11.

54. Charles Hodge, "Thornwell on the Apocrypha," *PR* 17 (1845):282; Hodge, "Idea of the Church," 277; Hodge, "Church of England," 380; Charles Hodge, "The Church — Its Perpetuity," *BRPR* 28 (1856):694; Charles Hodge, "Theories of the Church," *Essays and Reviews,* 211; Charles Hodge, "Rule of Faith," *BRPR* 14 (1842):611; Hodge, "Schaf's Protestantism," 630.

55. Hodge, "Is the Church of Rome a Part of the Visible Church?" 231, 237; Benjamin M. Palmer, *The Life and Letters of James Henley Thornwell* (Richmond, Va.: Whittet, Shepperson, 1875), 290.

56. Hodge, "Doctrine of the Reformed Church," *Essays and Reviews,* 359, 362; Hodge, "Tracts for the Times," 86, 105.

57. Hodge, *Systematic Theology,* 3:245; C. P. Krauth, *Infant Baptism and Infant Salvation in the Calvinistic System* (Philadelphia: Lutheran Book Store, 1874), 10, 13, 73; Hodge, "Tecnobaptist," 385.

58. Charles Hodge, "Voluntary Societies and Ecclesiastical Organizations," *BRPR* 9 (1837):102; Hodge, "Hamilton's Philosophy," 546, 553, 564; Palmer, *Thornwell,* 245; J. H. Thornwell, "Theology as a Life in Individuals and in the Church," *Collected Writings,* 2:48; Holifield, *Gentlemen Theologians,* 178, 204.

59. Holifield, *Gentlemen Theologians,* 197, 198; Palmer, *Thornwell,* 214; J. H. Thornwell, "Discourse Delivered by Dr. Thornwell Upon Being Inaugurated as Professor of Theology," *Collected Writings,* 1:582.

60. Palmer, *Thornwell,* 537.

61. John B. Adger, *My Life and Times* (Richmond, Va.: Presbyterian Committee of Publication, 1889), 77.

62. Thomas Cary Johnson, *The Life and Letters of Robert Lewis Dabney* (Richmond, Va.: Presbyterian Committee of Publication, 1903), 204–312.

63. Thornwell, "Inaugural Discourse," 575; Holifield, *Gentlemen Theologians,* 74; Douglas F. Kelley, "Robert Lewis Dabney," *Southern Reformed Theology,* ed. David F. Wells (Grand Rapids, Mich.: Baker Book House, 1989), 50.

64. J. H. Thornwell, "The Standard and Nature of Religion," *Collected Writings,* 3:86; J. H. Thornwell, "Theology, Its Proper Method and Its Central Principle," ibid., 1:470.

65. Thornwell, "Standard and Nature of Religion," 98; J. H. Thornwell, "Lecture on Miracles," *Collected Writings,* 3:227.

66. Thornwell, "Inaugural Discourse," 582; Thornwell, "Standard and Nature of Religion," 51, 61.

67. Palmer, *Thornwell,* 25, 222; Hodge, "Voluntary Societies," 102; Hodge, "Hamilton's Philosophy," 546, 553, 564.

68. J. H. Thornwell, "The Validity of the Baptism of the Church of Rome," *Collected Writings,* 3:347; J. H. Thornwell, "The Apocryphal Books," ibid., 3:746; Palmer, *Thornwell,* 296.

69. Palmer, *Thornwell,* 303; Thornwell, "Theology as a Life," 46; Charles Hodge, "The General Assembly," *BRPR* 31 (1859):617.

70. Thornwell, "Lectures in Theology," *Collected Writings,* 1:15–85.

71. J. H. Thornwell, "The Gospel, God's Power and Wisdom," *Collected Writings,* 2:321; J. H. Thornwell, "The Nature of Salvation," ibid., 2:377.

72. Thornwell, "Theology, Its Proper Method," 479; Adger, *Life and Times,* 313–25; Robert L. Dabney, *Lectures in Systematic Theology* (Grand Rapids, Mich.: Zondervan, 1972), 341–47, 348.

73. Adger, *Life and Times,* 311, 314, 326; Dabney, *Lectures,* 615–16, 810.

74. Thornwell, "Theology as a Life," 51; Thornwell, "Theology, Its Proper Method," 457; Thornwell, "Lectures in Theology," 37, 139; Thornwell, "Inaugural Discourse," 578.

75. Thornwell, "Lectures in Theology," 462; James Henley Thornwell, "Necessity of the Atonement," *Collected Writings,* 2:246.

Chapter 19. Lutherans: Reason, Revival, and Confession

1. Schaff, *America,* 150.

2. S. S. Schmucker, *Elements of Popular Theology* (1st ed. 1826; New York: Leavitt, Lord, 1834), 42–43.

3. Martin Luther, *A Treatise on Christian Liberty, Works of Martin Luther,* ed. H. E. Jacobs, 6 vols. (Philadelphia: General Council Publication Board, 1916), 2:312–48; Martin Luther, "Preface to the Complete Edition of Luther's Latin Writings," *Career of the Reformer IV,* ed. Lewis W. Spitz, *Luther's Works,* gen. ed. H. T. Lehmann, 54 vols. (Philadelphia: Muhlenberg Press, 1960), 327–38.

4. Heinrich Schmid, *The Doctrinal Theology of the Evangelical Lutheran Church* (1st ed. 1875; Minneapolis, Minn.: Augsburg, 1961), 31.

5. Ibid., 26–57; Robert D. Preus, *The Theology of Post-Reformation Lutheranism,* 2 vols. (St. Louis, Mo.: Concordia, 1970), 1:129–35.

6. P. J. Spener, *Pia Desideria,* trans. Theodore G. Tappert (Philadelphia: Fortress, 1988), 56, 100; A. H. Francke, "Autobiography," *The Pietists: Selected Writings,* ed. Peter C. Erb (New York: Paulist Press, 1983), 106; A. H. Francke, "Following Christ," ibid., 141; N. L. Count von Zinzendorf, "Account," ibid., 291–92.

7. Paul P. Kuenning, *The Rise and Fall of American Lutheran Pietism* (Macon, Ga.: Mercer University Press, 1988), 26.

8. Justus Falckner, *Grondlyche Onderricht* (New York: William Bradfordt, 1708), 1–2, 66, 69.

9. H. M. Muhlenberg, "Muhlenberg's Defence of Pietism," trans. C. W. Schaeffer, *Lutheran Church Review* 12 (1893):360, 361–62.

10. Kuenning, *Rise and Fall,* 35; J. J. Mol, *The Breaking of Traditions: Theological Conviction in Colonial America* (Berkeley, Calif.: Glendessary, 1968), 29.

11. Muhlenberg, "Defence," 362, 373; Kuenning, *Rise and Fall,* 35; Vergilius Ferm, *The Crisis in American Lutheran Theology* (New York: Century, 1927), 14; David A. Gustafson, *Lutherans in Crisis: The Question of Identity in Colonial America* (Minneapolis, Minn.: Fortress, 1993), 40.

12. Arthur C. Repp, Sr., *Luther's Catechism Comes to America* (Metuchen, N.J.: Scarecrow Press, 1982), 34, 51, 65.

13. Gustafson, *Lutherans in Crisis,* 55.

14. Hans Frei, *The Eclipse of Biblical Narrative* (New Haven, Conn.: Yale University Press, 1974), 55.

15. F. H. Quitman, *Evangelical Catechism* (Hudson, N.Y.: William E. Norman, 1814), 7, 9, 23, 33.

16. Ibid., 7, 38, 47, 174.

17. Ibid., 35, 48, 109–10, 113–14.

18. George Lochmann, *The History, Doctrine, and Discipline of the Evangelical Lutheran Church* (Harrisburg, Pa.: John Wyeth, 1816), 82, 87, 88, 102, 107, 124, 134–37.

19. Ferm, *Crisis,* 45–50.

20. Kuenning, *Rise and Fall,* 67.

21. S. S. Schmucker, "Intellectual and Moral Glories of the Christian Temple" (1824), 10, cited in Kuenning, *Rise and Fall,* 69; S. S. Schmucker, *Inaugural Address* (Carlisle, Pa.: Tizzard and Crover, 1826), 27; S. S. Schmucker, *Retrospect of Lutheranism in the United States* (Baltimore: Publication Rooms, 1841), 24; S. S. Schmucker, *The Patriarchs of American Lutheranism* (Baltimore: Publication Rooms, 1845), 22, 26.

22. Schmucker, *Elements of Popular Theology,* 41; Ferm, *Crisis,* 76, 79.

23. Schmucker, *Patriarchs,* 18; S. S. Schmucker, *Psychology, or, Elements of a New System of Mental Philosophy, on the Basis of Consciousness and Common Sense* (1st ed. 1842; New York: Harper, 1843), v.

24. Schmucker, *Psychology,* 21–30, 69–105.

25. S. S. Schmucker, ed., *An Elementary Course of Biblical Theology,* by C. G. Storr and C. C. Flatt, 2 vols. (1st ed. 1826; Andover, Mass.: Gould, Newman, 1826), 1:iii–iv.

26. Storr and Flatt, *Biblical Theology,* 1:37–50, 93–156, 102, 207.

27. Schmucker, *Elements of Popular Theology,* 10–16.

28. Ibid., 13, 15–33.

29. Ibid., 63, 64–80.

30. Ibid., 90, 99, 104.

31. Ibid., 128, 140.

32. Ibid., 199–218, 246, 251, 255; S. S. Schmucker, *Fraternal Appeal to the American Churches,* ed. Frederick K. Wentz (Philadelphia: Fortress, 1965), 34.

33. Schmucker, *Elements of Popular Theology,* 145, 168–82.

34. Ibid., 288–97.

35. Schmucker, *Fraternal Appeal,* 154, 158, 176–83; Gustafson, *Lutherans in Crisis,* 71; S. S. Schmucker, *Discourse in Commemoration of the Glorious Reformation of the Sixteenth Century* (New York: Gould, Newman, 1838), 12. See S. S. Schmucker, *The Papal Hierarchy* (Gettysburg, Pa.: Neinstadt, 1845), and S. S. Schmucker, *Elemental Contrast Between the Religion of Forms and of the Spirit* (Gettysburg, Pa.: Neinstadt, 1852).

36. S. S. Schmucker, *The American Lutheran Church, Historically, Doctrinally, and Practically Delineated* (Springfield, Ohio: Harbaugh, 1851), 252, 257; Kuenning, *Rise and Fall,* 97–228.

37. S. S. Schmucker, *Definite Platform, Doctrinal and Disciplinarian, for Evangelical Lutheran District Synods, Documents of Lutheran Unity in America,* ed. Richard C. Wolf (Philadelphia: Fortress, 1966), 44.

38. S. W. Harkey, *The Church's Best State; or Constant Revivals of Religion* (Baltimore: Publication Rooms, 1843), 29–30, 44; Samuel Sprecher, *Inaugural Address Delivered Before the Directors of Wittenberg College* (Springfield, Ohio: Halsey, Emerson, 1849), 8–9, 13; Gustafson, *Lutherans in Crisis,* 94.

39. Theodore Tappert, ed., *Lutheran Confessional Theology in America, 1840–1880* (New York: Oxford University Press, 1972), 6–30.

40. Gustafson, *Lutherans in Crisis,* 109–14.

41. Alton Ray Koenning, "Henkel Press: A Force for Conservative Lutheran Theology in Pre–Civil War Southeastern America" (Ph.D. diss., Duke University, 1972), 86–118.

42. David Henkel, *An Answer to Mr. Joseph Moore, the Methodist, with a Few Fragments on the Doctrine of Justification* (New Market, Va.: S. Henkel, 1825), 128, 179; David Henkel, *Against the Unitarians* (New Market, Va.: S. Henkel, 1830), 7–10.

43. John Bachman, *A Sermon on the Doctrines and Discipline of the Evangelical Lutheran Church* (Charleston, S.C.: Burges, 1837), 12, 14– 19; Adolph Spaeth, *Charles Porterfield Krauth,* 2 vols. (1st ed. 1898; New York: Arno Press, 1969), 1:194; Koenning, "Henkel Press," 200.

44. Spaeth, *Krauth,* 1:106.

45. David Henkel et al. "The Objections of the Committee Against the Constitution of the General Synod," *Documents of Lutheran Unity,* 76– 77; Henkel, *Answer to Moore,* 176; Ferm, *Crisis,* 238–39.

46. Charles Philip Krauth, "Review of Schmid's Dogmatik of the Lutheran Church," *Evangelical Review* 1 (1849):129; Charles Philip Krauth, "The Lutheran Church in the United States," *Evangelical Review* 2 (1850):1–3, 12–14.

47. W. J. Mann, *A Plea for the Augsburg Confession* (Philadelphia: Lindsay, Blakiston, 1856), 4; W. J. Mann, *Lutheranism in America* (Philadelphia: Lindsay, Blakiston, 1857), 133–34.

48. Charles Porterfield Krauth, *The Conservative Reformation and its Theology* (1st ed. 1871; Philadelphia: Lippincott, 1875), xiv; Charles Porterfield Krauth, "The Relation of our Confessions to the Reformation, and the Importance of their Study," *Evangelical Review* 1 (1849):240.

49. Mann, *Lutheranism in America,* 26; C. Philip Krauth, "The Lutheran Church in the United States," 12–14; J. A. Brown, *The New Theology: Its Abettors and Defenders* (Philadelphia: Ashmead, 1857), 12, 25, 36; Gustafson, *Lutherans in Crisis,* 140–42.

50. J. N. Hoffman, *The Broken Platform or a Brief Defense of Our Symbolical Books* (Philadelphia: Lindsay, Blakiston, 1856), ix; Brown, *New Theology,* 49–53; Mann, *Plea for the Augsburg Confession,* 40; Charles F. Schaeffer, "Symbolic Theology," *Evangelical Review* 4 (1850):483.

51. Lewis W. Spitz, Sr., *The Life of Dr. C. F. W. Walther* (St. Louis, Mo.: Concordia, 1961), 56–57, 84–85.

52. C. F. W. Walther, "Are We Guilty of Despising Scholarship?" (1875), *Selected Writings of C. F. W. Walther,* trans. H. J. A. Bouman (St. Louis, Mo.: Concordia, 1981), 135–36; C. F. W. Walther, "The Kind of Confessional Subscription Required," *Lutheran Confessional Theology,* 70.

53. Walther, "Confessional Subscription," 54–77, 70; Tappert, ed., *Lutheran Confessional Theology,* 34; Sigmund Fritschl, "The Doctrinal Agreement Essential to Church Unity," *Lutheran Confessional Theology,* 78–100.

54. Gottfried Fritschl, "Concerning Objective and Subjective Justification," *Lutheran Confessional Theology,* 141–65.

55. C. F. W. Walther, *Law and Gospel, Selected Writings,* 24–47.

56. Tappert, ed., *Lutheran Confessional Theology,* 33.

Chapter 20. Catholics: Reason and the Church

1. John Hughes, "Second Day's Speech Before the Board of Aldermen and Councilmen" (1840), *Complete Works of the Most. Rev. John Hughes,* ed. Lawrence Kehoe, 2 vols. (New York: Lawrence Kehoe, 1865), 1:160; John Hughes, "Reason and Faith" (1860), ibid., 2:330.

2. Robert Emmet Curran, S.J., "Introduction," *American Jesuit Spirituality: The Maryland Tradition, 1634–1900* (New York: Paulist Press, 1988), 14.

3. Joseph Greaton, "Method of Confessing," ibid., 88–92; Joseph Moseley, "On Saint Ignatius," ibid., 114–19; "The Pious Guide to Prayer and Devotion," ibid., 151–61; Peter Attwood, "The Incarnation," ibid., 78–85; Joseph Greaton, "Whipps and Thorns," ibid., 92–97.

4. The thirteen were Stephen Theodore Badin, Orestes Augustus Brownson, John Carroll, John Baptist Mary David, John England, Benedict Joseph Flaget, Demetrius Augustine Gallitzin, Isaac Thomas Hecker, John Joseph Hughes, Francis Patrick Kenrick, Anthony Kohlmann, John Purcell, Martin John Spalding.

5. John Hughes, "Lecture on the Present Condition and Prospects of the Catholic Church in the United States," *Complete Works,* 2:130; White, *Diocesan Seminary in the United States,* 29.

6. Peter Henry Lemcke, O.S.B., *Life and Works of Prince Demetrius Augustine Gallitzin,* trans. Joseph Plumpe (London: Longmans, Green, 1940), 194.

7. M. J. Spalding, *Miscellanea: Comprising Reviews, Lectures, and Essays* (Louisville, Ky.: Webb, Gill, Levering, 1855), 504; John Hughes, "Introduction . . . to Mr. Livingston's Book on Imputation" (1843?), *Complete Works,* 1:408; Anthony Kohlmann, *Unitarianism Philosophically and Theologically Examined* (Washington, D.C.: Henry Guegan, 1821), 83; John England, "Letters on the Calumnies of J. Blanco White Against the Catholic Religion," *The Works of the Right Rev. John England, First Bishop of Charleston,* ed. Ignatius A. Reynolds, 5 vols. (Baltimore: John Murphy, 1849), 1:304.

8. John Carroll, *An Address to the Roman Catholics of the United States of America*, *The John Carroll Papers*, ed. Thomas O'Brien Hanley, S.J., 3 vols. (Notre Dame, Ind.: University of Notre Dame Press, 1976), 1:113– 14; John England, "Letters to the Right Rev. Dr. Bowen," *Works*, 2:41; M. J. Spalding, *Lectures on the Evidence of Catholicity* (1st ed. 1847; Louisville, Ky.: Levering, 1857), 69; John Breckinridge and John Hughes, *Controversy Between the Rev. John Hughes . . . and the Rev. John Breckinridge* (Philadelphia: Whetham, 1833), 122.

9. Spalding, *Lectures*, 70, 265.

10. John England, "Letters on Various Misrepresentations of the Catholic Religion," *Works*, 2:213; "The Pastoral Letter of 1837, Third Provincial Council of Baltimore," *The National Pastorals of the American Hierarchy (1792–1919)*, ed. Peter Guilday (Washington, D.C.: National Catholic Welfare Council, 1923), 87; Hughes and Breckinridge, *Controversy*, 122.

11. Patrick Carey, ed., "Introduction," *American Catholic Religious Thought* (New York: Paulist Press, 1987), 6; Carla Bang, "John Carroll and the Enlightenment," *American Catholic Preaching and Piety in the Time of John Carroll*, ed. Raymond J. Kupke (Lanham, Md.: University Press of America, 1991), 107–36.

12. Carroll, *Address, Papers*, 1:84, 86.

13. England, "Calumnies," 142; John England, "An Essay and Letters on Infallibility," *Works*, 1:56; John England, "Letters on the Judicial Office of the Catholic Church," ibid., 1:87; Patrick Carey, *An Immigrant Bishop: John England's Adaptation of Irish Catholicism to American Republicanism* (Yonkers, N.Y.: U.S. Catholic Historical Society, 1982), 85–159.

14. Carroll, *Address*, 93; England, "Letters on the Judicial Office," 88–89; England, "Letters to Bowen," 67; England, "Calumnies," 295.

15. White, *Diocesan Seminary in the United States*, 136; Campbell and Purcell, *Debate on the Roman Catholic Religion*, 329; Francis Patrick Kenrick, *Theologiae Dogmaticae Tractus Tres, De Revelatione, De Ecclesia, et de Verbo Dei*, 4 vols. (Philadelphia: Johnson, 1839–40), 1:22; John Hughes, "Sermon Preached in the Cathedral Baltimore" (1851), *Complete Works*, 2:194.

16. John Hughes, "The Infallibility of the Church," *Complete Works*, 2:406; Hughes, "Reason and Faith," 330; John Hughes, "A Review of 'Kirwan' in Six Letters," *Complete Works*, 1:645, 658, 661; England, "Calumnies," 307.

17. Kohlmann, *Unitarianism*, 20, 33, 40; Spalding, *Lectures*, 42; Demetrius A. Gallitzin, *A Letter to a Protestant Friend on the Holy Scriptures* (Baltimore: Lucas, 1820), 139; Demetrius A. Gallitzin, "A Defence of Catholic Principles," *Gallitzin's Letters* (Loretto, Pa.: Angelmodde Press, 1940), 19; Spalding, *Lectures*, 403.

18. England, "Essay and Letters on Infallibility," 58; Spalding, *Lectures*, v.

19. Spalding, *Lectures*, 43, 55, 91, 131–41, 164, 194, 233.

20. Ibid., 134, 137–41; Kenrick, *Theologiae Dogmaticae*, 1:13; England, "Calumnies," 156.

21. John England, "The Substance of a Discourse Preached in the House of Representatives of the Congress of the United States," *Works*, 4:180; England, "Calumnies," 326; Breckinridge and Hughes, *Controversy*, 34; Hughes, "Reason and Faith," 331.

22. Hughes, "Infallibility of the Church," 438; John Hughes, "The Unity, the Univer-

sity, and Visibility of the Church," *Complete Works*, 2:289; Carey, *An Immigrant Bishop*, 147, 201.

23. England, "Essay and Letters on Infallibility," 74; England, "Letters on Various Misrepresentations," 238; Spalding, *Lectures*, 266; Campbell and Purcell, *Debate on the Roman Catholic Religion*, 71.

24. Francis Patrick Kenrick, *The Primary of the Apostolic See Vindicated* (New York: Edward Dunigan, 1848), v, 66–181.

25. Hugh J. Nolan, *The Most Reverend Francis Patrick Kenrick* (Washington, D.C.: Catholic University of America Press, 1948), 45, 238; Campbell and Purcell, *Debate on the Roman Catholic Religion*, 27, 215; Carroll, *Address*, 106; John England, "A Series of Controversial Pieces on Several Catholic Doctrines," *Works*, 2:291; Breckinridge and Hughes, *Controversy*, 55; Spalding, *Lectures*, 261; Gallitzin, *Gallitzin's Letters*, 14.

26. Campbell and Purcell, *Debate on the Roman Catholic Religion*, 235; Carroll, *Address*, 111; Gallitzin, *Letter to a Protestant Friend*, 39, 44; Breckinridge and Hughes, *Controversy*, 235.

27. Carroll, *Address*, 109, 111; Campbell and Purcell, *Debate on the Roman Catholic Religion*, 215; John England, "Letters in Reply to Essays, Controverting Several Statements," *Works*, 2:174.

28. Hughes, "Second Day's Speech," 160, 177; Breckinridge and Hughes, *Controversy*, 5; John Hughes, "Letters on the Catholic Church," *Complete Works*, 1:603; John P. Marschall, C.S.V., "Francis Patrick Kenrick, 1851–1863: The Baltimore Years" (Ph.D. diss., Catholic University of America, 1965), 209.

29. England, "Series of Controversial Pieces," 292; Hughes, "Letters on the Catholic Church," 593; Carroll, *Address*, 105; Kenrick, *Theologiae Dogmaticae*, 333–34; Gerald P. Fogarty, *Nova et Vetera: The Theology of the Tradition in American Catholicism* (Milwaukee, Wisc.: Marquette University Press, 1987), 8; Francis Patrick Kenrick, *A Vindication of the Catholic Church, in a Series of Letters Addressed to the Right Rev. John Henry Hopkins* (Baltimore: Murphy, 1855), 36; Fogarty, *American Catholic Biblical Scholarship*, 8–9.

30. Spalding, *Lectures*, 392; "The Pastoral Letter of 1840," *National Pastorals*, 131; Kenrick, *Vindication of the Catholic Church*, 38; Breckinridge and Hughes, *Controversy*, 302.

31. Breckinridge and Hughes, *Controversy*, 21, 69; Hughes, "Letters on the Catholic Church," 600; Campbell and Purcell, *Debate on the Roman Catholic Religion*, 31.

32. Breckinridge and Hughes, *Controversy*, 36; Gallitzin, *Letter to a Protestant Friend*, 95.

33. White, *Diocesan Seminary in the United States*, 135–39; John Tracy Ellis, *Essays in Seminary Education* (Notre Dame, Ind.: Fides, 1967), 146.

34. Carroll, *Address*, 94; England, "Calumnies," 308; Kohlmann, *Unitarianism*, 137–80; Kenrick, *Theologiae Dogmaticae*, 79, 89.

35. Kohlmann, *Unitarianism*, 41–45, 111; Spalding, *Lectures*, 41.

36. John Hughes, "Sermon" (1855), *Complete Works*, 2:256; John Hughes, "Influence of Christianity Upon Civilization," ibid., 1:352–54, 369.

37. Hughes, "Letters on the Catholic Church," 178; Kenrick, *Vindication of the Catholic Church*, 143, 150; James Hennesey, "Prelude to Vatican I: American Bishops and the

Definition of the Immaculate Conception," *Theological Studies* 25 (1964):414–15; Marschall, "Francis Patrick Kenrick," 206; Campbell and Purcell, *Debate on the Roman Catholic Religion,* 251; John Hughes, "Triumphs of the Catholic Church," *Complete Works,* 2:245.

38. Francis Patrick Kenrick, *A Treatise of Baptism* (Philadelphia: M. Fithian, 1843), 59, 61, 68; Francis Patrick Kenrick, *The Catholic Doctrine of Justification Explained and Vindicated* (Philadelphia: Cummiskey, 1841), 223.

39. Breckinridge and Hughes, *Controversy,* 183; Kenrick, *Justification,* 68, 70; Kenrick, *Theologiae Dogmaticae,* 279–80, 286, 295; England, "Letters in Reply to Essays," 106; John Hughes, "The Last Words of the Savior," *Complete Works,* 2:302.

40. Kenrick, *Justification,* 24, 25, 37, 39, 45; John England, "Letter to O'Connell on Liberality," *Works,* 2:355; John England, "Letter to the Right Rev. Dr. David, on the Definition of Faith," *Works,* 2:358.

41. Carroll, *Address,* 87; England, "Letter to O'Connell," 356; Breckinridge and Hughes, *Controversy,* 251; England, "Calumnies," 215.

42. Kenrick, *Justification,* 93.

43. Ibid., 93, 94–101, 112, 117, 173–74.

44. Ibid., 80, 104; England, "Calumnies," 214; Hughes, "Imputation," 414.

45. White, *Diocesan Seminary in the United States,* 139–40; Francis Patrick Kenrick, *Theologia Moralis,* 2 vols. (1st ed. 1841– 43; Mechliniae: H. Dessain, 1861), 1:5–36; L. Vereecke, "History of Moral Theology," *New Catholic Encyclopedia,* 15 vols. (New York: McGraw Hill, 1967), 9:1120–22.

46. White, *Diocesan Seminary in the United States,* 139; Hughes, "Imputation," 409; Spalding, *Lectures,* 208.

47. John England, "Letters on the Catholic Doctrine of Transubstantiation," *Works,* 1:417; Kenrick, *Justification,* 125; Kenrick, *Baptism,* 72.

48. John Hughes, "Sermon on the Occasion of the Dedication of St. Aloysius Church," *Complete Works,* 2:295; Kenrick, *Justification,* 127, 139.

49. Kenrick, *Vindication of the Catholic Church,* 85; John England, "Letter Addressed to a Lady," *Works,* 1:503, 505; Campbell and Purcell, *Debate on the Roman Catholic Religion,* 375; England, "Letters on the Catholic Doctrine of Transubstantiation," 354.

50. Gallitzin, *Gallitzin's Letters,* 59.

51. Constantine Pise, *Lectures on the Invocation of Saints, Veneration of Sacred Images, and Purgatory* (New York: H. G. Doggers, 1845), 8, 13, 44.

52. Hughes, "Influence of Christianity Upon Civilization," 353; John Hughes, "The Influence of Christianity on Social Servitude," *Complete Works,* 1:373, 380, 385.

53. Carey, "Introduction," 20; Spalding, *Miscellanea,* 77–95.

Chapter 21. The Transcendentalists: Intuition

1. R. W. Emerson, "An Address Delivered before the Senior Class of the Harvard Divinity School," *The Selected Writings of Ralph Waldo Emerson,* ed. Brooks Atkinson (New York: Modern Library, 1940), 72, 74.

2. William R. Hutchison, *The Transcendentalist Ministers: Church Reform in the New England Renaissance* (Boston: Beacon, 1959), 31.

3. Margaret Fuller, "Letter to William Henry Channing," *The Portable Margaret Fuller*, ed. Mary Kelley (Harmondsworth, England: Penguin, 1994), xix, 499–501.

4. Ralph Waldo Emerson, "The Transcendentalist," *Selected Writings*, 87, 93; Hutchison, *Transcendentalist Ministers*, 29.

5. Francis cited in Miller, ed. *The Transcendentalists*, 106; George Ripley, "To Andrews Norton," ibid., 163.

6. James Walker, "Foundations of Faith," ibid., 83.

7. James Marsh, "Preliminary Essay," *Aids to Reflection*, by Samuel Taylor Coleridge (London: George Bell, 1904), xlix.

8. Ibid., lxii; Samuel Taylor Coleridge, *Aids to Reflection*, 143–56.

9. Coleridge, *Aids to Reflection*, 134; James Freeman Clarke, "R. W. Emerson and the New School," *The Transcendentalists*, 203; James Freeman Clarke, *Autobiography*, ibid., 48.

10. Victor Cousin, *Elements of Psychology*, trans. Caleb S. Henry (New York: Ivison, Phinney, Blakeman, 1869), 414, 436.

11. Ibid., 154, 375.

12. C. S. Henry, "Introduction," *Elements of Psychology*, xiii, 80–81, 89; Ronald V. Wells, *Three Christian Transcendentalists* (New York: Octagon, 1972), 49–95; Charles Hodge, J. W. Alexander, and Albert Dod, "Transcendentalism of the Germans and Cousin," *PR* 11 (1839):37–101.

13. Orestes Brownson, *The Convert; or Leaves from My Experience, The Works of Orestes Brownson*, 20 vols. (New York: AMS Press, 1966), 5:19; Thomas R. Ryan, C.P.P.S., *Orestes Brownson* (Huntington, Ind.: Our Sunday Visitor, 1976), 38.

14. Orestes Brownson, *New Views of Christianity, Society, and the Church* (1836), *Works*, 14:32, 34.

15. Ryan, *Orestes Brownson*, 15–84, 208–15.

16. Orestes Brownson, "Victor Cousin," *The Transcendentalists*, 112–13.

17. Ibid., 112–13.

18. Ralph Waldo Emerson, "The Sovereignty of Ethics," *Lectures and Biographical Sketches, Emerson's Complete Works* (Riverside edition), ed. J. E. Cabot, 12 vols. (London: Routledge, 1883–1884), 10:196; David Robinson, *Apostle of Culture: Emerson as Preacher and Lecturer* (Philadelphia: University of Pennsylvania Press, 1982), 8.

19. Ralph Waldo Emerson, "Sermon IX," *Complete Sermons of Ralph Waldo Emerson*, gen. ed., Albert J. Von Frank, 4 vols. (Columbia: University of Missouri Press, 1989), 1:116; Ralph Waldo Emerson, "Worship," *The Conduct of Life, Complete Works*, 6:200; David Robinson, "The Method of *Nature* and Emerson's Period of Crisis," *Emerson Centenary Essays*, ed. Joel Myerson (Carbondale: Southern Illinois University Press, 1982), 91.

20. Ralph Waldo Emerson, "Sermon CLXII," *Complete Sermons*, 4:189, 193; Emerson, "Character," *Lectures, Complete Works*, 10:109; Stephen Whicher, *Freedom and Fate: An Inner Life of Ralph Waldo Emerson* (Philadelphia: University of Pennsylvania Press, 1953), 39, 41.

21. Merrill R. Davis, "Emerson's 'Reason' and the Scottish Philosophers," *New England Quarterly* 17 (1944):212–13.

22. Ralph Waldo Emerson, "Sermon XXXII," *Complete Sermons*, 1:249; "Sermon

XXXI," ibid., 1:252; "Sermon CXV," ibid., 3:152; "Sermon XVIII," ibid., 1:175; "Sermon CIII," ibid., 3:82; "Sermon CXIX, ibid., 3:181; "Sermon CXXXVI," ibid., 4:32.

23. Sampson Reed, "Oration on Genius" (1821), *The Transcendentalists,* 49–59; Ralph Waldo Emerson, *Representative Men, Complete Works,* 4:117, 130; Sydney Ahlstrom, "Ralph Waldo Emerson and the American Transcendentalists," *Nineteenth Century Religious Thought in the West,* ed. Ninian Smart et al., 2 vols. (Cambridge: Cambridge University Press, 1985), 1:33.

24. Emerson, *Representative Men,* 270; Robinson, *Apostle of Culture,* 84.

25. Ralph L. Rusk, ed., *The Letters of Ralph Waldo Emerson,* 10 vols. (New York: Columbia University Press, 1939), 1:412; Frank T. Thompson, "Emerson's Indebtedness to Coleridge," *Sketches in Philology* 23 (1926):66; Ralph Waldo Emerson, *The Journals of Ralph Waldo Emerson,* ed. E. W. Emerson and W. E. Forbes, 10 vols. (Boston: Houghton, Mifflin, 1909–14), 3:237; Ralph Waldo Emerson, *Nature, Selected Writings,* 23.

26. Emerson, *Representative Men,* 42, 57, 63; Stuart Gerry Brown, "Emerson's Platonism," *New England Quarterly* 18 (1945):335–37.

27. Emerson, *Nature,* 3, 6; Robinson, *Apostle of Culture,* 87.

28. Emerson, "Sermon CLX," *Complete Sermons,* 4:175; "Sermon LXXXVII," ibid., 2:247; "Sermon LXXXVIII," ibid., 2:254; "Sermon CLXV," ibid., 4:215; Emerson, *Nature,* 32.

29. Emerson, "Sermon LXXXVI," *Complete Sermons,* 2:233; Gustaf Van Cromphant, *Emerson's Ethics* (Columbia: University of Missouri Press, 1999), 57–89.

30. Emerson, "Sermon XXIII," *Complete Sermons,* 1:205; Emerson, *Nature,* 15, 34–35; Emerson, "The Over-Soul," *Selected Writings,* 261–62; Emerson, "Divinity School Address," ibid., 68; Robinson, *Apostle of Culture,* 133; Brown, "Emerson's Platonism," 325–45; Whicher, *Freedom and Fate,* 151.

31. Ralph Waldo Emerson, *Essays: First Series, Complete Works,* 2:107, 112; Ralph Waldo Emerson, *The Conduct of Life,* ibid., 6:12, 50; Robinson, "The Method of *Nature* and Emerson's Period of Crisis," 76–91; Robert D. Richardson, Jr., *Emerson: The Mind on Fire* (Berkeley, Calif.: University of California Press, 1995), 354.

32. Emerson, "Sermon CXXXI," *Complete Sermons,* 3:192; "Sermon CLXX," ibid., 4:238.

33. Emerson, *Lectures and Biographical Sketches,* 317; Emerson, "Sermon CLXX," *Complete Sermons,* 4:238.

34. Emerson, "Divinity School Address," 73, 75.

35. Ibid., 72.

36. Emerson, "Draft Sermon on the Evidences of Christianity" (1826?), *Complete Sermons,* 4:239, 257; "Sermon XIV," ibid., 1:152; "Sermon CIII," ibid., 3:82.

37. Emerson, "Sermon CIII," ibid., 3:82; "Sermon CX," ibid., 3:123.

38. William Henry Furness, *Remarks on the Four Gospels, The Transcendentalists,* 128.

39. George Ripley, "Herder's Theological Opinions and Services," ibid., 96, 101; George Ripley, "Martineau's Rationale," ibid., 131; Andrews Norton, "Ripley's Martineau," ibid., 159.

40. George Ripley, *The Latest Form of Infidelity Examined* (Boston: James Munroe, 1839), 13; George Ripley, *Defence of The Latest Form of Infidelity Examined* (Boston: James Munroe, 1840), 147.

41. Ripley, *Latest Form of Infidelity Examined,* 148; George Ripley, *Discourses on the Philosophy of Religion, The Transcendentalists,* 132– 40; Ripley, *Defence,* 158; George Ripley, "Jesus Christ the Same Yesterday, Today, and Forever," *The Transcendentalists,* 291–92.

42. Ripley, *Defence,* 83, 151; Ripley, "Jesus Christ," 286; Ripley, *Latest Form of Infidelity Examined,* 24.

43. Ripley, *Defence,* 43–44; Ripley, *Latest Form of Infidelity Examined,* 12–13; George Ripley, "Letter to the Church in Purchase Street," *The Transcendentalists,* 251–57.

44. Dewey, *Discourses and Reviews,* 232, 234; Frothingham, *Deism or Christianity?,* 13–14, 43; Walker, *Reason, Faith, and Duty,* 112.

45. Henry Steele Commager, *Theodore Parker: Yankee Crusader* (New York: Little Brown, 1936), 88; Theodore Parker, *Theism, Atheism, and the Popular Theology* (London: John Chapman, 1853), xxviii.

46. Theodore Parker, "The Previous Question Between Mr. Andrews Norton and His Alumni," reprinted in John Edward Dirks, *The Critical Theology of Theodore Parker* (New York: Columbia University Press, 1948), Appendix, 140, 151–52, 154.

47. Ibid., 155–56; Theodore Parker, "Strauss's Life of Jesus," *The Critical and Miscellaneous Writings of Theodore Parker* (1st ed. 1843; Boston: Little, Brown, 1856), 276, 290, 329–51; Commager, *Theodore Parker,* 71–73.

48. Theodore Parker, *A Discourse of Matters Pertaining to Religion* (London: J. Watson, 1849), 113, 175, 179; Parker, *Theism, Atheism, and the Popular Theology,* 182.

49. Theodore Parker, "A Discourse of the Transient and Permanent in Christianity," *Writings,* 156.

50. Ibid., 169.

51. Ibid., 172.

52. Parker, *Discourse of Matters Pertaining to Religion,* 14, 16, 104, 106, 112.

53. Ibid., 94, 138.

54. Theodore Parker, "Thoughts on Theology," *Writings,* 398.

55. Charles Cashdollar, *The Transformation of Theology, 1830– 1890: Positivism and Protestant Thought in Britain and America* (Princeton, N.J.: Princeton University Press, 1989), 96; Parker, *Discourse of Matters Pertaining to Religion,* 35–70; Parker, *Theism, Atheism, and the Popular Theology,* 122.

56. Cashdollar, *Transformation,* 90, 100–11.

57. J. W. Miles, *Philosophic Theology, or Ultimate Grounds of All Religious Belief Based in Reason* (Charleston, S.C.: J. Russell, 1849), 12, 86, 180, 188; Ralph Luker, "God, Man, and the World of James Warley Miles, Charleston's Transcendentalist," *Historical Magazine of the Protestant Episcopal Church* 39 (1970):101–36.

Chapter 22. Horace Bushnell: Christian Comprehensiveness

1. Horace Bushnell, *God in Christ* (Hartford, Conn.: Brown, Parsons, 1849), 93, 102; Horace Bushnell, *Christ in Theology* (Hartford, Conn.: Brown and Parsons, 1851), 86.

2. Robert Bruce Mullin, *The Puritan as Yankee: A Life of Horace Bushnell* (Grand Rapids, Mich.: Eerdmans, 2002), 136–49, 186.

3. Horace Bushnell, "Barbarism the First Danger" (1847), *Work and Play: Literary Varieties* (New York: Charles Scribner's Sons, 1883), 266.

4. Robert L. Edwards, *Genius of Singular Grace: A Biography of Horace Bushnell* (Cleveland, Ohio: Pilgrim Press, 1992), 36; Hodge, "God in Christ," *Essays and Reviews,* 471.

5. Edwards, *Genius of Singular Grace,* 100; Conrad Cherry, *Nature and Religious Imagination* (Philadelphia: Fortress Press, 1980), 157–230.

6. Horace Bushnell, "Christian Comprehensiveness" (1848), *Building Eras in Religion* (New York: Charles Scribner's Sons, 1881), 395, 412– 16, 419, 434, 450.

7. Mary Bushnell Cheney, *Life and Letters of Horace Bushnell* (New York: Harper and Brothers, 1880), 83; Horace Bushnell, "Living to God in Small Things" (1837), *Horace Bushnell: Sermons,* ed. Conrad Cherry (New York: Paulist Press, 1985), 141; Horace Bushnell, *Christian Nurture* (1st ed. 1847, 2nd ed. 1861; New Haven, Conn.: Yale University Press, 1967), 74– 101; Mullin, *Puritan as Yankee,* 67, 70, 125.

8. Hodge, "Bushnell on Christian Nurture," 333; Cheney, *Life and Letters,* 179; H. Shelton Smith, ed., *Horace Bushnell* (New York: Oxford University Press, 1965), 377.

9. Horace Bushnell, *Views of Christian Nurture, Horace Bushnell: Selected Writings on Language, Religion, and American Culture,* ed. David L. Smith (Chico, Calif.: Scholars Press, 1984), 113; David L. Smith, *Symbolism and Growth: The Religious Thought of Horace Bushnell* (Chico, Calif.: Scholars Press, 1981), 78.

10. Cheney, *Life and Letters,* 192; Horace Bushnell, "Christ the Form of the Soul," *Sermons,* 55–56, 59.

11. Bushnell, "Christ the Form of the Soul," *Sermons,* 55– 56; Horace Bushnell, "The Power of an Endless Life," ibid., 131; Horace Bushnell, "The Immediate Knowledge of God" (1872) ibid., 343.

12. Cheney, *Life and Letters,* 499; H. Shelton Smith, "Introduction," *Horace Bushnell,* 29–30; Mullin, *Puritan as Yankee,* 95–96.

13. Bushnell, *God in Christ,* 279–90, 302, 308.

14. Bushnell, *Christ in Theology,* 83–89.

15. Smith, "Introduction," *Horace Bushnell,* 28–29; Bushnell, "Immediate Knowledge of God," 218–26, 221.

16. Horace Bushnell, *Nature and the Supernatural as Together Constituting the One System of God* (1st ed. 1858; New York: Charles Scribner, 1863), 33, 323, 337–57; Bushnell, *God in Christ,* 74, 84.

17. Bushnell, *Nature and the Supernatural,* 507–08; Smith "Introduction," *Horace Bushnell,* 27; Horace Bushnell, "Darkness and Light," *Sermons,* 175; Horace Bushnell, "Revelation," *Selected Writings,* 31.

18. Bushnell, *Nature and the Supernatural,* 20, 333.

19. Bushnell, *God in Christ,* 102; Bushnell, *Christ in Theology,* 15; Smith, "Introduction," *Horace Bushnell,* 37; Bushnell, "Revelation," 30.

20. Bushnell, *God in Christ,* 46, 74; Bushnell, *Christ in Theology,* 74.

21. Bushnell, *God in Christ,* 57, 78; Horace Bushnell, "Our Gospel a Gift to the Imagination" (1869), *Building Eras,* 249, 256.

22. Bushnell, *Christ in Theology,* 69, 72, 91; Bushnell, "Gospel a Gift to the Imagination," 272.

23. Bushnell, *God in Christ,* 30, 78.

24. Bushnell, *Christ in Theology,* 69, 75.

25. Cheney, *Life and Letters*, 214, 234, 260.

26. Bushnell, *God in Christ*, 135, 137–74.

27. Ibid., 181; Bushnell, *Christ in Theology*, 117, 119, 133.

28. Bushnell, *Christ in Theology*, 120, 147; Horace Bushnell, "The Christian Trinity a Practical Truth" (1854), *Building Eras*, 119.

29. Bushnell, "Christian Trinity a Practical Truth," *Building Eras*, 119.

30. Bushnell, *God in Christ*, 148–63; Bushnell, *Christ in Theology*, 96, 110.

31. Bushnell, *Christ in Theology*, 91, 93.

32. Bushnell, *God in Christ*, 190, 269.

33. Ibid., 102–37; Bushnell, *Christ in Theology*, 256.

34. Bushnell, *Christ in Theology*, 248; Bushnell, *God in Christ*, 264.

35. Bushnell, *Christ in Theology*, 246, 259, 308–09, 313.

36. Bushnell, *God in Christ*, 258.

37. Horace Bushnell, *The Vicarious Sacrifice, Selected Writings*, 141.

38. Ibid., 144; Edwards, *Genius of Singular Grace*, 250.

39. Horace Bushnell, *Forgiveness and Law, Grounded in Principles Interpreted by Human Analogies* (New York: Scribner, Armstrong, 1874), 13, 35, 50.

40. Bushnell, *Nature and the Supernatural*, 39.

41. Ibid., 222, 446–92; Mullin, *Puritan As Yankee*, 198.

42. Bushnell, *God in Christ*, 63.

43. Bushnell, *Forgiveness and Law*, 201, 205, 212.

44. Bushnell, *God in Christ*, 93.

Chapter 23. The Mercersburg Theology: Communal Reason

1. J. W. Nevin, "Letter to Dr. Henry Harbaugh," *Reformed and Catholic: Selected Theological Writings of John Williamson Nevin*, ed. Charles Yrigoyen, Jr., and George H. Bricker (Pittsburgh, Pa.: Pickwick Press, 1978), 410; J. W. Nevin, "The Church" (1847), *The Mercersburg Theology*, ed. James H. Nichols (New York: Oxford University Press, 1966), 73; J. W. Nevin, "Introduction," Philip Schaff, *Principle of Protestantism* (1st ed. 1845; Philadelphia: United Church Press, 1964), 51; Schaff, *What is Church History?*, 9.

2. J. W. Nevin, *The Anxious Bench* (1844), *Selected Writings*, 13, 34, 43, 56, 93, 95; Schaff, *Principle of Protestantism*, 150.

3. Schaff, *Principle of Protestantism*, 224; Philip Schaff, *History of the Apostolic Church* (1853), *Mercersburg Theology*, 141; J. W. Nevin, "The Sect System," ibid., 100; Nevin, "The Church," 145.

4. Philip Schaff, "German Theology and the Church Question" (1855), *Philip Schaff: Historian and Ambassador of the Universal Church, Selected Writings*, ed. Klaus Penzel (Macon, Ga.: Mercer University Press, 1991), 102; Schaff, *Principle of Protestantism*, 98, 113–14, 225–26.

5. Schaff, *Principle of Protestantism*, 39; J. W. Nevin, "The Apostles Creed," *Mercersburg Review* 3 (1849):220; 4 (1849):318, 322, 338, 339.

6. J. W. Nevin, *My Own Life: The Early Years* (Lancaster, Pa.: Historical Society of the Reformed Church, 1964), 122.

7. Schaff, *What is Church History?*, 90–101.

8. F. A. Rauch, *Psychology: Or, a View of the Human Soul* (New York: Dodd, 1840), 18–44, 178–79; Nevin, *Mystical Presence,* 156–62; Schaff, *What is Church History?,* 91–94.

9. Penzel, ed., *Selected Writings,* xxvi.

10. Schaff, *History of the Apostolic Church,* ibid., 43.

11. J. W. Nevin, "Brownson's Quarterly Review," *Mercersburg Theology,* 336, 340; J. W. Nevin, "The Sect System" (1849), *Selected Writings,* 150.

12. Nevin, "Brownson's Quarterly Review," 330, 336, 339; Nevin, "Sect System," 150; Schaff, *Principle of Protestantism,* 113.

13. James Hastings Nichols, *Romanticism in American Theology* (Chicago: University of Chicago Press, 1961), 38; William DePuccio, "Nevin's Idealistic Philosophy," *Reformed Confessionalism in Nineteenth-Century America,* ed. Sam Hamstra, Jr., and A. J. Griffioen (Lanham, Md.: Scarecrow Press, 1995), 50–52; Nevin, "Brownson's Quarterly Review," 337.

14. Nevin, "Brownson's Quarterly Review," 334–38.

15. J. W. Nevin, "Faith, Freedom, and Reverence" (1850), *Mercersburg Theology,* 295; Nevin, "Brownson's Quarterly Review," 324.

16. Penzel, ed., *Selected Writings,* xxxi; Nichols, *Romanticism in American Theology,* 73–76.

17. J. W. Nevin, *The Anxious Bench* (Chambersburg, Pa.: Office of the Weekly Messenger, 1843), 29, 52; Nevin, *Anxious Bench,* 2d ed. (1844), *Selected Writings,* 12, 98, 100, 114; Nevin, "Letter to Harbaugh," ibid., 407.

18. J. W. Nevin, "Catholic Unity" (1844), *Mercersburg Theology,* 35–55.

19. George H. Shriver, *Philip Schaff: Christian Scholar and Ecumenical Prophet* (Macon, Ga.: Mercer University Press, 1987), 20.

20. Schaff, *Principle of Protestantism,* 121, 226–29; Penzel, ed., *Selected Writings,* xl.

21. Schaff, *Principle of Protestantism,* 124, 222.

22. Schaff, *What is Church History?,* 80–85, 113.

23. Schaff, "German Theology," 113; Schaff, *Principle of Protestantism,* 216.

24. Nichols, *Romanticism in American Theology,* 116–120; Schaff, *History of the Apostolic Church, Selected Writings,* 39; Schaff, *Principle of Protestantism,* 220.

25. Penzel, ed., *Selected Writings,* 25; Schaff, *History of the Apostolic Church,* ibid., 131.

26. J. W. Nevin, "The Vindication of the Revised Liturgy" (1866), *Selected Writings,* 372, 374; Nevin, "Letter to Harbaugh," 407–08; Schaff, *What is Church History?,* 11; Nevin, *Mystical Presence,* 52, 106.

27. Nevin, "Letter to Harbaugh," 408; J. W. Nevin, "Wilberforce on the Incarnation" (1850), *Mercersburg Theology,* 80; Nevin, "Vindication of the Revised Liturgy," 372; Nevin, "Apostles Creed," 337–38.

28. Nevin, *My Own Life,* 69–70; Nevin, "The Church," 65.

29. Nevin, "The Church," 60–61; Nevin, "Faith, Freedom, and Reverence," 287.

30. Nevin, "Catholic Unity," 40; Nevin, "Wilberforce on the Incarnation," 79, 80, 83; Nevin, *Mystical Presence,* 166.

31. Nevin, "The Church," 60, 65–66.

32. Ibid., 61, 64.

33. Nevin, *Mystical Presence,* 168, 213.

34. Ibid., 190, 191.

35. Ibid., 62.

36. Ibid., 156–61, 162.

37. Charles Hodge, "Doctrine of the Reformed Churches on the Lord's Supper," *BRPR* 20 (1848):230, 238, 247, 267, 272; J. W. Nevin, "Reply to Hodge," *Weekly Messenger of the German Reformed Church,* 31 May, 14 June, 28 June, 21 July, 9 August, 1848; J. W. Nevin, "Doctrine of the Reformed Church on the Lord's Supper," *Mercersburg Review* 2 (1850):437; Hodge, "What is Christianity?" 138, 158–59.

38. J. W. Nevin, "Noel on Baptism," *Mercersburg Review* 2 (1850):245, 249–50; Philip Schaff, *History of the Apostolic Church,* trans. E. D. Yeomans (New York: Charles Scribner's Sons, 1859), 570, 572.

39. J. W. Nevin, "Early Christianity" (1851), *Selected Writings,* 190, 198, 201–03, 269.

40. Schaff, *History of the Apostolic Church, Selected Writings,* 292; Nevin, "Early Christianity," 293.

41. Philip Schaff, *The Person of Christ, Philip Schaff,* 198, 200.

Chapter 24. Orestes Brownson and Isaac Hecker: Transcendental Catholicism

1. H. F. Brownson, ed., *The Works of Orestes Brownson,* 20 vols. (New York: AMS, 1966), 7; Marschall, "Francis Patrick Kenrick," 227–28.

2. Ryan, *Orestes Brownson,* 158, 163, 179; C. Carrol Hines, "Orestes Brownson: Jacksonian Literary Critic," *No Divided Allegiance: Essays in Brownson's Thought,* ed. Leonard Gilhooley (New York: Fordham University Press, 1980), 57.

3. Ryan, *Orestes Brownson,* 192, 193; Leonard Gilhooley, *Contradiction and Dilemma: Orestes Brownson and the American Ideal* (New York: Fordham University Press, 1972), 101; Orestes Brownson, "Aspirations of Nature" (1857), *Works,* 14:554, 569.

4. Orestes Brownson, *The Convert; or Leaves From My Experience, Works,* 5:2, 17, 175, 178; Orestes Brownson, "Protestantism in a Nutshell" (1849), *Works,* 6:148, 150.

5. Brownson, *The Convert,* 16, 153.

6. Ryan, *Orestes Brownson,* 294.

7. Brownson, *The Convert,* 125, 128; Ryan, *Orestes Brownson,* 245.

8. Brownson, *The Convert,* 129; Orestes Brownson, "Synthetic Philosophy" (1842–43), *Works,* 1:62, 68, 129.

9. Orestes Brownson, "Leroux on Humanity" (1842), *Works,* 4:119–22; Brownson, *The Convert,* 132, 148.

10. Orestes Brownson, "The Mediatorial Life of Jesus" (1842), *Works,* 4:154–72; Brownson, *The Convert,* 147.

11. Orestes Brownson, "The Church Against No-Church," *Works,* 5:331–89; Patrick W. Carey, "Orestes W. Brownson on Tradition and Traditionalism," *The Quadrilog: Tradition and the Future of Ecumenism,* ed. Kenneth Hagen (Collegeville, Minn.: Liturgical Press, 1994), iv.

12. Orestes Brownson, "Protestantism Ends in Transcendentalism" (1846), *Works,* 6:127; Brownson, "Protestantism in a Nutshell," 148– 52; Orestes Brownson, "The Mercersburg Hypothesis," *Works,* 14:17.

13. Brownson, "Church Against No-Church," 351; Orestes Brownson, "Maret on Reason and Revelation," *Works,* 1:438.

14. Orestes Brownson, "An A Priori Autobiography" (1850), *Works,* 1:234, 235; Orestes Brownson, "What Human Reason Can Do" (1855), *Works,* 1:310; Brownson, "Maret on Reason," 448.

15. Brownson, "A Priori Autobiography," 235; Brownson, "Maret on Reason," 454, 455.

16. Brownson, "Maret on Reason," 452; Orestes Brownson, "The Existence of God," *Works,* 1:257.

17. Brownson, "Maret on Reason," 440; Brownson, "A Priori Autobiography," 241; Orestes Brownson, "Vincenzo Gioberti" (1850), *Works,* 2:101–40; Orestes Brownson, "Philosophy of Revelation," ibid., 2:140–82.

18. Orestes Brownson, "Schools of Philosophy," *Works,* 1:298.

19. Ibid., 291; Brownson, "The Existence of God," 257.

20. Brownson, "The Existence of God," 261, 263; Brownson, *The Convert,* 169.

21. Brownson, "Maret on Reason," 476; Orestes Brownson, "Limits of Religious Thought," *Works,* 3:254, 269.

22. Orestes Brownson, "Synthetic Theology" (1873), *Works,* 3:552.

23. Orestes Brownson, "The Mysteries of Faith" (1863), *Works,* 8:37; Orestes Brownson, "Orthodoxy and Heresy Identical" (1849–51), *Works,* 7:27.

24. Brownson, "Maret on Reason," 498; Brownson, "Orthodoxy and Heresy," 52; Orestes Brownson, "Bishop Hopkins on Novelties" (1844), *Works,* 4:561.

25. George K. Malone, *The True Church: A Study in the Apologetics of Orestes Augustus Brownson* (Mundelein, Ill.: St. Mary of the Lake Seminary, 1957), 75; Ryan, *Orestes Brownson,* 386, 389.

26. Orestes Brownson, "Newman's Theory of Christian Doctrine" (1847), *Works,* 14:48; Orestes Brownson, "Newman's Development of Christian Doctrine," *Works,* 14:11–22.

27. Orestes Brownson, "Catholic Polemics" (1861), *Works,* 20:120.

28. Marschall, "Francis Patrick Kenrick," 214; Orestes Brownson, "Archbishop Spalding," *Works,* 14:505; Gilhooley, *Contradiction and Dilemma,* 149.

29. Ryan, *Orestes Brownson,* 533, 537.

30. Isaac T. Hecker, *Questions of the Soul* (New York: D. Appleton, 1855), 130, 282.

31. Orestes Brownson, "Questions of the Soul," *Works,* 14:540, 543.

32. Isaac T. Hecker, *Aspirations of Nature* (New York: James B. Kirker, 1857), 25, 208, 213.

33. Brownson, "Aspirations of Nature," 554, 557, 559, 562.

34. Ryan, *Orestes Brownson,* 541.

Chapter 25. The Dilemma of Slavery

1. Thornton Stringfellow, "The Bible Argument, or Slavery in the Light of Divine Revelation," *Cotton is King, and Pro-Slavery Arguments,* ed. E. N. Elliott (Augusta, Ga.:

Pritchard, Abbot, and Loomis, 1860), 503; Albert Barnes, *An Inquiry into the Scriptural Views of Slavery* (Philadelphia: Parry and McMillan, 1857), 381.

2. Samuel Sewall, *The Selling of Joseph: A Memorial* (1st ed. 1700; New York: Arno Press, 1969), 1, 2, 4, 6.

3. John Saffin, *A Brief and Candid Answer to a late Printed Sheet, Entituled, The Selling of Joseph* (1701), in George H. Moore, ed., *Notes on the History of Slavery* (New York: D. Appleton, 1866), 253, 254, 255.

4. Samuel Hopkins, *A Dialogue Concerning the Slavery of the Africans* (1st ed. 1776; New York: Arno Press, 1970), 26.

5. Thomas Bacon, *Two Sermons, Preached to a Congregation of Black Slaves* (1749), in *Religion in American History*, ed. Jon Butler and Harry S. Stout (New York: Oxford University Press, 1998), 84; Jon Butler, *Awash in a Sea of Faith* (Boston: Harvard University Press, 1990), 130–51.

6. Caroline L. Shanks, "The Biblical Anti-Slavery Argument of the Decade 1830–1840," *Journal of Negro History* 16 (1931):137; William Ellery Channing, *Slavery, Works*, 723–24; Barnes, *Inquiry*, 109.

7. William A. Smith, *Lectures on the Philosophy and Practice of Slavery* (Nashville, Tenn.: Stevenson and Evans, 1856), 140; John H. Giltner, "Moses Stuart and the Slavery Controversy," *Journal of Religious Thought* 18 (1961):33.

8. Albert Taylor Bledsoe, *Liberty and Slavery* (1856), *Cotton is King*, 301, 351; Stringfellow, "Bible Argument," 482; Richard Fuller and Francis Wayland, *Domestic Slavery Considered as a Scriptural Institution* (1st ed. 1845; New York: Lewis Colby, 1847), 189; Barnes, *Inquiry*, 248, 316; Francis Wayland, *The Elements of Moral Science*, ed. Joseph L. Blau (1st ed. 1835; Cambridge, Mass.: Harvard University Press, 1963), 191; Smith, *Lectures*, 137.

9. Bledsoe, *Liberty and Slavery*, 374; Fuller and Wayland, *Domestic Slavery*, 187, 195; Barnes, *Inquiry*, 226, 246, 326; Smith, *Lectures*, 144.

10. J. Albert Harrill, "The Use of the New Testament in the American Slave Controversy: A Case History in the Hermeneutical Tension between Biblical Criticism and Christian Moral Debate," *Religion and American Culture* 10 (2000):149–86.

11. Channing, *Slavery, Works* (1884), 723, 724.

12. Fuller and Wayland, *Domestic Slavery*, 89, 91.

13. Ibid., 172, 207; Bledsoe, *Liberty and Slavery*, 346–50; Stringfellow, "Bible Argument," 497.

14. Bledsoe, *Liberty and Slavery*, 343.

15. Charles Hodge, "The Biblical Argument on Slavery," *Cotton is King*, 857, 859; Charles Hodge, "Civil Government," *PR* 23 (1851):145.

16. Fuller and Wayland, *Domestic Slavery*, 49–53.

17. Bledsoe, *Liberty and Slavery*, 343; Stringfellow, "Bible Argument," 518; Fuller and Wayland, *Domestic Slavery*, 180, 210.

18. Fuller and Wayland, *Domestic Slavery*, 50, 181.

19. Barnes, *Inquiry*, 171–98; Shanks, "Biblical Anti-Slavery Argument," 142; Eugene D. Genovese, *"Slavery Ordained of God": The Southern Slaveholders' View of Biblical History and Modern Politics* (Gettysburg, Pa.: Gettysburg College, 1985), 7–23.

20. Hodge, "Biblical Argument," 875; Genovese, *"Slavery Ordained of God,"* 9.

21. Channing, *Slavery*, 723; Smith, *Lectures*, 176, 182; Bledsoe, *Liberty and Slavery*,

295; Mark A. Noll, "The Bible and Slavery," *Religion and the American Civil War,* ed. Randall M. Miller, Harry S. Stout, and Charles Reagan Wilson (New York: Oxford University Press, 1998), 66.

22. Jack P. Maddex, Jr., " 'The Southern Apostasy Revisited': The Significance of Proslavery Christianity," *Marxist Perspectives* 7 (1979):139; Hodge, "Biblical Argument," 866; Fuller and Wayland, *Domestic Slavery,* 148.

23. James Henley Thornwell, "The Christian Doctrine of Slavery," *Collected Writings,* 4:416; Wayland, *Elements of Moral Science,* 188; Genovese, *"Slavery Ordained of God,"* 15–23.

24. Fuller and Wayland, *Domestic Slavery,* 28, 34; Channing, *Slavery* (4th ed., Boston: James Munroe, 1836), 17; Smith, *Lectures,* 64.

25. S. W. S. Dutton, "Slavery and the Bible," *New Englander* 15 (1857), 134, cited in Robert Bruce Mullin, "Biblical Critics and the Battle Over Slavery," *Journal of Presbyterian History* 61 (1983):219; Barnes, *Inquiry,* 381.

Chapter 26: Afterword

1. Newman Smyth, "Orthodox Rationalism," *PR* 58 (1882):307, 312.

2. Henry Churchill King, *Reconstruction in Theology* (1st ed. 1901; New York: Macmillan, 1909), v, 19; George A. Gordon, "The Collapse of the New England Theology," *Harvard Theological Review* 2 (1908):127–68.

3. A. C. McGiffert, "The Progress of Theological Thought During the Past Fifty Years," *American Journal of Theology* 20 (1916):321–32 (hereafter *AJT*).

4. George A. Gordon, *Ultimate Conceptions of Faith* (Boston: Houghton Mifflin, 1904), 6–7.

5. William Adams Brown, "Changes in the Theology of American Presbyterianism," *AJT* 10 (1906):405.

6. Williston Walker, "Changes in Theology among American Congregationalists," *AJT,* 10 (1906):206; Brown, "Changes," ibid., 410.

7. George A. Gordon, "The Contrast and Agreement Between the New Theology and the Old," *The Andover Review* 19 (1893):1–18; Theodore T. Munger, "The New Theology," *The Freedom of Faith* (Boston: Houghton Mifflin, 1884), 3–44; William R. Hutchison, The *Modernist Impulse in American Protestantism* (Cambridge, Mass.: Harvard University Press, 1976), 76–110.

8. Carey, ed., "Introduction," *American Catholic Religious Thought,* 38; John Ireland, "The Church and the New Age," ibid., 179.

9. G. Stanley Hall, "Philosophy in the United States," *Mind* 4 (1879):90.

10. Henry C. Sheldon, "Changes in Theology Among American Methodists," *AJT* 10 (1906):34, 42; Brown, "Changes," 403; Albert H. Newman, "Recent Changes in the Theology of the Baptists," *AJT* 10 (1906):603; White, *Diocesan Seminary in the United States,* 144, 237–66.

11. Henry C. Sheldon, *System of Christian Doctrine* (1st ed. 1903; Cincinnati, Ohio: Jennings, Graham, 1912), 15, 237, 300, 432; G. S. Bishop, "The Testimony of the Scriptures to Themselves," *The Fundamentals,* 10 vols. (Chicago: Testimony Publishing, 1910), 7:38–54; see also 2:7– 28, 29–47; 3:7–41, 42–60, 86–97; 7:55–69; 10:18–25; 11:55–86.

12. Munger, "The New Theology," 4.

13. Ibid., 11.

14. Newman Smyth, *The Religious Feeling: A Study for Faith* (New York: Scribner, Armstrong, 1877), v, 18.

15. George Harris, "Ethical Christianity and Biblical Criticism," *Andover Review* 15 (1891):461–71; King, *Reconstruction*, v.

16. Munger, "The New Theology," 25.

17. Gordon, *Ultimate Conceptions*, vii.

Index